BLUES on CD

Charles Shaar Murray is the author of *Crosstown Traffic: Jimi Hendrix and Postwar Pop*, for which he received a 1990 Ralph J. Gleason Music Book Award, and a former Associate Editor of *New Musical Express*, in whose salt mines he laboured for more years than he cares to remember. Commencing his career in 1970 as a co-conspirator in the notorious Schoolkids' Issue of *OZ Magazine*, he has subsequently contributed to publications as diverse as *Vogue*, *Q*, *Rolling Stone*, *The Literary Review*, *The Daily Telegraph*, *The Guardian*, *The Observer*, *Guitar World*, *MacUser*, *The New Statesman* and *Time Out*. His favourite cult objects are the Fender Stratocaster, the Apple Macintosh and the Zippo lighter, and when not dodging creditors and editors, he terrorises London's blues bars as guitarist and vocalist with Blast Furnace. In 1991, Penguin Books published *Shots From The Hip*, a collection of two decades worth of his journalism, criticism and vulgar abuse; and at some time in the near future he hopes to complete *The Boogie Man*, a biography of John Lee Hooker. Born in London in 1951 and raised in Reading, Berkshire – where his parents moved in 1955 without seeking his advice or consent – he is married and inhabits a small, crowded flat in north London.

BLUES on CD

THE ESSENTIAL GUIDE

CHARLES SHAAR MURRAY

KYLE CATHIE LIMITED

First published in Great Britain in 1993 by
Kyle Cathie Limited
7/8 Hatherley Street, London SW1P 2QT

ISBN 1 85626 084 4

A Cataloguing in Publication record for this title is
available from the British Library.

Typeset by DP Photosetting
Printed by Clays Ltd, Bungay, Suffolk

This one's for Ruthie
– sorry!

"Blues ain't nothin' but a lowdown aching chill,
If you ain't had 'em, I hope you never will"
                                    – Son House

"Nothin' but the best, and later for the garbage"
                                    – John Lee Hooker

CONTENTS

CONTENTS

ACKNOWLEDGEMENTS

L adies and gentlemen, it's been a pleasure to be with you this evening, and please don't forget to tip your waiter or waitress, who's been working hard all night for you and your party.

Respect is due to all the various record companies who graciously disgorged entire truckloads of stuff for review in this book, but a special blues-power shout-out goes to the following: Ted Carroll and Gail Clarke at Ace Records, Karen Pitchford at Koch International, Samantha Richards at Charly (we got there in the end), Bruce Bastin at Interstate, John Martin at Topic, Colin Jones at Shanachie, Spike Hyde at Demon, Andy Gray at BGO, Pete Shertser at Red Lightnin', Billy Ray Gilliam at Bedrock, Malcolm Packer at Castle Communications and Kevin Grey at See For Miles. I also owe Big Fat Soulful Thanks to everybody who's put up with the delays to other projects caused by this book taking five times as long to write as originally intended. Y'all know who you are, and your forbearance has been greatly appreciated. *The Boogie Man* – soon come.

As stated in the Foreword, the torrent of blues releases (ancient and modern), various shifts in record company distributorship and the need to keep this book at a manageable length have made it impossible for *Blues on CD* to be as utterly definitive as I would have liked. Think of it as a time-lapse snapshot taken over a period of several months; a guide for listeners rather than an all-encompassing up-to-date catalogue. For example, let me turn you on to a couple of important records released too late for incorporation into the main body of the text. B.B. KING's *Blues Summit* (MCA MCD 10710) is the hardcore live-in-the-studio blues album which the big guy's fans have been awaiting for years; in order of appearance, its guest stars include – you ready for this? – ROBERT CRAY, KATIE WEBSTER, BUDDY GUY, JOHN LEE HOOKER, KOKO TAYLOR, ETTA JAMES, LOWELL FULSON, ALBERT COLLINS, Ruth Brown, Irma Thomas and JOE LOUIS WALKER. Cray and Walker appear with their own groups, Hooker with Cray's group plus ROY ROGERS, and everybody else with B.B.'s road band. The whole thing was cut in two five-day sessions – one in Memphis, one in Berkeley – during February and March of 1993; the repertoire brings vivid new life to a fistful of tried-and-trusted standards, and it's the first studio album B.B.'s made in well over a decade which sounds like he was singing, playing and thinking at the same time.

The second delves back over half a century, and gives CD buyers access to the first-ever recordings by MUDDY WATERS. *The Complete Plantation Recordings: The Historic 1941–42 Library Of Congress Field Recordings* (MCA/Chess CHD-9344 [US]) presents the 26-year-old McKinley Morganfield down home in Mississippi, as he sounded when Alan Lomax came down in search of ROBERT JOHNSON; it blends solo performances, interview material – in which Muddy acknowledges his considerable artistic debt to SON HOUSE – and string-band sessions with the Son Sims Four. It was hearing the playbacks of these recordings that finally persuaded Muddy that he had a future as a professional musician and which convinced him to pull up stakes and head for Chicago. To suggest that Chicago blues was simply Delta blues transformed into an electric ensemble music is a truism which this record forcefully validates: *The Complete Plantation Recordings* is the pivot between pre- and postwar downhome blues styles.

Despite the air of casual omniscience so painfully cultivated in the text, the accuracy of *Blues on CD* rests, somewhat precariously, on the formidable body of blues scholarship built up by many hands over the past several decades. I've leaned heavily on the liner notes to the discs reviewed, which means that yet another major shout-out goes to the Blues Mafia: Neil Slaven, Cliff White, Bruce Bastin, Norman Darwen, Mike Rowe, Andy McKaie, Billy Altman, Billy Vera, Jas Obrecht, Robert Palmer, Mary Elizabeth Alden and many others. Peter Guralnick's *The Listener's Guide to the Blues* (Blandford, 1982) was the book against which I invariably measured my tastes and my judgments, as well as the state of my blues collection. My first ports of call for basic biographical info on the artists discussed in this book were Sheldon Harris' *Blues Who's Who* (Arlington House, 1977), *The Penguin Encyclopedia of Popular Music*, edited by Donald Clarke (Viking, 1989), and Phil Hardy & Dave Laing's *The Faber Companion to 20th-Century Popular Music* (Faber & Faber, 1990). Robert Christgau's *Christgau's Guide: Rock Albums of the '70s* (Vermilion, 1982) and *Christgau's Guide: The '80s* (Pantheon, 1990) proved invaluable as a means of sorting out the major releases of the last couple of decades. A partial listing of the rest of the bookshelf looks sump'n like this:

Bessie, Christ Albertson (Abacus, 1975)

Rhythm Oil, Stanley Booth (Jonathan Cape, 1991)

The Poetry of the Blues, Samuel Charters (Avon, 1963)

The Bluesmen, Samuel Charters (Oak, 1967)

Stormy Monday: The T-Bone Walker Story, Helen Oakley Dance (Da Capo, 1987)

I Am The Blues, Willie Dixon with Don Snowden (Quartet, 1989)

Big Road Blues, David Evans (Da Capo, 1987)

The Bluesman, Julio Finn (Quartet, 1986)

Blues and the Poetic Spirit, Paul Garon (Eddison Bluesbooks, 1975)

Lost High, Peter Guralnick (Vintage, 1982/Penguin 1992)

Feel Like Goin' Home, Peter Guralnick (Omnibus, 1971/Penguin 1992)

Right on: From Blues To Soul In Black America, Michael Harambulos (Eddison Bluesbooks, 1974)

Urban Blues, Charles Keil (Chicago, 1966, 1991)

Mystery Train, Greil Marcus (Omnibus, 1977/Penguin, 1991)

Blues, Robert Neff & Anthony Connor (Latimer, 1976)

Deep Blues, Robert Palmer (PaperMac, 1981)

Chicago Breakdown, Mike Rowe (Eddison Bluesbooks, 1973)

B.B. King: The Authorized Biography, Charles Sawyer (Blandford, 1980)

Bluesland, ed. Peter Welding & Toby Byron (Dutton, 1991)

The Life & Legend Of Leadbelly, Charles Wolfe & Kip Lornell (HarperCollins, 1993)

Blues Fell This Morning, Paul Oliver (Cambridge, 1960)

ACKNOWLEDGEMENTS

By the way, assorted bits and pieces of this text have appeared, in different form, in *Q*, *The Daily Telegraph*, and *Guitar World*. For those who care about such things, this book was written on an Apple Macintosh IIxc using Microsoft Word 5.0 and 5.1 word-processing software. And the first-ever blues record to begin *'Woke up this mornin''* was BESSIE SMITH's 1928 'Empty Bed Blues'.

INTRODUCTION

I n an ideal world, the title *Blues On CD* would be entirely self-explanatory, and we could zip straight to the first chapter with a minimum of fuss, pausing only for ritual thanks to my wife, my mother, my agent, my accountant, my Macintosh™ guru, and all the people from all the record companies who provided the CDs reviewed in this book. Unfortunately, since this is – as you have probably observed in other contexts – far from being an ideal world, the title of this book requires some elucidation. The question of exactly what – in 1993 – constitutes 'the blues' is a sufficiently complex one to be worth a book in its own right (not this one, thankfully), but hopefully we can take a walk around that particular block in a moment or two. However, even locating a precise definition of 'on CD' poses certain awkward quandaries.

For a start, the CD market is a hi-tech descendent of 'album culture', a sensibility which has dominated jazz since the early 1950s and rock since the late 1960s. Albums – a suitably neutral term which can, I hope, serve here as an interchangeable synonym for both 'LPs' and 'CDs' – can contain extended performances far beyond the scope of a 45rpm or 78rpm single; a series of theme- or mood-linked pieces designed to be heard in sequence; or a mixture of both. Jazz musicians and rock musicians have both made use of the facilities offered by the long-playing format: jazz musicians took to it instantly because it suited the open-ended improvisation which is the cornerstone of their art; rock musicians, arguably, abused these facilities as a result of their infatuation with The Beatles' *Sergeant Pepper's Lonely Hearts Club Band*. The record business was delighted with the notion of album-as-package because it meant that the basic unit of sales was now something considerably more expensive than a mere single-play record. The end result of this process is that the single, or so they now tell us, is dead as anything other than a promotional tool to boost the sales of albums.

Jazz, then, has spent more than half of its recorded history – roughly, from 1920 to the present day – as an album music. Rock can make a similar claim if we date the birth of rock, as orthodoxy demands, from the 1954 release of Elvis Presley's first Sun single 'That's All Right Mama.' Blues, in its contemporary form, effectively remained a singles market as late as rock did, despite having begun its recorded life as a contemporary of jazz. The reason for this is plain: singles are cheaper than albums, and – until the '60s awakening of mass white acceptance of the music – those to whom blues records had always been sold were, mostly, the poorest people in America: working-class blacks. Singles were cheaper than albums: therefore, this audience bought singles, and the record companies whose source of income was that audience manufactured singles. Once the long-playing record established itself, the blues artists who made albums were those whose music appealed to the upper economic echelons of the blues audience: the sophisticated B.B. King and Bobby Bland were among the first. Albums by John Lee Hooker and Muddy Waters – whose rootsier 'electric downhome' blues sold to an older, more blue-collar market – didn't appear until a few years later, and those were both best-ofs, recycling previously successful singles. (Howlin' Wolf didn't make an album-as-album until 1968, and that was the legendarily dreadful 'psychedelic' experiment *The Howlin' Wolf Album*, a.k.a. *Howlin' Wolf's New Album*.) The only other blues performers who were recorded specifically as 'album artists' at that time were the older country bluesmen, whose music was targeted at affluent white folk-music fans.

So the vast majority of blues records made between the early '20s and the mid-'60s were singles, made by small, greedy record companies and designed to sell the maximum number of copies for the minimum financial outlay. The only blues recordings made simply because somebody thought that this music was worth preserving for its intrinsic historical and cultural importance were those cut for the Library Of Congress. Vocalion Records did not record Robert Johnson because they thought that he was a great artist whose work deserved to live forever: they recorded him because there was money to be made out of selling 78s of

Mississippi blues singers. (As a matter of fact, Robert Johnson was not especially successful in his lifetime: only one of his singles, 'Terraplane Blues', was anything more than a small regional hit, and many of his best-known songs were never released on record until the late-'50s folk boom prompted the compilation of an album of his songs.) This essentially pinpoints the fatuousness of the folkie fallacy that old blues 78s by rural, acoustic performers were 'pure' in a way that 45s and albums by urban, amplified performers were not. Both were made by artists and companies out to make money, using the best technology that could be afforded on a tight budget (i.e. low) and squeezing as many titles as possible out of one session. In other words, they were pop singles.

What this means, in practice, is that most CDs of music made during the first forty-odd years of recorded blues are compilations of singles cut over a period of several years: in some cases over more than a decade. They were not made to be heard back-to-back in bunches of twenty or more, and as a result many such anthologies may seem a little samey: a successful artist would stamp his or her aural signature on every tune, while an unsuccessful one would be searching for said aural signature. Some artists never made enough successful singles to fill up even a single CD, let alone a batch of 'em; which means that their half-dozen or so worthwhile tracks may be scattered across a variety of themed or shared anthologies.

Another problem for the modern CD listener confronting early blues is that the material which you'll find cluttering up the Blues section of your local chainstore outlet emanates from a bewildering variety of sources. The most desirable (and least complicated) option consists of British domestic releases (or full-distribution American imports) licensed directly from the legitimate copyright holders and digitally transferred (preferably by people with functioning ears) from the original master tapes or – in the case of the earliest country blues or jazz material, recorded before tape became the industry standard – from the original 78rpm metal stampers or treasured copies of the 78rpm singles. (A good cover and sensible liner notes don't hurt, either.) These do exist, but they can be found nestling side-by-side with American, Japanese or European imports from record companies which may or may not be legitimate, royalty-paying licensees of the material in question; and which may or may not have had access to first-generation masters. Consequently, the same repertoires – including the Chess and VeeJay catalogues which represent the finest Chicago blues of the '50s – seem to appear and reappear in a bewildering number of configurations: on different labels from different countries of origin, at different prices, with different artwork and different track selections. Making a choice may become a problem when something originating from Italy or Germany can offer a more generous running time and a more attractive combinations of tracks at a more competitive price than the 'authorised' British or American release.

Sometimes, it's a bargain. Often, it's a false economy. Unauthorised releases (bootlegs in all but name) abound and, naturally, such CDs have never been within shouting distance of the original master tapes. One Italian outlet, whose products offer theoretically good value, issues CDs which have actually been transcribed from previous vinyl editions. Since CD technology is a semi-exact science and not some form of technovoodoo whereby the simple act of digitising music automatically improves the sound quality, this would seem to negate all the advantages, other than durability and ease of use, of owning the material on CD in the first place. The authorised versions of any recording are therefore preferable on both aesthetic and moral grounds. They win aesthetically because they have been digitised from the original studio master tapes, and will therefore sound better: CDs have a wider frequency range than vinyl albums, and the use of copy master tapes which have been compressed and equalised for vinyl will inevitably fail to take advantage of CD's greater bandwidth. A CD master made from the original studio tape by an engineer who knows what (s)he's doing will offer perceptibly better sound quality than a slipshod digital transcription of a copy master optimised for vinyl, and if you can't tell the difference then you might as well have stuck with the vinyl version in the first place. They are superior morally because the original artist – or his or her estate – is receiving royalties from your purchases. Blues artists have, historically, been ripped off more than artists in any other field, and if you're going to spend your money on their music – as I sincerely hope you will – then (to quote J.R.R. Tolkien's cover note to the first authorised US paperback editions of *The Lord Of The Rings*) 'those who approve of courtesy to living authors will purchase this edition, and no other.' Replace 'to living authors' with 'to great bluesmen, living or dead, and their descendants' and (as they say at Burger King) you got it. With a legit issue, you get the best possible sound quality (thus reinforcing your self-image as a sussed consumer capable of seeking out top quality and high performance) along with a clear conscience (because some of your money is going to the people who actually did the work). Such a deal! So, Ground Rule Number One is this: wherever a legit version of a particular recording is available, that's the one which will be recommended. Better sound, better karma. You know it makes sense.

Before we leave the subject of CDs, allow me to add my two penn'orth (or, if you happen to be an American, my ten cents) to the still-raging controversy over the respective merits of digital and analaogue technology. Many neophobes, including Neil Young in a series of much-quoted diatribes, wax (no pun intended) lyrical over the superior warmth of vinyl, claiming that digital sound loses in harshness whatever it gains in clarity; and that the sampling rate is too low to provide true fidelity. It's undoubtedly true that many first-generation CDs did indeed suffer from overly bright highs and an unpleasantly thin mid-range, but these deficiencies had more too do with slipshod mastering techniques than any inherent limitations of the technology. Record companies have learned the hard way that the sound of a CD is exactly as good as that of the source from which it was mastered, and that nothing less than an uncompressed, unequalised studio master will do. Flaws in master-tape quality are far more apparent on a CD than they would be on vinyl, where the lower resolution can flatter such imperfections, and since blues recordings have almost invariably been made on a lower budget than their pop equivalents, it might be possible to make a case that blues 'belongs' on warm, funky vinyl rather than cold, clear CD. However, the upside is this: mastering technology is improving all the time, and the kind of techniques developed in the past few years have enabled the music of early greats like Bessie Smith or Robert Johnson to be heard with greater clarity and verisimilitude than at any time since the music was first made.

But what about the dreaded sampling rate? Well, movies are still projected at 24 frames a second, just as they were in the earliest days of film: not because any kind of impenetrable technological ceiling had been reached which would render it impossible to use a higher rate, but because, above 24 frames per second, the human eye is incapable of telling the difference. Digital sampling operates at 44,100 samples per second, which is about as high a rate as our ears can handle. Above 44,100 sps, distinctions are simply not cost-effective: anything more would be gilding the lily, over-egging the pudding, over-waxing the moustache. Maybe Neil Young can hear the difference: I can't, and if you're sufficiently enamoured of CD technology to have bought this book, then probably neither can you. Face it: if Neil Young's ears were *that* good, he'd be able to keep his guitar in tune.

Enough of this wirehead techie gibberish. Let's talk about the blues.

Firstly: what is 'the blues' and (possibly more important) what *isn't*.? And is it folk music, pop music or art music? Music identifiable as 'blues' was first heard around the turn of the century (according to contemporary accounts, anyway) and first recorded around 1920. The ubiquity of the influence of the blues on so many different areas of 20th century popular music means that the genre overlaps fairly freely with jazz, rock, soul, funk and folk music, creating a series of what we might call 'blue-grey areas.' For example, the blues shares the boogie-woogie pianists and 'classic blues' vocalists of the '20s (not to mention the 'jump' bands of the '30s and '40s, '50s soul-jazzers like Jimmy Smith and great anomalies like Mose Allison) with jazz; the post-jump novelty-blues singers of the '50s (Chuck Berry, Little Richard, Fats Domino, Bo Diddley, even James Brown) with rock 'n' roll; white '60s revivalists of the country-blues persuasion (John Hammond, Bonnie Raitt, Ry Cooder, even Bob Dylan) with folk music, and their electric contemporaries (Yardbirds, Animals, John Mayall, Eric Clapton, Peter Green's Fleetwood Mac) with British Invasion and progressive rock. Urban(e) 'Memphis synthesis' bluesmen like Bobby 'Blue' Bland, B.B. King, Little Milton and, first and foremost, Ray Charles shared, at least for a while, a consitituency first with swing and jump, and later with soul music; and so forth. What's more, many blues singers perform in styles not necessarily associated with their places of birth or primary residence, or frequently work within styles other than the one(s) with which they are principally associated.

A quick guide to the employed criteria, therefore. Unlike Paul Oliver's *Blackwell's Guide* to the same territory, I don't propose to bar *all* white musicians; if I created a definition of the blues which automatically excluded the likes of Stevie Ray Vaughan, Eric Clapton, Bonnie Raitt and John Hammond, I doubt that John Lee Hooker or Buddy Guy would ever speak to me again. Furthermore, how are we to explain the guitar duets cut by Lonnie Johnson and 'Blind Willie Dunn' at the dawn of blues recording once we know that 'Dunn' was actually the white jazz guitarist Eddie Lang? How about Johnson and Dunn/Lang's joint sessions backing the impeccably 'authentic' rural vocalist Texas Alexander, or the titanic 'classic' blueswoman Bessie Smith? Or 'singing brakeman' Jimmie Rodgers' 1929 'Blue Yodel No. 9' session with Louis Armstrong? There are indeed white performers in this book, but they've had to pay some serious dues to merit inclusion: to get in here, a white performer has had to have gained acceptance within the blues community itself, either by being a superb musician who has played the music well enough for long enough to gain the respect of the 'real guys', or else by contributing materially to the popularisation and perpetuation of the blues. Preferably, by doing both. This is why Vaughan, Clapton, Raitt and Hammond (not to mention Johnny Winter, John Mayall, Dr Feelgood and The Fabulous Thunderbirds) are in here while Ten Years After, Climax Blues Band, Savoy Brown and The Siegel-Schwall Blues Band aren't.

The fact is that the arrival of the white (Anglo-American) blues audience and a sizeable squad of dedicated white blues musicians saved the blues from (some of) the consequences of its steady loss of relevance to the African-American masses, but it also changed the blues – permanently. Early reactions to the 'white blues boom' from the blues veterans ranged from bemusement (why are they interested in this stuff?) through resentment (they're making more money off my song than I ever did) to gratitude (no white people in America ever heard of me until The Rolling Stones started to play my music); but ultimately, it was the white blues-rockers who created the mass audience which sustained the careers of most of the originators. Though certain styles – the Southern-soul/uptown blues fusion which is now typified (not to mention dominated) by the independent Malaco label (based in Jackson, Mississippi, and best-known for grooming Z.Z. Hill as the successor to Bobby Bland's throne, and then signing Bland himself when Hill died) – have never maintained a significant white constituency, and remain current purely because of the strength and loyalty of their rural Southern black support, blues today is primarily aimed at a white, album-buying audience. Or, to be precise, a white, CD-buying audience: you (or, if you don't happen to be white, someone very much like you who is).

Finally, a couple of *caveat emptors* and a few notes as to how this book is organised. Caveat the first: the available repertoire is in a perpetual state of flux. Previously unavailable CDs are released and currently available ones are deleted; and the distribution rights to various key catalogues may well change hands. A few examples: as this book as being prepared, a legal battle of considerable proportions is building over MCA and Charly's differing claims to control over European rights to the Chess catalogue. The UK distributorship of the Arhoolie catalogue shifted from Topic to Ace. Demon Records withdrew a couple of fairly tasty items – Johnny Winter's *Second Winter* and Taj Mahal's *Giant Steps/De Ole Folks At Home* – because the copyright holder required a larger payment for extension of their licensing arrangement than was justified by projected sales. Atlantic Records recently announced long-overdue steps for a comprehensive reissue programme of their awesome catalogue – including currently unavailable key works by Joe Turner, Ray Charles, Champion Jack Dupree, Professor Longhair, Jimmy Yancey and others – in conjunction with the repackaging virtuosi at Rhino Records, but very few items have thus far appeared, and none of them in the UK. Consequently, it is entirely possible that (a) items listed in this book as 'currently unavailable on CD' will actually be in stores by the time you read this; (b) items reviewed herein as available product could well have been deleted by the time you read this; or (c) a particular repertoire reviewed here may well have been transferred to a different company and be available in a differnt configuration to the one cited here.

Caveat the second: a lot of good stuff still hasn't emerged on CD. A few examples, once more: the only option for those interested in the post-'41 work of Sonny Boy Williamson I is an RCA compilation shared with Big Joe Williams, or a 4-CD set of the complete works in chronological order from the highly specialist Document label. Neither are satisfactory: the RCA is too skimpy and the Document set too indiscriminate. Ike Turner, in his pre-Tina incarnation, was an extremely important figure in the development of '50s Memphis blues, but much of his blues work is irritatingly unavailable. You will search in vain for any of the post-Sun recordings of Junior Parker, who was very popular during the '60s; and there has yet to be a significant revival of interest in the 'classic' female blues singers of the '20s and early '30s, with many of the most popular artists in that field very poorly represented on CD. Still, it's early days yet, and hopefully future editions of this book (if any!) will bring better news.

How this book is organised: after considering all the options (including a straight-up, all-in alphabetic listing; alphabetic listings within loose categories, and variations thereof) I've chosen to take the cowards' way out and adopt a customised version of the format devised by Peter Guralnick for his *Listener's Guide To The Blues* (Blandford Press). (Thanks, Peter. If your publishers had had the foresight to commission you to update your wonderful and indispensable tome for the CD era, I'd be dead.) I've sliced the blues into three time frames, each covered in one section of the book: Part One goes from the earliest blues recordings I can find up to the end of World War II; Part Two covers the period from the end of World War II to the mid-'70s, and Part Three brings the story up to the present day. Within each period, I've sliced the music yet again: this time by musical style, corresponding wherever possible to regional idioms. This creates certain unavoidable anomalies, since VE Day didn't automatically mark the disappearance of all pre-war styles and their replacement by post-war developments. For example, early 'jump' is covered in Part One because it is essentially a prewar idiom, inaugurated by Louis Jordan's first significant recordings in 1938; but popular jump records were made well into the '50s, some of them by artists whose careers didn't commence until well after World War II ended, so the bulk of the jump story is in Part Two. Similarly, T-Bone Walker's blues is listed as a postwar development, even though he made his first record in 1929 and began the significant phase of his recording career during the war years. Y'all are just going to have to bear with me on this one.

Within each style, I've sought to identify the leading performers and their best, most characteristic or most influential recordings. Less important (but still worthwhile) records, guest appearances, cover versions, mentions of key works currently unavailable on CD, works by related artists who don't rate their own entries, and general trivia are listed under the heading *Subjects for further investigation:* Song titles appear in single quotes 'Like So'; album references within each entry in ordinary italics *like so*; available albums under discussion in *Subjects for further investigation:* appear in bold italics **like so**. The first reference within each entry to a performer who has his, her or their own entry elsewhere will appear in small caps LIKE SO. Where an album is credited differently to the artist's name (let's say, J.J. Lonesome) as listed at the head of the entry, the heading for the discussion of that album (by J.J. Lonesome in collaboration with Texas Fred, or a Texas Fred album where J.J. Lonesome delivers significant performances as a sideman, or a collection which combines individual recordings by both) will appear like so:

- **J.J. LONESOME & TEXAS FRED:** *The Complete Rip-Off Sessions 1936–1941* (Blues Bore BB CD 015)

Or like so:

- **TEXAS FRED:** *Hard Times In Dallas* (Trainspotter TSCD 93729)

Within J.J. Lonesome's entry, an album entirely (or primarily) by him will appear like so:

- *Mean Old Highway* (Obsessive OBCD 61297)

However, if J.J.'s *Mean Old Highway* contains significant performances by Texas Fred, you may also find it in Fred's entry, this time discussed in the context of Fred's life and work, like so:

- **J.J. LONESOME:** *Mean Old Highway* (Obsessive OBCD 61297)

If, though, Fred and J.J. had spent the major part of their careers working as a duo, then their work would be discussed in a joint 'J.J. Lonesome & Texas Fred' entry, and only solo albums by one or the other of them would be differentiated. They would still have separate index entries, though.

A fully comprehensive index for a book as insanely heavily cross-referenced as this one would run to over thirty pages, so for reasons to do with the fragile sanity of both the author and the publisher, we've restricted it to a device for locating the principal biographical entries in the book. If we're all very lucky, future editions may include a heavyweight index which will enable you to trace the many eminently worthwhile minor artists (as well as the influences of the major ones) throughout the entire tract. As it is, one caveat: where an artist's surname (real or assumed) is part of their name (B.B. King, Muddy Waters), that is how they're indexed, but a *nom de blues* (Tampa Red, Lightning Slim) is indexed under the first letter of the first word. This, hopefully, solves the problem of whether to index-hunt for Memphis Slim next door to Memphis Minnie or Lightning Slim; or Little Milton next to Little Walter or Roy Milton. However, general usage among blues and R&B buffs means that Bo Diddley, Taj Mahal and Howlin' Wolf are the exceptions which prove the rule: look them up under DIDDLEY, BO; MAHAL, TAJ and WOLF, HOWLIN'.

One final thing. This book is unashamedly aimed at the blues fan who has come to the music via contemporary (or, at any rate, post-'60s consensus) rock and soul. My own tastes will be apparent, but not, I hope, overly intrusive. The more hardened blues buff may find the frequent references to blues-rockers and their cover versions of this hallowed material a trifle down-market, but . . . own up, aren't you glad that the rest of the world has finally caught up? If you're not, then fuck y'all and the Vocalion 78s you rode in on, because the rest of us are about to have a party. Now move everything breakable out of the room, roll back the carpet if it ain't nailed down, pour yourself a drink, fire up your CD player and get ready to turn the page and dance the mess around. In the words of Hound Dog Taylor, 'Let's have some fun!'

Charles Shaar Murray
Up against a deadline
London
1993

PART ONE: WALKIN' BLUES
(1920–1945)

E very journey needs to start somewhere; and if the journey is a long and complex one, the resourceful traveller brings a map. Most jazz or blues compilations conceived as study aids or history lessons face a severe trade-off between historicity and listenability, but there is one that doesn't; and a detailed examination of its contents can provide us with a comprehensive guide to much of the territory covered in Part One of this book.

- **VARIOUS ARTISTS:** *The Story Of The Blues*
  (Columbia 468992 2)

Blues historian Paul Oliver originally compiled this double album (now, of course, a double CD) in 1969, to illustrate his book of the same name. Theoretically, it carries the listener from traditional West African folk music – courtesy of Fra-Fra tribesmen from the Northern Territory of Ghana – through to the late-'60s 'present', but in practice its only concession to any postwar innovations comes from the inclusion of three (admittedly superb) examples of the post-MUDDY WATERS Chicago style from OTIS SPANN (1930–1970), JOHNNY SHINES (1915–1992) and ELMORE JAMES (1918–1963). Oliver's determinedly folkloric approach to blues may well indicate that his omission of both the late-'30s – mid-'50s jump idiom, codified by LOUIS JORDAN, and the mid-'40s-and-onwards style which T-BONE WALKER and his successors developed by juxtaposing jump and swing with electrified Texas blues guitar, is a deliberate attempt to exclude such vulgar pop music from the blues canon. I prefer to attribute it to a sensible compromise between an artistic preference for prewar rural styles (and the later urban styles most directly derived from them), a record company's desire to include at least *some* vaguely contemporary blues, and the practical problems of staying within a fixed budget for licensing outside material. Nevertheless, if we agree to scoop Spann, Shines and James off to one side while promising to deal with their work, and the work of their most distinguished contemporaries, in Part Two, we are left with a near-definitive collection; one which provides entry points to virtually every important area of pre-war blues.

The first section, corresponding to Side 1 of the original double-album, is entitled 'The Origins Of The Blues.' The snippet of 'Yarum Praise Songs', recorded in Ghana in 1964, which opens the anthology is a brief but intriguing one: the rhythm, shaken out on the rattle which serves as percussion, is remarkably similar to the maracca beats found on the BO DIDDLEY records of the '50s; the melodic line played on the fiddle bears an eerie similarity to time-honoured Mississippi Delta slide-guitar motifs; and the vocals find their echo in any number of field hollers and work songs. You can search almost in vain for traces of the blues in contemporary African music (I said 'almost' as a mark of respect to Ali Farka Toure, Mali's biggest JOHN LEE HOOKER fan), which conclusively demonstrates that the blues is an African-American creation, and that both sides of the hyphen are equally essential to the final result. Nevertheless, these traditional chants, some of which date back several hundred years to the days of the Middle Passage when millions of West African men, women and children were kidnapped into slavery, bear powerful witness to the ability of a people to protect and maintain their cultural identity through centuries of concerted effort to strip them of dignity, humanity and language.

In quick succession, we then meet five of the key figures in early rural blues. MISSISSIPPI JOHN HURT (1892–1966), a thoroughly atypical Mississippi bluesman if ever there was one, displays the sly delicacy of his singing and fingerpicking on a definitive 1928 version of the epic badman ballad 'Stack O'Lee Blues' (another variant of which provided a massive rock and roll hit for Lloyd Price almost three decades later), and the Georgia 12-string master BLIND WILLIE McTELL (1901–1959) uses his guitar to illustrate his assorted encounters on the journey described in the narrative talking blues 'Travelin' Blues' (1929). CHARLEY PATTON (1887–1934), who was HOWLIN' WOLF's primary influence, the first of the great Mississippi Delta stylists to record, and whose music was directly passed on to Muddy Waters and ROBERT JOHNSON by SON HOUSE, then roars through his 'Stone Pony Blues' (1934), demonstrating the slashing slide guitar and rich, gravelly chest tones which have characterised Delta blues ever since. He is followed by the great Texan singer/guitarist BLIND LEMON JEFFERSON (c1897–c1929), the first rural bluesman to become truly popular and influential through the recording medium: he was *massive* in the 1920s, and some of his single-string guitar lines have echoed down through the years in the work of T-Bone Walker and his many acolytes. 'Black Snake Moan' (1927) is Jefferson's adaptation of Victoria Spivey's original 'Black Snake Blues', which was one of the first of a whole series of 'snake' songs (including the 'Crawlin' King Snake' later popularised by John Lee Hooker). It's not altogether typical of Jefferson's work – he neither uses the knife with which he obtained so many of his chilling slide effects, nor does he sing in the piercing high register which obviously made such an impression upon ROBERT JOHNSON – but the power which he exerted upon public and peers alike is clearly discernible.

Huddie Ledbetter, best known as LEADBELLY (c1889–1949), is renowned primarily as both a walking treasure trove of American folklore and a decidedly folkloric figure in his own right, but even after his canonisation as a folkie icon, he still hankered after accepotance as a commercial bluesman. His 'Pig Meat Papa' (1935) is rolling 12-string thunder recorded the same year that he appeared with his discoverer John Lomax in a *March Of Time* newsreel. The sonorous-voiced and appropriately named Texas Alexander (1880–1955), an elder cousin of LIGHTNIN' HOPKINS, couldn't play guitar but always carried one in case he met someone who could. At various times his accompanists included Hopkins, Blind Lemon Jefferson, Josh White, Sam Chatmon and LOWELL FULSON, but the sparkling guitar on 'Broken Yo-Yo' (1929) is played by LONNIE JOHNSON (1889–1970), in his own right both one of the biggest blues stars, and one of the finest single-string guitarists, of his era. Oliver closes his 'first act' with a reminder of the blues fiddle tradition soon to be supplanted by the rising popularity of the harmonica: on 'Broke And Hungry Blues' (1929), the method- ical plod of Georgia guitarist Peg Leg Howell (1888–1966) is effectively counterpointed by the sobbing obbligato of an ano- nymous fiddler.

The second half of Disc 1 (or, in its original form, Side 2 of

Album 1) carries the catchall title of 'Blues And Entertainment': this is party music, dance music, drinking music. The Atlanta brother duo of Barbecue Bob (1902–1931) & Laughing Charley (1900–1963) hammer away at their 12-string guitars, cackle like lunatics and put each other in the dozens (trans: 'swap ribald badinage') on 'It Won't Be Long Now' (1927), while two associates of Peg Leg Howell, the guitar/fiddle duo of Henry Williams and Eddie Anthony, display thoroughly canny pop-craft by laying down an undulating dance beat, a string of flashy fiddle solos and a infectious, singable chorus on 'Georgia Crawl' (1928). Oliver's next two selections emphasise that the stereotype of country blues as essentially a solitary loner's music was not strictly accurate: there were plenty of string and jug bands, and The Mississippi Jook Band and The Memphis Jug Band, each represented here by an instrumental, were two of the best. The former present 'Dangerous Woman' (1936), an exhilarating boogie for piano, guitar and tambourine; while the latter's piano, jug, guitar and percussion plunk along behind the jauntily wailing harp of their leader Will Shade (1898–1966) on 'Gator Wobble' (1934), the first appearance on this collection of the classic shuffle beat which is still one of the most fundamental blues rhythms.

It has probably not escaped your notice that the earliest school of recorded blues (not to mention the most popular of its time) has gone thus far unacknowledged. The so-called 'classic' blues (a term invented by jazz critics, long after the fact, to distinguish it from all that degenerate jump trash) was primarily sung by women whereas the country blues is sung by men; primarily accompanied by piano and trumpet or clarinet, instead of guitar and harmonica or fiddle; primarily urban as opposed to rural; and mostly performed at stately, slow-drag tempos. It was hugely popular on record before anyone got around to marketing country blues; it was popular amongst the white intelligentsia (most of whom wouldn't – you should pardon the expression – *cotton onto* the country blues for another thirty-odd years) as well as with blacks; and it held commercial sway until the Depression. With its strong connections to both jazz and vaudeville, it was far better poised to affect the mainstream of white American pop than the rural blues would be until the dawn of the rock era. Why Oliver attempts to encapsulate an entire subgenre of this stature into a mere three songs is frankly beyond me: mind you, he picked a _great_ three songs. Above an ominously rolling piano and introduced by a piercing cornet, BESSIE SMITH (1894–1937) makes a vocal entry utterly commensurate with the title of 'Empress Of The Blues'. With 'In The House Blues' (1931), she wipes away any residual grin left on your face by the bucolic rollicking of Shade and his colleagues. It's a performance of stark drama, bottomless emotional depth, and consummate vocal authority; and it cannot be undermined even by percussion that sounds as if a pantomime horse has unaccountably been let loose in the studio.

Somewhat more jovial is the mysterious Texan Lillian Glinn, whose mildly lubricious 'Shake It Down' (1928) is set to a dignified ragtime trot with a more elaborate chord sequence than the three's-me-absolute-top-whack favoured by the rural guys. Bertha 'Chippie' Hill (1905–1950) strikes real sparks off Louis Armstrong's cornet on 'Pratt City Blues' (1926), or maybe he's striking sparks off her. Hill's performance is plain but immensely stirring; Armstrong dances around her with a fluency that would be almost insolent if it wasn't so blatantly good-humoured. It's almost as if he's trying to cheer her up. And then the sequence ends with a chunk of unreconstructed black vaudeville: Butterbeans & Susie's 'What It Takes To Bring You Back (Mama Keeps It All The Time)' (1930) is so theatrical you can smell the velvet curtains, and you just _know_ they got an encore.

Oliver resumes his story on the second disc, under the rubric of 'The Thirties: Urban And Rural Blues.' Right on that urban/rural cusp are the immensely popular duo LEROY CARR (1905–1935) & SCRAPPER BLACKWELL (1903–1962); their instrumentation (singing pianist accompanied by acoustic guitar) would not have been unusual in the country, but the smooth precision of their playing (especially Blackwell's stinging, immaculately phrased guitar) and Carr's crisp enunciation betrayed their city sophistication. 'Midnight Hour Blues' (1932) is a fair indication of their powers, and also of the way in which urban variants of rural styles trickled back to the country via records. 'East St Louis Blues' (1940) is significant less for Faber Smith's indifferent singing than the pianistics of boogie maestro Jimmy Yancey (1898–1951), while 'Good Whiskey Blues' (1935) is a comparatively mild example of the work of PEETIE WHEATSTRAW (1902–1941), the singer/pianist who called himself 'The Devil's Son-In-Law' or 'The High Sheriff Of Hell', and whose deadpan, homicidal songs were the '30s blues equivalent of modern 'gangsta rap'. He was reputedly an influence on singer/guitarist Casey Bill Weldon (1909-?), a former member of the Memphis Jug Band and one of Memphis Minnie's three ex-husbands, whose 'WPA Blues' (1936) indicates a profound scepticism towards FDR's New Deal. Oliver then leads us back to the Delta to meet Bo Carter (1893-1964), a member of the distinguished Chatmon family that dominated the Mississippi Sheiks. Chatmon's primary stock-in-trade was the double-entendre, but 'Sorry Feeling Blues' (1931) is a mournful ballad with deftly fingerpicked guitar and a delightful solo break.

The next two Delta bluesmen provide an instructive study in contrast: Robert Johnson (1911-1938) was the definitive Delta modernist, whose high, chilling voice, epigrammatic lyrics, funky syncopation and endless repertoire of fill-in guitar phrases have gained him authentically legendary status a half-century and more after his death and would undoubtedly have taken him far into the postwar era if he had lived significantly longer. 'Little Queen Of Spades' (1937) is far from being one of his masterpieces, but it demonstrates the artistic distance that already lay between him and an old-school Delta player like Booker T. Washington 'BUKKA' WHITE (1906-1977), only five years his senior but still, as 'Parchman Farm Blues' (1940) indicates, firmly adhering to the unreconstructed Charley Patton tradition. And we ride out with Memphis Minnie herself (1907-1973), picking guitar alongside her third husband Little Son Joe on her jaunty 'Me And My Chauffeur Blues' (1941), a perennial coffeehouse favourite during the folk boom.

Finally, we reach 'World War II And After' and historicity flies out the window, since the period between 1947 and 1963 is entirely unrepresented, and 'Roll 'Em Pete', the dazzling piano/vocal duet between (BIG) JOE TURNER and Pete Johnson, actually dates from 1938 and has absolutely nothing to do with postwar blues, except in the minds of nostalgic jazz critics. Never mind: the sequence is great fun to listen to, and by no means unenlightening. The first pair of songs introduces us to the longest-serving duo in folk blues, albeit not together. The popular finger-picking double-entendre merchant BLIND BOY FULLER (1908-1941) is represented by the mildly naughty 'I Want Some Of Your Pie' (1939), which features the extraordinary harmonica of SONNY TERRY

(1911–1986). After Fuller's death, Terry found a new partner, BROWNIE McGHEE (1915–), who had just had a hit of such major proportions with a song called 'The Death Of Blind Boy Fuller', that an unscrupulous promotor had actually sent him out on the road as 'Blind Boy Fuller No. 2'. McGhee is next up with the rather less impressive harmonica of Jordan Webb in support, on 'Millions Of Women' (1941), but the combination of Terry's big-toned harp and McGhee's neatly fingerpicked guitar was the sound that gave the duo a thirty-year career as a top attraction.

We're outta here on a couple of snapshots of different stages in the development of Chicago blues. Two of the most popular teams of the '40s are represented: 'Wild Cow Moan' (1947) juxtaposes the guitar and voice of BIG JOE WILLIAMS (1903–1982) and the thrilling harp of the original SONNY BOY WILLIAMSON (1914–1948) against a powerful bass-and-drum support which prefigures the sound of the Muddy Waters bands of the 1950s (indeed, Ransom Knowling, the bassist on this session, later played with the Waters band); while BIG BILL BROONZY (1893–1958) carols the raggy 'All By Myself' against Knowling's bass and the mighty piano of MEMPHIS SLIM (1915–1988). With a dizzying shift of time and space, it suddenly becomes 1968, but as Otis Spann sings the mournful slow blues 'Bloody Murder' to the sound of the piano that powered his half-brother Muddy Waters' various bands for almost twenty years, the only discernible sonic shift in the twenty-year leap is textural: the quality of the recorded drum sound, and the amplified harp blown by 'BIG' WALTER HORTON (1917–1981).

The sequence – indeed, the entire package – closes with another 1968 slow blues, 'I Don't Know', from Robert Johnson's old friend Johnny Shines, who is in devastatingly good voice and picks an unabashedly country-style blues on his modestly amplified electric guitar. However, on the penultimate selection, we finally get to hear an electric guitar – the instrument which has dominated the blues since the late '40s – used in anger; and in the hands of the raw-throated slidemeister Elmore James, it's electric in more than a merely literal sense. James brings his customary ragged incandescence to 'Sunnyland' (1963), a stomping, uptempo shuffle which is the only concession that _The Story Of The Blues_ makes to the way that blues has actually sounded since mass-produced electric guitars and amplifiers became affordable.

7

Subjects for further investigation: A second double, *The Story Of The Blues Vol 2*, has yet to appear on CD. A subsequent Oliver book/album project, *Savannah Syncopators: African Retentions In The Blues*, added both breadth and depth to our knowledge of the prehistory of the blues, but both are, sadly, currently unavailable in any form.

Now read on.

1. Pre-Blues

Our knowledge of what the blues was like before 1920, when the music was first recorded, is by definition anecdotal. We have written accounts (like W.C. Handy's tale of hearing a Mississippi guitarist playing slide with a knife in 1902); and we have lyrics and music, albeit transcribed by whites who may not have appreciated the finer points, cultural and musical, of what they were hearing. There were the blues hits which circulated via sheet music (Handy, again: his 'St Louis Blues was published in 1914), and there are the commercial recordings of older musicians whose style and repertoire were fixed in the late 19th century; but our most reliable source is the astonishing collection of recordings made for the Library Of Congress by John Lomax and, particularly, his son Alan. Recording singers who were too obscure or too old-fashioned for (or those who, like SON HOUSE and MISSISSIPPI JOHN HURT, had only had the surface of their repertoires skimmed by) the commercial companies, Alan Lomax went into the fields and the prisons in search of the real folk music of which, he firmly maintained, the commercial blues of the era was merely a caricature.

And, it must be said, he found it. The number of times that the Lomax name will surface during the first section of this book is no coincidence: it is almost entirely due to the pioneering work of the Lomaxes (*pere* as well as *fils*) that we understand as much about this music, and the lives and history of the people who made it, as we do. Their use of the folk-music convention of appending the collector's composer credit to work songs and field hollers, some of which date back to the nineteenth century and beyond, would have been uncomfortably close to the similar practice of record company bosses in the commercial sector (which remained widespread, as many aggrieved bluesmen have readily testified, well into the '60s) if there was even a shred of evidence that they did so for personal gain. (It has been pointed out that the Lomaxes copyrighted the songs of, among others, Leadbelly primarily to prevent others doing so.) Nevertheless, the bourgeois pur(ita-n)ism which leads Lomax A. to dismiss most commercial (and all electric) blues as the work of sell-outs is cultural myopia: distinctions between 'folk', 'commercial' and 'art' music are more profoundly blurred in the blues than in just about any other 20th century art form. Throughout the recorded history of the blues, much folk art now deemed invaluable was preserved for us only because somebody considered it commercially viable to do so. The 'folkists', on the other hand, captured material for which the commercial companies had no apparent use, and the extended length and comparative informality of many Library of Congress performances provide an invaluable account of how the music sounded when it was at home. The fruits of both philosophies thus combine to create a far richer, deeper picture of musicians and audiences alike, and the lives they led, than either could have done alone: it's as powerful an argument in favour of a mixed artistic economy as anything I can call to mind.

Nevertheless, Lomax's denunciation of the blues made for the market is a profound insult to both artist and audience. It demeans the artists by suggesting that they somehow betrayed their culture by seeking a route out of the limitations imposed by a corrupt and racist system which wanted them to stay poor and to aspire to nothing further than the backsides of their mules. And it insults the audiences by denying their emotional response to music which entertained and uplifted them by celebrating both the sorrows and the pleasures of their lives. Presumably Alan Lomax would have had more regard for a big-selling, money-spending blues star like BLIND LEMON JEFFERSON if he had remained a poverty-stricken street singer, known only to his local community, until his dying day.

- **VARIOUS ARTISTS:** *Roots Of The Blues* (New Note 80252-2)
- **VARIOUS ARTISTS:** *Murderers' Home* (Sequel NEXCD 121)
- **MEMPHIS SLIM, BIG BILL BROONZY & SONNY BOY WILLIAMSON:** *Blues In The Mississippi Night* (Sequel NEXCD 122 or Rykodisc RCD 90155)

Three Alan Lomax projects which approach the same subject from three different directions. *Murderers' Home*, recorded in 1947 at the dreaded Mississippi state penitentiary known as Parchman Farm (its alumni include SON HOUSE and 'BUKKA' WHITE), is a collection of chain-gang chants, work songs, field hollers and ballads, and it contains some of the richest and most deeply affecting vocal music you can find anywhere on record. (One of the reasons Lomax recorded in prisons was that longterm inmates had not recently been exposed to the corruptions of popular music.) *Blues In The Mississippi Night*, which dates from around the same time, is a paradox: an ethnological forgery which tells the truth. Lomax invited BIG BILL BROONZY, MEMPHIS SLIM and John Lee (the original SONNY BOY) WILLIAMSON to spend an afternoon in a New York studio talking openly about black life in the South, alternating their reminiscences with performances and spliced-in snatches of field recordings. The three bluesmen were so terrified by what they'd recorded that they insisted that Lomax remove their names from the issued product: their fears were not so much for their own safety as for that of family members still down South. It is only now that all three of them are dead that Lomax has felt free to restore their names to what is, by any relevant criteria, an awesome document.

Roots Of The Blues re-presents some of the *Murderers' Home* field recordings alongside some church music and recordings from Senegal, juxtaposed with country blues performances, mostly by MISSISSIPPI FRED McDOWELL. Again, it's fascinating both as music and as history – particularly the kind of historical baggage which modern white listeners can avoid bringing to the blues, but which African-American listeners (of any age) cannot – but Lomax loads his dice by selecting a mediocre electric blues by an undistinguished performer, Forest City Joe, as standard-bearer for an entire genre, and then launching into an extraordinary liner-note diatribe against contemporary blues. The commercial blues market, he writes, 'grew and prospered by teaching its mild-mannered country protagonists to cheapen themselves with gimmicks, insincere effects, poor arrangements and silly subject matter . . . the blues might have flowered so much more fully and richly if these men had not been forced to market themselves.' Yeah, right . . . they should have just stayed on the farm and waited for Massa Lomax to record all their songs and buy them a Coca-Cola for their trouble. 'Mild-mannered' these men might have been, especially around influential white people, but they certainly weren't dumb.

- **HENRY THOMAS:** *Texas Worried Blues: Complete Recorded Works 1927–1929* (Yazoo 1080/1)

Henry 'Ragtime Texas' Thomas was probably the oldest black musician ever to record. He was born sometime in 1874 in Big Sandy, Texas (no-one knows exactly where or when he died, but it's probably safe to assume he's not around any more), and was well into his fifties by the time of his first recording. By all accounts, his style and repertoire were fixed by the 1890s; a decade or so before the emergence of blues as a recognisable form (which is why the few formal blues tunes collected here were probably acquired later); and therefore his work provides unparalleled insight into the repertoire which might have been performed by an itinerant songster of the late 19th century. Thomas' 'Red River Blues' is an ancestor of ROBERT JOHNSON's 'Last Fair Deal Gone Down', which is why you can also find it on *The Roots Of Robert Johnson* (Yazoo 1073). The rock-oriented listener will undoubtedly recognise his 'Bull Doze Blues' as a direct forerunner, panpipes and all, of CANNED HEAT's 1968 hit 'Goin' Up The Country'; and Bob Dylan's second album (*The Freewheelin' Bob Dylan*, Columbia, 1962) included a version of Thomas' 'Honey Just Allow Me One More Chance', which Dylan speeded up from its relatively stately pace to a hectic sprint more characteristic of some of the other Thomas pieces included here.

Historians are divided as to whether Thomas' repertoire implies that he was more used to performing for white audiences than black, or simply that the distinctively African-American style which we call the blues was not yet codified during Thomas' musically formative years. In any case, Henry Thomas' music was not so much blues as a partial cross-section of the raw materials from which the blues was built. The music of the songster tradition, of which Thomas was the first recorded representative, drew on ballads, rags and hymns: 'set pieces', in other words. When Thomas learned his stuff, these songs had yet to fuse with the field hollers and work songs to create the 20th century African-American music we call the blues.

2. 'Classic' Blues

It is commonly agreed that the first identifiable 'blues' record was Mamie Smith's 1920 recording 'Crazy Blues', though by all accounts the song owed more to vaudeville than to blues, and its 'bluesiness' had more to do with the fact that Mamie Smith was audibly African-American than with any innate qualities of the song itself. Neverthless, its extremely healthy sales sparked off a boom in the recording of identifiably black artists, and launched the era of what has become known in retrospect as 'classic' blues, though – like much of the resulting music which followed – it had considerably more to do with early jazz and black vaudeville pop than it did to the rural blues (hence the inverted commas). To recap: 'classic' blues singers were generally women who – unlike almost all of their male counterparts – rarely played instruments; were accompanied principally by pianists and brass and reed players; and performed in urban theatres and cabarets, and touring vaudeville productions and tent shows. The heyday opf the 'classic blues' lasted all through the '20s, petering out in the early '30s, at the onset of the Depression. It was the first, last and only style of blues to be dominated by female performers: subsequent notables like MEMPHIS MINNIE, BIG MAMA THORNTON, ETTA JAMES and KOKO TAYLOR have been glorious but rare exceptions to the unwritten but widely observed rule that blues is men's business. The pop successes of JANIS JOPLIN and BONNIE RAITT have occasioned re-evaluations of this music: among contemporary performers, though only DANA GILLESPIE and SAFFIRE – THE UPPITY BLUESWOMEN have concentrated primarily on reworking and updating the 'classic' blues. *Antone's Women* (Antone's ANT 9902), featuring the likes of LOU ANN BARTON and SUE FOLEY, is the only extant compilation which specifically focusses on contemporary blueswomen.

By far the best-known, best-loved and best-remembered – in fact, the best by a mile, *period* – of the 'classic' blues singers was BESSIE SMITH, which is why she is also by far the best-represented on record. Many of her peers have fared less well, since this music is currently not particularly fashionable; which is why you can't find entire albums dedicated to their work and will therefore have to make do with compilations, many of which focus on the more ribald aspects of the music and also feature performances by the male rural singers of the era. It's an unsatisfactory state of affairs: I would love to be able to recommend definitive anthologies of the work of Sippie Wallace, Alberta Hunter, Bertha 'Chippie' Hill, Victoria Spivey or Ida Cox – hell, I would love to *own* such compilations – but as of right now there aren't any. It's therefore necessary to examine some of the greatest hits of that most legendary of blues performers, Various Artists. Apart from . . .

- **LOUIS ARMSTRONG:** *The Complete Recordings Of Louis Armstrong And The Great Blues Singers 1924–1930* (Affinity CD AFS 1018-6)

If we're going to explore the first great wave of urban blues recording, it might as well be with the first great jazz soloist of the century as our guide, though the privilege admittedly doesn't come cheap. During the second half of the '20s – before he became a star, a genius or the world's teddy-bear, and was simply a brilliant young trumpeter/cornetist on the way up – Armstrong supplemented an already busy musical schedule (including the epochal 'Hot Five' dates) by lending his golden horn to hundreds of blues sessions, first in New York City and later in Chicago. This brick-like 6-CD set collects 120 such sides, but please be aware that those responsible take the word 'complete' very literally: there are enough back-to-back alternate takes to have unwary listeners wondering if there's an echo in here. Armstrong worked with the front rank of 'classic' blues singers – BESSIE SMITH, MA RAINEY, Alberta Hunter, Sippie Wallace and Victoria Spivey – as well as with lesser names like Bertha 'Chippie' Hill, Butterbeans & Susie, Trixie Smith, Blanche Calloway (CAB CALLOWAY's sister) and

Margaret Johnson (LONNIE JOHNSON's wife); plus (the ringer!) country music legend and white-blues pioneer Jimmie 'The Singing Brakeman' Rodgers. (Any white guy who was singing blues in 1929 is my kind of country singer.) The difference between the great and the merely competent is underlined by the cruel juxtaposition of one Virginia Liston singing 'Everybody Loves My Baby' with the wonderful Alberta Hunter performing the same song with almost the same band.

Armstrong is, in many ways, an ideal accompanist: he knows that all the singers he was hired to back were not created equal. When a performance is strong enough to require minimal embellishment, he lays back; when a singer needs support, he's right there with just as little or as much as is necessary; and when the featured artist is truly dull, he pulls out an ear-catching flourish or two to prevent the track from dying the complete death. When Bessie Smith makes her entry, halfway through Disc 2, with a thoroughly imperious 'St Louis Blues' complete with eerie harmonium accompaniment, she turns everyone who preceded her – even the formidable likes of Hunter, Rainey and Wallace – into opening acts. It would have been an easier option for the collection to concentrate on the bigger stars and more durable names – certainly it would have made for a cheaper and more digestible package – but this way you get a real sense of the overall flavour of the era and the genre, as well as a clear understanding of exactly what qualities differentiated the real stars from the journey(wo)men. Most politically incorrect lyric: Trixie Smith's 'You've Got To Beat Me To Keep Me'.

- **Ladies Sing The Blues** (Living Era CD AJA 5092)

A superb budget-price anthology from a company I've never heard of, featuring many leading lights in fine form and distinguished company. Ida Cox's two contributions feature Charlie Christian on guitar and Lionel Hampton on drums, Mildred Bailey has the benefit of the great Johnny Hodges on alto sax, Adelaide Hall shows up with most of the Duke Ellington Orchestra including the great man himself, and Louis Armstrong blows a dazzling obbligato to that fabulous BESSIE SMITH version of 'St Louis Blues'. But naturally it's the singers who rule: Billie Holiday is especially welcome on two tracks where Lady really *does* sing the blues; Sippie Wallace leaves no doubt as to her opinion of her own erotic prowess on 'I'm A Mighty Tight Woman', and Lillian Glinn, Clara Smith, Ada Brown, Victoria Spivey (with the oft-anthologised 'Moaning The Blues'), MA RAINEY, Mamie Smith and others are all in full effect. At £8.99, this is a steal.

- *Better Boot That Thing: Great Women Blues Singers Of The 1920's* (RCA Bluebird 07863 66065 2)

Five tracks each by two major vocalists and two interesting minor ones: Alberta Hunter and Victoria Spivey were sophisticated city singers whose careers lasted well into old age, while Bessie Tucker and Ida May Mack were rural Texans about whom very little is known. Hunter (1895–1984) was born in Memphis, but ran away to Chicago at the age of 11; she became a major local attraction, performing alongside Louis Armstrong, and cut her first record as early as 1921. She was also a songwriter to be reckoned with: Bessie Smith's first-ever recording, 'Down Hearted Blues' (1923) was a cover of a Hunter original. Graduating to supperclubs and theatres, she was an international star (starring opposite Paul Robeson in the London production of *Showboat*, entertaining troops during World War II) until her retirement in 1957. After working as a nurse for twenty years, she was forced to retire when the hospital thought that she had reached the age of 70, though in fact she was 82. Coaxed back into performance, she played the Carter White House, wrote her autobiography and was lionised all over again. These 1927 tracks demonstrate Hunter's range: 'Sugar' is a straightforward sentimental pop song accompanied by the great Fats Waller on the organ, while the others are classic 'classic' blues.

Spivey's speciality was elaborate raunch: what else could we expect from a woman who originated the 'Black Snake Blues' (as customised by BLIND LEMON JEFFERSON, who learned the song from her in Houston, and JOHN LEE HOOKER) and was fond of performing it in a dress festooned with rubber snakes? Spivey (1906–1976) was born in Texas but launched her recording career in St Louis, achieving sufficient notoriety to become a popular touring attraction, record duets with Louis Armstrong and LONNIE JOHN-SON, and appear in King Vidor's 1929 musical *Hallelujah*. She retired to New York in 1951, but ten years later she started up her own record label, calling in young performers like Bob Dylan and JOHN HAMMOND to appear alongside well-known blues stars like BIG JOE WILLIAMS and WILLIE DIXON. She's represented here by a fistful of 1929–30 sides, including 'Dirty Tee Bee Blues', 'Telephoning The Blues' and 'Moaning The Blues', all of which showcase her flexible, piercing voice and wicked lyrics. Mack and Tucker cut their sides at the same 1928 Memphis session, and both are accompanied by the same pianist, one K.D. Johnson: my personal pick from that date is Tucker's rollicking title track, complete with emphatic oompah bass-line played on a tuba.

Subjects for further investigation: Spivey's original 'Black Snake Blues' appears on *Sissy Man Blues: 25 Authentic Straight & Gay Jazz & Blues Vocals* (Jass J-CD-13); this collection also includes Sippie Wallace's 'I'm A Mighty Tight Woman', and the first half of the two-part Victoria Spivey/Lonnie Johnson duet 'Toothache Blues', which can be found in its entirety on Johnson's *Steppin' On The Blues* (CBS 467252 2). Look for another two-part Spivey/Johnson duet, 'Furniture Man Blues', on *Raunchy Business: Hot Nuts & Lollipops* (Columbia 467889 2), and the uncompromising 'Dope Head Blues' on *News And The Blues: Telling It Like It Is* (CBS 467249 2). Hunter was herself no slouch at dropping a double-entendre, as proven on 'You Can't Tell The Difference After Dark', from *The Copulatin' Blues Compact Disc* (Jass J-CD-1), but the lyric's seeming apology for its protagonist's colour is deeply dispiriting. Sippie Wallace's autumnal revival is documented on *American Folk Blues Festival '66* (L&R/Bellaphon CDLR 42069); her '70s collaborations with BONNIE RAITT on *The Bonnie Raitt Collection* (Warner Bros 7599-26242-2).

- *Jazz Classics In Digital Stereo: The Blues 1923–1933* (BBC CD 683 [deleted])

Sad to say, this excellent collection – derived from a BBC radio series featuring Australian engineer Robert Parker's brilliant sonic cleanups of vintage 78s – is currently out of print, but if you ever see a copy around anywhere, snap it up. Featuring items by Ida Cox, Cleo Gibson, Rosa Henderson, Frances Hereford, MA RAINEY, BESSIE SMITH, Mamie Smith (not the historic 'Crazy Blues', unfortunately), Victoria Spivey (the same 'Moaning The Blues' as on the Bluebird collection reviewed above), Eva Taylor and Ethel Waters – as well as a fine contribution from the Memphis Jug Band, and another go-round for Jimmie Rodgers' epochal collaboration with Louis and Lil Armstrong on 'Blue Yodel No. 9' – it's an admirable introduction to the period.

- *Raunchy Business: Hot Nuts & Lollipops* (Columbia 467889 2)
- *The Copulatin' Blues Compact Disc* (Jass J-CD-1).
- *Sissy Man Blues: 25 Authentic Straight & Gay Jazz & Blues Vocals* (Jass J-CD-13)
- *Street Walkin' Blues: 25 Plaintive Paeans To The World's Oldest Profession 1924–1956* (Jass J-CD-626)
- *Them Dirty Blues* (Jass CD-11/12)

As the titles may suggest, the primary *raison d'être* of these collections is to document – and celebrate – treatments of sexuality in early blues (taking in work from artists rural as well as urban, and male as well as female) rather than to illustrate any specific style, but they nevertheless represent rich treasure trove for the seeker after some of the finest moments of the lesser-known early blueswomen (and some guys, too). The collective cast of characters includes MA RAINEY, Victoria Spivey, Bertha 'Chippie' Hill, Lil Johnson, Lucille Bogan, Ethel Waters, MEMPHIS MINNIE, Alberta Hunter, Blanche Calloway and Clara Smith: among the male participants are LONNIE JOHNSON, Bo Carter, TAMPA RED (featuring legendary female impersonator Frankie 'Half-Pint' Jaxon), CAB CALLOWAY, Jelly Roll Morton, The Mississippi Sheiks, Washboard Sam, Josh(ua) White and Jimmy Rushing. There's a considerable amount of overlap between these records, and the remorseless flow of double-entendres can get wearing if you try and listen to too much of this stuff at one sitting, but they're all both great blues and good fun. Start with *Raunchy Business:* and, if you want more copulatin', you can safely pick any of the Jass issues. They're the absolute duck's yas yas.

Subjects for further investigation: For years, Lucille Bogan was a legend among jazz fans on the strength of one 1935 performance which was never even released at the time. Her 'Shave 'Em Dry Pt 2', an incredibly filthy version of a well-known and already reasonably filthy song originally recorded in 1924 by Ma Rainey, was found on a test pressing and circulated for years on the collectors' market before it was finally issued to the general public. Born in Amory, Mississippi, on April 1, 1897, she was raised in Birmingham, Alabama, and made her earliest records in 1923, cutting for Okeh in New York City and Chicago, where she moved in the late '20s, returning to Birmingham in the mid-'30s. Usually accompanied after 1929 by pianist Walter Roland, she recorded both under her own name and as Bessie Jackson – it was 'Bessie' who was responsible for the notorious 'Shave 'Em Dry' – dying on August 10, 1948, in Los Angeles, where she had just moved with her new 29-year-old husband. *Lucille Bogan 1923–1935* (Story Of Blues CD 3535-2) and *Lucille Bogan & Walter Roland 1927–1935* (Yazoo 1017) collect a fair sampling of her work: I've no idea what Lucille Bogan did for a living when she wasn't earning her keep as a vocalist, but her primary source of subject-matter was prostitution. The Yazoo issue gives plenty of prominence to Roland, who was not only Bogan's studio accompanist, but a formidable performer in his right, singing and playing guitar as well as in his more familiar position at the 88s. Another high priestess of Classic Blues raunch was Lil Johnson: her history is obscure way beyond my humble powers of research. All that is reliably known is that she was a popular Chicago-based cabaret singer in the late '20s and enjoyed some recording success in the mid-'30s; and that the (almost) compleat Lil Johnson is found on *Hottest Gal In Town 1936–1937* (Story Of Blues CD 3513-2). Her variant on 'Shave 'Em Dry', more or less contemporary with Lucille Bogan's, can be found on *Street Walkin' Blues: 25 Plaintive Paeans To The World's Oldest Profession 1924–1956* (Jass J-CD-626). Four songs, three of them also available on *Hottest Gal In Town 1936–1937*, recur on *Raunchy Business: Hot Nuts & Lollipops* (Columbia 467889 2); the fourth is another variation on 'Get 'Em From The Peanut Man'. Two more, 'Press My Button, Ring My Bell' and 'You Stole My Cherry', are on *The Copulatin' Blues Compact Disc* (Jass J-CD-1) alongside *Hottest Gal*'s 'Stavin' Chain'. *Sissy Man Blues: 25 Authentic Straight & Gay Jazz & Blues Vocals* (Jass J-CD-13) is your port of call for 'Take Your Hand Off It'. For still more Lil, consult *Them Dirty Blues* (Jass CD-11/12).

Ma Rainey

Gertrude Pridgett, alias Ma Rainey, cut her first record in 1923 – the same year in which BESSIE SMITH made *her* debut – but they were by no means contemporaries. Billed as 'The Mother Of The Blues', Rainey was the elder (by some eight years), the more experienced and the better established, and had indeed worked alongside – if not actually tutored – the younger singer in more than one revue. Born in Columbus, Georgia, on 26 April, 1886, Gertrude was already performing in local talent shows by 1900, and singing blues by 1902. In 1904 she met her future husband, song-and-dance man and comedian William 'Pa' Rainey, and over the next dozen years they worked their way up the professional ladder to headlining status. Unlike many of her competitors who were essentially shake-dancing glamour girls, Ma Rainey – a short, dumpy woman with a gold tooth, plenty chins and a fondness for elaborate jewellery – made it on sheer personality and vocal ability, which gave her a massive advantage in the recording studio, where the ability to perform a stunning belly-dance counts for little. The ability to deliver a lyric in a clear, strong voice with a distinct individual personality, on the other hand, counted for a lot.

Rainey could sing the pop vaudeville of the time – indeed, she could sing virtually anything – but she was also thoroughly grounded in more downhome blues, and had the kind of rich, solid voice which could do that material justice. Professional to her toenails, she made a lot of money, but – unlike far too many other blues performers – she managed to hold onto most of it, and when her career faded in 1928 she was able to retire in comparative comfort and devote herself primarily to the church until her death on 22 December, 1939.

- *Ma Rainey's Black Bottom* (Yazoo 1071)

Ma Rainey cut something like 100 sides during her five-year recording career: this set, combined with the Rainey tracks on *The Complete Recordings Of Louis Armstrong And The Great Blues Singers 1924–1930*, gives you about a fifth of the total. The contexts range from the small jazz-band style most readily associated with the genre to more rural guitar backings and contributions from the guitar/piano duo of TAMPA RED & Georgia Tom, which emphasises her blend of authentic country-blues stylings and the pop and vaudeville touches popular at the time. This collection concentrates almost exclusively on blues material: her version of 'Stack O'Lee Blues' has more to do with 'Frankie & Johnny' than to the better-known variations ('Stagolee', 'Stagger Lee' et al) popularised by MISSISSIPPI JOHN HURT in the late '20s or Lloyd Price twenty or so years later. The CD's title, incidentally, derives from that of one of the songs, itself in turn named after a popular dance of the 1920s. Y'all should be ashamed of yourselves!

Subjects for further investigation: Another of Rainey's protèges was Mae Glover, known as 'Memphis Ma Rainey' or 'Ma Rainey II': a sample of her work under her own name, combined with a few titles by Lillian Glinn, can be found on *Lillian Glinn/Mae Glover 1929-1931* (Story Of Blues CD 3537 2). MEMPHIS MINNIE's 1940 tribute, 'Ma Rainey' is on *News And The Blues: Telling It Like It Is* (Columbia Legacy 467249 2)

Bessie Smith

More than a half-century after the fact, the towering figure of The Empress Of The Blues dominates our notion of the 'classic' blues just as ROBERT JOHNSON does contemporary perceptions of the Mississippi Delta blues of the '30s. The difference is that, in her case, she didn't have to wait for posterity to acknowledge her status. Johnson only had one regional hit ('Terraplane Blues') during his brief recording career, but Smith was a major star from the moment her first record 'Down Hearted Blues' went on sale in 1923. At the peak of her popularity she was the highest-paid black entertainer in America, the darling of '20s cafe society, and a figurehead of the Harlem Renaissance; her 45-strong troupe even travelled in Smith's very own 78-foot Pullman car. Like Johnson, she was blessed with the kind of vocal presence and authority of which lesser performers, however gifted, can only dream. It is not simply the size of the voice to which we respond, hugely miraculous though that voice indeed was, but the size of the personality which speaks through the voice: what attracts us is the music, but what transfixes us is Smith herself. She did not so much sings songs as inhabit them or wear them: W.C. Handy's celebrated 'St Louis Blues' will always be her personal property. So will "Tain't Nobody's Biz-ness If I Do' and, most poignant of all, 'Nobody Knows You When You're Down And Out', a song which she recorded in 1929, just as the popularity which had cushioned her against the initial effects of the Depression began to peter out.

Like Johnson, she had her myth: a big tough woman, fiercely proud of her race and gender, bisexually promiscuous and a notoriously heavy drinker, who took zero crap from anybody – black or white, male or female – and would cuss out or punch out anyone who offended her. (The sole exception was her husband and 'manager', Jack Gee, who was the only person capable of intimidating her one-on-one.) On one celebrated occasion, she outfaced half a dozen robed-and-hooded Ku Klux Klansmen who attempted to disrupt her tent show during her 1927 'Harlem Frolics' tour. She accepted the plaudits of wealthy, 'progressive' white admirers whilst making no concessions whatever to them; and she died a victim of the same racism from which she had never cowered, bleeding to death on a Mississippi roadside after a car crash because a white hospital would not consent to treat her.

And unlike Johnson, most of her myth is the actual, as well as symbolic, truth. The part that isn't is the legend of her death: at the time, no ambulance driver, black or white, would have even considered attempting to take her to a white hospital in segregated Clarksdale. Moreover, since the white and black hospitals were less than half a mile apart, there would have been no point in doing so even if the white hospital had had significantly better equipment than its black counterpart, which it hadn't. The doctor who was first on the scene opined, almost forty years later, that even if the ambulance had arrived promptly (which it hadn't), and even if either one of Clarksdale's hospitals had had access to contemporary medical facilities, her chances of survival would still have been no better than 50/50. It is therefore a matter of symbolism: if no African-American's life is unaffected by racism, how can their deaths be any different?

The real Bessie Smith – 'Bessie' was not a contraction of 'Elizabeth', but her actual Christian name – was born in Chatanooga, Tennessee, on 15 April, 1894. Orphaned at seven, she street-sang to her brother Albert's guitar accompaniment, but it was another brother, dancer Clarence, who was the first family member to make inroads into showbiz. He scored her an audition as a singer and dancer in the chorus of a couple of revues which also included MA RAINEY, but she was eventually fired because her complexion was considered too dark for a show whose motto was 'Glorifying The Brownskin Girl'. She did considerably better as a featured vocalist, and by the time open recording season on blueswomen was declared in 1923, she was already a popular in-person attraction in the South and the eastern seaboard. After a couple of false starts with producers who considered her 'too rough', Columbia released her first record, 'Down Hearted Blues'/ Gulf Coast Blues': it sold 750,000 copies. It also laid the first foundation-stone of one of the major creative achievements in the history of the blues, and one of the most spectacular successes of pre-war African-American showbiz. Almost incidentally, it also helped to establish one of the most recognisable labels in the Anmerican record industry.

Bessie Smith must have been something to see in her prime: some of her more elaborate outfits weighed as much as 50lb, and her spectacular revues – which had names like 'Harlem Frolics', 'Steamboat Days' and 'Midnight Steppers' – were constructed to showcase her as a dancer and comedienne, as well as the vocalist we know from her records. She hired the best dancers, comics and musicians she could find; her records sold like wildfire; her shows were always packed. For almost seven years – until her career began to falter and she and Jack Gee were divorced – they barnstormed their troupe around America, leaving a trail of empty bottles, wrecked hotel rooms and dressing rooms, bruised bimbos (of both sexes), colossal expenditures and delirious audiences in their wake. Quite like rock and roll, really.

Even with the onset of the Depression and the resulting fall in the general level of record sales, her singles remained among the most popular; and since Columbia wasn't in the habit of paying royalties, a slump in sales didn't worry her. A slump in show tickets, however, did – and a disastrous Broadway debut, in a production which even her presence could not dignify, didn't help either. She accepted more and more outside work, eventually even abandoning her traditional stipulation that she should always be the only blues singer on the bill. She was considered an old-timer, left over from a bygone era; her recording sessions were ever fewer and further between, and there is a certain grim symmetry in the fact that, three days after Bessie Smith's last session in 1933, the same studio and microphone were used for Billie Holiday's first. She was only forty and in no mood to quit, so she made strenuous attempts to update her music; by all accounts, these were well-received, especially a crucial date where she was a last-minute substitute for Holiday and took over the house. She adopted new costumes and dance steps, overhauled her repertoire, and worked with more swing-oriented musicians: the New York press hailed her for the 'comeback' she had managed without ever really being away, and fresh recordings, this time in her new contemporary style, were planned. And then, on the rainy night of 25 September, 1937, her chauffeur-driven car ploughed into the back of a parked but unlit truck ten miles out of Clarksdale. She died in hospital the following morning.

In 1938, the year after her death, Columbia began to reissue Bessie Smith's old records, the ones that had helped build the company a decade and a half before. Columbia is now been subsumed into the Sony *zaibatsu*, and Bessie Smith's records are still on sale. Like it says on the tombstone that her young admirer JANIS JOPLIN helped to buy, 'The Greatest Blues Singer In The World Will Never Stop Singing.'

- *The Complete Recordings Vol 1* (Columbia Legacy COL 467895 2)
- *The Complete Recordings Vol 2* (Columbia Legacy COL 468767 2)

Bessie Smith recorded consistently between 1923 and 1933, cutting some 160 complete sides over the full decade. The last complete reissue was a series of five vinyl double-albums released in the early '70s, which were – rather curiously – structured on the assumption that, since everybody used autochange turntables and ultimately wished to be able to listen to the complete works in chronological order, the best idea was to put Bessie's earliest and last recordings onto the first double-album and then continue the series by tunnelling towards her middle years simultaneously from both ends. This CD edition, rather more rationally, presents the complete, chronological Smith on a projected series of four 2-CD sets; the first two of which are already available, the third is about to be released as we go to press, and the fourth and last will be along, as they say, *real soon now*.

This is essentially a collector's approach, aimed at serious buffs who want the absolute full monty; and it means that anyone who wants Smith's greatest sides – which are spread across all the various phases of her career – is going to have to fork out out for all eight CDs. This is fine for me, because (a) I'm a fan, and (b) I get this stuff free, but it's bad news for the citizen who simply wants to find out if the Empress Of The Blues truly lives up to her billing, and to hear the most celebrated works from her ten recorded years. This approach worked fine for Robert Johnson, whose complete recorded catalogue consists of 29 songs and a dozen alternate takes and therefore fits neatly into a single package, but it's inappropriate for an artist as prolific as Smith. The current situation is frustrating because each set contains brilliant and less brilliant work: hopefully, by the time Columbia have completed their reissue of the *Complete Recordings* series, they might consider putting out a less intimidating one- or two-CD best-of StarterPak for civilians with finite disposable incomes.

That said, each of these sets admirably fulfils its brief: the remastering is state-of-the-art; the design is immaculate, and Chris Albertson's extensive liner notes are virtually a condensed, updated version of his definitive Smith biography, *Bessie: Empress Of The Blues*. The first volume takes us from February 1923 to April of 1924, where the second takes over to carry us onwards to November 1925, by which time the old horn-and-stylus method of recording had been replaced by 'electrical recording' (i.e. involving the use of a microphone) with a corresponding leap in fidelity. Those early sides are notable both for their starkness – Smith's first couple of dozen titles involved no accompaniment more elaborate than solo piano – and for the revelation that Smith's powers were already in full effect by the time she began recording. She'd been singing for years before she ever walked into a studio, and she was already 'Bessie Smith' from the first track of the first disk. Naturally, it's 'Down Hearted Blues': fewer performers have displayed greater authority from – literally – their first note.

Specific recommendations are nevertheless a problem. If you happened to be obscenely wealthy, I'd just say 'Don't ask questions, buy the lot', but since I suspect that this may not be the case, I'd suggest trying out *Vol 3* (which should be available by the time you read this), then *Vol 2*, and then simply flip a coin. Maybe Columbia's album programmers were right after all.

Subjects for further investigation: If you're put off by the scale of investment necessary to purchase the above and are therefore waiting for something a little easier on the comprehension and the pocket, remember the numerous fine performances by The Empress (including a few alternate takes not included in *The Complete Recordings*) featured on **The Complete Recordings Of Louis Armstrong And The Great Blues Singers 1924–1930** (Affinity CD AFS 1018-6). **The Beauty Of The Blues** (Columbia Legacy 468 768 2), a sampler disk for the fine 'Roots N' Blues' series, includes both 'T'ain't Nobody's Bizness' and 'St Louis Blues' (not to mention items by BLIND WILLIE McTELL, Robert Johnson, BIG BILL BROONZY, LONNIE JOHNSON, BLIND BOY FULLER and LEADBELLY); and **News And The Blues** (Columbia 467249 2) from the same series, contains her magnificent 1927 'Backwater Blues'.

3. *Country Blues*

Though the terms 'rural (or country) blues' and 'Delta blues' are often used as if they were freely interchangeable, country blues was already established as a recorded genre before any Delta artists ever made it into the studios. In the two seminal figures of '20s rural blues, we find the roots of the blues styles which continue to dominate more than sixty years later. BLIND LEMON JEFFERSON was the prime mover of the Texas and Southwestern blues tradition, with its emphasis on melodic single-string guitar lines, more relaxed and flexible rhythms, and cleaner, more precisely (but not much more precisely) enunciated singing; CHARLEY PATTON set the tone of the blues of the Mississippi Delta with his rough, growling voice, 'hard' rhythms, modal drones and bottleneck slide guitar. It was the Mississippi style, as extrapolated from Patton by SON HOUSE, ROBERT JOHNSON, HOWLIN' WOLF, MUDDY WATERS, JOHN LEE HOOKER and countless others, which formed the basis for the Chicago-dominated post-war 'electric downhome' school so beloved of early-'60s white blues boys like THE ROLLING STONES; but it was Jefferson's influence on his younger fellow-Texan T-BONE WALKER which, together with the dazzling guitar gymnastics of 'urbane' bluesman LONNIE JOHNSON, created B.B. KING's 'Memphis synthesis', and everything which subsequently sprang from that.

Blind Lemon Jefferson

The first true superstar of country blues, and – for the record – he really was blind and his first name really was Lemon. His antecedents are somewhat mysterious: all we can safely assume is that he was born somewhere in Texas (Couchman, a hamlet in Freestone County, is favourite) sometime between 1880 and 1897 (we have only LEADBELLY's word for the former date, which contradicts all other evidence); enjoyed massive popularity on record between 1926 and 1929, and froze to death in a Chicago blizzard sometime during the winter of 1929–1930: he suffered a heart attack while his car was snowed in, and his terrified chauffeur simply abandoned him right there. When Jefferson's best-selling, hugely influential records were made, ROBERT JOHNSON, HOWLIN' WOLF, and T-BONE WALKER were teenagers; LIGHTNIN' HOPKINS and MUDDY WATERS were adolescents; JOHN LEE HOOKER a child; B.B. KING a toddler; ALBERT COLLINS and BUDDY GUY still unborn.

Jefferson was firmly established as the most popular street-singer in Dallas when he was discovered by a Paramount Records talent scout, and his records were instantly successful, providing the first rural-blues challenge to the hegemony of the 'classic' blueswomen. His was therefore the first rural repertoire to be transmitted extensively on record, but since Lemon himself toured heavily, it's a moot point whether any given song of his was learned by any given bluesman via the traditional folk process or through the new medium. His music was characterised by an elasticised beat (in marked contrast to the driving rhythms of the Delta) which expanded and contracted to permit numerous guitar and vocal flourishes, and by his use of the guitar to answer his vocal lines with single-note passages – call (vocal) and response (guitar) – rather than as straightforward rhythm accompaniment.

(More traditional players, notably songster Mance Lipscomb, claimed that Lemon simply couldn't keep time: a criticism often levelled at 'irregular' players like John Lee Hooker) His vocal range encompassed everything from a rich, full-throated bellow to a piercing, nasal whine; his huge repertoire, derived from his years as a street entertainer and much of which was never recorded, included songs in all manner of styles other than the blues which Paramount's clientele demanded. This included gospel material; despite the licentiousness of both his lifestyle and much of his material, he was a religious enough man to refuse to perform on Sundays, even for considerable financial inducement.

Though his sales began to flag at the end of the '20s, Lemon was a highly successful artist: he wore immaculate suits, owned a fine car, and had a salaried chauffeur permanently on call, though the loyalty of his last chauffeur was, as events were to prove, somewhat questionable. What is beyond doubt is his influence on subsequent performers as diverse as Lightnin' Hopkins, B.B. King and John Lee Hooker: his celebrated 'Matchbox' even ended up in The Beatles' repertoire via Memphis rockabilly maestro Carl Perkins.

- *King Of The Country Blues* (Yazoo 1069)
- *Blind Lemon Jefferson* (Ace CDCH 399)

Two lovingly compiled and generously weighted (23 and 25 tracks, respectively, with a 9-track overlap between the two) options for your basic Blind Lemon primer. The Yazoo issue has better cover art and includes 'See That My Grave Is Kept Clean' (as covered by the young Bob Dylan on his very first album); the Ace boasts a superior liner note and both 'Black Snake Moan' and 'Jack O'Diamonds Blues'. 'Matchbox Blues', 'Broke And Hungry' and 'Bad Luck Blues' are common to both, as is 'That Crawlin' Baby Blues'; though the latter is, amusingly enough, listed on the Ace collection as 'That Growlin' Baby Blues', which sounds like it ought to have been part of the soundtrack to *The Exorcist*. Unfortunately, the poor condition of the original 78s from which both these collections were derived means that they're rather too noisy for comfortable listening: despite Lemon's genius, these wimpy hi-fi-trained ears cannot take more than half-a-dozen tracks at one sitting. Since those records sold in huge quantities

27

during the late '20s, we can but hope that either some cleaner copies eventually surface, or that the next generation of sound-restoration technology is able to remove the layer of interference which separates us from one of the true pioneers of the blues. (Folksinger Tom Paley, a former colleague of Leadbelly, Woody Guthrie, SONNY TERRY and BROWNIE McGHEE, recalls smashing a pile of old 78s, including a few of Lemon's, while playing with friends when a child in Brooklyn: he was heartbroken when, as an adult, he discovered exactly what it was that he'd destroyed.)

Subjects for further investigation: The Austrian Document label has issued a four-volume set of Lemon's 'Complete Recorded Works In Chronological Order'. *Volume 1 (1925–1926)* (Document DOCD-5017) kicks off with two gospel pieces, 'I Want To Be Like Jesus In My Heart' and 'All I Want Is That Pure Religion.' 'Matchbox Blues' reappears as the lead-off track for a fine compilation, *Blues Masters Vol 3: Texas Blues* (Rhino R2 71123), which traces Lone Star State blues all the way from Blind Lemon to STEVIE RAY VAUGHAN and beyond, also highlighting, among others, CHARLES BROWN, T-Bone Walker, PERCY MAYFIELD, BIG MAMA THORNTON, CLARENCE 'GATEMOUTH' BROWN, Mance Lipscomb and FREDDIE KING. Apart from vocalist Texas Alexander, far too much of whose work remains uncollected, Texas blues made its mark principally through the more sophisticated postwar artists like T-Bone Walker: the purest inheritor of Lemon's rural Texas tradition was probably Lightnin' Hopkins, who – together with Muddy Waters and John Lee Hooker – made his breakthrough in the years immediately following the end of World War II. 'Black Snake Moan', adapted by Lemon from Victoria Spivey's 'Black Snake Blues' is a principal ancestor of the 'Crawlin' King Snake' most frequently associated with John Lee Hooker; Lemon's 'Bad Luck Blues' was reincarnated during the '50s as B.B.King's 'Bad Luck Soul' (B.B.'s 'Bad Luck' is, however, a completely different song); hear it on *The Best Of B.B. King Vol II* (Ace CDCH 199).

Blind Willie McTell

Though he's often lumped in with fellow 'Atlanta 12-string' specialists like Barbecue Bob, the Georgian singer/guitarist Blind Willie McTell was *sui generis*. Bob Dylan paid him the supreme compliment of writing a song about him (and then didn't release it for almost a decade); the British folksinger Ralph McTell adopted his surname as a tribute; and his 'Statesboro Blues' became a late-'60s blues-rock standard, thanks to TAJ MAHAL and The Allman Brothers Band. McTell had one of the sweetest, most plangent voices in all recorded blues and he was an impressively powerful and versatile guitarist, adept at conjuring both intricate rags and driving bottleneck blues from the unwieldy 12-string. Amazingly, he recorded regularly for years despite never having anything even faintly resembling a hit. His material ranged from the savage misogyny of 'Southern Can Is Mine' to the insinuating charm of 'Statesboro Blues' or 'Mama 'Tain't Long 'Fore Day': discovering Blind Willie McTell is one of the great pleasures of the blues. Interestingly enough, his family name was actually 'McTier'; white incomprehension of Southern black pronunciation led to the misspelling on his first record label, and the name 'McTell' stuck.

He was born in Thomson, Georgia, on May 5, 1901 (or 1898): accounts disagree on whether he was born blind or lost his sight in childhood, but this disability didn't prevent him from receiving both musical training and Braille education. He learned guitar from his mother, who moved to nearby Statesboro in 1910; and ran away from home soon after to ply his trade as a travelling entertainer, making his first records in 1927. His occasional street-singing partners included fellow Georgian guitarist Curley Weaver, and the fearsome gospel-blues hellfire merchant BLIND WILLIE JOHNSON; and he lived long enough to record as late as 1949. His last years were spent as a preacher in Atlanta, and he died of a cerebral hemorrhage on August 19, 1959, in Milledgeville, Georgia, just a few years too early for the inevitable rediscovery which would have brought him the kind of late-blooming acclaim achieved by SKIP JAMES, MISSISSIPPI JOHN HURT or SON HOUSE. He was buried under his father's name: 'Eddie McTier.'

- *The Early Years 1927–1933* (Yazoo 1005)
- *1927–1935* (Yazoo 1037)

The essential Blind Willie: start with *The Early Years 1927–1933*, since it includes 'Statesboro Blues' and 'Mama 'Tain't Long 'Fore Day'. Both are packed with wonderful blues and devastating rags, and 'Southern Can Is Mine' is sort-of-common to both; it reappears, slowed down and – if anything – more threatening, as 'Southern Can Mama' on *1927–1935*. The latter album, equally entertaining if lumbered with a lower Title Recognition Factor, also benefits from a few charming 1931 sides on which McTell plays 6-string slide behind a female vocalist named either Ruth Day (according to the credits) or Ruth Willis (according to the liner note); I warmly recommend the mock-sanctimonious 'God Don't Like It' – punch line: 'and I don't either.'

Subjects for further investigation: More Blind Willie McTell – six 1949 sides from what was virtually his last session – can be found on *Three Shades Of Blues* (Biograph BCD 107), alongside titles by Skip James and BUKKA WHITE. His powers had declined somewhat by then, but it's a revelation to hear that booming 12-string so well-recorded: it sounds like an orchestra. 'Dying Crapshooter's Blues', from what purports to be McTell's last-ever session, is on *Bluesville Vol 1: Folk Blues* (Ace CDCH 247). McTell's sometime partner, guitarist Curley Weaver, takes his turn in the spotlight on *Georgia Guitar Wizard (1928–1935)* (Story Of Blues CD-3530-2); McTell himself appears on three 1935 titles. Taj Mahal's 'Statesboro Blues' is on *Taj Mahal* (Edsel ED CD 166), and also on the Taj compilations *Taj's Blues* (Columbia 471660 2) and *Taj Mahal – The Collection* (Castle Communications CCSCD 180), not to mention the all-star anthology *Q: The Blues* (The Hit Label AHLCD 1); The Allman Brothers Band give it their best shot on *The Allman Brothers Band At Fillmore East* (Polydor 823 273-2). To date, no-one has covered 'Southern Can Is Mine'. Dylan's 'Blind Willie McTell', recorded in 1983 during sessions for *Infidels*, finally emerged in 1991 on the cumbersomely titled *The Bootleg Series Vols 1–3 [Rare & Unreleased] 1961–1991* (Columbia 468086 2).

Robert 'Barbecue Bob' Hicks (1902–1931) was, incidentally, far more popular in his time than Blind Willie was. Solo or with his elder brother and fellow 12-stringer 'Laughing Charley' Hicks,

Bob was a consummate entertainer, pure and simple: he played blues, gospel, rags and pop with equal relish and commitment, hammering and sliding away at his 12-string with a rough verve that was essentially more Delta than Georgia. *Chocolate To The Bone* (Yazoo 2005) collects 20 of the 86 sides he cut between 1927 and 1931 – another, 'It Won't Be Long Now' featuring Laughing Charley, is on *The Story Of The Blues* (Columbia 468992 2) – and it includes his take on 'Poor Boy A Long Ways From Home' (one of the first versions ever recorded) and his thinly disguised variations on BLIND BLAKE's 'Diddy Wah Diddy' and TAMPA RED's 'Tight Like That.' The title track, an answer record to Lillian Glinn's 'Brownskin Blues', is affectionately parodied by MIKE BLOOMFIELD as 'I'm Glad I'm Jewish' on *I'm With You Always* (Demon FIEND CD 92).

THE MISSISSIPPI DELTA

Your starter for ten: where is the 'real' Home Of The Blues? Some say Chicago, some say Memphis, and some radicals now say Austin; but my money's still on Mississippi. To be precise, the Mississippi Delta: not that triangular epiglottis at the mouth of the Yazoo and Mississippi Rivers, but the area – incorporating parts of Mississippi, Arkansas and Tennessee – which, according to legend, stretches from the lobby of the Peabody Hotel in Memphis down to 'Catfish Row' in Vicksburg, Mississippi. The music of the Mississippi Delta is, I submit, 20th century African-American music in its purest form: it may be only one step away from the field holler, but that single step is a vitally important one. Delta blues is where a folk form develops the means to become both an art form and a commercial form, but does so without losing even a molecule of its human core. The blues can travel anywhere, but – to paraphrase ZZ TOP – its heart's in Mississippi.

Not surprisingly, Mississippi is the birthplace of, among others, MUDDY WATERS, B.B. KING, ROBERT JOHNSON, HOWLIN' WOLF, JOHN LEE HOOKER, SONNY BOY WILLIAMSON, SON HOUSE, SKIP JAMES, WILLIE DIXON,

ALBERT KING, BIG BILL BROONZY, ELVIS PRESLEY, JOHNNY WINTER, MOSE ALLISON and . . .

Charley Patton

Charley (or 'Charlie': the spelling varies from record to record) Patton was not the first Delta bluesman to immortalise his music on wax. That honour belongs to one Freddie Spruell (about whom virtually nothing is remembered, though a few of his songs, including the first known recorded version of 'Milk Cow Blues', still crop up on compilations), but Patton was the first one who matters. The basic Delta blues style – from which the post-war Chicago style was primarily derived – was, by all contemporary accounts, essentially Patton's style: SON HOUSE, BUKKA WHITE, MISSISSIPPI FRED McDOWELL and – by extension – ROBERT JOHNSON, MUDDY WATERS *et al* were following in his footsteps. According to his disciple HOWLIN' WOLF, the most ostentatiously Patton-patterned of all postwar bluesmen, Patton was a small, slight, wavy-haired, light-skinned 'Puerto Rican-looking' man of mixed European, African and Native American descent. Nevertheless, he is acknowledged as the first man to play the music we now know as Delta blues. Patton was renowned for the huge, raucous voice which emerged so incongruously from that meagre frame; and for his driving beat and extrovert performing style: he was fond of playing his guitar behind his neck or between his legs, in the manner later associated with T-BONE WALKER, GUITAR SLIM, JOHNNY GUITAR WATSON or JIMI HENDRIX. He was also a notorious hellraiser, given to slugging uncooperative women with his guitar, and forever getting himself into fights he couldn't win. His last recordings betray the audible effects of a barroom throat-slashing sustained in 1933.

Patton was born in 1887 or 1891 (accounts vary) in Edwards, Mississippi, and grew up on the huge Dockery plantation, where his parents moved around the turn of the century. In 1907 he took up the guitar under the tutelege of a local musician, and soon became an itinerant entertainer working the logging camps. This was something of an embarrassment to his parents, who had made sure that he received the kind of education which would have qualified him for the plantation's middle-managerial class. He made his first record in 1929, and cut regularly, first for Paramount and subsequently for Vocalion, until his death from a heart attack, brought on by chronic bronchitis and an overly strenuous performance at a white dance, on April 28, 1934, in Indianola, Mississippi. His signature songs, 'Pony Blues' and 'Banty Rooster Blues', are basic building blocks of Delta blues. He is also renowned as the originator of the standard 'Spoonful' (as popularised by Howlin' Wolf and numerous subsequent white folks), but Patton's 'Spoonful' bears less resemblance to Wolf's (or indeed, anybody else's) than it does to MISSISSIPPI JOHN HURT's 'Coffee Blues', a line of which provided '60s folk-rockers The Lovin' Spoonful with their name.

Throughout his life he fell victim to periodic but short-lived attacks of religion, and the duets with his last wife Bertha Lee, recorded at his final session in New York, bear an eerie resemblance to the work of the Texan gospel-blues giant BLIND WILLIE JOHNSON; in fact his first two releases, back in 1929, had been the hugely influential 'Pony Blues' and the gospel 'I'm Going Home'; the former as himself and the latter under the guise of 'Elder J.J. Hadley'. Patton's importance is literally impossible to overestimate: if any one artist could be truthfully described as the true Father Of Delta Blues, he's yer man.

- *Founder Of The Delta Blues* (Yazoo 1020)
- *King Of The Delta Blues* (Yazoo 2001)

Patton recorded something like 60 sides during his five recording years: by all accounts more than half of them were blues and the rest gospel and folk songs. Most of the key Patton songs which ultimately defined archetypal Delta blues are on *Founder*; but *King* is rather more than simply supplementary listening, since it's both more varied and more fun. It includes the massively influential 'Peavine Blues', and much of Patton's Blind Willie Johnson-styled religious work, including the scarifying 'Oh Death', a 'You're Gonna Need Somebody When You Die' which breaks down into an impassioned sermon, and 'Jesus Was A Dying Bed-Maker', originally recorded a few years earlier by Blind Willie himself; not to mention an enthusiastically pious 'I Shall Not Be Moved.' Patton's records can be hard going to all but the most devoted:

there's a limit to what even the most expert digital remastering can achieve with ancient 78s as chewed-up as these. Nevertheless, behind the crackles, pops, poots and clicks are the pounding, percussive rhythms, driving energy, singing slide fills and huge rough voice which changed the lives of Son House, Howlin' Wolf, Bukka White and Robert Johnson.

- **SON HOUSE/CHARLEY PATTON/WILLIE BROWN/ LOUISE JOHNSON:** *The Legendary Delta Blues Session* (Peavine PCD-2250[Japan])

When Patton travelled to Grafton, Wisconsin, for the marathon recording session scheduled for May 24, 1930, he took with him three companions. The first was his running buddy and performing partner Willie Brown; the second was a tall, lean, guitar-playing ex-con named Eddie 'SON' HOUSE, and the third was his then-girlfriend, singer/pianist Louise Johnson. The journey was complicated by the evident mutual attraction between House and Johnson, but the session – House's recording debut – was momentous. All four of Patton's contributions to this session – as well as the six of House's seven which were issued at the time, and Brown's and Johnson's two each – are available elsewhere, but it's fascinating to hear them in the context of the original session. The shrill-voiced Johnson paraphrases Cow Cow Davenport's oft-quoted classic 'Cow Cow Blues' as the stupefyingly salacious 'On The Wall'; a revival of Brown's wracked, string-snapping 'Future Blues' was a minor hit for Canned Heat in 1970. The liner notes will prove especially illuminating to those sufficiently fortunate to read Japanese fluently. The August 1992 edition of *Guitar Player* magazine carried a lengthy reconstruction by Jas Obrecht of the events surrounding this session, extracted from Obrecht's book *Early Blues: The Music Before Robert Johnson*, unpublished as this volume went to press.

- **VARIOUS ARTISTS:** *Masters Of The Delta Blues: The Friends Of Charlie Patton* (Yazoo 2002)

A generous 23-track, 70-minutes-plus sampling of the work of Patton's immediate peer group. It includes all of the non-Patton sides from the Grafton session: seven by House, including the previously-unreleased 'Walkin' Blues', and two each by Brown and Johnson, plus a couple by Patton's wife Bertha Lee (featuring himself on guitar), a couple by the ridiculously obscure Kid Bailey, and two powerful gospel-blues offerings in the Blind Willie Johnson manner by BUKKA WHITE. The most intriguing subset, though, is the quintet of titles by the excellent Tommy Johnson: he was the guy who first claimed to have obtained his musical mastery by cutting that deal-with-the-devil at the inevitable crossroads, thus indirectly starting the rumour that his young namesake Robert Johnson had done likewise. The 'Maggie Campbell Blues' he performs here is a development of one of Patton's favourite themes; his 'CANNED HEAT Blues' later helped out a young California bluesrock band in search of a name. This is probably the finest single document you can find of the first generation of recording Delta bluesmen: all it lacks is Patton himself.

Subjects for further investigation: Every other Delta blues record you can find. One Patton title you won't find on either *King or Founder* is 'Devil Sent The Rain Blues', included on **Mississippi Moaners 1927–1942** (Yazoo 1009), which also features SKIP JAMES' 'Cherry Ball Blues', a particular favourite of RY COODER's. **Lonesome Road Blues 1926–1941** (Yazoo 1038) introduces the mysterious Freddie Spruell: one of his two tracks is the earliest known version of 'Milk Cow Blues', later associated with KOKOMO ARNOLD, Robert Johnson and ELVIS PRESLEY. Of special interest is **Deep Blues** (Anxious 4509-9181-2), the soundtrack to the documentary-film adaptation of Robert Palmer's superb 1981 blues book, which uses performances by contemporary Delta blues artists like Lonnie Pitchford, Roosevelt 'Booba' Barnes and Jessie May Hemphill to demonstrate that the blues didn't vanish from Mississippi when Howlin' Wolf left for Chicago.

At the other extreme of early Delta music from Charley Patton were The Mississippi Sheiks: guitarist Walter Vinson (1901–1975) and fiddler Lonnie Chatmon (189?–1942/3), one of the Chatmon dynasty and, incidentally, Patton's half-brother. An offshoot of The Chatmon Brothers, a family string band with an eclectic repertoire designed principally for higher-paying and less vociferous white audiences, the Sheiks' music was light, swinging, jaunty and derived more or less equally from black and white rural folk sources. What Patton and the Sheiks shared musically was the admiration of the young Howlin' Wolf, who borrowed their biggest hit 'Sittin' On Top Of The World' a few decades later, and based his 'Smokestack Lightnin'' on a few lines from their 'Stop And Listen Blues'. Though the Sheiks' records were cut by Chatmon and Pickford with occasional extra guitar from another Chatmon brother, Armenter (1893–1964), better known as Bo Carter, their performing line-up was fairly volatile, often including yet another Chatmon, Sam, who recorded as a Sheik after the act's early-'30s peak. The original Mississippi Sheiks sides are on *Stop And Listen* (Yazoo 2008); **Banana In Your Fruit Bowl** (Yazoo 1064) showcases Bo's deft fingerpicking and relentless way with a single-entendre.

Son House

ROBERT JOHNSON was the man who brought the Mississippi Delta blues to its absolute peak of refinement, sophistication and self-conscious artistry. MUDDY WATERS was the man who transformed the Delta troubadour's art into an urban ensemble music. And Eddie James 'Son' House Jr was the man who inspired and tutored both of them. A singer and bottleneck guitarist of ferocious power and towering passion, House was born in Riverton, Mississippi, on March 21, 1902, and was preaching by the time he was fifteen. His relationship with the church was a complex one: his song 'Preachin' (The) Blues' – which he liked well enough to record several times during his career – begins 'I'm gon' get religion, I'm gon' join the Baptist church/I'm gon' be a Baptist preacher, and I don't want to have to work', but nevertheless, like many bluesmen including BIG BILL BROONZY, he moved back and forth throughout his life between the blues and the church. In his early '20s he taught himself guitar, but his musical career received a temporary setback when he was sentenced to fifteen years in Parchman State Farm for shooting a man in a barroom brawl. He served less than two years of his stretch, and on his release fell in with CHARLEY PATTON and his sidekick Willie Brown. The latter, who also tutored Robert Johnson, was to be House's best friend and performing partner on and off until Brown's death in 1957.

The three singles from his first session, cut for Paramount on

May 28, 1930 in Grafton, Wisconsin, when he'd only been playing guitar for three or four years, made him a guru to younger men like Johnson and Waters, and these – supplemented by 1941-2 Library Of Congress sessions for folklorist Alan Lomax – built his legend among later white blues fans. In 1964, a convocation of same, including scholar/entrepreneur Dick Waterman, tracked him down in Rochester, New York, where he had been living for the past twenty years, working as a railroad porter and barbecue chef. They introduced him to John Hammond, who recorded his *Father Of The Folk Blues* album in 1965 and presented him at the Newport Folk Festival, where he inspired a new generation of musicians, including BONNIE RAITT.

The astonishing influence Son House wielded can be demonstrated by reference to just one of his many songs. 'My Black Mama (Pt 1)' was developed from materials learned from an unrecorded older singer named James McCoy; and cut in Grafton. Its primal slide-guitar motif formed the basis for Robert Johnson's 'Walkin' Blues'; the lyrics for the second verse ('Ain't no heaven, ain't no burnin' hell/where I go when I die, can't nobody tell') provided the inspiration for 'Burnin' Hell', one of the most powerful songs in JOHN LEE HOOKER's capacious repertoire; and those of the third verse ('My black mama's face shines like the sun/ oh, lipstick and powder sure won't help her none') reappeared virtually intact – save for the word 'black' – in ALBERT KING's 'Oh Pretty Woman' as well as in subsequent versions of the same song by JOHN MAYALL and GARY MOORE. The fourth verse ('If you see my milk cow, tell her 'hurry home'/ain't had no milk since my milk cow been gone') recurred four years later in KOKOMO ARNOLD's 'Milk Cow Blues', and spread from there to Robert Johnson's 'Milk Cow's Calf Blues' (1937) and ELVIS PRESLEY's 'Milk Cow Blues Boogie' (1954). Even The Kinks recorded 'Milk Cow Blues' on *Live At Kelvin Hall* (1967), albeit as part of a medley with Ray Davies' own 'Tired Of Waiting For You' and the *Batman* theme. Isn't the folk process wonderful?

But I digress. Son House retired again in the mid-'70s, returning once more to the twin bosoms of the Baptist Church he had so sorely maligned, and his family, by then resident in Detroit, Michigan. He died there on October 19, 1988, and was buried in an unmarked grave. His admirers are currently attempting to raise money to purchase a headstone for the Father Of The Delta Blues.

- *Father Of The Delta Blues* (Columbia Legacy 471662)
- *Death Letter* (Edsel ED CD 167)

Two options for seekers after the epochal 1965 Son House comeback sessions, produced by John Hammond Sr and featuring the occasional musical support of future CANNED HEAT mastermind Alan Wilson on guitar and harmonica. The Edsel CD is a straightforward reissue of the '65 *Father Of The Folk Blues* album (complete with Dick Waterman's original liner note), while the Columbia Legacy package combines this material with a second disc of outtakes, including five alternate versions of songs from the '65 release, and seven unissued titles. With many of the mid-'60s 'rediscovery' recordings of great '30s bluesmen like SKIP JAMES, MISSISSIPPI JOHN HURT and others, there is a trade-off: what you gain in sound quality from thirty-odd years' worth of improvements in recording technology you often lose via a corresponding decline in the artist's powers. With Son House, this problem does not arise: though he required the reinforcement of Alan Wilson's presence and judicious quantities of whisky, House was as up for the downstroke during these sessions as he'd ever been. It requires little use of the imagination to understand why Johnson and Waters found House so inspiring: this is some of the most powerful Delta blues ever recorded, from the gospel holler of 'John The Revelator' to the driving, slashing slide-guitar of 'Death Letter.' Whether you prefer the single-album Edsel version or the deluxe Columbia Legacy edition, this is an essential item.

- *The Complete Library Of Congress Sessions 1941-1942* (Travelin' Man TM CD 02)
- *Delta Blues* (Biograph BCD 118)

Alan Lomax's 1941-2 Library Of Congress sessions produced Son House's second batch of recordings: six titles in string-band mode with Willie Brown (guitar), Fiddlin' Joe Martin (mandolin) and Leroy Williams (harp) from '41, and the rest cut solo a year or so later. The main difference between these sides and the earlier commercial recordings is the extended length – over six minutes

– of some of these performances. Some of this stuff is fantastic: I love 'Depot Blues' and the patriotic country-waltz 'American Defence' (neither of which House ever recorded again), and the extended string-band version of 'Walking Blues'; purists find this music lacking in vitality by comparison with the earlier sides, but the distinction isn't really cost-effective. The Biograph CD is more attractively packaged, and offers fractionally better sound quality: the Travelin' Man edition is easier to find and includes 19 titles as opposed to the Biograph's 15, so take your pick. Incidentally, House's only reward for all this was an ice-cold bottle of Co'-Cola. At least, I hope it was ice-cold. There's nothing worse than warm cola.

Subjects for further investigation: **The Legendary Delta Blues Session** (Peavine PCD-2250[Japan]) contains the May 28, 1930, Grafton sessions alluded to above, in their entirety. House contributes six sides, originally issued on three two-part singles: 'My Black Mama', 'Preachin' The Blues' and 'Dry Spell Blues', alongside songs by Charley Patton, Willie Brown and Louise Johnson. The original 1930 recordings of 'My Black Mama (Pt 1)' and 'Preachin' The Blues (Pt 1)' crop up again on **The Roots Of Robert Johnson** (Yazoo 1073) alongside songs by SKIP JAMES, KOKOMO ARNOLD, LEROY CARR & SCRAPPER BLACKWELL and CHARLEY PATTON; all of which were crucial source material for Robert Johnson. *Masters Of The Delta Blues: The Friends Of Charlie Patton* (Yazoo 2002) collects all six of Son's Grafton sides, plus a previously unissued version of 'Walkin' Blues' and material by BUKKA WHITE, Tommy Johnson, and others. *American Folk Blues Festival '67* (L&R/Bellaphon CDLR 42070) contains a slow, wracked live version of 'Death Letter' (retitled 'Got A Letter This Morning') by a Son who seems a shadow of his former self, but it's still an honourable, affecting performance.

Kokomo Arnold

James 'Kokomo' Arnold was suspicious about the whole notion of recording. If he made too many records, he reasoned, then other singers would be able to steal his songs. He was also fairly unimpressed with the business practices of the companies which recorded him; he could afford to be, thanks to an extremely lucrative bootlegging business. As a result, despite a successful run of singles commencing in 1934, he turned his back on the studio four years later and never recorded again. This was a pity, because he was a powerful and creative performer with a propulsive, well-defined bottleneck style and a real flair for composition; there's absolutely no reason to assume that his music had passed its sell-by date. His first hit single 'Milk Cow Blues'/'Old Original Kokomo Blues' (the B-side adapted from an earlier tune by another former bootlegger, pianist LEROY CARR's guitar alter ego SCRAPPER BLACKWELL; the A from a 1926 single by Freddie Spruell) was a major success, and both sides became standards; the problem was that they became standards not for Arnold, but for ROBERT JOHNSON, who rewrote them as 'Milkcow's Calf Blues' and 'Sweet Home Chicago.' Maybe Arnold had a point after all.

There isn't a lot of available information about Kokomo Arnold: he was born in Lovejoy, Georgia, on 15 February 1901, and spent time in Buffalo, New York, and in the Delta before settling in Chicago in 1929. He first recorded in 1930 (as 'Gitfiddle Jim' for Victor), but his main body of work was cut for Decca. After his retirement from recording, he continued to perform around Chicago until 1941, when he quit music entirely and let his guitar gather dust until the early-'60s revivalist movement brought him back to the stage for a few club performances. He still refused to record, though, and died in Chicago on 8 November, 1968, without adding anything new to his canon.

● *King Of The Bottleneck Guitar 1934–1937* (Black & Blue 59.250 2)

If this had more extensive liner notes and a better cover, it would be a model anthology: comprehensive, conscientiously remastered and generously weighted, with 23 tracks adding up to over 70 minutes of music. Apart from PEETIE WHEATSTRAW's piano on 'Mr Charlie', Arnold appears solo; and apart from LEROY CARR's 'How Long How Long Blues', it's all his own repertoire; albeit a repertoire loaded with 'common stock' motifs. Both his 'Sagefield Woman Blues' and 'Sissy Man Blues' are, effectively, precursors of Robert Johnson's 'Dust My Broom', though the latter inevitably concludes with the celebrated punch-line verse. We're not talking your-life-is-worthless-without-it here, but if your taste inclines towards prewar slide, then you'll be happy to make Kokomo Arnold's acquaintance.

Peetie Wheatstraw

If anything in the blues can truly be described as deliberate affront to all that is godly and decent, it would have to be the work – nay, the very existence – of Peetie Wheatstraw, who called himself 'The Devil's Son In Law' and 'The High Sheriff From Hell'. Celebrations of violence, brutality, drunkenness, diabolism and despair? He did 'em. Pianist/guitarist Wheatstraw – born William Bunch on 21 December, 1902, in Ripley, Tennessee, and based, for most of his career, in East St Louis, Illinois – was the blues equivalent of a 'gangsta rappa', the Ice-T or Ice Cube of his time. What's more, he was popular: he recorded 160 sides between 1930 and 1941, and you don't get to cut 80 singles in eleven years if no-one's buying them. Nevertheless, surprisingly little of his material has entered the standard blues repertoire.

He had a remarkably soft voice for such an alleged badass, and his piano playing was only slightly better than merely serviceable; his major calling card was his lyrical sensibility and the remarkable variety of threats, brags and sex jive he brought to his one basic framework: a medium-tempo rolling piano blues. His most lasting musical contribution was a vocal tic readily adopted by ROBERT JOHNSON and his successors: Wheatstraw was fond of bridging lines with a distinctive 'oohh, well,well', singing the 'oohh' in falsetto. He died in an East St Louis car crash on 21 December, 1941: it is to be hoped that the devil is taking good care of his most loyal relative by marriage.

● *The Devil's Son-In-Law (1930–1941)* (Story Of Blues CD 3541-2)

Wheatstraw was ambi-instrumental on guitar and piano, but this 20-track selection keeps him strictly behind the keys, except when Lil Armstrong or CHAMPION JACK DUPREE relieve him at the piano bench. The supporting cast also includes LONNIE JOHNSON and KOKOMO ARNOLD on guitars, plus – on a swing-oriented 1940 session – trumpeter Jonah Jones and drummer Big Sid Catlett. Check out 'Gangster Blues' and especially 'Chicago Mill Blues', wherein Peetie opines that the best way to score with lotsa women is to tell them that you have a job in the famously well-paying local steel mill.

Skip James

If SON HOUSE was the primary model for the rougher and more urgent Delta aspects of ROBERT JOHNSON's work, then Nehemiah 'Skip' James is the closest precursor of Johnson's eerie side. Though he's best-known to rock fans as the composer of Cream's 'I'm So Glad' (a children's song which he wrote in the '20s and first recorded in 1931), James' great achievement was the exquisitely desolate mood he could create with his high lonesome voice and minor-tuned guitar. Johnson may well be the most haunting of the prewar bluesmen, but Skip James runs him a very close second. His graceful, delicate music is the absolute antithesis of the raucous, barrel-chested school of Delta musicians who followed in the wake of CHARLEY PATTON.

James was born in Bentonia, Mississippi, on June 9, 1902, and for many years before his 'rediscovery' blues scholars constructed elaborate theories about a 'Bentonia school' of bluesmen playing special, locally-built guitars which couldn't be obtained elsewhere. However, when James re-emerged it was discovered that he played a perfectly ordinary guitar, and that 'special sound' was simply his E-minor tuning and his own personal touch. Similarly, the 'Bentonia school' was little more than a romantic myth: despite a few other Bentonia bluesmen with falsetto vocals and minor-tuned guitars, Skip James was *sui generis*. He had learned piano at high school and played organ in local churches, and his occasional keyboard excursions were as entrancing as his guitar pieces: his piano was as jauntily light-hearted as his guitar was melancholy and introspective. Religion played a major part in his life: after cutting his legendary early records in 1931 (in Grafton, Wisconsin, where Son House and Charley Patton had already recorded the year before), he relocated to Dallas, Texas, where he formed a successful gospel group before being ordained as a minister and moving back to Mississippi. He was 'rediscovered' in 1964, and returned to the blues with a triumphant appearance at that year's Newport Folk Festival. He remained a popular performer on the folk-blues circuit (though not as popular as his less unsettling contemporary MISSISSIPPI JOHN HURT) until his death on October 3,1969; he despised Cream's successful cover of 'I'm So Glad', but the $6000 realised from its royalties was just about enough to pay for his funeral.

Skip James was *spooky*, possums. His sound is as insubstantially spectral as anything in the blues; even Robert Johnson had more physicality, more solidity. Skip James' music drifts into your mind like a chill mist, and it clings long after you've switched it off.

● *Greatest Of The Delta Blues Singers* (Biograph BCD 122)

James' first post-rediscovery sessions, cut for the Boston independent Herwin label in 1964: not brilliantly recorded, but the thinness of the sound somehow adds to the effect. The Vanguard albums, which followed soon after and which contain much the same repertoire, are richer and fuller – far more 'professionally' recorded – but lack the emotional power James generates here. This album puts more of his post-rediscovery core repertoire onto one CD than anything else you'll find, though to be truly representative of his music it would have to include a piano piece, which it doesn't. Right from the opening 'Hard Time Killing Floor Blues', as affecting a performance as anything in recorded blues, James is casting his unique spell. He had been in hospital when his young admirers finally tracked him down, which adds a special poignancy to 'Sick Bed Blues' and 'Washington D.C. Hospital Blues'. There's also a characteristically distinctive treatment of the standard 'Catfish Blues', and a yearning 'Cherry Ball'. Two more cuts, including the delightful 'Drunken Spree', from the same session, alongside a reprise of 'I Don't Want A Woman To Stay Out All Night Long', have been exiled to *Three Shades Of Blues* (Biograph BCD 107), a collection which James shares with BUKKA WHITE and BLIND WILLIE McTELL: this seems a trifle miserly, as *Greatest* comes nowhere near to exhausting its available runtime.

- **Skip James/Today!** (Vanguard)
- **Devil Got My Woman** (Vanguard)

Between them, these two albums reprise most of what James cut for *Greatest Of The Delta Blues Singers*. The performances are by no means superior – indeed, the versions of 'Sick Bed Blues' and 'Devil Got My Woman' are, by comparison with the Biograph takes, about as close to throwaway as James ever got – but a far more rounded and detailed impression of his music emerges. For a start, James gets to play piano on these sessions: *Today!*'s reprise of 'All Night Long' transfers the song to the 88s – the intro gives you an idea of what Thelonious Monk would've sounded like playing Clarence 'Pinetop' Smith's 'Pinetop's Boogie Woogie' – and it sits very nicely alongside a version of LEROY CARR's 'How Long How Long Blues' which, by Skip James' standards, could almost be described as 'rollicking'. *Devil Got My Woman* features three more piano pieces, including a gorgeous 'Careless Love' and a menacing '22-20 Blues (the root of Robert Johnson's '32-20 Blues'). For a while, these were available as a vinyl double-album; unfortunately even the maximum runtime of a single CD couldn't cope with both of these at once.

Subjects for further investigation: James' reappearance at Newport '64 can be savoured on **Great Bluesmen/Newport** (Vanguard VCD 77/78), which features two excerpts from his performance, and **Blues At Newport** VCD 115/116), which includes his set-opener 'Devil Got My Woman.' James' influence on Robert Johnson is documented on **The Roots Of Robert Johnson** (Yazoo 1073), including the 1931 originals of 'Devil Got My Woman' and '22-20 Blues.' The prototype 'I'm So Glad' is on **Roots Of Rock** (Yazoo 1063); the post-discovery remake pales by comparison, though the microphone-stuck-by-a-pan-of-frying-bacon effect of the scratchy old 78 is infuriating. His original 'Cherry Ball Blues', as revived by RY COODER, is on **Mississippi Moaners 1927–1942** (Yazoo 1009); as we go to press, Yazoo are preparing *The Complete 1931 Session* for release in summer '93. A European concert performance of 'Hard Luck Child' is a highlight of **American Folk Blues Festival '67** (L&R/Bellaphon CDLR 42070).

'Bukka' White

Booker T. Washington White, one of the greatest of the spiritual descendants of CHARLEY PATTON, always hated the 'Bukka' soubriquet, but he was stuck with it. An ignorant white record producer billed Booker as 'Bukka' on the label of his first major batch of recordings in 1940, presumably because he'd never heard of the black leader Booker T. Washington (after whom both White and the Stax organist Booker T. Jones – of '& The MGs' fame – were named) and possibly also because he had problems with White's mile-deep Mississippi accent. 'Bukka''s earliest recordings had actually been made a decade earlier, when he'd been 'Washington White The Singing Preacher', and Washington White the blues singer, both of which entities released simultaneous debut records in 1930. White's other claim to fame – before his '60s rediscovery – was that he was B.B. KING's cousin, had sheltered his young relative on the latter's first trip to Memphis, and that B.B. had developed his hugely influential finger vibrato as a means of mimicking the tremulous vocalisms which 'Bukka' achieved with his slide.

White was born in Houston, Mississippi, on 12 November of either 1906 or 1909, and by 1919 was living with an uncle near Greneda, Mississippi. Falling under Patton's spell he took up guitar, and at 20, he cut his first records in Memphis. They weren't notably successful, and a few months later he was back farming in the Delta. A 1937 barroom altercation ended with 'Bukka' shooting a man; he jumped his bail and fled to Chicago, where he managed to talk his way into a recording session. According to legend, he managed to cut two titles – including his signature piece 'Shake 'Em On Down', later revived by LED ZEPPELIN – before the Mississippi sheriff's men came and got him. Not surprisingly, there was no bail this time, and 'Bukka' wound up in the notorious Parchman Farm 'correctional facility'. There he was found by (surprise!) Alan Lomax, but contributed only a couple of songs to the Library of Congress: he was saving his best material for his next commercial session. This wasn't long in coming: a combination of record company pressure and a re-examination of the evidence (suggesting that White had acted in self-defence) got him sprung from the slammer and back in the studio by 1940. Washington White was now 'Bukka' White: the

45

name on a powerful series of songs, formed in the crucible of Parchman, which formed the foundation for his legend. 'Parchman Farm Blues' (no relation to the MOSE ALLISON song of the same name), 'Fixin' To Die' (a favourite of the young Bob Dylan), and 'When Can I Change My Clothes' eventually achieved near-Grail status for devotees of rural blues, but a favourable commercial climate no longer existed for Delta blues of such arresting starkness. No more sessions were forthcoming, and, after a two-year stint in the Navy, 'Bukka' finally settled in Memphis, where blues enthusiasts Ed Denson (later manager of Country Joe & The Fish) and avant-folk guitarist John Fahey finally tracked him down – via relatives in Aberdeen, Mississippi – in 1963.

The resulting album, *Mississippi Blues* – released that same year on Fahey and Denson's Takoma label and reissued some years later as part of Samuel Charters' *Legacy Of The Blues* series – was virtually White's testament. He had not recorded for almost a quarter of a century and – as far as he knew – there was no guarantee that he would ever record again. So he poured everything he had into the afternoon's worth of songs Fahey and Denson recorded in his Memphis boarding-house, reprising much of his classic early repertoire and revealing aspects of his music which the single-length recordings of the '30s and '40s had proved unable to accomodate. His return to professional music-making wasn't an instant, overnight success, but later that same year he recorded again, this time for Arhoolie Records, consolidating his position as a true elder statesman of Delta blues. He made it to Carnegie Hall and the Newport Folk Festival, toured Europe with the 1970 and 1972 American Folk Blues Festivals and cut several more albums before ill-health finally forced his retirement in the mid-'70s. He died in Memphis, of cancer, on 26 February, 1977.

- *Legacy Of The Blues Vol 1* (Sonet SNTCD 609)

The Return Of 'Bukka' White: his propulsive, clangorous steel-bodied guitar still pounding, his slide still wailing, his singing as urgent as ever. He revisits 'Shake 'Em On Down', 'Poor Boy Long Way From Home'(the venerable Delta theme he recorded in Parchman for Alan Lomax) and 'When Can I Change My Clothes', here mistitled 'Parchman Farm Blues': the intervening quarter-century hadn't dimmed the intensity and immediacy of his classic prisoner's lament. He also includes a couple of train songs – 'New Orleans Streamline' and 'The Atlanta Special' – the first of his lengthy recorded improvisations, and a spoken reminiscence of his mentor ('I wanted to come to be a great man like Charley Patton, but I didn't want to die like he did'). This is one of the classic 'rediscovery' albums, on a par with the great 'comeback' records of SKIP JAMES, SON HOUSE and LIGHTNIN' HOPKINS.

- *Sky Songs* (Arhoolie CD-323)
- *Baton Rouge Mosby Street* (Blues Beacon BLU-10032)

Neither the pre-war singles nor the Takoma album did real justice to White's phenomenal capacity for improvisation, an art at which he was equalled only by JOHN LEE HOOKER and Lightnin' Hopkins. *Legacy Of The Blues Vol 1* consisted mainly of set-pieces, with little hint of the kind of songs which he would 'just reach up and pull out of the sky'. *Sky Songs* is a single-CD filleting of a pair of albums White cut later in 1963; *Baton Rouge Moseby Street* was cut nine years later in Munich, Germany, but both feature White simply winging it, giving himself a groove and letting his life flow out for as long as it took until he'd said or sung everything he need to say or sing. *Sky Songs*' piano-backed blues monologue 'Sugar Hill' finally fades out at 12:25 with 'Bukka' still going. Even the songs which start out with formal structures soon dissolve: the 'Poor Boy' he sings on *Baton Rouge* is, naturally, an entirely different song from the 'Poor Boy Long Way From Home' on *Legacy Of The Blues Vol 1*; similarly Baton Rouge contains two different versions of 'Tippin' In', one retitled 'Stone'. *Sky Songs* is probably the one to get, but *Baton Rouge* is the one to get next.

Subjects for further investigation: At the moment, there isn't a readily available CD collection of 'Bukka' White's pre-war sides, which is severely annoying since Peter Guralnick, who should know, described the long-deleted vinyl anthology, *Parchman Farm* (Columbia), as 'one of the pinnacles of recorded blues'. A few of those key early titles have been compiled, though: 'Washington White' contributes 'The New 'Frisco Train' to **Mississippi Moaners 1927–1942** (Yazoo 1009); that 'Shake 'Em On Down' that 'Bukka' just about managed to record before the sheriff's men came and got him in 1937 is on **Roots Of Rock** (Yazoo 1063); the scarifying

47

1940 'Parchman Farm Blues' appears both on *Legends Of The Blues Vol 1* (CBS 467245 2) and on *The Story Of The Blues* (Columbia 468992 2); and two slide *tours de force* from the same year, 'Bukka's Jitterbug Swing' and 'Special Stream Line', appear, appropriately enough, on *The Slide Guitar: Bottles, Knives & Steel* (CBS 467251 2). At the other end of his career, his two American Folk Blues Festival stints are represented on *American Folk Blues Festival '70* (L&R/Bellaphon CDLR 42021) and *American Folk Blues Festival '72* (L&R/Bellaphon 42018). *Three Shades Of Blues* (Biograph BCD 107), which he shares with Skip James and BLIND WILLIE McTELL, contains what are probably his last recordings: five shorter songs recorded in 1974 in West Memphis, Arkansas.

Robert Johnson

The revisionists are already gnawing at Robert Johnson's reputation, possibly on the grounds that any artist who attracts such universal admiration just *has* to be crap. Charles Chaplin wasn't funny, Otis Redding wasn't really a great soul singer, and Robert Johnson is – ahem – *overrated*. The objections to Johnson's towering status are generally based on the notion that impressionable young whites, giddy with the romantic myth of Johnson's haunted life and mysterious death, and generally ignorant of prior developments in rural blues, have deified Johnson by attributing to him the innovations of others. With all due respect to Johnson's great predecessors and influences, like CHARLEY PATTON, SON HOUSE, SKIP JAMES, KOKOMO ARNOLD, LEROY CARR and LONNIE JOHNSON – all of whom created guitar riffs, lyrical motifs and even near-complete songs which found their way into Johnson's repertoire – his work was indeed the fullest, finest pre-war flowering of the great Delta tradition. Surprise! He really *was* that good. And even though three decades of dedicated research have stripped away much of the fog surrounding the mundane events of Johnson's life, his music seems, if anything, even more impressive than it did back in the days when all that was known of Johnson was the legend of the faceless drifter who, at some moonless Delta crossroads, allegedly sold his soul to Satan in exchange for his extraordinary musical powers.

The mythic Johnson was a mysterious travelling bluesman who had never (as far as anyone knew) been photographed, who had somehow (through a deal with the devil, it was said) transformed himself overnight from a mediocre performer to one of the most powerful anybody had ever heard, and who died in strange circumstances, rumoured to be the victim of a voodoo curse. His ectoplasmic presence seemingly left little trace of his passage other than those 29 songs of rage, regret, terror and despair that he recorded in Texan hotels and storerooms in 1936–7. If those songs had been less remarkable, his story would simply have remained an anecdotal blues curio of interest only to blues fanatics, but his subsequent deification among blues-rock aficionados – signposted by two key cover versions, ERIC CLAPTON's 'Crossroads' (with Cream, 1968), and THE ROLLING STONES' 'Love In Vain' (1969) – transformed Johnson into a 20th-century Faust who stole the fire and paid not only with his life, but his immortal soul.

The real Johnson had a real history and a real background: one of the reasons that his life proved so difficult to reconstruct was that, when he was born in Hazlehurst, Mississippi, on May 8, 1911, his mother was married to someone other than his natural father, and he was born 'Robert Leroy Dodds.' The couple separated, and young Robert was raised – and resented – by Charles Dodds who, for reasons which need not concern us, had changed his name to 'Spencer'. Later Robert Leroy Dodds Spencer rejoined his mother and her new husband Willie 'Dusty' Willis, thus acquiring yet another stepfather and yet another surname. When he was 17, he learned of his real father, Noah Johnson, and became Robert Johnson. Along the line, he had also discovered music and sex: as soon as he was old enough he was hanging around the juke joints watching local stars like Son House and Willie Brown at work, blowing fair harmonica but attracting massive derision whenever he picked up a guitar; and by the time he was 18 he was married. Sadly, his 16-year-old wife died in childbirth the following year; Robert was away on his wanderings at the time, and the local community never forgave him. From then on he was an pariah, perpetually on the move for the rest of his life: his occasional travelling companions and jamming colleagues included Rice Miller (later better-known as SONNY BOY WILLIAMSON II, but then calling himself Little Boy Blue), HOWLIN'

WOLF, ELMORE JAMES, (BIG) WALTER HORTON and MEMPHIS SLIM, but his closest associates were JOHNNY SHINES, Robert Jr Lockwood (his stepson despite a mere four-year gap in their ages) and David 'Honeyboy' Edwards. Somewhere along the the line 'Little Robert' not only got good with a guitar, but he got great.

Those who knew Johnson have admiringly described his 'phonographic memory': how he could be in the middle of a conversation while a song was playing on a radio or jukebox, and – even though he was paying no discernible degree of attention to the song – he would later be able to sing and play it flawlessly, with every musical and lyrical detail intact. Johnson was the first bluesman who systematically learned from records (as opposed to reworking his local traditions); and he seemingly conceived his songs as records in the first place. Rather than simply string out a series of common-stock verses over standard riffs and changes, he composed tight, set-piece songs custom-designed for the three-or-so-minute limits of a 78rpm single. He didn't have a big voice in the sense that BESSIE SMITH or Charley Patton had big voices; it wasn't huge, round and chesty as their were. Instead, it was high and keening: a thin, piercing sound that could cut through any distraction; his guitar backgrounds literally explode with ideas; and his lyrics evocatively depict a man beset by inner as well as external demons. Johnson could never escape the 'Hellhound On My Trail' because it was part of him. Songs like that – and 'Me And The Devil' and 'Crossroads' and 'Stones In My Passway' – depict a man in flight from himself.

All of Johnson's 29 songs were recorded in 1936–7, during three sessions in Texas: only one, 'Terraplane Blues', was any kind of significant success during his lifetime. Nevertheless, the New York producer/entrepreneur John Hammond was aware of Johnson's reputation and sought to book him for the epochal From Spirituals To Swing at Carnegie Hall. Unhappily, by the time Hammond sent for Johnson – to give him the kind of metropolitan showcase which would, undoubtedly, have changed the course of 20th century popular music – Johnson had already fallen into the hellhound's foetid embrace. He died in Greenwood, Mississippi, on 16 August, 1938, after being slipped a bottle of poisoned whisky at a dance he was playing with Honeyboy Edwards. It is still not known exactly who was responsible; the current theory is that the poisoner was a male relative (brother or father) of a girlfriend of Johnson's whom he habitually abused. The all-important rural blues slot at Hammond's concert eventually went to BIG BILL BROONZY, by then already far better-known and more popular with black audiences than Johnson.

Robert Johnson's music lacks all trace of the majestic repose which characterise so many other Delta giants, musical ancestors and offspring alike. Every note, whether played or sung, is taut and sinewy; edgy and propulsive. His music actually feels *driven*: going to a Robert Johnson record for relaxation is like drinking six double espressos just before midnight and expecting a good night's sleep. But since music is not necessarily supposed to be a tranquiliser, and because great art is that which allows us not only to share the experiences of others but to use the knowledge thus gained to reexamine our own inner lives, Robert Johnson remains the greatest artist that the pre-war blues ever produced.

- *The Complete Recordings* (CBS 467246 2)
- *Delta Blues Legend* (Charly CD BM 13-2)

What it says it is: these two editions – differing only in packaging and price (£4 or so cheaper for the Charly) and absolutely indistinguishable once they've been inserted into your player – contain all of Johnson's 29 recorded songs, plus 11 alternate takes. The CBS issue comes with an analytical and biographical account by Steve LaVere, the American archivist who is currently the aristic executor of the Johnson estate, plus LaVere's occasionally dubious transcriptions of, and commentaries on, Johnson's lyrics. In those 29 songs, Johnson absorbed and synthesised virtually all of the previous achievements of the blues masters, gave them his own personal stamp and, in the process, created an entirely new set of possibilities which, six and a half decades later, his successors are still exploring. Whichever version takes your fancy, you should not be without this music: if you only ever own one Delta blues album, make it this one. In fact, get up and go out and buy it. *Now*. It's okay, I'll wait . . .

- **VARIOUS ARTISTS:** *The Roots Of Robert Johnson* (Yazoo 1073)

This fine compilation, which would be an exemplary early blues anthology even without its Johnson connection, documents

Johnson's sources and his borrowings from artists as diverse as the sophisticated Lonnie Johnson or Leroy Carr & SCRAPPER BLACKWELL to Delta ancestors like Charley Patton or Henry Thomas, plus the expected Skip James, Kokomo Arnold, and Son House. Paradoxically, one's admiration for Johnson is increased rather than decreased by the resulting comparisons. For example, Leroy Carr's 'When The Sun Goes Down' is a wonderful song, but it's not a patch on the epic 'Love In Vain' which Johnson created from its raw material; and while Hambone Willie Newbern's 'Rollin' And Tumblin'' is a majestic account of one of the staple Delta themes, Johnson's 'If I Had Possession Over Judgement Day' uses its framework to construct something uniquely powerful and terrifying.

Subjects for further investigation: The Johnson legacy extends far and wide. His most prominent disciples in postwar blues were Muddy Waters and Elmore James: 'Walkin' Blues' and 'Kind Hearted Woman' were staples of Muddy's early repertoire, and James turned 'Dust My Broom' into a signature tune. Shines and Lockwood lived with Johnson's ghost for the rest of their careers: their highly individual gifts overshadowed by their illustrious mentor. Of all the white blues-rockers who have attempted to take Johnson's music on board, the most determined was probably Eric Clapton, who has spent over a quarter of a century slowly working his way through the Johnson songbook ever since, as a member of JOHN MAYALL's BluesBreakers, he chose 'Ramblin' On My Mind' for his first-ever studio lead vocal. The fascinating Honeyboy Edwards album *Delta Bluesman* (Indigo IGO CD 2003) combines a 1942 Library of Congress session (recorded in Clarksdale, Mississippi, by – you guessed – Alan Lomax) with material cut almost half a century later in Chicago. Many other artists, including TAJ MAHAL, have cut superb Johnson-derived material, but I'll leave you to discover that stuff for yourself. Nominating an all-time favourite Johnson cover is a hellish task, but while jointly awarding the Gold Medal in the 'rock' division to the Stones' live version of 'Love In Vain' and Cream's 'Crossroads', allow me to recommend you a marvellous reinterpretation of 'Terraplane Blues' by JOHN LEE HOOKER (vocals) and ROY ROGERS (slide guitar). You can find it on Rogers' *Slidewinder* (Blind Pig BP

72687), or on the Hooker career best-of *The Ultimate Collection 1948–1990* (Rhino R2 70572 [US]).

Tommy McClennan

When Delta singer/guitarist Tommy McClennan arrived in Chicago in 1939, the good-natured BIG BILL BROONZY warned him that local audiences might not take particularly kindly to the couplet 'nigger and the white man playing seven-up/nigger won the money, scared to pick it up' which McClennan was fond of inserting into his version of the staple 'Bottle Up And Go.' McClennan disregarded Broonzy's advice, sang the lines when he performed the song at a house party, and ended up leaving via a first-floor window with the remnants of his guitar still round his neck.

McClennan was an archetypal hard-living, hard-travelling, hard-drinking, hard-strumming Delta bluesman. Born in Yazoo City, Mississippi, on 8 April, 1908, he worked his way to pro status via the usual round of activities: he started out street-singing, graduated to house-parties and country dances (usually in the company of Robert Petway and subsequent ROBERT JOHNSON associate Honeyboy Edwards) and finally moved to Chicago, where entrepreneur Lester Melrose recorded him for the Bluebird label. Presumably Melrose did so simply to cover his bets: Delta blues – especially served up as raw as McClennan's music – was well past its commercial peak, and the postwar downhome revival sparked by Muddy Waters, LIGHTNIN' HOPKINS and JOHN LEE HOOKER was still the best part of a decade away. Even so, McClennan's career missed both the electric-downhome and folk-revival boats: he died a destitute alcoholic in Chicago sometime between 1958 and 1962.

- *Travelin' Highway Man 1939–1942* (Travellin' Man TM CD 06)
- *I'm A Guitar King 1939–1942* (Wolf WBCD-001)

The complete Tommy McClennan: between them, these round up all of the 41 sides recorded by McClennan during his three-year heyday. He was first on record with the standard 'Cross Cut

Saw Blues' (nowadays indelibly associated with ALBERT KING), and the eerie modalities of his work in 'Spanish' (open-G) tuning irresistably recall John Lee Hooker: in fact, many of the songs by SONNY BOY WILLIAMSON I which later turned up in Hooker's repertoire – notably 'Sugar Mama' and 'Bluebird Blues' – seem derived from McClennan's versions rather than from William-son's originals, and Hooker's various versions of 'Bottle (It) Up And Go' are based on McClennan's. The Wolf set is the one to get if you want to explore the McClennan/Hooker connection; otherwise *Travelin' Highway Man* is the more enticing of the pair.

Subjects for further investigation: McClennan's buddy Robert Petway has the distinction of being the first bluesman to record the Delta staple 'Catfish Blues' (a.k.a. 'Still A Fool' or 'Two Trains Running'), as popularised in the '50s by MUDDY WATERS and memorably revived on a 1967 radio session by JIM HENDRIX. Hear it, and him, on *Mississippi Blues (1935–1951)* (Wolf WBCD-005), which also includes the complete prewar recordings of Robert Johnson's stepson Robert Jr Lockwood, plus a 1951 Lockwood session which included the first postwar recording of 'Dust My Broom'.

(Mississippi) Fred McDowell

Like the songsters Mance Lipscombe and Jesse Fuller, Fred McDowell managed the difficult feat of getting 'rediscovered' without ever really having been discovered in the first place. Despite being a talented musician of the CHARLEY PATTON school who was part of the the early blues generation – he was born in Rossville, Tennessee, near Memphis, on 12 January , 1902 – McDowell remained unrecorded until 1959, when he was located in Como, Mississippi, where he had been living since the late '20s, by the ubiquitous Alan Lomax. Lomax recorded a few tracks with him, which surfaced on various Atlantic and Prestige anthologies. What surfaced was a fully realised post-Patton downhome style, complete with irresistably propulsive rhythms, a decisive slide stroke, a strong yet flexible baritone voice, and a huge repertoire of personal variations on local staples. Some of his material was indeed derived from half-remembered snatches of records, but much of it had been acquired the traditional way: from other local singers, most notably Eli Green, a few years McDowell's senior and a fellow Patton devotee.

He recorded again in 1962 (for the same collectors who, two years later, taped SKIP JAMES' first session since 1931), and finally turned pro after a rapturous reception at the University Of Chicago Folk Festival in 1963. From then on until his death from cancer in Memphis on 3 July, 1972, he worked a lucrative round of clubs and festivals, touring Europe several times and even becoming the subject of a sgort documentary film. Fred McDowell was pretty much a one-riff guy – for variation, he plays his standard slide lick fast or slow, or forcefully or delicately – but he sings superbly, his groove is awesome and once he gets The Riff fully cranked, it hurtles along like an express train.

- *Fred McDowell* (Flyright FLY CD-14)
- *Mississippi Delta Blues* (Arhoolie CD 304)

There's not an awful lot to choose between these: they were recorded at around the same time – in '62 and '64–5, respectively – and feature much of the same repertoire. The Arhoolie set has a slightly better song selection, including the original of 'You Gotta Move' (which THE ROLLING STONES borrowed for *Sticky Fingers*), a BLIND WILLIE JOHNSON-style gospel performance with his wife, and a couple of duets with McDowell's mentor Eli Green, but the Flyright set, recorded live in McDowell's home and the homes of various friends and relatives, with enthusiastic appreciation from anybody who happened to be in the room at the time, has considerable immediacy and charm.

Subjects for further investigation: Mid-'60s McDowell in concert can be found on *Great Bluesmen At Newport* (Vanguard VCD 77/78) and *American Folk Blues Festival '65* (L&R/Bellaphon LRCD 42025); Big Mama Thornton's *Ball N' Chain* (Arhoolie CD 305) features a couple of fabulous Thornton/McDowell duets.

Memphis Minnie

Beware of generalisations, like the one about male and female roles in the blues: Lizzie Douglas, better known as Memphis Minnie, was as close a female equivalent as we're ever likely to find to the great male performers of Delta blues. She wrote her own material, played her own guitar, and matched all but the very best of the men at their own game: she once beat BIG BILL BROONZY in a 1933 Chicago contest. Her career eventually spanned almost three full decades of blues, three husband/collaborators, hundreds of sides and not a few hits. However, the tune for which her name is best known to rock fans – LED ZEPPELIN's 'When The Levee Breaks', for which they generously allowed her to share composer credits with the four members of the band – was in fact originally written and sung by 'Kansas Joe' McCoy, Minnie's second husband and performing partner. (The first was guitarist Casey Bill Weldon of the Memphis Jug Band; the third Ernest 'Little Son Joe' Lawler.) Still, hey! what's a few hundred thousand dollars between friends?

Born in Algiers, Louisiana, on 3 June, 1897, and raised in Walls, Mississippi, she learned banjo and guitar from her parents and, at the age of thirteen, ran away to the city which provided her soubriquet. As 'Kid Douglas', she was already a well-known local street singer: she must have been out there nickel-and-diming as soon as she learnt her first two chords. She even performed with the Ringling Brothers Circus (in what capacity is not known), and linked up with Joe McCoy during the '20s when they were both members of the Memphis-based Beale St Jug Band. Her first recordings were made in 1929 and her last exactly 30 years later, though she'd been in near-retirement for most of the '50s. In her prime she played an extremely snappy lead guitar – ever the maverick, she was already playing electric by 1942 – and sang in a powerful voice which contrived to be both rounded and edgy. Her best-known songs were probably 'Chauffeur Blues' (a.k.a. 'Me And My Chauffeur'), a coffee-house favourite during the early '60s, and 'Bumble Bee', the inspiration for MUDDY WATERS' better-known 'Honey Bee'.

For most of her recording life, she'd commuted between Memphis and Chicago, and it was in the former city, appropriately enough, that she died of a fatal stroke on 6 August, 1973. She was buried, equally appropriately, in Walls, Mississippi; a true heroine of the blues. Any woman for whom the words 'Goddammit, who says I can't?' have any resonance should hoist a glass of something potent to her memory.

- *Hoodoo Lady (19333–1937)* (Columbia Legacy 467888 2)
- *Early Rhythm & Blues 1949* (Biograph BCD 124)

Currently, these are the only two Memphis Minnie CDs you can get, and neither of them is the one you need. *Hoodoo Lady* spans the mid-'30s, and very enjoyable most of it is, too: it ought to be retitled *More Songs About Sex And Food*, what with 'Keep On Eatin'', 'Good Biscuits', 'My Butcher Man' and more. There's a thinly disguised rewrite of 'St Louis Blues', entitled 'I Hate To See The Sun Go Down', and a foreshadowing of 'Little Red Rooster' in 'If You See My Rooster (Please Run Him Home)', plus a lot of fiery, sensual singing and neat, punchy guitar. The Biograph set earns the first of the Disingenuousness In Packaging awards which this book will periodically hand out to CDs which, intentionally or not, mislead the public: this is actually a compilation of 1949 sides from the pioneering but defunct Regal label. Minnie appears on only five of the 16 selections (making it a mini-Minnie rather than a full-length showcase), and the other artists, including JIMMY ROGERS, 'St Louis Jimmy' Oden (best-known as the composer of the classic 'Goin' Down Slow') and pianists Sunnyland Slim and Little Brother Montgomery, deserve rather better billing than they receive here. This caveat aside, Minnie plays powerhouse electric guitar and sings as richly and lasciviously as ever on these prototype Chicago blues-band sides, which feature Sunnyland Slim on piano: if the then-neophyte Muddy Waters had been a woman, he'd've sounded very much like this. The problem is that the really cool Memphis Minnie stuff comes from the late '20s/early '30s, and from the late '30s/early '40s; to find that stuff you have to root around the compilation albums. A forthcoming Arhoolie CD should, hopefully, solve the problem.

Subjects for further investigation: Memphis Minnie wasn't the only exception to the men-only rule, though she was by far the most distinguished: more sisters can be found doin' it for themselves on **Mississippi Girls 1928–1931** (Story Of Blues CD 3515-2) and **Female**

Country Blues Vol 1: The Twenties 1924–1928 (Story Of Blues CD 3529-2). The invaluable compilation *Roots Of Rock* (Yazoo 1063) leads off with the original 1929 'When The Levee Breaks' by Kansas Joe & Memphis Minnie; 'My Wash Woman's Gone', of the same vintage, pops up on *Country Blues Bottleneck Guitar Classics 1926–1937* (Yazoo 1026). McCoy sings lead on both tracks, but Minnie is the featured guitarist. 'Ma Rainey', an affecting 1940 tribute to a spiritual forebear, is on *News And The Blues: Telling It Like It Is* (Columbia Legacy 467249 2); for another fine piece from the same year, 'Nothing In Ramblin', seek out *Legends Of The Blues Vol 1* (Columbia Legacy 467245 2). 'Me And My Chauffeur Blues' is on *The Story Of The Blues* (Columbia 468992 2), which is about where we came in.

4. Urban(e) Blues

Lonnie Johnson

Because the earliest urban bluesmen used the same basic instrumentation (piano, acoustic guitar) as their downhome counterparts, it's all too easy to lump all pre-war acoustic blues into one category, ignoring the vast gulf which – though they were near-contemporaries – separated a Delta bard like SON HOUSE and a cosmopolitan polymath like Lonnie Johnson. To describe him as 'sophisticated' would be an understatement: as a vocalist and entertainer his affinity was to the vaudeville tradition of the 'classic blues'; as an instrumentalist he was nothing less than a primary architect of jazz guitar. Yet he, too, was a bluesman; and one of the most successful and influential of his time.

He was a dazzlingly dextrous and inventive guitarist who contributed landmark solos to early Louis Armstrong and Duke Ellington sides; his duets with jazz guitarist Eddie Lang (who had to be credited as 'Blind Willie Dunn' in order to placate neanderthal whites who couldn't handle the idea of interracial musical collaboration) are still considered high points of jazz guitar. As a featured vocalist, he was one of the biggest blues stars to emerge in the late '20s; recording everything from drastically rude 'classic blues' duets with VICTORIA SPIVEY to pop ballads like 'Tomorrow Night.' His compositions have entered the repertoires of ROBERT JOHNSON, ELVIS PRESLEY and B.B. KING: the latter, for what it's worth, considers Lonnie to have been far more important to his own development than Robert. As a studio musician, he performed on hundreds of sessions – playing piano and violin as well as guitar – accompanying everyone from itinerant bluesman Texas Alexander to leading blueswomen like Spivey, Clara Smith and Bertha 'Chippie' Hill.

Alonzo Johnson was born into a large, intensely musical New Orleans family on February 8, 1894. In 1917 he toured Europe with a jazz revue, but settled in St Louis after returning to New Orleans to find that most of his family had perished in a 'flu epidemic. He played in local bands and on the odd studio date; in 1925 he entered a local blues talent contest and won for 18 successive weeks. His reward was a recording contract, and – for better or for worse – he was a bluesman for the rest of his life, enjoying several distinct periods of success, interspersed with periods working at low-paid jobs outside music. He toured as BESSIE SMITH's costar, and hosted his own radio show; his career thrived until the onset of the Depression. By the late '30s he was in Chicago, recording for the Bluebird label; when that bubble burst he recorded booting post-jump in the T-BONE WALKER style. However, he was too sophisticated for downhome and too old for rock and roll, so after a few years as a hotel janitor, he spent the '60s as an honoured monument of the jazz age. He died in Toronto on June 16, 1970, after a heart attack sustained as the result of being struck by an out-of-control car which mounted the pavement.

● *Steppin' On The Blues* (Columbia Legacy 467252 2)

The early Johnson (1925–1932) in a variety of guises: the virtuoso guitarist is liberally represented, playing either solo, with various pianists or, on three devastating duets, with Eddie Lang (and, on two selections, backing Texas Alexander): skip straight to 'Playing With The Strings' as an example of why Lonnie Johnson is easily as important to early jazz guitar as Charlie Christian or Django Rheinhardt. Also on hand is the popular entertainer, hammering home the double-entendres with Victoria Spivey on the two-part 'Toothache Blues'. The most impressive and individual work of his long and varied career. Fetch!

● *He's A Jelly Roll Baker* (RCA Bluebird 07863 66064 2)

Mostly guitar/piano duets a la TAMPA RED & Georgia Tom or LEROY CARR & SCRAPPER BLACKWELL, recorded in Chicago between 1937 and 1942 with accompanists like Joshua Altheimer and Lil Armstrong. Apart from the raggy ballad 'In Love Again', most of the material is in the relaxed, jazzy 'Bluebird' vein which dominated Chicago blues before the advent of MUDDY WATERS and the domination of the Chess school of South Side electric downhome.

● *Me And My Crazy Self* (Charly CD CHARLY 266)

In 1947 Johnson signed to the Cincinnati-based King label – later the home of jump kings like WYNONIE HARRIS, Eddie 'Cleanhead' Vinson and ROY BROWN and subsequent R&B stars like FREDDIE KING, LITTLE WILLIE JOHN and JAMES BROWN, but then best-known for country music – and brought himself up-to-date with a vengeance. Playing electric guitar with tough big-band ensembles that rivaled T-BONE WALKER's backup crews, he scored big with the 1948 ballad 'Tomorrow Night', a favourite of Elvis Presley's. It's not included here, unfortunately: you can allegedly find it on the compilation *Tomorrow Night* (King KS 1083) and may you have better luck locating that particular item than I've had.

Subjects for further investigation: If *Steppin' On The Blues* doesn't deliver enough of Johnson's work from that prolific period, then further examples of his mastery are scattered throughout many other titles. **Raunchy Business: Hot Nuts & Lollipops** (Columbia 467889 2) teams him up once again with Victoria Spivey on the two-part 'Furniture Man Blues' and keeps the double-entendres coming on 'Wipe It Off' and 'Best Jockey In Town'. The 1927 'Life Saver Blues' is on **The Roots Of Robert Johnson** (Yazoo 1073); **Great Blues Guitarists: String Dazzlers** (Columbia 467894 2) collects three more wonderful duets with Eddie Lang as well as two fine solo performances; **Them Dirty Blues** (Jass CD-11/12) includes the intriguing 'Once Or Twice' and the 'You Rascal You' variant

'Uncle Ned, Don't Lose Your Head'; the first part of the Johnson/
Spivey 'Toothache Blues' is also available on *Sissy Man Blues: 25
Authentic Straight & Gay Blues & Jazz Vocals* (Jass J-CD-13), while
Street Walkin' Blues (Jass J-CD-626) re-presents 'Crowin' Rooster
Blues' from his Bluebird period alongside the previously unre-
leased 1931 'Your Love Is Cold'. 'Fine Booze And Heavy Dues', a
1961 sample of his work during the folk-blues revival, appears on
Bluesville Volume 1: Folk Blues (Ace CDCH 247). For a taste of
Johnson's piano work, there's 'Sam, You're Just A Rat' on
Barrelhouse Blues 1927-1936 (Yazoo 1028). Elvis Presley's version of
'Tomorrow Night' is on *Reconsider Baby* (RCA PD 85418) and *The
King Of Rock'N' Roll: The Complete '50s Masters* (RCA PD 90689(5));
Bob Dylan's on *Good As I've Been To You* (Columbia 472710 2);
SNOOKS EAGLIN's on *The Legacy Of The Blues Vol 2* (Sonet SNTCD
625).

Leroy Carr & Scrapper Blackwell

Piano/guitar teams were big news in the late '20s and early '30s:
the Chicago-based TAMPA RED & Georgia Tom, of whom more
later, were one of the most successful such duos: the other and
most likely the more influential was, improbably enough, a pair of
bootleggers from Indianopolis, Indiana. Pianist/vocalist Leroy
Carr was the composer of such celebrated blues standards as
'How Long Blues' (their very first hit and one of the top blues
tunes of 1928; the source of the 'Come Back Baby' most
frequently associated with LIGHTNIN' HOPKINS), '(In The Evening)
When The Sun Goes Down' (the basis for ROBERT JOHNSON's
immortal 'Love in Vain'), 'Mean Mistreater', 'Sloppy Drunk' and
'Blues Before Sunrise'. Guitarist Francis 'Scrapper' Blackwell, who
also freelanced as an accompanist to others and, occasionally, as a
vocalist in his own right, rivalled the celebrated LONNIE JOHNSON for
his clean, dextrous, imaginative acoustic lead-lines, just as Carr
challenged him as a pioneer of sophisticated but soulful blues
balladry. It was Blackwell, in his solo incarnation, who originated
'Kokomo Blues', later passed on by KOKOMO ARNOLD to Robert
Johnson, who transformed it into the familiar 'Sweet Home
Chicago.' Between 1928 and 1935, when Carr died of – ironically

– severe alcohol abuse, and Blackwell, as a result, flipped out, they were one of the most popular 'race' acts in America. They were certainly among Robert Johnson's favourites: it's been suggested, intriguingly enough, that Johnson's complex guitar arrangements partially derive from an attempt to match the interplay of Carr's piano and Blackwell's guitar.

Leroy Carr – born in Nashville, Tennessee, on 27 March, 1905 – had clear urban diction and a rich, mellifluous voice admirably suited to the slow-to-medium-tempo blues the duo favoured: he was undoubtedly a more resourceful pianist than the majority of the duo's records would suggest, but he preferred to keep his piano work fairly straightforward, concentrate on his singing, and let his gifted partner Blackwell – born in Syracuse, North Carolina, on 21 February, 1903 – take care of the solos and fills. He could play uptempo when the material demanded it, but he plainly sounded more comfortable with a relaxed groove. They were introduced in 1927 by the owner of an Indianapolis record store and, after an initial period of reluctance to exchange their lucrative bootlegging interests for of the uncertainties of the music business, they duly teamed up, cut 'How Long Blues' for Vocalion Records, sold shitloads of records and almost instantly became a top attraction, touring almost continuously from 1928 to 1932. Even during the two-year recording hiatus enforced on them by the Depression, they hibernated comfortably in a St Louis club residency; returning to the studio in 1934 to resume business as usual. Scrapper Blackwell took his partner's death very hard indeed, possibly because he had stormed out of what turned out to be their final session together, leaving Carr to finish the date solo. Scrapper quit fulltime music until 1959, and what could have been a distinguished '60s blues comeback was terminated when he was shot in the back in an Indianapolis alley and died on 7 October, 1962.

The extent to which Carr was loved and mourned can be gauged by the success of Bill Gaither's tribute 'Life Of Leroy Carr'; the fact that Blackwell effectively 'disappeared' from the scene when Carr died only accentuated the sizeable gap he left in the blues landscape. The Carr-Blackwell sides were slick enough for the city but accessible enough for rural listeners because they refined the blues without diluting it; in doing so, they provided an invaluable signpost to its eventual future.

- **LEROY CARR:** *1930–1935* (Magpie PYCD 07)
- **LEROY CARR:** *Vol 2:1929–1935* (Magpie PYCD 17)

Your basic Leroy Carr & Scrapper Blackwell kit: The original 'How Long Blues' is missing, but they re-recorded it four more times, and two later versions are featured on *1930–1935*. Of the other Carr standards, the first volume includes 'Sloppy Drunk Blues' (as well as the poignant solo performance 'Going Back Home' from his last session in 1935), while you have to go to Vol 2 for 'Blues Before Sunrise' and 'When The Sun Goes Down'. It would be nice if there was a single-CD Leroy Carr compilation with all his best-known tunes on it, but life would be meaningless without a little adversity.

- **SCRAPPER BLACKWELL:** *The Virtuoso Guitar Of Scrapper Blackwell* (Yazoo 1019)

Blackwell had a dusty, unassuming voice – far more country-sounding than Carr's even though his diction was not significantly less crisp – and his guitar still dazzles even without piano accompaniment. As well as singing lead, he also appears here as accompanist to the terrifyingly (and justifiably) obscure Black Bottom McPhail, to one Tommie Bradley (though there is, apparently, some controversy among buffs as to whether the guitar on Bradley's track is actually Blackwell at all), and to someone called Leroy Carr, though both the Carr/Blackwell collaborations included here also appear on *1930–1935*. More to the point, it also includes his 'Kokomo Blues': this selection is highly recommended to guitar buffs.

Subjects for further investigation: **Leroy Carr & Scrapper Blackwell** *1930–1958* (Story Of Blues CD 3538-2) fleshes out the material on the two Magpie collections without adding anything particularly essential. Its principal draw is a quartet of comeback tracks – including a devastatingly poignant 'Nobody Knows You When You're Down And Out' retitled 'Once I Lived The Life Of A Millionaire' – recorded by Blackwell in 1958; **Bluesville Vol 1: Folk Blues** (Ace CDCH 247) adds two more from the following year: one a reprise of 'Down South Blues' (from *Virtuoso Guitar*), the other a remake of Carr's 'Blues Before Sunrise.' 'When The Sun

Goes Down' also appears on **The Roots Of Robert Johnson** (Yazoo 1073).

5. 'Folk' Blues

'All songs is folk songs – I never heard no horse sing 'em,' quoth the great BIG BILL BROONZY: the line's always good for a laugh even if it isn't actually very helpful. Nevertheless, the point is a valid one: the blues is simply one of many strands of rural folk music to emerge into the twentieth century (even though it is first among equals) from the American heartlands. Many performers were skilled at a variety of musics – a 'songster' prided himself on being able to play songs in any style a listener might request – delivering anything from hillbilly to polkas for white audiences, as well as several flavours of blues to blacks, and gospel to both. For sound commercial reasons, a black artist would be far more likely to be recorded exclusively as a bluesman by entrepreneurs catering to black record buyers: Robert Johnson's contemporaries maintain that he had several different repertoires, but only his 'blues' repertoire was recorded. However, academics and devotees, notably those – like John and Alan Lomax – employed by the Library Of Congress, sought out and preserved the older forms which predated the 1920s' 'blues boom.' Men like Broonzy, Huddie 'LEADBELLY' Leadbetter, MISSISSIPPI JOHN HURT, SONNY TERRY & BROWNIE McGHEE were living treasuries of African-American oral culture: they not only enriched our collective musical vocabulary, but made irreplaceable contributions to our understanding of how life was lived amongst the rural poor.

'Folk' blues of what is generally classified as 'Piedmont', 'East Coast' or 'Carolina' style used a very different set of stylistic devices from those of the Delta or Texas-style 'country' blues. More closely related to Anglo-Celtic folk music, it places a far greater emphasis on the structural integrity of the melody line, meter and chord sequence than the freer, rougher, more modal blues of Texas and the Delta. Guitarists of this school are far more likely to play neatly fingerpicked ragtimey chord sequences in standard tuning, using the keys of C, D and G; while their 'country' counterparts favoured the 'Spanish' (open G or A) or 'Vastopol' (open D or E) retunings for bottleneck pieces, and the keys of E or A when playing in regular tuning. Where a Delta singer would improvise a song by stringing a mixture of 'common stock' and original verses together around a particular theme, the 'folk' bluesman would be far more likely to perform a narrative ballad with a set beginning, middle and end; taking as much care to preserve a song's lyrical as structural integrity.

The connection with white folk music was more than simply a musical one: whereas black audiences – and the (mostly) white entrepreneurs who catered to their tastes – weren't interested in any but the most deeply coded social protests or songs about oppression, crusading leftist folkies like Woody Guthrie and Pete Seeger encouraged their black counterparts, like Broonzy, Lead-belly, and Terry & McGhee, to address these issues directly. Characteristically, many of these musicians – Broonzy and McGhee particularly – maintained parallel careers recording city blues (featuring electric guitar, piano, drums and saxophone) for black audiences until the mid-'50s, and Terry & McGhee cut *I Couldn't Believe My Eyes* (BGO BGOCD), a rocking urban blues album co-featuring Chicago slide modernist EARL HOOKER, as recently as the late '60s. In the end, the most powerful argument is the one in favour of a mixed economy of the blues: one which recognises both its dual status as folk and popular art, and the unique and valuable parts played by commercial and academic sectors alike.

Leadbelly

The career of Huddie Ledbetter – the first name rhymed with 'moody' rather than 'muddy' – qualifies as a true American legend both because of the extraordinary wealth of vernacular song which 'Leadbelly' (the nickname was both a pun on his surname and an acknowledgement of his toughness) donated to the world, and because of what his equally extraordinary career tells us about America in the first half of the 20th century. Whether or not Leadbelly actually 'wrote' (in a formal European sense) songs like 'Goodnight Irene', 'Cotton Fields', 'Midnight Special', 'Have A Whiff On Me', 'Rock Island Line', 'Pick A Bale Of Cotton' or 'Ella Speed', it's through him that they entered the standard vocabulary of American music. And then there's the myth: the leather-lunged iron man with the ear-to-ear scar and 12-string guitar who knew 500 songs; the convicted felon who twice sang himself out of the toughest jails in the South to become first the pet of New York cafe society and finally an icon of the Left. Leadbelly was a dangerous, violent man, but he wasn't a gangster or a crook: the only money he ever made came from picking cotton or making music. He was simply a bayou brawler with awesome physical strength, an omnipresent clasp knife, a hairtrigger temper and an inability to stay out of trouble.

Huddie Ledbetter was born on 15 January, 1888, by Caddo Lake near Shreveport, Louisiana, just where the Texas, Louisiana and Arkansas state lines intersect, though when he was five his parents moved to Leigh, Texas, just across the state line. His parents doted on him: he was a big tough boy who could pick more cotton than anybody else on the farm, and who was profoundly fond of women, booze and fighting in more or less any combination. His father was a musician and taught him accordion; later on he learned guitar, harmonica and piano. Early in the new century, he set off on a decade's worth of itinerant music-making around Louisiana and Texas, and it was during this time that he acquired both the formidable repertoire which sustained him through the years, and the 12-string guitar which was to become his trademark instrument. In Dallas he met up with BLIND LEMON JEFFERSON, starting out as the genius' 'lead man' – a position also filled at various times by T-BONE WALKER and Josh(ua) White – before graduating to full-fledged running buddy and performing partner. It is mildly intriguing to speculate on what might have been had the partnership lasted, but Leadbelly's musical career was rudely interrupted when he was jailed for assault in 1916. His parents mortgaged their farm to pay for a lawyer, but he didn't serve even his comparatively light three-month sentence: Lead-belly escaped and spent a couple of years living under the alias of 'Walter Boyd'. Unfortunately, 'Boyd' got busted too: this time for murder, and in 1918 Leadbelly went down for a thirty-year spell in Harrison Country Prison in Texas. A musical plea to Governor Pat Neff had him back out seven years later, but Leadbelly's temper got the better of him once again, and he was back in jail by 1930, this time for attempted murder.

In 1933, a crucial encounter took place: John Lomax arrived at Louisiana State Penitentiary (better known as 'Angola', one of the heaviest jails in the South) on his ceaseless quest for real-life American folk music; he found Leadbelly and recorded him for the Library of Congress. One of those songs, 'Governor O.K. Allen', was widely credited for getting Leadbelly sprung the following year – as 'Governor Pat Neff' had done nearly a decade earlier – but the Louisiana authorities insist that, with time off for good beahvious, Leadbelly would have been released anyway. However, the upshot was that as soon as Leadbelly was back in the world, he sought out Lomax and signed on as his chauffeur, bodyguard and client. The relationship between the altruistic Southern paternalist and the brawling, unlettered Southern genius forever changed American music. The question of who was manipulating who is an intriguing one: the spectacle of Lomax hauling Leadbelly, sometimes clad in stylised convicts' garb, around the society salons is not a pleasant or comfortable one for moderns to contemplate, and the temptation is to consider Lomax as an exploiter, but the traffic went both ways. Basically, Leadbelly simply 'yassuh'ed Lomax to death, and as a good paternalistic Southern gent with the welfare of the the Nigra at heart, Lomax fell for it. It was Lomax who made Leadbelly famous, and if he attempted to force his interpretation of Leadbelly on the artist himself as well as on the world at large, then that was simply because of the man he was and the times in which he lived.

The first problem was that of turning Leadbelly's notoriety and artistry into something they could take to the bank. They attempted to translate his fame and eminence into cash (and to establish himself with the contemporary black audience) by recording him as a commercial blues man, and collected a healthy advance on the basis of contracting to record forty sides for the ARC label, but the venture was a failure: as far as most black record-buyers were concerned, his music was ten years out of date, and only a handful of titles were ever issued. Leadbelly became irritated at Lomax's desire to keep him away from the black communities and to prevent him from spending his meagre earnings on booze and partying (instead of, as Lomax wanted him to do) saving his money to buy a house for himself and his young wife Martha); Lomax was sorely puzzled because Leadbelly was no longer the sweet, humble man he had seemed to be when Lomax met him in prison: it never seemed to occur to him that a man in prison will become whatever he needs to become in order to gain his freedom, and that once Leadbelly was no longer in prison, he saw no need to continue behaving as if he was. The two eventually parted company – though for the rest of Leadbelly's life he stayed on cordial terms with Lomax's son Alan – around 1939, the time Leadbelly served his last jail term: a year in New York's Riker's Island for assault.

During his final decade, Leadbelly's home in New York was a centre for folk and blues activity: his intimates and housemates included SONNY TERRY, BROWNIE McGHEE and Woody Guthrie. He remained active, performing and recording (notably for the small Folkways independent) to steadily increasing success and acclaim, but time was running out for him: he died in New York, after a battle with Lou Gehrig's disease, on 6 December, 1949, barely a year before folk group The Weavers took his 'Goodnight Irene' to the top of the pop charts, beginning the process that made his repertoire the cornerstone of the folk revival of the '50s. It is said that only time anyone ever saw Leadbelly cry was the day he realised that he could no longer play his guitar.

- *The Very Best Of Leadbelly* (Music Club MCCD 106)

A handy budget-price starter-pack, nicely annotated and rounding up 20 tracks with a playing time of 65 minutes for – at the time of writing – £5.99. Drawn from the Library of Congress and Folkways catalogues, it includes, from his 'folk' repertoire, 'Midnight Special', 'Careless Love', 'Goodnight Irene', 'Rock Island Line' and 'Bourgeois Blues', as well as blues pieces like 'Match Box Blues' and the fabulous LoC version of 'C.C. Rider.' As an affordable beginners' guide to Leadbelly, it could hardly be improved upon, but if you develop a taste for Mr Ledbetter, you're going to want to move on to . . .

- *Midnight Special* (Rounder CD 1044)
- *Gwine To Dig A Hole To Put The Devil In* (Rounder CD 1045)
- *Let It Shine On Me* (Rounder CD 1046)

The Library of Congress recordings: 46 songs, recorded by John and/or Alan Lomax between 1935 and 1942, which represent the greatest single storehouse of American folk song available anywhere; and – despite sound quality which was primitive even for its time – the definitive document of Leadbelly and his music. These aren't the records by which Leadbelly was best known in his lifetime, but they're the ones by which he deserves to be remembered. *Midnight Special* contains the greatest number of Leadbelly's signature songs: 'Midnight Special', 'Take A Whiff On Me', two versions of 'Irene', a gorgeous 'Careless Love' and 'Governor O.K. Allen', dedicated to obtaining his release from his second major jail term. Apart from *The Very Best Of*, it's probably the best general introduction to his work, but my personal favourite of the three is *Gwine To Dig A Hole To Put The Devil In*, the one to go for if you've already bought the Music Club set. It contains his blues masterpiece 'C.C. Rider', which magically combines a foot-stomping boogie beat worthy of JOHN LEE HOOKER himself with a breathtakingly delicate and lyrical slide line, and a couple of startling pieces which reinterpret Anglo-Celtic folk balladry in a bold blues context. 'Mama Did You Bring Any Silver' (a.k.a. 'Gallis Pole') is the source for LED ZEPPELIN's 'Gallows Pole'; but the astonishing (and rather unpromisingly titled) 'If It Wasn't For Dicky' comes as close as anything ever recorded to providing an idea of how HOWLIN' WOLF would've sounded if he'd hung out as Cecil Sharp House. Then there's 'Governor Pat Neff', with which he drastically shortened his first jail term, and the taut, raging 'Bourgeois Blues', written at the urging of Alan Lomax who, even if he contributed nothing else to the song, certainly taught Leadbelly the word 'bourgeois'. *Let It Shine On Me* features a heaping handful of gospel songs and sacred fragments, plus a couple more of Leadbelly's later topical ballads, including the acrid 'The Scottsboro Boys'.

- *King Of The Twelve-String Guitar* (Columbia Legacy 467893 2)

Leadbelly as commercial bluesman, 1935: in market terms, a complete and utter flop, since the contemporary black audience at whom the records were aimed no longer had any significant interest in such old-timey stuff. This in itself should create no problem for the modern listener, since in the 1990s it matters little whether this material was recorded in 1935 or 1925 as long as it sounds good now; but sadly this stuff isn't great blues, great Leadbelly, or even the best possible selection from the available material. Though it draws on the same sessions, has the same number of tracks and even boasts a six-out-of-sixteen overlap, *King* isn't a patch on *Leadbelly* (Columbia CK 30035 [US]), the collection it displaces. Leadbelly's musical canvas was a spectacularly broad one: conventional blues was simply one of its many details, and not even the most intriguing one.

The musician depicted on *King Of The Twelve-String Guitar* is an interesting minor Gulf Coast bluesman whose work has something of the barrel-chested weight and rhythmic drive of CHARLEY PATTON, a hint of the 12-string thunder of Georgia stars like Barbecue Bob, and – most prominent of all – the influence of Leadbelly's old Dallas street partner Blind Lemon Jefferson, from whom he borrowed 'Black Snake Blues' and 'Matchbox Blues', and of whom the older CD contains an enchanting reminiscence. *Leadbelly* is also the better bet, if you can find it, because it includes a version of his loveliest blues piece 'C.C. Rider' – not as good a version as the one on *Gwine To Dig A Hole To Put The Devil In*, however – a sturdy 'Death Letter' to rival SON HOUSE, and the powerful, autobiographical 'Mr Tom Hughes's Town'. *King* does, however, include 'Packing Trunk Blues', which features a very similar background to 'C.C. Rider', but then so does the highly recommended compilation *The Slide Guitar: Bottles, Knives & Steel* (Columbia Legacy 467251 2).

- *Alabama Bound* (RCA Bluebird ND 90321)

Amazingly, these 1940 Victor sessions with The Golden Gate Jubilee Quartet, who appear on eight out of 16 tracks, were both Leadbelly's first recordings for a major record company, and his first collaborative studio efforts. Some of the tracks with the gospel quartet are stilted and contrived – bearing in mind the backbreaking realities of black Southern rural life, the jollity of 'Pick A Bale Of Cotton' seems both incongruous and disingenuous – but 'Good Morning Blues', with its spoken introduction ('Never was a white man had the blues, because no problems') is one of the most powerful blues pieces he ever recorded, and there is a delightful irony to be savoured in the fact that the title track shares its melody and structure with the great ribald 'classic' blues 'Don't You Feel My Leg'. 'Easy Rider' is essentially the same as 'C.C. Rider', but performed on 'straight' guitar rather than slide; the versions of 'Can't You Line 'Em' (a.k.a. 'Linin' Track', as revived in the '60s by TAJ MAHAL) and 'Rock Island Line' are effective enough and there's real power and poignancy to 'I'm On My Last Go-Round', but, despite the considerable plus-factor of professional-quality recording, this remains Grade B Leadbelly and should not take purchasing preference over the Library of Congress material. Or, for that metter, over . . .

- **_Leadbelly Sings Folk Songs_** (Smithsonian/Folkways CD SF 40010)

The Library of Congress continued by other means: like his friends Woody Guthrie and Sonny Terry (both of whom show up on this collection, as does Cisco Houston, another New York crony), Leadbelly recorded frequently for Moses Asch's Folkways indie during the '40s, but – unlike the Library of Congress stuff – this material was actually released during Leadbelly's lifetime. Peculiarly enough, one of the songs listed on the front cover ('Alabama Bound') doesn't appear on the disk despite a stingy runtime of only 32-and-a-bit minutes, itself inexplicable when one considers how much Leadbelly material Asch recorded. Nevertheless, it's worthwhile because the LoC aesthetic remains intact: the backing voices of Terry, Guthrie and Houston provide a funkier 'Stewball' than do the Golden Gate Jubilee Quartet on the RCA sides, and the overall sound is pleasingly raw and clear. There are even brief samples of Leadbelly's accordion work and his (very rare) preaching, a powerful 'Linin' Track', an exhilarating blast of Terry's harp and whooping on a rocking 'Outskirts Of Town', and the dazzling one-two punch of the gospel 'The Blood Done Signed My Name' and a tribute to the recently-deceased Jean Harlow. In lieu of conventional liner notes, you get Guthrie's essay 'Leadbelly

Is A Hard Name'. There's nothing wrong with this CD that couldn't've been cured by doubling the runtime.

Subjects for further investigation: In 1988, Columbia issued an album entitled *Folkways: The Vision Shared*, in which contemporary stars ranging from LITTLE RICHARD and Taj Mahal to Bruce Springsteen and Bob Dylan reinterpreted some of the bestknown songs of Leadbelly and Woody Guthrie as a tribute to, and fundraiser for, the Smithsonian/Folkways project. Folkways' own *Folkways: The Original Vision* (Smithsonian/Folkways CD SF 40001) gathers up the 'originals' of the reinterpreted songs: Leadbelly's contributions include 'Midnight Special', 'Goodnight Irene', 'Bourgeois Blues' and 'Rock Island Line', as well as – on '4,5 And 9' – a teamup with Sonny Terry & Brownie McGhee. *Good Morning Blues* (Biograph BCD 113) presents, alongside excellent material by REV. GARY DAVIS and the ebullient harp-blowing gospel bluesman Dan Smith, a 12-minute 1940 pilot tape for a proposed radio show, in which Leadbelly performs a half-dozen songs (including Good Morning Blues', 'Worried Blues' and 'Boll Weevil') with Guthrie as MC. Both the Library of Congress and Smithsonian/Folkways are sitting on vast amounts of unavailable-on-CD Leadbelly, and EMI presumably hold the tapes of his '40s sessions for Capitol, so keep watching the skies for further releases.

To create a context for John Lomax's discovery of Leadbelly, check out *Red River Blues* (Travelin' Man TM CD 08), a collection of LoC recordings made by the Lomaxes and others (including the great African-American poet and folklorist Zora Neale Thurston) in prisons and elsewhere in Georgia and Virginia, between 1934 – the year after Lomax first recorded Leadbelly – and 1943. Few of the various performers (Blind Joe, Reese Crenshaw, Booker T. Sapps and others) ever distinguished themselves in civilian life – singer/harpist Buster Brown (1911–1956), of 'Fannie Mae' and 'Dr Brown' fame, was the main exception – but it certainly wasn't because of shortage of talent: Jimmie Strothers, in particular, delivers some fabulous slide on 'Goin' To Richmond'.

Big Bill Broonzy

When producer/entrepreneur John Hammond was assembling the cast for the first of his all-star 'Spirituals To Swing' Carnegie Hall concerts in 1938, ROBERT JOHNSON was his first choice as standard-bearer for the rural blues singer/guitarist tradition. However, as Hammond discovered, Robert Johnson was dead; and his second choice, BLIND BOY FULLER, was in jail. (Inexplicably, LEADBELLY was never approached.) Hammond ended up booking Fuller's sidekick, harpman SONNY TERRY, and Big Bill Broonzy: the paradox was that Broonzy, a popular and versatile Chicago-based entertainer, was far better-known to black audiences and record-buyers than Johnson ever was. He had already been recording for almost a decade as both sideman and featured artist, and was to enjoy success in a variety of different careers – country bluesman, city bluesman, folk singer and finally Beloved Entertainer – before his death in 1958.

It is no exaggeration to state that William Lee Conley 'Big Bill' Broonzy, born in Scott, Mississippi, on June 26, 1893, was one of the best-loved and most-travelled bluesmen of all. During the 1950's, he toured Europe, South America. Africa and Australia to rapturous receptions, and he was virtually a demigod to British folk and jazz fans. (Cannily, he had informed his hosts that he was the last living _real_ blues singer; knowing no better, they believed him.) His first instrument was the violin, and his first calling was as a preacher in Arkansas, but after a brief spell in the Army right at the tail end of World War I, he moved to Chicago. He came to the guitar late (in 1924) and made his first record a mere four years later. Possibly because he learned guitar in the city rather than the country, his playing was far more slick and urban than that of his Delta contemporaries, and he could move effortlessly from slick, raggy novelties to downhome deep blues. He was similarly gifted as a singer: his voice was as rich, deep and sonorous as that of any big-chested Mississippi shouter, but his enunciation was city-crisp and he had enviable flexibility and vocal control; he was also a prolific composer with nigh on 300 copyrighted songs to his credit. By temperament he was a gregarious, genial man, and it was not surprising that he became the best-selling bluesman of the immediate pre-war era, and the virtual godfather of the first wave of Chicago blues: the 'Bluebird' years of TAMPA RED, MEMPHIS SLIM, MEMPHIS MINNIE and the original SONNY BOY WILLIAMSON. This geniality is clearly apparent in his music, which has as much, if not more, to do with pleasure as with pain.

By the time MUDDY WATERS and WILLIE DIXON transformed the blues of the Windy City into the electric-downhome ensemble music which ate the world, Broonzy had adroitly shifted his ground before it collapsed under him: two 1947 tracks included on *Big Bill Broonzy 1934-1947* (Story Of Blues CD 3504-2) feature him playing electric guitar in an emphatically postwar-styled setting. (He had, in fact, spent a year or so working as a janitor at an Iowa university.) He was now Big Bill The Folk Singer, shucking his slick city suits in favour of the overalls which he hadn't worn since he left the South three decades earlier. Some claim that he was taking the opportunity to discard vulgar commercialism and return to the 'authentic' music of his youth; others that there was something demeaning about this sophisticated urbanite masquerading as an illiterate sharecropper, but there was no doubting the passion and commitment which he brought to the older-style blues and the pre-blues ballads; nor the power of such explicit social commentaries (I refuse to use the term 'protest songs') as 'Get Back' and 'When Will I Be Called A Man?'

Sadly, he didn't live long enough to cash in on what could have been the biggest jackpot of all: the 1960s 'rediscovery' of great acoustic bluesmen like Mississippi John Hurt, Skip James and Son House, from which other experienced performers like JOHN LEE HOOKER and SONNY TERRY & BROWNIE McGHEE had benefited. Broonzy's voice was destroyed by throat and lung cancer in 1957, and he died in Chicago on August 15, 1958. His easy adaptability has ultimately counted against him: since his music was neither as eerie and mesmeric as that of Robert Johnson and Skip James, nor as funky and muscular as that of LEADBELLY or Waters, his reputation as a performer has suffered. Nevertheless, his best-known songs, including 'Just A Dream', 'I Feel So Good', and the much-covered 'Key To The Highway', live on.

- *Good Time Tonight* (CBS 467247 2)

A well-chosen and easily accessible cross-section of Broonzy's work from 1930–1940, covering everything from raggy novelties like 'Flat Floot Suzie With A Yas Yas' (which Slim Gaillard's fans will probably recognise) to the deeper blues of 'Worry You Off My Mind.' This period is covered in rather more detail (and with surprisingly few overlaps) on *Do That Guitar Rag 1928–1935* (Yazoo 1035), *The Young Big Bill Broonzy 1928–1935* (Yazoo 1011), *Big Bill Broonzy 1935–1940* (Black & Blue 59.253 2) and *Big Bill Broonzy 1934–1947* (Story Of Blues CD 3504-2)

- *Remembering Big Bill Broonzy: The Greatest Minstrel Of The Authentic Blues* (BGO BGCD 91)

These 1951 sessions capture Broonzy at his most self-consciously folkloric, performing folk material like 'John Henry' and 'The Blue Tail Fly', alongside tougher blues like 'Get Back', a diplomatically retitled version of his uncompromising 'Black, Brown And White' ('If you're white, all right/if you're brown, stick around/if you're black, get back'). Some unintended mirth may be gleaned from the listing of a track allegedly entitled 'Leroy Carr': what actually happens is that Broonzy strums a chord, inquires 'You remember this? It's LEROY CARR', and launches into a rendition of the great pianist's 'When The Sun Goes Down', the song upon which ROBERT JOHNSON based 'Love In Vain'. Presumably the producers were unfamiliar not only with the song, but also with the name of the one of the most prominent performers in pre-war blues.

- *Big Bill Broonzy Sings Folk Songs* (Smithsonian Folkways CD SF 40023)
- *The 1955 London Sessions* (Sequel NEXCD 119)

The last, more or less, of Big Bill. The Folkways album combines studio and concert sides (including a duet of 'John Henry' with Pete Seeger) from shortly before his death, when intimations of mortality brought him back to gospel material like 'This Train' (the 'original' upon which Wille Dixon based LITTLE WALTER's 'My Babe') and 'Tell Me What Kind Of Man Jesus Is'; the London album is mostly solo, with four songs featuring a British 'trad jazz' ensemble, and is chiefly noteworthy for a stunning, passionate 'When Will I Be Called A Man?'

Subjects for further investigation: Broonzy's 1938 Carnegie Hall appearance is documented on *From Spirituals To Swing* (Vanguard VCD2-47/48); Muddy Waters' tribute album *Muddy Waters Sings Big Bill* is doublebacked with *Muddy Waters, Folk Singer* on MCA/ Chess CHD-5907. Alan Lomax's celebrated 'ethnological forgery' *Blues In The Mississippi Night* (Sequel NEXCD 122), which features Broonzy alongside Memphis Slim and the original Sonny Boy Williamson, tells you as much as you could want to know about the rigours of black life in the racist South in the early 20th century. Broonzy's work as a studio guitarist would take pages and pages to list, but you can find him on a staggering proportion of the blues records cut in Chicago during the '30s and early '40s. Hear him on fine form behind his half-brother Robert 'WASHBOARD SAM' Brown (1910–1966), who specialised in cheerful hokum, on *Rockin' My Blues Away* (RCA/Bluebird ND90652), *Washboard Sam (1935–1947)* (Story Of Blues CD 3502-2) and *JAZZ GILLUM/WASHBOARD SAM: Harmonica and Washboard Blues 1937–1940* (Black & Blue 59.252 2). The last-cited is probably the best bet, since it's shared by Sam and singer/harpist Gillum; it includes Broonzy's celebrated composition 'Key To The Highway', albeit sung by (and credited to) Gillum. Incidentally, the Story Of Blues collection includes, on 'It's Too Late Now' (1938), an electric guitar solo by the white jazz guitarist George Barnes which anticipates many of the later developments most frequently associated with T-BONE WALKER.

Blind Blake

It would be unfair to the memory of REV. GARY DAVIS to state categorically that Arthur 'Blind' Blake was the greatest ragtime guitarist of his time, but not *that* unfair. The mysterious Blind Blake – born somewhere in Florida sometime in 1890; died somewhere else in Florida sometime in 1933 – cut immensely popular novelty singles for Paramount between 1926 and 1932, and his music is notable both for its sheer good humour and for the boggling virtuosity of his guitar work. There's not a lot to say about Blind Blake: he lived, he played, he died. And he was brilliant.

● *Ragtime Guitar's Foremost Fingerpicker* (Yazoo 1068)

The pick – no pun intended – of Blake's six-year recording career, from wonderful raggy novelties like 'Diddie Wa Diddie' and 'Skeedle Loo Doo' to decidedly less light-hearted fare like 'You Gonna Quit Me' and 'Bad Feeling Blues'. There's nothing in pre-war blues as jauntily beguiling as Blind Blake in a good mood.

Mississippi John Hurt

Proof, if any were needed, that regional classifications are neither infallible nor inflexible. John Hurt was born in Mississippi and spent almost his entire life there, but his conversational singing and delicate, intricate fingerpicked guitar had little or nothing to do with the Delta blues archetype of driving, declamatory CHARLEY PATTON-derived stylings. His repertoire certainly included blues, but also encompassed rags, spirituals and ballads. Hurt made a small but celebrated group of recordings in 1928, but – until his 'rediscovery' in the '60s – he had never performed to any audience other than small local gatherings in his home village of Avalon, Mississippi. It's worth considering the possibility that a songster as muted and intimate as Mississippi John Hurt could not have performed outside the studio for an audience of any significant size until the era of amplification. Considering that electricity was not a commonplace amongst the rural poor until considerably later, the most popular performers were those who could pump their lungs and thrash their guitars hard enough to keep a shack full of hearty partygoers dancing all night without the use of a PA system. Under these circumstances, a whispering finger-picker like John Hurt could not have comfortably entertained anywhere larger or noisier than a front porch. He was the original shoe-gazer – his vocals are not so much projected as allowed to drip from his nose – but he was also an utterly charming performer who beguiled every audience he faced.

77

'Mississippi' John Smith Hurt was born in Teoc, Mississippi, on July 3, 1893. His family moved to Avalon when he was two, and, apart from trips to Memphis and New York City to record for OKeh in 1928, Hurt remained in Mississippi working his farm until his 'rediscovery' in 1962. He spent the last four years of his life as a celebrity, working every major folk club and festival in North America, and basking in his recognition as a major cultural resource before he died in Greneda, Mississippi on 2 November, 1966.

- *1928 Sessions* (Yazoo 1065)

At 36, Hurt's seamed, nasal voice already seemed that of a much older man, one in which you could hear a lifetime of aiming a thousand-yard stare from his back porch. These early sides are so remarkably well-preserved you'd imagine that someone stored a complete, unplayed set of them in tissue paper until Yazoo could get hold of them and transcribe them to DAT. Here's where you find staples like 'Stack O'Lee Blues (the original badman ballad, and an ancestor of the better-known 'Stagger Lee', a New Orleans relative which became a rock and roll hit for Lloyd Price thirty-plus years later), the enchanting 'Candy Man' and the powerful 'Spike Driver Blues', a.k.a. 'Take This Hammer', the 'answer song' to 'John Henry.' Recorded in two sessions – one in Memphis, the other in New York – in February and December of 1928, these sides represent a brief brush with the music business by a man who considered himself a farmer by trade. It was thirty-five years before his chance to record came round again.

- *Worried Blues 1963* (Rounder CD 1082)
- *Avalon Blues* (Flyright FLYCD 06)

Both of these claim to be John Hurt's first post-rediscovery sessions: in a way, they're both right. The Rounder CD was taped in early '63 at what sounds like either a crowded living room or a small club while Hurt was limbering up for his festival debut; the Flyright is the celebrated Library Of Congress session from July of the same year. Both feature Hurt in relaxed, informal settings with a fair amount of chat between songs, and since he wasn't exactly a fireball of youthful energy even back in 1928, the intervening three-and-a-half decades did little damage and much good to his music. His singing was, if anything, even more slyly understated than it had been in 1928, and his fingerpicking no less deft and delicate. This is folk blues at its most truly intimate: an integral part of Hurt's magic was his ability to bring the confidentiality and relaxation of an impromptu back-porch to a recording studio or an audience of any size, and here the illusion is so fine that you're almost afraid to cough in case you distract him. They reprise many of the best-known tunes from his '28 sessions and, if historicity is not a priority for you, you may prefer these to the originals, since they have the benefit of superior technical values and the charming introductions.

- _The Best Of Mississippi John Hurt_ (Vanguard VMCD 7304)
- _Last Sessions_ (Vanguard VMD 79327)

The misleadingly entitled former is a live album from a 1965 club show; the Advertising Standards Authority-friendly latter was recorded in New York City in February and July of '66. Hurt had always sung the odd gospel tune alongside his secular material but, like many older bluesmen, he recorded more and more such songs in his last years: intimations of mortality presumably prompting a desire to get right with God. _Best Of_ opens up with no less than three of 'em, including 'I Shall Not Me Moved'. The best way to indicate the span of _Last Sessions_ is to say that it begins with 'Po' Boy Long Ways From Home' and ends with 'Goodnight Irene': like _Best Of_, it's a 'supplementary', rather than a first-call, Mississippi John album: as superbly performed as everything else he did, but exploring the nooks and crannies of his repertoire rather than the keynote tunes available elsewhere.

Subjects for further investigation: Hurt's triumphant '60s comeback is documented on _Blues At Newport_ (Vanguard VCD 115/116) – which also contains enough superb material by the likes of SKIP JAMES, JOHN LEE HOOKER, REV. GARY DAVIS and SONNY TERRY & BROWNIE McGHEE to qualify as an essential purchase – and its near-equal _Great Bluesmen/Newport_ (Vanguard VCD 77/78). The first opens up with Hurt performing three of his best-known sonmgs 'Candy Man', 'Coffee Blues' (from which the '60s folk-rock hitmakers The Lovin' Spoonful derived their name) and, of course, 'Stack O'Lee

Blues', the latter appearing here as 'Stagolee'; the second includes 'Slidin' Delta' and 'Trouble, I've Had It All My Days'.

Two other gifted songsters of approximately Hurt's generation – Mance Lipscomb (1895 P1976) and Jesse 'Lone Cat' Fuller (1896P1976) – had to wait until the arrival of the postwar folk boom before their music made even the slightest impact on the outside world. Lipscomb, a demon slide-and-fingerpicker and splendidly laconic vocalist who spent all his life around his birthplace of Navasota, Texas, may have sounded like the missing link between Mississippi John Hurt and LIGHTNIN' HOPKINS, but his music clearly inhabited the same universe as fellow Texas pickers BLIND LEMON JEFFERSON and LEADBELLY, with whom he had a considerable amount of repertoire in common. Chris Strachwitz founded Arhoolie Records specifically to release the 1960 tapes which make up the first half of *Texas Songster* (Arhoolie CD 306), and they're truly delightful, as are the 1964 live tracks which complete the package.

There was rather more to Georgia-born Jesse Fuller than the riotous, kazoo-tooting folkie favourite 'San Francisco Bay Blues' – most recently exhumed by ERIC CLAPTON on *Unplugged* (Reprise 9362-45024-2) – for which he is best-known. For a start, there was his one-man-band approach: not just simultaneous guitar, harp and kazoo, but a pedalled bass he called a footdella, and a foot-operated washboard for percussion. Then there was his harmonica style, which may sound familiar to fans of Bob Dylan, and his ability make a 12-string dance. *Frisco Bound* (Arhoolie CD 360, mostly recorded in 1955 with the addition of a few 1963 live tracks, presents a born entertainer with a more serious side: alongside the rags and novelties are some shiveringly powerful deep blues and gospel pieces. Fuller's takes on 'Po' Boy Long Way From Home' (here retitled 'Cincinnati Blues') and 'Motherless Children' stand up beside any you can find, and his hair-raising slide medley of 'Amazing Grace' and 'Hark From The Tomb' would have won an amen from BLIND WILLIE JOHNSON himself. Fuller also appears on *Blues At Newport* (Vanguard VCD 115/116), banging out another version of 'San Francisco Bay Blues.'

While we're on the subject, *Furry Lewis In His Prime 1927–1928* (Yazoo 1050) collects the early recordings of Memphis songster Walter 'Furry' Lewis (1893–1981): definitive showcases for his sweet, clear voice and inventive guitar. After 40-odd years as a street cleaner in Memphis, he was rediscovered and lionised – Joni Mitchell even wrote a song about him – but his comeback records demonstrated that the voice had lasted considerably better than his guitar-playing. Lewis was a much-loved local personality in Memphis, but his days as a front-rank music maker were effectively over.

Blind Boy Fuller

Ace fingerpicker Fulton Allen – better known as Blind Boy Fuller – was one of the most successful downhome stars of the mid-to-late '30s: equally adept at jaunty, salacious novelty rags and deep blues, he was the man who – in his delightful 'Truckin' My Blues Away' – coined the phrase 'Keep On Truckin'', as later immortalised by cartoonist and old-timey music nut Robert Crumb. He was, above all, a startlingly inventive guitarist, willing to embellish a composition by beating out a percussion break on the top of his instrument or plinking the strings behind the bridge. During his brief but illustrious recording career – from 1935 and 1940 – he also helped to launch the careers of REV. GARY DAVIS, SONNY TERRY and BROWNIE McGHEE. Davis (at that time unordained and simply plain Blind Gary Davis) had been Fuller's street-singing partner and occasional studio accompanist (Fuller claimed to have tutored Davis, though Davis tells it the other way round); Terry had played harp on some of Fuller's later recordings, and McGhee was a protege of Fuller's who, when the great man pegged out, was given Fuller's guitar and sent out on the road as 'Blind Boy Fuller No 2'.

Fulton Allen was born in Wadesboro, North Carolina, on 10 July, 1907. He was sighted at birth, but an unspecified infection began to erode his vision when he was in his late teens, and he was registered as blind in 1929, when he and his young wife went on welfare. Like many another blind Southern black, he turned to street-singing and became a familiar figure in Durham, North Carolina – where he first encountered Sonny Terry and Gary Davis – deriving the bulk of his income from playing outside the Bull Durham tobacco factory as the workers clocked off on payday. A fortuitous 1935 encounter with a talent scout led to

Fuller and Davis being taken to New York to record: somewhere *en route* Fulton Allen became Blind Boy Fuller, and Blind Boy Fuller became the last of the the the top-selling pre-war rural bluesmen. That didn't prevent him from dying broke, however: according to Brownie McGhee, Fuller was a pauper when a kidney ailment took him out on 13 February, 1941.

Things could conceivably have gone better for Fuller if he hadn't been in jail when John Hammond came to Durham in 1938 to get him for the 'From Spirituals To Swing' show. Fuller had been charged with shooting at his wife: according to Hammond's memoirs, he'd done so by standing in the middle of a room and turning slowly in a circle, firing all the while. Instead, Hammond took Sonny Terry.

- *East Coast Piedmont Style* (Columbia Legacy 467923 2)
- *Truckin' My Blues Away* (Yazoo 1060)
- *Blind Boy Fuller 1935–1940* (Travelin' Man TM CD 01)

The 22-track *East Coast Piedmont Style* is, by an extremely short head, the Fuller to get, though it doesn't include 'Truckin' My Blues Away' or very many contributions from Sonny Terry. 'Truckin'' is, however, included on *Legends Of The Blues Vol 1* (Columbia Legacy 467245 2), which contains so much excellent material by other artists – BESSIE SMITH, BLIND LEMON JEFFERSON, MISSISSIPPI JOHN HURT, SON HOUSE, BUKKA WHITE, MEMPHIS MINNIE, ROBERT JOHNSON, LEADBELLY, BLIND WILLIE McTELL and CHARLEY PATTON amongst them – that buying it is hardly an imposition. The 20-track Travelin' Man issue has no less than seven Terry cameos, six of which are drawn from Fuller's final session in 1940; that session also includes some interesting gospel material – intimations of mortality, anyone? – unissued elsewhere. Fuller's washboard man Bull City Red takes the vocal on the final '(Take My Hand) Precious Lord', which features both Sonny Terry and Jordan Webb on harps. The Yazoo has a Robert Crumb cover but only 14 tracks, and all three CDs overlap considerably. *East Coast* is an admirable showcase for his warm wit and finger-picking chops of doom: rock fans be warned that Fuller's 'Rag Mama Rag' is only the most distant of ancestors to Robbie Robertson's composition of the same name on The Band's second album.

Sleepy John Estes

Another hero of the '60s blues rediscovery boom was 'Sleepy' John Estes, a major influence on both TAJ MAHAL and RY COODER, whose nickname is variously attributed to a 'lazy' eye blinded in his childhood, and a tendency to doze off due to low blood pressure. He has a highly distinctive sound – a highpitched, wiry voice riding dissonantly over the piano and mandolin accompaniments he favoured – which many (including, I confess, the auithor) can either take or leave alone. Nevertheless, his songbook is a rich one, and his material has proved exceptionally durable: his 'Someday Baby' was an ancestor of Maceo Merriwether's standard 'Worried Life Blues', and in its original form it also provided sterling service for MUDDY WATERS and BIG TOM WILLIAMS. Taj Mahal posed with Estes on the cover of *Recycling The Blues And Other Related Stuff* (Columbia, unavailable on CD), and recorded his 'Diving Duck Blues' and 'Everybody's Got To Make A Change' (as 'Everybody's Got To Change Sometime'). His funk-blues masterpiece 'Leavin' Trunk' is almost entirely derived from an Estes song inexplicably (and confusingly) labelled as 'Milk Cow Blues'. The same song is also the source for Cooder's 'Ax Sweet Mama', which you can find on Cooder's *Boomer's Story* (Reprise 7599-26398-2), also featuring a rather dilapidated and timeworn cameo from Estes himself on his own 'President Kennedy'.

John Adam Estes was born in Ripley, Tennessee, on 25 January, 1899, though some sources date his birth as late as 1904. His closest associates were mandolinist James 'Yank' Rachell (1910–) and harpist Hammie Nixon (1908–), the latter a profound influence on a younger hanger-on, John Lee (the first SONNY BOY) WILLIAMSON. Estes' earliest stab at professional music was a jug trio co-featuring Rachell and pianist Jab Jones. Working picnics, dances and anything else he could find with Rachell, Jones and Nixon in various combinations, he made his first records in Chicago in 1929, the most successful of which was the intriguing 'Rollin' And Tumblin'' variant 'The Girl I Love, She's Got Long Curly Hair'. Any initial success was, however, damped by the Depression; though he and Nixon toured with the Rabbit Foot Minstrels in 1939, he was effectively out of professional music by 1941. In an abortive comeback, he and Nixon cut a few sides for the pre-Sun Sam Phillips in 1950, but it came to virtually naught.

By the time of his rediscovery in 1962, he had lost the sight of his remaining eye and done considerable work on his guitar playing. He worked steadily through the '60s and '70s, touring Japan as late as one year before his death, on 5 June, 1977, in his adopted home of Brownsville, Texas, the source of the subject matter for so many of his songs.

- *I Ain't Gonna Worry No More 1929–1941* (Yazoo 2004)
- *Brownsville Blues* (Delmark DD 613)

The basic originals and basic rediscovery albums: the Yazoo set has the historicity and it also has the 'originals' of Estes' most celebrated songs; the Delmark, mostly recorded in 1962 with cameos from Nixon and Rachell (the latter appearing this time on electric lead guitar), has vastly superior singing and guitar work. I still consider Estes far more important as a composer than as a performer, but here's where you'll find the evidence to prove me wrong.

Subjects for further investigation: As befitted his status as a reigning elder statesman, Estes made the statutory appearances at the Newport Folk Festival and on the American Folk Blues Festival tours of Europe. The former shows are recalled on **Blues At Newport** (Vanguard VCD 115/16) and **Great Bluesmen/Newport** (Vanguard VCD 77/78); the latter on **American Folk Blues Festival '64** (L&R/Bellaphon CDLR 42024) with Hammie Nixon, and **American Folk Blues Festival '66** (L&R/Bellaphon CDLR 42069) which teamed him with Yank Rachell. His footnote to the story of Sun Records, 'Policy Man', is included on **The Sun Blues Years Vol 6: Too Blue To Cry** (Sun CD SUN 38).

Sonny Terry & Brownie McGhee

The longest-serving duo in the history of the blues was composed of one consummate entertainer and one rough-hewn genius; contrary to myth and their public proclamations, guitarist Walter 'Brownie' McGhee and harpist Saunders 'Sonny Terry' Terrell were not only far from the best of friends, but they cordially disliked each other and each would cheerfully have broken up the act if circumstances and public demand had not kept forcing them back together. Nevertheless, their association lasted, on and off, for over forty years, during which time they were the hardest-working and most visible representatives of the Southeastern folk blues tradition. Sonny Terry played Carnegie Hall in 1938 as part of John Hammond's trailblazing 'From Spirituals To Swing' presentation, and during the 1950s both men appeared in Broadway shows: Brownie both performed and acted in Langston Hughes' *Simply Wonderful*; Terry was in *Finian's Rainbow*, and they teamed up in the original production of Tennessee Williams' *Cat On A Hot Tin Roof*. They both began their careers as proteges of Sonny's Carolina homeboy BLIND BOY FULLER: Terry made his recording debut in 1937 as a sideman for Fuller, and McGhee was groomed as Fuller's successor when the great fingerpicker's health began to fail. During the 1940s they were prominent members of the New York leftist folk-blues circle which coalesced around the formidable figure of LEADBELLY, and which also included Woody Guthrie and Pete Seeger: they were still performing 'Pick A Bale Of Cotton' when they contributed a pickin'-and-grinnin' cameo to Steve Martin's 1979 movie *The Jerk*.

Though Terry was the virtuoso of the pair, they were both formidable talents with distinctive personal sounds: McGhee was the smoother and more versatile vocalist, though Terry's rougher, plainer sound was arguably the more affecting. McGhee's Carolina-style guitar picking was neat, driving and funky: even though the duo's format awarded the bulk of the soloing to Terry's fabulous harp, Brownie's solo recordings demonstrate that he could knock out a more than fair lead. Sonny Terry's trademark was the falsetto whoop with which he decorated his tricky, ornate harmonica work, and the mind-boggling ease with which he would alternate his blowing and whooping invariably provided the highlight of any of the duo's shows. Still, it was the more urbane, outgoing McGhee who introduced the songs, set the audience at their ease and provided the context in which his taciturn partner could thrive.

Sonny Terry was the older of the two, born in Greensboro, North Carolina, on 24 October, 1911. At the age of 11, he lost the sight of his left eye in a farmyard accident; five years later, his right was put out in another. Blindness provided him with a powerful incentive to work harder on the harmonica with which he'd been fooling since he was eight, and in 1928 he left home to work as an itinerant musician, street-singing or working in a touring medicine show. In 1934 he met Blind Boy Fuller working the other side of a street in Durham, North Carolina, and it was his association with Fuller that took him to Carnegie Hall and introduced him to his long-time partner and nemesis, Brownie McGhee. McGhee was from Knoxville, Tennessee, where he was born on 30 November, 1915. Afflicted with polio as a child, he'd learned guitar from his father and was playing before he was 10; after his parents separated he, like Terry, set off to earn his living from music. In the late '30s, he drifted into Fuller's orbit where he first encountered Sonny Terry. In 1940, he accompanied Terry to Washington DC, where the harpist was due to cut a session for the Library of Congress and to play a civil rights benefit concert organised by Paul Robeson. They ended up performing and recording together for the first time, and at the concert they met Leadbelly, their second mentor.

After his now-legendary tour of duty as 'Blind Boy Fuller No 2', McGhee settled in New York; he and Terry lived at Leadbelly's house for a time, and they worked together sporadically through-out the '40s and '50s, appearing with the Almanac Singers (the ancestors of The Weavers, who had the huge hit with Leadbelly's 'Goodnight Irene' just after Leadbelly died), backing each other up on record, in concert and on the streets. They finally formalised the partnership in the late '50s, and remained a blues institution – pally in public, fighting in private – until they finally played their last job together in 1982. Sonny Terry died on 11 March 1986; Brownie McGhee is alive and well in Oakland, California. They have been criticised for presenting a sanitised, showbizzy account of their music, but they have simply remained true to the street-singer ethos with which they started out: you play what the public wants to hear. Brownie's sensibility dominated the duo, which was only fair since he did the bulk of the lead singing (Terry's tastes were more downhome, as his 1984 solo album *Whoopin'* suggests), but the concessions to public taste were in the presentation rather than the music. Moreover, their exposure to metropolitan white audiences came early in their careers. They remain the definitive folk-blues harp-guitar duo, and the best of their records still make wonderful listening.

- **BLIND BOY FULLER:** *Blind Boy Fuller 1935–1940* (Travelin' Man TM CD 01)
- **VARIOUS ARTISTS:** *From Spirituals To Swing* (Vanguard VCD2 47/48)

The earliest readily available Sonny Terry recordings: *From Spirituals To Swing* finds Sonny onstage at Carnegie Hall in 1938, accompanied only by Fuller associate Bull City Red on washboard, for six-and-a-half minutes of unearthly falsetto and pungent harp. Most of the Fuller/Terry sides on the Travelin' Man CD were cut in Chicago during Fuller's last session in June 1940, and while Terry sounds less assured than on his later recordings – either because he had not yet grown accustomed to the studio or because he was there to back up his mentor – his signature sound, with its distinctive vibrato, was already in place.

- **BROWNIE McGHEE:** *Brownie McGhee 1944–1955* (Travelin' Man TM CD 04)
- **BROWNIE McGHEE:** *The Folkways Years 1945–1959* (Smithsonian Folkways CD SF 40034)

The earliest Brownie McGhee side I can find is 'Million Lonesome Women' (1941), included in *The Story Of The Blues* (Columbia 468992 2), but these CDs provide two contrasting accounts of Brownie McGhee's studio years in New York. The Travelin' Man CD contains his commercial blues recordings as both leader and sideman, while the Folkways set documents the consciously folk sides he cut for Moses Asch before moving to the West Coast in the late '50s. Sonny Terry is prominently featured on several tracks of both discs, and the Travelin' Man CD also features pianists CHAMPION JACK DUPREE and Big Chief Ellis, both of whom take lead vocal turns. It's pleasant but non-classic, though there's a cute anecdote attached to 'Drinkin' Wine Spo-Dee-O-Dee', recorded in 1947 and sung by McGhee's brother Granville 'Stick' McGhee (1919–1961). In 1949, a bored DJ began playing the record, by then long out-of-print, and a distributor anxious to take advantage of the airplay called Ahmet Ertegun, boss of the then-fledgling Atlantic label, to inquire after stocks of the record. Ertegun offered to cut a new version of the song for him, and called Brownie to ask him to make the record. However, Stick happened to be in New York staying with Brownie at the time, so Stick, with Brownie on second guitar, recut his own song. The new record sold 400,000 copies and established Atlantic as a major player in the R&B market, which is considerably more than it did for Stick, none of whose subsequent sides had any appreciable impact.

The Folkways disk is rather more to the point, though the title seems a bit of a misnomer: according to the individual session details, these songs were recorded between '55 (rather than '45) and '59. The repertoire includes a couple of standards associated with BIG BILL BROONZY ('Careless Love' and 'Just A Dream'), several pointed originals, and older pre-blues songs like 'Long Gone', 'Betty And Dupree' and 'Raise A Ruckus Tonight'. Brownie plays lovely guitar throughout (including some raunchy electric on the sardonic 'Pawn Shop Blues'), though there's a Sonny Terry-sized gap in many of these sides which only disappears when the harp man sits in. Interestingly enough, one track on which Terry does *not* appear is 'Me And Sonny', in which Brownie attests to their undying love and friendship.

- *Hometown Blues* (Mainstream MDCD 902)

Recorded between 1948 and 1951, this collection mixes acoustic duo performances with small-band sides cut for a variety of labels under a variety of names. Even at this early stage, much of the repertoire which would last them for the next thirty or so years was already in place: Broonzy's 'I Feel So Good' and 'Key To The Highway', 'Bulldog Blues' (a.k.a. ''Fore Day Creep' and best-known to Eric Clapton fans as Cream's Blind Joe Reynolds-derived 'Outside Woman Blues'), plus venerables like 'C.C. Rider', 'Sittin' On Top Of The World' and 'Goin' Down Slow', and McGhee's own 'Pawn Shop Blues'. LIGHTNIN' HOPKINS, at that time one of the leading lights in the downhome revival, would probably not have been best pleased by the challenge Brownie throws down in 'Lightnin's Blues'. (As was the custom for releases on Mainstream and its sister label Sittin' In With, all the songs were copyrighted in the name of one 'R. Ellen', who must be a gifted writer indeed when one considers how many fine songs he appears to have written for the likes of Sonny & Brownie, Lightnin' Hopkins and JOHN LEE HOOKER.) Though this doesn't represent the fully-developed partnership that was still almost a decade away, it's still an entertaining record, with a full, raw, reverby sound which compromises effectively between ambience and clarity.

- **BROWNIE McGHEE & SONNY TERRY:** *Brownie McGhee & Sonny Terry Sing* (Smithsonian Folkways CD SF 40011)
- *California Blues* (Ace CDCH 398)

These late-'50s albums cemented the collaboration, and remain the freshest of a whole pile of albums which recycle much of the same material and approach. They contain the first sides on which Sonny and Brownie functioned as a true duo, singing together as opposed to simply taking turns to back each other up. The vocal blend is a more arresting sound than either of them singing individually, and both sets are superbly recorded: this is, literally, Sonny and Brownie getting their act together. The Folkways CD includes light, sympathetic drumming on a few tracks, while *California Blues* is unadorned; it's also the more immediate and contains fractionally better repertoire, though at only half the length of its competitor it's not fantastic value for money. Both represent 'classic' Terry & McGhee: the sound that they took around the world for the next quarter-century. The Folkways highlights include 'Old Jabo', a pre-blues chant which audibly draws on the same sources as much of BO DIDDLEY's deeper material, and the lovely duet 'Heart In Sorrow', a hardy perennial of their live performances. 'Best Of Friends' is 'Me And Sonny' rewritten as a tribute to Leadbelly: 'John Henry' appears on both albums, but only *California Blues* includes the 'answer', 'Take This Hammer.' Among the latter's other highspots: the duo's variants on 'Motherless Child' and Poor Boy From Home', the lovely blues ballad 'Sportin' Life', and their perennials 'Cornbread and Peas' and 'Louise.'

- *The 1958 London Sessions* (Sequel NEXCD 120)

Sonny & Brownie went international in 1958, when they depped for a seriously unwell Big Bill Broonzy on a European tour. They recorded two sets of sessions in London: one with members of Chris Barber's jazz band, and the other either alone or with guest pianist Dave Lee. These are the latter, thankfully: Lee justifies his presence on the opening 'Just A Dream', written by the absent Broonzy. Terry's fabulous 'train harp' on 'Southern Train', a kind of cross between Arthur 'Big Boy' Crudup's 'Mean Old Frisco' and Junior Parker's 'Mystery Train', benefits from some judicious echo: he also shines on a fine and frisky previously unreleased version of 'Fox Chase'. Otherwise it's business as usual, with a 'Cornbread, Peas And Black Molasses' that almost equals the one on *California Blues*; McGhee himself plays some more than creditable piano on 'Brownie's Blues'. From '59 and '60, *Midnight Special* (Ace CDCH 951) and *Back To New Orleans* (Ace CDCH 372) represent more of the same. Terry & McGhee were remarkably consistent performers, and there's actually very little record-to-record variation in quality. The criterion therefore becomes repertoire: the ones to get are the ones with the songs you want to hear. Most of the best material on these two is available elsewhere, performed at least as well.

- **BROWNIE McGHEE, SONNY TERRY WITH EARL HOOKER:** *I Couldn't Believe My Eyes Plus . . .* (See For Miles SEECD 92)

The original *I Couldn't Believe My Eyes* album, recorded in 1969 with Chicago slide whiz Earl Hooker on board, but unreleased until 1973, was a surprisingly successful return to band recording. This reissue pads out the original album with selections from another '69 recording, *Long Ways From Home*. The sessions took place in L.A., but the aesthetic is pure Chicago: this rocking, boisterous album sits very comfortably alongside the MUDDY WATERS records of the '50s and '60s, and Earl Hooker is particularly outstanding on the country-rag title track. My only quarrel is with the mix: some of Brownie's songs, including 'Tell Me Why', boast lyrics that deserve better than burial below the piano and drums.

- **SONNY TERRY WITH JOHNNY WINTER, WILLIE DIXON:** *Whoopin'* (Alligator ALCD 4738)

Sonny Terry's last recording, apart from a session for Quincy Jones' soundtrack to *The Color Purple* (Qwest, unavailable on CD), provides an indication of how his music might have sounded if he'd wound up in Chicago, rather than New York, during the early '50s. Recorded in 1984, it took him right back to the downhome blues of his youth in the company of guitarist-producer JOHNNY WINTER and bassist WILLIE DIXON, both of whom knew a thing or two about amped-up Delta blues, and it's a revelation. Terry blossoms outside McGhee's shadow; in turn, Winter demonstrates, on both electric and National steel guitars, the restraint and idiomatic fidelity which he always displays in the company of older bluesmen who tame his penchant for arena-rock excess. *Whoopin'* is one of those rare records that tells us something we didn't know about the music of someone who'd virtually been part of the furniture of the blues since before Winter was born. There's a cookin' version of Lee Dorsey's New Orleans hit 'Ya Ya', a deep, sensual 'Roll Me Baby', a reprise of the Terry/McGhee standard 'Hooray That Woman Is Killin' Me' (retitled 'Whoee Whoee') and all manner of good stuff: this exemplary album is loose where it needs to be loose and tight where it needs to be tight. Sonny Terry went out in style.

Subjects for further investigation: Sonny and Brownie toured Europe with the annual American Folk Blues Festival package on no less than three occasions: the aural evidence is on *American Folk Blues Festival '62* (L&R/Bellaphon CDLR 42017), *'67* (L&R/Bellaphon CDLR 42070) and '70 (L&R/Bellaphon CDLR 42021). They also perform a snappy one-two of 'Long Gone' and 'Key To The Highway' on the indispensable *Blues At Newport* (Vanguard VCD 115/16): apart from John Lee Hooker and REV. GARY DAVIS, all of the other featured veterans – MISSISSIPPI JOHN HURT, Rev. Robert Wilkins, Jesse Fuller and SKIP JAMES – had been away from active music for decades. Sonny and Brownie were in practice, and it shows. My all-time favourite Sonny & Brownie material was on a budget album entitled *Lightnin', Sonny & Brownie* (Saga, long unavailable), an early-'60s in-concert recording shared, as the title might suggest, with a drastically on-form Lightnin' Hopkins, and I'm still waiting for a CD reissue of it. The duo's last noteworthy album was the mid-'70s *Sonny & Brownie* (A&M, unavailable), on which they introduced Brownie's song 'The Blues Had A Baby' (later co-opted by Muddy Waters), squeezed every last drop of irony from Randy Newman's 'Sail Away' and brought on JOHN

MAYALL for a tune called 'White Boy Lost In The Blues.' Supplementary listening for fans of Brownie McGhee and Blind Boy Fuller should include *East Coast Blues* (Yazoo 1013); even though the only well-known name featured is BLIND BLAKE, who contributes the typically dazzling 'Blind Arthur's Breakdown', watch out for Willie Walker, one of the few guitarists whom Rev. Gary Davis acknowledged as a master.

GOSPEL BLUES

The implacable rivalry between gospel and the blues is one of the central truisms of blues lore. Gospel is the music of The Lord; blues, as a(n extremely) worldly music, belongs to 'Im Downstairs. However, almost three decades before RAY CHARLES consigned himself to eternal damnation by hi-jacking gospel songs and coupling them with bluesy lyrics (thereby creating soul music), guitar-toting preachers had performed a mirror-image of the same operation by using the devil's instruments for the Lord's purpose. Men like BLIND WILLIE JOHNSON – the connoisseurs' slide player, RY COODER's ultimate hero – and REV. GARY DAVIS roared out their warnings in huge, rasping baritones: these guys are *scary*. *Preachin' The Gospel: Holy Blues* (Columbia 467890 2) is an excellent introduction to the field, including practitioners like Washington Phillips – another Cooder favourite – Sister O.M. Terrell, Josh(ua) White wearing yet another of his many hats, the splendidly named pianist Arizona Dranes and, naturally, Blind Willie Johnson. POP STAPLES (a.k.a Roebuck Staples, founder of The Staple Singers) is just about the only contemporary practitioner of this intriguing subgenre, but as *Peace To The Neighborhood* (PointBlank VPBCD 8) eloquently testifies, his worldview is – thankfully – considerably sunnier and more benevolent than Blind Willie's. Mind you, so is Ian Paisley's.

Blind Willie Johnson

It would not be overly fanciful to suggest that that the damnations which so terrified ROBERT JOHNSON are those with which his namesake, Blind Willie, threatens sinners: if, as one friend of mine suggested, Blind Willie Johnson's thunderous growl sounds like the voice of the devil, that is almost the point. If he can't scare you sinners into righteousness, his music suggests, he'll quite happy to sit there and laugh while you burn for all eternity. There is no humour and precious little compassion in Blind Willie Johnson's music: this is Christian fundamentalism at its most nakedly vengeful. With the possible exceptions of Robert Johnson and SKIP JAMES, there is little in pre-war rural blues which is as bleak and terrifying: yet Blind Willie's blasted landscape is illuminated by moments of transcendant beauty. His eerie modal slide guitar demonstrates an uncannily sharp ear for precise microtonal pitching, and awesome control of his instrument.

In what was a comparatively brief studio career (roughly speaking, between late 1928 and mid-1930), Blind Willie recorded several memorable songs which are still in circulation. His instrumental-with-humming 'Dark Was The Night, Cold Was The Ground' is an essential rite-of-passage for post-RY COODER country-blues slide stylists; 'Mother's Children Have A Hard Time' was reworked by ERIC CLAPTON as 'Motherless Children'; 'Nobody's Fault But Mine' provided the peg for one of LED ZEPPELIN's finest exercises in blues monumentalism; 'You're Going To Need Somebody On Your Bond' was adopted by folk singer Buffy Sainte Marie and subsequently became a staple for TAJ MAHAL. Though that ringing slide and deep, growling voice sound like pure Mississippi Delta, Blind Willie Johnson was actually from Marlin, Texas, where he was born in 1900. He apparently wanted to be a preacher at as early an age as five; two years before he was blinded by his stepmother during a furious row with his father. He made a living performing both sacred and secular material on the streets of Dallas, whence he was first brought into the recording studio, generally with his wife Angeline as vocal support. The couple settled down in Beaumont, Texas, after Blind Willie's last session in 1930, and he continued to perform there – both in church and on the streets – for the rest of his life. He died there, in 1949, from pneumonia contracted from the cold water used to put out a house fire.

- *Praise God I'm Satisfied* (Yazoo 1058)
- *Sweeter As The Years Go By* (Yazoo 1078)

The two Blind Willie Johnson collections: the first, and more essential, concentrates on his remarkable slide work, (though the latter includes one such masterpiece 'Lord, I Just Can't Keep From Crying') and features, among others, 'Dark Was The Night, Cold Was The Ground', 'Nobody's Fault But Mine' and 'Mother's Children Have A Hard Time'. His 'natural' voice is a surprisingly light baritone, but most of his menacing hymns are croaked in a rasping basso offset by that high keening slide and the vocal counterpoints provided by his wife. It's instructive to compare his version of the gospel standard 'John The Revelator' with SON HOUSE's, and to note the influence that his records had on subsequent performers like BUKKA WHITE and MISSISSIPPI FRED McDOWELL. Be aware that Blind Willie's music is not for the fainthearted, but if you're after an emotional experience that you won't forget in a hurry, then *Praise God I'm Satisfied* deserves a high placing on your want list.

Subjects for further investigation: If you want to hear 'Dark Was The Night, Cold Was The Ground' without buying the full tour ticket to Blind Willie's apocalyptic universe, seek out *The Slide Guitar: Bottles, Knives And Steel* (Columbia Legacy 467251 2), which also includes wicked slide showcases for TAMPA RED, CHARLEY PATTON, BUKKA WHITE, Robert Johnson and SON HOUSE. Other collections in the same series which include notable Blind Willie Johnson tracks include *Preachin' The Gospel: Holy Blues* (Columbia Legacy 467 890 2), *Great Blues Guitarists: String Dazzlers* (Columbia Legacy 467894 2), *Legends Of The Blues Vol 1* (Columbia Legacy 467245 2) and *News And The Blues Telling It Like It Is* (Columbia Legacy 467249 2). Ry Cooder's version of 'Dark Was The Night, Cold Was The Ground' appeared on his first solo album *Ry Cooder* (Warner Bros., 1970, unavailable on CD); Brit slidemeister Mike Cooper takes it on (with saxophone replacing the voice) on *Slide Crazy!* (Sky Ranch SR 652324), while Australian maverick DAVE HOLE takes a hotwired electric approach on *Short Fuse Blues* (Provogue PRD 70362). Eric

Clapton's 'Motherless Children' was premiered on **461 Ocean Boulevarde** (Polydor 827-576-2) and reprised on **Crossroads** (Polydor 835 261-2); Zeppelin's 'Nobody's Fault But Mine' first appeared on **Presence** (Swan Song 289 402) and was recycled on the **Led Zeppelin** boxed set (Atlantic 7567-82144-2); and Taj Mahal's 'You're Gonna Need Somebody On Your Bond' is on **Giant Step/De Ole Folks At Home** (Columbia CGK 18 [US]). There was also a version of 'I Just Can't Keep From Crying' by Ten Years After, but let's leave that particular barrel unscraped for as long as possible.

Reverend Gary Davis

According to his one-time street-singing partner Reverend Gary Davis, BLIND BOY FULLER was only a fairly good guitarist. 'He would have been alright,' Davis was fond of saying, 'if I had kept him under me long enough.' Considering that Fuller was a very nifty picker indeed, this remark would have been blatantly and absurdly self-serving coming from anybody other than the Rev. Davis, who was the only ragtime picker whose name can safely be mentioned in the same breath as that of the acknowledged all-time champ, Arthur 'BLIND' BLAKE. From the same Carolina blues scene which produced Blind Boy Fuller, SONNY TERRY & BROWNIE McGHEE, Davis – born in Laurens, South Carolina, on 30 April 1896, and blind from the age of two – learned to sing and play guitar in his local Baptist church. From the age of 15, he was on the road throughout the Carolinas; by 1931, he had settled in Durham, North Carolina, where he met Fuller and Terry. When Fuller made his 1935 trek to cut his debut sides in New York, Davis went with him and played second guitar on some of the Fuller sides as well as recording some titles of his own, but he and the producer fell out over the then-unordained but already highly devout Davis' unwillingness to record more than a couple of blues tunes. Hias other 1935 titles were all gospel tunes: the scarifying 'Lord I Wish I Could See' – released under the name 'Blind Gary Davis' and included on *Preachin' The Gospel Holy Blues* (Columbia Legacy 467 890 2) – dates from that session.

Davis was ordained two years later, and – true to his principles – did not record again until he'd finally moved North. By 1944, he had arrived in the Bronx, New York City, where he eked out a living teaching guitar – to, among others, RY COODER and Stefan Grossman – and evangelising on the street: the original Manic Street Preacher. He recorded occasionally and began performing in more formal settings: in 1950 he played LEADBELLY's memorial concert at New York's Town Hall, and by 1957 was performing and recording with ever-increasing regularity. When he first returned to recording, Rev. Davis would only consent to perform instrumental versions of some of his saltier secular songs. After awhile he unbent sufficiently to recite, rather than sing, the lyrics, which he did with the nanosecond timing and self-deprecating intonation of a master standup comic. What emerges from his recordings is not just the mind-boggling drive, precision and elegance of his guitar-picking, but the humanity, warmth and wit of the man himself. I don't know about you, but I find the humour and compassion of the Rev. Davis a far more potent advertisement for the Lord than the terrifying imprecations of BLIND WILLIE JOHNSON. Until the end of his life, he combined his performance activities with pastoral duties at his local church.

Rev. Davis suffered a fatal heart attack while en route to a show, and died in Hammonton, New Jersey, on 5 May, 1972. By all accounts, he was a genuinely lovable man and, unless every note he ever played was a lie, those accounts were true.

- *Pure Religion And Bad Company* (Smithsonian/Folkways SF 40035)

Seeing as how there is no currently available compilation of the Rev. Davis' rare and scattered pre-war sides, this is where we come in: the 1957 session which represents the earliest full-length recording date of his currently available on CD. He was still uneasy with secular material when this was cut, which is why the version of 'Hesitation Blues' included here is strictly instrumental, but there is a real freshness to these performances of his staples 'Cocaine Blues' and 'Candy Man'; the instrumental 'Buck Dance' is nothing short of stunning, and he brings a powerful fervour to the terrifying blues 'Moon Going Down' and to the numerous gospel pieces. Needless to say, the selection also includes both 'Pure Religion' and 'Bad Company': the story of his life, really.

- *Blues & Ragtime* (Shanachie 97024)

Many of the Rev. Davis records available today derive from tapes made by his students, most notably guitarist/teacher Stefan Grossman, who recorded these titles in New York between 1962 and 1966. This particular selection draws on the same pool of material as *Reverend Gary Davis* (Heritage HT CD 02) and *I Am A True Vine* (Heritage HT 07) but, as the title suggests, it omits most of the gospel songs in order to concentrate on Davis as secular entertainer. Naturally, the selection includes the staples 'Candy Man' and 'Cocaine Blues' without which no Davis performance was ever really complete, and – O embarrassment of riches! – a twelve-minute live version of 'Hesitation Blues' that keeps the audience audibly creased up and almost lasts the course even on a home hi-fi. (There's also some wonderfully loopy slide on 'Whistlin' Blues'.) Thanks to judicious remastering, the sound is an improvement on the Heritage discs; it would be nice if some more of those tracks – particularly the gospel pieces – were to receive similar treatment in the future. In fact, an all-gospel set compiled from the Grossman tapes would make a dandy companion piece: they could call it *Gospel & Gospel*. In the meantime, the keyword for this album is either 'staggering' or 'delightful'. When I decide, I'll let you know.

- *From Blues To Gospel* (Biograph BCD 123)
- **LEADBELLY, REV. GARY DAVIS, DAN SMITH:** *Good Morning Blues* (Biograph BCD 113)

Recorded in a single day in 1971 with the Rev. Davis working out on a brand-new custom-built (but hastily-tuned) 12-string guitar, *From Blues To Gospel* finds the good humour still intact but the picking slightly laboured. He performs the statutory 'Cocaine Blues', blows a wheezing harp on 'Lost John', and revisits his astonishingly powerful 1935 song 'Lord, I Wish I Could See' as part of an extended gospel selection which is the album's strongest suite. Three and a half decades have mellowed the song, and Davis generates the greatest intensity on the closing 'I Will Do My Last Singing'. Five more tracks from the same session appear on *Good Morning Blues*, alongside a fascinating Leadbelly snippet (a 1940 pilot for a proposed radio show in which Leadbelly sang a few songs and was introduced and interviewed by Woody Guthrie), and three songs from the ebullient harp-blowing gospel bluesman Dan Smith. The star turn is a sublimely witty 'Hesitation Blues' which improves on the *Blues And Ragtime* version only because it clocks in at a rather more manageable 4'54": the class clown is an instrumental 'Candy Man' marred by a faltering second guitar from one of the Rev. Davis' pupils. If Biograph really wanted to be nice to us, they could reunite the complete contents of the 1971 session on one single CD.

Subjects for further investigation: Rev. Davis performs a powerful 'Death Don't Have No Mercy' on *Blues At Newport* (Vanguard VCD 77/78); and there's a 1961 version of 'You Got To Move' on *Bluesville Vol 1: Folk Blues* (Ace CDCH 247). Another guitar-picking preacher, Rev. Robert Wilkins (1896–?), is best-known for THE ROLLING STONES' cover – as 'Prodigal Son', on *Beggars' Banquet* (London 800 084-2) – of 'That's No Way To Get Along', his variant on the Delta staple generally known as 'Po' Boy Long Ways From Home'. *The Original Rolling Stone* (Yazoo 1077) rounds up his original recordings, including 'That's No Way To Get Along' and the two-part 'Rollin' Stone'; the combination of the two just about validates the title. Wilkins (1896–?), from Hernando, Mississippi, was based in Memphis and recorded for Victor and Vocalion between 1929 and 1935; he took up the ministry in 1950, and remained in the church thereafter, though he would still perform seculart material after hius rediscovery. His admirers dote on his brooding tenor, unusual song-structures and instrumental blend of blues and rag styles: those unwilling to invest in a whole CD of his bleak stylings should be advised that Wilkins' original 'That's No Way To Get Along' is collected on the invaluable *Roots Of Rock* (Yazoo 1063), and that a very long (9'39') '60s live version, under the 'Prodigal Son' title, appears on *Blues At Newport* (Vanguard VCD 115/16).

6. Barrelhouse, Jumpin' Jive and the Sound of the City

THE BOOGIE PIANISTS

So riddle me this: was boogie a piano style later adapted by guitarists, or *vice versa*? I'm afraid it's a split decision: though first-generation blues piano was esentially derived from what the guitarists were already doing, pianists and guitarists effectively cross-pollinated each other ever since, striving to overcome the inbuilt limitations of their instruments in order to mimic each others' effects and techniques. (Ragtime guitar virtuoso REVEREND GARY DAVIS used to claim, for example, that he 'had a piano round [his] neck'.) Both guitarists and pianists often took to the highways: one crew carried their instruments on their backs, while the other generally stood a fair chance of finding a piano somewhere at their destination. Halls, bars and sportin' houses which included a piano among their furnishings became known as 'honky-tonks' or 'barrelhouses'; and the terms 'barrelhouse' or 'honky-tonk' were thus generally applied to rocking blues piano pieces with sexy, danceable rhythms.

'Boogie-woogie' was formalised as a genre by the 1928 success of 'Pine Top's Boogie Woogie' by Clarence 'Pine Top' Smith (1904–1929), who unfortunately wasn't around long enough to benefit from what his hugely influential record unleashed on the world. He didn't 'invent' the music – it had, after all, been around at least since the turn of the century, and records in related styles already existed – but once people heard Pine Top, they suddenly knew what it was they'd been listening to. (Unfortunately, I've been unable to locate a CD including this epochal performance, but any of the numerous subsequent versions of it by Joe Willie 'PINETOP' PERKINS – who was awarded Smith's nickname by his friends because he played the piece so well – will give you a fair idea of what was going on.) Before then, the style had been known as 'Dudlow', after an unrecorded Mississippi pianist named Dudlow Joe.

Like 'classic' blues, the barrelhouse/honky-tonk/boogie-woogie family of piano styles is criminally under-represented on CD (as is ragtime, its second cousin), though hopefully the situation will improve as the silver disk remorselessly eats up every single musical performance ever recorded. Since I can't point you in the direction of readily available editions of the wonderful work of the likes of Jimmy Yancey, Eurreal 'Little Brother' Montgomery, Pete Johnson, Charles Edward 'Cow Cow' Davenport, 'Cripple' Clarence Lofton and Albert Ammons, allow me to do the next best thing.

- **VARIOUS ARTISTS:** *Barrelhouse Blues 1927–1936* (Yazoo 1028)

Here's where you start. This collection of early blues piano kicks off beautifully on Cow Cow Davenport's rollicking 'State Street Jive', with his sly, high-pitched monologue floating over his tumultuous piano; and Little Brother Montgomery's mournful, stately 'Vicksburg Blues' (1935), his variation on the theme of '44' (recorded in 1929 by ROOSEVELT SYKES), a piano equivalent to the Delta slide-guitar motif most frequently associated with 'Rollin' And Tumblin''. Elsewhere, we can marvel at the rolling muscularity of Charley Taylor's slow-blues bass-riffing on 'Heavy Suitcase Blues', or wallow in Louise Johnson's euphorically sexual 'On The Wall'. And Joe Dean's 'I'm So Glad I'm Twenty-One Years Old Today' (1930) is a direct ancestor of CHUCK BERRY's 'Back In The USA' (just sing Dean's title to Berry's melody, and you got it figured out).

- **VARIOUS ARTISTS:** *From Spirituals To Swing* (Vanguard VCD2-47/48)

These massively influential concert, promoted by John Hammond and staged at Carnegie Hall in 1938 and 1939, not only introduced the likes of BIG BILL BROONZY and SONNY TERRY to 'polite' 'society', but also gave pride of place to some major keyboard sorcerers. James P. Johnson performs two pieces on his own and also appears as one of the New orleans Feetwarmers and as part of the ensemble backing 'classic blues' singer Ida Cox; Pete Johnson pumps it for all he's worth behind JOE TURNER on 'It's All Right Baby', and the aptly-titled 'Cavalcade Of Boogie' pits Albert Ammons against Meade Lux Lewis with a Basie rhythm section as referees. These shows gave the music a new lease of life and a new audience; it was probably the most important event in the boogie-woogie calendar since Pine Top Smith entered the studio a decade before. Its success even persuaded Lewis (1905–1964), whose 'Honky Tonk Train Blues' is one of the enduring classics of the genre, to come out of retirement. The version included on *Meade Lux Lewis (1939–1954)* (Story Of Blues CD 3506-2) is a 1944 remake, but it's still wonderful, as is everything else on the collection. *Sissy Man Blues* (Jass J-CD-13) also provides the opportunity to hear Lewis accompanying the alleged hermaphrodite George Hannah on 'The Boy In The Boat' (think about it) and Hannah's theme song 'Freakish Man Blues.'

Roosevelt Sykes

Roosevelt Sykes – nicknamed 'The Honeydripper' as a tribute to his mastery of jivey seduction – lived a long time, played a hell of a lot of piano, travelled all over the world and died happy. Born in Elmar, Arkansas, on 31 January, 1906, he was raised in St Louis, Missouri, learned to find his way around a keyboard playing organ in church, and was barrelhousing around Louisiana and the Delta by the time he was out of his teens. He first entered the studio in Chicago to cut the humungously influential '44' (1929); despite its success and that of subsequent singles, he remained based in St Louis until the early '40s, when he moved to Chicago before finally relocating to New Orleans in 1954.

A genial man-mountain whose playing was as lithe and graceful as his corporeal form was obese, Sykes went international with a vengeance from the '60s onwards; by the end of his life he must've played every major club, college and festival in the North America, and made several forays into Europe. At some point he converted to Islam: his Muslim name was (logically enough) Roosevelt Sykes Bey. He died on 11 July, 1983, in New Orleans, a piano man's town if ever there was one.

- *The Honeydripper 1929–1941* (Story Of Blues CD 3542-2)

Roosevelt Sykes made records all his life, but keyboard cognoscenti tend to prefer the early ones. This collection is utterly delightful: it ranges from the soulful and sombre to the ribald and rollicking, and virtually every song throws up a line or a lick familiar from subsequent recordings by others. For example, 'Dresser With The Drawers' (1933), sung by one Carl Rafferty, shares its central metaphor with one of the more celebrated verses of ROBERT JOHNSON's subsequent 'From Four Till Late'; 'Dirty Mother For You' (originally released as by 'The Honeydripper') is one of the oldest back-alley blues around: JOHNNY GUITAR WATSON was still singing a barely cleaned-up version in the '70s. However, the bragging title track 'The Honeydripper' (1936) bears no relation to the well-known Joe Liggins instrumental, but on the other hand it does feature a dazzling guitar cameo from KOKOMO ARNOLD. There's even, on 'Let The Black (Cat) Have His Way' (1941), a rare example of overt racial anger in commercial blues.

Subjects for further investigation: Seemingly like every other bluesman of any repute who could still function well enough to find his instrument, Roosevelt Sykes toured Europe with the American Folk Blues Festival in 1965 and 1966: *American Folk Blues Festival '65* (L&R/Bellaphon CDLR 42025) and *'66* (L&R/Bellaphon CDLR 42069) will furnish the gory details.

An intriguing slice of blues piano 'prehistory' can be found on Fats Waller's *Low Down Papa* (Biograph BCD 114); its contents aren't actual performances by Waller, but 'hand-played' piano rolls dating from 1923–1931. (The 'piano roll', designed for automatic 'player pianos', was probably the earliest form of sequencer software, and thus naturally has no place in such an emphatically organic music as the blues.) The repertoire's blend of popular songs, rags and blues places it perfectly in the 'classic blues' tradition which links Tin Pan Alley with the Delta, and the wit, elegance and relaxed jauntiness of the playing makes me want to hear Waller doing it for himself. For some of the background activity to the major practitioners, you could do considerably worse than *Piano Blues Vol 1: The Twenties (1923–1930)* (Story Of Blues CD 3511-2), *Piano Blues Vol 2: The Thirties (1930–1939)* (Story Of Blues CD 3512-2), *Piano Blues Rarities (1933–1937)* (Story Of Blues CD 3507-2) and *Texas Blues Piano (1929–1948)* (Story Of Blues CD 3509-2).

This music was, of course, the direct ancestor of the postwar blues piano of such distinguished citizens as OTIS SPANN, MEMPHIS SLIM, CHAMPION JACK DUPREE and Pinetop Perkins, on whose records the music lived on. Right on the cusp was Cecil Gant (1915–1951), a Nashville-born singer pianist who enjoyed a 1945 pop hit with 'I Wonder', but whose heart was definitely closer to the 1944–7 dirty blues and boogie-woogie sessions found on *Cecil Gant* (Krazy Kat KK CD 03). *Specialty Legends Of Boogie-Woogie* (Specialty/Ace CDCHD 422) rounds up an assortment of 1947–1951 tracks by, among others, ROY MILTON, Joe Liggins, Camille Howard and Joe Lutcher to demonstrate that boogie-woogie was still both boogie-ing and woogieing in the immediate postwar period. For a glimpse of the tradition in its dignified old age, try the anthology *Boogie Woogie Masters* (Black & Blue 59.063 2). Recorded between 1969 and 1986, it features performances by MEMPHIS SLIM, Lafayette Leake, and – taking a rare turn at the 88s – Joe Turner himself. Appropriately enough, it opens with a rousing 'Pinetop's Boogie Woogie' performed by Pinetop Perkins, and ends with Memphis Slim's 'Boogie For Pinetop'.

THE JUMP GENESIS

In the beginning there was Basie. To be precise, in the beginning there was the sophisticated, artful post-vaudeville of CAB CALLO-WAY, but before you could say 'Hi-de-hi-de-ho!' the Count Basie Orchestra came striding out of Kansas City with flags waving, brass blazing, and huge, jovial men like Jimmy Rushing, JOE TURNER and Joe Williams (the latter not to be confused with country bluesman BIG JOE WILLIAMS) bellowing the blues up front. (The invaluable *From Spirituals To Swing: Carnegie Hall Concerts 1938/39* (Vanguard VCD2-47/48) provides an idea of just how powerful Basie's 'Band That Plays The Blues' sounded back then, but only an idea: the Basie band was cut down to a mere seven pieces for that show.) Essentially, jump was uptempo, small-band swing with novelty-blues vocals, and its godfather was LOUIS JORDAN, who had thoroughly defined the genre by the time America entered World War II. More than any other music, it was the common ground between the vastly different aesthetics of the swing and rock-and-roll eras. Its heyday lasted from the imme-diate postwar era until the early '50s, when it drained into the twin channels of rock-and-roll and 'Memphis synthesis' blues.

Jump enjoyed a minor revival in London during the mid-'80s, helped along by the success of ex-New Waver Joe Jackson's *Jumpin' Jive* album. For a while, you couldn't move on clubland for baggy suits, stand-up basses, saxophones and young men with red faces and redder braces bellowing songs like Jordan's 'Choo Choo Ch'Boogie' or WYNONIE HARRIS' 'My Big Ten Inch'.

Cab Calloway

To contemporary audiences, Cab Calloway is the black-suited janitor who taught John Belushi and Dan Aykroyd their blues lore in John Landis's 1980 cult romp *The Blues Brothers* before magically metamorphosing into a white-suited vaudevillean to perform an enchanting 'Minnie The Moocher'. In fact, Cabell Calloway – born in Rochester, New York, on Christmas Day of 1907 – was an early superstar of black entertainment: he and his orchestra succeeded Duke Ellington as the house band at New York's legendary Cotton Club. (Ellington's *Playing The Blues 1927–1929* (Black & Blue 59.232 2) will give you some idea of exactly what kind of act Calloway had to follow). Calloway would swagger around in a white satin tail-suit, hair flailing, doing his immaculate rubber-legged dance moves while conducting his band and singing his sly jive novelties: he was immensely popular on radio, records and movies throughout the '30s. Nowadays, people have decided that this stuff is part of 'jazz'; at the time, it was simply popular music, and had an immense effect on the more sophisticated bluesmen of the time. After all, what they were doing was pop, too: Calloway was having fun and making money, and they wanted some of both.

- *The Jumpin' Jive!* (Classic Jazz CDCD 1075)

This generous budget-price hour-plus of Calloway's music comes sans liner notes or session credits, so I'll stick my neck out and opine that most of it comes from the '30s. 'Minnie The Moocher' (and its sequels 'Minnie The Moocher's Wedding Day' – a.k.a. 'Kicking The Gong Around – and 'Keep That Hi-De-Hi In Your Soul'), 'St James Infirmary', 'Reefer Man', 'The Scat Song', a riotously uptempo 'Corrina Corrina', and the keynote 'Hep-Hep! The Jumpin' Jive' are still Big Fun.

Louis Jordan

If Louis Jordan's roots were in CAB CALLOWAY, Count Basie and Duke Ellington, his branches included CHUCK BERRY, B.B. KING, Bill Haley & The Comets, JOE TURNER's '50s successes with Atlantic Records, and even Kid Creole & The Coconuts. The 'jump' school of witty, uptempo novelty blues founded by Jordan had an incalculable, indelible effect on both postwar blues and the early rock of the '50s. In a sense, Jordan's music is the pivot between the swing era and rock and roll: the swinging, danceable hits this sax-blowing, jive-talking 'Clown Prince Of Rhythm And Blues' released between the late '30s and the early '50s found musical echoes in the post-T-BONE WALKER 'Memphis synthesis' school led by B.B. King (as well as in the numerous jumpers whose work is discussed in Part 2), and his jivey, Runyonesque tales of party-hearty mishaps and misadventures evidently lit a spark in the young Chuck Berry.

Born in Brinkley, Arkansas, on July 8 1908, Jordan learned clarinet from his father, studied at Arkansas Baptist College and tried his hand at professional baseball before settling on a musical career: his work experience included touring with the Rabbit Foot Minstrels behind MA RAINEY. In 1936, he joined drummer Chick Webb's band (then featuring vocalist Ella Fitzgerald), as an all-round saxophonist, singer, dancer, comic and MC: leaving the band shortly before Webb's death in 1938, Jordan formed his own band (which eventually became 'Louis Jordan & His Tympany Five'), brushing aside any quibbles about there being at least eight band members, none of whom was a tympanist. The following year he commenced a recording career which made him one of the most successful recording artists of the '40s, and lasted well into the 1950s. As well as supplying black jukeboxes with an endless supply of hits – eleven in 1946 alone! – he duetted with Bing Crosby, Ella Fitzgerald and Louis Armstrong, and starred in innumerable soundies as well as a few legit Hollywood movies. Whether Jordan's music was 'really' jazz, blues, pop or 'rhythm and blues' (a category he almost singlehandedly forced into being), the most important thing to remember is that it was great entertainment.

Jordan died in Los Angeles on February 4, 1975: even though his moment had passed, he remained musically active right up until a year or so before his death.

- **Five Guys Named Moe: Louis Jordan's Golden Greats** (MCA MCLD 19048)

Your basic single-disc, twenty-track, 60-minute introduction to the wonderful world of Louis Jordan. Released to capitalise on the success of the highly-praised West End musical *Five Guys Named Moe*, it features 'Five Guys Named Moe', 'Saturday Night Fish Fry', 'Choo Choo Ch'Boogie', 'Ain't Nobody Here But Us Chickens', 'Is You Is Or Is You Ain't My Baby', 'Let The Good Times Roll', 'Caldonia' (so beloved of B.B. King, ALBERT KING, ALBERT COLLINS, BUDDY GUY and CLARENCE 'GATEMOUTH' BROWN), 'Beans And Cornbread' (recently featured in Spike Lee's *Malcolm X*), 'Early In The Morning', and plenty more.

Subjects for further investigation: A slenderised budget-price equivalent of *Five Guys Named Moe* is **Jump Jive! The Very Best Of Louis Jordan** (Music Club MCCD 085). Four tracks and twelve minutes lighter with a mere six-track overlap, it omits 'Caldonia' but includes 'Open The Door Richard', 'Mop Mop', 'If You're So Smart, How Come You Ain't Rich', 'Run Joe' and 'Fat Sam From Birmingham', so why not treat yourself to both? **Louis Jordan, His Elks Rendezvous Band & Tympany Five: The Complete Recordings 1938–1941** (Affinity CD AFS 1033-2) is a nicely packaged 2-CD set which enables you to eavesdrop as Jordan refines his sound into the vehicle for his '40s triumph: Ella Fitzgerald's 3-CD set *The Complete Recordings 1935–1939* (Affinity CD AFS 1020-3) features Jordan on alto sax as a member of Chick Webb's band and Fitzgerald's own Savoy Eight. Pay special attention to the 1938 'Rock It For Me': it's a good one to pull out of the hat if you're ever stuck in one of those name-the-first-ever-rock-and-roll-record conversations.

CHICAGO: THE BLUEBIRD BEAT

Blues and jazz have been recorded in Chicago almost long as they've been recorded, *period*. Even before the the genesis of the distinctive post-war strain of Windy City most frequently associated with Chess Records and epitomised by MUDDY WATERS, Chi-town was a major regional recording centre, and many of the great rural blues artists came there to make their records. Inevitably, some of them decided to settle there; equally inevitably, a distinctive local sound began to emerge. Georgia transplant Hudson 'TAMPA RED' Whittaker soon became one of the kingpins of the pre-war South Side scene, and BIG BILL BROONZY was its primary figurehead, but the Godfather of pre-war Chicago blues recording was entrepreneur Lester Melrose: imagine a WILLIE DIXON who didn't actually compose or perform but simply decided who got to record and who didn't, and you've got it. For Chess – Chicago's leading post-war blues independent label – read Bluebird, the Chicago-based 'race records' subsidiary of the formidable Victor label.

Melrose ran Bluebird as a personal fiefdom: it was Melrose, not the artists, who had the contract with Victor. Some folks still blame ELVIS PRESLEY because Crudup never received the massive royalties accrued by Presley's versions of his 'That's All Right Mama', 'My Baby Left Me' and 'So Glad You're Mine': their complaints could be more profitably addressed to the executors of Lester Melrose's estate, which received the monies but somehow neglected to pass them on while poor old Arthur was in a position to derive some benefit from them. At various times the Melrose stable of blues stars included Broonzy, Tampa Red, MEMPHIS MINNIE, MEMPHIS SLIM, BIG JOE WILLIAMS, Arthur 'Big Boy' Crudup, Jazz Gillum, John Lee 'SONNY BOY' WILLIAMSON and Washboard Sam. In a tightknit system which was later adopted by Dixon at Chess, many of these artists played on each others' sessions, with the result that a distinctive 'house sound' readily emerged: not surprisingly, it was known as the 'Bluebird Beat.'

Tampa Red

Hudson 'Tampa Red' Whittaker's name might be rather more familiar today if his singing – pleasantly creaky, but hardly memorable – had been as distinguished as his slide-guitar work and his songwriting talents. He was, after all, a central figure in the Chicago blues mafia of the '30s ands early '40s, whose apartment served as a clubhouse and rehearsal room for what must have seemed like most of the musicians on the South Side. He was renowned for his extraordinarily rich and accurate bottlenecking, and his frequent team-ups with pianist Georgia Tom (who, after co-writing 'It's Tight Like That', later metamorphosed into the gifted and prolific gospel composer/publisher Rev. Thomas A. Dorsey) set the standard for post-LEROY CARR & SCRAPPER BLACKWELL piano-guitar duos. He is credited with the composition of blues standards ranging from the ribald hokum of 'It's Tight Like That' (one of the most-covered songs of the late '20s and early '30s) and 'Let Me Play With Your Poodle' to the limpid beauty of the blues ballad '(When Things Go Wrong) It Hurts Me Too'. His 'Black Angel Blues', transformed by Robert Lee McCollum (a.k.a. Robert Lee McCoy and best-known as Robert Nighthawk) into 'Sweet Black Angel', lives on as 'Sweet Little Angel', one of B.B. KING's most durable songs.

Born in Southville, Georgia, on 25 December, 1900, he acquired the 'Tampa Red' nickname because of his light colouring and reddish hair, and his residence in Tampa, Florida, where he moved to live with his grandmother after the death of his parents. He eventually settled in Chicago in 1925, and by 1929 was recording prolifically both as leader of Tampa Red's Hokum Jug Band (or 'Hokum Jazz Band'), and as an accompanist to others, including the titanic MA RAINEY and the cross-dressing, female-impersonating comic Frankie 'Half-Pint' Jaxon (1895–?). Red continued to record after World War II, but his postwar recordings failed to maintain his early momentum. By all accounts, he was profoundly distressed by the death, in 1953, of his wife Frances: as a result, he became an alcoholic and suffered a calamitous decline in both his musical and mental powers. In 1974 he entered a Chicago nursing home; either he's still alive there, or else his passing has remained unnoticed.

- **Bottleneck Guitar 1928–1937** (Yazoo 1039)

The first two tracks of this collection demonstrate the extremes of Tampa Red's music: the curtain-raiser is the salacious 'It's Heated', sung by Frankie 'Half-Pint' Jaxon, but it's followed by 'You Got To Reap What You Sow', a gorgeous solo bottleneck instrumental version of the theme which served as the music for 'It Hurts me Too' before Red himself takes over the vocals for 'What's That Tastes Like Gravy?'. He was an astonishingly sympathetic accompanist – whether the vocalist was a clownish goodtimer like Jaxon, a newcomer like Madlyn Davis or a walking monument like Ma Rainey (heard here on 'Black Eye Blues') – and a sufficiently savvy musician to integrate the slide guitar, most often featured by solo singer/guitarists, with other instruments.

Subjects for further investigation: **It's Tight Like That (1928–1942)** (Story Of Blues CD 3505-2) puts the lion's share of the spotlight on Tampa Red the hokum man, co-starring with Georgia Tom, Frankie Jaxon and such long-forgotten troupers as Papa Too Sweet and Sweet Papa Tadpole, though it also includes a characteristically lyric solo instrumental version of Leroy Carr's 'How Long How Long Blues'. **Guitar Wizards 1927–1935** (Yazoo 1016) includes his dazzling 'Boogie Woogie Dance'. The Tampa Red records you need but can't get are *The Guitar Wizard* (RCA, unavailable) and, confusingly, *The Guitar Wizard* (Blues Classics, unavailable), which contain later works including Bluebird-and-after versions of 'It Hurts Me Too' and 'Black Angel Blues.' Those intrigued by Jaxon's shenanigans can gorge themselves on **Frankie 'Half-Pint' Jaxon (1927–1940)** (Story Of Blues CD 3533-2); it doesn't feature Tampa Red, but where else can you hear songs like 'I'm Gonna Dance Wit De Guy Wot Brung Me', 'You Got To Wet It' and 'Can't You Wait (Till You Get Home)'?

Rather more to the point is Robert Nighthawk (1909–1967), a shadowy, itchy-footed figure originally from Helena, Arkansas, who pops up in some highly unlikely places. We first log him in 1939 as Robert Lee McCoy, playing harp behind pianist Lee Brown on 'My Driving Wheel' – included on **Harmonica Blues: Great Harmonica Performances Of The 1920s and '30s** (Yazoo 1053) – and guitar on some of the SONNY BOY WILLIAMSON I Bluebird sides collected on **Throw A Boogie Woogie** (RCA Bluebird ND 90320).

Between 1948 and 1964, he cut the Chess sides collected on **Black Angel Blues** (Chess CD RED 29), an anthology shared with harpist Forest City Joe, a fervent admirer of Sonny Boy Williamson I who, sadly, didn't bring very much of his own to the party. Nighthawk's biggest hits were with the Tampa Red-derived 'Sweet Black Angel' and 'Annie Lee Blues', but – as documented on **Live On Maxwell Street** (Rounder CD 2022) – he was, by 1964, reduced to playing in the street for tips, a fate which also befell the great harpist BIG WALTER HORTON. Nighthawk was a superb musician often favourably compared to MUDDY WATERS and ELMORE JAMES, but the blues life can be merciless to those whose talent exceeds their strength of character.

Big Joe Williams

For a while, Big Joe Williams was one of the major stars of the Bluebird stable, despite being as rough and unreconstructed a Delta bluesman as it would be possible to find this side of BUKKA WHITE or MISSISSIPPI FRED McDOWELL. He was born (on 16 October, 1903) and died (on 17 December, 1982) in the small town of Crawford, Mississippi: his music stayed as stubbornly rooted in the soil of the Delta as he did. The land he bought there after his return from Chicago, and indeed whatever comfort he enjoyed in his old age, were earned by his copyrighting of the classic 'Baby Please Don't Go', one of the most durable of all blues tunes and a hit for Big Joe in 1941. That the song was a favourite of MUDDY WATERS and JOHN LEE HOOKER, Delta musicians from the next generation, should not be surprising, since Hooker's guitar and Waters' voice demonstrate the extent to which both have plainly drunk from the same well as Williams. Nevertheless, Big Joe's sound was utterly distinctive and deeply personal, and only partly derived from the mandolin-like ring of his famous 9-string guitars, which were home-converted from 6-stringers so that the upper strings are doubled like those of a 12-string guitar, and tuned to an open chord of G. The crucial difference between Big Joe Williams and the more sophisticated and adaptable younger generation represented by Waters and Hooker was that they were committed to the evolution of their music and Williams to its preservation. Whereas all three left Mississippi, it was Williams who came back.

One of 15 children, he left home at 12 to seek his fortune playing music and working a series of back-breaking manual jobs in logging and turpentine camps. By the time he made his first records in 1929 (as a member of the Birmingham Jug Band), he was a real tough guy: an iron man in the LEADBELLY mould, but without the violent history. In 1932 he recorded at the same Grafton, Wisconsin, studio which had earlier recorded CHARLEY PATTON, SON HOUSE and SKIP JAMES, but it wasn't until 1935, when he reached Chicago and and joined Lester Melrose's Bluebird blues factory that he was able to support himself entirely through music. Like most blues stars of the period, he never got rich; but unlike many of them, he managed to stay in the game throughout the '50s and early '60s. Big Joe Williams didn't need to be rediscovered because he never really went away: he never made it to the Newport Folk Festival, but in 1962 and 1965 he played Carnegie Hall. He remained the ultimate platonic ideal of a rural bluesman: tough, illiterate and permanently on the move, criss-crossing the US with his home-modified 9-string guitar and a suitcase, while making periodic forays into Europe and Scandinavia. His audiences were white folkies and the older patrons of ghetto bars, for whom his music still provided nostalgic pleasure. Big Joe cut back his musical activities after he fell ill in 1974, but occasionally still performed, albeit locally, as late as 1980. A video of his appearance at a local blues festival held in that year shows him still a powerful and imposing presence: battered and stooped, but full-voiced and unbowed.

● **SONNY BOY WILLIAMSON & BIG JOE WILLIAMS:** *Throw A Boogie Woogie* (RCA Bluebird ND 90320)

Since Lester Melrose liked to maintain a cohesive house sound (not to mention saving time and money) by using his stars as sidemen on each others' sessions, this compilation is remarkably coherent as well as highly enjoyable: six of the first eight songs feature Big Joe backing up Sonny Boy, before Williamson moves into the accompanist's chair for six of the second eight, on which Big Joe takes the lead. Scooping up both men's early hits, this is a marvellously convenient way to get acquainted with two major practitioners of the immediately pre-Chess school of Chicago blues. As far as Big Joe is concerned, this is where you find the prototype for all subsequent versions of 'Baby Please Don't Go', including those of Van Morrison (with Them), Muddy Waters and John Lee Hooker, whose signature song 'Crawlin' King Snake' was also recorded by Williams in 1941. Williams' singing is rich and inventive (PEETIE WHEATSTRAW-style '*oohh*-well-well' and all), his plunky guitar is deft and driving, and Sonny Boy blows his brains out even more enthusiastically on the Williams sides than he does on his own. Incidentally, there's a very strong resemblence between Williams' title piece and Sonny Boy's 'Got The Bottle Up And Gone'.

- *Shake Your Boogie* (Arhoolie CD 315)
- *The Legacy Of The Blues Vol 6* (Sonet SNTCD 635)

The major postwar albums: the first half of *Shake Your Boogie* derives from sessions recorded in California during 1959 and 1960. During some of the sessions, Williams was out on bail from the 'Greystone' unit of the local slammer after an incident involving a knife, and the churning emotion of the situation seems to channel directly into the music, and not simply the 'explicit 'Greystone Blues'. The rest dates from 1969, with a young CHARLIE MUSSELWHITE sitting in here and there on harmonica and Big Joe experimenting with a slide: the performances areunderstandably less driven, but overall it's a powerful set of moans, stomps, boogies and ballads, plus the odd gospel piece. One of the latter, 'I Want My Crown', features a powerful vocal by Williams' wife Mary which irresistably recalls the old BLIND WILLIE JOHNSON records. Throughout, but especially on the remake of the Bluebird-era 'Throw A Boogie Woogie', Williams' guitar simultaneously recalls the heavy but dextrous picking of Leadbelly and the mesmeric drones of John Lee Hooker. The Sonet set was recorded in Stockholm in 1972, and it has a thinner sound than the Arhoolie disk, but if anything it has an even starker and more rough-hewn elegance than the earlier music. There is a bleakness to this music which was wholly absent from the more playful Bluebird stuff: no-one could accuse Big Joe Williams of mellowing with age and, as far as I know, no-one ever did.

Subjects for further investigation: Big Joe's turn with the American Folk Blues Festival came in 1963, which put him in the company of his old Bluebird colleague MEMPHIS SLIM and, ironically enough, SONNY BOY WILLIAMSON II, not to mention Muddy Waters, OTIS SPANN and WILLIE DIXON. Unfortunately, ***American Folk Blues Festival '63*** (L&R/ Bellaphon CDLR 42023) features only one brief performance by Big Joe.

Sonny Boy Williamson I

The humble Hohner harmonica (the 'French harp' in blues-speak) began to replace the fiddle in the blues armoury around the same time as the steel-string guitar supplanted the banjo, and by the time country blues recording commenced, the harp men were already in place. However, since the instrument isn't particularly loud, they appeared primarily as part of an ensemble rather than as featured artists, and it wasn't until the advent of electrical recording and P.A. systems that the harp player was able to become the front man. As the 1928–36 sides on *Harmonica Blues: Great Harmonica Performances Of The 1920s and '30s* (Yazoo 1053) demonstrate, early players like Jaybird Coleman, DeFord Bailey and BIG BILL BROOZY's half-brother Jazz Gillum had already developed radical note-bending and tonguing techniques as embellishments to the 'cross harp' style – using a harmonica tuned to the relative fourth of the key of the song – which is the most basic technique of blues harp. Nevertheless, the first real blues harmonica star was John Lee 'Sonny Boy' Williamson.

In the decade between his first recording and his murder in a Chicago street fight, he bequeathed to posterity a wealth of licks and techniques, a handful of classic songs and even – to Alex 'Rice' Miller, an older musician from Mississippi who had forty years of musical experience under his belt before he ever recorded – his name. His most important legacy, however, was the concept of harmonica as a lead instrument with comparable resources to a saxophone or guitar. Before Sonny Boy Williamson, the harmonica had been first a respectable 'parlour' instrument and then a party-time ensemble instrument only a couple of steps up from the kazoo. After Sonny Boy, it became one of the major 'voices' of the blues; Chicago became Harptown, and no South Side ensemble was complete without one. He set the precedent for everybody from LITTLE WALTER to CHARLIE MUSSELWHITE, and his influence is most readily discernible in the playing of HOWLIN' WOLF and, inevitably, SONNY BOY WILLIAMSON II. It's a shame that his distinguished *nom de blues* is most frequently associated with an elderly imposter who was undoubtedly sufficiently gifted to have made it on his own ticket.

John Lee Williamson was born in Jackson, Tennessee, on 30 March, 1914; he taught himself the basics of blues harp when still a child and refined his craft at the knees of SLEEPY JOHN ESTES, mandolinist Yank Rachell and Estes' harp-playing buddy Hammie Nixon, with whom he hoboed through the South as a teenager and who gave him his nickname. He wound up in Memphis, working with pianist Sunnyland Slim, before settling in Chicago during the mid-'30s. Working his way up from sideman status in clubs to studio gigs, he made his studio debut as a featured artist in 1937; a string of successful singles made him one of the city's kingpin bluesmen. If he hadn't been murdered on 1 June, 1948, by thieves attempting to relieve him of his night's wages after a gig, he would undoubtedly have become a significant voice in the postwar 'electric downhome' movement which was just about to get into gear. And Rice Miller would either have had to use his own name or stay out of recording studios.

- **SONNY BOY WILLIAMSON & BIG JOE WILLIAMS:** *Throw A Boogie Woogie* (RCA Bluebird ND 90320)
- *1938–1940* (Black & Blue 59.251 2)

Sonny Boy recorded more or less continuously until his death (mostly for Victor but with a few late-'40s sides for Columbia) but it's only the early work which has so far received the attention of the repackagers. This is about as good an introduction to his work as you can get: Williamson's half of this collection includes many of his signature songs, and his presence is also strongly felt on most of the Williams sides which complete the package. 'Good Morning Little Schoolgirl' is one of the hardiest perennials in the blues songbook: it was, naturally, speedily adopted by Rice Miller and became a subsequent favourite of MUDDY WATERS, as well as '60s blues-rockers like THE YARDBIRDS and JOHNNY WINTER; 'Sugar

Mama' was later adopted by Howlin' Wolf and JOHN LEE HOOKER. Unfortunately, it omits his 'Decoration Day' and 'Bluebird Blues' (also recycled by Hooker and Wolf), but you can find versions of those on the Black & Blue set, which draws on two early sessions, with Big Bill Broonzy on guitar. The repertoire also includes a remake of 'Sugar Mama': 'Baby I've Been Your Slave' has resurfaced (as 'How Many More Years') in the repertoires of Howlin' Wolf and LIGHTNIN' HOPKINS, and the collection is jam-tight with early showcases for Sonny Boy's talky harp and jovial presence.

Subjects for further investigation: Alongside Big Bill Broonzy and MEMPHIS SLIM, Sonny Boy was one of the participants in *Blues In The Mississippi Night* (Sequel NEXCD 122 *or* Rykodisc RCD 90155), Alan Lomax's epic anecdote-and-performance portrait of the rural South; the interaction of the three personalities provides an unmatchable insight into the man behind the harp. The best single-volume introduction to early harmonica blues is the collection cited above, *Harmonica Blues: Great Harmonica Performances Of The 1920s and '30s* (Yazoo 1053); its postwar equivalent is undoubtedly *Blues Masters Vol 4: Harmonica Classics* (Rhino R2 71124), which is loaded with masterful performances by, among others, Little Walter, JIMMY REED, JAMES COTTON, Sonny Boy Williamson II, JUNIOR WELLS, PAUL BUTTERFIELD, Howlin' Wolf, BIG WALTER HORTON, SLIM HARPO and Charlie Musselwhite. The story is continued on *Low Blows: An Anthology Of Chicago Harmonica Blues* (Bedrock BEDCD 15), a collection focussing on later work by lesser-known names of whom the most prominent are Big Walter Horton and Cary Bell; the single overlap with the Rhino CD is a performance of Robert Jr Lockwood's 'Take A Little Walk With Me' by one-armed harpist Big John Wrencher.

PART TWO: BRIGHT LIGHTS, BIG CITY
(1945–1974)

The period immediately following the end of World War II effectively marks the watershed between the decline of the older blues forms and their superseding by the styles which, even today, continue to define the form. The first of these latter was what critic Charles Keil has dubbed 'the Memphis synthesis', because Memphis was traditionally a cultural crossroads where rural bluesmen from the Delta could rub shoulders (and trade licks) with their 'jazzier', more sophisticated contemporaries from Texas and the Southwest Territories. The Delta begins, it is said, in the lobby of the Peabody Hotel; and in the early 1950s the city simultaneously nurtured the progressive blues of B.B. KING, Johnny Ace and BOBBY BLAND; and the cruder, more urgent rural blues that Sam Phillips was recording at Sun with HOWLIN' WOLF, JUNIOR PARKER, IKE TURNER and LITTLE MILTON. The 'Memphis synthesis' was a swinging meld of jumpin' jive and the increasingly common electric blues guitar, equally derived from, on the one hand, Kansas City big-band jazz and LOUIS JORDAN; and, on the other, the effects of amplification on the single-string guitar lines of BLIND LEMON JEFFERSON, SCRAPPER BLACKWELL, and LONNIE JOHNSON. Its avatar was T-BONE WALKER, but by the mid-'50s B.B. King had assumed the mantle.

The second was a Northern industrial-metropolitan transformation of the music of the Mississippi Delta diaspora: downhome blues electrically heated into an urgent, streamlined distillation of its rural ancestor. Its signpost was 'Short Haired Woman', a surprise 1947 hit by LIGHTNIN' HOPKINS (from Texas: regional boundaries aren't infallible, after all), which sold 50,000 copies for a tiny Houston indie. A year later came MUDDY WATERS' 'I Can't Be Satisfied', the foundation stone on which Chess Records' Chicago empire was built; and then, a few months after that, the million-selling 'Boogie Chillen' by the Detroit-based Delta expat JOHN LEE HOOKER. Hooker and Hopkins remained defiantly maverick, musical laws entirely unto themselves, but Waters rapidly became the godfather not only of a regional scene, but of an entire subgenre beloved of musicians and listeners all across America and, later, the world. In his hands, the Electric Downhome style became the 'Chicago Blues' musical idiom, and its parameters were essentially defined by the work of the various editions of the band which he led for over three decades.

Essentially, all the ingredients for what became 'rhythm and blues' – the funky, danceable, uptempo sound which is rock and roll's most immediate ancestor – were in place by 1948. T-Bone Walker was at the height of his fame; B.B. King, Muddy Waters and John Lee Hooker were just embarking on their recording careers. In West Memphis, Arkansas, Howlin' Wolf was leading his first band; in St Louis, pianist Johnnie Johnson's group, fronted by a young singer-guitarist named CHUCK BERRY, was working the clubs and bars; and in New Orleans, a pudgy young man named FATS DOMINO was coming to the attention of talent scouts from Imperial Records. Thanks to AMOS MILBURN, WYNONIE HARRIS and, of course, Louis Jordan, jump was still jumping; the second of two US Musicians' Union bans on recording had just ended; the first all-black radio station, WDIA, had just commenced broadcasting from Memphis; and audiences, musicians and record labels alike were ready to roll. And they did.

1. Electric Downhome: Chicago and Elsewhere

Muddy Waters

There had been blues in Chicago long before McKinley Morgan-field, a.k.a. Muddy Waters, arrived from Mississippi in 1943. The city had, after all, been a major regional recording centre, its studios attracting performers and companies from hundreds of miles around; and performers like BIG BILL BROONZY, TAMPA RED, SONNY BOY WILLIAMSON, MEMPHIS SLIM, Sunnyland Slim and many others were already established in the city before Muddy ever disembarked from the Greyhound bus. What Muddy Waters created was a distinctive Chicago style, built around his own tastes and his own strengths: a style with instant relevance and appeal to the massive influx of his fellow Delta migrants: a transformation of his (and their) idiom into a clamorous, rumbustious urban blues style which paralleled their experiences. As they became urban beings and their culture adapted with them, the music of Muddy Waters described the changes in their lives: as they moved from their scattered shacks in flat expanses of Delta countryside to crowded apartments in teeming South Side tenements, the blues found its sense of solitude and wide open space replaced with the jostling clamour of the ghetto.

Muddy Waters is one of the most important musicians in this book, because he, more than anyone else, linked the straight-no-chaser Delta blues of CHARLEY PATTON, SON HOUSE and ROBERT JOHNSON to the R&B-based rock with which THE ROLLING STONES, and their successors, took over western youth. He oversaw the creation of postwar Chicago blues, first as an idiom and then as an institution. Waters' influence did not depend solely on his musical skills, vast though they were, but on his stature as an individual human being: a man with equivalent gifts could still have achieved infinitely less without the outstanding personal qualities which made Muddy a perfect ambassador for the Chicago blues scene. Waters was a natural leader, a man of immense charm, dignity and authority; he was disciplined, reliable, intelligent, and loyal both to his employers and to his employees. Unlike HOWLIN' WOLF, JIMMY REED, or SONNY BOY WILLIAMSON II, he was professional to his fingertips. His bands attracted first-class talent, and he allowed his sidemen the freedom to hone their skills, strut their stuff and build their reputations, encouraging them to record their own music on his studio time, training them to become leaders in their own right. When musicians like LITTLE WALTER, JIMMY ROGERS, OTIS SPANN or JAMES COTTON set off on their own, he wished them luck and replaced them. There was never any doubt as to who was the *auteur*: if Rogers was replaced by Pat Hare, or Walter by JUNIOR WELLS and then by Cotton, or even Spann by PINETOP PERKINS, the sound of the Muddy Waters Blues Band remained constant and distinctive.

McKinley Morganfield was born in Rolling Fork, Mississippi,

on 4 April 1915, and acquired his nickname in childhood. He worked as a field hand, but his ambitions went far beyond that: by his late teens he was running his own whisky still and playing music, starting out blowing harp and then graduating to guitar. His mentor and tutor was Son House, but his hero was Robert Johnson, whom he never met but once saw play: an indelible experience which changed the course of his life. Waters' mature style drew freely on their influences: he reworked themes derived from both of them; his rich, chesty voice and spikily adroit bottleneck guitar displaying both House's weight and drive, and Johnson's intensity and detail. What distinguished him from other Delta singers with the same influences and heritage was the unmistakable personal authority with which he transformed the music of itinerant loners into the sound of a bustling, unified community. Another turning point came in 1941, when the seemingly ubiquitous Alan Lomax visited the plantation where Muddy worked. Lomax, having already recorded House, was anxious to record Johnson for the Library of Congress, unaware that the enigmatic genius was already in his grave. Once enlightened, he inquired after ELMORE JAMES, already performing locally in a Johnson-derived style; finally, Lomax ended up recording young Muddy Waters, both solo and in a string-band setting with the Son Sims Four. Even though the recordings were non-commercial and – bearing in mind Lomax's slender budget – virtually unpaid, Muddy was sufficiently impressed with his own played-back sound to decide on a career as a professional musician. By 1943, he was in Chicago, staying with a cousin and driving a truck for a local paper factory.

In the Windy City, he set about making a name for himself in the local taverns, encouraged by Broonzy and Sunnyland Slim. His first few recording sessions went nowhere, though on the evidence of 'Hard Day Blues', cut for Columbia in 1946 and unreleased until 1990, when it finally surfaced on *Legends Of The Blues Volume One* (CBS 467245), the Waters sound was already in place despite attempts to urbanise his defiantly rural style. The break came in 1948 when Aristocrat Records, a small label started up by Polish emigré club-owners Leonard and Phil Chess, recorded Muddy, playing electric slide guitar accompanied only by the standup bass of Ernest 'Big' Crawford, performing 'I Can't Be Satisfied', adapted from a song he'd cut for Lomax seven years before. The first pressing sold out in 24 hours. Muddy put together the first of his classic bands, though Chess (as the Aristocrat label was speedily renamed) initially preferred to record him with minimal accompaniment. One by one, guitarist Jimmy Rogers, harmonica whiz Little Walter and pianist Otis Spann joined the team, and the package was completed in 1954 when Chess hired the gargantuan bassist/composer/studio fixer Willie Dixon to oversee their blues recordings. Even though he was often outsold by competitors like Jimmy Reed and protégés like Rogers and Walter, Muddy was The Godfather Of Chicago Blues. Hit followed hit: Waters' repertoire, composed either by Willie Dixon or Muddy himself, was adapted wholesale both by successive generations of bluesmen, and by the white kids who discovered his music in the '60s. British groups like the The Rolling Stones, The Mojos, The Hoochie Coochie Men and The Manish Boys (featuring a very young David Bowie) even named themselves after his songs. Amusingly enough, his first British tour had been greeted with anguished hauteur by British jazz critics who had never before heard electric blues and who regarded Waters' music as little better than rock and roll.

By the end of the 1950s, when the bottom dropped out of the traditional city blues economy, Waters adroitly repositioned himself: he starred in a blues afternoon at the 1960 Newport Jazz Festival and Chess, who had hitherto regarded him as a singles artist whose only extant album was a best-of, released two albums that year. One was *Muddy Waters At Newport* (MCA/Chess CHD-31269), which showed off the in-person power of the current edition of his band; the other a respectful tribute to the late Big Bill Broonzy. Waters was thus introduced to jazz and folk audiences, further courted by 1964's all-acoustic *Muddy Waters, Folk Singer*. In the wake of the success of the Stones and their ilk, he returned to Europe with his acoustic guitar, only to be greeted by hordes of longhaired kids ready to rock. Waters received the young whites who courted him with his customary easy warmth and magisterial aplomb, and soon some of them, like The Rolling Stones, PAUL BUTTERFIELD and ERIC CLAPTON were in a position to repay their debts to him. He became a much-loved elder statesman, but in the early '70s, he was seriously injured in a car crash; and then insult was added to injury by the Chess brothers' decision to sell out to a New York corporation for vastly more money than any of their artists could even imagine. In the late '60s, Chess' attempts to keep Waters 'current' had forced him into ridiculously inappropriate recording strategies like the 'psychedelic' *Electric Mud* album.

Help was at hand: Texan blues-rocker JOHNNY WINTER lured Waters away from Chess to his own Blue Sky label, and set about recreating the raunchy purity of the '50s recordings, aided and abetted by members of Waters' past and present bands, including James Cotton, WALTER HORTON, Luther Johnson, Jimmy Rogers, Pinetop Perkins and the great drummer Willie 'Big Eyes' Smith. Four albums, *Hard Again*, *I'm Ready*, *Muddy 'Mississippi' Waters Live* and *I'm A King Bee*, were released between 1977 and 1980. (The same strategy was to prove even more successful, more than a decade later, for JOHN LEE HOOKER.) By 1980, Waters was an honoured prophet in his own land and many others; he had finally left the South Side and moved into a comfortable suburban home with his 25-year-old wife and numerous grandchildren. He died peacefully in his sleep on 30 April 1983; it was only after his death that it was discovered that he had developed cancer. His music, needless to say, is still alive and well: it is doubtful that a night passes without someone, somewhere, playing a Muddy Waters song and an audience getting up onto its collective hind legs and shaking several tail feathers.

The Waters songbook includes 'Hoochie Coochie Man', 'I Just Want To Make Love To You', 'You Shook Me', 'You Need Love' (a.k.a. 'Whole Lotta Love', Zep fans), and 'I'm Ready' (all composed by Willie Dixon, and all superb), but rather more to the point are his own songs and adaptations: 'Got My Mojo Working', 'Walking Through The Park', 'Long Distance Call', 'Manish Boy' (a straight lift of Bo Diddley's 'I'm A Man', but still . . .), 'Rolling Stone', 'I Can't Be Satisfied', 'You Can't Lose What You Ain't Never Had' and his personal variants of Delta staples like 'Baby Please Don't Go', 'Walkin' Blues', 'Catfish Blues' (retitled 'Still A Fool') and 'Rollin' And Tumblin''. The Stones covered one of his tunes for the B-side of their debut single and included one on each of their first two albums: his songs have been recorded by everyone from JIMI HENDRIX to JIMMY SMITH.

- **The Chess Box** (MCA/Chess CHD3-80002 [US])

As good a place to start as any, if you can find it: UK distribution of this and the other *Chess Box* collections (by Willie Dixon, Howlin' Wolf, CHUCK BERRY and BO DIDDLEY) has been patchy and inconsistent due to a legal dispute between MCA and Charly (formally unresolved as this book goes to press) over who holds UK distribution for the Chess catalogue. A great many individual Chess/MCA discs, however, are currently available alongside the Charly issues.

But I digress. *The Chess Box* is everything you'd want from a 3-CD boxed set: it's panoramic, selective and gorgeously packaged, running from Muddy's earliest Chess sides cut in 1947 (when they recorded him in a more urbane, T-BONE WALKERish bag than the citified country blues which made him a star) up to 1973's 'Can't Get No Grindin''. Hard decisions are made – the well-known 1960 Newport Jazz Festival live recording of 'Got My Mojo Workin'' is supplanted by the rarely-repackaged original 1956 studio single version – but generally all the calls are good ones. Every highspot in Muddy's thirty-year association with Chess is hit with plenty of room left for further exploration. As Robert Palmer's superb analytical essay points out, this collection goes a long way towards gainsaying the critical cliché that the late-'50s Waters bands (featuring guitarist Pat Hare and harpmen James Cotton and Big Walter Horton) were of necessity inferior to the more famous line-up with Little Walter and Jimmy Rogers: the first band may have had stronger soloists but the later combos were superior as ensembles. Even when performers who are stars in their own right (like RORY GALLAGHER, Mitch Mitchell, PAUL BUTTERFIELD, MICHAEL BLOOMFIELD, EARL HOOKER or BUDDY GUY) drift in and out of the various studio groups, there's absolutely no question as to who's in charge.

- **They Call Me Muddy Waters** (Instant CD INS 5036)

A generously weighted, sensibly compiled and sensibly priced budget best-of, concentrating on the early-'50s classics and including 'I Just Wanna Make Love To You', 'Rollin' Stone', 'I'm Ready', 'Hoochie Coochie Man', 'Louisiana Blues', 'Manish Boy', 'Long Distance Call', 'Walking Blues', 'Rolling And Tumbling' and plenty more. As an affordable launch-pad into the Waters *oeuvre*, it just cain't be beat.

- *Rock Me* (Charly CD BM 10)

The later greatest hits, not necessarily designed as a complement to the preceding entry but coincidentally picking up just about where *They Call Me Muddy Waters* leaves off. With a lower title recognition factor and less famous sidemen but absolutely no appreciable drop in quality, it includes 'I Live The Life I Love' (memorably covered by MOSE ALLISON), 'Walking Through The Park', 'Mojo', 'Mean Mistreater' and 'She's Into Something'.

- *Muddy Waters Sings Big Bill Broonzy/Muddy Waters, Folk Singer* (Chess/MCA CHD-5907)

Two of Muddy's first three albums-as-albums (the third being the 1960 Newport live set) thoughtfully doublebacked onto one fine CD: the Broonzy tribute was cut in 1960 with the Cotton/Hare line-up, and 1964's all-acoustic *Folk Singer* features Muddy with Willie Dixon's standup bass, Clifton James's sympathetic brushed drumming and Buddy Guy on second acoustic guitar. Both may seem like the kind of contrived 'concepts' that record companies dream up to broaden fading artists' appeal, but the integrity and enthusiasm of the music is undeniable. The Broonzy material comes out sounding like pure Muddy Waters, and there's nothing sterile about the acoustic 'roots move' of *Folk Singer*.

- **MUDDY WATERS, BUDDY GUY, HOWLIN' WOLF, SONNY BOY WILLIAMSON & WILLIE DIXON:** *Live Action!* (Charly CD BM 15)

As part of their rearguard action against the erosion of the traditional blues market, Chess Records set up this 1963 supersession, originally released on vinyl in the UK as *Folk Festival Of The Blues* and, in the US, as *Blues From Big Bill's Copacabana* (the Chicago club at which it was recorded). True to its billing, this is as explosively live as any '60s Chicago blues album you can find – just listen to the rhythm section falling apart at the beginning of 'Got My Mojo Working' – with one puzzling anomaly: Sonny Boy

Williamson's sole contribution, 'Bring It On Home', sounds as if the studio take of the song had simply been spliced into the performance tape. In the midst of such a boisterous live show, with a highly vocal audience audibly enjoying themselves throughout, the sudden shift to studio ambience is doubly incongruous. Muddy and the Wolf are both on superb form, but the star is Buddy Guy: the anarchic edge which he brings to these blues patriarchs is the factor that convinced a young English rockabilly fan named Jeff Beck that there might just be something to this blues stuff after all.

- *THE SUPER SUPER BLUES BAND: The Super Super Blues Band* (Charly CD BM 26)

Continuing their safety-in-numbers strategy, Chess wheeled Muddy, Little Walter and BP DIDDLEY (with Guy on guitar and Spann on piano) into the studio to record *Super Blues*, a triple-header jam album in which they would perform each other's songs, insult each other and generally recreate the atmosphere of a prime head-cuttin' session in a South Side tavern. The session took place in January 1967, selling well enough to justify a follow-up, *The Super Super Blues Band*. So they reconvened later that same year, with Howlin' Wolf (his faithful guitarist companion Hubert Sumlin in tow) lumbering in to take Little Walter's place. Sumlin's presence necessitated Guy's switching to bass, which is never a great idea. This CD fillets both of these albums and it's a mess, though a hugely entertaining one. The selections are titled after whatever song the performers start out with, though it's rarely the one with which they end up. The opener, nominally Muddy's 'Long Distance Call', sets the tone: Wolf starts the proceedings by throwing the song away before he's finished the first verse, turning it into his own 'I Asked For Water', and remorselessly insulting Bo, who's funking around making space noises with his battery of effects while a backing singer periodically screams (possibly to make it a little, ummm, *groovier* for the white kids), and Muddy makes occasional attempts to grab his song back. *The Super Super Blues Band* conclusively proves that (a) Buddy Guy is not a bass player, (b) Little Walter was pretty much burned out towards the end, (c) nobody except Muddy Waters could upstage Bo Diddley, and (d) that no one except Howlin' Wolf could upstage both of them at once. Most of it goes nowhere, but it's a pleasure to go nowhere in such distinguished company.

- *Hoochie Coochie Man* (Epic 461186 2)
- *Blues Sky* (Columbia Legacy 467892 2)

Two competing 12-track filletings of *Hard Again*, *I'm Ready*, *Muddy 'Mississippi' Waters Live* and *I'm A King Bee*, the four Johnny Winter-produced 'comeback' albums for Blue Sky Records which restarted Muddy's career in the late '70s. The first was originally compiled in 1983 as a memorial album, the second dates from 1992: the overlap is minimal, with only two songs ('I Can't Be Satisfied' and 'Screamin' And Cryin'') common to both. In a straight fight, I'd back the earlier package (though I have to declare an interest: I wrote the liner note) because it includes *Hard Again*'s killer opening, 'Manish Boy' (as featured in a 1988 Levi's commercial), plus 'I'm Ready', 'Champagne And Reefer', 'Hoochie Coochie Man' (obviously) and 'The Blues Had A Baby And They Named It Rock And Roll'. Rich in good humour and sheer whomp, these later recordings complement rather than displace the original Chess sides, and are eminently worthwhile in their own right: not least for several new compositions which prove that Muddy had retained his songwriting skills as well as his performing powers. Winter is both a sympathetic producer and a marvellously supportive guitar presence: if he'd made no records whatsoever as a featured artist, these albums alone would have earned him the gratitude of blues fans everywhere. Check out *Hoochie Coochie Man*, and then explore the currently available Blue Sky albums: *Hard Again* (Blue Sky CDSKY 32357), *I'm Ready* (BGO BGOCD 108) and *Muddy 'Mississippi' Waters Live* (BGO BGOCD 109).

Subjects for further investigation: **The Complete Muddy Waters 1947–1967** (Charly CD RED BOX 3) is exactly what it says it is: a humungous 9-CD set for the truly committed Muddite. Johnny Winter's **Nothin' But The Blues** (BGO BGOCD 104) was cut during the *Hard Again* sessions with Cotton and Perkins in full effect: Muddy himself takes a fine lead vocal on his own 'Walking Through The Park'. **Fathers And Sons** (Chess/MCA CHD-92522) is an all-star half-studio-half-live 1969 team-up including Michael Bloomfield (guitar), Paul Butterfield (harp), Duck Dunn (bass), Sam Lay & Buddy Miles (drums) and the ubiquitous Otis Spann (piano); despite Bloomfield's occasionally limp and inappropriate B.B. KING-style leads, it's pretty wonderful, and Butterfield gives it plenty of Walter throughout. Storming 1970 live performances of 'She's 19 Years Old', 'Hoochie Coochie Man' and 'Got My Mojo Working', with the Buddy Guy/Junior Wells band, can be found on *18 Tracks From The Film 'Chicago Blues'* (Red Lightnin' RLCD 0080) alongside notable performances from KOKO TAYLOR, J.B. Hutto, Guy & Wells and others. His ego never inhibited him from accompanying other people: he and his 1966 band can be heard backing John Lee Hooker on *Live At Cafe Au Go-Go* (BGO BGOCD 39), and giving Otis Spann his turn as frontman on Spann's *The Bottom Of The Blues* (BGO BGOCD 92). Muddy also appears performing 'Manish Boy' at The Band's allstar farewell concert on *The Last Waltz* (WEA K266076), the soundtrack to Martin Scorsese's famous 'rockumentary'. And the eerie, legendary, more-talked-about-than-heard 1950 duet with Little Walter on Baby Face Leroy's 'Rollin' And Tumblin'' surfaces on *Blues Masters Vol. 2: Postwar Chicago Blues* (Rhino R2 71122), the best single-volume introduction to the subject that you can possibly buy.

Lightnin' Hopkins

It has been said, not entirely in jest, that Sam 'Lightnin' Hopkins was the only great postwar bluesman who suffered from being over-recorded. He was certainly prolific: Prestige Records' 112-song, 7-CD set *The Complete Prestige-Bluesville Recordings* (Prestige 7PCD-4406-2) covers a mere four years of his career, and no less than 28 of the 43 selections on *The Complete Aladdin Recordings* (EMI CDP-7-96843-2) were cut at a single session. Like JOHN LEE HOOKER, he was adept at creating songs almost out of thin air (or, in BluesSpeak, creating 'air music'): he was never at a loss for a topical improvised lyric or an old song – either his own or somebody else's – to customise and adapt for any record company willing to pay cash up front. Also like Hooker, Hopkins habitually wrong-footed his accompanists by never allowing the formal niceties of timing or structure to interfere with the mood he was attempting to create. A titan of postwar downhome blues, an astonishingly deft and inventive guitarist, and a sly, pointed lyricist with a matchingly wry vocal delivery, Hopkins was the truest inheritor of BLIND LEMON JEFFERSON's rural Texan tradition. And it was his 1947 hit with 'Short Haired Woman' which blasted a path for the subsequent successes of Hooker and MUDDY WATERS, though the darker, heavier Delta-derived sounds eventually proved more durably popular than the dryer, lighter Texas lilt of Lightnin's blues.

The younger cousin and occasional accompanist of Texas Alexander, Hopkins was born in Centerville, Texas, on 15 March 1912 and spent most of his life streetsinging for tips in the Houston area. At the age of eight, he jammed with, and was encouraged by, Blind Lemon Jefferson, but he was in his 30s by the time he decided to take his musical career seriously. In 1946 he was whisked off to Los Angeles to record as a duo with pianist Wilson 'Thunder' Smith for Aladdin Records, and the label thought it would be cute to credit the record to 'Thunder & Lightnin''. Even though the partnership didn't last, the nickname did; Sam remained 'Lightnin' Hopkins' for the rest of his life. For the next few years, Hopkins's records were staples of the rural black jukebox market, never selling less than 40,000 copies and often as many as 80,000, but by the mid-'50s he seemed to have worn out his welcome with audiences and patrons alike by recycling the same material through too many hasty sessions. Having halted the downward spiral of the late '50s with a consciously 'folk' album, *The Roots of Lightnin' Hopkins* (Folkways, unavailable), he thereafter worked the white market (on albums) and his traditional audience (on singles) with equal enthusiasm.

Despite the '60s interest in his music, Hopkins only toured Europe twice (in 1963 and 1977), and travelled extensively within the US only with the greatest reluctance. He hated to fly and rarely left Houston; many of his Prestige sides were made by recording him in Houston and then flying the tapes to the East Coast for generally bewildered rhythm sections to overdub. This lack of adventurousness was mirrored in his music: once his style was set (as it already was by the time he made his first recordings) it never changed that much. Even though he varied his context – slow songs and fast, solo and accompanied, acoustic guitar and electric – there was little actual development; no sense that he shared Waters' and Hooker's intense desire to expand the possibilities of unreconstructed country blues styles. While his songs were superbly suited to his own needs, Hopkins never created a standard which, like Waters' 'Got My Mojo Working' or Hooker's 'Boom Boom', could retain the composer's individual stamp even when separated from the composer's performance. His influence was thus limited by comparison with that of Waters and Hooker (let alone the relentlessly eclectic, peripatetic and inquisitive B.B. KING), yet on his own terms and within his self-imposed restrictions, he played some of the deepest and most gripping downhome blues to be found anywhere on record.

Lightnin' Hopkins died of cancer in Houston on 30 January 1982. His health had been deteriorating steadily for several years: he had not toured since 1977 or recorded since 1974, and his ferocious gambling habit meant that he rarely had any money. His music was both a diary, and a means of sustaining him in his chosen lifestyle (that of a successful hustler from Houston's Third Ward district): if he'd had the character, discipline and sheer professionalism of a Waters, Hooker or BIG BILL BROONZY, he would undoubtedly have been a more successful and more influential performer. But then he wouldn't have been Lightnin' Hopkins. A famous anecdote from the late '60s concerns a Houston jam session involving Hopkins and some future members of ZZ TOP: drummer Frank Beard committed _lèse-majesté_ by telling Hopkins that he'd changed chord in the wrong place. 'Lightnin' change,' riposted Hopkins, 'when Lightnin' want to.' The point, of course, was that, deep down, Lightnin' never wanted to change at all.

- _The Complete Aladdin Recordings_ (EMI CDP-7-96843-2)
- _The Complete Gold Star Sessions Vol. 1_ (Arhoolie CD-330)
- _The Complete Gold Star Sessions Vol. 2_ (Arhoolie CD-337)

Cut between November 1946 and February 1948, Aladdin's 43-song double-CD finds Lightnin' at the outset of his recording career, fresh out of Houston and ready to decant onto disc the distillation of a couple of decades of street-singing. Just how ready he was can be deduced from Aladdin's willingness to release around 20 Hopkins singles in less than a year and a half despite the fact that he was recording prolifically for others during the duration of the contract. (To add insult to injury, a couple of weeks after recording the version included here, he recut 'Short Haired Woman' for the tiny Houston indie Gold Star, and their version was the hit.) This is the working repertoire of a highly resourceful Texas street-singer immediately after the war: blues, boogies and ballads, mostly solo. The Gold Star collections come from the same period and just about have the edge, possibly because Lightnin' was more comfortable recording in Houston. *Vol. 1* is the best representation of Young Lightnin' in action: it contains the scarifying 'Tim Moore's Farm', which pillories a notoriously vicious and callous white prison boss; the extraordinary 'Zologo Blues' (prototype zydeco – hence the title – with Lightnin' mimicking accordion sounds on the Hammond organ); and the hit version of 'Short Haired Woman'.

- *Blues Train* (Mainstream MDCD 901)
- *Sittin' In With Lightnin' Hopkins* (Mainstream MDCD 905)

1950–1 sessions for Bob Shad's Mainstream and Sittin' In labels: *Blues Train* includes a brace of early '50s hits ('Coffee Blues' and 'Hello Central'), and the added tightness of focus developed since the Aladdin records indicates the extent to which Hopkins was adapting to the demands of the studio. *Sittin' In With* finds Lightnin' working with amplified guitar and rhythm section some of the time, which adds some much-needed light-and-shade: a variation of 'Bald Headed Woman' was later immortalised by HOUND DOG TAYLOR under the intriguing title 'Give Me Back My Wig'. As a bonus, there's 'New York Boogie', in which Lightnin' takes an potshot at some of the mannerisms of his rival John Lee Hooker.

- *Lightnin' Hopkins* (Smithsonian/Folkways CD SF 40019)

The turnaround: Lightnin', down on his luck in 1959 after outstaying his welcome with the black Southern jukebox audience, is tracked down to a one-room apartment in Houston by Sam Charters, who rents him a guitar, buys him a bottle of gin, and records him in the apartment with a single hand-held microphone, moving the mike upwards when Lightnin' sings and down again for the guitar fills and solos. The result – bleak, lonesome and as intense as anything Lightnin' ever cut – was released by Folkways Records under the title *The Roots Of Lightnin' Hopkins* and was Lightnin's first-ever album-as-album, and introduced him to the folk audience which sustained him for much of the rest of his career. On a strict pound-per-minute basis, its 32-minute runtime is not fabulous value for money, but it's the purest distillation of Lightnin' Hopkins' music you can find.

- *The Complete Prestige-Bluesville Recordings*
  (Prestige 7PCD-4406-2)

This weighty 7-CD set reassembles, in chronological order, the complete contents of no less than eleven previously released albums (including the spoken-word *My Life In The Blues*) and throws in a previously unreleased 13-song 1964 live recording. (However, Ace Records – Prestige's UK licensees – are not utterly devoid of mercy: *Double Blues* (Ace CDCH 354) pairs up the original *Down Home Blues and Soul Blues* albums; *Blues In The Bottle* and *Walkin' This Road By Myself* appear back-to-back on Ace CDCHD 930, though neither CD is able to accommodate full double-album runtime and thus omits some of the original material.) Needless to say, you really need to love Lightnin' Hopkins to spring for a collection on this scale, especially since the clunkers are at least as numerous as the gems, but said gems include a wonderful session with SONNY TERRY sitting in on harp (originally released as *Late Night Blues*), some superb live recordings, including the uproarious 'What'd I Say' pastiche 'Me And RAY CHARLES', and two contrasting rhythm section approaches: the brushes-and-standup-bass favoured on the New Jersey sides, and the full-tilt stomp of Lightnin's Houston club band. A single- (or even double-) CD best-of drawn from this box would be, like, *toadly ahhhhhhsum, doooood*, but few other than Lightnin's most devoted fans would have the stamina even to attempt the task.

- *Morning Blues* (Charly CD BM 8)
- *The Legacy Of The Blues Vol. 12* (Sonet SNTCD 672)

Later Lightnin': *Morning Blues* is split half-and-half between very fine '65 Houston sessions with mysterious but magnificent pianist Elmore Nixon (1933–1975) and an uncredited but uncannily empathetic rhythm section; and '69 Muscle Shoals sessions featuring a houseband more accustomed to cutting with ELVIS PRESLEY or Aretha Franklin than with a cantankerous, idiosyncratic Texas songster. (A note on the folk process: 'Fishin' Clothes' (from *Morning Blues*) has absolutely nothing to do with taking the piscine, but a common phonetic misinterpretation of the line 'I would go home but I ain't got *sufficient* clothes'; the song itself is simply Blind Lemon Jefferson's 'Bad Luck', revived in the '50s by B.B. King as 'Bad Luck Soul'.) The high-point of the '65 tracks is the eerie 'Lonesome Dog Blues', where Hopkins's guitar mimics the howling hound so evocatively that you'll swear he's using a slide. The Muscle Shoals sides never satisfactorily resolve a basic groove mismatch between Hopkins and the backup musicians and Eddie Hinton's farcical 'psychedelic' guitar on 'Mr Charlie Pt 2' is in the finest tradition of CANNED HEAT's Henry Vestine, Big Brother's James Gurley or Country Joe & The Fish's Barry Melton. *The Legacy Of The Blues Vol. 12* (1974) was recorded in Houston with a local rhythm section by Sam Charters, who produced the Folkways relaunch album: the inescapably autumnal ambience adds poignancy, if nothing else.

Subjects for further investigation: Lightnin' plays for them Yurrupeans (in the company of SONNY BOY WILLIAMSON II, HOWLIN' WOLF, WILLIE DIXON, SLEEPY JOHN ESTES, Sugar Pie Desanto and Sunnyland Slim) on ***American Folk Blues Festival '64*** (Bellaphon/L&R CDLR 42024).

John Lee Hooker

The last of the great electric downhome triumvirate who broke through in the late '40s, John Lee Hooker's music is simultaneously the quintessence of the blues; and utterly unlike anything else in the field. Hooker is a mass of contradictions: he is the very soul of Mississippi though he left that state for good whilst still in his mid-teens; his music is the deepest, most stubbornly traditional and challenging blues of any major artist currently performing, yet his popularity and hi-profile visibility are matched only by the far more 'progressive' B.B. KING and ROBERT CRAY; he is a complete original whose songs spin off those of others. His power lies in his unrivalled ability to evoke an atmosphere and tell a story: when you give yourself up to his mesmeric, melismatic baritone vocals, his hypnotically tapping foot and the eerie modal drone of his guitar, you are irresistably drawn into his world, and utterly in his power. Though his recording career only commenced in November 1948, when he cut his first sides in the back room of a Detroit record store, John Lee Hooker's blues sound 'earlier' than even the '20s recordings of BLIND LEMON JEFFERSON, made when Hooker was a child. Listening to him, you almost believe that this music is the first blues, the primal blues, the blues on which all other blues are based.

The core of Hooker's art is the manner in which he hot-wired this utterly primal blues with the crackling, reverberant electricity of the Motor City ghettoes, seemingly skipping three decades of 'development' while still remaining up-to-date. Hooker equates beauty with truth: he sets up a groove and tells you a story or describes his feelings, happily flouting rhyme and metre in the interests of conveying an emotion, staying on a chord until he's ready to move on, forcing structure to serve him rather than dictate to him. Utimately, Hooker makes music to communicate his feelings, whether it is the sorrow and desolation of the abandoned lover or the rambunctious joy of the boogie. He believed as firmly as did MUDDY WATERS in the sanctity of rhythm'n'groove, but – unlike Muddy and WILLIE DIXON – he preserved spontaneity at all costs. He could write a tight, rhymed, rocking hit like 'Boom Boom' or 'Dimples', but it is with the 'deep' downhome blues that he has always felt most at home.

One of ten children, John Lee Hooker was born on 22 August 1920 on a farm somewhere on the outskirts of Clarksdale, Mississippi, and spent his formative years in and around the nearby small town of Vance (where his playmates sometimes included JIMMY ROGERS and SNOOKY PRYOR). His deeply religious father disapproved of the blues and its attendant lifestyle, but young John Lee was vastly intrigued by the music of local bluesman Tony Hollins, his elder sister's boyfriend. Hollins showed John Lee some guitar rudiments – including songs he still plays to this day, like 'Crawlin' King Snake' – and gave him his first instrument. When John Lee's parents separated, he stayed with his mother and her new husband, himself a guitarist who taught John the essence of the boogie which gave him his first hit some two decades later. In his mid-teens, John ran away to Memphis to stay with an aunt, but she turned him in and he was taken back to Mississippi. The early '40s found him in Detroit. Working in the great Motor City auto plants by day and the bars and taverns by night, Hooker set about the twin tasks of raising a family, and forging a reputation as a bluesman. By the end of World War II he was a popular local attraction; no less a personage than T-BONE WALKER gave him his first electric guitar. The golden age of electric downhome blues was just beginning, with the early Muddy Waters and LIGHTNIN' HOPKINS records massively popular with Southern migrants newly arrived in the big cities, and in 1948 Hooker recorded for local entrepreneur Bernard Besman. His first record 'Boogie Chillen' was leased to the Los Angeles-based Modern label, and sold over a million copies the following year. Three years later, 'I'm In The Mood For Love' equalled its predecessor's success.

Since Modern's accounting practices meant that Hooker's earnings failed to keep pace with his sales, he recorded promiscuously and pseudonymously for virtually every blues and R&B label in the nation before settling down with the Chicago-based Vee Jay label; this may help to explain why any reasonably comprehensive blues CD rack will contain more items by John Lee Hooker than by any bluesman, even B.B. KING, his good friend and fellow veteran of Modern and ABC. (This is why CDs from virtually every stage of Hooker's long and prolific career will generate their own *Subjects for further investigation*: notice.) He had his share of hits throughout the '50s, and when the tastes of the R&B audience shifted, Hooker moved smoothly into the folk scene, reverting to his acoustic roots at the Newport Folk Festival and – during one memorable Greenwich Village folk-club stint – giving an untried young singer named Bob Dylan his first professional engagement. Riding a new wave of European enthusiasm for the blues, the Coast To Coast Bluesman went international: his 1956 recording of 'Dimples' charted in the UK eight years later as young admirers like Steve Winwood, Pete Townshend, Van Morrison and Eric Burdon came to learn from the master: Winwood's very first professional recording (as a member of The Spencer Davis Group) was a version of 'Dimples'. The same song was one of three Hooker compositions featured on Burdon's first album with The Animals; Morrison's debut with Them was with a Hooker-derived version of the standard 'Baby

Please Don't Go' (a single these days best-known for 'Gloria', its original B-side).

Back in the US, the triumphant *Hooker'N Heat.* (a link-up with the chart-riding CANNED HEAT, who had been unashamedly booglarising his music for years) gave Hooker the best-selling album of his career; a return to early form and early style featuring Hooker solo (complete with heavily amplified footstomp), duetting with Canned Heat's virtuoso Alan Wilson, and rocking along with the full band. It easily outclassed – and outsold – the 'psychedelic-supersession' albums into which his then-current label, ABC (to whom he'd signed after Vee Jay's mid-'60s collapse) later shoehorned him, but it was almost twenty years later before anybody had the bright idea of once more cutting Hooker in his native musical habitat. In 1970 he left chilly, gritty Detroit for the sunnier climes of California; relocating to the San Francisco Bay Area, he settled into a comfortable old age as an elder statesman of the blues, recording rarely (and even more rarely cutting anything memorable), touring the nation and the world with his Coast To Coast Blues Band. He became a reliable but predictable fixture on the blues circuit, occasionally surfacing via on-(and off-) screen cameos in movies like *The Blues Brothers* and *The Color Purple*, or bizarre one-offs like the title role in Pete Townshend's rock-opera version of Ted Hughes's *The Iron Man*. Then came *The Healer*: Hooker's new management decided that it was time that he made a prestigious, high-profile album which reinterpreted his classic repertoire in the company of well-known likeminded souls. Hooker's famous admirers, including Carlos Santana, Robert Cray, Los Lobos, BONNIE RAITT, GEORGE THOROGOOD, CHARLIE MUSSELWHITE and Canned Heat, piled in to help out, and the result – released in late 1989 – was a smash hit. The following summer, Hooker toured the blues festival circuit and grossed over $3,000,000.

A followup album, 1991's *Mr Lucky*, did even better, this time with the assistance of ALBERT COLLINS, JOHN HAMMOND, THE ROLLING STONES' Keith Richards, Van Morrison, JOHNNY WINTER, CHUCK BERRY's piano partner Johnnie Johnson, and return engagements by Cray and Santana. By this time, Hooker was a familiar media face, appearing in several TV commercials (and being imitated in several more); *Mr Lucky* gained him not one but two entries in *The Guinness Book Of Records*: for the highest UK chart position ever attained by a blues album, and the oldest performer ever to reach the Top Five. He collaborated with his old friend Miles Davis on the score for Dennis Hopper's movie *The Hot Spot*; he was honoured by an all-star tribute concert at Madison Square Gardens, and, when he guested on the last Stones tour, virtually turned ERIC CLAPTON and The Rolling Stones into his backing group.

At the time of writing, the Hook is more visible than ever: the re-working of 'Boom Boom' which provides his latest album with its title track reached Number 16 in the UK singles chart and provided the theme for a Lee Jeans commercial. All in all, Hooker has made more money in the last four years than in the previous forty. He travels less and less these days – sadly, his European fans have probably seen the last of him – but he's made his point: by sticking to his guns, he has finally eclipsed many more biz-savvy bluesmen who have attempted to succeed by compromising with pop style and fashion. John Lee Hooker takes it easy ... but he takes it.

- *The Ultimate Collection 1948–1990* (Rhino R2 70572 [US])

Filleting John Lee's massive and widely-spread output into one manageable compilation is a herculean task, and my Delta Blues Museum baseball cap is hereby doffed (for neither the first nor last time) to Rhino for even attempting to clean these particular stables. This 2-CD set gives you a heaping handful of early-'50s Detroit sides (including both sides of Hooker's very first single), plenty of Vee-Jay material (naturally including both 'Dimples' and 'Boom Boom'), a judicious selection of circa-1960 'folk blues' tracks, some Chess and ABC material from the '60s, a heady blast of *Hooker 'N Heat* and a couple of genuine collectors' items: Hooker singing ROBERT JOHNSON's 'Terraplane Blues' accompanied by ROY ROGERS's impeccably Johnsonian slide, and a rousing 1990 live version of 'I'm In The Mood For Love' with Rogers and Bonnie Raitt. Considering the complexity and expense of licensing so much material from so many different sources, this is about as representative a Hooker selection as can possibly be squeezed into two discs.

- *The Detroit Lion* (Demon FIEND CD 154)
- *Half A Stranger* (Mainstream MDCD 903)

By an extremely short head, the best entry points into the confusing world of Hooker's first half-decade in the record biz, mainly because they both include the important early hits 'Boogie Chillen', 'I'm In The Mood For Love' and 'House Rent Boogie' (*The Detroit Lion* scores an extra point for also including Hooker's earliest recording of his staple 'Crawlin' King Snake'). Due to the deadly combination of Hooker's promiscuous recording habits and his early mentor Bernard Besman's equally promiscuous licensing habits, it's almost impossible to acquire a decent cross-section of this stuff without buying the same titles several times over: for example, purchasers of *Blues Brother* (Ace CDCHD 405) will find 13 of its 24 tracks duplicated on the 20-track *Graveyard Blues* (Speciality/Ace CDCHD 421).

- *House Of The Blues* (Charly CD RED 5)
- *Don't Turn Me From Your Door* (Atco 82365-2[US])

Two more fine early '50s Hooker albums: dank, echoing, scary and exhilarating by turns. The original 10-track *House Of The Blues* album (available in an MCA/Chess incarnation as CHD-9258) dates from 1951, as does most of the material on *Don't Turn Me From Your Door*, which is filled out with a few '61 tracks. If you prefer Hooker at his most introvertedly menacing, these are the ones to get. (This Charly issue of *House Of The Blues* is pumped up with 1966 band tracks from *The Real Folk Blues*, of which more later, and thus represents excellent value for money: committed Hookerphiles may prefer to pick up the MCA issue – with the original artwork – alongside the expanded version of *The Real Folk Blues* ... of which, as you may have guessed, more later.)

Subjects for further investigation: More early '50s Detroit Hooker, and, yes, there is an awful lot of it: *Detroit Blues* (Flyright FLYCD 23) contains 12 examples of the young(ish) Hook alongside five by his occasional studio sideman and running buddy Eddie Burns (the latter playing mainly harp, having not yet acquired his 'Guitar' nickname), and a couple by pianist Baby Boy Warren. *Boogie Awhile* (Krazy Kat KK CD 05), *No Friend Around* (Red Lightnin' RLCD

0093), *That's Where It's At!* (Stax CDSXE 064), *Don't You Remember Me* (Charly CD CHARLY 245), *John Lee Hooker Plays & Sings The Blues* (Chess CD CHESS 1008) and the two above-cited Ace sets – *Blues Brother* (Ace CDCHD 405) and *Graveyard Blues* (Speciality/ Ace CDCHD 421) – also flesh out Hooker's formative years as a recording artist. *Introducing ... John Lee Hooker* (MCA MCLD 19165) combines a good selection of '50s and '60s Chess tracks juxtaposed with some late-'60s Bluesway material and, ahem, a liner note by your humble servant. For a sardonic 'answer record' to Hooker's 'I'm In The Mood For Love', check out Helen Humes's 'I Ain't In The Mood' on *60 Great Blues Recordings* (Cascade CBOXCD 3).

- *Boogie Chillen* (Charly CD CHARLY 4)

This 22-song gem is the best single-volume account of Hooker's years with Chicago's Vee Jay Records (Chess's hottest local competition), where he first came to grips with the problem of recording his idiosyncratic blues with full backup bands other than his own custom-trained Detroit crews. Hooker recorded (almost) exclusively for them between 1955 and 1965 (apart from a brief fling with Riverside around the turn of the decade), and so this should be your first port of call for the likes of 'Dimples' and the unsurpassed original version of 'Boom Boom'. The remakes of Hooker staples like 'Crawlin' King Snake', 'I'm In The Mood For Love', 'Bottle Up And Go' and 'Hobo Blues' are nothin' but fine, but the recut 'Boogie Chillen' featured here is, as far as I'm concerned, definitive: purists who believe that first versions are invariably best are welcome to disagree. *Boogie Chillen* also includes 'No Shoes' (a sizeable R&B chart hit), 'Maudie' (dedicated, not altogether complimentarily, to his then wife), 'I Love You Honey', the striding 'This Is Hip', the lascivious 'Big Legs, Tight Skirt' and the marvellous slow blues 'It Serves Me Right To Suffer'. If you don't have some Vee Jay material in your John Lee Hooker collection, you don't *have* a John Lee Hooker collection.

Subjects for further investigation: Charly provide more Vee Jay-derived Hooker on *Let's Make It* (Charly CD Charly 170); *This Is Hip* (Charly CD BM 7) and *Mambo Chillun* (Charly CD BM 19) are the budget-price equivalents. Vee Jay's current US licensee is Chameleon Records, who have reissued all of Hooker's Vee Jay albums in facsimiles of the original packaging. Since US albums of that time seldom ran over half an hour apiece, none of these are particularly good value; though I recommend *Concert At Newport* (Vee Jay VJD 81078 [US]) for its documentation of Hooker's appearance at the 1964 Newport Folk Festival, accompanied only by the acoustic bass of Bill Lee (yes, Spike's dad). *Blues At Newport* (Vanguard VCD 115/116) and *Great Bluesmen/Newport* (Vanguard VCD 77/78) each provide two tracks from that same acoustic set, alongside performances by SONNY TERRY & BROWNIE McGHEE, REV. GARY DAVIS, MISSISSIPPI JOHN HURT, SON HOUSE, SKIP JAMES, John Hammond and Lightnin' Hopkins. *The Best Of John Lee Hooker* (Music Club MCCD 020) combines a good-value 12-track fillet of the Vee Jay years with eight Chess titles from the early '50s and mid-'60s; Chameleon's Vee Jay-era Hooker compilation is *The Hook* (Chameleon D2-74794, US only). The ultimate collectors' wet dream is, of course, *The Vee Jay Years 1955-1964* (Charly CD RED BOX 6), a 6-CD set which documents this key period in as much detail as even the most obsessive Hooker freak could desire.

- *That's My Story/The Folk Blues Of John Lee Hooker*
  (Ace CDCHD 927)
- *Live At Sugar Hill Vols. 1 & 2* (Ace CDHD 938)

Hooker in acoustic 'folk blues' mode. Each of these CDs pairs up two vinyl albums: the first (studio) disc combines solo performances with a session featuring Cannonball Adderley's rhythm section, while the second finds him in concert. The 'folk' designation is decidedly double-edged: *That's My Story*'s first two tracks, 'I Need Some Money' and 'I'm Wanderin'', are adaptations of pop-blues hits: respectively, Barrett Strong's then-current Motown hit 'Money' (just about the only song to be covered by both The Beatles and The Rolling Stones, as well as by JLH), and the CHARLES BROWN urbane-blues standard 'Driftin' Blues'. Not surprisingly, Hooker's touch on the acoustic guitar is not that different from his approach to the electric: what *is* different is the production, the ascetic, documentary approach of which contrasts dramatically with the reverb-soaked electricity of the Detroit recordings or the rocking early '60s band grooves. John Lee himself is, as always, John Lee; and the repertoire is more or less the standard Hooker set. Those with a predilection for acoustic blues will probably prefer their Hook in this flavour; me, I enjoy it any way it comes. The US equivalent of *Live At Sugar Hill Vols. 1 & 2* is *Boogie Chillun* (Fantasy FCD-24706-2); it combines the two original vinyl albums by omitting 'Matchbox' instead of 'I Was Standing By The Wayside', but is otherwise identical.

Subjects for further investigation: **The Country Blues Of John Lee Hooker** (Riverside OBCCD-542-2) is the 'solo' half of *That's My Story/The Folk Blues Of John Lee Hooker* (Ace CDCHD 927). For the usual playing-time reasons, the combined package omits three of these tracks, so if you want *Country/Folk Blues Of* in its entirety, here's where you get it.

- **The Complete Chess Folk Blues Sessions** (MCA MCD-18335)

The *Real Folk Blues* title is something of a misnomer: Chess had previously used it as a catchall title for a series of singles anthologies by Muddy Waters, SONNY BOY WILLIAMSON and HOWLIN' WOLF albums; these are rocking band sides in the Vee Jay mould, chiefly remarkable for spirited and exuberant performances by Hooker himself, and – despite the presence of steady Eddie Burns – for the total confusion into which the studio musicians are often thrown by Hooker's idiosyncratic timing. Chess recorded two albums' worth of material but only released one: this edition blows the dust off the outtakes, some of which are wonderful. The original *Real Folk Blues* album is combined with some superfine early-'50s sides on *House Of The Blues* (Charly CD RED 5).

- **Live At Café Au Go-Go** (BGO BGOCD 39)

The latter part of Hooker's ABC-Bluesway period (1966–1974) was spent working harder and harder to light a fire under progressively less and less sympathetic bands. *Live At Café Au Go-Go* (1967) presented him in concert in New York with one of the best bands of his career. Unfortunately, the group wasn't his but Muddy Waters', featuring OTIS SPANN on piano and Muddy himself on guitar. The repertoire includes fine versions of 'One Bourbon, One Scotch And One Beer', 'Jesse James' and 'I'll Never Get Out of These Blues Alive'; and the result is the kind of deep, deep, *deep* blues – Hooker singing 'for people who feel the way I do' – which makes you wonder what would have occurred if Hooker had put as much effort and energy as Waters did into maintaining a first-class full-time band.

- *Urban Blues* (BGO BGOCD 122)
- *Simply The Truth* (BGO BGOCD 40)

A highly listenable if mostly non-epochal pair of late '60s studio sessions. The first, from 1967, features an unusual line-up: two basses on some of the tracks (played by Phil Upchurch and JIMMY REED's sidekick Eddie Taylor), plus lead guitar contributions from Hooker's sometime partner Eddie Kirkland, BOBBY BLAND's 6-string foil Wayne Bennett and, on the apocalyptically gripping topical blues 'The Motor City Is Burning', an uncredited BUDDY GUY. Other high points: a very cool remake of 'Boom Boom', and the original versions of 'Mr Lucky' and 'Think Twice Before You Go'. The second, cut the following year with a New York studio band, wins out on inspired juxtapositions of both topic – the Vietnam war (he's ag'in it) is immediately followed by the mini-skirt (he's for it) – and mood: the joyful boogie of 'I Wanna Bugaloo' and '(Twist Ain't Nothin But) The Old Time Shimmy' alternates with the eerie desolation of 'Tantalizin' With The Blues' and 'One Room Country Shack'. Trivia note: Hele Rosenthal, who plays harp on *Simply The Truth*, resurfaced almost twenty years later as the *eminence gris* behind Paul Simon's *Graceland*.

- **CANNED HEAT & JOHN LEE HOOKER:** *Hooker 'N Heat: The Best Of ... Plus* (See For Miles SEE CD 234)

The most successful album of Hooker's first two decades came at a time of considerable turbulence. Following the break-up of his marriage, Hooker had uprooted himself from Detroit – where he had lived for almost thirty years – and relocated to the San Francisco Bay Area. It wasn't too long before his disciples Canned Heat 'borrowed' him from ABC to record with them for Liberty; and, what's more, they had the sense to stay out of his way for most of the session. The approach chosen by the band (specifically: vocalist Bob Hite and manager Skip Taylor, who produced; and presiding genius Alan Wilson, who played guitar, harmonica and piano) was to make a John Lee Hooker album featuring Canned Heat, rather than a Canned Heat album featuring John Lee Hooker. Cut during a three-day session which recreated the ambience of the Besman-era Detroit sides by equipping Hooker with a knackered vintage amplifier and a clearly-miked platform on which to stomp, this approach paid off, big time. Hooker had refined his craft considerably since he last recorded in his classic style, and recording technology had evolved to the point where fidelity and raunch could be reconciled. The results were stunning: Hooker, still raw from the upheavals in his life, responded with one of the finest sustained studio performances of his career. A deep blues like 'The Feeling Is Gone' is soaked through with the pain and loneliness of separation; the original one-man groove machine rocks boogies like 'Send Me Your Pillow' until they achieve a literally trance-like intensity. Novelties like 'Bottle Up And Go' rub shoulders with homilies like 'The World Today' and Charley Patton echoes like 'Peavine', but the album's true masterpiece is a remake of the 1949 'Burning Hell', where Hooker's exultant celebration of freedom from an afterlife is matched every step of the way by Wilson's virtuoso harp. Indeed, the rapport between Wilson and the notoriously unpredictable Hooker verges on the uncanny: the mood remains unbroken until a slow blues with the fully assembled band is disrupted by Henry Vestine's sour, fuzz-boxed guitar. Still, *Hooker 'N Heat* culminates in a thunderously good-humoured 'Boogie Chillen No 2', and remains the best album-as-album in the first four decades of Hooker's recording career. This single-CD edition omits two solo Hooker performances from the original double-album – hence the cumbersome and unenlightening subtitle – but the 2-CD US equivalent is the full monty. Alan Wilson died even before these sessions were mixed; hence the sombre cover shot of Hooker and the surviving band members in a dingy hotel room, with a black-bordered portrait of Wilson hanging on the wall.

Subjects for further investigation: After the success of *Hooker 'N Heat*, one might have expected ABC to have learned something. They had, but it was the wrong lesson: they attributed its triumph less to the unvarnished 'classic' Hook which Hite, Wilson and Taylor had presented than to the presence of high-profile rock stars. The result was a series of 'super-sessions' like 1970's aptly-named

Endless Boogie (BGO BGOCD 70) and 1971's *Never Get Out Of These Blues Alive* (See For Miles SEECD 89), which smothered Hooker in plodding rhythm sections, superfluous instrumentation and over-eager whiteboy hotshots. (Incidentally, the current See For Miles issue of *Never Get Out Of These Blues Alive* – the high point was probably Van Morrison's duet with Hooker on the title track – incorporates three tracks from 1969's never-reissued *If You Miss 'Im ... I Got 'Im*, John Lee's only recorded collaboration with his younger cousin, the slide-and-wah-wah master EARL HOOKER, who, sadly, died the following year.) The process culminated in the extraordinary *Free Beer And Chicken* (BGO CD 123), which – despite some fine keyboards by John Lee's son Robert, a couple of intriguing funk experiments and a lovely 'Bluebird Blues' – finally collapses under the weight of producer Ed Michel's pretensions. A tired and emotional Joe Cocker shows up for a couple of guest 'vocals'; a fine, heartfelt version of 'Sittin' On Top Of The World' is gradually overlaid with absurd kalimba and flute; and if you think that John Lee Hooker would title a song '(You'll Never Amount To Anything If You Don't Go To) Collage (A Fortuitous Concatenation Of Events)' of his own accord, then you'n me better have us a little talk. Nevertheless, I am compelled to acknowlege that, out of all Hooker's albums, this is the one to which he most frequently chooses to listen in his car. *Tantalizin' With The Blues* (MCA DMCL 1686) fillets the ABC period tolerably well, omitting both the worst excesses of the super-session and psychedelic periods (yeahhh!) and 'The Motor City Is Burning' (boooo!). John Lee's reaction to his time with ABC was to record virtually nothing for the next fifteen years.

- *Alone* (Tomato 2696602)
- *The Cream* (Charly CD CHARLY 106)

A pair of live albums, respectively recorded in 1976 and 1977: the first is a 2-CD set documenting a solo performance in New York, while the second catches Hooker in a California club with the then-current edition of the Coast To Coast Blues Band plus guest harpist Charlie Musselwhite. The boogies on *Alone* are almost perfunctory, but the slow, ruminative pieces – including stunning readings of 'Dark Room', 'Jesse James', 'Never Get Out Of These Blues Alive' and 'T.B. Sheets' – are amongst Hooker's most powerful. *The Cream* presents Hooker on reasonable fettle with a so-so band: for completists only.

- *The Healer* (Silvertone ORE CD 508)
- *Mr Lucky* (Silvertone ORE CD 519)
- *Boom Boom* (PointBlank VPBCD 12)

The autumnal triumphs: these albums have taken considerable stick from Hooker purists, but – the occasional misstep notwith-standing – the power and individuality of Hooker's music remains uncompromised. Producer Roy Rogers, an alumnus of the Coast To Coast Blues Band and an impressive country blues stylist in his own right, had evidently learned the right lessons from *Hooker 'N Heat*: the numerous guest stars come to celebrate Hooker, not to bury him; to jam *with* him, not over him. The combined guest list for the three albums is somewhat intimidating (Carlos Santana, Robert Cray, Bonnie Raitt, Albert Collins, George Thorogood, Canned Heat, Van Morrison, Keith Richards, John Hammond, Los Lobos, Charlie Musselwhite, Jimmy Vaughan, Ry Cooder, Booker T, Johnnie Johnson and more), but the music isn't: without exception, all the participants know that they're there to play Hooker's music in his style and on his turf; and that's what they do. The only real breaks with the tradition come from Santana – the title track of *The Healer* is a masterpiece, the rather more fusoid 'Stripped Me Naked' (from *Mr Lucky*) isn't – but rather than list the plentiful highlights of the individual albums, I'll simply issue a blanket recommendation for all three.

- **ORIGINAL MOTION PICTURE SOUNDTRACK:** *The Hot Spot* (Antilles ANCD 8755)

John Lee Hooker meets Miles Davis meets TAJ MAHAL, with Roy Rogers and a fine rhythm section in attendance. The occasion was a Jack Nitzche soundtrack for a poorly-received Dennis Hopper movie, and the result is a haunting collection of ominous moans and slow shuffles which enables Hooker to prove that he doesn't need words to sing the deepest and most emotionally complex blues; Miles to demonstrate that he was as much at home in Hooker's menacing dreamscape as in any of the other territories he explored during his long and extraordinary career; and Taj to recycle the 'Wild Ox Moan.' The rocking 'Bank Robbery' is unique in the annals of contemporary music: after all, where the hell else are you going to hear Miles Davis do the boogie?

Subjects for further investigation: Hooker is far from being a compulsive jammer, but he has been known to bestow his benign presence on close friends, and on those who offer him something genuinely intriguing. He appears with John Hammond on *Got Love If You Want It* (PointBlank VPBCD 7); with his old buddy Eddie Kirkland on *All Around The World* (Deluge/Sky Ranch 652331); and singing Robert Johnson's 'Terraplane Blues' with his producer and former sideman Roy Rogers on *Slidewinder* (Blind Pig BP 72687). The limited-edition JIMI HENDRIX CD *Red House: Variations On A Theme* (Jimi Hendrix Reference Library/Hal Leonard Publishing: no c/n) presents several examples of Hendrix working over his signature slow blues 'Red House' in a variety of contexts, and it's capped by the same song performed by Hooker with a studio group including Randy California (guitar) and Booker T. Jones (organ). Last, and weirdest, he portrays the title character in Pete Townshend's rock-opera adaptation of Ted Hughes's novel *The Iron Man* (Virgin CDV 2592).

Willie Dixon

Willie Dixon had minimal influence as a performer, but as house songwriter and bassist-in-residence for Chess Records during much of the '50s and '60s, he provided HOWLIN' WOLF and MUDDY WATERS with much of their best-known repertoire. BO DIDDLEY, SONNY BOY WILLIAMSON II, LITTLE WALTER, OTIS RUSH and KOKO TAYLOR also benefited from custom-tailored Dixon material, as did the bluesrockers who learned the songs from their favourite records and re-popularised them in the '60s. Even CHUCK BERRY, who had no need of bought-in compositions, benefited from Dixon's expertise: the bearlike bassist's pumping bottom-lines contributed immeasurably to the danceable groove of Berry's hits. Dixon's compositions include 'Back Door Man', 'My Babe', 'Hoochie Coochie Man', 'Little Red Rooster', 'I Just Want To Make Love To You', 'I Can't Quit You Baby', 'You Need Love' (a.k.a. 'Whole Lotta

Love' after LED ZEPPELIN got through with it), 'You Shook Me','Bring It On Home', 'I Ain't Superstitious', 'Spoonful', 'Wang Dang Doodle', 'You Can't Judge A Book By The Cover' and hundreds more; he may well be the most-recorded blues composer of them all.

A 6'5", 250-lb man-mountain born in Vicksburg, Mississippi, on 1 July 1915, Dixon was writing poetry and dabbling in music (particularly gospel singing, to which his rumbling *basso profundo* lent itself particularly well) from an early age. Moving to Chicago in 1936 to box, he was the 1937 Golden Gloves amateur heavyweight champion and Joe Louis' sparring partner before taking up bass and concentrating on his music. Dixon and pianist/vocalist Leonard 'Baby Doo' Caston formed The Five Breezes, but his career was interrupted by a lengthy wartime courtroom battle for conscientious objector status. 'I am not a citizen,' he told the court, 'I am a subject'; and, eventually, he won. After the war he and Caston reunited to form The Big Three Trio. They became a popular cabaret-blues attraction, but Dixon frequently moonlighted as bassist for more rough-edged acts like TAMPA RED, SONNY BOY WILLIAMSON I, MEMPHIS MINNIE, or a new guy in town called Muddy Waters.

After playing on a 1948 Robert Nighthawk session for Chess Records, he began an association which made Dixon a legend and the Chess brothers a fortune. He recorded as a featured artist after The Big Three broke up in 1951, but soon moved into writing and arranging for other performers; initially drawing on his Big Three experience to cut swinging, sophisticated records for the likes of JIMMY WITHERSPOON, LOWELL FULSON and Willie Mabon. The breakthrough came in 1954 when he wrote 'Hoochie Coochie Man' for Muddy Waters: the song encapsulated not only Muddy's sound, but the house style of the label and, ultimately, the entire Chicago blues genre. In its wake, he created a library of unforgettable Chess blues hits for Muddy, Howlin' Wolf, Little Walter and anybody else on the label who was short of material or whose records weren't selling. In 1957 Dixon left Chess because the Chess brothers were not only severely underpaying him, but had shown poor aesthetic sense by rejecting Otis Rush, whom Dixon thought was sensational. He proved both points by setting up a new indie, Cobra/Artistic Records, with local 'businessman'

Eli Toscano, signing Rush, and scoring him a first-time R&B Top Ten hit with 'I Can't Quit You Baby.'

Cobra turned out to be extremely important: masterminded by Dixon, its roster – led by Rush, 'MAGIC SAM' Maghett, and a young Louisianan named BUDDY GUY – developed the city's new blues sound: a dramatic blend of the dominant Waters-style idiom, and a frenetic vocal and lead guitar style drawn primarily from early B.B. KING. Cobra was an artistic success but a financial failure (mainly due to Toscano's habit of gambling away the proceeds) and by 1960 Dixon was back at Chess, bringing Rush and Guy with him: the latter's hot streak was already beginning to cool, but Guy was coming into his own. Dixon also played a leading rle in bringing bluesmen like Sonny Boy Williamson II, JOHN LEE HOOKER and T-BONE WALKER to Europe – and thereby perpetuating the music's popularity among an important generation of musicians and listeners – by organising the American Folk Blues Festivals for German promoter Horst Lippman. He kept his hand in as a performer by forming a duo with pianist Memphis Slim, and recording his first solo album: not for Chess, but for Prestige, for whose financial practices he had rather more respect. He remained at Chess for much of the '60s, but since the Fender bass had replaced the old standup doghouse on all but the most self-consciously traditional blues sessions, he rarely played in the studio any more; and with the shift from blues to soul and rock, he was no longer crucial to the company's strategy.

His health suffered in the '70s and '80s: he contracted diabetes and eventually had a leg amputated. He recorded the occasional solo album; continued to encourage younger artists; set up the Blues Heaven Foundation to inform the public about the blues and to support ageing R&B artists who had fallen on hard times; wrote an autobiography (*I Am The Blues*, co-written with Don Snowden), and scored a highly gratifying autumnal 1991 Grammy with *Hidden Charms* (Silvertone ORECD 515). He died in California on 29 January 1992: a giant in every sense of the word.

● *The Chess Box* (MCA/Chess CHD2 16500 [US])

There was more to postwar blues than the Chicago style; more to Chicago blues than Chess Records; and more to Chess Records than Willie Dixon. Nevertheless, this comes dangerously close to being a definitive anthology of classic Chi-town blues. Remember Dixon's 'library of unforgettable Chess blues hits'? This is it. Currently hard to find but well worth seeking out, it includes all his major Chess hits, as performed by Muddy, Walter, Wolf, Bo Diddley et al, plus a few of his own performances. If you can't find it, try the single-disc fillet *A Tribute To Willie Dixon: 1915–1992* (Charly CD RED 37), which begins, appropriately enough, with Robert Nighthawk's 'Sweet Black Angel' from the 1948 session which introduced Dixon to Chess. Otherwise, you'll just have to settle for a bunch of the Waters, Wolf and Walter collections recommended elsewhere in this chapter. My heart bleeds for you.

- *The Big Three Trio* (CBS 467248 2)

Twenty-one 1947–52 Chicago sides from Dixon's Big Three: Dixon himself on bass, Leonard 'Baby Doo' Caston on piano, and, on all but two of the tracks, Ollie Crawford on guitar; plus the odd rented drummer. The material (mostly original) is a mix of blues, ballads, jump and novelties, much of it delivered in fabulously tight three-part close harmony and affording plenty of opportunities for instrumental flash. This is about as smooth and sophisticated as small-group blues ever got: a far cry from the rough, bustling downhome-gone-to-big-town blues which Dixon made at Chess and Cobra. Standouts: the breakneck pace and ragtime changes of 'Don't Let That Music Die', and Caston's stunning piano on '88 Boogie'.

- **WILLIE DIXON WITH MEMPHIS SLIM:** *Willie's Blues* (Ace CDCHD 349)

Because Dixon and Slim were such slick old pros, this near-impromptu 1960 session – cut at such short notice that Dixon wrote some of the material in the cab *en route* to the studio – almost comes off. The performances are considerably better than the material, but the music is relaxed, swinging and sounds like it was a lot of fun to play; certainly exceptionally pleasant, if inessential and somewhat low-key, listening. The original session is plumped up to CD length with nine Memphis Slim tracks of approximately the same vintage: no complaints there.

● *Hidden Charms* (Silvertone ORE CD 515)

Willie Dixon's career climaxed with the belated arrival of what had eluded him ever since he bought his first bass: recognition as an artist in his own right. Produced by T-Bone Burnett and featuring a rock-solid studio band including pianist Lafayette Leake, harpist Sugar Blue, guitarist Cash McCall and the deluxe rhythm section of Red Callender (bass) and Earl Palmer (drums), *Hidden Charms* won him a Grammy with a blend of new and old material including 'I Love The Life I Live' (originally recorded by Muddy Waters and revived to great effect by Mose Allison) and the tongue-twisting 'Don't Mess With The Messer'. Talk about going out on a high note . . .

Subjects for further investigation: Track Dixon's involvement with the American Folk Blues Festival tours of the '60s on *American Folk Blues Festival '62* (Bellaphon/L&R CDLS 42017), *American Folk Blues Festival '63* (Bellaphon/L&R CDLS 42023), *American Folk Blues Festival '64* (Bellaphon/L&R CDLS 42024) and *American Folk Blues Festival '70* (Bellaphon/L&R CDLS 42021). His last gig as a session bassist was in 1984, for Johnny Winter's production of harpist SONNY TERRY's farewell album *Whoopin'* (Sonet/Alligator SNTCD 915). For further enlightenment, just keep buying blues albums and see how often Dixon's name pops up.

Howlin' Wolf

When IKE TURNER first introduced Sam Phillips to a huge Arkansas farmer known as Big Foot Chester, the Sun Records mastermind listened to him sing and thought to himself, 'This is where the soul of man never dies'. Whereas JOHN LEE HOOKER appears vulnerable even in moments of triumph or joy, the man they called Howlin' Wolf seemed utterly indestructible even at his extremes of grief or pain, and powerful enough to overload every microphone through which he ever sang: that's why his voice was as 'electric' as anything else on the records, including the amplified guitars and harps. Wolf sounded like an untameable force of nature that no tape could contain, some irreducible human core no microphone could capture: his recorded voice became something compressed and distorted until it resembles a hurricane attempting to squeeze through a letterbox. The blues can boast finer guitarists, finer composers, finer harmonica players and, even, finer singers; but it has no recorded voice more memorable, and no human presence more compelling.

Unfortunately, dealing with The Mighty Wolf was apparently a lot less enjoyable than listening to him. Some of his associates alleged that he was 'bone stupid': illiterate, slow-witted, chronically suspicious that absolutely everybody was out to cheat him, and utterly convinced that MUDDY WATERS was his most deadly enemy, even though Muddy had helped get him work when he first came to Chicago. (WILLIE DIXON, who wrote and arranged much of Wolf's Chess material, claimed that the only way he could get the Wolf to record a song was to tell him that Muddy wanted it.) Furthermore, the legendary structural irregularity of some of Wolf's records is attributed to the fact that Wolf simply never knew when to come in unless somebody prodded him (unlike Hooker, who knows exactly what he's doing even when his accompanists are tearing their hair out in fistfuls). Never mind – however it was created, Howlin' Wolf's music is one of the most precious jewels in the blues crown. Wolf's songs – both his own compositions and those crafted for him by Dixon – have found their way into the repertoires of Sam Cooke, ALBERT KING, JIMI HENDRIX, TAJ MAHAL, KOKO TAYLOR, LONNIE BROOKS, ROBERT CRAY, ETTA JAMES, THE ROLLING STONES, JAMES COTTON, The Doors, ERIC CLAPTON, PAUL BUTTERFIELD, Manfred Mann, THE YARDBIRDS, Dave Edmunds and Love Sculpture, Little Feat, CANNED HEAT, JOHN HAMMOND, Jeff Beck with Rod Stewart, DR FEELGOOD, STEVIE RAY VAUGHAN, DR JOHN, The Pointer Sisters, Z.Z.Hill, The Grateful Dead, BIG MAMA THORNTON, THE FABULOUS THUNDERBIRDS, DANA GILLESPIE and even Megadeth.

Chester Arthur 'Howlin' Wolf' Burnett (born 10 June 1910, in West Point, Mississippi) had learned guitar directly from CHARLEY PATTON, briefly travelled with ROBERT JOHNSON (during which time he passed on some of Patton's 6-string wisdom to Johnson's stepson Robert Jr Lockwood), and received harmonica tuition from his brother-in-law SONNY BOY WILLIAMSON II, but until his late thirties he was content to remain a farmer by trade and play music for recreation. The local success of his band, through which Junior Parker and James Cotton both passed, gained him a DJ slot on a radio station based in West Memphis, Arkansas, which brought him to the attention of Ike Turner, who in turn took him to Sam Phillips in 1951. His first single paired 'Moaning In The Moonlight' and 'How Many More Years', the latter being quite the heaviest – in the 'metal' sense of the term – blues record thus far, complete with Turner's stomping piano and guitarist Willie Johnson's murderously distorted power chords. Phillips sold the masters to Chess, and a bidding war soon erupted, with Modern Records (Phillips's contracted outlet) and Chess both demanding Wolf masters and both (thanks to Phillips's cheerful entrepreneurism) receiving them. Eventually, the Bihari brothers, who ran Modern, started recording Wolf themselves in West Memphis under Turner's supervision, generally on retitled versions of songs also cut for Phillips. When the dust settled, Chess's issue of 'Moaning In The Moonlight' and an alternate take (retitled 'Morning At Midnight') which Phillips had sold to Modern's RPM subsidiary had both charted very healthily, and Wolf was one of the hottest names in downhome blues. In 1952 he sold out his interest in the family farm, signed exclusively to Chess, and relocated to Chicago, leaving behind his hometown band, which had refused to make the trek with him.

Making his initial recordings with Chess studio players while terrorising the local blues bars to let them know that the Wolf was in town, he slowly assembled a band of his own and became part of the furniture of the South Side scene. His records never sold as well as they had during his initial breakthrough, but Chess was making plenty of money from the rock and roll success of CHUCK BERRY and BO DIDDLEY and could well afford to keep the Wolf in business to maintain their core ghetto audience. Eventually Wolf went back down home long enough to pick up some Delta musicians (including guitarist Willie Johnson, who'd played on the Sun sides) but his greatest acquisition was from James Cotton's band: a teenage guitarist named Hubert Sumlin (born 16 November 1931, in Greenwood, Mississippi). Sumlin trained up by playing rhythm, mostly behind lead guitarist Jody Williams, before moving into Wolf's lead guitar chair in 1956. Despite initial conflict (legend hath it that in one epic fight they punched out each others' front teeth), Sumlin virtually became Wolf's adopted son, remaining at his side for the rest of his career. His jagged note-bursts and slicing tone made him a demigod to subsequent blues-rock guitarists like Clapton, Hendrix, Beck and Vaughan, and he was almost as much a part of Wolf's sound as the great man's mouth-harp.

Wolf went down slow between 1969 – when he suffered first a heart attack and then a kidney ailment which left him permanently dependent on dialysis treatment – and his death from cancer in Hines, Illinois, on 10 January 1976, though his last years included one final magnificent bellow of defiance at a world which had never understood him, in the form of 'Coon On The Moon', from the 1971 album *Message To The Young*: sadly, it's never been reissued or anthologised. Whether you want to classify the Wolf as a Delta bluesman or a Chicago titan, the fact remains that there's no music like this anywhere else in the blues. Chester Burnett really *was* the Howlin' Wolf, and nobody else could ever have been.

- *The Chess Box* (MCA/Chess CHD3-9332 [US])
- *Smokestack Lightnin'* (Instant CD INS 5037)

The Chess Box presents three CDs, luxuriously packaged and annotated, of the Mighty Wolf at his mightiest, while *Smokestack Lightnin'* is about as much bang-for-the-buck as you can possibly squeeze onto one budget-price 28-track disk. The big box contains 72 tracks from 1951–71, while the less ambitious Instant CD gives up the ghost in 1962, but both packages demonstrate the Wolf's extraordinary power. Most of the hits are represented on both items; it's just that The Chess Box offers so much superb additional material that's as powerful as the high-title-recognition-factor songs. 'Smokestack Lightnin'', 'Back Door Man', 'Spoonful', 'Evil', 'Sittin' On Top Of The World', 'Red Rooster', 'How Many More Years', 'Wang Dang Doodle' . . . all those wonderful examples of what ROBERT CRAY calls Wolf's 'Martian reggae' are present in all their glory, though the Instant CD omits 'I Ain't Superstitious' and 'Built For Comfort'.

- *Howlin' Wolf Rides Again* (Ace CDCHD 333)
- *Howlin' For My Baby* (Sun CD CHARLY 66)
- *Cadillac Daddy: Memphis Recordings 1952* (Rounder CD-SS-28)
- *The Wolf Is At Your Door* (Charly CD BM 5)

Early Wolf, recorded in Memphis in 1950–1: the roughest, rawest and most primal music of his career. The Ace package is drawn from the Modern repertoire; the Sun collection contains three tracks which were leased to Chess plus a bunch of stuff which hung in the vaults for a while; the 12-cut Rounder disc recycles much the same Sun tracks as the 18-selection *Howlin' For My Baby*; and the Charly set is a blend of Chess and Sun material. Willie Dixon was fond of saying that Chicago blues was simply Delta blues electrified, but most of the Chess recordings Dixon supervised for the Wolf sound positively genteel by comparison. You want real electric Delta blues with the accent firmly placed on both 'electric' and 'Delta'? This is it.

- *The London Howlin' Wolf Sessions* (MCA/Chess CHLD 19167)

Wolf Lite: this 1969 supersession was recorded in London at the behest of The Rolling Stones, and it finds the vulpine patriarch debilitated by ill-health and armpit-deep in whiteboy guest stars including Eric Clapton (guitar), Steve Winwood (keyboards), Bill Wyman and Klaus Voorman (bass), and Charlie Watts and Ringo Starr (drums), though the presence of familiar faces like Hubert Sumlin and pianist Lafayette Leake must have reassured the Wolf as much as it stabilised the music. Starr, incidentally, is something of a blues buff on the quiet: when, in pre-Beatles days, he briefly considered emigrating to the US, he chose Houston as his destination simply because LIGHTNIN' HOPKINS lived there; and, a couple of years after backing Wolf on this remake of 'I Ain't Superstitious', he and Voorman reappeared sitting in with B.B. KING on *In London* (BGO BGOCD 42). A sedate canter through the classic Wolf repertoire, reprising 'Red Rooster', 'Rockin' Daddy', 'Who's Been Talkin'', 'I Ain't Superstitious', 'Sittin' On Top Of The World','Wang Dang Doodle',' 'Built For Comfort' and other Wolf staples, it's respectful as hell and represents a rationalised, but by no means charmless, version of Wolf's music, shorn of its bonecrushing power and exhilarating randomness.

153

Most illuminating moment: Wolf attempts to teach 'Red Rooster' to the musicians (two of whom had already had a worldwide hit with a cover of it) by bottlenecking his part from the original version – one of the few songs he ever recorded which prominently featured his own guitar – on a National steel, creating a huge, scary sound worthy of Patton himself. Clapton attempts to persuade him to play guitar along with the band for the take: Wolf refuses, and counts along with his riff, confusing them still further. Cut to the take itself, without Wolf's guitar: though it has a nice groove, it's not the groove that Wolf had played. It should have been.

Subjects for further investigation: Chester Burnett wasn't the first bluesman to call himself 'Howlin' Wolf'. That honour belongs to J.T. Smith (1890–?), who was also known as 'Funny Papa' or 'Funny Paper' (nobody was ever quite sure), and it was Smith who wrote the song 'Howling Wolf', which Wolf recorded as 'The Wolf Is At Your Door', and which remained in Muddy Waters' repertoire until the end of his life. A sampling of Smith's work, including 'Howling Wolf Blues Pts 1 & 2', can be found on *Funny Papa Smith 1930–1931: The Original Howling Wolf* (Yazoo 1031); LIGHTNIN' HOPKINS's 1948 performance of the song is on *The Complete Aladdin Recordings* (EMI CDP-7-96843-2); for Muddy's late-'70s live rendition, seek out *Muddy 'Mississippi' Waters Live* (BGO BGOCD 109); more of 'Funny Paper' is available on *Texas Blues Guitar (1929–1935)* (Story Of Blues CD 3532-2). *Who Will Be Next?* (Charly CD BM 30) is an intriguing budget collection salting lesser-known excerpts from the mid-'50s Chess repertoire, many of which are unavailable elsewhere on CD, with a few hits like 'Smokestack Lightnin'' and 'Who's Been Talkin'?' Wolf also appears in mixed company alongside Muddy Waters, Willie Dixon and BUDDY GUY on *Live Action!* (Charly CD BM 15), and with Waters, Guy, Bo Diddley and LITTLE WALTER on *The Super Super Blues Band* (Charly CD BM 26); not to mention the European shot on *American Folk Blues Festival '64* (L&R/Bellaphon CDLR 42024), which also features Hubert Sumlin playing behind Sonny Boy Williamson, Sugarpie DeSanto and Sunnyland Slim. Sumlin never recovered from Wolf's death: he still performs and records, but the Wolf-sized hole in his music is unfillable. Sumlin is not much of a vocalist, and even less of a songwriter: the aptly-titled

My Guitar And Me (Black & Blue 59.248 2), recorded in France in 1975 with a stalwart Chicago band including LONNIE BROOKS on second guitar, leaves Sumlin's still-superb guitar work seemingly unanchored. Two late-'80s albums, *Hubert Sumlin's Blues Party* (Black Top CD BT-1036) and *Healing Feeling* (Demon/Black Top FIENDCD 193), attempted to solve the problem by drafting in guest vocalists – BOBBY BLAND soundalike Mighty Sam McClain, and the late James 'Thunderbird' Davis, respectively – but groovy though they were, the end result was to make Sumlin a sideman on his own records. The best of the solo Sumlins is *Heart And Soul* (Blind Pig BP7 3389), a stomping, go-for-it 1989 team-up with fellow Wolf homeboy James Cotton.

Elmore James

The partial truth of the familiar assertion that Elmore James built a career on one ROBERT JOHNSON lick ('Dust My Broom', to be precise) should not obscure the fact that he is one of the most underrated of blues instrumentalists. The raucous, scything tones he produced with his monstrously over-amped Johnson riffs laid the foundations for entire schools of electric slide, from the downhome boogie of J.B. Hutto, HOUND DOG TAYLOR, GEORGE THOROGOOD and LI'L ED & THE BLUES IMPERIALS to the Chicago progressive EARL HOOKER and the various superheated rococo white blues (-based) slide guitarists, including Duane Allman, JOHNNY WINTER, Lowell George (of Little Feat) and RY COODER when he turns his amp up. He was also a wonderful singer with a riveting, passionate intensity which is as impossible to resist as it is to ignore. And when FLEETWOOD MAC started out in 1967, they devoted almost half their stage show to Jeremy Spencer's hamfisted Elmore James impresssions.

Elmore James was born in Richland, Mississippi, on January 27, 1918, and took up guitar in his teens after hearing Robert Johnson in nearby Belzoni. Following a spell in the Navy, he gigged with Alex 'Rice' Miller (a.k.a. SONNY BOY WILLIAMSON II) and worked on the latter's popular radio show. Accompanying Sonny Boy to a 1952 Trumpet Records session, he overcame his microphone fright and, with Williamson blowing harp beside him, recorded his version of 'Dust My Broom', which made the R&B Top 10. Signed to the Los Angeles-based Bihari brothers' group of labels, he released 'I Believe' (another 'Dust My Broom' variant, this time with a rocking sax-and-piano accompaniment and a cranked-up groove) and saw that go Top 10 too. Relocating to Chicago, he recorded prolifically for both the Biharis (on their Flair and Meteor labels) and for Chess, often cutting the same songs with the same musicians for both companies. However, he never repeated his early success, and – since a combination of ill-health and heavy drinking rendered him progressively less reliable – the Biharis dropped him in 1956.

He continued to record, cutting both for Chess and the Fire/Enjoy labels, but with steadily diminishing returns. He died in Chicago on 24 May 1963, just a few years too early to reap the rewards of the acclaim and popularity (let alone the Fleetwood Mac royalties) that the Blues Boom would have brought him. Thirty years after his death, his mixture of barely controlled emotion and rocking good humour is as immediately engaging as ever.

- *Let's Cut It: The Very Best Of Elmore James* (Ace CDCH 192)

The best of the early-'50s Flair/Meteor period, anyway: these were James's most successful years and this is certainly a fair cross-section of his repertoire. What is surprising – to those overly swayed either by his imitators or his detractors – is not how many 'Dust My Broom' variants this includes, but how few. James can be heard playing 'straight' (i.e. non-slide) guitar and working over Latin beats as well as his trademarked shuffles and slow blues, but everything is sung with that patented throat-searing intensity.

- **ELMORE JAMES & JOHN BRIM:** *Whose Muddy Shoes* (MCA/Chess CHD 9114)

The rest of the early '50s: this combines nine Elmore tracks (seven of them from 1953) with six by John Brim, five of which, including the Van Halen-covered 'Ice Cream Man', also appear on *Vintage Blues* (Chess CD RED 9) alongside material by ALBERT KING, OTIS RUSH and OTIS SPANN. As well as the inevitable rerun of 'Dust My Broom', this selection includes the rocking 'Madison Blues' (a favourite of George Thorogood and Fleetwood Mac's Jeremy Spencer), the wracking slow blues 'The Sun Is Shining', and a decidedly individual take on T-BONE WALKER's 'Stormy Monday'.

● *The Immortal Elmore James: King Of The Bottleneck Blues* (Music Club MCCD 083)

Guess what song this one begins with: from '57 until the end, the rest of Elmore James. If anything, this music is even more powerful than the earlier, more successful stuff. James was still adding to his songbook during this period: these selections include the heartbreaking 'The Sky Is Crying', various items popularised by well-known blues-rockers, including the immortal 'Shake Your Moneymaker' (Fleetwood Mac), 'Done Somebody Wrong' (THE YARDBIRDS), 'Look On Yonder Wall' (PAUL BUTTERFIELD), 'Can't Stop Loving' (George Thorogood) and 'Bleeding Heart' (JIMI HENDRIX); plus Elmorised versions of blues standards like 'Rollin' And Tumblin'', 'It Hurts Me Too' (particularly wonderful, this), and 'Every Day I Have The Blues'. Ry Cooder maintains that Elmore's classic sound – with the 'good' amplifier – is to be found on the Fire/Enjoy's Chicago sessions: you'll find plenty of 'em here. Recommended!

Subjects for further investigation: That original '52 Trumpet 'Dust My Broom' with Sonny Boy Williamson is included on Sonny Boy's *King Biscuit Time* (Arhoolie CD 310). The later years covered on *The Immortal Elmore James* are explored in considerably more detail on *Standing At The Crossroads* (Charly CD BM 28), *Come Go With Me* (Charly CD CHARLY 180), and *The Sky Is Crying* (Charly CD BM 12). If you've already popped for *The Immortal Elmore James*, the first-cited is favourite for two reasons: it includes some fine songs ('Person To Person', 'One Way Out') which the Music Club disc omits; and it's the only Elmore James CD you can buy which *doesn't* include a version of 'Dust My Broom'. Elmore's legacy is explored on just about any record you can find by Hound Dog Taylor or George Thorogood; not to mention J.B.Hutto, Hutto's nephew Li'l Ed (& The Blues Imperials), or the blues-band incarnation of Fleetwood Mac.

Johnny Shines

Always a bridesmaid, never a bride (1): Johnny Shines was a talented artist who spent his entire professional life under the shadow of a genius; a great artist eclipsed by a greater. He was ROBERT JOHNSON's travelling companion between 1934 and 1937, and knew Johnson better than anyone, with the possible exception of Johnson's stepson, Robert Jr Lockwood. John Ned Shines was born near Memphis in Frazier, Tennessee, on 26 April 1915; and grew up in Memphis and Arkansas. His first musical model was HOWLIN' WOLF, five years Shines's senior and himself heavily under the influence of CHARLEY PATTON. They met in 1932, and the teenage Shines so thoroughly mastered the older man's style that he was briefly known as 'Little Wolf'. The real turning point was Shines's encounter with Robert Johnson, with whom he soon teamed up, venturing as far north as Detroit and into Canada. After Johnson's death, Shines planned to travel to Africa, but made it no further than Chicago, where he worked in construction; leading an eight-piece jazz group in his spare time, but soon drifting back to the blues.

Like his contemporary MUDDY WATERS, he was rejected by Columbia in 1946, but when – also like Muddy – he recorded for Leonard Chess, his sides were rarely released: for artistic and commercial reasons (according to Chess) or personal reasons (according to Shines). A few sessions for J.O.B. – a second-rank Chicago indie which specialised in recording those artists who couldn't get onto (or didn't get on with the bosses of) Chess and Vee Jay – produced some powerful but unsuccessful extensions of the Johnson legacy. So in 1958 Shines pawned all his guitars and amps for $100; not returning to music until 1966, when Vanguard commissioned a session for their *Chicago/The Blues/Today!* series. After a spell alongside WALTER HORTON in WILLIE DIXON's Chicago Blues All-Stars, he moved to Alabama and from then until his death on 22 April 1992, he worked steadily, mainly as a soloist (and, occasionally and reluctantly, as a duo with Robert Jr Lockwood), not so much replicating Robert Johnson as expanding their common heritage. If Johnson had lived, Shines would have been seen as his own man; as it was, he spent most of his professional life as an unwilling surrogate for a dead friend and mentor. He was also as incisive, eloquent and politically conscious a spokesman as the blues has ever had – as demonstrated on the spoken introductions on the 1971 live album *Hey Ba-Ba-Re-Bop!* – and, if given the chance, could have projected the Johnson legacy into the future rather than simply reproduce its past.

● **JOHNNY SHINES & ROBERT JR LOCKWOOD:** *Johnny Shines & Robert Jr Lockwood* (Flyright FLYCD 10)

The Johnson inheritors in separate sessions for the J.O.B. label: Shines's 1952-3 tracks feature him in a similar style to the earliest Muddy Waters records, backed by standup bass and, on some of the material, the gorgeous harp of Walter Horton. 'Ramblin'' is his intense, slashing take on Johnson's 'Walkin' Blues', while 'Fish Tail' revisits the same 'Terraplane Blues' that he was later to transform into 'Dynaflow Blues'. Lockwood appears both as a leader – most notably on the first postwar recording of 'Dust My Broom', which preceded ELMORE JAMES's version by some months and might conceivably have beaten him to the R&B Top 10 if J.O.B. had ever released it, and on 'Aw Aw Baby', a retitled 'Sweet Home Chicago' – and backing pianist Sunnyland Slim.

● **VARIOUS ARTISTS:** *Chicago/The Blues/Today! Vol. 3* (Vanguard VMD 79218)

Shines's 1966 return to music-making: he later claimed that, until a week before the session, he had not held a guitar in his hands for seven years. This 13-track disk is split 50-50 between Shines and Johnny Young, with Walter Horton prominent throughout and taking the spotlight on a serious blowout with fellow-harpist Memphis Charlie (a.k.a. CHARLIE MUSSELWHITE). Some of these performances are decidedly ragged (drummer Frank Kirkland takes quite a while to figure out what Shines is up to on the justifiably legendary 'Dynaflow Blues'), but undeniably powerful and deeply affecting.

● *Hey Ba-Ba-Re-Bop!* (Rounder CD 2020)

This is the about the best straightforward acoustic Johnny Shines record you can buy. On these 1971 live recordings, the repertoire is half Shines's own material and half covers, but – thank God – he only plays three Johnson songs. With characteristic audacity, he includes an interpretation of the Lionel Hampton big-band classic which gives the album its title track and blends his customary post-Johnson approach with a JOHN LEE HOOKER-style boogie on the arresting 'I Will Be Kind'. Alternative highlight: a terrifyingly intense version of Kokomo Arnold's 'Milk Cow Blues'.

● *Traditional Delta Blues* (Biograph BCD 121)

Shines in straight revivalist mode, performing solo with a National steel guitar in 1972. The anti-drug 'Glad Rags' demonstrates rarely-displayed songwriting chops, but the overall sterility of the performances suggests that the strain of having to be Robert Johnson, when he really wanted to be Johnny Shines, was beginning to tell. Of all the material recorded for this album, the producers typically decided to hold back most of Shines's own songs in favour of the Johnson interpretations, but thankfully these appear on . . .

● *Mr Cover Shaker* (Biograph BCD 125)

. . . which matches *Hey Ba-Ba-Re-Bop!* as an example of Johnny Shines being, for once, Johnny Shines. The rest of the album was recorded in 1974 with a big band led by David Bromberg, and features one of the few recorded instances of Shines's music played the way he wanted to play it, complete with horns, piano, rhythm section,backing vocals and even fiddle and mandolin. The band sides, with their prominent clarinet and mandolin, recall the jazz of the '30s: the session climaxes on a deeply-felt reading of the gospelly 'Stand By Me'.

Subjects for further investigation: One Chess side which was released, 1950's 'Joliet Blues' (recorded under the *nom de blues* of 'Shoe Shine Johnny' with most of Muddy Waters' sidemen as back-up), surfaces on the 4-CD set *Chess Blues* (MCA/Chess CHD4-9340). Another pair of 1953 J.O.B. titles, 'Living In The White House' and 'Please Don't' appear on J.B. Lenoir's *His J.O.B. Recordings 1951–1954* (Flyright FLYCD 04); Shines's last recordings – a W.C. Handy Award-winning team-up with harpist Snooky Pryor and guitarist John Nicholas on which Shines restricts himself to vocals and includes yet more Johnson songs – are on *Back To The Country* (Blind Pig BP 74391). The most frequent canard aimed at Johnny Shines was that he was a mere footnote to Robert Johnson; unfortunately the best that a book of this scope can offer his contemporary Robert Jr Lockwood is to render him a footnote to Johnny Shines. Lockwood – born 37 March 1915, in Marvell, Arkansas – was Johnson's stepson, though 'dad' was only three years older than 'Junior'. A versatile, ambitious and highly influential lead guitarist whose personal tastes leaned closer to jazz than to downhome blues, he tutored the young B.B. KING and was one of Chess Records' busiest studio musicians, with a particular aptitude for backing harpists. He can be heard on any number of records by WILLIAMSON and LITTLE WALTER, where his adventurous chord voicings added urban sophistication to even the most determinedly downhome music. On *Steady Rollin' Man* (Delmark DD-630), he fronts a Chicago rhythm section on an overly restrained 1970 session, while *Robert Jr Lockwood Plays Robert & Robert* (Black & Blue 59.740 2) features him solo on 12-string guitar playing a mixture of Johnson songs and his own material. The instrumentals are better than the vocals (on the Delmark album you keep expecting Sonny Boy or one of the Walters to come soaring in), the electric guitar is better than the acoustic (though the 12-string slide on the likes of 'Walkin' Blues' is intriguing) and the Johnson songs are better than his. His most influential early hit, 'Take A Little Walk With Me' (1941), can be found on *Lonesome Road Blues 1926–1941* (Yazoo 1038), and also on *Mississippi Blues 1935–1951* (Wolf WBCD-005), which combines six Lockwood tracks – four from 1941, two from 1951 – with material from Robert Petway and the terrifyingly obscure Otto Virgial.

Sonny Boy Williamson II

If Alec 'Rice' Miller had had a little more faith in his own considerable abilities as vocalist, songwriter, harmonicist and hustler, his name would have been one of the most venerated in postwar blues. However, he decided in 1941 to borrow the *nom de blues* of an established fellow harpist, John Lee 'SONNY BOY' WILLIAMSON; and after the latter's death in 1948, Miller claimed that he actually was the original Sonny Boy Williamson, much to the confusion of record buyers then and since. Miller, born in Glendora, Mississippi, on 5 December 1899 (or 1894, 1897 or 1909, depending on which story he happened to be telling at the time), was a unique stylist: he sang his songs of paranoia and betrayal in a quavering baritone, and blew a piercing, flamboyant harp in which every single note appeared to be individually shaped by those fluttering hands before being allowed to reach the microphone. The ultimate irony was that he was a much more powerful performer than the man whose name he appropriated.

By the time he made his first records in 1951, Rice Miller was already a veteran. He had knocked around the South, played with ROBERT JOHNSON and taught harmonica to his brother-in-law, a hulking CHARLEY PATTON acolyte better known as HOWLIN' WOLF: his path frequently crossed those of men like ELMORE JAMES, JOHNNY SHINES, SUNNYLAND SLIM, and Robert Jr Lockwood, with whom he worked frequently during the '30s, and who played lead guitar on many of his Chess recordings in the late '50s. (Contrariwise, he also picked up a few licks from a young prodigy named Walter Horton.) He became Sonny Boy Williamson in 1941, when he began hosting 'King Biscuit Time', a daily 15-minute show sponsored by the King Biscuit Boy flour company and broadcast by KFFA Radio from West Helena, Arkansas. The real Sonny Boy Williamson, stuck all the way up in Chicago, could do little or nothing about this elderly interloper (even when the company took advantage of his popularity to launch a new line called Sonny Boy Meal) but the fact remains that Miller did not record until Williamson was safely dead and buried. For all his reputation as a mean, bitter man, he was often generous to up-and-coming musicians: B.B. KING owes his start to a guest spot on Sonny Boy's radio show, and for a while, JAMES COTTON was virtually his adopted son.

It would be nice to say that the success of his early records for Trumpet led to his move to Chicago to record for Chess: but what actually happened was that Trumpet found him so hard to deal with that they sold his contract: Chess ended up buying it from a third party, and by 1955 he was in their studio with MUDDY WATERS, OTIS SPANN, JIMMY ROGERS and WILLIE DIXON backing him up. His first single, 'Don't Start Me Talkin'', was a hit, and he recorded prolifically before, and sporadically, after the late-'50s blues downturn. Other bluesmen survived the Blues Recession by becoming 'folk singers': Sonny Boy did it by becoming a cult figure in Europe. Crossing the pond with the 1963 American Blues Festival, he stole the show from Muddy Waters, MEMPHIS SLIM and LONNIE JOHNSON, and elected to stay in London. He recruited the likes of The Animals and THE YARDBIRDS as backup bands, commissioned a Savile Row suit in black and grey checkerboard, and delighted in sporting a bowler hat, a furled umbrella and a briefcase (containing his harps and a bottle of whisky). After a second American Folk Blues Festival the following year, he returned to the Delta, resuming his old radio show and telling tall tales of his travels in Europe, which, apparently, no one believed. He was found dead in his bed by drummer Peck Curtis on 25 May 1965.

- *The Best Of Sonny Boy Williamson* (Chess CD CHESS 35)

Start here: this is where you find the great Chess hits and near-hits, cut under Willie Dixon's supervision between 1955 and 1963, with Chess studio stalwarts including Robert Jr Lockwood and assorted members of the various Muddy Waters bands. This is one of the great repertoires of postwar blues: the best-known is probably the Willie Dixon composition 'Bring It On Home' (as, heh heh, 'borrowed' by LED ZEPPELIN), but you find the real Sonny Boy (or the real Rice Miller) on tunes like 'Fattenin' Frogs For Snakes', '99', 'Don't Start Me Talkin'', 'Help Me', 'Nine Below Zero', 'One Way Out', 'Your Funeral And My Trial', 'By Bye Bird' (which, believe it or not, was covered by The Moody Blues on their very first album) and 'All My Love In Vain'. That deep, bitter, tremulous voice carries the unmistakable emotional authenticity of a real man in real situations, and the lyrics carry that juxtaposition of the cliche and the aper u which is at the very heart of great blues writing. The mouth harp's pretty good, too.

- *King Biscuit Time* (Arhoolie CD 310)

The 1951 Trumpet sessions: so downhome that the Chess material is sophisticated by comparison. Sonny Boy, making a late-blooming debut when well into his fifties, performs with the assurance of a veteran and the eagerness of a man on the verge of a breakthrough. Added bonuses: Elmore James's original 'Dust My Broom', cut at a Sonny Boy session; the original cut of 'Eyesight To The Blind' (later re-recorded for Chess as 'Born Blind') which so impressed Pete Townshend that he incorporated it into The Who's *Tommy*; and a chaotic 'King Biscuit Time' radio session in which Sonny Boy assays T-BONE WALKER's 'Stormy Monday Blues'.

Subjects for further investigation: **Nine Below Zero** (Charly CD BM 22) is a more than acceptable budget-price 18-track alternative to the 22-track *Best Of*, while **Work With Me** (Chess CD RED 14) supplements both with some of the lesser-known titles. At the other extreme, **The Chess Years** (Chess CD RED BOX 1) is the absolute 4-CD full monty, outtakes and all, covering the full decade of Sonny Boy's association with the label. The great and the good, the mediocre and the dreadful: they're all here. Hear him conquering Europe on **American Folk Blues Festival '63** (L&R/ Bellaphon CDLR 42023) and **American Folk Blues Festival '64** (L&R/ Bellaphon CDLR 42024). He's also the secret hero of a Yardbirds tribute collection credited to ERIC CLAPTON, Jeff Beck & Jimmy Page: **Blue Eyed Blues** (Charly CD BM 20) documents Sonny Boy's London adventures with two 1963 live tracks backed by the Clapton-era Yardbirds, and two more with a 1965 studio band led by Page. **Keep It To Yourself** (Alligator ALCD 4787) is an exquisite acoustic album cut in Sweden with guitarist Matt Murphy (of *Blues Brothers* fame) and Memphis Slim during a one-day break from the '63 American Folk Blues Festival.

(Big) Walter Horton

If nothing else, harmonica virtuoso Walter Horton will be remembered for having more nicknames than almost any other bluesman: Walter 'Shakey' Horton, Walter 'Mumbles' Horton and – to distinguish him from his illustrious disciple, Marion 'LITTLE WALTER' Jacobs – Big Walter. Plus, of course, variations like 'Big Walter "Shakey" Horton', etc, etc. Naturally, there was a lot more to him than amusing soubriquets: despite the greater fame and popularity of Little Walter, SONNY BOY WILLIAMSON II, JAMES COTTON,

JUNIOR WELLS and PAUL BUTTERFIELD, many connoisseurs regard Horton as the finest of all the great post-war harp men. (As a matter of fact, he hated being called either 'Shakey' or 'Mumbles'. Wouldn't you?)

Walter Horton was born in Horn Lake, Mississippi, on 6 April 1918, and moved to Memphis as a child. The decision to opt for a career in music was essentially made for him, because he lacked both the physical strength for menial work and the education for anything else. He had been given his first harmonica when he was five, and was playing on the street not too long after that. Learning his trade around the clubs and bars, he met (and taught) Little Walter and James Cotton during the late '40s, travelled briefly to Chicago, where he played for tips on Maxwell Street, and by 1951 was back in Memphis recording as a sideman (and occasionally as a featured artist) for Sam Phillips's Sun Records, blowing a piercing, articulate harp very much in the manner associated with Rice (Sonny Boy Williamson II) Miller, though it was actually Horton who had taught Miller (who, in turn, taught HOWLIN' WOLF. So it goes). In 1953 he finally relocated to Chicago, replacing Junior Wells (who had just replaced Little Walter) in MUDDY WATERS' band before himself being displaced by Cotton, who held down the Waters harp chair well into the '60s. Both Walters did, however, alternate with Cotton on Waters' studio dates throughout the late '50s, and Horton and Waters reunited for 1978's *I'm Ready* (BGO BGOCD 108), the second in the series of 'comeback' albums produced for Waters by JOHNNY WINTER.

Despite poor health, Horton became one of the busiest harpists in Chicago, participating in the American Folk Blues Festival tours of Europe at the behest of WILLIE DIXON, and performing and/or recording with JOHNNY SHINES, JIMMY ROGERS, Robert Nighthawk, BIG MAMA THORNTON (no mean harpist herself, as it happens), TAMPA RED, OTIS RUSH, Sunnyland Slim and later, during the late-'60s blues boom, with Johnny Winter and FLEETWOOD MAC. His reunion with Muddy Waters was one of the very few bright spots of the '70s, as far as the increasingly alcoholically-challenged Horton was concerned: in his last years he was actually back playing for tips and drinks on Maxwell Street (in John Landis's 1980 movie *The Blues Brothers*, he can be seen doing exactly that, blowing behind JOHN LEE HOOKER on 'Boom Boom'). He died in Chicago on 8 December 1981.

- **WALTER 'MUMBLES' HORTON:** *Mouth Harp Maestro* (Ace CDCH 252)

The 1951 Modern sessions cut at Sun: the band sides are reminiscent of the earliest Memphis HOWLIN' WOLF tracks, and both the team-ups with one-man-band Joe Hill Louis (not to be confused with the contemporary guitarist JOE LOUIS WALKER) and the solo numbers are absolute *tours de force*; some of these songs remained in Horton's repertoire for the rest of his career. The superb second take of the solo 'What's The Matter With You' – listening to Horton's mushmouthed vocals on this, the first track he ever cut for Sun, it's easy to guess why Sam Phillips nicknamed him 'Mumbles' – can also be heard on the excellent anthology *The Fifties: Juke Joint Blues* (Ace CDCH 216); 'Black Gal' and 'Hard Hearted Woman' resurface on *60 Great Blues Recordings* (Cascade CDBOX 3).

- **BIG WALTER HORTON WITH CAREY BELL:** *Big Walter Horton With Carey Bell* (Alligator ALCD 4702)

The second album from Bruce Iglauer's then-fledgling Alligator Records (the first was by HOUND DOG TAYLOR) was cut in 1972, with Horton's harmonica protégé Carey Bell and JIMMY REED's veteran backup guitarist Eddie Taylor in attendance. The production is pretty stark, and Horton is in fairly subdued form, but the music has an affecting strength and dignity. The powerful Horton/ Taylor duet 'Trouble In Mind' reappears on *The Alligator Records 20th Anniversary Collection* (Alligator ALCD 105/6).

- **BIG WALTER 'SHAKEY' HORTON:** *Live At The El Mocambo* (Red Lightnin' RLCD 0088)

Horton did some touring in the wake of the Alligator album, and this was recorded in Toronto on 25 July 1973, with an uncredited band backing Horton on a hot night when he was clearly having a good time. It's a good account of his mature sound – much bigger and rounder than in the '50s – but the technical quality of the recording is atrocious. Guess we hadda be there.

*Subjects for further investigation: **Johnny Shines & Robert Lockwood*** (Flyright FLYCD 10) includes a fine 1953 Shines/Horton session in which Horton demonstrates exactly how much Little Walter learned from him (and Shines exactly how much he learned from ROBERT JOHNSON). ***American Folk Blues Festival '65*** (L&R/Bellaphon CDLR 42025) finds Horton performing with J.B. LENOIR and BUDDY GUY; and ***American Folk Blues Festival '70*** (L&R/Bellaphon CDLR 42021) catches him with Willie Dixon's Chicago Blues All Stars. ***Chicago/The Blues/Today! Vol. 3*** (Vanguard VMD 79218) splits its 13 1966 tracks between The JOHNNY SHINES Blues Band and Johnny Young's South Side Blues Band, both featuring Horton on harp. On one track, the Shines band magically transforms itself into 'Big Walter Horton's Blues Harp Band With Memphis Charlie' (the latter being a youthful CHARLIE MUSSELWHITE) for the dual-harp instrumental 'Rockin' My Boogie'. Horton and Willie Dixon make a guest appearance on ***Johnny Winter*** (Edsel ED CD 163), backing Winter on a 1969 version of Muddy's 'Mean Mistreater'; Carey Bell, accompanied by his guitarist son Lurrie, appears as a leader on four tracks from ***Living Chicago Blues Vol. 1*** (Alligator ALCD 7701), the first of a series intended as an '80s counterpart to Vanguard's massively influential mid-'60s *Chicago/The Blues/Today!* albums.

Little Walter

As JIMI HENDRIX was to the electric guitar and JIMMY SMITH to the Hammond organ, so stands Marion 'Little' Walter Jacobs to the harmonica. He was by no means the first harpist to cup his instrument into a microphone, but he was the first to accept the challenge of a head-on confrontation with the possibilities of amplification; to modernise the old-time country harp styles just as T-BONE WALKER or JOHN LEE HOOKER had transformed the guitar styles of Texas and the Delta. He had the imagination of a first-class bebop saxophonist, a purist's sense of line, and lips and lungs of leather; enabling him to craft a rich, powerful, reverb-soaked tone which he could shape into anything from the piercing wail of an alto sax or the thick simmer of a Hammond organ to the brassy punch of a full horn section or the percussive chop of a great rhythm guitarist. (Incidentally, Walter actually *was* a great rhythm guitarist, as you can hear on early '50s MUDDY WATERS sides like 'Honey Bee' and 'Still A Fool'.) He was never a great singer – he always used to claim that he only started to sing as a means of catching his breath between harp choruses – but he had a light, insinuating vocal approach which lent itself perfectly to songs like 'My Babe' (WILLIE DIXON's adaptation of the old gospel standard 'This Train', set to a swinging JIMMY REED-style shuffle). At the peak of his popularity, when he emerged from the Muddy Waters band just as his colleague JIMMY ROGERS had done a few years earlier, he decisively outsold his old boss: in 1954, there was at least one Little Walter record (and sometimes two) in the R&B charts every single week.

Walter was born in Marksville, Louisiana, on 1 May 1930. He started on harp when he was eight, and ran away from home to learn his craft, first in New Orleans and subsequently in the Delta. By the time he arrived in Chicago in 1947, he was already a veteran, having played in streets, clubs and radio since he was 12. Before he was out of his teens he'd worked with TAMPA RED, BIG BILL BROONZY and MEMPHIS SLIM, been tutored by BIG WALTER HORTON and both SONNY BOY WILLIAMSONs, and established himself as the Most Valuable Player in the Muddy Waters band. His break came when, at the tail end of a 1952 Muddy Waters session, the band cut a harmonica instrumental which they had been using as an on-bandstand signature tune. While the Waters band were touring the South, Chess released the track under the title of 'Juke' and credited it to 'Little Walter & His Night Cats'. It was an instant smash, and Walter didn't even wait for the tour to finish before hightailing it back to Chicago to start his own band by hiring young JUNIOR WELLS's musicians away from him, and bequeathing the Waters job to Wells by way of compensation. At Chess's insistence, he continued to record with Waters until 1958, by which time the incumbent, JAMES COTTON, was finally deemed acceptable.

Walter was universally admired by his peers, and equally universally detested. He was cocksure, combative and truculent, given to storming out of studio dates and drinking heavily on the bandstand. (The technical term is 'a pain in the ass'.) Despite his huge popularity and awesome talents, he was unable to keep a permanent band together, and his unreliability meant that bookings gradually became more and more scarce. He died in Chicago on 15 February 1968, from injuries sustained in a brawl outside a club he'd been playing. Despite the excellence of players like Junior Wells, James Cotton, his mentor Big Walter Horton, and their white disciples PAUL BUTTERFIELD and CHARLIE MUSSELWHITE, Little Walter remains the definitive Chicago harp.

● *Blues With A Feeling* (Charly CD BM 23)

Little Walter cut over a hundred sides for Chess Records between 1952 and 1968: this well-chosen Instant Little Walter Kit presents 16 of the best. I miss the storming 'It Ain't Right' and the sly 'Boom Boom (Out Go The Lights)' – the latter no relation whatsoever to John Lee Hooker's more celebrated 'Boom Boom' – but here are affecting slow blues like the title track, the T-Bone Walker-derived 'Mean Old World', and 'Last Night'; the snappy, swinging instrumentals like 'Juke' and 'Off The Wall' (both rite-of-passage set-pieces for wannabe blues harpists), and uptempo shuffles like 'You Better Watch Yourself' and 'Everything's Gonna Be Alright'; plus, of course, 'My Babe'. This selection covers the first seven years of his solo career (1952–9) and features him with his Jukes (guitarists David and Louis Myers, and later Robert Jr Lockwood; Fred Below on drums), the Waters band (Muddy and Jimmy Rogers on guitars), and various studio groups bossed and bassed by Willie Dixon. Blues harp doesn't get significantly better than this.

Subjects for further investigation: Walter built his reputation and did some of his finest work as a sideman to Muddy Waters. He was a member of Muddy's working band from 1948 until 1952, but recorded with Muddy from 1950 until 1958, despite having been replaced by harpists of the calibre of Junior Wells and James Cotton. Waters' *They Call Me Muddy Waters* (Instant CD INS 5036) is a judicious selection of Muddy's early-'50s sides, most of which feature Walter; seekers after something more elaborate are directed to a 4-CD Waters set, *The Chess Box* (MCA/Chess CHD-80002 [US]) or, for the 9-CD *absolute* full monty, *The Complete Muddy Waters 1947–1967* (Charly CD RED BOX 3). Hear Walter working in the more modern 'West Side' idiom on an OTIS RUSH session with players nearer his own age on *Double Trouble* (Charly CD BM 24).

Jimmy Rogers

Another mainstay of the great 1950s Muddy Waters band, guitarist Jimmy Rogers (born James A. Lane in Ruleville, Mississippi, on 3 June 1924) also enjoyed several hits as a performer in his own right, though most of his early successes were recorded with Waters' band during Waters' studio sessions, and his solo career has been pursued but intermittently. Rogers lacked the kind of distinctive vocal or instrumental 'signature' which redered a HOWLIN' WOLF or ALBERT COLLINS so instantly compelling, but he was (and is) a performer of considerable taste, skill and resource as well as a gifted composer, and his solo work remains intensely enjoyable. Rogers – occasionally referred to as 'Chicago Jimmy Rogers' to distinguish him from the phonetically identical 'Singing Brakeman', white country icon Jimmie Rodgers – arrived in Chicago in 1941 after a childhood and adolescence spent in Atlanta and Memphis, where he had cut his musical teeth playing with Robert Nighthawk, SUNNYLAND SLIM and SONNY BOY WILLIAMSON II, and soon became one of the city's most dependable sidemen, working with Williamson, HOWLIN' WOLF and SUNNYLAND SLIM in addition to his duties with Muddy Waters.

Rogers's run of solo hits, beginning with 'That's Alright' (1950) were undoubtedly successful – at times, like fellow Waters alumnus LITTLE WALTER, he outsold his boss – but even though he had a frontman's talent, he lacked a frontman's temperament, remaining a member of Muddy's band until 1957, when he was replaced by Pat Hare. Unwilling to tour regularly because of his family commitments, he spent much of the '60s running a clothing store, though his guitar was periodically dusted off for the odd gig or studio date. He still performs; and when he does, he rocks the house.

- *That's All Right* (Chess CD RED 15)
- *Hard Workin' Man* (Charly CD BM 3)

Jimmy Rogers's finest hour – or, to be precise, his finest 69 minutes and 55 seconds – is on *That's All Right*: These Chess sides were cut between 1950 and 1958, with Grade-A backup crews including Little Walter and BIG WALTER HORTON (harps), Elgin Evans and Fred Below (drums), OTIS SPANN (piano), WILLIE DIXON and Big Crawford (basses), and Robert Junior Lockwood and Muddy Waters (guitars). It includes Rogers' best-known songs: 'That's Alright', 'Ludella', 'Walking By Myself', 'The World's In A Tangle' and 'Money, Marbles And Chalk'; though for his celebrated 'Sloppy Drunk', you have to go to *Hard Workin' Man*, a slimmer but also eminently listenable compilation drawn from lesser-known 1951–8 Chess sides. In its unassuming way, this is some of the most enjoyable Chicago blues around.

- *Ludella* (Bedrock BEDCD 13)

The Austin house bands assembled by Clifford Antone for his club and label – whence this was licensed – are always superb, and the crew here includes FABULOUS THUNDERBIRDS harpist Kim Wilson (who also produced these 1990 live-and-studio sessions), pianist PINETOP PERKINS (Otis Spann's successor in the Muddy Waters band), drummer Ted Harvey (from HOUND DOG TAYLOR's House-Rockers), guitarists Hubert Sumlin (of Howlin' Wolf fame) and local legend Derek O'Brien. These people are all steeped in the Chicago tradition and it shows, big time; plus Rogers's voice has grown larger and grainier with age. Including such Rogers staples as 'Chicago Bound', 'Sloppy Drunk', 'You're Sweet' and 'Gold Tailed Bird', this is the best post-Chess Jimmy Rogers record you can get.

Subjects for further investigation: Rogers's musical rapport with Muddy Waters has been described as 'telepathic': judge for yourself on Waters' *They Call Me Muddy Waters* (Instant CD INS 5036) (24 early '50s sides); or on the two seriously heavy-duty Waters collections, *The Chess Box* (MCA/Chess CHD3-80002 [US]) and *The Complete Muddy Waters 1947–1967* (Charly CD RED BOX 3). In 1977, Waters and Rogers reunited for *I'm Ready* (BGO

BGOCD 108), the second of four 'comeback' albums produced for Waters by JOHNNY WINTER. *Chicago's Jimmy Rogers Sings The Blues* (Sequel NEXCD 142) contains comeback sides from 1972–3, which straddle the uncomfortable divides between relaxed and listless, pleasant and plodding. Look for the original 'Walking By Myself' on *The Best Of Chess Blues Vol. 1* (Chess/MCA CHD-31315) or on the hideously hard-to-find *Chess: The Rhythm And The Blues* (Charly CD SAM 500); the latter also includes 'Chicago Bound', itself also available on *Comin' Home To The Blues Vol. II* (Music Club MCCD O26).

Junior Wells

Singer/harmonicist Amos Wells Jr (a.k.a. Junior Wells) is still best-known for his twenty-year partnership with BUDDY GUY. Born in Memphis, Tennessee, on 9 December 1934, his family moved to Chicago in 1946, and he took up harmonica in his early teens. Wells lost control of his band The Aces when LITTLE WALTER, freshly departed from MUDDY WATERS' ensemble in the wake of his 1952 solo hit 'Juke', scooped them up to serve as his backing group. Wells, not to be outdone, promptly stepped into Walter's freshly-vacated job with Muddy and played live with him for a season, but army service intervened before he could record anything significant with the Waters band. Back in civvies, Wells resumed his musical career in earnest, cutting hits like 'Messin' With The Kid' and 'Little By Little' for entrepreneur Mel London. In the mid-'60s he teamed up with Buddy Guy, who played guitar on virtually all of Junior's subsequent records (though Junior rarely appeared on Buddy's) as well as working prolifically as a duo during the '70s. Times have been harder for Junior since Guy cut out on his own: the irony was always that, while Buddy was the greater draw (and certainly the greater artist), Junior always dominated the shit out of him on stage. Wells has a distinctive vocal presence: a jivey, hustler's demeanour, alternately arrogant and wheedling. As an instrumentalist, he remains one of the definitive Chicago harps, and the best of his records are the epitome of Grade A Chicago barroom blues.

- *Messin' With The Kid 1957–1963* (Flyright FLYCD 03)
- **JUNIOR WELLS WITH EARL HOOKER:** *Messin' With The Kid* (Charly CD CHARLY 219)

Two alternative packages of the same six years' worth of singles originally cut for Mel London's Chief and Age labels, with stellar session crews including EARL HOOKER (guitar), WILLIE DIXON (bass), Lafayette Leake (piano), Billy 'The Kid' Emerson (organ) and Fred Below (drums). Wells's key early hits – 'Messin' With The Kid' and 'Little By Little', both of which he's recut on numerous subsequent occasions – are present and highly correct, as well as a definitive cover of ELMORE JAMES's 'It Hurts Me Too', a fine duet with Hooker on 'Calling All Blues' and no shortage of others. Both variants are highly acceptable, though the Charly issue has the edge: its 24 tracks include Hooker's fine 'Blues In – Natural' and 'Blue Guitar', and it has an excellent liner note by Neil Slaven.

- *It's My Life, Baby!* (Vanguard VMCD 7311)
- *Comin' At You* (Vanguard VMD 79262)

Two '60s sessions, both prominently featuring Buddy Guy. The first – and by far the better – dates from 1964 and presents Wells both in a small-group context, recorded live at Pepper's Lounge with a quartet including Below on drums, and in the studio with added rhythm guitar and the funkier, more soul-influenced Little Al replacing Below. The sound quality on the live tracks is less than pristine – Wells sounds as if he's singing through the same Fender guitar amp with which he amplifies his harp – but the music is pungent, urgent and as serious as a heart attack. *Comin' At You* was recorded five years later with a big, brass-heavy band (tenor sax, trombone and three trumpets, one of which is jazz great Clark Terry) and a repertoire of blues standards including 'Hoochie Coochie Man', 'Five Long Years', 'Mystery Train' and – of course – 'Little By Little'.

- *Hoodoo Man Blues* (Delmark DD-612)
- *South Side Blues Jam* (Delmark DD-628)

Wells's most important mid-to-late-'60s material wasn't cut for Vanguard, but for the Chicago independent Delmark: *Hoodoo Man*

Blues (1966) and *South Side Blues Jam* (1970) are as loose and live as studio blues ever gets. Both feature guess-who on guitar, and the latter was OTIS SPANN's last studio recording. *Hoodoo Man Blues* finds Junior in the early stages of the JAMES BROWN obsession which dominated much of his non-blues solo work in the '60s – he cut a few currently-out-of-print funk albums for the now-defunct Blue Rock – and the repertoire here includes 'Hound Dog' reworked as a hustling minor-key blues, and a couple of songs associated with SONNY BOY WILLIAMSON I: a funkified 'Good Morning Little School-girl', and the title track. *South Side Blues Jam* is even better: an astonishingly powerful record which is as close to personal testimony as anything recorded in the idiom. It came at a time of crisis in the blues: MAGIC SAM was dead, HOWLIN' WOLF had suffered a serious heart attack, Muddy Waters had barely survived a major car accident, and Spann himself didn't even live long enough to see the album released. It must have felt like the South Side's Last Stand. The repertoire revisits ROBERT JOHNSON and Muddy Waters, but the best of it is original, notably 'I Could Have Had Religion', 'Blues For Mayor Daley' and Guy's 'Trouble Don't Last Always'. Wells discards his jive, putting himself on the line to a greater extent than on any of his records, before or since; and Spann and Guy give musical blood in response. *South Side Blues Jam* was a defiant hymn of pride and belief in the power and value of a music then facing a seemingly inevitable commercial decline. If this had been the last Chicago blues album ever made – thankfully it wasn't, by a *very* long chalk – the music would still have gone out with its head held high. *South Side Blues Jam* is the sound of men, literally, playing for their lives.

Subjects for further investigation: The Junior Wells Chicago Blues Band (a quartet line-up featuring Guy) contributes five songs (including a lovely reading of the then recently-deceased SONNY BOY WILLIAM-SON's 'Help Me'; the gung-ho and hugely controversial 'Vietcong Blues', and a remake of 'Messin' With The Kid') to *Chicago/The Blues/Today! Vol. 1* (Vanguard VMD 79216). Wells and saxopho-nist A.C. REED guested on BONNIE RAITT's 1971 debut album *Bonnie Raitt* (Warner Bros, unavailable); an edited version of 'Finest Lovin' Man' from that album opens up *The Bonnie Raitt Collection* (Warner Bros 7599-26242-2). A couple of riffs from *Hoodoo Man Blues'* 'Snatch It Back And Hold It' were sampled by the Georgia rap posse Arrested Development for their 'Mama's Always On Stage', from 3 *Years, 5 Months And 2 Days In The Life Of* (Cooltempo CCD 1929 3219292).

James Cotton

Always a bridesmaid, never a bride (2): James Cotton learned harmonica as a child at the knee of SONNY BOY WILLIAMSON, came of musical age in Memphis under the wing (or paw) of HOWLIN' WOLF, succeeded LITTLE WALTER and JUNIOR WELLS in the harmonica chair of the MUDDY WATERS band, and – after taking off as a bandleader in his own right – enjoyed the patronage of rock stars like Steve Miller, MIKE BLOOMFIELD, Todd Rundgren and JOHNNY WINTER, all of whom have played on, or produced, his records. Nevertheless, he's never quite cracked the mainstream, which may well be because – even though he's a superb harpist and an ingratiating, immensely hard-working live entertainer – he's a journeyman vocalist with no distinctive original material.

Born in Tunica, Mississippi, on 1 July 1935, he started playing harp as a child after hearing Sonny Boy Williamson on the radio; at seven he was already playing streets and parties, and at nine he ran away from home to find Sonny Boy. The older man took him in and tutored him, bequeathing him his band when he moved North. The band didn't last long, and Cotton ended up in Howlin' Wolf's band, cutting a few Sun singles as a vocalist before heading up to Chicago and joining Muddy Waters. He played on many of the great late-'50s Waters records (even though Chess preferred to use LITTLE WALTER or WALTER HORTON in the studio), and performed with Muddy at the pivotal 1960 Newport Jazz Festival gig, which finally rendered contemporary Chicago blues acceptable to white jazz and folk audiences. Cotton struck out on his own in 1966, and he's been there ever since. I have to declare an attitude here: while I admire his fabulous harp technique, his steadfast devotion to the blues, and his warm-hearted, crowd-pleasing presence, I've rarely found his records satisfying. Please feel free to disagree: any one of the following could well be the answer to your bluesy prayers.

- *Live And On The Move* (Sequel NEXCD 123)
- *Live From Chicago – Mr Superharp Himself!* (Alligator ALCD 4746)
- *Live At Antone's Nightclub* (Antone's ANTCD 0007)

Cotton has always been good value in concert, and the first two (from 1974 – with Matt 'Guitar' Murphy – and 1986, respectively) sound like they were big fun on the night: the big, brassy bands are tight and driving, if generic, and Cotton blows his head off throughout. The third, from 1988, is the one, though: it reunites surviving members of the last great Muddy Waters band – including drummer Willie 'Big Eyes' Smith, bassist Calvin Jones and pianist Pinetop Perkins, plus Murphy again – for a pro- gramme of songs associated with Muddy, Little Walter and Sonny Boy Williamson. *Take Me Back* (Blind Pig BP 72587) is a slightly earlier exercise, studio-based but basically similar, in re-evoking past glories, also with Perkins on board. The Antone's live album wins.

- *High Compression* (Alligator ALCD 4737)
- *Mighty Long Time* (Antone's ANTCD 0015)

Studio Cotton: the 1984 Alligator set is split between tracks cut with the *Live From Chicago – Mr Superharp Himself!* road band, and an allstar studio group featuring Pinetop Perkins and guitarist Magic Slim. It's likeable, if unmemorable; Cotton's best-ever studio album is also his most recent. *Mighty Long Time* enlists the Waters vets heard on the Antone's live album, plus the cream of Austin's blues mafia, plus assorted drop-ins – including guitarists Jimmy Vaughan (from the FABULOUS THUNDERBIRDS), Hubert Sumlin, Matt 'Guitar' Murphy and BOBBY BLAND alumnus Wayne Bennett; and pianists Pinetop Perkins and STEVIE RAY VAUGHAN's former keyb- man Reese Wynans) – and it smokes.

Subjects for further investigation: Cotton's best shot for Sun was the mordant 'Cotton Crop Blues': it's included on **JUNIOR PARKER, JAMES COTTON & PAT HARE:** *Mystery Train* (Rounder CD SS 38). This is as good a time as any to discuss Herman 'Little Junior Parker' (1932–1971), one of the Great Lost Bluesmen: he was a young singer/harpist from Clarksdale who passed through Howlin' Wolf's band before Cotton. He aspired to the sophistication of jump and blues-balladry, but made his recording debut as 'Little Junior's Blue Flames', with the decidedly downhome sounds of 'Feelin' Good' – a derivation from JOHN LEE HOOKER's then-recent hit 'Boogie Chillun' which later attained some renown in its own right, becoming one of MAGIC SAM's live showstoppers – and, of course, 'Mystery Train' itself, later recycled by ELVIS PRESLEY. After Sun, he signed to Houston's Duke/Peacock combine, recording the same kind of material as Bobby Bland, with whom he briefly toured as Blues Consolidated. At the end of his career, he was reduced to covering such unsuitable songs as George Harrison's Beatles B-side 'The Inner Light', and died before attaining the kind of breakthrough which would have kept his later – and more representative – music in print. Prominently featured throughout this disc is guitarist Pat Hare (with whom Cotton was later reunited in the Waters band), who takes the spotlight on the scarifying 'I'm Gonna Murder My Baby'. Eight years later, he did just that, so they locked him up and threw away the key; he died of cancer, still in jail, in 1980. The originals of 'Cotton Crop Blues' (plus Little Junior's 'Feelin' Good' and 'Mystery Train', can also be found on *The Sun Story Vol. 1: Sunrise* (Instant CD INS 5039), which also includes Jackie Brenston's 'Rocket 88', and 'Easy' by Jimmy & Walter (Horton). Cotton revisited 'Cotton Crop Blues' in the company of OTIS SPANN on Chicago/The Blues/Today! Vol. 2 (Vanguard VMD 79217). *Cut You Loose!* (Vanguard VMD 79283) was Cotton's major-label solo debut, and a sorry mess it was too; marred by fussy arrangements, inappropriate material and *not enough harp*. His period with Muddy is documented on *Rock Me* (Charly CD BM 10), and the best of the late-'70s reunion sessions can be sampled on *Hoochie Coochie Man* (Epic 461186 2). Cotton also plays some fabulous harp on Hubert Sumlin's *Heart And Soul* (Blind Pig BP7 3389). Some six years after the Grammy-winning success of the ALBERT COLLINS/ROBERT CRAY/JOHNNY COPELAND jam session *Showdown!*, Alligator attempted to pull off the same stunt a second time by teaming Cotton up with Junior Wells, Carey Bell and Billy Branch for a four-man blowout entitled *Harp Attack!* (ALCD 4790). Unfortunately, it succeeded only in proving that it's easier for three guitarists to stay out of each others' way than four harmonica players.

Jimmy Reed

In the rock world, the byword for lousy record company judgement was the decisions, by executives of Decca Records, to reject The Beatles in 1962 and JIMI HENDRIX in 1966. There are a few equivalents in bluesland (the Chess brothers refused to record OTIS RUSH in 1956, and Alligator's Bruce Iglauer turned down ROBERT CRAY in the late '70s), but the most spectacular was Chess's willingness to allow Jimmy Reed to slip through their fingers. Reed's astonishing run of hits between 1957 and 1963 (13 R&B chart entries, 12 pop hits) made him by far the most commercially successful of all the downhome Chicago bluesmen, and was almost solely responsible for establishing the fledgling Vee Jay label as Chess's principal local competitor. Reed himself (born Mathis James Reed in Dunleith, Mississippi, on 6 September 1925) was an utterly distinctive stylist with as acute a pop sensibility as any of his blues contemporaries. His work was tailor-made for singles: like CHUCK BERRY and BO DIDDLEY, most of his records were seemingly made to the same template, but each song boasted a memorable hook of its own, or some intriguing variation which cut it out from the pack. Listening to Jimmy Reed records is like eating peanuts: they're all pretty much the same, but you can't stop with just one.

Reed favoured relaxed shuffle rhythms – partway between a lope and a lurch – picked and strummed by himself and his alter ego, guitarist/bassist Eddie Taylor, and punctuated with squeaky harmonica riffs tootled on a harp worn in a harness around his neck. (Bob Dylan has claimed that he derived his harp style from Reed, as well as copping the idea of using the harp holder.) Reed's epigrammatic, slyly self-deprecating lyrics (mostly written by his wife, Mary Lee 'Mama' Reed, who whispered the words into his ear just before he sang them) were delivered in a lazy, slurred drawl; and the resulting combination proved so popular in Louisiana that a whole school of laid-back 'swamp blues' (centred around Jay Miller's Excello label and spearheaded by SLIM HARPO, LIGHTNIN' SLIM, and LAZY LESTER) arose in his image. His most popular songs – 'Bright Lights, Big City', 'Shame Shame Shame', 'Big Boss Man', 'Ain't That Lovin' You Baby', 'Honest I Do', 'Baby What You Want Me To Do', and not a few others – are still part of the standard blues repertoire, thanks to covers by the likes of

ELVIS PRESLEY, MUDDY WATERS, THE ROLLING STONES, THE YARDBIRDS, The Pretty Things, Aretha Franklin, JOHNNY WINTER, Steve Miller, ELVIN BISHOP, KOKO TAYLOR, SON SEALS, GEORGE THOROGOOD *et al.*

Reed himself was illiterate, like many other Southern bluesmen of his generation; dearly loved a drink or seventeen, and had suffered from epilepsy since 1957. Still, he hung in there even after his Golden Era was up, scraping the R&B charts with 'Knockin' On Your Door' in 1966; and, even as late as the mid-'70s, he retained enough of a place in the affections of older black record buyers for a collection of his oldies to materialise briefly in the R&B album chart. Reed had quit drinking by the time he died (in his sleep, on 29 August 1976, in Oakland, California), but this new-found sobriety came too late to restore his shattered health. He remains one of the most charming of all bluesmen, the originator of some of the music's catchiest songs, and a welcome counterweight to its overwhelmingly macho tradition.

- *Big Boss Blues* (Charly CD Charly 3)

The most readily available beginners' guide to the insinuating charms of Jimmy Reed's blues. 'Ain't That Lovin' You Baby', 'Honest I Do', 'Big Boss Man', 'I Ain't Got You', 'Shame Shame Shame', 'Baby What You Want Me To Do', 'Goin' To New York' and 'Take Out Some Insurance' and, of course, 'Bright Lights, Big City' itself (Jay McInerney fans please note) are all included here, which means that it's worth anybody's blues money. A budget-price fillet appears as *Bright Lights, Big City: His Greatest Hits* (Charly CD BM 17), but the grownup version is preferable unless financial constraints are truly pressing. This is some of the friendliest, most relaxed and most utterly charming blues ever recorded, and I'd truly hate to be without it.

Subjects for further investigation: Reed's final recordings from the mid-'70s are available, alongside tidbits from EARL HOOKER, BIG JOE WILLIAMS, LIGHTNIN' HOPKINS, Homesick James and ROOSEVELT SYKES, on *Big Boss Men* (Red Lightnin' RLCD 0092): on the old-timey tracks he seems listless, and the interpolation of funk beats and (Earl Hooker's?) wah-wah guitar simply make him sound acutely uncomfortable. Reed's devotees will almost certainly enjoy the work of the Louisiana bluesmen he inspired: check out anything you can find by SLIM HARPO, LIGHTNIN' SLIM, and Lazy Lester.

J.B. Lenoir

The problem with classifying blues singers by era, region or style is that occasionally you run into brilliant anomalies like J.B. Lenoir. Unlike most Chicago bluesmen of his generation, he preferred to play acoustic guitar, though he never chased the white folkie audience until comparatively late in his career; and he freely blended good-time jump-ups like 'Mama, Talk To Your Daughter' (his most famous and most-covered song) with religious material and acrid social commentary. One example of the latter, his 1952 single 'Eisenhower Blues', attacked the newly-elected Republican administration in such uncompromising terms that it prompted direct intervention by the White House, forcing the label to pull the record out of the shops less than two months after its release.

He was born in Monticello, Mississippi, on 3 March 1929 ('J.B.' is not an abbreviation, but his actual given name), played around the South with SONNY BOY WILLIAMSON II and ELMORE JAMES, and moved to Chicago in 1948, performing with BIG BILL BROONZY, JOHNNY SHINES and SUNNYLAND SLIM, as well as working the usual round of clubs and studios and taking the occasional day job. Until 1965, when German promoter Horst Lippman, for whom he had toured Europe as part of the American Folk Blues Festival, commissioned Willie Dixon to produce a Lenoir album, he had recorded nothing but singles; but those singles had endeared him to the likes of JIMI HENDRIX and JOHN MAYALL. His high, clear voice, deft guitar and tough, pointed lyrics would undoubtedly have made him a much bigger star had he lived a little longer, but he died in Urbana, Illinois, on 29 April 1967, of a heart attack following massive injuries sustained in a road accident.

● *Alabama Blues!* (L&R/Bellaphon CDLR 42001)

Lenoir's one and only album-as-album, recorded in Chicago in 1965 by Willie Dixon and featuring Lenoir more-or-less solo, accompanied only by occasional drums from Freddie Below and the odd vocal intervention by Dixon himself. It's an uncommonly powerful piece of work, opening up with the uncompromising title track and smiting the ungodly (the US government, mainly) from Vietnam to Mississippi. The other side of Lenoir is represented too, though, with the signature 'Mama, Talk To Your Daughter' and the bouncy, good-humoured 'Mojo Boogie'.

● *His J.O.B. Recordings 1951–1954* (Flyright FLYCD 04)

Lenoir as jobbing (no pun intended) bluesman, cutting singles with pianist Sunnyland Slim. Playing electric guitar and singing mainstream commercial-blues lyrics, Lenoir loses much of the distinctive character of his music: the most powerful pieces are the tracks where Lenoir and Slim back up JOHNNY SHINES.

Subjects for further investigation: 'Eisenhower Blues' can be found on *The Best Of Chess Blues: Vol. One* (Chess/MCA-CHD 31315); the original 'Mama, Talk To Your Daughter' is on *Blues Masters Vol. 2: Postwar Chicago* (Rhino R2 71122-2 [US]). Lenoir's participation in the American Folk Blues Festival is documented on *American Folk Blues Festival '65* (L&R/Bellaphon CDLR 42025). John Mayall's '67 tribute 'The Death Of J.B. Lenoir' appears on *Crusade* (Deram 820 537-2), and he returned to the theme in 1969 with 'I'm Gonna Fight For You J.B.' on *The Turning Point* (BGO BDOCD 145). Mayall had also essayed two Lenoir numbers during the 1966 *A Hard Road* sessions with PETER GREEN, but the rocking 'Mama Talk To Your Daughter' and Green's courageous but inadequate solo version of 'Alabama Blues' did not emerge until the outtakes-and-rarities collection *Thru The Years* (Deram 844 028-2) was released in 1971. 'Mama Talk To Your Daughter' was also the title track of a now-deleted 1988 Warner Bros release by Robben Ford; and LONNIE BROOKS does the same song his way on *Sweet Home Chicago* (Black & Blue 59.554 2). JOHN LEE HOOKER 'hookerised' the song for Vee Jay in 1958 as 'Mama, You Got A Daughter', but it remained unreleased until 1986, when it appeared on the anthology *Blues Upside Your Head* (Charly CD CHARLY 26). Confirmed Hooker-ites can also locate it on *The Hook* (Chameleon D2-74794, US only); MAGIC SAM's fans can find his version on *West Side Soul* (Delmark DD-615).

Koko Taylor

Given the status disparity between male and female blues singers, it should come as little surprise to learn that the position of 'Queen Of The Blues' is far from a precise equivalent to the 'King Of The Blues' position enjoyed by B.B.KING. The present incumbent is undoubtedly Koko Taylor, born Cora Walton in Memphis, Tennessee, on 28 September 1935. A leather-lunged Chicago blues diva who's as tough as you want her to be and then some, she has, as far as I know, yet to receive any phone calls from U2 or GARY MOORE. After the obligatory round of club-gig dues-paying and indie-label recording dates during the '50s and early '60s with, amongst others, J.B. LENOIR, BUDDY GUY & JUNIOR WELLS) she came under the capacious wing of WILLIE DIXON and, with his sponsorship, toured Europe with the 1967 American Folk Blues Festival, and recorded for Chess throughout the '60s. Her biggest score was with a smouldering '65 update of HOWLIN' WOLF's 'Wang Dang Doodle' which managed the difficult feat of stealing a Wolf song so convincingly that it's now entirely hers; since 1975, she's recorded several albums for Alligator; and, while Taylor is hardly the most versatile blues singer around, she's certainly one of the most powerful: still stone guaranteed to heat up any stage within seconds of setting foot on it.

- *Love You Like A Woman* (Chess CD RED 25)

The Koko Taylor '60s Chess collection, produced and mostly written by Dixon, and featuring a feral young Koko clawing her material apart in the company of the likes of Lafayette Leake or Sunnyland Slim (piano), Buddy Guy, Robert Nighthawk or JOHNNY SHINES (guitars) and WALTER HORTON (harp). The repertoire ranges from traditional Chess-style South Side blues to more contemporary soul-inflected material: 'Wang Dang Doodle' takes pride of place, but it's by no means all that this collections has to offer; and some of these songs – including 'I Got What It Takes' (a variant of MUDDY WATERS's 'The Same Thing') and 'Love You Like A Woman' itself – have stayed with Koko throughout her career. The punchline to the title track, incidentally, is '. . . but I'll fight you like a man.' Bet she would, too.

- *Queen Of The Blues* (Alligator ALCD 4740)
- *Live From Chicago: – An Audience With The Queen* (Alligator ALCD 4754)

From 1985 and 1987 respectively, the best of Taylor's Alligator albums. Queen Of The Blues boasts excellent material (the return of 'Love You Like A Woman', Howlin' Wolf's 'Evil', Albert King's 'The Hunter', an answer-to-SLIM HARPO 'Queen Bee'); fine cameos (by ALBERT COLLINS, SON SEALS, LONNIE BROOKS and JAMES COTTON) augmenting an already excellent band including Johnny B. Gayden on bass; and La Taylor herself in terrifyingly good voice. The live album features no special guests or hot studio players: just Taylor and her road band The Blues Machine, and it's an absolute joy, with a climactic 'Wang Dang Doodle' that hits like a ten-ton truck.

Subjects for further investigation: 1975's *I Got What It Takes* (Alligator ALCD 4706) was Taylor's Alligator debut; *From The Heart Of A Woman* (Alligator ALCD 4724) and *Jump For Joy* (Alligator ALCD 4784) are her most recent albums. *American Folk Blues Festival '67* (Bellaphon/L&R CDLR 42070) depicts the summit meeting between Koko and Europe.

Hound Dog Taylor

Not many people know this, but Theodore Roosevelt 'Hound Dog' Taylor had six fingers on each hand. One shudders to think what, say, John McLaughlin or Yngwie Malmsteen would have done with their bonus digits, but those rudimentary little fingers which graced each mitt did absolutely nothing for (or to) Hound Dog's defiantly downhome slide-guitar playing. One night, after rather more Canadian Club than usual, he hacked off the right-hand superfluity with a razor, but the process was so painful that he decided to leave the left one where it was, and there it remained until his death. Apparently extra fingers, toes and nipples ran in his family.

Hound Dog Taylor (born in Natchez, Mississippi on 12 April 1917) was an anachronism, and proud of it. Though he remained virtually unrecorded until 1971, his music was an utterly unmodified representation of the earliest electric rural blues, exactly as it might have been heard in a Delta jook joint twenty or more years earlier. Rough, raw, yeasty and utterly unselfconscious, Taylor's blues was a rowdy, joyful noise which made absolutely no concessions to anybody or anything. A near-contemporary of MUDDY WATERS, HOWLIN' WOLF, JOHN LEE HOOKER and his greatest influence ELMORE JONES; he played around the Delta in his youth and moved to Chicago in 1942. He held day jobs as a carpenter and a short-order cook, before becoming a fulltime musician in 1957, playing bars and street markets either solo or with his House-Rockers (guitarist Brewer Phillips and drummer Ted Harvey), and releasing the odd single for long-vanished Chicago indies. (FREDDIE KING's trademark instrumental 'Hideaway' is based on a riff King copped from Taylor.) Until 1970, they attracted absolutely no attention outside the South Side (despite Taylor's participation in the 1967 American Folk Blues Festival, where he performed alongside LITTLE WALTER, KOKO TAYLOR, 'BUKKA' WHITE, SON HOUSE, SONNY TERRY & BROWNIE McGHEE), but, at one lounge where Hound Dog Taylor & The HouseRockers had a residency, the regular clientele included a young clerk from the local blues label Delmark, and he was sufficiently moved by their raucous, old-timey electric blues to quit his job and start his own company specifically to record them. His name was Bruce Iglauer, and *Hound Dog Taylor & The HouseRockers* was the first release on Iglauer's Alligator label, which eventually eclipsed Delmark as Chicago's top blues indie.

It sold 10,000 copies: enough to make Taylor, Phillips and Harvey a national and international touring attraction. Their second album, Natural Boogie, followed two years later, but Taylor died of cancer on 17 December 1975, just before the release of their third, the live *Beware Of The Dog*. His most prominent disciples are GEORGE THOROGOOD & THE DESTROYERS – formed as a direct result of Thorogood's admiration for Hound Dog Taylor & The HouseRockers – and the ebullient Chicago quartet LI'L ED & THE BLUES IMPERIALS. Blues has its enduring monuments: the titanic achievements of artists like ROBERT JOHNSON, SMITH, MUDDY WATERS, WILLIE DIXON, JOHN LEE HOOKER or B.B. KING. But its heroes are also men like Hound Dog Taylor, playing the blues in local bars for their own pleasure and that of their friends, neighbours and fellow drinkers. Blues can survive without the patronage of MTV, university sociology departments, rock megastars, book publishers and makers of television commercials: it has done so in the past and will do so again. But its real home is elsewhere: the blues will never die until the day the last blues bar goes out of business.

- *Hound Dog Taylor & The HouseRockers* (Alligator ALCD 4701)
- *Beware Of The Dog* (Alligator ALCD 4707)

The first album because it was first; the live album because it's live. You got a problem with that?

*Subjects for further investigation: **Natural Boogie** (Alligator ALCD 4704) and **Genuine Houserocking Music** (Alligator ALCD 4727) complete the Taylor dossier: if you loved the other two you'll probably want these because they're simply more of the same. Genuine Houserocking Music,* compiled and released after Taylor's death in 1975, collects outtakes from the first album and *Natural Boogie.* It's somewhat flawed, but what the hell: this is Hound Dog Taylor we're talking about. You want perfection? Go listen to Whitney Houston. That '67 European tour is recalled on *American Folk Blues Festival '67* (Bellaphon/L&R CDLR 42070).

CHICAGO PIANO

Pianists were vastly important in the prewar blues scene – as the success of LEROY CARR, Georgia Tom, Roosevelt Sykes and many others will attest – but though it was a key instrument in postwar downhome ensembles, the pianist was seldom the main guy: that honour mainly belonged to guitarists and harp men. Comparatively few pianists made significant recordings as leaders, which was hard cheese on fine musicians like Andrew 'Sunnyland Slim' Luandrew, Eurreal 'Little Brother' Montgomery and Lafayette Leake, all of whom earned the bulk of their crusts performing behind other artists, amassing hundreds of session credits but earning little money and even less mass acclaim. OTIS SPANN was the lynchpin of the first twenty years' worth of MUDDY WATERS bands – second only in importance to Muddy himself – and the likes of ELMORE JAMES and CHUCK BERRY leaned heavily on the contributions of their respective pianists, Johnny Jones and

Johnnie Johnson, but city blues possessed few equivalents to FATS DOMINO, RAY CHARLES, LITTLE RICHARD or CHARLES BROWN. Those who did emerge generally owed their eminence to stints behind guitar-playing leaders and, when times were tough, they were often glad of their ability to make a buck in someone else's band. (In New Orleans, the situation was entirely different: piano players ruled the roost – Fats Domino, PROFESSOR LONGHAIR, JAMES BOOKER and, a little later, Art Neville, Allen Toussaint and DR JOHN – and most guitarists, other than Snooks Eaglin and Earl King, were simply hired help.) The exceptions included . . .

Memphis Slim

Despite making his name in Chicago and (for his last three decades) his home in Paris, Peter Chatman – no relation to the Chatman family which included Bo Carter and THE MISSISSIPPI SHEIKS – would always be Memphis Slim, 6'2" of rolling, soulful blues piano. Born in – you guessed – Memphis, Tennessee, on 3 September 1915, he spent much of the '30s on the road playing Southern juke joints and work camps until he settled in Chicago in 1937 and struck up an occasional partnership with BIG BILL BROONZY, which lasted on and off throughout the '40s. His composition 'Every Day I Have The Blues' became a standard in the early '50s thanks to recordings by LOWELL FULSON, the Count Basie Orchestra (featuring Joe Williams) and, most notably, B.B. KING, for whom it became a virtual signature tune. Often in tandem with guitarist M.T. (better known as Matt 'Guitar') Murphy – of *Blues Brothers* sort-of-fame – or with WILLIE DIXON, he was a fixture on the Chicago scene both as a leader and sideman, but in the '60s he opted to become a solo performer on the folk-blues scene and took up residence in Paris, where he died on 24 February 1988. He was a warm, dignified stage presence and a hellaciously fine pianist. He recorded prolifically (though much of his work remains unavailable on CD) and toured regularly almost until the end of his life: one late highlight was a reunion tour with Murphy, of which more later.

- *Rockin' The Blues* (Charly CD BM 21)

Slim's farewell to Chicago: these aptly titled '58-9 Vee Jay sessions, with various small groups prominently featuring Matt 'Guitar' Murphy, were among his last before hopping the pond. The version of 'Mother Earth' included here is inferior to the 1950 Chess version, but not that inferior; and 'Steppin' Out', an instrumental spotlighting Murphy, became one of ERIC CLAPTON's party pieces during his tenure with JOHN MAYALL. Not a vastly important collection but a highly enjoyable one, and warmly recommended to lovers of piano blues.

- *The Legacy Of The Blues Vol. 7* (Sonet SNTCD 647)

This relaxed, reflective session (featuring Slim on organ as well as piano) was recorded in the early '70s, with New York studio musicians, as part of Sam Charters's ambitious 'Legacy Of The Blues' series. Kicking off with an easy-up, lo-cal version of 'Every Day I Have The Blues' (inexplicably saddled with one of the most graceless fade endings in all recorded blues), Slim moves on to Broonzy's 'I Feel So Good', here retitled 'Ballin' The Jack'; the rolling, anecdotal 'Only Fools Have Fun'; an exuberant 'Broadway Boogie'; two powerful black-consciousness pieces ('I Am The Blues' and 'Freedom'), and more. Go 'long with your bad self, Slim.

- **MEMPHIS SLIM & MATT 'GUITAR' MURPHY:** *Together Again For The First Time*/**EDDIE TAYLOR**: *Still Not Ready For Eddie* (Antone's ANT0305CD)

Slim and Murphy mix it up on a 1985 live reunion at Cliff Antone's club in Austin, Texas: available doublebacked with a rare stage-centre endeavour by Chicago studio guitarist Eddie Taylor, renowned for his contributions to JIMMY REED's Vee Jay sessions. The Slim/Murphy tracks are raw and riotous, loose and euphoric: Murphy picks like a madman on 'Steppin' Out' and 'My Babe'. Does the phrase 'it boogies like a bastard?' mean anything to you?

- **Boogies For All My Friends** (Black & Blue 59.741 2)

The regal expat making music in his adopted home: *Boogies For All My Friends* - mostly instrumental, mostly solo - is, as the title suggests, a series of blues and boogie tributes to the great pianists who make up Slim's peer group: ROOSEVELT SYKES, Pete Johnson, Albert Ammons, Meade Lux Lewis, Jay McShann, Lloyd Glenn, Sammy Price, Pinetop Smith (or is it PINETOP PERKINS?), Jimmy Yancey and OTIS SPANN, plus maybe a couple for Memphis Slim. The musical portraits are witty, apposite, and affectionate: this delightful album, custom-tailored for late-night listening, is the finest piano showcase of his career.

Subjects for further investigation: **Memphis Blues: The Paris Sessions** (Stash ST-CD-11) is something of a curio which starts with Slim hosting a rather haphazard jam session: the rhythm section remain uncredited, possibly at their own request. One of the participants, saxophonist/singer Evelyn Young, is a former member of B.B. KING's band who used to be known as 'Mama Nuts' on account of her behaviour after a few drinks; the others – guitarist Don McMinn, harpist Sunny Blake, singer Booker T. Laury – don't bring a hell of a lot to the party, and it's a relief when the guests step back halfway through and Slim takes over. The album effectively starts there: I recommend programming your player to start at track 12. For Slim over Europe in 1963 (with Willie Dixon, Matt 'Guitar' Murphy, MUDDY WATERS, Otis Spann and SONNY BOY WILLIAMSON II), there's the inevitable **American Folk Blues Festival '63** (L&R/Bellaphon CDLR 42023); for an account of his partnership with Willie Dixon, check out **Willie's Blues** (Ace CDCHD 349), which also includes nine tracks from Slim's unavailable *Just Blues* album. Along with Big Bill Broonzy and SONNY BOY WILLIAMSON I, Slim participated in the recording of the extraordinary documentary **Blues In The Mississippi Night** (Sequel NEXCD 122 or Rykodisc RCD 90155); for a sample of his work as a Chicago studio pianist in the early '40s, hear him behind Broonzy on **Big Bill Broonzy (1934–1947)** (Story of Blues CD 3504-2), and check out both of them behind Broonzy's half-brother WASHBOARD SAM on **Rockin' My Blues Away** (RCA/Bluebird ND 90652) and **Washboard Sam (1935–1947)** (Story Of Blues CD 3502-2). After Slim's death, the underrated Matt 'Guitar' Murphy finally got around to cutting his own highly enjoyable solo album, *Way Down South* (Antone's ANT0013), roping in his brother Floyd for a few guitar cameos, and revealing a bluff, gruff vocal style that perfectly complements his deft guitar. Why didn't he do it years ago?

Otis Spann

Fifties-style Chicago blues piano essentially means Otis Spann. Half-brother to MUDDY WATERS and the anchor of the Waters bands of the '50s and '60s, Spann (born on 21 March 1930, in Jackson, Mississippi) was by no means the only great pianist ever to work in the idiom, but he represented its purest distillation: his left hand laying down rock-solid bass-lines while his right played fluid, glistening fills and obbligatos. A fine, if understated, vocalist, he recorded sporadically as a featured artist and had recently left the Waters fold to strike out on his own when, at the height of his musical powers, he died in Chicago on 24 April 1970.

● *The Bottom Of The Blues* (BGO BGOCD 92)

The best, by a country mile, of all Spann's solo recordings. It's not the only one – a promising session for Prestige Records (currently unavailable on CD, so don't worry about it) was effectively capsized by producer Sam Charters's decision to hire Barry Melton of Country Joe And The Fish to play lead guitar; a favour to Melton but a disservice to Spann – but it's easily the most powerful. Recorded in 1968 with Spann's wife Lucille helping out on the vocals and the full majesty of the Waters band, including the leader's stirring slide-guitar, it peaks on 'Looks Like Twins', a towering minor-key blues composed by Waters, but never recorded by him, which links sexual passion and racial pride in a lyric every bit as affecting as the music. The rest of the album is wonderful, but 'Looks Like Twins' is worth the price of admission all by itself.

Subjects for further investigation: Spann can be heard to excellent effect on most of the Muddy Waters sides recorded between 1953 and

1969; as part of the Waters band backing JOHN LEE HOOKER in a 1966 club appearance on *Live At Café Au Go-Go* (BGO BGOCD 39), and behind BUDDY GUY on *A Man And The Blues* (Vanguard VMD-79272 [1967]), as well as on a fair amount of CHUCK BERRY's '50s sides. *Vintage Blues* (Chess CD RED 9) includes four mid-'50s Spann tracks featuring WALTER HORTON (harp) and Robert Jr Lockwood (guitar); and *Chicago/The Blues/Today! Vol. 1* (Vanguard VSD 79216) presents Spann accompanied only by drummer S.P. Leary. *Raw Blues* (London 820 479-2) contains real treaure trove: four numbers (outtakes from the currently unavailable Decca album *The Blues Of Otis Spann*) recorded in London during a 1964 Muddy Waters tour, where Spann is backed by Muddy's own rhythm section plus Muddy himself (playing guitar under the transparent pseudonym of 'Brother' and sharing the vocals, albeit off-mike, on 'You're Gonna Need My Help'), and a guest appearance by ERIC CLAPTON on 'Pretty Girls Everywhere'. 'You're Gonna Need My Help' can also be found on *The Blues Guitar Box 2* (Sequel NEXT CD 185). He teamed up with Fleetwood Mac for *The Greatest Thing Since* Colossus (Blue Horizon, unavailable); his last session – and one of his best-ever – was JUNIOR WELLS's *South Side Blues Jam* (Delmark DD628).

Eddie Boyd

Edward Riley Boyd, born in Stovall, Mississippi, on 25 November 1914, was never a particularly memorable performer: he had a muted, mournful voice best suited to slow, intimate blues; and a pedestrian piano style with little of the urgency and range of Memphis Slim or OTIS SPANN. Still, he was a popular Chicago bluesman during the '50s, and left his permanent mark on the music with his early-'50s hits 'Five Long Years', 'Third Degree' and '24 Hours', all well-loved and oft-played compositions which are part of the standard blues repertoire. He arrived in Chicago via Memphis in 1941; playing piano behind, among others, SONNY BOY WILLIAMSON I, MUDDY WATERS, JOHNNY SHINES and LITTLE WALTER, before recording as a featured artist for J.O.B. and Chess. He came to Europe with the American Folk Blues Festival in 1965 as part of the house band led by BUDDY GUY, and subsequently toured and recorded with JOHN MAYALL's Bluesbreakers and FLEETWOOD MAC: like Memphis Slim and CHAMPION JACK DUPREE, he eventually opted for permanent expat status, settling first in France and finally in Finland.

- *The Legacy Of The Blues Vol. 10* (Sonet SNTCD 670)

The only Eddie Boyd album you can currently buy was recorded in Scandinavia in the early '70s: it's not particularly impressive, but it does contain 'Black, Brown And White', a fine, scornful version of BIG BILL BROONZY's 'Get Back'.

Subjects for further investigation: Boyd's original 'Five Long Years', cut for J.O.B. in 1952, is on *Blues Masters Vol. 2: Postwar Chicago* (Rhino R2 71122); look for the original '24 Hours' on *The Best Of Chess Blues Vol. 1* (MCA/Chess CHD-31315), and a later live performance of the same song, with Buddy Guy playing guitar, on *American Folk Blues Festival '65* (L&R/Bellaphon CDLR 42025). 'Third Degree', which Boyd cowrote with Willie Dixon, is most readily available on *A Tribute To Willie Dixon 1915-1992* (Chess CD RED 37). His album with Fleetwood Mac was 7936 *South Rhodes* (Blue Horizon, 1968, unavailable): two tracks from those sessions appear on *Fleetwood Mac: The Blues Years* (Essential ESBCD 138).

Pinetop Perkins

Joe Willie 'Pinetop' Perkins replaced OTIS SPANN in the MUDDY WATERS band in 1969, where he remained until Waters' death in 1983. His nickname derives from that of an older musician, Alabama boogie pianist Clarence 'Pinetop' Smith (1904–1929), whose signature piece was 'Pinetop's Boogie Woogie'. Perkins (born 7 July 1913, in Belzoni, Mississippi) recorded Smith's tune for Sun in 1951, and as a result was awarded the 'Pinetop' nickname by his suitably impressed friends. After working around the Delta with Robert Nighthawk, BIG JOE WILLIAMS and SONNY BOY WILLIAMSON II, he moved to the Chicago area in 1949, playing with EARL HOOKER, LITTLE MILTON, ALBERT KING and others before filling Spann's chair with Muddy Waters. Ever since

Muddy died in 1983, Pinetop's been a roving elder statesman of blues piano, recording extensively as a leader in the last few years; and last time I saw him – in March 1992 – he was in Cliff Antone's nightclub in Austin, wearing a slick suit and a Stetson hat, having his shoes shined by an awestruck white student, and looking very pleased with himself.

- **PINETOP PERKINS/LUTHER JOHNSON JR:** *Boogie Woogie King* (Black & Blue 233520)

I believe 'rollicking' is the appropriate term: this 12-songs-in-a-day session features Pinetop working out with his colleagues from the 1976 edition of the Waters band. The first eight songs feature Perkins accompanied only by the rhythm section and Johnson's guitar, stomping, whooping and rolling his way through staples like 'Pinetop's Boogie Woogie', TAMPA RED's 'Sweet Black Angel' and Robert Junior Lockwood's 'Take A Little Walk With Me' before Johnson takes over the vocals and brings in the rest of the band for the finale.

- *After Hours* (Blind Pig 73088)

Pinetop cut his first US album as a leader in 1988, backed by New York-based Chicago revivalists Little Mike & The Tornadoes, a good tough white blues posse in the style of the 1960s PAUL BUTTERFIELD and CHARLIE MUSSELWHITE bands. The ensemble tracks are tight and rocking, if not always overly distinctive, and the highlights are the solo (or almost) versions of pianists' delights like Avery Parrish's title track, Jimmy Yancey's 'Yancey Special' . . . and, oh yes, 'Pinetop's Boogie Woogie'.

Subjects for further investigation: That 1953 verion of 'Pinetop's Boogie Woogie' turns up, confusingly enough, on *The Sun Blues Archives Vol. 1: Guitar Blues* (Sun CD SUN 29) at the tail end of a shared session by Perkins and EARL HOOKER. Four 1978 tracks, cut with more or less the same Muddy sidemen who appeared on *Boogie Woogie King*, feature on *Living Chicago Blues Vol. II* (Alligator ALCD 7702). The 1991 live and studio sessions presented on *Pinetop Perkins With Chicago Beau And The Blue Ice Band* (Platonic BEDCD 22) team the genial pianist with an Icelandic rhythm section. Don't laugh: they swing, albeit in a manner that suits the more aggressive approach of Pinetop's co-star, harpist Chicago Beau, rather better than it does Pinetop himself. Opening with Eddie 'Cleanhead' Vinson's 'Kidney Stew' (credited to Perkins), they crash through a programme of the kind of ELMORE JAMES, Muddy Waters and Sonny Boy Williamson standards to which blues bands always resort when rehearsal time and studio budgets are tight. Best shot: Pinetop's in-concert tribute to Chicago piano godfather Sunnyland Slim. If nothing else, 1992's *On Top* (Deluge/ Sky Ranch SR 652330) demonstrates Pinetop's range: it opens with 'Kidney Stew' (again! At least this time it's credited to Vinson) and closes with the hardy perennial 'Just A Gigolo'. In between, the repertoire borrows from EDDIE BOYD, Maceo Merri-wether, Jimmy Yancey, Elmore James and Muddy Waters; it has its moments, but Pinetop sounds considerably more subdued than on the Black & Blue or Blind Pig sets.

This is as good a time as any to talk about Sunnyland Slim, without whom everything in the above section might have been completely different. It was Slim – born Andrew Luandrew in Vance, Mississippi, on 5 September 1907 – who, when asked to supply a guitarist for an Aristocrat Records session, brought along young Muddy Waters. The resulting partnership between Waters and Aristocrat (which soon renamed itself Chess, after its bosses) was the foundation upon which postwar Chicago blues was built; Slim went elsewhere. He'd got his start as a protege of the Georgia-born singer pianist Peter 'Doc' Clayton (1898–1947), best-known for his extravagant falsetto whoops, white-rimmed specs and his composition 'Hold That Train', later updated by BUDDY GUY as 'Hold That Plane'. After Clayton's death, Slim recorded as 'Doctor Clayton's Buddy': *Doctor Clayton And His Buddy (1935–1947)* (Story Of Blues CD3539-2) features both the last of the master and the d but of the student, with Big Bill Broonzy in attendance on guitar throughout. Understandably, Slim adopts Clayton's whoop on these sides – his 'own' voice was a sharp, edgy tenor which could probably have stood more studio exposure – but it's his piano playing which earned him his living. Slim has appeared as a sideman on literally too many Chicago blues records to mention, straddling the eras of Broonzy and TAMPA RED, and the post-Muddy years. *Legacy Of The Blues Vol. 11* (Sonet SNTCD 671) is a majestic, meditative solo showcase dating from 1971; perfect for contemplative late-night listening and, on 'Days Of Old', in which Slim recalls his rural childhood, deeply affecting and illuminating. Miraculously, Slim is still alive, though not exactly working extensively.

CHICAGO WEST SIDE: THE YOUNG TURKS

West Side blues was a late-'50s update on the classic South Side sound epitomised by Chess Records: it replaced slide guitar by grafting a modification of the B.B. KING/T-BONE WALKER school of lead guitar onto the South Side verities, favoured horns over harp, experimented with uptempo funk beats and emphasised overtly churchy vocals. Whereas classic Chess-style Chicago blues was the music of first-generation migrants from Down Home, West Side was indigenously urban: most of its practitioners were Southern-born, but they were a decade (or several) younger than the transplanted Delta patriarchs in whose footsteps they were following, and their preoccupations, attitudes and outlook were correspondingly far more thoroughly citified. Nowadays, the West Side sound is effectively the mainstream of the blues: BUDDY GUY is currently its most prominent standard-bearer, but its founder was OTIS RUSH, its British Ambassador FREDDIE KING, and MAGIC SAM and EARL HOOKER its Lost Princes.

Buddy Guy

On the right night, Buddy Guy is not just the most exciting blues artist you can find: he's the most exciting blues artist you can imagine finding. On the wrong night, he's almost an embarass-ment. This Edge City approach to performance is what enables him to walk onto the same stage as ERIC CLAPTON, Jimmy Vaughan, ROBERT CRAY and ALBERT COLLINS, and (almost) effortlessly steal the show: it's also what kept him virtually unrecorded for almost twenty years. It's not even a matter of 'temperament' – the offstage Buddy Guy is as modest, relaxed and genial a man as you could possibly hope to meet – but simply that Guy, like his rock opposite number Jeff Beck, literally has more talent than he knows what to do with. His inconsistency is both his greatest strength and his greatest failing.

At his best, he's an absolute monster. For its sheer passion and emotional intensity, his first hit 'First Time I Met The Blues' (1960) has been compared to the work of ROBERT JOHNSON; he was a major influence on Clapton, Cray, Beck, JIMI HENDRIX and STEVIE RAY VAUGHAN. In concert, he's fond of cutting his volume down to just above zero, singing chorus after chorus while standing off the microphone, and then – once the entire audience is leaning forward, straining to hear him – he'll kick his volume up to 11 and plaster everybody against the back wall. In his younger days, he was the absolute master of guitar theatrics: playing guitar with a handkerchief or a drumstick, using an extra-long cable to play from the middle of the room, or even outside it; the works. His range stretches from whispers to screams, from needlepoint delicacy to meatcleaver assault.

George 'Buddy' Guy was born in Letchworth, Louisiana, on 30 July 1936, and gleaned his first bluesical inspiration from JOHN LEE HOOKER's 'Boogie Chillun'. He then discovered B.B. KING, upon whose early style the Guy approach is based, and local hero GUITAR SLIM; after gigging with the likes of LIGHTNIN' SLIM, SLIM HARPO and LAZY LESTER, he relocated to Chicago in 1957 and set about carving his way into the scene by participating in jams and 'Battles Of The Blues' with the likes of OTIS RUSH and MAGIC SAM. On one memorable occasion, no less a personage than MUDDY WATERS found him about to go on stage ravenous with hunger after three days without food. Muddy cussed him out, slapped him around and forcefed him sandwiches in the back of a Chevrolet: Guy went on stage and won the contest. He cut a few records for WILLIE DIXON's Cobra label; when Cobra went under, Dixon took him to Chess, where he hit with his debut, 'First Time I Met The Blues'. Thereafter he combined a day job as a truck-driver with frequent studio work for Chess and a string of singles under his own name, toured Europe with the 1965 American Folk Blues Festival, and struck up a partnership with harpist JUNIOR WELLS which lasted, on and off, for over a quarter of a century.

This team-up generally proffered rather more Wells and rather less Guy than many listeners would have desired: I will never cease to wonder why anyone with Buddy Guy's vocal, instrumental and theatrical resources allowed himself to be so thoroughly dominated onstage for so long by a less gifted performer. Their biggest theoretical break was an allstar session produced by Eric Clapton in the wake of his 1970 *Layla* sessions, but they were unable to cut a full album's worth of tunes: the tapes stayed in Atlantic's vault until someone had the bright idea of plumping it up by commissioning a few new sides by Buddy and the J. GEILS BAND. It was finally released in 1972, and even with Clapton, Geils and DR JOHN on board, didn't sell well enough for Atlantic to keep them on its roster. Thus they entered the wilderness: they ran their Chicago clubs, cut the occasional disappointing low-budget album, and toured, toured, toured.

Fast-forward to the late '80s: thanks to Robert Cray, Stevie Ray Vaughan and a few others, blues was back on the agenda. B.B.King was riding high with U2, John Lee Hooker was flavour of the month, and Eric Clapton was playing blues again. Thanks to a couple of barnstorming appearances with Clapton at the Royal Albert Hall, Guy was brought back into the studio – without Junior Wells – to record a high-profile comeback album, *Damn Right I've Got The Blues*. It made the pop charts and, at long last, the mercurial Buddy Guy finally became a star.

- *The Very Best Of Buddy Guy* (Rhino R2 78020[US])

A more than reasonable career CV, this even includes a couple of the tracks Guy cut in Louisiana before making the trek to Chicago; and it manages to hit most of his high-spots, though it does peter out on some less-than-distinguished late-'80s material from just before *Damn Right*. However, since many of Guy's best performances are lo-o-ong ones, the 'Greatest Hits' format doesn't flatter him, and some of the longer tracks have been edited.

- *Stone Crazy* (Chess CD RED 6)

A highly intelligent filleting of Guy's Chess years (1960–7) and thus better value than the rather more elaborate *The Complete Chess Studio Recordings* (MCA/Chess CHD2-9337), which gives you the dross alongside the gems: the best stuff stands alongside the great Otis Rush sides as West Side blues at its most compelling. It showcases Guy's take on the basic West Side materials: the strong

Delta roots of the lyrics, the revved-up, tremulous, gospel-charged vocals, and a post-B.B. King approach to the guitar which emphasised and exaggerated the rough edges which B.B. himself had so conscientiously sanded off as he refined his craft. Cut while Guy was alternating truck-driving with a position as Chess's house guitarist, the material ranges from agonised Rush-style slow blues epics ('First Time I Met The Blues', 'Stone Crazy' – the long version, praise Jah – 'Ten Years Ago', 'When My Left Eye Jumps', 'I Got A Strange Feeling' and 'Leave My Woman Alone', as covered by Stevie Ray Vaughan, and no relation either to the RAY CHARLES/Everly Brothers number or to John Lee Hooker's 'Leave My Wife Alone') to rocking shuffles like 'Let Me Love You' and plenty of get-down boogaloo fluff. The full monty version ranges from the oh-wow to the ho-hum; this one from the entertaining to the downright riveting.

- *A Man And The Blues* (Vanguard VMD 79272)
- *Hold That Plane!* (VanguardVNP 7315)

Vanguard's late-'60s foray into Chicago blues scooped up JAMES COTTON, CHARLIE MUSSELWHITE and Junior Wells as well as Guy: but Buddy got the best results. The deal yielded these two studio sessions and a currently unavailable live album: the first, featuring Otis Spann on piano, is the better of the two, though the title track of *Hold That Plane!* (derived from Doc Clayton's 'Hold That Train') is one of Guy's best slow blues. Both albums follow the Chess format of wracked slow blues alternated with novelty boogaloos and leavened with the odd shuffle: they're clearer and more measured than the Chess sides, if generally of lower voltage. They have their moments, but if Vanguard can ever be bothered, a judicious filleting of all three albums onto a single full-length CD would be much appreciated.

- **BUDDY GUY & JUNIOR WELLS:** *Drinkin' TNT 'N' Smokin' Dynamite* (Red Lightnin' RLCD 0076)
- **BUDDY GUY & JUNIOR WELLS:** *Play The Blues* (Rhino/Atco R2 70299[US])

When is a team not a team? When they're Junior Wells and Buddy Guy, as documented in concert (with an allstar band, including

THE ROLLING STONES's Bill Wyman and pianist PINETOP PERKINS, at the 1974 Montreux Festival), and in the studio (alongside Eric Clapton, Dr John and the J. Geils Band on various 1970–2 sessions). *Play The Blues* is neat, snappy, relaxed and funky and emphasises the incongruity of the partnership: Wells dominates five of the eight Clapton-produced tracks, and is entirely absent both from two of the three on which Buddy sings lead, as well as from the two makeweight tracks recorded two years later with the J. Geils Band. He also hogs the spotlight on the bulk of the Montreux set, but not on the ones that count: Guy's slow-blues performances on 'Ten Years Ago' and 'When You See The Tears From My Eyes' are positively incendiary; Wells struts through his old hits and a few standards mundane by comparison. An inferior 1977 sequel, *Live At Montreux* (Black & Blue 59.350 2), further documents the disparity between Guy's passion and Wells' perfunctoriness, as well as the latter's relentless hogging of the lead vocal mike; *Alone And Acoustic* (Isabel 59.910 2) is the duo's 1981 roots move: it has its moments (notably the three John Lee Hooker tunes) but as acoustic-guitar-and-harp teams go, it wouldn't lose SONNY TERRY & BROWNIE McGHEE any sleep.

- *The Blues Giant* (Isobel 59.900 2)

Cut during a one-day break from a 1979 French tour with a quartet including his brother Phil Guy on rhythm guitar, this underrated curio is the only Buddy Guy album of any merit recorded between the early '70s and the late '80s, and it's strongly recommended to Stevie Ray Vaughan fans. Big, loud, guitaro-centric and blustery, it's as ferocious as anything Guy has ever put on record, if not as eloquent; and spikes a selection of snarling, raging slow blues – including a hair-raising rewrite of 'Stone Crazy' entitled 'Are You Losing Your Mind?' – with an intriguing post-Hendrix funk-rock workout. (Alligator licensed it for US release in 1981 under the title *Stone Crazy*: confuse that edition with Charly's similarly-titled Chess collection at your own peril.)

- *Damn Right I Got The Blues* (Silvertone ORE CD 516)

The grand slam. The backdrops are very much in the blues-heard-as-big-rock Gary Moore vein, but the material – ranging from fresh originals by Guy himself and John Hiatt to selections from the repertoires of LOUIS JORDAN, Big Jay MacNeely, Wilson Pickett and EDDIE BOYD – plays straight to Guy's strengths, and his performances are positively incandescent. There are the obligatory big-star cameos for the benefit of those who are impressed by the presence of Eric Claptron, Jeff Beck and Mark Knopfler, but the only one who is actually noticeable is Beck, who contributes an archetypally loopy solo to 'Mustang Sally'. There's hardly a slack moment from end to end of this album, from the walloping title track to the finale, an elegiac instrumental tribute to Stevie Ray Vaughan.

● *Feels Like Rain* (Silvertone ORE CD 516)

The followup to the grand slam. Guy spreads his wings on tributes to JAMES BROWN ('I Go Crazy'), Marvin Gaye (a stunning 'Trouble Man'), Muddy Waters ('Nineteen Years Old'), RAY CHARLES ('Mary Ann'), Junior Wells ('I Could Cry') and Guitar Slim ('Sufferin' Mind'); enlists the support of Bonnie Raitt (on John Hiatt's title track), JOHN MAYALL (on 'I Could Cry') and Paul Rodgers (on Soul Brothers Six's 'Some Kind Of Wonderful'), and swarms all over his wah-wah pedal just like Jimi or Stevie. With its leonine confidence and surging propulsion, this is the work of a man who knows his time has come; not 'after awhile', but *now*.

Subjects for further investigation: If *Stone Crazy* has whetted your appetite whetted for early Chess Guy but you don't want to replace it with the *The Complete Chess Studio Recordings*, you might try *The Treasure Untold* (Charly CD BM 11) or *I Cry And Sing The Blues* (Charly CD BM 27), both of which include stuff *Stone Crazy* omits. As a Chess studio musician, Guy can be heard playing guitar and occasional bass on records by KOKO TAYLOR, HOWLIN' WOLF and numerous others, but his best shots as a sideman were both with Muddy Waters: playing downhome acoustic on *Muddy Waters, Folk Singer* (doubled with *Muddy Waters Sings Big Bill Broonzy* on MCA/Chess CHD-9507) and with Muddy and Wolf on *Live Action!* (Charly CD BM 15). *American Folk Blues Festival '65* (L&R/ Bellaphon CDLR 42025) has Guy all over it, both as a featured artist and playing guitar and bass behind others including John Lee Hooker; Guy is prominently featured on *Antone's Tenth*

Anniversary Anthology Vol. 1 (Bedrock BEDCD 8) and *Vol. 2* (Antone's ANTCD 0016); and rather less prominently on Eric Clapton's *24 Nights* (Reprise 7599-26420-2). Clapton's soundtrack from the film *Rush* (Reprise 7599-26794-2), in which his justly celebrated 'Tears In Heaven' was premiered, features a (very) good ten-minutes-plus of Guy blasting away on 'Don't Know Which Way To Go', with the Clapton band in support. Some moderately hot live 1970 Buddy-and-Junior stuff, including three jams with Muddy Waters, appears on *18 Tracks From The Film 'Chicago Blues'* (Red Lightnin' RLCD 0080), and Buddy's also on various Junior Wells albums listed elsewhere. Phil Guy, Buddy's younger brother and a much brusquer performer than his voluble sibling, has a decent enough album of his own, *Tina Nu* (JSP JSPCD 622).

Otis Rush

One of the Big Six post-T-BONE WALKER blues guitarists (for the record, the others are the Three KINGS – B.B., ALBERT and FREDDIE – plus BUDDY GUY and ALBERT COLLINS), Otis Rush has had rather more influence than success. There is a considerable case to be made that ERIC CLAPTON's guitar (and vocal) style owes far more to Rush than to the more frequently cited Buddy, B.B. and Freddie: indeed, playing Rush's original of 'Double Trouble' to dyed-in-the-wool Claptomaniacs is one of life's more satisfying minor pleasures. Rush is one of the most intense bluesmen ever to record: no one wrings the last possible emotional drop from a minor-key slow blues the way he does. Much of his '50s material (written either by WILLIE DIXON or by Rush himself) has entered the standard blues repertoire: JOHN MAYALL recorded 'All Your Love' (with Eric Clapton), and 'I Can't Quit You Baby' (with Mick Taylor); Clapton himself later assayed 'Double Trouble'; Led Zeppelin cut 'I Can't Quit You Baby' on their first album; and, more recently, DR FEELGOOD dallied with 'Violent Love'.

Born on 29 April 1934, in Philadephia, Mississippi, Rush picked up his first guitar at the age of eight: left-handed as he is, Rush plays a conventionally strung guitar upside down, like Albert King, Bobby Womack and Bob Geldof. Relocating to Chicago in his mid-'teens, he began entering (and winning!) local 'cutting contests' and came to the attention of Willie Dixon, who wanted to record him for Chess. The Chess brothers felt differently about it, and so Dixon – already peeved with Chess – took Rush to his fledgling Cobra label. Here, Dixon evolved a Cobra house style based on the West Side group of up-and-coming younger bluesmen – including Buddy Guy and MAGIC SAM Maghett – of whom Rush was the doyen. Between 1956 and 1958, Rush recorded a string of astonishing singles for Cobra (including 'Double Trouble', 'All Your Love' and 'I Can't Quit You Baby'); after the label's demise, he and Dixon cut a few more for Chess (including the shattering 'So Many Roads') but since Rush has rotten luck, worse advice and a reputation for poorly developed interpersonal skills, he has been criminally underrecorded ever since. A few tracks on *Chicago/The Blues/ Today! Vol. 2* (Vanguard VSD 72917) revived matters somewhat, leading to a deal with Atlantic's Cotillion subsidiary. (The session was productive in its own right: its highlights included the version of 'I Can't Quit You Baby' on which the Mayall and Zeppelin covers were based, and Rush's instrumental version of the old IKE & Tina TURNER hit 'It's Gonna Work Out Fine' – here retitled 'Everything's Gonna Work Out Alright' – bears a remarkable resemblence to the one cut some years later by RY COODER for *Bop 'Til You Drop*). The Cotillion album (1969's *Mourning In The Morning*) was, unfortunately, negligible and is, fortunately, currently unavailable.

A rather better 1971 session for Capitol remained unissued until 1976; since then we've seen a few (mostly disappointing) further albums, and many intermittently brilliant live performances. Album titles like *Right Place, Wrong Time* and *Lost In The Blues* are proving sadly appropriate.

● *Double Trouble* (Charly CD BM 24)

If this also included the 1960 Chess single 'So Many Roads' – as did the frustratingly no-longer-available *The Classic Recordings* (Charly CD CHARLY 217) – it would be virtually all the Otis Rush you'll ever need: it collects the Cobra sides on which Rush's reputation rests, and they still sound terrific. Cobra's recording facilities were not the finest, but Willie Dixon knew how to run a session, and Rush is on fabulous form. Here are the originals of 'All Your

Love', 'I Can't Quit You Baby' and the title tune; the backup crews Dixon assembled for these sessions include IKE TURNER and Wayne Bennett as second guitars; both LITTLE WALTER and BIG WALTER HORTON sit in on harmonica; and Dixon himself anchors the rhythm section on bass. This is some of the most scarifying blues ever recorded: the emotional intensity is literally frightening. Paradoxically, the uptempo tunes are the most relaxed, but since Rush's forte is the slow blues, they're also the least individual.

Subjects for further investigation: The most accessible source for Rush's 1960 Chess sides is *So Many Roads* (Charly CD BM 2), jointly bylined to Rush and Albert King; it features eight tracks by each of them, naturally including the wracked, smouldering title track which is, in many ways, Otis's masterpiece. Those same sixteen tracks are also part of *Vintage Blues* (Chess CD RED 9), where they are bundled with worth-having material by OTIS SPANN and John Brim: *Vintage Blues* is harder to find than *So Many Roads*, but it's considerably better value. Seek out 'So Many Roads' itself on *The Blues Guitar Box* (Sequel TBB CD 47555), or *The Best Of Chess Blues Vol. 2* (MCA/Chess CHLD 19094). *Right Place, Wrong Time* (Edsel EDCD 220) is the '71 Capitol session: its high points are the anguished title track (which, by a process of 'organic sampling', cops its basic groove and horn arrangement straight from Albert King's 'You Sure Drive A Hard Bargain') and a very soulful take on Tony Joe White's 'Rainy Night In Georgia'. *Lost In The Blues* (Sonet SNTCD 1045) was a slack session of standards recorded during a two-day break in a 1977 Swedish tour. This 1991 remix, with LUCKY PETERSON's keyboard overdubs supervised by Alligator's Bruce Iglauer, does little to enliven a drab and tired performance. *Live In Europe* (Isabel 59.921 2) and *Tops* (Demon FIENDCD 143) are live albums from 1977 and 1985, respectively: both demonstrate the extent to which a once-unique performer has allowed himself to become so thoroughly derivative of more successful peers (Albert and B.B. King, to be precise), but the latter is the easy winner, thanks both to expertly driving backup from a brassy six-piece band led by guitarist Bobby Murray (no relation to the author, more's the pity) and featuring future ROBERT CRAY keyboard op Jimmy Pugh; and to an enthusiastically committed performance from Rush himself.

Freddie King

Though he was born and raised in Texas and cut his most memorable records for a label based in Cincinnati, Freddy (the spelling changed in the late '60s) King was, for all practical purposes, an honorary West Sider. After all, he'd left Gilmer, Texas – where he was born on 3 September 1934 – as a lad of 16, and spent the next ten years refining his youthful chops in the taverns and Blues Battles of the West Side. Though Texans, who are patriotic to the point of arrant chauvinism, claim him by citing his indubitable links to the Texas guitar tradition of T-BONE WALKER, CLARENCE 'GATEMOUTH' BROWN and ALBERT COLLINS, his singing betrays its affinity with the gospelly post-B.B. KING style of BUDDY GUY and OTIS RUSH.

No relation to any other large Gibson-wielding gentlemen with the same surname, Freddy King was a popular and respected local live performer, but Chess declined to record him on the grounds that he was too similar to B.B.: the nearest he got to a recording deal during the '50s was the opportunity to cut a few unreleased sides for Cobra Records. Finally, he was recommended to the Cincinnati-based King/Federal label and he was on his way, scoring several Pop and R&B hits with a series of snappy trademarked instrumentals, commencing with 'Hideaway' – which he and pianist/collaborator Sonny Thompson put together out of a HOUND DOG TAYLOR lick, the main riff from Jimmy McCracklin's 'The Walk', a snatch of the Peter Gunn theme, and a hip diminished chord King had just learned from Robert Junior Lockwood – and slightly fewer with his vocal releases. His early records found a sympathetic audience among British blues boomers: along with Hubert Sumlin, Buddy Guy and the other two Kings, he was a primary influence on ERIC CLAPTON. Three successive JOHN MAYALL albums featured versions of his instrumentals: Clapton assayed 'Hideaway' on *Blues Breakers*; Peter Green took on 'The Stumble' on *A Hard Road*, and Mick Taylor attempted 'Driving Sideways' on *Crusade*; while Stan Webb of Chicken Shack adopted 'San-Ho-Zay'. The vocals had their following also: his 'Have You Ever Loved A Woman' was a favourite of Clapton's, and 'The Welfare' later showed up in the repertoires of Albert Collins and ROBERT CRAY.

Unlike many of his contemporaries, Freddie did well out of the late '60s and early '70s: after leaving King/Federal in 1966, he cut a couple of pretty decent albums for Atlantic (both, like most vintage Atlantic stuff, currently unavailable) and spent the '70s on Shelter and RSO, under the respective patronage of Leon Russell and Eric Clapton, with whom he frequently toured. None of his subsequent records had the influence and impact of the epochal King/Federal sides, but they sold steadily and he enjoyed high-profile concert work right up until just before his death, of hepatitis and other complications, in Dallas, Texas, on 28 December 1976. His creative years were seemingly behind him, but he was still a consummate entertainer.

- **FREDDY KING:** *Texas Sensation* (Charly CD CHARLY 247)

This may not be the only Freddy King album you'll want, but it's the only one you need. A generous, 20-track hour or so's worth of King/Federal tracks, mostly from 1960–2 plus one each from '64 and '66. All the great instrumentals – 'Hideaway', 'The Stumble', 'Driving Sideways', 'San-Ho-Zay', 'Sen-Say-Shun') and his best-known vocals – 'Have You Ever Loved A Woman', 'I'm Tore Down', 'The Welfare', 'You've Got To Love Her With A Feeling' – easily available in one place, along with wondrous oddities like the country ballad 'Teardrops On Your Letter', and 'Lonesome Whistle Blues', with its haunting backing vocal line.

Subjects for further investigation: For a straightforward reissue of the classic early-'60s all-instrumentals album that Clapton, Green, Mayall *et al* wore out in the '60s, consult *Let's Hide Away And Dance Away With Freddy King* (King KCD-773). *Boy-Girl-Boy* (King KCD-777), jointly credited to King, singer Lula Reed, and Sonny Thompson, is an entertaining early-'60s exercise in teenage-dance-party pop by a team of blues people. '70s F. King: *Gettin' Ready* (Sequel NEX CD 126), produced by Leon Russell and Don Nix, is an engaging set of mostly standards (Nix's 'Going Down' is the killer original) plus outtakes including Steve Winwood's 'Gimme Some Lovin''; *The Texas Cannonball* (Sequel NEX CD 175), also produced by Russell and padded with outtakes to a whopping 77 or so minutes, is similarly funky, tasteful and includes a sensitive mixture of blues standards and well-chosen soul and rock covers from the repertoires of Bill Withers and Creedence

Clearwater Revival, but it rarely catches fire. **Burglar** (BGO BGOCD 137), produced in the UK by Brit-blues godfather Mike Vernon (who'd recorded all those Freddie King covers by Mayall & Co) and featuring British funksters Gonzalez as the backing band, packs a groove that kicks like a Mississippi mule: no shortage of fire, but a dearth of first-class material. Small World Note: Steve Ferrone, heard here drumming with Gonzalez on nine of the ten tracks, went on to join the Average White Band and then Eric Clapton's group; the '74 edition of Clapton's band supplies the backup on the tenth, 'Sugar Sweet'.

Magic Sam

Sam Maghett (a.k.a. 'Magic Sam') is one of the great lost heroes of postwar blues. The third, and youngest, of the triumvirate of singer/guitarists who graduated from Cobra Records to define the West Side school of blues (the other two being, of course, OTIS RUSH and BUDDY GUY), he was poised for a major mainstream breakthrough after a triumphant performance at the 1969 Ann Arbor Jazz & Blues Festival, but died in Chicago of a heart attack only a few months later at the age of 32, on 1 December 1969. Many believed that the handsome, well-spoken, quick-witted Maghett, a keen admirer of JIMI HENDRIX and TAJ MAHAL, was the true heir of the Chicago blues tradition, and the man best qualified to take the blues into the '70s and beyond; to accomplish the kind of commercial feats eventually pulled off a decade later by ROBERT CRAY. Born in Grenada, Mississippi, on 14 February 1937, Sam moved to Chicago in 1950, sang gospel and played in bars with his harpist uncle 'Shakey Jake' Harris's band; by 1957 he was recording for Cobra under the wing of WILLIE DIXON, both with Harris and as a featured artist. Throughout the '60s, as the music struggled to redefine itself in the wake of the defection of its original audience and the growth of the white market, he cut formularised singles for local labels while occasionally playing second guitar behind Otis Rush, but his reputation rested on his stunning club performances, a couple of which were preserved on amateur recordings and eventually issued, alongside his '69 Ann Arbor set, on *Magic Sam Live*.

At its purest, as at the Ann Arbor show, Sam's take on the West Side sound was stripped to the bone (no harps, horns or piano). His music demonstrated a thorough-going awareness of current developments in rock and soul without any pandering to their demands; and his 1968 Delmark album *West Side Soul* was a genuine landmark, both defining the subgenre and staking Sam's claim as its new figurehead. His music had a lighter, more antic spirit than that of Rush (who was at his best when at his gloomiest), and his death gutted the blues community: Magic Sam was deemed the artist most likely to reverse the music's commercial and artistic decline. Listening to his music over twenty years after his death, there's no doubt that he could well have achieved just that, a full decade before the arrivals of Robert Cray and STEVIE RAY VAUGHAN. Indeed, Sam anticipated both of them: his blend of deep blues and uptown soul is not dissimilar from the Cray formula; and the staggering intensity of the Ann Arbor trio performance is an obvious precursor of SRV's tidal-wave approach to the blues. Magic Sam was well-named.

- *West Side Soul* (Charly CD BM 29)

Charly's titling of this album should qualify for some kind of award for sheer disingenuousness in packaging: it's a collection of Sam's 1957–60 Cobra sides travelling under the papers of the legendary 1968 album of the same name. It's well worth having in its own right, just as long as you know what you're getting: the sound of a gifted young player searching for a voice, rather than the voice itself. Sam's guitar and vocals are recorded 'hot', the guitar shimmering with shrieking treble, and the vocal microphone's distortion reminiscent of a younger, lighter-voiced HOWLIN' WOLF: Sam is still audibly under the influence of his mentor Otis Rush (incidentally, Sam's 'All Your Love' is not the well-known Rush standard of the same title, but an original song), though it's difficult to imagine Rush attempting something like the hectic rockabilly of '21 Days In Jail', or the sheer jauntiness of the aptly titled instrumental 'Magic Rocker'. Magic Sam had more of a rock-and-roll edge to his music than did any of his blues contemporaries, and this album proves it.

- *West Side Soul* (Delmark DD-615)

The genuine article. Backed by bass, drums, rhythm guitar and the odd splash of piano (from the visiting 'Stockholm Slim'), Sam emerges from the shadows of Rush and Guy with an eclectic set which stretches from the opening BOBBY BLAND-style gospel-blues swing of 'That's All I Need' to the uproarious canters through 'Sweet Home Chicago' and J.B. LENOIR's 'Mama Talk To Your Daughter'; and the exhilarating JOHN LEE HOOKEResque boogie of JUNIOR PARKER's 'Feelin' Good'. Steeped as it is in the verities of postwar blues, *West Side Soul* has a youthful freshness and urgency which contributes to its immense charm and more than compensates for the odd out-of-tune guitar. Yet this album has considerably more than just charm: it's exceptionally powerful and atmospheric, and the closest Sam ever got to putting his music on record thy way he wanted it.

- *Magic Sam Live* (Delmark DE-645)

The energy is as hi as the fi is lo: if this 73-minute diamond-in-the-rough had been professionally recorded it would be a better album than *West Side Soul*; a live '60s blues document to rival B.B. KING's *Live At The Regal* or ALBERT KING's *Blues Power*. As it is, it's merely fantastic. Derived from amateur location recordings, it brings together '63-'64 material from Chicago's now-defunct Club Alex (with five-piece bands including A.C. REED and Howlin' Wolf's hornman Eddie Shaw on tenor saxes) and that show-stopping '69 appearance at the Ann Arbor Blues Festival (all the more remarkable when it's considered that Sam and his bassist appeared with borrowed gear and Sam Lay, formerly with Howlin' Wolf and PAUL BUTTERFIELD, as a last-minute sittin'-in drummer). That show must have been the blues equivalent of Jimi Hendrix's eruption at the '67 Monterey Pop Festival – Sam was the acknowledged hit of an event which also featured MUDDY WATERS, Howlin' Wolf, B.B. King, SLEEPY JOHN ESTES, BIG JOE WILLIAMS, FREDDIE KING, Roosevelt Sykes, MISSISSIPPI FRED McDOWELL, LIGHTNIN' HOPKINS, CLIFTON CHENIER, Luther Allison, T-BONE WALKER and Otis Rush – but in every performance included here, Sam goes the limit, tearing the maximum intensity both from his guitar strings and vocal chords. Treasures include rocking versions of Freddie

King's 'Tore Down' and 'San-Ho-Zay', plus Hooker-style boogie well and truly kicked into Chicago overdrive on 'Feelin' Good' and two encores of 'Lookin' Good' (reprised from *West Side Soul*). The music is superb; the sound is about as good as we have a right to expect from amateur recordings made between 25 and 30 years ago. No doubt about it: Magic Sam had the keys to the kingdom.

● *Give Me Time* (Delmark DD-654)

At home with Magic Sam, singing and playing solo one afternoon in 1968 for his guests (including EDDIE BOYD, who donates some impromptu backing vocals) with his kids in the background. A few blues standards ('Sweet Black Angel', 'I Can't Quit You Baby'), a few aching soul ballads; some new, some previously recorded, like *West Side Soul*'s 'That's All I Need'. We can only be grateful that Delmark resisted the temptation to overdub bass and drums on these tapes, but Sam's timing is so immaculately steady that they could probably have gotten away with it. Not recommended as anybody's first Magic Sam album, but once you've fallen in love with the man's music, you won't want to be without it.

Earl Hooker

In a blues community where artists routinely claim kinship with more illustrious performers to whom they are no verifiable blood relation, it's worth noting that Earl Zebedee Hooker really *was* JOHN LEE HOOKER's younger cousin. Another lost hero whose premature death terminated an exceptionally promising career, Earl Hooker's speciality was progressive slide guitar which drew on country, jazz, soul and funk as well as the blues: unlike the more traditionally-based slide stars, from CHARLEY PATTON to RY COODER, who played in open tunings, Hooker used standard tuning, augmented in later years with frequent doses of wah-wah pedal. No one except JIMI HENDRIX would match Earl Hooker at the recondite art of wah-wah blues, and only Jeff Beck has even approached his unique wah-wah/slide combination. (Jimmy Page? Fergeddaboudit!)

Born in Clarksdale, Mississippi – wasn't everyone? – on January

15, 1930, and raised in Chicago, where his parents moved before he was a year old. A wild boy in his teens, he ran with Chicago street gangs and, in later life, was as renowned for his reluctance to pay his musicians as for his startling instrumental prowess. He went to the same school as Ellas 'BO DIDDLEY' McDaniel; learned slide guitar in his teens from Robert Nighthawk and, at 19, was back down south with a group led by IKE TURNER. By the early '50s he was leading his own band, cutting the odd session here and there, including a few 1953 sides for Sun; by 1960 he was a regular member of Mel London's studio crew, recording both as a featured artist and behind JUNIOR WELLS.

His 1961 instrumental, 'Blue Guitar', based on Arthur Crudup's 'Rock Me Baby' (itself made famous by B.B. King), was purchased by Chess for use as the backing track to Muddy Waters' celebrated 'You Shook Me', with lyrics composed by WILLIE DIXON. The song was later covered by The Jeff Beck Group (featuring Rod Stewart) and by LED ZEPPELIN. Zeppelin's 'Whole Lotta Love' was based on another Waters/Dixon/Hooker collaboration, 1962's 'You Need Love.' Both featured organ solos by Johnny 'Big Moose' Walker,the first time that organ was featured on a blues recording: another Hooker innovation. A 1969 American Folk Blues Festival tour took him to Europe in the company of MAGIC SAM, CLIFTON CHENIER and Carey Bell, but the tuberculosis with which he'd battled for the previous few years finally took him off the set on April 21, 1970. Never much of a singer, he was nevertheless enormously influential: however, he had more impact on his peers than on the public. To this day, bluesmen will still tell you that Earl Hooker was one of the greats.

- **JUNIOR WELLS & EARL HOOKER:** _Messin' With The Kid_
  (Charly CD CHARLY 219)

Those Wells/Hooker sides, cut for Mel London's Chief, Age and Profile labels in the early '60s. Wells's contributions are discussed elsewhere; what's relevant here is the uniquely clear, ringing tone which Hooker brings, on both slide and 'straight' guitar, to every tune on which he appears. Naturally, 'Blue Guitar' is included.

- *Two Bugs And A Roach* (Arhoolie CD-324)

A combination of late-'60s Chicago sessions and 1952/3 Memphis tracks, added to the original abum for CD reissue: the common factor, other than Hooker himself, is pianist PINETOP PERKINS. The title cut is a tuff-enuff funk boogaloo; the 'bug' of the title is TB. 'I got to get rid of this bug, it's gon' kill me' jives Hooker: if only he'd been kidding. The '68/'69 titles demonstrate that, like Jimi Hendrix, Hooker had both the grounding in blues tradition necessary to play the music 'from the inside', and the sonic imagination and eclectic tastes required to create something fresh and new with it; the Sun sessions that his distinctive personal 'touch' was there almost from the beginning. If these tracks languished in the vaults, it's probably because of the vocals, which are less than enticing, but there's no arguing with the breakneck bluegrass/jazz licks on 'Guitar Rag.'

Subjects for further investigation: Eight previously unreleased 1953 Sun sides, featuring Hooker, again with Pinetop Perkins, surfaced on *The Sun Blues Archives Vol. 1: Guitar Blues* (Sun CD SUN 29): six are instrumentals (including an early version of 'Blue Guitar'), with Hooker and Perkins taking one vocal apiece. Hooker's combination of blues, Latin and country licks on 'Mexicali Hip-Shake' anticipates many of the trademarks of the then-unrecorded CHUCK BERRY; more of his bizarre country chops are aired on 'Red River Variations.' 'Blue Guitar' is also available on *Blues Masters Vol. 2: Postwar Chicago Blues* (Rhino R2 71122). *Big Boss Men* (Red Lightnin' RLCD 0092) includes another late-'60s wah-funk instrumental, 'Blues For Dancers' with some fine harp, possibly by Junior Wells; *American Folk Blues Festival '69* (L&R/ Bellaphon CDLR 42071) is where you find Hooker live at the Royal Albert Hall. His 1969 team-up with SONNY TERRY & BROWNIE McGHEE on *I Couldn't Believe Me Eyes . . . plus* (See For Miles SEE CD 92) is far less incongruous than you'd imagine: Hooker's tough slide puts McGhee back into the solid urban blues style of his '40s commercial recordings, while the country changes of McGhee's title song suit Hooker down to the ground. Irritatingly enough, Hooker's only recorded collaboration with his cousin John Lee of that ilk, *If You Miss 'Im, I Got 'Im* (Probe, 1969) is currently out of print: the nearest you can come to it is checking out the excerpts from it included on the CD edition of John Lee's *Never Get Out Of These Blues Alive* (See For Miles SEE CD 89). Contemporary Texas hotshot SUE FOLEY reworks Hooker's 'Off The Hook' and 'Hooked On Love' on *Young Girl Blues* (Antone's ANT CD 0019).

2. Memphis, Texas and All Points In Between

T-Bone Walker

Contemporary blues starts here. Aaron Thibeaux 'T-Bone' Walker did indeed have influences of his own – notably BLIND LEMON JEFFERSON (whose 'lead boy' he was as a child in Texas), Charlie Christian (with whom he had a street-singing duo as a youth in Oklahoma), SCRAPPER BLACKWELL, LONNIE JOHNSON and LOUIS JORDAN – but what is far more important is the influence which he had on others. The first to adapt the single-string improvisatory flourishes of the progressive country blues guita-rists to the electric instrument and juxtapose the resulting joyful noise with the brassy blare of a swing band, Walker created a style and a repertoire which has long outlived him: wherever electric blues guitar is played, you're still hearing what T-Bone Walker developed in the '30s and '40s. Like Chuck Berry and B.B. King, he perfected the art of the signature intro: an instantly recognisable guitar lick that announced 'Hi, this is a new T-Bone Walker record' within the first few bars. His virtuoso phrasing, adroit use of double-time licks – wherein he plays eight or sixteen beats to the bar while the rhythm section plays four – and sliding sixth and ninth chords speedily became permanent foundations of the musical vocabulary of the new blues guitar.

Born in Linden, Texas, on 28 May 1910 and raised in Oklahoma, 'Bone' cut his first record 'Trinity River Blues' in 1929 under the soubriquet of 'Oak Cliff T-Bone' – the curious can find it on *Legends Of The Blues Vol. II* (Columbia Legacy 468770 2) – and was playing electric guitar by 1935. His 'T-Bone Blues' was first recorded in 1940, and he cut 'Mean Old World' and a few others for the then-tiny Los Angeles-based Capitol label in 1942, but it was the seminal sides recorded between 1946 and 1948 for Capitol's Black & White subsidiary that caused the revolution. In Memphis, the young B.B. KING heard Walker's 'Stormy Monday Blues' and went straight out to buy himself an electric guitar: others like CLARENCE 'GATEMOUTH' BROWN, LOWELL FULSON and ALBERT KING soon followed, and the word soon spread to hundreds and thousands of others. His mellifluous crooning vocals, sly lyrics, dry woody guitar tone and jumping jazzy backdrops made him the role model for an entire generation of bluesmen. A former dancer, he was also a hugely extrovert performer, copyrighting many of the guitar-badman stunts (favourite: playing the guitar behind his head while sinking into a perfect splits) which subsequently provided such sterling service for CHUCK BERRY, BO DIDDLEY, GUITAR SLIM, BUDDY GUY, ALBERT COLLINS, JOHNNY GUITAR WATSON, JIMI HENDRIX and STEVIE RAY VAUGHAN. 'Stormy Monday' itself became part of the core repertoire of the blues: it's been recorded by B.B. King, Albert King, Albert Collins, LITTLE MILTON, BOBBY BLAND, JUNIOR WELLS (with Buddy Guy), JAMES COTTON, JIMMY WITHERSPOON, JOHN MAYALL, ELMORE JAMES, The Allman Brothers Band, Eddy Clearwater and countless others.

An intensely creative four-year stint with Imperial Records consolidated Walker's achievement, but a combination of deterio-rating health (due principally to overwork and incipient alcoho-lism) and shifts in black record-buyers' tastes (away from blues in favour of doo-wop, soul and rock) meant that his glory days were over. He continued to perform and record until his death from cancer in Los Angeles on 16 March 1975, but the results were mostly lacklustre: attempts by well-meaning record producers either to stage grandiose recreations of the T-Bone heyday, or to render him sufficiently far-out and groovy for the Now Genera-tion, both met with abject failure. Nevertheless, his contribution had been made: the hundred or so tracks he cut for Black & White and Imperial between 1946 and 1954 permanently altered the way that popular music is heard and played. Others who have drawn on the single-line, string-bending blues guitar school may look tall, but that's because they're standing on T-Bone Walker's shoulders.

- *Low Down Blues* (Charly CD CHARLY 7)
- *T-Bone Shuffle* (Charly CD BM)

The late '40s Black & White recordings that changed the world. Naturally including '(Call It) Stormy Monday', 'T-Bone Shuffle' and 'T-Bone Jumps Again', Low Down Blues is the place to start: its companion, drawing on the same catalogue, overlaps minimally but serves mainly to flesh out our picture of an entire genre in the making. Like all compilations constructed from singles by artists with definite musical signatures, it risks sameness, but the deftly swinging backdrops and the sheer wit and elegance of T-Bone's performances make it easy to imagine the impact of these sides on audiences and musicians who had never heard anything like it before for the simple reason that there never *had* been anything like it before. These are among the most influential blues sides ever recorded: virtually every urban bluesman borrowed something from here.

- *The Complete Imperial Recordings 1950–1954* (Imperial/EMI CDP-7-96737-2)
- *The Hustle Is On* (Sequel NEXCD 124)

The Black & White sessions defined T-Bone's approach; the Imperial years refined it. The bands get bigger, the arrangements more elaborate, and T-Bone gleefully rises to meet the occasion with increasing confidence and resourcefulness. It is a never-ending source of delight to hear T-Bone's guitar emerge – like a stunt flier from a deep cloud – out of the orchestral flourishes with which the solos on the up-tempo tunes almost invariably begin. Here's where you find 'Cold Cold Feeling', 'Tell Me What's The Reason' and 'Glamour Girl'; unfortunately, it's also where you find 'Pony Tail' and 'Teenage Baby' (no middle-aged man, with the possible exceptions of JOHN LEE HOOKER and Lemmy, has any business singing about pony tails and teenage babies). Never mind: like all the sets in this series, *The Complete Imperial Recordings 1950–1954* is beautifully packaged and annotated. *The Hustle Is On* is the same Imperial repertoire, filleted. Containing 28 of the 52 selections from the luxurious EMI double-pack, it's a less intimidating (as well as a less expensive) proposition, and it hits most of the high-spots, but – carp, carp, carp – it omits the superb 'Too Lazy' and 'I Walked Away'.

Subjects for further investigation: ***T-Bone Blues*** (Atlantic, 1960, unavailable) draws on sessions from 1955, 1958 and 1959 featuring guests ranging from Barney Kessel to Junior Wells, and was T-Bone's last best shot in the studio. ***American Folk Blues Festival '62*** (L&R/Bellaphon CDLR 42017) finds Bone as part of an all-star blues package touring Europe, performing 'I Wanna See My Baby', as well as playing guitar behind MEMPHIS SLIM and harpist Shakey Jake, and piano behind John Lee Hooker. 1968's ***Funky Town*** (BGO BGOCD 116) places Bone under the wing of producer Bob Thiele, manfully attempting to cope with the brave new world of Stax and JAMES BROWN, but whatever claims to the contrary the liner notes may make, the remake of his Imperial-era 'Party Girl' makes plain that he clearly wasn't comfortable with funk-accented beats and heav-*ee* guitar sounds.

Ike Turner

If Ike Turner had fallen under a bus sometime in 1959, he would ave gone down in cultural history as one of the most important figures in the development of '50s rhythm and blues. A notable performer (on both guitar and piano), bandleader, producer and talent scout, he became a key player in the Memphis scene of the early '50s and was instrumental in launching the careers of HOWLIN' WOLF (that's Ike's piano on Wolf's 'How Many More Years'), BOBBY BLAND and B.B. King, bringing them to the attention of Sam Phillips's Sun label and thence to Modern and Chess. With his band The Kings Of Rhythm, he recorded 'Rocket 88', released in 1951 under the name of The Kings' saxophonist Jackie Brenston (who wrote and sang it), which was not only an R&B chart Number One, but considered by many eminent musicologists to be the first true rock and roll record. (Others award that honorific to FATS DOMINO's 'The Fat Man', which came out at around the same time.)

Born on 5 November 1931, in Clarksdale, Mississippi, hometown to not a few other R&B greats, Turner played piano behind

Robert Nighthawk and SONNY BOY WILLIAMSON II while still in his teens. In 1954, he relocated to St Louis, where he was later to discover a brass-lunged young singer named Anna Mae Bullock, whom he hired, renamed 'Tina Turner' and later married. The rest of that particular story is too familiar to require retelling here, except to point out that the grim soap-opera of the Turners' professional and married life has somewhat overshadowed Ike's credentials as one of the great performer/entrepreneurs of the blues. He played a mean, spiky Stratocaster guitar style reminiscent of BUDDY GUY, OTIS RUSH (at least two of whose classic Cobra sides, 'All Your Love' and 'Double Trouble' – both later covered by JOHN MAYALL – feature Ike on second guitar) and his old pal ALBERT COLLINS (who, incidentally, ghosted some of the guitar solos on Ike & Tina's 1969 blues album *Outta Season* [Blue Thumb, unavailable] and inherited I&TT drummer Soko Richardson when the Ike & Tina Turner Revue went out of business); and sang/rapped in a threatening deadpan which he played for comedy as well as menace.

- **IKE TURNER'S KINGS OF RHYTHM:** *Trailblazer* (Charly CD CHARLY 263)

At these 1956–7 Cincinnati sessions, jump turns into rock and roll before your very ears. Vocalists Jackie Brenston (back, tail-between-legs, after his failure to follow up 'Rocket 88'), Billy Gayles and The Gardenias are the nominal frontpeople, but the real stars are Ike's guitar and band: check out the devastating bursts of Stratocaster abuse on Gayles's 'Just One More Time', 'I'm Tore Up' and 'No Coming Back'.

- **IKE & TINA TURNER:** *Too Hot To Hold* (Charly CDCD 1042)

This skimpily packaged budget collection is, regrettably, about as good as it currently gets. A few tracks from Outta Season are recycled here, including B.B. King's 'Rock Me Baby' and 'Please Love Me', and Bobby Bland's 'I Smell Trouble'; the latter, despite being a *tour de force* showpiece of I&TT's live concerts (and live recordings), featuring Albert Collins's guitar rather than Ike's.

Subjects for further investigation: Ike Turner the bluesman is, at the moment, poorly represented on CD. Apart from the bulk of the Kings Of Rhythm sides, key stuff you currently can't get on silver disk includes *Outta Season* and *The Hunter*, the two late-'60s blues albums he cut with Tina for Blue Thumb; and two solo albums, *Blues Roots* and *Bad Dreams*, recorded for Liberty in the early '70s and compiled in 1987 into Stateside's *Rockin' Blues*, though his version of Jimmy Liggins' brilliant 'I Ain't Drunk' (later revived by Albert Collins) can be located on *20 Great Blues Recordings Of The '50s and '60s* (Cascade CDROP 1005). His 'Cuban Getaway' (revived in the '90s by SUE FOLEY) is on *R&B Confidential No. 1: The Flair Label* (Ace CHCD 258), and two more sides are included in *20 Great R&B Hits Of The '50s* (Cascade CDROP 1001). His superb 1962 instrumental 'Prancin'' can be located on *The Blues Guitar Box* (Sequel TBB CD 47555), and 'Twistin' The Strings' can be hunted down either on *The Blues Guitar Box 2* (Sequel NXT CD 185), or on *Blues Guitar Blasters* (Ace CHCD 232). 'Rocket 88' is on *The Sun Story Volume 1: Sunrise* (Instant CD INS 5039) and, of course, on Jackie Brenston's *Rocket 88* (Chess CD RED 30); two tracks by 'Ike & Bonnie Turner' – an early shot at the Tina Experiment – are on *The Sun Blues Archives Vol. 6: Too Blue To Cry* (Sun CD SUN 38).

B.B. King

Let's hand this one over to the MC who does the honours on the Big B's 1966 live album *Blues Is King*: 'Ladies and gentlemens, at this time I'd like to introduce to you the biggest name in blues today. Ladies and gentlemens, the undisputed king of the blues, the world's greatest blues singer . . . let's hear it for Mr B.B. King!' That's about right, apart from the understatement. Despite the autumnal triumph of court shaman JOHN LEE HOOKER and the Roman spring of crown prince ROBERT CRAY, it's still B.B. King who is – just as surely as JAMES BROWN is still the Godfather Of Soul – the Chairman Of The Board Of Blues Singers, and – as the title of his 4-CD career-retrospective boxed set insists – the King Of The Blues. And if – as when he was the subject of an extraordinarily bilious diatribe in America's *Guitar World* magazine from CLARENCE 'GATEMOUTH' BROWN, his friend over a four-decade span – the head that wears that particular crown sometimes rests a trifle uneasily, then that simply comes with the territory.

To younger rock fans, B.B. King is the jovial, Falstaffian patriarch with the bullhorn voice and Lucille, the dancing guitar who beamed in a short but memorable Live Aid set back in '85, and practically stole U2's 'When Love Comes To Town' from under them. To blues buffs and guitar mavens, he's the man who literally wrote the book on postwar electric blues lead guitar; the man who knows more ways to bend and vibrate a note on his guitar Lucille than Madonna does to undress; who combines the roles of master musician and Beloved Entertainer more gracefully than anyone since Louis Armstrong. He grew up behind a plough in the Mississippi Delta, and he has been received in the White House by the President of the United States (pity it was only George Bush, though). To B.B. King himself, however, he is a man who has not yet fulfilled either his artistic or his commercial potentials; and, despite all his success and acclaim, he is still dissatisfied at 67. To the rest of the world, B.B. King is a titan, a legend, a demigod. To himself, he's an underachiever.

Born near Itta Bena, Mississippi – a place so small that you only find on the most highly detailed maps – on 25 September 1925, Riley 'Blues Boy' King arrived smack in the middle of the Blues Generation: he's a generous quarter-century younger than BIG BILL BROONZY or SONNY BOY WILLIAMSON II, fifteen years younger than HOWLIN' WOLF, ROBERT JOHNSON or T-BONE WALKER, ten years younger than MUDDY WATERS, five years younger than John Lee Hooker, a near-contemporary of ALBERT KING and Clarence 'Gatemouth' Brown, five years older than LITTLE WALTER and a decade or so older than BUDDY GUY or OTIS RUSH, not to mention having some twenty years or more on the likes of Keith Richards and ERIC CLAPTON and being a full three decades clear of STEVIE RAY VAUGHAN or Robert Cray. He began his musical career singing in church and on the streets, rapidly discovering that blues tunes gained him more tips than gospel songs.

When he was 23, he left Mississippi for a brief sojourn in Memphis, Tennessee, staying with his uncle, country bluesman Booker T. Washington 'BUKKA' WHITE'. Before long he was back to stay and within a couple of days, he was appearing on SONNY BOY WILLIAMSON's local radio show; and soon parlaying that into a show of his own. (During those early Memphis years, one of the faces on the scene was this funny-looking white boy named ELVIS PRESLEY.) B.B. cut his first record in 1949, and 'Three O'Clock Blues' – cut, like most of his records at the time, at the Sun studios in Memphis – gave him his first hit in 1951. He's been on the road ever since, as one of black America's favourite entertainers, regularly playing 300 or more shows a year, an astonishing total only recently cut back to a mere 250 or so. He moved from Modern Records to a major, ABC, in 1960; ABC already had RAY CHARLES and hoped that B.B. would follow Brother Ray into the affections of white record-buyers, but it took until 1968 – when MIKE BLOOMFIELD introduced him at San Francisco's Fillmore Auditorium and 'The Thrill Is Gone' put him into the pop charts and, eventually, onto *The Ed Sullivan Show* – before B.B. King was truly on his way. Since then, you name it and he's done it. He became the first blues star to play the major venues in Las Vegas; now he lives there, which means – according to some of his colleagues in the blues world – that he can be nearer the gambling tables which allegedly represent his only known vice.

What drove his music was the quest for self-improvement, the desire to beat the white world by becoming more than anybody could expect an unschooled Mississippi farmboy to be; what shaped it was a canny deejay's ear which enabled him to blend a new style of blues from the influences not only of bluesmen like BLIND LEMON JEFFERSON, T-Bone Walker and LONNIE JOHNSON, but those of jazz greats like Charlie Christian, Django Rheinhardt and Count Basie, blues balladeers like ROY BROWN, and pop ballad singers like Frank Sinatra and Tony Bennett. His absorption of these early inspirations enabled him to create vocal and guitar styles which were both instantly, distinctively recognisable, and capable of enormous variation. The guitar sound was thick and rich, but also agile and liquid, capping time-honoured blues riffs with elegant, jazzy embroideries; his formidable array of vocal techniques stretched from rough, tough Delta hollering to matinee-idol crooning and preacherly gospel fervour. His early repertoire demonstrated both his song-finding knack and his ability to convert the near-hits of others – LOWELL FULSON's 'Three O'Clock Blues', MEMPHIS SLIM's 'Every Day I Have The Blues', TAMPA RED's 'Sweet Black Angel' ('Sweet Little Angel' in B.B.'s version), LOUIS JORDAN's 'How Blue Can You Get', John Lee Hooker's 'It's My Own Fault', Arthur 'Big Boy' Crudup's 'Rock

Me' – into his own smashes. Even 'The Thrill Is Gone', the signature smash which transformed his career, was an old Roy Hawkins tune which B.B. had sat on for almost twenty years, eventually transforming it from a pleasant blues ballad into a string-enriched soul-cry which simultaneously contrived to be both silky-sophisticated and aching-raw.

He's recorded with everybody from the Duke Ellington Orchestra to Living Colour's Vernon Reid; from Leon Russell to his old Memphis chum BOBBY BLAND; from GARY MOORE to The Crusaders: his warm, expansive personality, dazzling guitar, rich, full-throated singing, eclectic tastes and sheer capacity for hard work have made him a true grandmaster of the blues: one of the pillars upon which the edifice of the music continues to rest. B.B. King began as an innovator and has become an institution; it is to his everlasting credit that institutional status is not enough for him. Though his live show has remained more or less the same for decades (give or take a new song here or there), his studio music continues to develop. After more than 40 years, he's still looking forward to the next record. And so are we.

- *King Of The Blues* (MCA MCAD4-10677)

The 4-CD full monty, stretching all the way from B.B.'s first-ever single (1949's 'Miss Martha King') to a swaggering live 1991 throwdown with GARY MOORE. On that first session, he sounds country as hell, despite the thickly amplified guitar; and the studio musicians are utterly confused by his downhome sense of time and metre. Nevertheless, he learned fast, and what's most apparent from this collection's four-decade sweep is the sheer consistency of his work. Not every single side he's ever cut could be described as 'great', but each and every period of his work has produced some wonderful music. Niggles: it's only natural that MCA – as inheritors of B.B.'s ABC catalogue – have somewhat under-represented the '50s Modern Records repertoire (which they've had to license from elsewhere), but there's no reason to edit out the guitar introduction to 'Gambler's Blues', one of the most exquisite choruses King has ever played (never mind, you can hear the whole thing on *Blues Is King . . . plus*), nor to avoid rescuing the gorgeous 'You Are Still My Woman' from the otherwise disappointing *Indianola Mississippi Seeds* album. Still, that's just carping: B.B.'s is one of the great stories of the blues, and the collection tells virtually all of it, letting us eavesdrop as the brash Delta farmboy becomes 'the Dynamic Gentleman Of The Blues'.

- *The Best Of B.B. King Vol. 1* (Ace CDCH 908)
- *The Best Of B.B. King Vol. 2* (Ace CDCH 199)

The Big B's '50s hits: some of the time he's a raunchy electric downhomer; at others he's a relaxed, swinging sophisticat; here he's the handsome young matinée proclaiming his devotion with lush ballads; there the jilted lover, either bitter or lachrymose. And everywhere the rhythm sections kick, the brass blares, and Lucille talks back. B.B. established both his repertoire and his reputation during these years: the first volume boasts 'Three O'Clock Blues', 'Every Day I Have The Blues', 'Sweet Sixteen', 'You Upset Me Baby' and 'Please Love Me'; the second 'Rock Me Baby', 'It's My Own Fault' and 'Bad Luck Soul', all of which reappear over and over again throughout his career, especially on his live albums. The sound of a legend not only being built, but earned.

- *Live At The Regal* (MCA MCAD-31106 [US])
- *Blues Is King . . . plus* (See For Miles SEECD 216)

The two great mid-'60s live albums, respectively from '64 and '66. It is a ludicrous state of affairs that *Live At The Regal*, one of the most famous and influential blues albums ever released, is only available in the UK as an import, but as a budget reissue its import price-tag is no greater than that of a full-price domestic release. Both albums were recorded in Chicago during a comparative career lull during which B.B. had cut his usual big band back to a six-piece; both feature him at his most extrovert, working over a delighted audience who're obviously loving every second; both feature his then-current repertoire done to an absolute turn; and both beat the crap out of all but the very best of his studio work. And both albums deserve every molecule of *Live At The Regal*'s exalted reputation. It's certainly the better-known of the pair, but I'd give *Blues Is King* the edge for a variety of reasons, some of them good ones: it was recorded in a club rather than a theatre and the audience response is thus that much more immediate; B.B. had a particularly gorgeous guitar sound that night, and his playing on the various slow blues selections is a personal best; and lastly because it was the first B.B. King album I ever owned, and in many ways it's still my favourite. The current issue of *Blues Is King* includes, as a bonus, both sides of a 2-part live single featuring an extended version of 'Sweet Sixteen' cut at the same show, but they remain tacked onto the end of the album as two separate cuts: neither edited back together nor integrated into the programme. For a fully restored version, you have to go to the *King Of The Blues* boxed set. Nevertheless, if you want to hear B.B. at his most powerful, this is where you go: he was never tougher.

- *Lucille* (BGO BGOCD 36)
- *Blues On Top Of Blues* (BGO BGOCD 69)

These two fine '68 studio albums are never less than solid, and occasionally they're positively inspired. Lucille is relaxed, charming, intimate: it opens with B.and his guitar delivering an autobiographical dialogue over a late-night blues groove; elsewhere he tackles LITTLE WILLIE JOHN's 'Need Your Love So Bad' – the version from which FLEETWOOD MAC's Peter Green learned the song – and LITTLE WALTER's 'Watch Yourself'. *Blues On Top Of Blues* is a bold, brassy mule-kick of an album, featuring the same road band as *Blues Is King* plus some extra horns for B. to shout at. This album, with a studio guitar sound considerably less subdued than it later became, spawned the R&B hit 'Paying The Cost To Be The Boss': still its best shot, though not by much.

- *His Best: The Electric B.B.King* (BGO BGOCD 37)
- *The Best Of B.B. King* (MCA CMCAD 31040)

Respectively, a pair of best-ofs filleting the early and late '60s, and compiled in 1968 and 1972. They track B.B.'s progress as he restocks his eroding fanbase of black adults: first with young white rock fans (documented on *His Best*), and then, capitalising on the resulting success of 'The Thrill Is Gone' by moving into Vegas casinos and plush nightclubs, with affluent white adults (as you can hear on *The Best Of*). *His Best* delivers bona-fide R&B chart hits like 'Paying The Cost To Be The Boss' and 'Don't Answer The Door'; some deep(ish) blues, and a couple of soundtrack excerpts from the Sidney Poitier vehicle *For The Love Of Ivy* which don't sound as if they overtaxed the combined compositional talents of Quincy Jones and Maya Angelou. *The Best Of* juxtaposes the traditional and the transitional: the new, suave 'The Thrill Is Gone' B.B. rubs studio shoulders with Leon Russell, Joe Walsh and sundry British rockers, while his timeless in-concert equivalent socks home 'How Blue Can You Get' to a captive audience at Cook County Jail and remakes 'Sweet Sixteen'.

- *Midnight Believer* (MCA DMCL 1802)

B.B.'s best studio shots of the '70s came from an alliance with The Crusaders: the veteran soul-jazzers turned jazz-funkers, working with lyricist Will Jenkins and producer Stewart Levine, gave him a mink-lined nightclub funk crisp enough to kick the ballads in the ass, and smooth enough not to frighten the white folks when the temperature starts to rise. *Midnight Believer* (1978) was first; *Take It Home*, released the following year and, annoyingly, currently unavailable on CD, was almost as good. (A full-length CD of the best of both is long overdue.) The Crusaders did everything right except neglecting to insist on simultaneous recording of B.B.'s guitar and vocal tracks: B. and Lucille don't quite sound as if they're in the same conversation. Nevertheless, these songs fit yer man like so many $1000 suits, and some are still in his live show. 'Hold On' is one of the most moving songs he's ever recorded, and 'Never Make A Move Too Soon' one of the funniest.

- *There Must Be A Better World Somewhere* (BGO BGOCD 124)

With material custom-composed by Mac 'DR JOHN' Rebennack (who plays exemplary piano throughout) and lyricist Doc Pomus, this 1981 session is one of the most satisfying studio album-as-album projects of B.B.'s entire career. The six-piece horn section includes former Ray Charles vets David 'Fathead' Newman (tenor) and Hank Crawford (alto), but it's deployed with considerable restraint and the focus is entirely on B.B. himself, rising splendidly to the occasion of his best batch of songs since the Crusaders sessions. It's a spare, committed performance: I wish he'd sink his teeth into songs as meaty as 'The Victim', the title track, and the bitterly ironic 'Life Ain't Nothin' But A Party' rather more often.

- *Live At San Quentin* (MCA DMCG 6103)
- *Live At The Apollo* (GRP GRD 9637)

B.B.'s most recent live albums, recorded in 1990 and 1991: the former, cut with his road band at one of his prison concerts, is a blast from start to finish. It's not only a fine account of his current performances – complete with 'Let The Good Times Roll', 'Every Day I Have The Blues', 'Sweet Little Angel', 'Never Make A Move Too Soon', 'The Thrill Is Gone', 'Sweet Sixteen' and 'Rock Me Baby' – but it benefits both from terrific audience rapport and the kind of thrillingly dirty guitar sound he rarely gets in the studio. The second, with an all-star 17-piece jazz band including Harry 'Sweets' Edison (trumpet), Kenny Burrell (guitar), Plas Johnson (tenor) and Ray Brown (bass), shares some repertoire with *San Quentin*; it has its moments but suffers both from an excess of gravitas and from a band which, despite its awesome collective gifts, simply doesn't speak B.B. King as its native language.

- *There Is Always One More Time* (MCAD 10295)

This 1991 reunion with Stewart Levine, Will Jennings and ex-Crusader Joe Sample is B.'s most recent studio date at the time of writing. It has less mink and more muscle than their first go-round, not to mention an elegiac spirit and a fine sense of drama. These days, B.B. does his best singing in the studio and his best guitar playing on stage, so it's as well that the songs amply repay the effort he puts into them. Apart from 1982's decidedly retro *Blues 'N' Jazz* (MCA, unavailable), it's his best studio album for over a decade. Songs like 'I'm Movin' On', the title piece, and 'The Blues Come Over Me' are nostalgic in content rather than form: for B.B. King, there *is* always one more time.

Subjects for further investigation: The more than adequate budget-price *The Fabulous B.B. King* (Ace CDFAB 004) provides a quick, inexpensive method of hitting the young King's highspots: seekers after '50s-style B. can also wallow in *Singing The Blues/The Blues* (Ace CDCHD 320), which doublebacks his first two albums;

the ballad-intensive *Heart & Soul* (Ace CDCH 376); the all-instrumental *Spotlight On Lucille* (Ace CDCH 187), and the outtake-crammed *My Sweet Little Angel* (Ace CDCHD 300). *In London* (BGO BGOCD 42) is a 1971 supersession involving – among others – Ringo Starr, ALEXIS KORNER, Dr John, Steve Marriott and his Humble Pie colleagues, Pink Floyd's Rick Wright, and a few overdubbed ringers from from NY and LA. Despite the novelty value of hearing B.B. do a few things he normally avoids, like playing acoustic guitar and working with a harp player, its best moments come from the Louis Jordan flagwaver 'Caldonia', and post-'The Thrill Is Gone' sophistifunkers like 'Ghetto Woman' and 'Ain't Nobody Home'; the first and third of these can be heard to better effect on *The Best Of B.B. King* (MCA CMCAD 31040). *Guess Who* (BGO BGOCD 71) and *Friends* (BGO BGOCD 125) are, respectively, second- and third-rate studio B.B. from the early '70s. B. is a consummate professional, and thus sounds good even when he's virtually 'phoning the parts in; but he's also a bluesman, and thus only sounds great when his heart is in the material. *Friends*, recorded in Philadelphia back when the Philly sound was hip, clocks in at a miserable 26 or so minutes: rotten value even on vinyl, and inexcusable on CD. His two mid-'70s team-ups with Bobby Bland – *Together For The First Time . . . Live* (BGO BGOCD 161) and *Together Again . . . Live* (BGO BGOCD 162) – catch musical fire only intermittently, but present an intriguing picture of the pressures placed on two close friends, both accustomed to absolute control of their performing environment, when they attempt to share the same stage.

Guitar Slim

One of the jobs RAY CHARLES did during a six-month New Orleans sojourn in 1953 was to arrange and play piano on a session for local bluesman Eddie 'Guitar Slim' Jones, who'd recently scored with 'The Story Of My Life'. The result was 'The Things That I Used To Do': a massive 1954 R&B hit, a much-covered (by, among others, JAMES BROWN, BUDDY GUY, MUDDY WATERS, IKE TURNER, LITTLE MILTON, ALBERT COLLINS, CHUCK BERRY, LONNIE BROOKS, and STEVIE RAY VAUGHAN) permanent addition to the standard blues repertoire. It was also a major vindication for Brother Ray's churchy take on the blues – with this under his belt, he had the clout to take far more control over his own Atlantic sessions, with stunning effect – and an introduction to the extrovert Mississippi-born guitarist whose contemporaries described him as the 'performin'est' bluesman of all. Guitar Slim (born in Greenwood, Mississippi on 10 December 1926) thought nothing of dyeing his hair blue and going on stage with suit and shoes to match, complete with 250-foot guitar cord. Enormously influential to young Louisiana bluesmen like Buddy Guy, Earl King and LONNIE 'Guitar Junior' BROOKS, his heyday was the early '50s, but a combination of ill-health and changing tastes lost Slim the kind of career momentum which even a label switch from Specialty to Atlantic couldn't cure. Sadly, Slim lacked both the physical stamina and the musical resources which enabled contemporaries like Ray Charles and B.B KING to develop and sustain their careers past the mid-'50s. He died in New York City on 7 February 1959.

- **_The Things That I Used To Do_** (Specialty/Ace CDCHD 318)

All the hits (well, 'The Things That I Used To Do' and 'The Story Of My Life', plus a bunch of other stuff both slow and anguished, and jumping and jivey). An entertaining package built around one hit and its variants, this is excellent value and thoroughly blues-approved. Slim's sawtoothed guitar sound, horn-driven backings and huge, urgent voice are impeccably commemorated on this collection.

Subjects For Further Investigation: **GUITAR SLIM JR: _The Story Of My Life_** (Sky Ranch SR 652311) or, to be more precise, 'The Story Of My Father's Life'. Rodney Armstrong, a.k.a. Guitar Slim Jr, is indeed the true, authentic son and heir of Eddie Jones, and the bulk of this album is dedicated to reinterpretations of Senior's catalogue (though, interestingly enough, he avoids 'The Things That I Used To Do'), which was probably a sound commercial decision as well as a deeply-felt personal project. However, he's a fine singer and guitarist in his own right; and now that he's got this heritage move out of the way, he's presumably ready to step out and explore his own identity. Trivia note: Slim's widow later married another distinguished singer/guitarist, LOWELL FULSON. By

225

the way, if you're certain that 'The Things That I Used To Do' is all the Guitar Slim you need, you'll find it on *Creole Kings Of New Orleans* (Specialty/Ace CDCHD 393) nestling alongside exemplary material from Lloyd Price, PROFESSOR LONGHAIR, PERCY MAYFIELD, Art Neville, CLIFTON CHENIER, Joe Liggins *et al*. But it's not.

Bobby 'Blue' Bland

Bobby Bland is unique among major-league bluesmen because he neither composes nor plays an instrument: his gifts are purely vocal. Nevertheless, to state that Bland is 'only' a singer is as misleading as it would be to claim that Yehudi Menuhin is 'only' a violinist: he is one of the true vocal virtuosi of this music, and while the blues is the emotional and musical centre of his work, he's equally comfortable with soul, gospel, jazz, country and the 'quality' ballad. The Bland style is sophisticated and dramatic while the Bland voice is huge, warm, grainy: on the more intimate pieces the power is held in reserve, and when the brassy powerhouse bands he favours crank up, Bland can crank right up there with them. Yet, for all his intimidating vocal muscle, what has made Bland a firm favourite of Southern black audiences for three and a half decades has been the quality and intensity of his emotional expression. He's a big fat man with a big fat soul: when Bobby Bland says he loves you, you *know* he loves you. And when he lets loose with the choked *skrrawwk* that is his most distinctive (and most frequently parodied) vocal device, you know that he's either feeling very good or very bad. And you feel it right along with him.

Robert Calvin Bland was born on 27 January 1930 in Rosemark, Tennessee; he moved to Memphis as a teenager, sung some gospel and hung out with fellow aspirers like B.B. KING (as whose on-the-road chauffeur/valet he served for a short while in the early '50s), Johnny Ace and Rosco Gordon. In 1951 he cut a few tracks for the pre-Sun Sam Phillips; the masters were sold to Chess and subsequent sessions ended up on Modern. A deal with Don Robey's Houston-based Duke label followed, and this arrangement stood until ABC purchased Duke in 1973, by which time Bland was one of the biggest stars in rhythm and blues. (Only RAY

CHARLES, JAMES BROWN and FATS DOMINO have bettered his score of forty R&B chart entries in eighteen years.) ABC was, in turn, absorbed by MCA, who didn't know how to handle a major R&B artist with no significant white following. Currently, Bland records for the Mississippi-based Malaco label, playing to the constituency who have always supported him: any night he plays the Clarksdale Civic Auditorium is a major event in the Delta social calendar.

● *The '3B' Blues Boy: The Blues Years 1952–1959* (Ace CDCHD 302)

The '3B' tag refers to Bland's original byline of 'Bobby "Blue" Bland': they might as well have made it '4B' since he was often known as 'Big Bobby "Blue" Bland'. Here we find a gifted neophyte struggling to locate and define a unique voice and style of his own: about halfway through this selection of tracks cut for the Modern and Duke labels, he finds it. With his 1957 recordings of 'I Smell Trouble' (revived in the early '70s by IKE & Tina TURNER, and again in the mid-'80s by JOHNNY WINTER) and 'Further (On) Up The Road' (later a favourite of, among others, FREDDIE KING and ERIC CLAPTON), the boy became the man . . . and I mean The Man! The fabulous guitar is by Clarence Holliman: the wonderful Wayne Bennett can be heard giving it some serious B.B. on Bland's '60s sides.

● *The Voice: Duke Recordings 1959–1969* (Ace CDCHD 323)

If you only acquire one Bobby Bland CD, this is the one to get. It refrains from calling itself *The Best Of Bobby Bland*, but only the niggliest purist would possibly complain if it did. Crammed full of R&B chart smashes (and not a few pop hits), this 26-track goodie-box is the ideal one-disc Bobby Bland primer: an absolute feast of swinging, soulful, brass-backed ballads and blues. 'Turn On Your Lovelight', 'Ain't Nothin' You Can Do', 'I Pity The Fool', 'Call On Me', 'Two Steps From The Blues', 'That Did It', 'Chains Of Love' – they're all here and they're all sublime.

- *His California Album* (BGO BGCD 64)
- *Dreamer* (BGO BGCD 63)

From 1973 and 1974 respectively, these two ABC albums set the style for the '70s Bland oeuvre: heavily orchestrated deep soul performed by the cream of the Los Angeles studio mafia under the supervision of Steve Barri and Michael Omartian. There's plenty of fluff here alongside gems like 'Ain't No Love In The Heart Of The City' and 'I Wouldn't Treat A Dog (The Way You Treated Me)', the glorious one-two punch which opens *Dreamer*: these albums, plus the intermittently excellent but currently unavailable *Reflections In Blues* (ABC,1977), would reduce down to a superb compilation. Maybe one of these days someone will get around to doing it.

- *First Class Blues* (Malaco MAL-5000-CD)

Though it hedges its bets by borrowing 'Two Steps From The Blues' and 'St James Infirmary' from the Duke era, this 1987 compilation is a more than satisfactory update on Bland's Malaco years. The Malaco aesthetic – a richly earthy Southern fusion of '60s-style deep soul and urban blues: without a doubt the dominant blues idiom of the contemporary rural South – was essentially derived from Bland's work, so it's fitting that that's where he ended up. Despite markedly coarsened pipes, some of these records, like 'Members Only' and 'After All', are among the sweetest of his entire distinguished career.

Subjects for further investigation: The most celebrated album-as-album of Bland's entire career was 1961's *Two Steps From The Blues* (BGO BGOCD 163), which was the most successful blues album extant until the arrival of ROBERT CRAY's *Strong Persuader*: six of its twelve tracks reappear on *The Voice* and one more on *The '3B' Blues Boy*. The first thing ABC did upon acquiring Bland's services was to team him up with B.B. King for *Together For The First Time . . . Live* (BGO BGOCD 161) and *Together Again . . . Live* (BGO BGOCD 162): not so much great music as an intriguing documentary of the tension between personal friendship and professional rivalry. The definitive one-volume guide to Malaco is *The Best Of Blues And Soul* (Malaco MAL CD341) which opens up, appropriately enough, with Bland's 'Members Only' and includes contributions from the late Z.Z. Hill ('I'm A Blues Man' and 'Cheatin' In The Next Room'), the huge, salty-voiced Denise LaSalle ('Don't Mess With My Man' and 'Down Home Blues') and LITTLE MILTON ('The Blues Is Alright' and 'Nobody Sleepin' In My Bed But Me') as well as fine stuff from Latimore, Johnnie Taylor, McKinley Mitchell and Dorothy Moore. B.B. King's decidedly pre-Malaco 'Sweet Sixteen' also shows up: God knows why, but it never hurts to hear it again. Hill, the prime inheritor of the Bland legacy, a major influence on Robert Cray, and Malaco's flagship act during the early '80s, is splendidly represented by *The Best Of Z.Z. Hill* (Malaco MAL CD342), which collects 17 examples of his work, including the anthems 'Down Home Blues', 'I'm A Blues Man' and, of course, 'Cheatin' In The Next Room'; his '60s Kent recordings can be found on *The Down Home Soul Of Z.Z. Hill* (Kent CDKEN 099). Two early-'70s Denise LaSalle albums are paired on *On The Loose/Trapped By A Thing Called Love* (Westbound CDSEWD 018). The nearest contemporary equivalent is the work of Robert Cray: if pop and rock audiences ever abandon Young Bob (which, at the moment, seems pretty unlikely), Malaco will fit him like a glove.

Lowell Fulson

Always a bridesmaid, never a bride (3): singer/guitarist Lowell Fulson (or 'Fulsom', as some sleeve- and label-copy occasionally had it) was often so far ahead of his time that it's almost pitiful. At the tender age of 18, he joined the long line of distinguished guitarists to accompany country blues singer Texas Alexander – his predecessors had included BLIND LEMON JEFFERSON, LIGHTNIN' HOPKINS and LONNIE JOHNSON – and after emerging from the US Navy in 1945, began recording country blues on the West Coast with his brother Martin. One of his songs from that period, 'Three O'Clock Blues', later became the basis for B.B. KING's first big hit. Correctly assuming that unreconstructed country blues had little immediate future, he shifted to jump; it was his 1950 hit version of MEMPHIS SLIM's 'Every Day I Have The Blues' which was adapted by B.B. as a perennial signature tune; and his early

sidemen included the then-unknown saxophonist Stanley Tur-
rentine, and a young pianist/singer named RAY CHARLES. In 1954, he
composed and recorded the enduring 'Reconsider Baby', later
covered by ELVIS PRESLEY and BOBBY BLAND, for Chess; his 'Blue
Shadows Falling' became a staple for Junior Parker; his 'Talkin'
Woman' (retitled 'Honey Hush') is a keystone of ALBERT COLLINS's
repertoire, and his guitar style undoubtedly influenced Collins.
Switching styles to soulful, funky R&B in the mid-'60s, he
returned to the charts with 'Tramp', which soon became a
worldwide hit for Otis Redding & Carla Thomas, and was revived
a quarter-century or so later by rappers Salt 'N' Pepa. So why isn't
this man a star?

Well, it's certainly nothing to do with shortage of talent, though
it takes more than just talent to be a B.B. Fulson – born in Tulsa,
Oklahoma, on 31 March 1921, of Native American and African-
American parentage – is a Southwestern bluesman in the grand
manner: big voice, sharp thumbpicked guitar, hip songs. It may be
because he never attracted the patronage of influential white
bluesrockers; or because his various record companies never
applied serious promotional leverage to establishing him outside
the traditional R&B market; or perhaps because, for all his
manifest talents, he lacks the sheer charisma of a B.B. King,
MUDDY WATERS, BUDDY GUY or JOHN LEE HOOKER. He's still active,
currently commuting between Texas and California, and recording for the Black Top label, and he's still good value.

● *Reconsider Baby* (Chess CD RED 15)

With its loping groove, droning horns, angular guitar, evocative
lyric and passionate vocal, the 1954 title track of this collection is
an absolute masterpiece. There's literally not a false move from
end to end, and the interplay between Fulson's guitar and Paul
Drake's piano is the equal of anything that Fulson does elsewhere
on this disk with the rather more celebrated Lloyd Glenn. It was
a considerable hit, which is why it casts a fairly long shadow over
the other 23 tracks, recorded in Dallas, L.A. and Chicago between
1954 and 1962; the most extreme example is the sequel song 'So
Glad You Reconsidered'. The occasional variants, like the rolling
Nwawlins groove of 'I Want To Make Love To You' or the
barnstorming 'Rock This Morning', are therefore welcome

changes of pace from the regular shuffles-and-ballads fare, but it's soulful, swinging, sophisticated and generally a fine showcase for Fulson's approachable voice and tricky guitar.

- *Tramp/Soul* (Ace CDCHD 339)

Two doublebacked albums, comprising material from 1966–7 and 1965–6 respectively, presumably sequenced this way so that the CD leads off with the title track of *Tramp*. At this point, Fulson (billed, incidentally, as 'Lowell *Fulsom*') was being marketed as a contemporary soul man, and these albums mix forays into ALBERT KING-style funk-blues with pretty much the mixture as before, only with a less interesting band. He handles the '60s grooves with considerable aplomb, but still sounds more at home with the shuffles and slow blues. Big fun: 'My Achin' Back'.

Subjects for further investigation: The earliest Fulson currently in catalogue is on *San Francisco Blues* (Black Lion BLCD 760176): small-group sides from 1946–51 and highly enjoyable, too; but the crucial postwar country blues and small-combo stuff will have to wait until Ace, the current distributors of Arhoolie Records, who control this material, recompile and reissue it for CD. If you want 'Reconsider Baby' but not *Reconsider Baby*, there's no shortage of options: it's on *Blues Masters Vol. 1: Urban Blues* (Rhino R2 71121); *The Blues Guitar Box* (Sequel TBB CD 47555); *Comin' Home To The Blues Vol. II* (Music Club MCCD 0226); *The Best Of Chess Blues Vol. 1* (MCA/Chess CHD-31315); and *Chess Blues* (MCA/Chess CHD4-9340). Elvis Presley's version is, not surprisingly, on *Reconsider Baby* (RCA PD 85418). The '88 sessions on *It's A Good Day* (Rounder CD 2088) take a relaxed, enthusiastic, spry-sounding Fulson back both to his late '40s/early '50s sound, and to the funk-blues '60s. The guitar has aged better than the voice, but it's engaging if not exactly indispensable. Otis Redding & Carla Thomas's dozens-trading version of 'Tramp' is on *The Otis Redding Story* (Atlantic 781 762-2): Salt 'N' Pepa's on *The Greatest Hits* (ffrr 828291 2).

Clarence 'Gatemouth' Brown

The word according to Gate: the Louisiana-born, Texas-bred multi-instrumentalist Clarence 'Gatemouth' Brown says that he isn't a blues musician. He also says that he isn't a country musician, a jazz musician, a zydeco musician, a calypso musician, or anything else: he's simply an American musician who plays world music, Texas-style. Nevertheless, he made his name in the late '40s as one of the first wave of electric blues guitarists to emerge in the wake of T-BONE WALKER, recording a string of brash, brassy post-jump singles very much in the T-Bone mould for Don Robey's Houston-based Peacock label. A formidable entertainer who taught the likes of GUITAR SLIM, ALBERT COLLINS and BUDDY GUY a thing or two about how to work an audience, Brown was even able to give T-Bone himself a run for his money: his first break came when he leapt onto the bandsdtand at Robey's Bronze Peacock club, picked up the guitar recently discarded by a 'temporarily indisposed' T-Bone, and tore up the house.

Never one to be trapped in one bag, Gate used his formidable expertise on fiddle and harmonica to establish a presence in country music (becoming a regular on Roy Clark's *Hee-Haw* TV show in the '60s; in performance he's quite likely to follow a Louisiana fiddle tune with an Ellington number with a brassy, swinging Texas blues. Gate cuts an impressive, Mephistophelean figure: tall, cadaverously lean, goateed, always immaculately decked out in black Stetson and designer cowboy duds, and with an ever-present pipe clenched between his teeth. Born in Vinton, Louisiana, on April 18, 1924, he currently divides his time between touring on the blues, jazz and country circuits; fulfilling his duties as an honorary deputy sheriff in his local police force; and giving cantankerous-old-sod interviews denouncing all blues singers both for their alleged musical limitations and for the sexual immorality of their music. Incidentally, his brother – also a singer/guitarist – was known as James 'Widemouth' Brown.

● *The Original Peacock Recordings* (Rounder CD 2039)

The classic '50s Gate: blazing horns, tricky licks and an immaculate sense of when to respect the eternal verities of Texas swing and when to drop-kick them into the middle distance. The range stretches from the wailing, anguished slow blues 'Dirty Work At The Crossroads' and the LOUIS JORDAN-style post-jump of 'Hurry Back Good News' to the bouncy country-ish 'That's Your Daddy Yaddy Yo' and Gate's trademark instrumental showstopper 'Okie Dokie Stomp.' He flashes the harp on 'Gate's Salty Blues' and the fiddle on 'Just Before Dawn'; in its way, it's as solidly entertaining as sophisticated '50s blues ever gets. Special 'disingenuousness in packaging' caveat: Charly Records released some of this material on vinyl under the highly appropriate title *San Antonio Ballbuster*: they're currently using that title, complete with splendid 1940's cover shot of Young Gate in a Big Suit, for a perfectly adequate set of '65 Nashville recordings (Charly CD BM 6), including two takes of the country novelty 'May The Bird Of Paradise Fly Up Your Nose', a remake of 'Gate's Salty Blues' (with some highly swinging fiddle) and three SONNY BOY WILLIAMSON tunes. Nothing wrong with this material, but it ain't what it looks like.

- **Texas Swing** (Rounder CD 11527)

A thoughtful 17-cut single-CD fillet of two of Gate's most successful contemporary recordings: the 1982 Grammy-winner *Alright Again!* (Rounder CD 2028) and the following year's Grammy-nominated sequel *One More Mile* (Rounder CD 2034). *Texas Swing* manages to round up nine out of ten tracks from the first (unfortunately, the loser is the liting Louisiana groove of 'Honey In The Be-Bo'), and eight out of ten from the second (sadly, not the rollicking fiddle feature 'Sunrise Cajun Style' or the Basie-esque instrumental blaster 'Flippin' Out'). This is one of those collections where 'highlights' are the rule rather than the exception, but respect is due to Gate's all-time slow-blues fiddle masterpiece 'Song For Renée', originally from *One More Mile*; and the marvellous double-whammy of Albert Collins's 'Frosty' and T-Bone Walker's 'Strollin' With Bones' which leads off both the compilation and *Alright Again!* In an ideal world, anyone with a weakness for hard-charging, brassy Texas blues would have the complete editions of both *Alright Again!* and *One More Mile*; but, bearing in mind that life is full of small disappointments, *Texas Swing* is a bargain and a half.

- **Real Life** (Rounder CD 2054)

Gate live in '85, playing PERCY MAYFIELD ('Please Send Me Somone To Love'), Duke Ellington ('Take The A Train', *wicked*), W.C. Handy ('St Louis Blues') and Gatemouth Brown (yep, 'Okie Dokie Stomp', among others); plus an insane reggae-fied chicken-pickin' instrumental version of 'Frankie And Johnny.' Plenty of priceless moments – and Gate's 'beloved entertainer' schtick is never less than engaging – but the studio albums win on focus.

- **Standing My Ground** (Alligator ALCd 4779)
- **No Looking Back** (Alligator ALCD 5904)

From '89 and '92, the latest and Gate-est: *Standing My Ground* opens up with a ridiculously bumpy funk take on MUDDY WATERS's 'Got My Mojo Working' (based, perversely, on JIMMY SMITH's version, and credited to 'Foster' – who he?); it also includes his manifesto 'I Hate This Doggone Blues', and Gate compensates for the absence of harmonica by playing indifferent drums on 'She Walks Right In' and banging out a creditable piano solo on 'Never Unpack Your Suitcase'. He then tops it by playing a guitar solo. *No Looking Back* leads with 'Better Off With The Blues' (composed by Nicholson, Fritz & [presumably Delbert] McClinton), as sophisticated a slow blues about the mixed feelings with which a relationship ends as anyone has ever written. It also boasts one piquant Nwawlins funk instrumental ('Stop Time'), an Ellington ('C Jam Blues'), a fine original blues in 'My Own Prison', a duet with Michelle Shocked, and a song about Gate's dog. Both very cool albums, but don't even think about buying either until you've checked out *The Original Peacock Recordings* and *Texas Swing*.

Albert King

Few bluesmen exerted as powerful an influence over both contemporaries and juniors as Albert King. ERIC CLAPTON, JIMI HENDRIX, MICHAEL BLOOMFIELD, ROBERT CRAY, STEVIE RAY VAUGHAN, JOE LOUIS WALKER and GARY MOORE have all fallen helplessly under the spell that the late Albert King cast with his big, warm, foggy croon and his merciless, clawing guitar: JIMI HENDRIX used to sing Albert

King's solos note-for-note as a party trick. 'How can he sing so sweet and play so dirty?' a bystander is reported to have asked at one of King's '60s ghetto shows, before he made his breakthrough to 'the love crowd' with a 1968 Fillmore West concert where he opened the show for Hendrix and JOHN MAYALL. A huge man with a quietly commanding stage presence, he was fond of wandering onstage with a pipe in his mouth, unhurriedly sorting out his cables and adjusting his amp while his backing band played his warm-up theme, Herbie Hancock's 'Watermelon Man'. What rendered his work so mesmeric is a pair of twinned tensions: on the one hand between the furry, reassuring voice and that mean, vicious guitar, and his unique combination of reticence and aggression on the other. Perhaps we can add a third: the tension between the monumental simplicity of his vocal and instrumental stylings and the sophistication of the funk-blues backdrops against which he invariably works. The fact that his most successful and memorable records were cut for the Stax label in the latter half of the '60s with the participation of Booker T & The MGs and The Memphis Horns – the same firm responsible for the great Sam & Dave and Otis Redding sides of the same period – hasn't hurt much, either.

Albert King, who died of a heart attack in Memphis, Tennessee, on 21 December 1992, was born Albert Nelson in Indianola, Mississippi, on 25 April 1923: just two years before his more illustrious near-namesake Riley 'B.B.' KING put in his first appearance in nearby Itta Bena. For a time, Albert's record companies' PR hacks claimed that he and B.B. were half-brothers: this claim is utterly unfounded, despite the facts that Albert's guitar is nicknamed 'Lucy' in thinly disguised *hommage* to B.B.'s 'Lucille', the name 'Albert' is a popular one within B.B.'s family, and that B.B.'s own father's name was . . . Albert King. Raised in Forrest City, Arkansas, he spent some time in Chicago before settling in St Louis, driving bulldozers and moonlighting as a drummer – for JIMMY REED, amongst others – while honing his utterly distinctive approach to electric blues guitar and fighting it out in the clubs with other local attractions like IKE TURNER's Kings Of Rhythm and LITTLE MILTON. (Ironically enough, SON SEALS – now established as one of the preeminent stylists of Chicago blues guitar – himself spent some time as Albert King's drummer.) A self-taught, left-handed guitarist, King's unique sound derives in part from his unusual techniques: he played his Gibson Flying V guitar strung back-to-front (i.e. with the high strings uppermost and the bass strings at the bottom), and open-tuned to the chord of C minor. He recorded for the King, Bobbin and Chess labels throughout the '50s and early '60s before signing to Stax in 1966 and making that all-important breakthrough to the contemporary rock and soul audiences: simultaneously scoring R&B hit after R&B hit on the soul charts and wowing the San Francisco hipoisie at the Fillmore Auditorium. King moved to Tomato Records after Stax's demise, and cut two unmemorable albums for Fantasy Records in the early '80s: *San Francisco '83* – reissued on CD, with extra tracks, as *Crosscut Saw: Albert King In San Francisco* (Stax CDSXE 076) – and the following year's *I'm In A Phone Booth, Baby* (Stax CDSXE 083), featuring his version of the then little-known ROBERT CRAY's 'Phone Booth'. He recorded infrequently in his latter years – his last album was the lacklustre *Red House* (Essential ESSCD 147 [1991]) – and the heart seemed to have gone out of his most recent performances. Nevertheless, he was one of a handful of musicians who can truly be said to have made irreplaceable contributions to the basic vocabulary of modern blues guitar: Clapton regurgitated King's principal solo from 'Oh Pretty Woman' note for note on Cream's 'Strange Brew' [1967], and Mark Knopfler and Stevie Ray Vaughan played unadulterated Albert King pastiches on, respectively, Bob Dylan's *Slow Train Coming* [1979] and David Bowie's *Let's Dance* [1983].

The essentials of the Albert King guitar style are tone and phrasing. Playing without a pick and sounding every note with downstrokes of his thumb, he coaxed the broadest, richest sound of any blues guitarist from his Flying V and his big old Acoustic amplifier. He was never a fast, fluent, flashy guitarist: his power derived from his impeccable timing rather from the kind of voluble frenzy beloved of white rock guitarists. In-concert albums like 1968's *Live Wire/Blues Power* demonstrate his unparalleled mastery of dynamics: his ability to build remorselessly to a raging climax and cut everything back to barely a whisper before repeating the same stunt two or three times, each time with greater and greater impact, within the space of a single song. (Is there anything *sexual* in this? Discuss, writing on only one side of the paper.) King's rhythmic flexibility also stood him in good stead by time and time again enabling him to adapt to changes in musical fashion without ever compromising the fundamental values of his music: he has shifted effortlessly from the basic swing, jump, shuffle and slow-blues tempi of the bluesmen of the '40s and '50s to the syncopated country funk of the '60s Stax house band and beyond to the lush bedroom soul and sophisticated street-funk of the '70s. Despite the tremendous contributions made by BUDDY GUY, OTIS RUSH, FREDDIE KING and ALBERT COLLINS, Albert King's primacy as an architect of contemporary blues guitar could be challenged only by B.B. KING and the late T-BONE WALKER. He is one of the dozen or so artists in this book whom you most urgently need to hear.

- *King Of The Blues Guitar* (Atlantic 8213-2 [US])

. . . and this is where you start. 'I'm gonna give every disc-jockey the blues across the country,' announces Albert in 'Cold Feet'; 'if you don't dig this you got a hole in your soul.' You know what? He's right. *King Of The Blues Guitar* gathers together the fruits of Albert's first two years with Stax: dance-your-ass-off funk epics like 'I Love Lucy' and 'Cold Feet', blues guitar primers like 'Oh Pretty Woman', 'Crosscut Saw' and 'Born Under A Bad Sign', snappy instrumentals like 'Overall Junction' and 'Funk-Shun', heart-wrenching love-gone-bad melodramas like 'As The Years Go Passing By', 'I Almost Lost My Mind', 'You're Gonna Need Me' and 'You Sure Drive A Hard Bargain', plenty of killer slow blues like 'Personal Manager' and 'Laundromat Blues' and even a straight cabaret-blues reading of 'The Very Thought Of You'. This CD repackage bulks up the original vinyl release with an extra five tracks drawn from B-sides and other sources, adding up to a 17-track, 53-minute delight. Albert's guitar sizzles like a hot iron suddenly shoved into a bucket of ice-water, while Booker T & The MGs (guitarist Steve Cropper, bassist Duck Dunn, drummer Al Jackson Jr, and Booker T himself on keys) and The Memphis Horns alternate the kicking grooves which they put behind Sam & Dave and Otis Redding with classic Memphis-synthesis swing-blues moves. It's not currently available in the UK on a domestic release, but your nearest branch of Tower Records will be delighted to sell it to you for around the price of a regular British product. Trust me: if you only have one Albert King album, make it this one. Hell, if you only have one blues album from the '60s, make it this one. If I was in the business of star-rating the albums in this book from one to five, this would rate a six.

- *I'll Play The Blues For You: The Best Of Albert King* (Stax CDSX 007)

. . . or 'What Albert Did Next'. It's not quite 'The Best Of Albert King' for the simple reason that it's not *King Of The Blues Guitar*, but after a curtain-raising reprise of the original version of 'Born Under A Bad Sign' it picks up where the earlier album left off: in other words, after Stax switched their distribution from Atlantic to Gulf & Western in 1968. The rights to material from the two Stax 'eras' are controlled by different companies, which is why the two catalogues remain separate, but the two albums dovetail quite neatly: Albert revisits early material like 'Laundromat Blues' and 'Crosscut Saw' (the former opens up with a menacingly misogynistic monologue worthy of either Peetie Wheatstraw or Ice Cube, while the latter gets a popping, syncopated '70s funk attack) and takes his street-funk blues into the lusher orchestral pastures of his Stax stablemate Isaac Hayes. Not to be confused with a 1972 album also called *I'll Play The Blues For You* (currently available, coupled with 1971's *Lovejoy*, on Stax CD-SXD 969), from which it borrows four tracks including the title tune.

- *Live Wire/Blues Power* (Stax CDSXE 022)
- *Live* (Charly CD BM 18)

Live Wire/Blues Power was Albert's meet-the-hippies triumph, complete with a cover shot of the great man with a flower in his mouth looking for all the world like Ferdinand The Bull. It abstains from revisiting King's core repertore or Greatest Hits, instead concentrating primarily on powerhouse instrumentals, fast and slow; and cosy homilies on the expressive and curative powers of the blues. King gives a disgracefully hammy and manipulative performance which is nevertheless outrageously enjoyable: the album depicts a man at the height of his powers, joyfully aided and abetted by a band and audience prepared to go the distance with him. *Live* catches him almost a decade later at the Montreux Jazz Festival, steaming through his standard '70s repertoire (plus the venerable chestnuts 'Stormy Monday' and 'Kansas City') with titanic zest. A double-LP cut down to a single CD, this reissue loses the equivalent of a full side of the vinyl original (which is why I'll be keeping mine despite welcoming this CD), and it's the side with King's reworking of BLIND LEMON JEFFERSON's 'Matchbox', and 'Jam In A Flat': the latter a sprawling 15-minute throwdown featuring RORY GALLAGHER, LOWELL FULSON and Louisiana Red. Still, *Live* presents 67 minutes of The Baddest Of Albert King, which means it's *plenty* bad.

● *Blues For Elvis* (Stax CDSXE 073)

Whose idea *was* this, anyway? Originally released in 1969 under the somewhat unwieldy title of *King Does The King's Things*, this relaxed saunter through the ELVIS PRESLEY repertoire is something of an oddity, though an entertaining one. One distinguished adopted Memphian pays sly, funky tribute to another, though Albert seems to be amusing himself by attempting to turn every song into 'Crosscut Saw'. The highlights include a severely rocking 'Don't Be Cruel' and a gorgeous instrumental reading of 'One Night'; an extra bonus for veteran Elvis-watchers is a sleeve-note by none other than Albert Goldman, who rhapsodises about 'Elvis' novacaine [sic] lip, his pale poached face, with the sweat drippin' down on that black leather jacket'. I love it when he talks dirty like that . . .

● *I Wanna Get Funky* (Stax SCD 8536-2 [US])

Of all the Albert King studio recordings post-dating the 'classic Stax' era, this wide-screen epic of funk-blues-as-psychodrama is easily the finest. Cut in 1976 with the next-generation Stax studio crew – The Bar-Kays – augmented by guitarist Donald Kinsey (the album's only formally credited rhythm section player, albeit with his surname misspelled as 'Kenzie') who went on to play with Bob Marley, Peter Tosh and his own KINSEY REPORT, plus a veritable battalion of string and horn players, it opens with a masterpiece of latenight smoochiness – the title track – and thereafter juxtaposes moments of high drama (a rework of LITTLE MILTON's 'Walking The Back Streets And Crying' which easily eclipses the original), wry humour ("Til My Back Ain't Got No Bone'), genuine pathos ('I

Can't Hear Nothin' But The Blues'), cynical realism ('That's What The Blues Is All About') and lots of general funking around.

- *The Big Blues* (King KCD 852)

Apart from a few 1953 and 1961 Chess numbers, the crucial pre-Stax Albert King tracks can be found here on this collection of mid-'50s-through-mid-'60s tunes cut for the Bobbin and King labels. Strutting his searing stuff against rather more mainstream jump-blues backdrops than on the various Stax issues, King hones his vocal and instrumental chops on standard swing, shuffle, slow-blues and rhumba grooves, laying repertoire foundation-stones like 'Don't Throw Your Love On Me So Strong', 'Goin' To California', 'I Get Evil' and 'Let's Have A Natural Ball' (this last borrowed from T-BONE WALKER, but who's keeping score?) This is the sound of a giant in embryo: the bluesical equivalent of finding a youthful incarnation of your favourite actor starring in a generic but well-made B-movie on late-night TV.

Subjects for further investigation: **Wednesday Night In San Francisco** (Stax CDSXE 031) and **Thursday Night In San Francisco** (Stax SXCDE 032) represent the outtakes from the *Live Wire/Blues Power* Fillmore West sessions: the repertoire is loaded with standards – both King's and other people's – and a blues-approved good time is had by all. 1973's **Blues At Sunrise** (Stax CDSXE 017) is an earlier shot at the Montreux Jazz Festival, backed by one of his finest-ever road bands (including a three-piece horn section and the indefatigable Donald Kinsey); three extra titles from the same show pop up on **Montreux Festival** (Stax CDSXE 070), alongside performances by Chico Hamilton and Little Milton; and there's yet more live Albert on **Wattstax: The Living Word** (Stax CDSXE2 079), where he lines up with, among others, Isaac Hayes, Rufus Thomas, The Staple Singers, and The Bar-Kays. **Vintage Blues** (Chess CD RED 9) and **So Many Roads** (Charly CD BM 2) both juxtapose the remaining early A.K. material (three 1953 tracks from his first-ever session, plus five 1961 sides) with some rather more essential 1960 OTIS RUSH titles, but since *Vintage Blues* also throws in four fine OTIS SPANN cuts and five from the incredibly obscure John Brim – one of which, 'Ice Cream Man', was covered by, of all people, Van Halen – it's the one to get. **The Lost Session**

(Stax CDSXE 106), recorded in 1971 but unreleased until 1986, is an intriguing curio: arranged and produced by John Mayall on a single studio day with an all-original book co-composed by King and Mayall, it features a looser, jazzier band than the usual King accompanists, and is genuinely exciting when it gels, which isn't nearly often enough. *The Blues Don't Change* (Stax CDSXE) is a prudently retitled and repackaged reissue of 1977's *The Pinch*, a gorgeously lush cinerama-blues epic cut in 1973–4 and, by the time the overdubs were done, not dissimilar to *I Wanna Get Funky*. The two-part original title track has such lovely music that it takes a while to register that what Albert is actually suggesting is that the best way for a man to get a woman to fall in love with him is to pinch her butt. (Maybe this works if you're 6'4" and weigh 300lbs: personally, I'm sceptical.) Elsewhere: the fabulous 'The Blues Don't Change' itself; a remake of 'Oh Pretty Woman'; covers of 'Feel The Need In Me' and 'I Can't Stand The Rain'; and an instrumental, 'King Of Kings', which is a virtual lexicon of Albert's Greatest Licks. And a nice black-and-white shot of Albert to replace the improbably pneumatic butt-shot which graced the original LP.

Albert Collins

One of the most prominent bluesmen of the '90s is a Texas-born veteran who's been out there since the mid-'50s, slugging away at his own defiantly individualistic approach to the post-T-Bone Walker tradition of blues lead guitar, based on an F-minor tuning and the CLARENCE 'GATEMOUTH' BROWN-style use of *a capo* to shift keys. 'The Master Of The Telecaster''s calling card is sheer tone – make that T.O.N.E: no electric guitarist who's ever lived can pack as much sheer power into a single note as Albert Collins. You can imagine Collins's strings snapping right off his guitar under the onslaught of that savage bare-thumb-and-fingers attack while the loudspeakers of his amplifier catch fire.

Born in Leona, Texas, on 1 October 1932, Collins has variously claimed to be, and to have been taught by, LIGHTNIN' HOPKINS' cousin. Originally, he wanted to be a hot soul-jazz organist in the tradition of JIMMY SMITH, Jimmy McGriff, Richard 'Groove' Holmes and Big John Patton, but eventually realised that a Fender Telecaster was considerably more portable than a Hammond B-3. He began playing around the Houston area in the late '50s, and made his name with a series of snappy, catchy FREDDIE KING-style guitar instrumentals, with 'cold'-themed titles like 'Frosty', 'Frostbite', 'Thaw Out' and 'Sno-Cone'. (These were collected into the 1962 album *The Cool Sound Of Albert Collins* (Crosscut Records, currently unavailable on CD), and were a major influence on the young JIMI HENDRIX, whose job in LITTLE RICHARD's band Collins temporarily inherited.) In the late '60s he cut three albums for Imperial Records at the behest of his admirers in CANNED HEAT, but they were neither commercial nor artistic successes and Collins was sufficiently discouraged to retire from music for a time. However, he soon returned, gigging all over the country with local bands (including, in the Pacific Northwest, the young ROBERT CRAY Band) backing him in each area. In 1978 he joined the Chicago-based Alligator label, and it's been onwards and upwards ever since: jamming at Live Aid with GEORGE THOROGOOD & THE DESTROYERS, costarring in TV commercials with Bruce Willis, appearing in the Disney movie *Adventures In Babysitting*, adding lead guitar to David Bowie's single 'Underground', sharing a Grammy with Robert Cray and JOHNNY COPELAND for *Showdown!*, touring extensively with GARY MOORE, and even putting the fear of God into BUDDY GUY at one of ERIC CLAPTON's Albert Hall blues nights. Currently signed to PointBlank Records, he is now one of the world's top blues attractions; a status which is both hard-earned and thoroughly deserved.

- *Ice Pickin'* (Alligator ALCD 4713)
- *Cold Snap* (Alligator ALCD 4752)

To this day, the finest Albert Collins records you can buy. *Ice Pickin'* was Collins's 1978 Alligator debut, and a triumph for Bruce Iglauer's productorial instincts: he rounded up some excellent material, drafted in a first-class studio band (most of whom, including stellar bassist Johnny Gayden, later became Collins' permanent road band, The Icebreakers), and recorded Collins' guitar right in your face: so loud and trebly that every note *hurts*. Collins is at home with three basic grooves – uptempo jump shuffles; deep slow blues; and bouncing, bumping funk – and all three are served up barbecue-hot. It was also the album with which Collins finally came into his own as a vocalist, demonstrating a warm, foggy ALBERT KING-style approach and a slyly humourous way of delivering the right lyric. *Cold Snap* features a larger horn section, which sets off Collins's guitar beautifully but does rather less for his voice, but the material is excellent throughout. It's generally the quality of the material – much of his best stuff has been written by his wife Gwen – which makes the difference between great and adequate Collins; the man himself is always impeccably blues-approved.

- **ALBERT COLLINS, ROBERT CRAY & JOHNNY COPE-LAND:** *Showdown!* (Alligator ALCD 4743)

This 1985 three-man summit smokes from start to finish. The original notion was a state-of-the-Texas-bluesmens'-art jamdown with Collins, Copeland and CLARENCE 'GATEMOUTH' BROWN, but Cray stepped in as a substitute when it turned out that Gate, for one reason or another, wasn't up for the downstroke. It's definitely Collins's show, which is appropriate enough since Copeland and Cray had both been his protégés at various times: out of nine tracks, Cray is absent from two and Copeland from three. All three are on blistering form – those who find Cray's playing too smooth generally end up eating their words with hot sauce after a blast of this – and *Showdown!* eminently deserved its 1986 Grammy award.

- *The Complete Imperial Recordings* (Imperial/EMI CDP-7-96740-2)

Theoretically, Collins's big break should have come at the cusp of the '60s and the '70s with *Love Can Be Found Anywhere Even In A Guitar*, *Trash Talkin'* and *The Compleat Albert Collins*, the three Canned Heat-sponsored albums which this compilation rescues from the vinyl bargain bins. In practice, and with hindsight, it's easy to see why they didn't do the job. Both material and backings are off-the-peg generic, and the production is decidedly thin, dissipating much of the power of Collins's inimitable guitar sound. It's not surprising that The Master Of The Telecaster spent most of the next decade in the wilderness, and serves to emphasise that Alligator did not only Collins, but also the rest of us, a hell of a favour by recording him in a context which played straight to his strengths. *Caveat*, except the most fanatical Collins completists, *emptor*.

- *Molten Ice* (Red Lightnin' RLCD 0089)
- *Frozen Alive* (Alligator ALCD 4725)
- *Live In Japan* (Alligator ALCD 4733)

Albert Collins live: *Molten Ice* was recorded in 1973 at a Canadian club gig and, despite being decidedly lo-fi, it's a burner: the best possible antidote to the inhibited, antiseptic Imperial sides of approximately the same vintage. Backed by The Moe Peters Band (what, if anything, ever happened to them?) Collins blazes through his standard concert repertoire, including Jimmy McGriff's 'All About My Girl', GUITAR SLIM's 'The Things That I Used To Do', his wife Gwen's composition 'Got A Mind To Travel' and his own 'Frosty'. (Trivia note: 'Wah Heat' – one of Collins' rare performances with a wah-wah pedal – ended up giving its name to a now-forgotten post-punk band from Liverpool.) Flash forward eight years to *Frozen Alive* – recorded in Minneapolis with The Icebreakers, including A.C. REED on tenor and the Very Great Johnny B. Gayden on bass – and 'Frosty', 'Got A Mind To Travel' and 'The Things That I Used To Do' are still on the setlist, along with rousing shots at ALBERT KING's 'Angel Of Mercy' and LOUIS JORDAN's 'Caldonia', plus a slamming Gayden showcase called 'Cold Cuts'. The same Icebreakers line-up appears on 1984's *Live In Japan*, this time with Reed taking his own vocal showcase; it features a marvellous 'Stormy Monday' and a blazing take on Jimmy McGriff's 'All About My Girl', but the definitive Albert Collins live album has yet to be recorded.

- **JOHN ZORN:** *Spillane* (Elektra Nonesuch 979 172-2)

A strange brew indeed: sandwiched between a splendidly mock-*noir* tribute to Mickey Spillane and an astonishingly irritating workout for the Kronos Quartet, a Japanese opera singer and a scratch-mix deejay, we find 'Two-Lane Highway' – subtitled 'Concerto For Albert Collins' – an eerie blues dreamscape in which Collins's guitar moves from scenario to scenario backed by an allstar band including guitarist Robert Quine (more familiar to fans of Lou Reed, Lloyd Cole and Richard Hell than to blues lovers), organist Big John Patton, bassist Melvin Gibbs and drummer Ronald Shannon Jackson. Albert also finds time to recite a brief, scarifying road anecdote about checking into a motel and finding a corpse in his bed. It's probably true, too.

Subjects for further investigation: **Frostbite** (Alligator ALCD 4719) is almost as good as _Ice Pickin'_ and _Cold Snap;_ **Don't Lose Your Cool** (Alligator ALCD 4730) and **Iceman** (PointBlank VPBCD 3) are almost as good as _Frostbite._ Collins cameos: check out his guest spots on JOHN LEE HOOKER's **Mr Lucky** (Silvertone ORE CD 519) and **Boom Boom** (PointBlank VPBCD 12); Gary Moore's **Still Got The Blues** (Virgin CDV 2612) and **After Hours** (Virgin CDV 2684); Jack Bruce's **A Question Of Time** (Epic 465692 2); and KOKO TAYLOR's **Queen Of The Blues** (Alligator ALCD 4740). The original version of 'The Freeze' is on **Blues Masters Vol. 3: Texas Blues** (Rhino R2 71123).

Little Milton

Let no one deny 'Little' Milton Campbell's talent for being in the right place at the right time: in the '50s he recorded for Sun and Bobbin; in the '60s for Chess; in the '70s for Stax and TK; and in the '80s and '90s for Malaco. Milton's problem has always been lack of a distinctive musical personality; in the '50s he tried just about every current blues style on for size, and in the '60s he remained under the enormous shadows of his models, B.B. KING and BOBBY BLAND. His mature guitar style is as blatantly Kingoid as anything in the blues, his vocal approach is an effective synthesis of those of King and Bland, and he shares their fondness for bellowing against big brassy backdrops. No innovator he, but living proof that, in the blues universe, originality often counts for less than believability and emotional commitment to the material; and in those departments he yields to no man. Born on 7 September 1934, in Inverness, Mississippi, Little Milton – so named not because of any diminutiveness of stature, but because his dad was also named Milton – started out in Memphis, recording for Sun in the early '50s as a protege of IKE TURNER and eventually following Turner to St Louis. There he, like ALBERT

KING, recorded for the Bobbin label, which was eventually bought out by Chess.

Between '62 and '69 he scored no less than 29 R&B chart entries; during the '70s he moved to Stax (as an understudy to Albert King). He remains enormously popular in the Deep South and still records prolifically for the Mississippi-based soul indie Malaco label. It's generally accepted that his best stuff – including soul-blues masterpieces like 'Grits Ain't Groceries' and 'We're Gonna Make It' – was cut for Chess in the '60s. Milton has remained loyal to the audience that gave him those hits, and they've remained loyal to him. He's never had a discernibly original idea in his life (unless you count those '50s Sun sides, which anticipated the West Side school of OTIS RUSH, BUDDY GUY and MAGIC SAM by quite a few years), but he gets enviable mileage out of other people's old ones.

● *We're Gonna Make It* (Chess CD RED 18)

The first-pick Little Milton album is the easily the best record Bobby Bland never made; by which I mean that Milton sings so wonderfully that you can almost overlook the fact that he plays virtually no guitar. This loads up 24 tracks from the '60s, beginning in 1962 with some bought-in Bobbin sides and ending up in 1969, and includes his magnificent signature hits 'We're Gonna Make It' (1965), the stupefyingly funky 'Grits Ain't Groceries' (1968) and the rocking 'If Walls Could Talk' (1969). Factor in superb covers of everything from GUITAR SLIM's 'The Things That I Used To Do' and the venerable 'Kansas City' to Johnnie Taylor's 'Who's Cheating Who', Rosco Gordon's 'Just A Little Bit', and a powerfully affecting take on Robert Parker's 'Blues Get Off My Shoulder', and you have a deep-dish blend of archetypal Memphis-to-Chicago blues and gospelly Southern soul that's as captivating as it's derivative, which is plenty.

● *The Sun Masters* (Rounder CD SS 55)

A gifted, determined young man in search of a sound in early '50s Memphis, working out a heartful of undigested influences against primo grooves provided by Ike Turner's Kings Of Rhythm. Blazing with restless energy, driven by the Turner band's eloquently sleazy jump and swing, and garnished with the most devastating guitar Milton ever recorded, these sides are short on content but long on fun. The first half-dozen tracks are the As-and-Bs of his only three Sun singles; the previously unreleased material includes the goofy LOUIS JORDAN-style jump novelty 'Re-Beat', and the not-altogether-goodhumoured ELVIS PRESLEY piss-take 'Ooo Wee, Wee Baby'.

Subjects for further investigation: **Waiting For Little Milton/Blues 'N' Soul** (Stax CDSXD 052) doublebacks two early-'70s Stax albums: *Blues 'N' Soul* is by far the better of the two, but since you get *Waiting For Little Milton* chucked in as a bonus, who's complaining? Here Milton seems to be mutating into ALBERT KING: the '70s Stax team give Milton the same big sweeping settings of the Albert K. records of the same period, and he responds in kind, most notably on the majestic 'Woman Across The River' and the almost-but-not-quite bathetic 'Behind Closed Doors'. *The TK Sessions* (Sequel NEXCD 168) scoops up two eminently listenable but less than epochal self-produced albums, *Friend Of Mine* (1976) and Me For You, You For Me (1977), originally intended for Stax release before the company went bust ,and mixing the Shaft-era Stax style (wah-wah guitar, fatback grooves, lavish orchestration) with gospelly blues ballads. While you're picking up **The Best Of Blues And Soul** (Malaco MAL CD341) in order to catch up with Mr Bland's current activities, you can also find Milton in the same location, still satisfying that Southern audience which has sustained him throughout his career.

Johnny 'Guitar' Watson

To borrow a brag from Ice-T, this guy is 'the dopest, flyest, O.G. pimp hustler gangster player hardcore motherfucker alive today' in the blues. The self-styled 'Gangster Of Love' is a fire-breathing, audience-eating showman in the grand tradition of T-BONE WALKER, CLARENCE 'GATEMOUTH' BROWN and GUITAR SLIM (in other words, one of those guys with a legit claim to have been 'doing JIMI HENDRIX 15 years before Jimi Hendrix'); he has the distinction of being Frank Zappa's original electric guitar hero; and he is unique amongst postwar bluesmen in that he enjoyed a highly successful spell as a legit '70s funkateer, scoring hits like 'Ain't That A Bitch', 'A Real Mother For Ya', 'It's All About The $ Bill' and a funked-up remake of his early-'60s hit 'Gangster Of Love'.

Born in Houston, Texas, on February 3, 1935, his folks moved to L.A. in 1950, and Johnny was off to an early start. Starting out on piano, his other main instrument, he cut his earliest sides as Young John Watson, but by the mid-'50s he was Johnny 'Guitar' Watson for life, and recording for Modern. His biggest hits for them were both fairly derivative – 'Those Lonely, Lonely Nights' was a note-for-note copy of Earl King's original, and 'Three Hours Past Midnight' was a thinly-disguised rewrite of B.B. KING's hit 'Three O'Clock Blues', but his spiky Houston guitar and wheedling, hustler's vocals made his work as distinctive as any of his better-known counterparts. Johnny Otis took him to King Records in 1961, where he enjoyed hits with 'Cuttin' In', 'Those Lonely Lonely Feelings' and his signature 'Gangster Of Love.' He toured the UK in the mid-'60s as a team with Larry Williams (a contemporary of LITTLE RICHARD whose bank balance has been considerably fattened by The Beatles' '60s covers of his 'Slow Down' and 'Bad Boy'), and benefited from San Francisco rocker Steve Miller's cover of 'Gangster', but his greatest latter-day success was his '70s funkmeister period, which utilised his multi-instrumental talent – he played bass as well as guitar and keyboards – and his enthusiasm for computer technology. He's still out there in L.A., looking hale and hearty, and no doubt waiting for his next opportunity.

- *3 Hours Past Midnight* (Ace CDCH 909)
- *Gangster Of Love* (Charly CD CHARLY 267)

From the mid-'50s to the early '60s, this is Watson the bluesman in full effect. The Ace album is packed with jump novelties and anguished slow blues, and considerably more worthwhile than its dearth of well-known song titles might suggest. So – if my memory serves me well – is the Charly issue, which is currently in catalogue, but out of stock. If you enjoy *3 Hours Past Midnight*, you'll like *Gangster Of Love* even more.

● *Listen/I Don't Want To Be Alone, Stranger* (Ace CDCHD 408)

A doubleback of two early-'70s Fantasy albums: Mr Watson in transit from R&B to his sarky-disco phase and temporarily incarnated as a luurrrrve-man (and I'm talkin' 'bout *luuurrrve*, baby) with rather more guitar than you'd find on an Isaac Hayes record. *Listen* is lush and low-key in a Shaft-era sort of way; *I Don't Want To Be Alone, Stranger* edges closer to the kind of sound that he was getting on the DJM hits, with 'Trippin'', the title track, and the jivey 'You Can Stay But The Noise Must Go'. My first instinct would be to say that you'd be better off with Fantasy's deleted *Greatest Hits* compilation, but most of that defunct LP's ten tracks are here, anyway.

Subjects for further investigation: DJM's long-gone 1981 vinyl compilation *The Very Best Of Johnny Guitar Watson* showcased the hitmaking late-'70s JGW in all his gold-toothed, designer-shaded glory. If it ever emerges on CD, it's equally recommended to disco nostalgists and those who want to see how a bluesman with open ears and commercial smarts can go from washed-up to cleanin'-up. *The Larry Williams Show Featuring Johnny Guitar Watson and The Stormsville Shakers* (Edsel EDCD 119) is a souvenir of the Williams-Watson team's 1965 UK tour: Larry scores big with 'Slow Down', but JGW takes the honours with 'Looking Back' (later revived by JOHN MAYALL and DR FEELGOOD) and something called 'Two Hours Past Midnight'; they also duet on, of all things, The YARDBIRDS' 'For Your Love'.

Big Mama Thornton

Willie Mae 'Big Mama' Thornton was an utter anomaly: an uncompromisingly downhome blues artist who was (a) female and (b) based on the West Coast. The roughest, toughest blueswoman to emerge between MEMPHIS MINNIE and KOKO TAYLOR, Thornton is best-known for cutting the original version of 'Hound Dog', as custom-composed by Jerry Leiber and Mike Stoller (or by JOHNNY OTIS, depending on whether you get your story from Otis or from Leiber and Stoller), and later immortalised by ELVIS PRESLEY; and for her own composition 'Ball 'N Chain', which became JANIS JOPLIN's signature tune in the late '60s. In her prime, she weighed well over 300 lbs, had a voice capable of derailing an express train, played vicious harmonica and adequate drums, and could probably have punched out HOWLIN' WOLF with either hand. Even the notoriously brutal and intimidating Don Robey, boss of the Houston-based Duke/Peacock labels, was allegedly scared of her.

She was born in Montgomery, Alabama, on 11 December 1926, and ran away from home to seek her musical fortune after winning a local talent contest in 1940. Her first exposure to blues came through hearing BESSIE SMITH and Memphis Minnie, and continued their legacy through work in Atlanta and Houston before signing with Don Robey under the production wing of Johnny Otis, who kitted her out with 'Hound Dog'. When her Duke/Peacock contract expired she left town on a tour with CLARENCE 'GATEMOUTH' BROWN and relocated to the West Coast, where she cut 'Ball 'N Chain' for a small local label not given to precise accounting of royalties. She toured Europe with the 1965 American Folk Blues Festival, recorded for Mercury and Vanguard and remained in constant demand for live work: she played her last show a mere few months before her death in Los Angeles on 25 July 1984, by which time various alcohol-complicated ailments had stripped her of all but 95 pounds of her legendary bulk. Blues could have done with a couple of dozen more like Willie Mae Thornton: a monstrous regiment of women to challenge its male hegemony.

- *The Original Hound Dog* (Ace CDCHD 940)

Leading off with exactly what the title suggests, this is a judicious selection of the early '50s Peacock sides: swinging southwestern jump boogie in which this inexorable human tank ruthlessly wipes out any traces of incipient sophistication. 'I Smell A Rat' and 'I Ain't No Fool, Either' aren't as memorable as 'Hound Dog' but they're even more belligerent, if that's possible.

- *Ball 'N Chain* (Arhoolie CD 305)

These mid-'60s sessions find Big Mama in fine voice and fast company: the eight tracks recorded in Britain in 1965 during a break from the American Folk Blues Festival tour include six with BUDDY GUY's band (two of these with dazzling cameos from WALTER HORTON, and one in which the redoubtable Mama plays simultaneous harp and drums), and two astonishingly powerful deep-blues collaborations with MISSISSIPPI FRED McDOWELL. Then there are another five cut the following year in San Francisco with the MUDDY WATERS band, featuring JAMES COTTON and OTIS SPANN as well as the Big Mud himself: these titles *roar*. And as if that's not enough, there are two more from 1968 with her own hard-punching soul-rock band. And you've still got your money in your pocket? The versions of 'Hound Dog' and 'Ball 'N Chain' included here aren't the originals, but if you only ever own one Big Mama Thornton record, make it this one.

Subjects for further investigation: Jail (Vanguard VMD 109) is a mid-'70s live album cut, as the title might suggest, in a couple of prisons: it features rather more of an indifferent band (led by George 'Harmonica' Smith) than it does of a rather subdued-sounding Big Mama. *American Folk Blues Festival '65* (L&R/Bellaphon CDLR 42025) features Big Mama performing 'Hound Dog' with the same Buddy Guy-led band that appeared on *Ball 'N Chain*: the same track reappears on *The Best Of The American Folk Blues Festivals 1963–1967* (L&R/Bellaphon CDLR 42066). Her considerable debt to Memphis Minnie gets paid off with a lovely 'Me And My Chauffeur' on *20 Great Blues Recordings Of The '50s And '60s* (Cascade CDROP 1005). Both sides of her 1966 single 'Life Goes On'/'Because It's Love' reappear on *All Night Long They Play The Blues* (Ace CDCHD 440). That original 'Hound Dog' is included in *Blues Masters Vol. 5: Jump Blues* (Rhino R2 71125): God knows why, because, wonderful as it is, it sounds like a real country cousin in such sophisticated company.

Etta James

If anyone alive today is capable of challenging KOKO TAYLOR's divine right to the Queen Of The Blues crown, it's Etta James, probably best-known as the originator (and, by her own account, the composer, whatever the credits may say) of the soul-blues standard 'I'd Rather Go Blind'. Starting out in the mid-'50s as a plump teenage R&B prodigy, she became a deep-soul diva in the late '60s and, even as we speak, she's probably on a stage somewhere in the USA stewing up a blistering blend of blues, rock, soul and gospel. A decades-long battle with drug addiction has periodically brought her down, but – thankfully – never laid her out.

The illegitimate daughter of a teenage mother and the celebrated pool hustler Minnesota Fats, Jamesetta Hawkins was born in Los Angeles on January 25, 1938, and raised there by foster parents before rejoining her natural mother in San Francisco. There's a choice of stories concerning her 1954 'discovery' by Johnny Otis: the better one has her talking her way into Otis's hotel room and waking him out of a sound sleep by singing to him; the more prosaic one involves Otis spotting her as part of a vocal group at a Fillmore Auditorium talent contest. The upshot, however, was that Etta had two 1955 hits for Modern Records with 'The Wallflower' (a.k.a. 'Roll With Me Henry', an answer record to Hank Ballard & The Midnighters' 'Work With Me Annie'), and 'Good Rockin' Daddy.' (It's illuminating that 'Roll With Me Henry' had to be retitled to avoid censorship; by modern standards it's fairly innocuous.) The hits dried up after that, but in 1960 Harvey Fuqua of The Moonglows took her to Chess, for whom she scored intermittent hits – including a particularly hot streak of Muscle Shoals sessions between 1967–70 – until the company went out of business in the mid-'70s.

Since then, she's undergone the inevitable ups-and-downs of the R&B life. Atlantic's studio guru Jerry Wexler produced 1977's ambitious, eclectic *Deep In The Night* (Warner Bros, unavailable), which juxtaposed pop standards by the likes of The Eagles and Alice Cooper with blues, deep-soul and gospel material, but unfortunately it bombed. Her most recent manifestations have included a swaggering guest shot in Chuck Berry's Hail! Hail! Rock 'N' Roll movie, and a series of gorgeous soul diva albums for Island and Elektra. She remains a true original: a rotund fireball ready to burn down any house with the kind of raw emotional heat which can neither be simulated nor learned. You either got it or you don't got it, and Etta James emphatically do got it.

- **R&B Dynamite** (Ace CDCH 210)

This is what it says it is: rocking, approachable '50s pop for blues people, drawing on jump and doo-wop as well as the classic West Coast R&B moves. Young Etta's voice is powerful, untrained and deeply soulful; what comes over is both the enthusiasm and the ingenuity of the participants. Harold Battiste blows some seriously obscene sax around Etta's jive on 'The Pick Up', and material comes from Leiber & Stoller, Richard Berry and Berry Gordy as well as from James herself. Don't underestimate this collection simply becasuse it only includes two big hits ('Roll With Me Henry' and 'Good Rockin' Daddy'); the tracks that didn't hit are as good as the ones that did. Harvey Fuqua provides the link between late Modern and early Chess; he duets with Etta on the last track here . . .

- **Tell Mama** (Chess CD RED 7)

. . . and the first track here. The story continues seamlessly on this Chess collection, though it inexplicably omits key early-'60s hits like 'At Last', 'All I Could Do Was Cry', 'Pushover' and 'Stop The Wedding'. Nevertheless, it demonstrates the increasing bluesiness and the simmering sexuality of the mature Etta James style – not surprisingly, since this was Chess – and provides a heaping handful of her '67-and-onwards Muscle Shoals Southern-soul epics, including 'I'd Rather Go Blind' and the blistering title track, which is fully entitled to stand tall beside the great Aretha Franklin sides of the same period. Unfortunately, this collection omits 'In The Basement', her awesome duet with Sugar Pie DeSanto, but you can find that, plus 'Do I Make Myself Clear', another DeSanto/James soul summit, on DeSanto's *Down In The Basement – The Chess Years* (MCA/Chess CHD-9725); notable in its own right for Sugar Pie's sizzling 'Slip-In Mules' (an answer record to Tommy Tucker's 'Hi Heel Sneakers'), and 'Soulful Dress' (an answer record to 'Slip-In Mules'). Eclecticism alert: Etta covers both Howlin' Wolf's 'Spoonful' and Sonny & Cher's 'I Got You Babe,' as well as goodies by Rosco Gordon and Otis Redding.

- **The Right Time** (Elektra 7559-61347-2)

From 1992, this uncompromising roots-move is Etta's most recent at the time of writing: produced by Jerry Wexler and packed with hi-protein guests (guitarists Steve Cropper, LUCKY PETERSON and JIMMY JOHNSON; tenor sax hero Hank Crawford; even a duet with Steve Winwood) and classic songs (Wilson's Pickett's 'Ninety Nine And A Half', Z.Z. Hill's anthemic 'Down Home Blues', Al Green's 'Love And Happiness', RAY CHARLES' title tune). What's more it doesn't disappoint: it's been years – hell, *decades* – since Etta's done this good a job of reconciling her twinned aspects of tough, salty done-it-all blueswoman and wounded, had-it-all-done-to-me deep-soul queen. It's about as funky as any record cut in 1992 has a right to be; a class act.

Subjects for further investigation: There's a fair amount of cool Chess material still under wraps: the early-'70s 2-LP vinyl collection *Peaches* (Chess, unavailable) includes some of the hits that *Tell Mama* misses out; and *Come A Little Closer* (Chess, 1974, unavailable), including everything from urgent, *Shaft*-era funk to burning Lowell George slide-guitar and a killer version of 'St Louis Blues', would also be a welcome reissue. 1990's **Stickin' To My Guns** (Island CID 9955) is certainly aptly titled: produced by her former Muscle Shoals sideman Barry Beckett, it's squarely in the tradition of their '60s collaborations *circa* 'Tell Mama', though at a lower temperature. Guest-starring Red Hot Chili Pepper Arik Marshall and ex-Meter Leo Nocentelli (guitars), ROBERT CRAY keyb-op Jimmy Pugh and even rapper Def Jef, this smoulders rather than blazes, but there's no shortage of good moments if you don't demand the nonstop Vesuvius of some of her stage shows.

So who, you may be wondering, is Johnny Otis? A Greek-American singer/drummer/pianist/bandleader/songwriter/entrepreneur/vibraphonist/DJ swarthy enough to pass for a light-skinned African-American, John Veliotes (1921–) was one of the real movers and shakers in the California R&B scene of the '50s; he was instrumental in launching the careers of Little Esther (Phillips), BIG MAMA THORNTON and JOHNNY 'GUITAR' WATSON as well as that of Etta James, and for a while his Johnny Otis Show revue included guitarist Jimmy Nolen, later to make his mark slice-and-dicing the 4/4 with JAMES BROWN. **Creepin' With The Cats** (Ace

CDCHD 325); *Dig These Blues* (Ace CDCHD 334) and *Dapper Cats, Groovy Tunes & Hot Guitars* (Ace CDCHD 351) mine the vaults of his '50s label Dig Records for a whole bunch of cool jump and boogie, though none of them includes 'Harlem Nocturne', 'Willie And The Hand Jive' or 'Ma, He's Making Eyes At Me', his biggest hits of the decade. He's currently a pastor and community organiser in L.A., and still occasionally rounds up a revue and plays some rhythm and blues, as 1981's *The New Johnny Otis Show* (Alligator ALCD 4726) and 1990's *Good Lovin' Blues* (Ace CDCH 299) eloquently testify.

3. Goin' Down Louisiana: Swamp Fever and Mardi Gras Mania

Louisiana music in general – and New Orleans music in particular – is a law utterly unto itself. Its location and history made it the womb of jazz at the turn of the century, but after 1949, when R&B recording began in earnest in the Crescent City, a unique postwar R&B style emerged: rhythms with a Latin tilt, vocals with a Caribbean lilt. Is New Orleans R&B 'really' blues, jazz, funk, rock or all of the above? The answer is 'Yes . . . *please*'. Defiantly localised music is often parochial in its concerns and appeal, but the sheer eclecticism of the city's sound enabled it to go pop with very little modification: it's bouncy, friendly, hook-laden, rhythmically irresistible, happier than any other variety of blues, and virtually unmistakable for anything else. Native son FATS DOMINO and visiting fireman LITTLE RICHARD (imported from Georgia) took New Orleans music into the chart heart of the '50s; elsewhere in Louisiana, a new flavour of Southern blues was bubbling. For a bunch of painless primers to the byways of the bayou, consult *The Story Of Goldband Records: Eddie's House Of Hits* (Ace CDCHD 424), which includes a couple of fine tracks by LONNIE BROOKS in his '50s guise of 'Guitar Junior', plus the young Dolly Parton's 1959 version of 'Puppy Love'; *We Got A Party!: The Best Of Ron Records Vol. 1* (Rounder CD 2076), featuring the likes of

Irma Thomas, Robert Parker and PROFESSOR LONGHAIR; and the more contemporary **Louisiana Scrapbook** (Rykodisc RCD 20058), which includes JAMES BOOKER, The Dirty Dozen Brass Band, WALTER 'WOLFMAN' WASHINGTON, CLARENCE 'GATEMOUTH' BROWN and the New Orleans piano patriarch Tuts Washington.

SWAMP BLUES

One of the most delightful subgenres from a state positively crawling with them was 'swamp blues': laid-back and wide-open where urban blues was aggressive and clamorous; as languorous and sticky as Delta blues was harsh and dry. This basically meant the sides which producer J.D. 'Jay' Miller – Baton Rouge's answer to Sam Phillips and the Chess brothers – supplied to the Nashville-based Excello label. *Sounds Of The Swamp: The Best Of Excello Records Vol. 1* (Rhino R2 70896 [US]) provides a fair idea of what Miller was up to: a reverb-drenched Louisiana equivalent of the kind of records JIMMY REED was cutting up in Chicago, the groove relaxed to a point just on the safe side of soporific but still distinctly kickin', topped off with drawled, nasal vocals and lashings of tootling mouth-harp. The difference was that the Louisiana guys could sleaze their way around a rhumba as easily as Reed could somnambulate through a shuffle. LIGHTNIN' SLIM and LAZY LESTER were two of Miller's main guys, but his star act was . . .

Slim Harpo

Like his model JIMMY REED, Slim Harpo – born James Isaac Moore on 11 February 1924 in Labdell, Louisiana – was, in his own quiet way, one of the most successful bluesmen of the late '50s and early '60s. 'Rainin' In My Heart' and 'Scratch My Back' were both pop Top 40 hits (in 1961 and 1966, respectively) and thanks first to Brit R&B icons like THE ROLLING STONES, THE YARDBIRDS, Them (featuring Van Morrison), The Kinks and The Pretty Things; and later to Austin bluesrockers like THE FABULOUS THUNDERBIRDS and LOU ANN BARTON – who recycled Harpo hits like 'I'm A King Bee', 'Got Love If You Want It', 'Scratch My Back', 'Rainin' In My

Heart', 'Shake Your Hips', 'Tip On In' and 'Te-Ni-Ne-Ni-Nu' – his repertoire is still performed today.

Slim didn't consider a musical career until the mid-'50s when, under the name of Harmonica Slim, he started working as a sideman with his pal Otis (LIGHTNING SLIM) Hicks. Hicks introduced him to Jay Miller and – after the existence of another 'Harmonica Slim' prompted a swift *nom de blues* change to 'Slim Harpo' – his first session, in 1957, produced 'I'm A King Bee' and 'Got Love If You Want It'. Playing Reed-style rhythm guitar and rack harp, he oozed his way into the hearts and minds of his countrymen and, by 1967, had abandoned Miller to start recording in Nashville. Overcoming his reluctance to tour outside the South, he played in New York and Los Angeles and set his sights on the rock marketplace, but a fatal heart attack took him off the set on 31 January 1970.

- *The Best Of Slim Harpo* (Ace CDCHM 410)

This is exactly what it says it is: all the above hits and lots, lots more. Laid-back but kickin' music that generates as much propulsion with as little apparent effort as anything you're likely to hear, this is memorable, danceable, unpretentious and plenty big fun.

Subjects for further investigation: If you fall under Harpo's languorous spell, *I'm A King Bee* (Flyright FLYCD 05) will supply you with numerous outtakes and extras, plus almost-as-cool-as-the-original alternates of hits like the title track and 'Don't Start Crying Now'. As noted above, Harpo covers abound: one of the most interesting (and most obscure) is 'Tina Nu' – a sensible retitling of 'Te-Ni-Ne-Ni-Nu' – by BUDDY GUY's younger brother Phil Guy, who claims to have played lead guitar on Slim's original. Find it on Phil's *Tina Nu* (JSP JSPCD 226); Lou Ann Barton takes on the same song, back-to-back with 'Shake Your Hips', on *Read My Lips* (Antone's ANT0009CD). The Stones hit 'I'm A King Bee' on *The Rolling Stones* (Decca 820 047-2), and 'Shake Your Hips' on *Exile On Main Street* (Rolling Stones 450196 2); The CLAPTON-era Yardbirds essay 'Got Love If You Want It' on *Five Live Yardbirds* (Decal CD CHARLY 182); The Fabulous Thunderbirds work out on 'Scratch My Back' and 'Tip On In' on *Portfolio* (Chrysalis MPCD

1599). Trust me: you don't need the Kinks and Pretty Things stuff.

Lightning Slim

If Slim Harpo was Excello's biggest swamp blues act, Harpo's brother-in-law Otis 'Lightning Slim' Hicks was its first, and the one of whom Jay Miller was fondest. Hicks was so defiantly rural that Harpo seems a veritable urban sharpie by comparison. His brooding baritone was set against Electric Downhome backdrops firmly rooted in Delta soil, but distinctively Louisianan in ambience and pace. Otis Hicks was born outside the Bayou – in St Louis, on March 13, 1913 – but his family moved to Louisiana before he reached his teens. By the early '50s he was playing regularly around Baton Rouge, earning his nickname by his obvious devotion to the music of LIGHTNIN' HOPKINS. Between 1954 and 1963 his records – including 'Bad Luck', 'Tom Cat', G.I. Blues' and Wintertime Blues' were notable regional successes, but the strutting 'Rooster Blues', which reached No 23 in the R&B charts in 1959, was his only national hit.

He survived the mid-60s downturn in his recording fortunes – his career revived to the extent that he toured Europe in the early '70s – but ill-health caught him out: he died of cancer in Detroit on July 27, 1974. Never a major hitmaker, he illustrates one major joy of exploring the blues: the constant reminders of how intensely satisfying even an obscure practitioner of a regional subgenre can be. By all means develop your acquaintance with the work of the frontline of blues stars; just remember that every so often you'll encounter something by someone you've never heard of which will affect you just as deeply.

- *Rollin' Stone* (Flyright FLY CD 08)

The hits plus the others, and the odd outtake. Slim's pet mode was the Hopkins-style slow blues – he even alludes to himself as 'Po' Lightnin'' ocasionally – but there's no shortage of variation. There's the uptempo 'Rooster Blues',which would be rock and roll if it could have been bothered, as would 'Bugger Bugger Boy' (I'm sure Slim meant 'Boogie Boogie Boy'; aren't you?); some insane grooves which suggest that HOWLIN' WOLF had moved to Baton Rouge rather than Chicago, and that the food and climate had improved his temper; and a couple of talking blues, 'Trip To Chicago' and 'Lightnin' Blues', which display a way with narratives that recalls JOHN LEE HOOKER as well as Lightnin' Hopkins. Plus lotsa slow blues in E.

Subjects for further investigation: **King Of The Swamp Blues** (Flyright FLYCD 47) contains more outtakes, including remakes of the hits, and some unvarnished acoustic blues, including a 'Paper In My Shoe' borrowed from a 1954 local hit by zydeco man Boozoo Chavis, and featuring some exotic bayou percussion. **Blue Lightnin'** (Indigo IGO CD 2002) catches Slim at a 1972 London concert with the slightly overbearing accompaniment of a lovably rumbustious home-grown Chicago-style blues band who play, as Brit blues guys generally do, as if they were accompanying a full-throated extrovert like MUDDY WATERS or Howlin' Wolf. One of Slim Harpo's successors as the man at whom Lightnin' Slim hollered 'Blow your harmonica, son!' was the ebullient Leslie Johnson, a.k.a Lazy Lester (1933–), a versatile sessioneer who played harp, guitar and percussion on a variety of Jay Miller sessions as well as cutting in his own right. Due to the vagaries of licensing, it's easier to find Lester's outtakes than his released masters, but the eminently listenable late-'50s-to-late-'60s **Lazy Lester** (Flyright FLY CD 07) includes a more than acceptable version of 'Sugar Coated Love', as covered by Texan swamp-blues aficionados LOU ANN BARTON – on **Read My Lips** (Antone's ANT0009CD) – and THE FABULOUS THUNDERBIRDS on **Portfolio** (Chrysalis MPCD 1599); the released version of his other pick-to-click, 'I Hear You Knockin'' (not the SMILEY LEWIS tune that was a 1970 hit for Dave Edmunds), is on **Sounds Of The Swamp: The Best Of Excello Records Vol. 1** (Rhino R2 70896 [US]). **Harp And Soul** (Alligator) is a lively 1988 rediscovery job with lead guitar by KENNY NEAL: it revisits the chilling '50s 'Bloodstains (On The Wall)', includes a strong, affecting take on 'Dark End Of The Street', and romps through some routine standards. Generally, all concerned do a fine job of sounding like the Thunderbirds trying to sound like Lazy Lester.

NEW ORLEANS (PROPER)

Champion Jack Dupree

William Thomas 'Champion Jack' Dupree earned his nickname through his skills as a boxer: fortunately he quit the fight game in 1940 with his hands still intact. He took New Orleans piano all over Europe before settling down to voluntary European exile, spending several years as quite the most famous bluesman in Halifax, Yorkshire, as well as living in Switzerland and Germany. In his later years he took up painting (one work selling for as much as $7,000), but his principal achievements were a lifetime of ambassadorship for his personal take on his hometown piano tradition; and the influence of his early records on later Crescent City keyboard titans like FATS DOMINO and PROFESSOR LONGHAIR.

That blues artists have led hard lives is a commonplace (and, considering the endemic poverty and racism with which they have had to contend, an eminently justifiable one), but Jack Dupree's life was harder than most. Born in New Orleans on 4 July 1910 (or 1909, as the case may be), he was orphaned as a small child when the Ku Klux Klan burnt down his family's home, and grew up, like Louis Armstrong ten years earlier, in the city's Colored Waifs Home. When, with his recording career barely launched, he joined the U.S. Navy to fight in World War II, he was captured by the Japanese and spent two years in one of their world-famous prison camps. His most celebrated subject matter was the street-life of the African-American underclass; his music was always patently the work of a tough guy with a generous heart and a sense of humour. His style was thoroughly Nwawlean, albeit modified by extensive travel. Even before he'd relocated to Indianapolis in 1940, he spent time in New York City (his adopted hometown between 1945 and 1960) and his vocal approach incorporated the 'ooh-well-well' near-falsettos of the Delta. The title of his UK-recorded 1964 album *From New Orleans To Chicago* is an appropriate one: Dupree's piano has taken exactly that musical journey without him ever doing more than pass through the Windy City.

Dupree died in his home in Hanover, Germany, on 21 January 1992; fortunately, he returned to New Orleans a couple of times in his last years and recorded a pair of fine autumnal albums produced by Ron Levy. Jack Dupree finally came home, and so did his music.

- **1945–1946 (The Joe Davis Sessions)** (Flyright FLYCD 22)
- **1945–1953** (Krazy Kat KK CD 08)

Early Dupree, recorded in New York City: the 20 solo Davis sides are preponderantly blues, but the '46 batch manifest the Dupree who inspired the young Domino and Longhair. The tough, rocking ensemble tracks on the Krazy Kat album heavily feature the expert city blues electric guitar of BROWNIE McGHEE, moonlighting from his folkie activities and, on one decidedly Chicago-style 1953 session, bringing SONNY TERRY along with him. 'Shake Baby Shake' and the closing 'Shim Sham Shimmy' rock considerably harder than you'd expect from New York City blues; McGhee's guitar isn't as ferociously distorted as Willie Johnson's on HOWLIN' WOLF's Memphis sides, but it's still a long way from the clean Carolina finger-picking with which his name is generally associated.

- **Champion Jack Dupree Sings The Blues** (King KCD-735)

Whoever supervises the packaging of King Records' reissues clearly can't be bothered with unnecessary trimmings like liner notes or session details; so all I can offer is that these tracks were (probably) cut in Cincinnati and New York between 1953 and 1955. Good-humoured, light-hearted small-band sides which demonstrate how polished and confident an entertainer Dupree had become, they concentrate on comic monologues like 'Tongue Tied Blues', 'Hair Lip Blues' and 'Me And My Mule', despite the occasional deeper blues like 'Camille', a first cousin to the 'Louise' beloved of JOHN LEE HOOKER and MISSISSIPPI FRED McDOWELL. Burning question: is the (excellent) guitar and harp by Brownie and Sonny? Alternative title: *Having A Hoot With Champion Jack Dupree.*

- **Back Home In New Orleans** (Bullseye Blues NET CD 9502)
- **Forever And Ever** (Bullseye Blues NET CD 9512)

The homecoming albums, recorded in 1990 and 1991 under the watchful ear of Ron Levy, Roomful Of Blues' keyboardist/leader and former ALBERT KING and B.B. KING sideman. Dupree coasts through the first one genially enough, but *Forever And Ever* is the one which really delivers: all the way from the scarifying autobiographical deep blues 'They Gave Me Away' through to 'Yella Pocahontas', the most overtly Nwawlean piece he's ever recorded, it's a fine swan song for a true prodigal son of the Crescent City.

Subjects for further investigation: More late-'40s Dupree/McGhee sides are included on ***Brownie McGhee 1944–1955*** (Travelin' Man TM CD 04): the Champ takes lead vocals on two of them. Dupree's most celebrated album is *Blues From The Gutter* (Atlantic, 1958, currently unavailable) which includes a terrific 'Junker's Blues'. ***Raw Blues*** (London 820 479-2) includes a couple of outtakes, featuring JOHN MAYALL on harp and ERIC CLAPTON on guitar, from *From New Orleans To Chicago* (Decca, 1964, unavailable) one of several well-regarded Dupree albums cut in London. Others include *When You Feel The Feeling You Was Feeling* (Blue Horizon, 1968, unavailable), and ***The Legacy of The Blues Vol. 3*** (Sonet SNTCD 626); the latter, recorded in 1971, features ex-Bluesbreaker Hughie Flint on drums with his McGuinness-Flint colleague Benny Gallagher (later of Gallagher and Lyle, etc.) partnering him on bass: its best shot is the uncompromisingly militant curtain-raiser 'Vietnam Blues'.

Fats Domino

In chart terms, Antoine 'Fats' Domino was New Orleans' Big Kahuna. He transcended both Nwawlins and the R&B scene to become one of the most consistent sellers of the rock and roll era, scoring 36 Top 40 hits in eight years, and selling 65 million records between 1955 – when 'Ain't It A Shame' 'crossed over' from the R&B charts to the pop audience – and 1963. Like JIMMY REED in Chicago, only on a vastly bigger scale, he outsold his homeboys thanks to catchy material, a relaxed but irresistible rhythm, and a winning vocal style which radiated charm. PROFESSOR LONGHAIR was the hipsters' pick as top Crescent City piano man, but Domino – born guess where on 26 February 1928 – was the people's choice.

Like just about everybody else in New Orleans, he was raised up in a musical family, discovering the piano around the same time he learned to speak. Schooled on jump champs like LOUIS JORDAN, AMOS MILBURN, ROY MILTON and JOE TURNER, and boogie-woogie masters like Albert Ammons, Pete Johnson and MEADE LUX LEWIS (not to mention local heroes CHAMPION JACK DUPREE, Isadore 'Tuts' Washington and Professor Longhair), the 5'5", 200lb Domino acquired his nickname and his first recording contract before he was 21. The nickname came from his first bandleader, Billy Diamond, and the contract from the ubiquitous Dave Bartholomew (born 24 December 1920, in Edgard, Louisiana), New Orleans' equivalent to Memphis's IKE TURNER or Chicago's WILLIE DIXON. Domino's very first session produced a 1949 R&B chart smash with 'The Fat Man' (an almost-unreconstructed reworking of Dupree's 1940 'Junker's Blues'), and he continued to rack up frequent R&B hits for another five years. He also kept his hand in by playing a few sessions for Bartholomew's other artists, including Smiley Lewis: the signature piano intro to Lloyd Price's 'Lawdy Miss Clawdy' – hear it on _Lawdy!_ (Ace CDCHD 360) – is Domino's work. In 1955, 'Ain't It A Shame' fought Pat Boone's exploitative whitebread cover version to a draw and put Domino into the pop charts, where he stayed until the early '60s, when the British Invasion (spearheaded by The Beatles, whose Paul McCartney was a devoted Domino fan) relegated him to the oldies shows.

Unlike CHUCK BERRY, whose rock and roll success was founded on sly, witty songs written around specifically teen topics, Domino didn't so much modify his basic Nwawlins R&B as simply emphasise the pop qualities which were already there. Domino has added little to his songbook since his first flush of success – apart from The Beatles' 1968 'Lady Madonna', originally composed by McCartney as a Domino tribute, and a minor country hit, 'Whiskey Heaven', in 1982 – but then he hasn't had to. He's still a popular live attraction because advancing age hasn't affected his show: the legends of Berry or JAMES BROWN both depend on continued physical agility, but Fats doesn't need to do anything except sit behind his piano, and play, sing and smile. Which, to this day, he does.

- *My Blue Heaven: The Best Of Fats Domino Vol. 1* (EMI CDP-7-92808-2)
- *They Call Me The Fat Man: The Legendary Imperial Recordings* (EMI E2-7 96784-2)

Two options for catching up with the Fat Man: the first is a tasty snack and the second a four-course meal. The 20-track, single-disk *My Blue Heaven* includes all Fats's biggest pop hits; the 100-song, 4-CD boxed set doesn't contain absolutely *everything* the great man recorded as a featured artist between 1949 and 1962 – 260 tracks total – but you'd have to be a *very* serious Domino nut to complain. Both track – the big box with five times as much detail – Domino's progression from blues to R&B to pop with what was, essentially, the same music. 'If you just want the hits – 'The Fat Man', 'Ain't It A Shame', 'I'm In Love Again', 'Blueberry Hill', 'Blue Monday', 'My Blue Heaven', 'I'm Walkin'', 'I'm Ready', 'Walkin' To New Orleans', 'Let The Four Winds Blow', and not a few others – then the single CD should be just your speed. (There isn't a Volume II; not yet, anyway.) If you want more, then the big box has it.

Professor Longhair

They called Henry Roeland 'Roy' Byrd – a.k.a. Professor Longhair, or ''Fess' for short – 'the Bach of rock'; I hear him as the (Thelonious) Monk of R&B. Longhair was the definitive New Orleans pianist – just ask DR JOHN, Allen Toussaint or Art Neville – and his eccentric sense of space, wicked sense of humour and laudable refusal to allow his formidable technique to run away with him simply reinforce the comparison. Byrd was born in Bogalusa, Louisiana, on 19 December 1918, and commenced his career as an entertainer by whistling and tap-dancing on the streets of New Orleans. Somewhere along the line he formulated, under the guidance of local 88s guru Isadore 'Tuts' Washington, his one-of-a-kind piano style, mingling the standard blues and barrelhouse progressions with the pan-African lilts and cadences of New Orleans, and a vocal approach to match. Scoring a job with FATS DOMINO's bandleader Dave Bartholomew, he got in on the ground floor of Nwawlins R&B recording with 'She Ain't Got No Hair'.

'Fess had an excellent '50s but a rotten '60s: by 1964, his music had gone out of style, and he was reduced to supporting himself as a cardsharp and a janitor: ironically, he was sweeping up in a record store, and hearing his early records – for which he received no royalties – played every year at Mardi Gras. Like many another bluesman, he was 'rediscovered': he was welcomed as a conquering hometown hero at the 1971 New Orleans Jazz And Heritage Festival, and spent his last decade happily recording (and re-recording) his classic hits and the new repertoire he'd developed while he'd been away from studio and bandstand. Tributes like *Gumbo* (by his disciple Dr John who, as studio guitarist Mac Rebennack, had backed him up in the '50s) did his reputation no harm at all, and he remained his own weird self until the end, still whistling his unpredictable but oh-so-right lead lines and kicking out the backbeat through the front of his pianos as he hammered out his unique syncopations. He died in New Orleans on 30 January 1980; just after he'd finished recording *Crawfish Fiesta*, possibly the best album of his entire career, for – appropriately enough – Alligator Records.

● *Mardi Gras In New Orleans* (Nighthawk NHCD-108)

The original stuff, mostly: cut 1949–57 with 'Fess's notorious bands The Blues Jumpers, The Blues Scholars and, best of all, The Shuffling Hungarians for Mercury, Atlantic and various lesser-known labels, and including a couple of tracks featuring the most hog-whimperingly out-of-tune 12-string guitar you've ever heard in your life. The voice is happily bemused, the piano always knows exactly what is going on, the repertoire includes 'Tipitina' (the cool version, not the better-known but inferior alternate version), 'Mardi Gras In New Orleans' (the first version, but not the best), 'She Ain't Got No Hair' (a hit the following year retitled as 'Bald Head'), 'No Buts No Maybes' and 'Baby Let Me Hold Your Hand', and those snaky beats will kick you in the ass every time . . . and make you like it. However, it's light on piano features, the horn section overplay, and the sound quality is somewhere between so-so and dreadful. Purists will nevertheless want to make this their first port of call, but everybody else stay on board for . . .

- *House Party New Orleans Style: The Lost Sessions 1971–2* (Demon FIENDCD 189)

Cut in Baton Rouge and Memphis, with SNOOKS EAGLIN's fabulous guitar on all 15 tracks and The Meters' drummer Zig Modeliste slice-and-dicing the beat on four, these were Longhair's comeback sides, recorded in the wake of a triumphant reappearance at the 1971 New Orleans Jazz And Heritage Festival after seven years in the wilderness. The full richness of quintessential Nwawlins often requires a larger band than the quartets heard here, but these sessions lack neither force nor subtlety . . . nor, for that matter, mischievous good humour and audible enthusiasm. A revitalised 'Fess careens through his classic repertoire, including 'Tipitina', 'Junko Partner', 'No Buts No Maybes', 'Cabbagehead' and an instrumental 'Big Chief': if this had been released at the time (instead of languishing in various vaults until the early '80s) Dr John might never have bothered making *Gumbo*. Special note to Demon's art department: on the back of a 12" LP sleeve, 9pt type is clearly legible. When the artwork is then photographically reduced to the size of a CD inlay card, it is not. I shall keep my vinyl copy of this for its superior Graphical User Interface rather than its sound.

- *Crawfish Fiesta* (Alligator ALCD 4718)

Despite a version of 'Big Chief' that's played way too fast for comfort, the omission of 'Tipitina', and a careless bit of CD mastering that not only gets the original LP 'sides' mixed up but doesn't acknowledge the fact on the track listing, this is (by a nose) the best Professor Longhair CD you can buy. Taken from his very last sessions (he didn't live to see the album released) with Dr John dusting off his guitar specially for the occasion, it's about as much fun as anything in recorded rhythm and blues – anything since the heyday of LOUIS JORDAN, anyway – and proves beyond a doubt that the good Professor still had more than enough of the Right Stuff clear up to the end. If 'Whole Lotta Lovin'' and 'Bald Head' don't make you laugh, you're sick; if 'Cry To Me' and 'Her Mind Is Gone' don't make you want to dance, you're dead. *Mardi Gras In New Orleans* is the classicists' Longhair; this and *House Party New Orleans Style* are for civilians. The civilians get a better deal.

Subjects for further investigation: Highly regarded by 'Fess buffs but currently unavailable on CD (why?) are the live **Last Mardi Gras** and the early-singles compilation *New Orleans Piano* (Atlantic,1982 and 1972). If you want to stick with the post-rediscovery Longhair albums, you can catch up with the 1957 sides 'Baby Let Me Hold Your Hand' and 'No Buts No Maybes' on **Creole Kings Of New Orleans** (Specialty/Ace CDCHD 393), which also includes a pre-Dr John Mac Rebennack as the mastermind behind Jerry Byrne's 'Light Out', and other fine Nwawlins fare from GUITAR SLIM, PERCY MAYFIELD, CLIFTON CHENIER, Lloyd Price, Larry Williams and Art Neville. The current state of New Orleans piano is surveyed on **Keys To The Crescent City** (Rounder CD 2087), featuring Neville, Eddie Bo, Willie Tee and CHARLES BROWN.

Smiley Lewis

If my name was Smiley Lewis, I'd want to change it to something more interesting, like Overton Amos Lemon. Instead, Overton Amos Lemon – born in DeQuincey, Louisiana, on 5 July 1913 – changed his name to Smiley Lewis. He was playing guitar alongside Isadore 'Tuts' Washington in a jazz band when Dave Bartholomew, FATS DOMINO's other half, decided to check him out as a singer. Lemon became Lewis for his first release, and was revealed to have a big, bluff voice which lent itself admirably to the generic but enjoyable jump novelties with which Bartholomew kept him plentifully supplied. His records, cut for Imperial, for whom Bartholomew was already recording Domino, were second-string Bartholomew compositions (Fats Domino got the best ones), but they were immaculately arranged and performed – the likes of Washington, Domino and Huey 'Piano' Smith played piano on his sessions – in the genial, ear-catching Domino tradition, though they often rocked considerably harder. Smiley's records always sold well in the South, but the songs most frequently associated with him are 'I Hear You Knocking' (recycled by Bartholomew on a Fats Domino record in 1958, and a No. 1 hit for Dave Edmunds in 1970), and 'One Night' (which created a minor scandal when covered by ELVIS PRESLEY, albeit in slightly bowdlerised form). Even 'Blue Monday', one of Domino's signature tunes, made its debut a year or two earlier on a Lewis record. Smiley Lewis's career declined steadily throughout the early '60s: he died in New Orleans, of stomach cancer, on 7 October 1966, two years after his final, unsuccessful session.

- *New Orleans Bounce: 30 Of His Best* (Sequel NEXCD 130)

The (almost terrifyingly) Compleat Smiley Lewis, 1950–60. A minor performer, for sure; but this collection is a salutory reminder of just how engaging some minor R&B performers could be. It includes 'I Hear You Knocking', 'Blue Monday' and 'One Night' (of course!), and mingles me-too jump novelties like 'Caldonia's Party' (sung to the melody and chord changes of Lloyd Price's 'Lawdy Miss Clawdy') with specially-for-the-home-folks stuff like 'Gumbo Blues', complete with reference to Rampart Street, 'Down Yonder' and 'Tee Nah Nah'. And from his very first Imperial session, there's 'Slide Me Down', a deeply-felt showcase for Lewis's severely underrated blues singing and some lead guitar which wouldn't have disgraced GUITAR SLIM.

Subjects for further investigation: Earl King was another singer-guitarist brought to Imperial by Dave Bartholomew. King – born Silas Johnson in New Orleans on 6 February 1934 – already had one hit, 'Those Lonely, Lonely Nights' (Ace, 1955), to his credit when Bartholomew scooped him up in 1959; but at Imperial he started having them again. His guitar playing sparkled considerably more than his singing, but his later compositions like 'Come On' and 'Trick Bag' became favourites of JIMI HENDRIX and STEVIE RAY VAUGHAN, and Robert Palmer and The Meters. The Earl King album you need is *Trick Bag* (Stateside, unavailable), a 1987 vinyl compilation of Imperial sides; the one you can get is *Glazed* (doublebacked with *Ron Levy's Wild Kingdom* on Demon FIENDCD 712). It's pleasant and enjoyable enough: King even reprises 'Those Lonely, Lonely Nights', long since thought ceded to JOHNNY GUITAR WATSON; and THE FABULOUS THUNDERBIRDS' Kim Wilson and Jimmy Vaughan guest on the Levy sides. In their civilian identity as Roomful Of Blues, Ron Levy's Wild Kingdom supply King's back-up, which means that it's essentially their album rather than his. This wouldn't be a problem if you could get the Imperial sides, which are extremely snappy. But you can't.

James Booker

James Carroll Booker III was such an accomplished musical mimic that, while still in his teens, he used to 'ghost' FATS DOMINO's piano parts so that Dave Bartholomew could stockpile backing tracks while the Fat Man was out on the road. Similarly, since Huey 'Piano' Smith was not fond of touring, Booker would be sent out to front Smith's band The Clowns in his stead, and no one ever complained. Born guess-where on 17 December 1939, Booker was a teen piano prodigy who supplemented classical tuition with extra-curricular boogie-woogie studies and had his own local radio show by the time he was 14. Unfortunately, he also acquired a lifetime heroin habit: given morphine after being struck by a hit-and-run driver at the age of nine, he learned to love the drug almost as much as he loved the piano. 'Junco Partner', indeed.

He was a popular R&B sideman, touring and recording with the likes of BOBBY BLAND, Joe Tex, Wilson Pickett and Ringo Starr: his biggest success as a featured artist was the 1960 instrumental 'Gonzo'. A regular at the New Orleans Jazz & Heritage festivals while playing both lounges and dives at home, he became a major touring attraction in Europe during the '70s. Nevertheless, he only recorded three album-as-albums before his death in 1983. A dazzling eclectic who could follow Chopin with LEADBELLY or PROFESSOR LONGHAIR with Roger Miller without turning a hair, his sly hustler's voice, flamboyant stage presence (check out that silver-star eye-patch), raconteurial skills and insolent keyboard flash have proved utterly irreplaceable.

● *Junco Partner* (Hannibal HNCD 1359)

Booker's first and most startling album, recorded solo in New Orleans in 1976 and unavailable in any format for most of the intervening period, has been a legend among Nwawlins piano fanciers for years: all I can say is that it lives up to its reputation. He covers Earl King; gives the title tune a decidedly different twist from either Professor Longhair, DR JOHN or its composer CHAMPION JACK DUPREE; does ungodly things to 'On The Sunny Side Of The Street' and Chopin's 'Minute Waltz'; plays the most unusual version of 'Goodnight Irene' imaginable and generally puts on one of the greatest one-man studio shows you'll ever hear.

● *New Orleans Piano Wizard: Live!* (Rounder CD 2037)

Live in Switzerland in 1977, Booker turns a fistful of standards – ranging from blues chestnuts like 'Please Send Me Someone To Love' and 'Black Night' to 'On The Sunny Side Of The Street' and 'Come Rain Or Come Shine' – inside out for the benefit of a highly appreciative audience. You may think that you never want to hear anyone play 'Something Stupid', but Booker could well change your mind.

● *Classified* (Rounder CD 2036)

In the studio in 1982 with a rhythm section and Alvin 'Red' Tyler's tenor sax: the repertoire includes Titus Turner's 'All Around The World' (as immortalised by LITTLE WILLIE JOHN, but better known as LITTLE MILTON's 'Grits Ain't Groceries'), a Professor Longhair medley and staples like 'Hound Dog' and 'Lawdy Miss Clawdy-'(not to mention 'Baby Face' and Roger Miller's 'King Of The Road'). The bass and drums smooth out some of Booker's left-hand caprices, which makes for a more conventional, though still satisfying, ride.

Dr John

The veteran New Orleans saxophonist/arranger Harold Battiste was responsible for two great '60s scams: the first was to convince the world that Sonny Bono (the shorter, uglier half of Sonny & Cher) was a genius record producer; the second – and the marginally less risible – was to transform a white Nwawlins session musician named Malcolm 'Mac' Rebennack into the

DR JOHN

fearsome voodoo priest Dr John Creaux, The Night Tripper. Rebbennack, born in New Orleans on 21 November 1941, was a jack-of-all-trades who'd been playing guitar and piano on sessions for the likes of PROFESSOR LONGHAIR, Earl King and Huey Smith since the early '50s; he'd written Jerry Byrne's rock'n'roll classic 'Lights Out' (most recently revived by DR FEELGOOD and JOHNNY WINTER).

The first Dr John album, *Gris-Gris* (Atlantic, unavailable) was a masterpiece of psychedelic hokum, but once the voodoo schtick wore thin in the early '70s, Rebbennack embarked on his real life's work: to dedicate his formidable pianistic skills and uniquely twisted voice – exactly halfway between a whine and a croak – to interpreting and extending his hometown's R&B heritage. It's still what he does today, alternating solo-album exercises in New Orleans classicism with lucrative studio work for anyone who needs some serious bayou fonk (which means everyone from B.B. KING and Johnny Winter to Ringo Starr and Marianne Faithfull). He's one of the very few white musicians discussed in this book who, as far as the black musicians with whom they work are concerned, are only white on the outside. The 'authenticity' question simply doesn't arise with Dr John: he's been playing this music for nearly forty years, and has contributed as much to its growth as any man living.

- *Gumbo* (Atco 7006-2[US])
- *Goin' Back To New Orleans* (Warner Bros 7599-26940-2)

Two full decades separate these wonderful musical travelogues, but nothing else does. In each case, Dr John assembled Grade-A Nwawlins crews to work out on Grade-A Nwawlins material. *Gumbo* (1972) concentrates on material associated with Huey 'Piano' Smith, Earl King and Professor Longhair: songs like 'Big Chief', 'Junko Partner', 'Don't You Just Know It', 'Come On Let The Good Times Roll', 'Iko Iko' and 'Tipitina'. Anyone who can't party to this record can't party, *period*. *Goin' Back To New Orleans* (1992), the most ambitious record Dr John has ever made, is broader in both scope and sound: it draws its keynote from JOE LIGGINS's title tune; includes gorgeous backing vocals from The Neville Brothers, and refers back to Buddy Bolden, Jelly Roll Morton and beyond. There is an undeniable aura of self-

271

consciousness about these albums – respectively reconstruction and fantasia – but you'll only notice it when you're sitting down. *HINT!*

- *Dr John Plays Mac Rebennack* (Demon FIEND CD 1)
- *The Brightest Smile In Town* (Demon FIENDCD 9)

The mixture as before, only solo and (mostly) instrumental. Whereas *Gumbo* and *Goin' Back To New Orleans* respectively focus on the Crescent City's '50s pop/R&B tradition and on that tradition's roots in the early years of this century, these two are ruminative piano showcases from '81 and '82, the first featuring mainly original material in the Longhair/Smith tradition, and the second drawing on an eclectic bag of songs ranging from Jimmie Rodgers's 'Waiting For A Train' to W.C. Handy's 'Didn't He Ramble' and Harold Arlen's 'Come Rain Or Come Shine'. If *Gumbo* and *Goin' Back To New Orleans* take you to New Orleans team-handed for, respectively, a rocking street party and some weird combination of a street parade and a voodoo ceremony, these take you there alone, at night, for a contemplative stroll down the Bourbon Street of your dreams. Not as mind-boggling as the JAMES BOOKER solo albums, but considerably more relaxing.

- **BLUESIANA:** *Bluesiana Triangle* (Windham Hill Jazz WD-1025)
- **BLUESIANA:** *Bluesiana II* (Windham Hill Jazz 01934 10133-2)

The original Bluesiana were a dream team: the good Doctor on piano, guitar and vocals, alongside saxophonist David 'Fathead' Newman, and jazz patriarch Art Blakey on drums (and, miraculously, playing piano and singing 'For All We Know' as the album's closer). They do everything from post-bopping the blues on Newman's 'Heads Up' to taking standards like 'When The Saints Come Marching In' and the traditional 'Shoo Fly Don't Bother Me' for a street parade. Reconvening after Blakey's death with Living Colour's Will Calhoun in the drum chair, they played up the fonk quotient of their bluesy jazz (complete with appropriate titles like 'Fonkalishus' and 'Skoshuss'). Dr John's 'Doctor Blooze' could almost serve as a career credo.

Subjects for further investigation: The nearest you'll get to a basic Dr John best-of is *The Ultimate Dr John* (Warner Special Projects 9-

27612-2 [US]), which includes the eerie 'Walk On Gilded Splinters' (from *Gris-Gris*) and a heaping handful of *Gumbo*. If I attempted to provide a Dr John sessionography we'd both be here all night; so suffice it to say that B.B. King's ***There Must Be A Better World Somewhere*** (BGO BGOCD 124), with Dr John playing piano throughout, contains an entire programme of songs composed (with one exception) by Dr John and the late lyricist Doc Pomus. For more Rebennack piano (and another superb Pomus/Rebennack composition, 'Hello Stranger'), seek out Marianne Faithfull's ***Strange Weather*** (bundled with *Broken English* as Island ITSCD 10), and Johnny Winter's ***Third Degree*** (Alligator ALCD 4748). The 'Bluesiana' name no longer implies the presence of Rebennack or Newman: it's currently being used by the young rhythm section featured on New Blueser John Mooney's ***Travelin' On*** (Crosscut CCD 11032).

Snooks Eaglin

The current king of Nwawlins guitar is Fird – yes, *Fird* – 'Snooks' Eaglin, a Great Uncategorisable who once got mistaken for a blues singer and finally learned to live with it; the best story I ever heard about him concerns the time Eaglin (who is blind) walked out on some PROFESSOR LONGHAIR sessions in upstate New York because the sound of snowfall was keeping him awake at night. Born in New Orleans on 21 January 1936, he lost his sight before he was a year old as the result of a botched glaucoma operation, and found the guitar at age six in his local Baptist church. In the late '50s folklorist Harry Oster heard him street-singing and, impressed by his deft guitar-playing and eclectic repertoire, recorded him as a solo acoustic bluesman. In fact, Snooks had been street-singing to raise money to start up an R&B band, and indeed spent much of his subsequent career leading a small group through club gigs ranging from blues dives through to the New Orleans Playboy Club, where his charm and versatility made him a perennial favourite. Eaglin can sing and play just about anything a customer was likely to request, all the way from supperclub standards to country and western, from downhome blues to hometown R&B.

His earliest attempts at commercial recording (ten 1960–1 sides for – how did you guess? – Dave Bartholomew at Imperial Records) went nowhere; so, apart from an early-'70s solo session for Sam Charters's *Legacy Of The Blues* series, he stuck to local live work until Black Top Records boss Hammond Scott tempted him back into the studio in 1987. The resulting albums are among the most unselfconsciously enjoyable New Orleans R&B created in the past decade: Snooks earns his tag as 'the Professor Longhair of the guitar' not simply because of his dazzling guitar technique, amiably eccentric vocal style and overt Nwawlins roots; but because his records are just so much fun. Live long and prosper, Fird.

- *The Legacy Of The Blues Vol. 2* (Sonet SNTCD 625)

If Sam Charters expected to find the acoustic street-singer of the Oster sessions when he commissioned this solo session in 1971, he had another think coming. Playing (and occasionally thumping on) electric guitar throughout, Eaglin juxtaposes JOHN LEE HOOKER-style boogie with JAMES BROWN funky-drummer beats; adapts the piano standard 'Pine Top's Boogie Woogie' to guitar and the nightclub-flamenco 'Malaguena' to funk; and covers everything from LITTLE RICHARD's 'Lucille' to LONNIE JOHNSON's 'Tomorrow Night'. In fact, this album is a virtual primer in advanced funk rhythm guitar: even Nile Rodgers could probably learn something from it.

- *Baby, You Can Get Your Gun!* (Demon FIENDCD 96)
- *Out Of Nowhere* (Demon/Black Top FIENDCD 146)
- *Teasin' You* (Black Top CD BT-1072)

The most recent items in Snooks's CV are these considerably-more-than-fine late-'80s band albums. The third-time-lucky law makes *Teasin' You* the pick of the litter: partly because The Meters' George Porter is putting maximum bass in your face, and partly because there's no second guitarist to clutter the proceedings. No disrespect to Ronnie Earl and Anson Funderburgh, who rhythmed the first two, but Snooks Eaglin needs a rhythm guitarist like B.B. KING needs a lead guitarist. Deep blues, classic New Orleans R&B, hard bop, hard rock, blues-balladry and on-

the-one funk: Eaglin takes them all in his stride. Start with *Teasin'*
You and then sample to taste.

Subjects for further investigation: **Country Boy Down In New Orleans**
(Arhoolie CD-348) collects Snooks's late-'50s/early-'60s country
blues sessions. Featured on both 6- and 12-string guitars, Snooks
demonstrates his range, skill and willingness to entertain on
everything from country blues standards to cunningly rear-
ranged New Orleans R&B staples; but unless acoustic blues is
your very favourite thing or you've decided to become an Eaglin
completist, this one can wait. For a real Crescent City summit
(and a rare example of Snooks as sideman), check out Professor
Longhair's **House Party New Orleans Style: The Lost Sessions 1971–2**
(Demon FIENDCD 189). Another excellent solo album, *Down*
Yonder (Sonet, 1977), remains irritatingly unavailable.

Clifton Chenier

We can't leave Louisiana without a quick word about 'zydeco': the
name derives from the phrase 'les haricots sont pas sale' (meaning
'the beans ain't salted'), and the music is the black Creole side of
Louisiana's tradition of accordion-driven Francophone two-steps.
(When white guys from a country music background do it, it's
called 'cajun'; itself derived from 'Acadian', though I prefer to
think that it's a pun on 'accordion'.) Zydeco's master musician,
Clifton Chenier (born in Opelousas, Louisiana, on June 25, 1925)
blended classic zydeco with downhome blues (as might be
expected from one of the many cousins of LIGHTNIN' HOPKINS), and
recorded for Specialty (for whom he cut his first hit 'Ay-Tete Fee'
– that's 'Hey Little Girl' to us; catching on yet? A rewrite of Lionel
Hampton's 'Hey-Ba-Ba-Re-Bop', incidentally – in 1955) and Chess
subsidiaries Argo and Checker during the '50s. However, his most
consistent recordings were the series of albums he cut for
Arhoolie during the '60s and '70s. (Naturally, he continued to cut
small-label singles for the local market at the same time.)

As well as being a virtuoso who could bludgeon his squeeze-box
into sounding like an amplified mouth-harp, a Hammond organ or
an entire horn section, Chenier was a showman to the back teeth.

Like soul giant Solomon Burke, 'The King Of Rock And Soul', Chenier styled himself 'King Of Zydeco' and made his onstage entrances robed and crowned. He carried it off, too: his popularity extended way beyond the South, enabling him to tour nationally and internationally; even making the mandatory European jaunt via an American Folk Blues Festival tour in '69. Chenier died in Louisiana on December 12, 1987 – three years after winning a Grammy for his next-to-last-album *I'm Here* – of the diabetes-related kidney ailments which had laid him low since 1979 and necessitated the amputation of a foot in 1982; his son C.J. Chenier subsequently took over the band and carries on the family tradition.

- *Zodico Blues & Boogie!* (Ace CDCHD 389)

The best of the '50s Speciality sides plus a bunch of unreleased stuff from the same sessions: nothin' but the raw stomp, including both the original 'Ay-Tete Fee' master and an outtake that's almost as good; not so much zydeco as a zydeco-flavoured take on the R&B materials of the time: more blues and boogie than 'zodico'. Personally, I have no problem with this: it's these tracks which made Chenier a big enough star to do three-month-plus tours with the likes of JIMMY REED, ETTA JAMES and LOWELL FULSON.

- *Bon Temps Roulet!* (Arhoolie CD-345)
- *Louisiana Blues And Zydeco* (Arhoolie CD-329)
- *King Of The Bayous* (Arhoolie CD-339)

Over an hour's worth of '60s sessions on each of these, all of which feature cousin Lightnin's piano guy Elmore Nixon: the first two albums cover '64–'67 (though *Bon Temps Roulet!* includes a ringer from '73), and the third '65–'70. The first – and easily the best – features a variety of line-ups, ranging from simple piano and drums, plus bigger bands including fiddle (played by Chenier's uncle Morris), bass, guitar, and Chenier's brother Cleveland on rub-board (a a sort of ridged metal T-shirt played with thimbles); the material includes blues standards ranging from the title track (a Francophonisation of LOUIS JORDAN's 'Let The Good Times Roll') to BLIND LEMON JEFFERSON's 'Black Snake Blues' and BIG BILL BRONZY's

'Key To The Highway', as well as homegrown Louisiana fare. The severely rootsy *Louisiana Blues And Zydeco* leads off with a quintessential 'Zydeco Sont Pas Sale' with only drums and rubboard accompaniment, and includes a remake of 'Ay-Tete Fille'; Engelbert Humperdinck wouldn't believe the funky version of 'Release Me' on *King Of The Bayous*, but hopefully he'd get off on its 'Zodeco Two-Step,' if not its rocking variant on 'Dust My Blues.'

- *Live At St Marks* (Arhoolie CD-313)
- *The King Of Zydeco Live At Montreux* (Arhoolie CD-315)

So how do you like your live Chenier: playing a dance for a bunch of homesick bayou expats in California, or doing the biz for a stadium-full of European jazz fans? One guess only, folks. If the lo-fi location recording on *Live At St Marks* (1971) didn't dissolve the bass and drums into oatmeal, it would be not only Chenier's best album, but one of the finest live blues albums of its decade. It's only fractionally rawer than his studio recordings, but the palpable sense of connection between artist and audience makes it considerably richer. The Montreux album, from '75, is a well-recorded, well-performed, and well-received (especially when Clifton tells the crowd that he speaks French too, but it's a little different) 'live greatest hits' album, but *St Marks* cuts it cold on the vibe-o-meter. (Personal highlight: 'Mama Told Papa', a steaming boogie variation of Junior Parker's 'Feelin' Good', itself derived from JOHN LEE HOOKER's 'Boogie Chillun'.)

- *Bogalusa Boogie* (Arhoolie CD-347)
- *I'm Here!* (Sonet SNTCD-882)

Arhoolie boss Chris Strachwitz says in his liner note that, as far as he's concerned, *Bogalusa Boogie* was the best thing he ever cut on Clifton Chenier. Dating from 1975, it's both crisply recorded and exuberantly performed, and deserved to win the Grammy that eventually went to 1982's *I'm Here!* The unspoken subtitle of that album would be 'I'm (Still) Here!', because it marked Chenier's return to recording after severe health problems which necessitated the use of an electronic accordion because his dialysis treatments had left him too enervated to pump his old piano accordion. It's a poignant, courageous record, but the sound of the new instrument is unsatisfying, and the strain tells on Chenier's performance. His very last sessions, cut in 1984 for a small Lafayette label, appear on *King Of Zydeco* (Ace CDCHD 234); I prefer not to remember him that way.

Subjects for further investigation: **Out West** (Arhoolie CD 350) is a California semi-super-session featuring ELVIN BISHOP on slide guitar; the original 'Ay-Tete Fee' is also included on *Creole Kings Of New Orleans* (Ace/Specialty CDCHD 393); the American Folk Blues Festival live recordings are on *American Folk Blues Festival '69* (L&R/Bellaphon LRCD 42071). Zydeco is a whole musical sub-universe of its own and I'm not necessarily the best person to guide you through it, but the compilation *Zydeco Party!* (Ace CDCHD 430) includes contributions from Rockin' Dopsie, Rockin' Sidney (the 'My Toot Toot' man) and Boozoo Chavis as well as Chenier and a whole host of other accordion-strangling good-timers. Chavis has his own album, *Boozoo Chavis* (Elektra American Explorer 7559-61146-2); and you can check out a more contemporary zydeco sound from Buckwheat Zydeco (led by the scene's young hotshot, Stanley 'Buckwheat' Doral) on *On Track* (Charisma CDCUS 13).

4. *The Jump Legacy*

Jump was the last new blues style introduced before World War II – thanks, principally, to LOUIS JORDAN – and accordingly it was the first off the blocks when the war ended. Even after Electric Downhome and the Memphis Synthesis, West Coast jump remained the mainstream of working-class African-American entertainment until the mid-'50s. Basically, jump was cut-down swing-band stuff (the archetypal jump combo would drop three horns onto a piano-bass-and-srums rhythm section) with kicking, danceable beats and novelty lyrics: it was rock and roll before rock and roll was (as was its white counterpart, 'Western Swing', with which it freely exchanged repertoire); whether it remained so after the arrival of CHUCK BERRY, ELVIS PRESLEY and LITTLE RICHARD is another matter entirely. However, once rock and roll arrived in its post-Presley form, jump atrophied; those of its constituent parts not swallowed by rock were seamlessly absorbed by urban blues, the small-group end of populist jazz, and the new gospel-inflected R&B of RAY CHARLES and JAMES BROWN, which they ended up calling 'soul'.

The best available one-volume introduction to jump is *Blues Masters Vol. 5: Jump Blues Classics* (Rhino R2 71125); there's no shortage of honking and shouting from the likes of ROY BROWN, ROY MILTON, WYNONIE HARRIS, CLARENCE 'GATEMOUTH' BROWN, JOE TURNER, Ruth Brown, JIMMY LIGGINS and BULLMOOSE JACKSON, but AMOS MILBURN is unaccountably absent. *Jumpin' The Blues* (Ace CDCHD 941) showcases a platoon of lesser-known performers (of whom the least obscure is probably Cecil Gant) to scarcely lesser effect; while *Shoutin' Swingin' And Makin' Love* (MCA/Chess CHD 9327) concentrates on a smaller group of performers, including Jimmy Rushing and JIMMY WITHERSPOON, but its prize is a triad of tunes from Wynonie Harris's last session, with a B.B. KING-styled studio band featuring either BUDDY GUY or someone who sounds very much like him. Jump reminds us that contemporary critical demarcations between blues, jazz, rock and pop were definitely not observed at the time, and a damn good thing too.

Come! Let us return to a time when men were men, suits were suits, saxophones were saxophones, and guitarists were admitted only if they promised to behave.

Roy Brown

Roy Brown's plummy voice, exaggerated vibrato and mock-British vowel sounds weren't to everybody's taste, but they certainly made an impression on the young JAMES BROWN and B.B. KING; the latter's early style owed almost as much to Brown's vocal mannerisms – and to the unusually prominent guitar on his records – as it did to T-BONE WALKER's pioneering licks. Born on September 10, 1925, in New Orleans, his best shot came when he composed 'Good Rockin' Tonight' in 1947 and had the song taken off him by WYNONIE 'Mr Blues' HARRIS, who had a bigger hit with it the following year, and from whose version ELVIS PRESLEY borrowed it. Brown struck back with the almost identical 'Rockin' At Midnight' (a No 2 R&B hit), only to have Harris co-opt it into

'Rock Mr Blues'. 'Mr Blues' also lifted Brown's 'Lollypop Mama' and 'Miss Fanny Brown'; no wonder they were didn't get on.

Brown was born in New Orleans on September 10, 1925,and raised in Los Angeles. He made his first records in 1947 for the Texas-based Gold Star label, and enjoyed a decade or so's worth of R&B hits on various labels. He resurfaced in the late '70s as a guest artist with Johnny Otis's revue, and was in the process of relaunching himself when he died on May 25, 1981. He could at least console himself with the thought that he outlived Wynonie Harris.

- **WYNONIE HARRIS/ROY BROWN:** *Battle Of The Blues Vol. 1* (King KCD-607)
- **EDDIE 'CLEANHEAD' VINSON/WYNONIE HARRIS/ROY BROWN:** *Battle Of The Blues Vol. 4* (King KCD-668)

These slim-line budget collections currently represent all the Roy Brown you can get on CD: he and Harris split the 14-track *Vol. 1* down the middle; and they take three each (to shaven-headed saxophonist Eddie 'Cleanhead' Vinson's six) on the 12-track *Vol 4*. You can hear the young B.B. taking notes on 'Big Town' (not just to Brown's vocal tricks but to the uncredited guitarist's muted-but-funky fills). 'Boogie At Midnight' is another variation on 'Rockin' At Midnight', but this time it's Brown who gets to sing 'Lollypop Mama' and 'Fanny Brown'; his best shot is the epic 'Love Don't Love Nobody' (as covered by James Brown), but dig the taunting tone of his ride-out to 'I Got The Last Laugh Now.'. All the Harris tracks included here, except 'Shake That Thing', are also on Harris's *Good Rocking Tonight* collection (Charly CD CHARLY 244), but they include most of the biggies; if you're in a hurry *Vol. 1* will do sterling service as a summary of both men's work. *Vol. 4*, adorned with the most garish imaginable example of '50s sexist kitsch cover art, displays Brown's smooth way with a slow blues on 'Trouble At Midnight' as well as his mock-operatic excess on 'Queen Of Diamonds'; seekers after more of Vinson can find him trading tracks with JIMMY WITHERSPOON on *Battle Of The Blues Vol. 3* (King KCD-634), though his signature song 'They Call Me Mr Cleanhead' slips through the net. The *Battle Of The Blues* title is ironically appropriate, considering how cordially Brown and Harris allegedly disliked each other.

Wynonie Harris

Wynonie 'Mr Blues' Harris was almost the perfect jumpster archetype: a slick-suited, pencil-moustached, eye-rolling self-mythologiser surrounded by moonlighting jazz players blowing their brains out on big-fun swing shuffles. Clearly, Wynonie didn't believe in false modesty (or, indeed, any other kind); he closes out 'Keep On Churnin' ('Til The Butter Come') with 'Hey, heifer – here comes your bull'. 'Bull' is, quite possibly, the appropriate word.

Born in Omaha, Nebraska, on August 24, 1915, he was outta there by the time he was 18; studying great blues shouters like Jimmy Rushing and Joe Turner in Kansas City and scuffling in Los Angeles as a singer, dancer, drummer, comedian, MC or movie extra. By 1944, he was a featured vocalist with Lucky Millinder's band before cutting under his own name for a variety of labels; his golden era was with the Cincinnati-based King label, which he joined in 1947. 'Mr Blues' suffered a career downturn after the mid-'50s; recording dates were fewer and further between, and when he died on June 14, 1969, in Los Angeles, he had not performed for two years. Unlike his Fellow Lucky Millinder grad, Benjamin 'BULLMOOSE' JACKSON, Harris wasn't around long enough for his music to come back into favour, but the best of his records eminently deserve their classic status.

- *Good Rocking Tonight* (Charly CD CHARLY 244)

The basic Wynonie Harris record: covering assorted 1947–1953 King sessions, and including the inevitable title track plus the country borrowings 'Bloodshot Eyes' and 'Good Morning Judge'. Outside the better-known cuts are subtler joys: self-referential brag songs like 'Rock Mr Blues' and 'Mr Blues Is Coming To Town'; the broadest double-entendres since the heyday of LUCILLE BOGAN on songs like 'I Won't Like My Baby's Pudding', 'Keep On Churnin' ('Til The Butter Come)', and 'Lollipop Mama'; and some serious saxophone and trumpet abuse on, respectively, 'She Don't Sell No More' and 'Baby, Shame On You'.

281

Amos Milburn

Amos Milburn liked a drink, or several. More important, he liked songs about drink – or several. His 1950 hit 'Bad Bad Whiskey' was eventually followed by 'Good Good Whiskey', 'Vicious Vicious Vodka', 'Juice Juice Juice', 'Rum And Coca Cola' and – for the busy drinker in a hurry – 'One Scotch, One Bourbon, One Beer'. The booze he sang about probably contributed as much to his eventual career decline as the booze he drank: his increasingly specialised target audience was probably too pissed to find the record store even if they still had enough money to buy a record.

A gifted singer/pianist/composer who wore his influences – LOUIS JORDAN's party-time swing novelties and CHARLES BROWN's soulful, sophisticated blues balladry – on both sleeves, Milburn was born in Houston, Texas, on April 1, 1926; was discovered leading a band there shortly after his demob from World War II,and by 1946 he was in L.A. recording for Aladdin. He did well, too: his versatility enabled him to score equally high with jolly-up novelties like 'Chicken Shack Boogie' or 'One Scotch, One Bourbon, One Beer'; coolly anguished ballads like 'Empty Arms Blues', 'Bewildered', or the blatantly Charles Brown-derived 'Let's Make Christmas Merry, Baby'. Milburn at his most raucous was still considerably smoother and more laid-back than WYNONIE HARRIS or BULLMOOSE JACKSON, but he still ran out of steam after a smouldering 1956 remake of 'Chicken Shack Boogie'; even the intervention of Berry Gordy Jr, who commissioned a 1962 Motown album complete with a Little Stevie Wonder cameo – could salvage him. Milburn's heavy drinking was complicated by epilepsy, and after a series of strokes, he lost the use of one hand. Six months after relapses necessitated the amputation of a leg, he died in Cleveland on January 3, 1980. His songs are still in circulation: JAMES BROWN had a 1961 R&B smash with 'Bewildered'; 'One Scotch' is probably best known in its 1966 JOHN LEE HOOKERised incarnation 'One Bourbon, One Scotch, One Beer'; and BUDDY GUY cut a fine, reflective 'Bad Bad Whiskey'.

- *Blues & Boogie: His Greatest Hits* (Sequel NEX CD 132)

A full decade's worth from 1946–56: out of these 23 tunes, no less than 18 made the R&B Top 10; 13 of those went Top 5; and four of *those* ('Chicken Shack Boogie', 'Bewildered', and 'Roomin' House Boogie') made Number 1. Idiotically, the compilers sequence the 1954 'Good Good Whiskey' before the original 1950 'Bad Bad Whiskey', but otherwise it's a generously-laden, judiciously-selected and consistently entertaining assortment of slow blues, jivey jumps and intriguing mid-paced items. Oh yeah – they haven't bothered with 'Vicious Vicious Vodka', 'Juice Juice Juice', or 'Rum And Coca Cola'.

Subjects for further investigation: James Brown's fabulous version of 'Bewildered' is included in *Star Time* (Polydor 849 108-2), though it would have been more appropriate alongside his take on ROY BROWN's 'Love Don't Love Nobody' on *Messin' With The Blues* (Polydor 847 258-2); Hooker's 'One Bourbon, One Scotch, One Beer' made its debut on 1966's *The Real Folk Blues*: find it on either *The Complete Chess Folk Blues Sessions* (MCA/Chess MCD-18335) or *House Of The Blues* (Chess CD RED 5); Buddy's 'Bad Bad Whiskey', cut in 1970 with ERIC CLAPTON producing and playing slide, is on *Buddy Guy & Junior Wells Play The Blues* (Rhino R2 70299); Amos's old pal and role model CHARLES BROWN does it on *All My Life* (Bullseye Blues NET CD 9501).

Roy Milton

Roy Milton was a ridiculously successful elder statesman of jump: he cut his first hit record in 1945 – when he was thirty-eight years old – and then proceeded to rack up a total of 18 Top 10 R&B hits within the next five years. As a result he was, at least until the blossoming of Phil Collins, the most successful drummer/front-man in postwar popular music (and let's leave Dave Clark out of this): and, as one of the first artists signed to Specialty Records, his hits ensured the longevity of the label that later brought the world LITTLE RICHARD and Sam Cooke. His secret weapon was his band's brilliant pianist, Camille Howard (also a more than competent vocalist and a featured attraction in her own right), whose praises he sang in 'Camille's Boogie'; and he had a sharp enough ear for changing trends to hire an electric blues guitarist in 1949.

Born in Oklahoma sometime in 1907, Milton was a swing-band

vocalist who was unexpectedly forced to double on drums one night in 1929 when the regular incumbent got arrested just before a show: he decided he liked it, and sang from behind his kit for the rest of his career. He hit L.A. in 1935 and kept afloat as a musician, movie extra and (briefly) nightclub proprietor until he cut his first record in 1945. After a few false starts, he hit the jackpot with 'R.M. Blues' (which hit in '46) and he and Speciality Records were very happy together until the inevitable post-rock decline set in. Under the good auspices of Johnny Otis, he had a late-blooming comeback (sadly without Howard, who'd joined the church and forsworn worldly music) in the '70s, but poor health eventually got to him, and he died in L.A. on September 18, 1983. His biggest hits were 'Milton's Boogie' and 'R.M. Blues' (1946), 'True Blues' (1947), 'Everything I Do Is Wrong' and 'Hop, Skip And Jump' (1948), 'The Hucklebuck' and Information Blues' (1949), 'Oh Babe' (1950), 'Best Wishes' (1951) and 'Night And Day' (1952), all of which made the R&B Top 5.

- *Roy Milton & His Solid Senders* (Specialty/Ace CDCHD 308)
- *Vol. 2: Groovy Blues* (Specialty/Ace CDCHD 435)

Since Roy Milton's repertoire was never extensively covered by other artists, the distinction between these two albums has very little to do with title recognition factor. The hits are all on the first album, which means that the material is slightly snappier, but the quality of the performances is laudably consistent across both CDs, which cover 1945–52 and 1946–53, respectively. In other words, plenty of powerful and inventive piano (and the occasional lead or duet vocal) from Howard; underrecorded drums and smooth vocalising from Milton himself; material ranging from unreconstructed swing to low-down blues to jump novelties to glutinous ballads; plenty of fine cameos from the horn players and (on the later tracks) some rousing blues guitar from Johnny Rogers.

Subjects for further investigation: Eight scintillating Camille Howard solo features, plus a rerun of Roy's 'Milton's Boogie', are among the crown jewels of *Specialty Legends Of Boogie-Woogie* (Specialty/Ace CDCHD 422).

Bullmoose Jackson

The big-voiced and over-saxed Benjamin Clarence 'Bullmoose' Jackson was both a legitimate jazz guy with a wicked line in tenor-sax stylings, and the lascivious singer best-known for the immortal jump standard 'My Big Ten-Inch (Record Of The Band That Plays The Blues)'. Born in Cleveland, Ohio, sometime in 1919, he'd played with Lena Horne, Freddie Webster and Big Sid Catlett before joining Lucky Millinder's band: his vocal talents were only revealed when WYNONIE HARRIS, the Millinder band's featured vocalist, refused to sing one night and Jackson stepped into the breach. Since the Millinder band was exclusively contracted elsewhere,they used Jackson's name – as well as those of other members, like drummer Panama Francis – for extracurricular recording sessions for King. The upshot was that Jackson soon became an attraction in his own right and, inevitably, started his own band.

Like many another jumpster, Bullmoose enjoyed his greatest successes between the mid-'40s and mid-'50s. Times were lean for him after that, and Bullmoose had to wait for a mid-'80s jump revival before he could lumber back into the spotlight. He died, happy and lionised – June 21, 1985 had been declared 'Bullmoose Jackson Day' in Pittsburgh – on 31 July 1989.

- **Badman Jackson, That's Me** (Charly CD CHARLY 274)

Many of Jackson's biggest hits were with ballads, including 'I Love You, Yes I Do', a big favourite of B.B. KING's which was a hit not once but twice: Jackson almost kickstarted a second career with a 1961 remake. This 1945–1955 collection concentrates mainly on the jumps, both original and borrowed. Complete with 'I Wanna Hug, Kiss Ya, Squeeze Ya' (heisted from one Buddy Griffin and subsequently JOHN LEE HOOKERised), 'Meet Me With With Your Black Dress On' (a.k.a. 'Meet Me With Your Black Drawers On'), 'Nosey Joe' (composed by the young Leiber & Stoller), 'Why Don't You Haul Off And Love Me' (lifted from country star Wayne Raney) and no less than two versions of 'My Big Ten Inch' (Aerosmith, you should be ashamed of yourselves), this is one of the most flat-out enjoyable jump collections you can buy.

Subjects for further investigation: If you develop a taste for this kind of mess-around, Oklahomans Joe Liggins and his younger brother Jimmy Liggins should be high on the list of other jump guys you might dig. Pianist Joe Liggins (1915–) got started first, racking up ten hits – notably 'The Honeydripper' and 'I've Got A Right To Cry', on Exclusive Records – but guitar-playing Jimmy Liggins, seven years Joe's junior and Big Bro's former on-the-road chauffeur/valet, had taken the results of his own songwriting bug to Specialty after Exclusive turned him down. By 1948 he'd placed three singles of his own in the R&B Top 20 (1947's 'Cadillac Boogie' the source for Jackie Brenston's subsequent 'Rocket 88'; allegedy the first-ever rock and roll record, not amongst them), so he was in a good position to cast Joe a lifeline when Exclusive went under. Joe immediately re-recorded his two biggest songs, but it was the new ones which counted: 'Pink Champagne', Billboard's #1 R&B single of 1950, was only the most successful of the four singles he put into the R&B Top 5 that year. Both faded from view in the mid-'50s, despite Jimmy salvaging the family honour by scoring one final hit, 'Drunk' (R&B No4), despite having been shot in the mouth in 1949.

Joe's music was smoother and more sophisticated: check it out on *Joe Liggins And The Honeydrippers* (Specialty/Ace 307) and, if needs must, *Vol 2: Dripper's Boogie* (Ace/Specialty CDCHD 436). Jimmy's was rougher and more downhome, thanks to his prominent guitar: he's on *Jimmy Liggins And His Drops Of Joy* (Specialty/Ace CDCHD 306) and *Vol. 2: Rough Weather Blues* (Ace/Specialty CDCHD 437). Purists please note: the first Jimmy album includes the overdubbed version of 'Drunk', which was the hit, while *Vol. 2* includes an undubbed version. Who said it's only dance music that's remix crazy? 'Drunk''s sequel, Jimmy's hilarious 'I Ain't Drunk' (as covered by IKE TURNER and ALBERT COLLINS) was cut for Aladdin after Jimmy left Speciality, and has never been reissued. 'Cadillac Boogie' is also included on *Blues Masters Vol. 5: Jump Blues Classics* (Rhino R2 71125).

The only white jumpster who mattered (apart from Johnny Otis) was Louis Prima: his work is collected on *Jump, Jive And Wail* (Charly CD CHARLY 252), but further to that, since this CD was 'out of stock' during the writing of this book, deponent sayeth not.

5. *Blues & Jazz*

Discussions of the relationships between jazz and the blues are
the kind of stuff to which entire books are devoted, and since we
don't want to be here all night (let alone all year), let's simply cut
to the chase: not all blues players can play jazz (though a few can,
and many more enjoy listening to it) but no jazz player can truly
qualify as 'great' if they can't play the blues. Blues is the heartbeat
of jazz: it may not be on the surface of all jazz; but whenever that
heartbeat ceases, the music is dead. From Louis Armstrong to
Duke Ellington, from Count Basie to Charlie Parker, from Billie
Holiday to Miles Davis, from Charlie Christian to Wynton
Marsalis: even when they weren't playing the blues, they were
playing *with* the blues.

As a snapshot of how the relationship sometimes works, I've
nominated four musicians whose work exists on that blue-grey
area between the two. Whether they're bluesmen who've made a
mark in jazz, or jazz musicians who've made major contributions
to the blues, is open to debate. That all four of them are giants in
both fields, is not.

(Big) Joe Turner

A case in point: the great Joe Turner could as easily appeared in
the 'rock' section (because his '50s Atlantic sides were massively
influential and contributed key repertoire to the first generation
of white rock and rollers) or in the 'jump' section (because, after
all, those same sides were simply hopped-up jump) than here.
Alternatively, he could have been listed in the pre-war chapter
since he first recorded in the late '30s and, as the founding father
of the Kansas City school of blues-shouting, blazed the path later
followed by Jimmy Rushing, Joe Williams and JIMMY WITHERSPOON.
Born – on May 18, 1911 – and raised in K.C., he was street-singing
for coins before he was out of short pants, and used to love to
hang around a local bar to hear boogie piano genius Pete Johnson
at work. Eventually, he and Johnson ended up as a team in another
tavern: Johnson played piano while Turner bounced, bartended

and bellowed. In 1938, entrepreneur John Hammond heard them and whisked them off to New York for his legendary 'From Spirituals To Swing' show at Carnegie Hall – also featuring Count Basie, BIG BILL BROONZY, SONNY TERRY and Benny Goodman – and they were away: commencing with the classic 'Cherry Red', Turner recorded prolifically for a variety of labels throughout the '40s.

Unbelievably, considering his popularity and influence within the jazz and blues communities, Turner had to wait until 1950 to enjoy his first hit, 'Still In The Dark', cut for the Freedom label. But then the dam burst and he romped through the '50s with a string of R&B hits for Atlantic Records whiuch straddled the jump/rock fence with enviable equilibrium. He never had any further hits, but he was firmly established as a leading presence on the concert circuit, and he remained a top attraction almost until the end. Big Joe (by this time 'Unfeasibly Gynormous Joe') finally gave up the ghost in Inglewood, California, on November 23, 1985.

- **JOE TURNER, SMILIN' SMOKEY LYNN:** *Shoutin' The Blues* (Specialty/Ace CDCHD 439)

A 22-track compilation leading off with eight '49–'50 Turner sides, including the R&B chart hit 'Still In The Dark', which immediately preceded his Atlantic sojourn. Most of the rest of it is taken up by Turner imitator Smokey Lynn, but it also includes four sides of similar vintage by Big Maceo Merriwether, recorded shortly after the stroke which eventually caused his death, with TAMPA RED on guitar and Elmore James' pianist Johnnie Jones ghosting the keys. The contrast between these Turner tracks and the Atlantic period which commenced the following year illustrate exactly what kind of frosting Ahmet Ertegun and his chief arranger/composer Jesse Stone applied to the Turner cake: tougher backbeats, catchier songs. There's nothing wrong with this material: it's just that the Atlantic sides are classics and these are merely fine.

- *Texas Style* (Black & Blue 59.547.2)

Relaxed, good-humoured stuff, cut in France in 1971 with a trio led by pianist Milt Buckner and enlivened by the distinctive bowed-bass-and-vocal-unison of Slam Stewart. Big Joe revisits earlier triumphs like 'Cherry Red' and 'TV Mama' – but where are the goddam horns?

Subjects for further investigation: Turner is one of those artists who absolutely define their idiom, and one of the great frustrations of this book is that none of the records on which he does it are currently available. If you could get 'em on CD, I'd steer you towards *Early Big Joe* (MCA, unavailable) for its fabulous early-'40s sides with Johnson and other piano maestri; and then to *His Greatest Hits* (Atlantic, unavailable), which contains everything from 'Shake Rattle And Roll', 'Flip Flop And Fly, 'Corrina Corrina' and 'Chains Of Love' to 'Honey Hush' and 'Sweet Sixteen' (later adopted by, respectively, ALBERT COLLINS and B.B. KING), and the uncharacteristic but wonderful 'TV Mama', cut in Chicago with ELMORE JAMES and his band. The original 1938 Turner/Johnson version of 'Roll 'Em Pete' is on *The Story Of The Blues* (Columbia 468992 2); the soundtrack album to Spike Lee's *Malcolm X* (Qwest/Reprise 9362-45130-2) contains a later, undated version. An excerpt from their Carnegie Hall debut is preserved on *From Spirituals To Swing* (Vanguard VCD2-47/48). Of the Atlantic sides, you can hear 'Chains Of Love' on *Blues Masters Vol. 1: Urban Blues* (Rhino R2 71121) and 'Shake Rattle And Roll' on *Blues Masters Vol. 5: Jump Blues Classics* (Rhino R2 71125).

Jimmy Witherspoon

Albert Einstein once said something to the effect that 'if I succeed, the Germans will say I am a German and the French will say that I am a Jew. If I fail, the French say that I am a German, and the Germans will say I am a Jew.' Jimmy Witherspoon has a similar problem: blues fans say he's a jazz singer and jazz fans that he's a blues singer. Both factions will happily turn out to see him, though, and so they should: Witherspoon may not be splitting the atom, but he sounds as if he is.

The most powerful living practitioner of the lost art of Kansas City-style blues shouting, Spoon blows a big bad full-chested baritone equally capable of sonorously intoning over an intimate chamber-blues ensemble, or cruising around or through a swaggering big-band horn section. Born in Gurdison, Arkansas, on August 8, 1923, he followed the classic path West to L.A., emerging from the US Army in 1945 in time to replace Walter Brown in Jay McShann's band. (Charlie Parker was also a McShann grad; Brown and McShann were the co-composers of the standard 'Confessin' The Blues', as beloved of CHUCK BERRY and THE ROLLING STONES.) He rapidly established himself with a personalised version of the standard 'Ain't Nobody's Business' (with which he had a hit in 1949) and his own perennial composition 'Times Gettin' Tougher Than Tough'. Hard-working and prolific, he's been an indestructible fixture on the jazz and blues scene ever since, recording for just about every R&B and jazz label around: Spoon material lurks in the vaults of Chess, King, Modern, RCA, Prestige, Atlantic, Reprise and so on *ad infinitum*. Even throat cancer couldn't put him out, thanks to the NHS, and he's still at it today: his most recent album, *The Blues, The Whole Blues, And Nothing But The Blues*, was released in 1992.

- *Jimmy Witherspoon & Jay McShann* (Black Lion BLCD 760173)
- *Blowin' In From Kansas City* (Ace CDCHD 279)

Early Spoon from the late '40s and early '50s: the Black Lion is split between McShann sides featuring Spoon, instrumentals and tracks showcasing other, less interesting, vocalists, but it's exciting as hell, and you get your 'Ain't Nobody's Business' and 'Times Gettin' Tougher Than Tough' (even though the former precedes the hit version and the latter is retitled 'Money's Gettin' Cheaper'. The Ace set is hot, distorted and riotous – someone buy the guitarists a drink – and it features Spoon with Johnny Otis's band as well as McShann's, but it doesn't include any of Spoon's signature songs.

- *Rockin' With Spoon* (Charly CD BM 25)

Remember what I said about great jazzmen playing the blues? Since I ain't gonna shut up, this is where I put up: these '59 live sessions – one at the Monterey Jazz Festival, one in an L.A. club – present Spoon working through his classic repertoire in the company of Ben Webster and Mel Lewis (respectively on tenor and drums throughout) alongside Coleman Hawkins (tenor), Roy Eldridge (trumpet), Woody Herman (clarinet) and Earl Hines (piano) on the Monterey set; and Gerry Mulligan (baritone sax) in the club. (The rhythm sections aren't bad, either.) With songs like ROY BROWN's 'Good Rockin' Tonight', Leiber & Stoller's 'Kansas City', LEROY CARR's 'How Long', JOE TURNER & Pete Johnson's 'Roll 'Em Pete', MEMPHIS SLIM's 'Every Day I Have The Blues' (done a la Count Basie and Joe Williams) and Spoon's own 'Times Gettin' Tougher Than Tough' on the menu, this is the absolute quintessential Jimmy Witherspoon album. Here he is, shouting the blues over a bunch of jazz players going hog-wild, and generating enough energy to light up half of California. Not a guitarist in sight.

Subjects for further investigation: **Jimmy Witherspoon And Panama Francis' Savoy Sultans** (Black & Blue 59.177 2) combines two '79/'80 sessions: one finds Spoon working through a Basie-derived repertoire with a septet led by drummer Francis; the other uses an organ-guitar-drums trio to explore more recent standards like 'Every Day I Have The Blues' and 'Stormy Monday'; both are longer on expertise than vitality. **Battle Of The Blues Vol. 3** (King KCD-634) comprises eight sides apiece by Witherspoon and saxophonist/singer Eddie 'Cleanhead' Vinson; the chart-aimed Spoon titles include rather too much of a mooing vocal group and rather too little first-class material. The highlight of the three '50s Spoon tracks on **Shoutin' Swingin' And Makin' Love** (MCA/Chess CHD-9327) is a gorgeous 'Goin' Down Slow' with McShann on piano, but his most celebrated Chess side was Willie Dixon's composition 'When The Lights Go Out': find it on **A Tribute To Willie Dixon 1915–1992** (Chess CD RED 37) or on Dixon's **The Chess Box** (MCA/Chess CHD2-16500. Just in case you may need another version of 'Ain't Nobody's Business', there's a previously unissued '56 take on **Chess Blues** (MCA/Chess CHD4-9340). The contemporary **The Blues, The Whole Blues, And Nothing But The Blues** (Indigo IGO CD 2001) is a classy collection of sophisticated soul-blues ballads, with a frayed but resonant Spoon squeezing every ounce of juice from some good new songs.

Mose Allison

Most white guys who sing the blues attempt to sound black: in fact, the holy grail for most white blues guys is to 'pass' in a blindfold test. One who didn't was Mose Allison, a jazz pianist born in Tippo, Mississippi, on November 11, 1927; he sang the blues as himself, in a huskily conversational manner which was his and his alone, though others – notably GEORGIE FAME – have mimicked it. He was also a composer with a formidable library of epigrammatically sardonic songs, including 'Your Mind Is On Vacation', 'Parchman Farm' (a favourite of Georgie Fame and JOHN MAYALL), 'A Young Man' (a.k.a. 'Young Man Blues', as featured by The Who), 'Fool Killer', 'If You Live', 'Days Like This', 'Everybody's Cryin' Mercy' and 'If You're Going To The City'. As a vocal interpreter, he has performed songs like WILLIE DIXON's 'Seventh Son' and 'I Live The Life I Love', CHARLES BROWN's 'Fool's Paradise', PERCY MAYFIELD's 'Lost Mind' and Mercy Dee Walton's 'One Room Country Shack' with such distinction that unwary listeners think they're his.

Allison got his start in New York City during the mid-'50s, emerging from college and the Army to play with the likes of Gerry Mulligan and Stan Getz, who loved his muscular, bluesy post-bop piano style. He began recording as a featured artist for Presige Records ('56–'59) and Columbia ('59–'61) before settling down for a lengthy sojourn with Atlantic, who have, naturally, allowed his finest work to go out of print. A further couple of early-'80s albums for the now-defunct Elektra Musician label, one of which featured Jack Bruce (bass) and Billy Cobham (drums) as rhythm section, demonstrated that his powers were utterly undiminished. It would be nice if Sony and WEA would get up offa the Allison thangs they're currently holding; and even nicer if someone would record him again. Mose Allison is about as funky as a white guy can get without wearing audio blackface: we need more of him.

● *Mose Allison Sings And Plays* (Prestige CDJZD 007)

The 1963 collection *Mose Allison Sings* (itself a filleting of various vocal tracks from three years' worth of albums, including the legendary *Back Country Suite*) pumped up to a satisfactorily CD-filling 77 minutes or so. It does full justice to Mose the interpretative pianist-vocalist – he does just fine by Willie Dixon, SONNY BOY WILLIAMSON, George & Ira Gershwin, Duke Ellington, Percy Mayfield, JOE LIGGINS and JIMMY ROGERS – but rather less for Mose the songwriter; his classic repertoire reflected here only by 'Parchman Farm', 'If You Live' and 'A Young Man.' This isn't the compilers' fault – most of those great songs were written after he left the label – but this disk's unfortunate status as the only Mose Allison CD in the rack contributes to an inadequate depiction of a great talent. If you ever see anything on Atlantic claiming to be a Mose Allison best-of, buy it. We can worry about the details later.

Jimmy Smith

'The Incredible' Jimmy Smith was neither the first nor the only jazz organist – Fats Waller and Wild Bill Davis had been there a long time before him, and the likes of Big John Patton, Jimmy McGriff, Richard 'Groove' Holmes and Shirtley Scott were all in there pitching for his crown – but more than anyone else, he was the guy who got the Hammond out of church and into the bars during the mid-'50s: almost as subversive a gesture as the grand larceny of gospel songs and devices perpetrated at around the same time by RAY CHARLES and JAMES BROWN. Smith's music was utterly funky; whether he was working out on a pop ballad, a jazz standard, a funk-blues instrumental or one of his idiosyncratic vocal interpretations of songs like 'Hoochie Coochie Man' or 'Got My Mojo Working', the man was playing nothin' but the blues. The galvanic energy with which The Incredible attacks what's basically a fairly rinky-dink instrument is astonishing; the intense excitement he can generate with it even more so.

Born in Norristown, Pennsylvania, on December 8, 1925, James Oscar Smith started out on piano, turning pro in 1952. By '56 he'd discovered the glories of the Hammond and commenced recording for Blue Note; a whole slew of organ-guitar-drums trios springing up in his wake all across black America. In the '60s he recorded for Verve under the supervision of pop-jazz entrepreneur Creed Taylor, who cleaned Smith up so that they could both clean up. Smith has ridden trends up and down, and he's still playing: in 1987, he even cropped up on the title track of Michael Jackson's *Bad*. Jimmy Smith invented a new way to play the blues, and virtually a new instrument to play it on. Just as LITTLE WALTER reinvented the harmonica and, in their different ways, T-BONE WALKER, Charlie Christian and JIM HENDRIX reinvented the electric guitar, Jimmy Smith is the *onlie begetter* of the way we hear the electric organ today.

● *Compact Jazz* (Verve 831 374-2)

An excellent budget-price sampler of Smith's pop-jazz '60s Verve catalogue: there's the visceral kick of hearing him punch it out with arranger Oliver Nelson's platoons of brass on the likes of 'Walk On The Wild Side' or 'Who's Afraid Of Virginia Woolf?', but for our purposes it's the blues tunes which make the running: 'The Organ Grinder's Swing' and 'Blue Bash' (the title tunes of two annoyingly-unavailable small-group albums; the former feauring a gorgeous 9-minute slow blues called 'Oh No Babe'), 'Blues In The Night', 'Night Train' (with Wes Montgomery on guitar) and Duke Ellington's 'C-Jam Blues.' Then there's 'Got My Mojo Working', heh heh. If this is pop-jazz, it's about as unglossy as it ever gets. (For pre-cleanup Jimmy Smith, listen to The Incredible on 1958's live-in-Harlem *Cool Blues* (Blue Note CDP 7 84441 2); and *Open House/Plain Talk* (Blue Note CDP 7 84269 2) and *Back At The Chicken Shack* (Blue Note CDP 7 46402 2), both from 1960.)

6. The Blues Balladeers

Nat King Cole may not have been a blues singer – though he was a fine jazz pianist – but he certainly influenced his fair share of bluesmen. The success of his piano-bass-and-guitar trio not only sparked an explosion of such groups – WILLIE DIXON's Big Three and Johnny Moore's Three Blazers (featuring pianist/singer CHARLES BROWN) were but two of them – but launched a school of sophisticated nightclub blues balladry which retained the blues form (albeit with some jazzy variations) while infusing it with more than a touch of Cole's mellifluousness. Most of them were fronted by piano-playing smoothies who were as much descendants of LEROY CARR as of Cole. RAY CHARLES, who originally launched his career imitating Cole by way of Brown, emerged from this school to carve a very different swathe through popular music: B.B. KING adored the smooth-blues school – as the '50s anthology *Heart And Soul* (Ace CDCH 376) clearly demonstrates, and so did JAMES BROWN, though comparatively little of the ease and cool of the great blues balladeers audibly rubbed off on his sandpaper gospel shriek. Like the jumpsters, the first-generation blues balladeers ran into severe career roadblocks with the advent of rock, soul and the Memphis/Southwest Territories blues synthesis, but their music retains both its charm and its effect.

Charles Brown

During his original mid-'40s-to-mid-'50s hey-day, they used to call Charles Brown 'the black Bing Crosby': this flatters Crosby and demeans Brown. To ears attuned to rawer, rootsier blues, Charles Brown's tinkling arpeggios and greasy croon can seem cloying and dated, but the artistry is immaculate. First as the pianist/vocalist frontman of guitarist Johnny Moore's Three Blazers, and then as a solo artist, Charles Brown – born September 13, 1922, in Texas City, near Houston, Texas – was the doyen of the blues-ballad subgenre. His material, notably 'Driftin' Blues', 'Black Night', 'Fool's Paradise' and the immortal 'Merry Christmas, Baby', remains in common currency (thanks to, among others, CHUCK BERRY, MOSE ALLISON, ELVIS PRESLEY, BOBBY 'BLUE' BLAND, Junior Parker, RAY CHARLES and ERIC CLAPTON) and so does he: he's released two excellent albums in the past few years and toured with BONNIE RAITT. In civilised homes where Christmas songs are *verboten*, 'Merry Christmas Baby' is the honourable exception. Brown was held in such high esteem that when he came to New Orleans for a session in the '50s, one of the guitarists (a young fellow named Mac Rebennack, later known as DR JOHN) was so nervous that he got drunk and had to be sent home.

He was that *rara avis*: a blues singer from the African-American middle-class. The proud owner of a B.Sc in chemistry, he was a high-school teacher before following the call of the wild piano to L.A. and hooking up first with Johnny Moore's band, and then with Aladdin Records. Brown's composition 'Driftin' Blues' (with Johnny Otis on drums) was a smash, and the boys done well – three more R&B Top 10 hits – before Brown went solo in 1949, maintaining a similar sound to the Three Blazers' records but with prominently featured tenor sax. He continued to prosper, perhaps because Moore continued to play on some of Brown's sessions until 1953; and held off post-rock decline until 1961, when he had his last hit with 'Please Come Home For Christmas'. Since then, he's simply been out there earning a living, though the last few years have seen a considerable upturn in his fortunes: his 1986 album *One For The Road* and its 1990 successor, *All My Life*, leading to renewed interest in his smoothly anguished sweet blues. In the piano-bar of my dreams, Charles Brown still holds court.

- *Driftin' Blues: The Best Of Charles Brown* (EMI CDP-7-97989-2)
- *Hard Times & Cool Blues* (Sequel NEX CD 133)

Two alternative fillets of the classic Charles Brown era, 1946–56: EMI offer 20 tracks to Sequel's 25, with a 12-track overlap. The essential titles – 'Driftin' Blues', 'Homesick Blues', 'Trouble Blues', 'Black Night', 'Hard Times', 'Seven Long Days' and 'Fool's Paradise' – are present and correct in both cases (though both albums, for some no doubt vital reason, include Brown's '56 remake of 'Merry Christmas, Baby' rather than the Three Blazers' 1946 original). Given a choice, I'd pick the EMI: despite its shorter runtime its selection and packaging are vastly superior. Either way, you're in for a treat: laid-back lugubriousness has never sounded so hip.

- *All My Life* (Bullseye Blues NET CD 9501)

Fractionally the stronger of Brown's 'comeback' albums, though *One For The Road* (Demon FIEND CD 88) certainly has its merits. This one, from 1990, features duets with Dr John and Ruth Brown (who, incidentally, would easily have rated an entry in her own right if her crucial '50s Atlantic sides were available), liner notes by Jerry Wexler and Bonnie Raitt; remakes of Amos

Milburn's 'Bad Bad Whiskey', Brown's own 'Fool's Paradise', 'Early In The Morning' and 'Seven Long Days'; plus a great new tune, 'A Virus Called The Blues', which deserves classic status of its own.

Subjects for further investigation: 1964's **Boss Of The Blues** (Mainstream MDCD 908) is best avoided except by those who dislike Brown's piano playing and blues singing, and would prefer to hear Brown interpret pop standards while leading a small studio band on organ for six tracks and fronting hideous string arrangements for another ten. Three latter-day Charles Brown solo performances can be found on **Keys To The Crescent City** (Rounder CD 2087); Chuck Berry's 'Merry Christmas Baby' is on **Fruit Of The Vine** (Chess CD RED 9) and Elvis Presley's on **Reconsider Baby** (RCA PD 85418); 'Hard Times' is performed by Ray Charles on **The Birth Of Soul** (Atlantic 82310 2), and by Eric Clapton on **Journeyman** (Reprise 926 074-2) and **24 Nights** (Reprise 7599-26420-2). B.B. KING and BOBBY BLAND square up to 'Driftin' Blues' on **Together For The First Time . . . Live** (BGO BGOCD 161) and JOHN LEE HOOKER, for neither the first or last time, does it his way on **Don't Turn Me From Your Door** (Atco 7 82365-2 [US]). Mose Allison does a wonderful 'Fool's Paradise', but since it's on Atlantic, you can't get it.

Percy Mayfield

If CHARLES BROWN was 'the black Bing Crosby', then Percy Mayfield was 'the sepia Sinatra.' Songwriter supreme and matinee idol *par excellence*, he was on course for a brilliant career after seven straight hits hits commencing with 1950's No 1 'Please Send Me Someone To Love', but a serious car crash in 1952 left him facially scarred and robbed of his self-confidence. Despite a few more '50s hits as a performer, he settled down to earn his crusts as a composer, working as an in-house songwriter for RAY CHARLES's Tangerine organisation during the '60s, and providing his boss with hits like 'Hit The Road, Jack'. Early Mayfield compositions like 'Please Send Me Someone To Love', 'Memory Pain' (the basis for JOHN LEE HOOKER's 'It Serves Me Right To Suffer'), 'Strange Things Happening' and 'River's Invitation' remain blues standards to this day.

Mayfield was born in Minden, Louisiana, on August 12, 1920, and earned his first break in 1949 when he wandered down to an L.A. studio to try and sell some songs to JIMMY WITHERSPOON. Instead, the company signed him up as an artist in his own right. He had a few scattered hits after his accident – the most recent in 1974 – but it's as 'The Poet Of The Blues' that he will be remembered. He died in L.A. on August 12, 1984: his 64th birthday.

- *The Poet Of The Blues* (Specialty/Ace CDCHD 283)

Mayfield sings in the archetypal baritone croon of the blues balladeer, but with an underlying astringent nasality to cut the grease somewhat: this was just as well considering how downbeat most of his material was, but he could still be witty ('Lost Mind') and effervescent ('I Dare You Baby'). It's not surprising that he did so well as a songwriter: you'll tire of his voice before you tire of his lyrics. And the voice'll hold you for quite a while. A sequel, *Vol 2: Memory Pain* (Specialty/Ace CDCHD 438), includes alternate takes of most of the hits but, for others than Percy's nearest and dearest, it's most noteworthy for its inclusion of Percy's acapella demo of 'Hit The Road, Jack.' Johnny Adams' **Walking On A Tightrope** (Rounder CD 2095) is an entire programme of Mayfield songs.

Little Willie John

Little Willie John was one of those 'got-it-all' guys – he was young, he was cute, he had a fabulous voice, he'd sung with the Duke Ellington and Count Basie bands before he was seventeen, and he had his first hit at 19 – but he ended up a Lost Hero. After he died (in prison, of pneumonia) in 1968, JAMES BROWN recorded a tribute album to him, *Thinking Of Little Willie John . . . And A Few Nice Things*. A decade or several younger than the jumpsters and the blues balladeers, he reworked their idioms for the emerging soul era: if RAY CHARLES was the new sound's secular preacher and Brown its whirling dervish, Little Willie John was its love man. His youthful tenor was as sweetly insinuating as that of any blues balladeer, but it was fresh and funky, and in a music dominated by older singers, his youthfulness was almost attractive in itself, even without his plangent emotionalism. ROBERT CRAY is but one of many singers who learned a thing or two from Little Willie John.

His best-known songs were the original version of 'Fever' (later recorded by, among others, Peggy Lee, ELVIS PRESLEY and Madonna) and his own composition 'Need Your Love So Bad' (rerun by B.B. KING and FLEETWOOD MAC). Born Mertis John Jr, in Lafayette, Arkansas, on November 15, 1937, and raised in Detroit, he was spotted at a talent show in 1951 by the ubiquitous Johnny Otis, who recommended him to King Records. The label turned him down, but signed him four years later: his first single, Titus Turner's 'All Around The World' (later cut by LITTLE MILTON as 'Grits Ain't Groceries') went R&B Top 5 in 1955, 'Need Your Love So Bad' did likewise in January 1956, and 'Fever' made No 1 that May. In theory, he should have been ideally placed to become a power in '60s soul, but something went wrong (possibly due to his fondness for booze and dope), and the hits dropped off after 1961's 'Take My Love'. He killed a man in a 1966 tavern brawl, and went down for it; he then contracted pneumonia behind bars and died there, in Walla Walla, Washington, on May 29, 1968.

- *Fever* (Charly CD CHARLY 246)

A real gem, this: you can hear jump and blues-balladry turning into rock and soul before your very ears. Mainly recorded in New York and Cincinnati 1955–63, this keeps that gorgeous voice right up front – except on the inexplicable 'Bo-Da-Ley Didd-ley', a yakety-sax instrumental tribute to guess-who – restating John's jump roots with a swinging take on BULLMOOSE JACKSON's 'Why Don't You Haul Off And Love Me', and a feast of deep blues ballads, of which 'Suffering With The Blues' is merely the most gorgeous. Why don't you haul off and buy it?

Subjects for further investigation: **Mister Little Willie John** (King KCD-603) was the man's third album: this straight-up 12-track reissue includes stuff also on the Charly compilation and thus represents less than wonderful value, but if you fall for Little Willie's considerable vocal charms, it's the only available next stop. James Brown's versions of 'Suffering With The Blues', 'Talk To Me, Talk

To Me' and 'Need Your Love So Bad', borrowed from the original *Thinking About Little Willie John . . .* album) are on **Messin' With The Blues** (Polydor 847 258-2). A couple of other blues balladeers you may want to check out before we move on are Jesse Belvin (1932–1960) and Ivory Joe Hunter (1914–1974); the problem is that neither of them are particularly well-represented on CD. Neither Belvin's **The Blues Balladeer** (Specialty/Ace CDCHD 305) nor **Ivory Joe Hunter Sings Sixteen Of His Greatest Hits** (King KCD-605) contain much of the work that made them famous, so it's as well to wait a little longer.

7. The '50s: Hail Hail Rock 'n Soul

BROWNIE McGHEE said it first, but MUDDY WATERS said it loudest: 'The Blues Had A Baby And They Called It Rock And Roll'. The earliest true rock and roll record – according to purists – was Jackie Brenston's 1951 hit 'Rocket 88', a piece of cranked-up jump loosely based on Jimmy Liggins's 'Cadillac Boogie' (1947), produced by Sam Phillips for what later became Sun, and arranged by IKE TURNER, of whose Kings Of Rhythm Brenston was then a member. Despite the existence of a late-'40s crossover school known as 'hillbilly boogie', rock-as-we-know-it began when Southern white boys like Jerry Lee Lewis, Carl Perkins and ELVIS PRESLEY used the musical language of hillbilly to decode jump and country blues via the common ground of gospel, and started playing their guitars as loud and cranked as the bluesmen did.

Apart from the above, the best of the postbilly whiteboy rockers were Buddy Holly, Eddie Cochran, Gene Vincent and The Everly Brothers. They were the kings of *something*, sure enough: the best of their records retain an utterly timeless power. But even though the branch eventually outgrew the tree, it could never be truly independent of its roots. Neither could soul: as formulated by RAY CHARLES and JAMES BROWN, it brought the gospel roots of R&B onto the surface and into the light.

Chuck Berry

So who really was the King Of Rock and Roll? It wasn't ELVIS PRESLEY: he may have been elected its President (with Lewis, Holly, Cochran, Vincent, and The Everlys as his cabinet), but the search for the true-born king leaves you with a straight choice between LITTLE RICHARD and Chuck Berry. Charles Edward Anderson Berry, born 18 October 1926, in San José, California, gave rock its smartest, slyest lyrics; its hottest guitar licks – his compositions have been recorded by, to name but four, Elvis Presley, The Beatles, JIMI HENDRIX, and THE ROLLING STONES – and its most crucial iconography; he was also a presence on the national pop charts a full year before Presley. Yet his music came from Chess Records in Chicago – to whom he'd been recommended by no less a sage than MUDDY WATERS – and his '50s recordings featured the same sidemen as the classic South Side blues tracks of the same period. Pianist Johnnie Johnson, Berry's longtime St Louis sidekick, alternated keyboard duties with the likes of OTIS SPANN and Lafayette Leake; the rhythm section was usually WILLIE DIXON and drummer Fred Below; and when a second guitar was required Chess enlisted Matt 'Guitar' Murphy or BO DIDDLEY.

Presley's formulation of rock depended on approaching blues via country music: Berry's on travelling in the opposite direction. His 'Chuck Berry beat' – the basic *runka-runka* rhythm guitar which the Stones's Keith Richards developed into rock's most recognisable *lingua franca* – and his clean, clear diction both derived from country music. But Berry shared basic materials with many more orthodox black entertainers: he loved LOUIS JORDAN's work, both for the lively wit of the saxophonist's tall tales, and for the innovative licks of his guitarist Carl Hogan; he borrowed guitar techniques from T-BONE WALKER and from jazz greats Django Rheinhardt and Charlie Christian; and he simultaneously appreciated the sophisticated balladry of Nat 'King' Cole and CHARLES BROWN; the Caribbean novelties of Harry Belafonte; the searing electric downhome blues of Muddy Waters and ELMORE JAMES; and the Grand Ole Opry. In his music, you can hear it all.

The manically hopping black rockabilly of 'Maybellene' – boy meets girl, girl meets car, boy's car chases girl's car – burst into the charts in 1955, almost simultaneously with the Hot 100 debuts of FATS DOMINO and LITTLE RICHARD. Unlike Fats and Richard, Berry emerged fully grown on his first-ever recording: he had paid zero dues on the R&B market. His performing experience had all been local; after a few years in jail for auto theft, he'd worked around St Louis in a band initially led by pianist Johnnie Johnson, but soon taken over by Berry. He'd come to Chicago to meet Waters; Muddy had recommended him to Chess, and the rest is a sex'n'jail'n'rock 'n' roll legend which requires no retelling here. Suffice it to say that the pop success of Berry's unique country/ R&B hybrid, and the lesser (but still significant) sales of Bo Diddley's records, kept Chess in the big time after the subsidence of the initial impact of the label's South Side blues stars; and that the link between youth-oriented rock and roll and Chicago blues provided by Berry's music was what enabled the Stones to create the new blues audience which sustains the music to the present day.

So was Chuck Berry a bluesman? Yes, he was, among many other things: from the B-side of 'Maybellene', a stone blues called 'Wee Wee Hours', to 1970's 'Have Mercy Judge', the blues is never far from the surface of Berry's music, and the scattering of blues-standard covers from the repertoires of GUITAR SLIM ('The Things I Used To Do'), Muddy Waters ('I Got To Find My Baby'), Charles Brown ('Merry Christmas Baby'), Jay McShann ('Confessin' The Blues') and 'Big Maceo' Merriwether ('Worried Life Blues') scattered through his catalogue simply demonstrate the fact. Even teen-oriented songs like 'School Days' or 'Rock And Roll Music' contain references to juke-joints and home-brew which belong to Southern black, rather than suburban white, experience.

Despite enjoying the biggest hit of his career with the ludicrous 'My Ding-A-Ling' (1972), and also despite the brilliant 1970 diptych of 'Tulane' and 'Have Mercy Judge' (from *Back Home*, 1970), Berry has been a spent creative force for much of the past 30 years. Whatever generosity of spirit Berry retains has all gone into his work; his finest music overflows with it.

- *Hail! Hail! Rock 'N'Roll* (Instant INS CD 5035)
- *Fruit Of The Vine* (Chess CD RED 9)

The great twenty-eight and the next twenty-four, respectively; with a mere two-track overlap. Every single track on *Hail! Hail!*

Rock 'N'Roll, from 1955's 'Maybellene' to 1964's 'The Promised Land', is an acknowledged classic, and whether you call it blues, R&B, rockabilly, rock 'n'roll or just plain pop, it remains a cornerstone of postwar popular music. I mean: 'Roll Over Beethoven', 'Johnny B. Goode', 'Sweet Litle Sixteen', 'Reelin' And Rockin'', 'Carol', 'Back In The USA'' 'Memphis Tennessee', 'No Particular Place To Go' ... the hits just keep on comin'. (Incidentally, listen out for ETTA JAMES, Marvin Gaye and The Moonglows providing the vocal backup on 'Almost Grown' and 'Back In The USA'.) *Fruit Of The Vine* is less consistent and its contents are less familiar, but it holds up remarkably well, since second-string Berry titles include the likes of 'It Wasn't Me', 'Tulane', 'Jo Jo Gunne' and 'Jaguar And The Thunderbird', all of which would be top-of-the-range items on anybody else's best-of.

Subjects for further investigation: The 3-CD, 71-track Chuck Berry career CV is *The Chess Box* (MCA/Chess CHD3-80001 [US]); it's as meticulously researched, lovingly compiled, beautifully designed and exquisitely annotated as you'd expect from this series, but if you can live without 'Betty Jean', 'Run Rudolph Run', 'Down The Road Apiece' and 'My Ding-A-Ling', you'd be (several pounds) better off sticking with the two Charly collections cited above. Further selections from the same set of Greatest Hits (plus a few tracks uncollected elsewhere) can be found on *The EP Collection* (See For Miles SEECD 320), while *Rock 'N' Roll Rarities* (MCA/ Chess CHD-92521) scoops up the kind of outtakes and alternative mixes over which collectors drool. After his exposure alongside Berry (and Keith Richards, ERIC CLAPTON, ROBERT CRAY *et al*) in the enormously revealing rockumentary *Hail! Hail! Rock 'N'Roll*, Johnnie Johnson became something of a cult hero in his own right; performing at Clapton's Albert Hall blues summits for two successive years, as documented on *24 Nights* (Reprise 7599-26420-2); guesting on JOHN LEE HOOKER's *Mr Lucky* (Silvertone ORE CD 519) and finally cutting a highly entertaining album of his own, *Johnnie B. Bad* (Elektra Nonesuch American Explorer 7559-61149-2), with both Clapton and Richards among the guest stars. You don't seriously expect a listing of great Chuck Berry covers, do you? Just one, then: you ain't lived 'til you've heard Jimi Hendrix do 'Johnny B. Goode' – on *Hendrix In The West* (Polydor 831 312-2).

Bo Diddley

Bo Diddley will probably be pissed off to find himself in a blues book, since he's always considered himself to be, first and foremost, a rock'n'roller. In fact, his music is the purest African-American rock and roll ever recorded, and during the '50s this master of trash-talkin' and guitar toys, this avatar of JIMI HENDRIX and Ice-T alike, also somehow managed to invent both rap music and psychedelic guitar. Still, the blues (and the pre-blues of field hollers and the dozens) remains the spine of his extraordinary Afro-rock: Bo may not have been the biggest rock and roll star of the '50s, but – in cultural terms – he was definitely the blackest.

Bo Diddley was actually Ellas McDaniel, born in McComb, Mississippi, on 30 December 1928, to a family with strong Louisiana connections. When he was six he was taken to Chicago (one of his schoolmates, two years his junior, was EARL HOOKER), and his music draws on bayou, Delta and ghetto alike. Check it out: the principal characteristics of Bo Diddley's music include an unmistakeable signature beat, an Afro-Cuban 'hambone' clave like a New Orleans rhumba choreographed for elephants and emphasised with shaken maraccas for extra percussive value; an open-tuned guitar pounding out riff-laden, one-chord trance-dance rhythms, with primitive effects devices pulsing along with the beat and taking the place of the Delta bluesman's slide; and a songbook full of the kind of boasting, taunting brag-chants that resound in every inner-city playground or street-corner. And you say this stuff ain't the blues?

Apart from anything else, Ellas McDaniel was a tweak: he designed his own guitars and built his own amplifiers. Like any modern rapper, he went by a street handle rather than a legal name, and half his songs were about telling the world how totally bad-ass Bo Diddley was. There was little hostility in it, though: it was just that he was having a great time being Bo Diddley and wanted to tell the world about it. 'Bo Diddley'/'I'm A Man', his first hit, was followed by 'Hey! Bo Diddley', 'Diddley Daddy', 'Bo's A Lumberjack', 'Bo Diddley's A Gunslinger', 'Bo Meets The Monster', 'Bo Diddley Is Loose' plus, just for variety, 'The Greatest Lover In The World' and '500% More Man'. He'd studied classical violin as a child and played trombone in church, but by the late '40s he had fallen under the spell of JOHN LEE HOOKER's 'Boogie Chillen', learned to box, and started street-singing with a guitar. Some-where along the line Ellas McDaniel, fiddle student and church boy, had become Bo Diddley, the baddest cat alive.

In 1955 he and his band, including harpist Billy Boy Arnold, auditioned simultaneously for Chess and Vee Jay. Vee Jay got Arnold – whose biggest hits, 'I Wish You Would' and 'I Ain't Got You', were covered by THE YARDBIRDS in 1964 – but Chess got Bo. They also got a steady stream of R&B hits, and a couple of nibbles at the pop chart; plus a publishing catalogue that bands like THE ROLLING STONES (and The Yardbirds, JOHN HAMMOND, ERIC CLAPTON, The Animals, The Pretty Things, Manfred Mann, The Kinks, Quicksilver Messenger Service, The New York Dolls, GEORGE THOROGOOD, DR FEELGOOD, and others less distinguished would take to the bank just as the US hits dried up.

His tough, extrovert stage act influenced Elvis Presley, JIMI HENDRIX and Bruce Springsteen: the Bo Diddley hitlist includes his own compositions 'Bo Diddley' (naturally), 'I'm A Man' (a.k.a. 'Manish Boy'), 'Diddley Daddy', 'Say Man', 'Crackin' Up', 'Road Runner' and Willie Dixon's 'You Can't Judge A Book By Its Cover'; those are just the ones that charted. His album tracks and B-sides were mined by his devoted British admirers, and songs like 'Bring It To Jerome', 'I Can Tell', 'Who Do You Love', 'Mona' and 'Before You Accuse Me' became part of the standard repertoire of early-'60s UK R&B. In the late '50s Buddy Holly covered 'Bo Diddley' by playing it as if it were a Buddy Holly song; in 1964 the Stones – who'd slept on Bo's hotel room floor during much of their first UK tour – played Holly's 'Not Fade Away' as if it were a Bo Diddley song. If Bo hadn't signed away all his Chess royalties and copyrights during the early '70s, he'd be a rich man today (and if 'feel', 'sound' and 'groove' were as copyrightable as melodies and lyrics, he'd be richer still). Instead he's a bitter one, and with some reason. He was last seen sharing a Nike commercial with athlete Bo Jackson; punch line: 'Bo, you don't know Diddley'.

- *The Chess Box* (MCA/Chess CHD2-19502[US])

Since this is as luxurious and elaborate as any other *Chess Box*, it comes as something of a let-down when only two CDs fall out of the package: there's at least another disc's worth of Grade-A Diddley left in the vaults. Nevertheless, each CD is indeed packed to bursting with Bo's weirdest and most wonderful stuff; and despite the presence of OTIS SPANN, WILLIE DIXON, Lafayette Leake and other Chess stalwarts, it's still Bo's show all the way. Remember: you got no Bo, you ain't got Diddley.

Subjects for further investigation: The filleted version is *Hey! Bo Diddley* (Instant CD INS 5039), a budget-price domestic single-disc which does as good a job of providing a basic Diddley primer as you could reasonably expect for the money. *The EP Collection* (See For Miles SEECD 321) mingles some of the hits with a few esoteric items ('She's Fine, She's Mine', 'Hey Good Looking' – written for Bo by CHUCK BERRY, as it happens – and 'Hong Kong Mississippi') omitted from both the Instant and MCA sets.

Little Richard

If 'Little' Richard Penniman has a spiritual ancestor it may well have been Frankie 'Half Pint' Jaxon, the 5'2" transvestite whose good-humoured campness enlivened so many of the old TAMPA RED records, but his music sounded as if it had just crash-landed in a flying saucer from the planet Revlon, combining the screaming passion of secularised Deep South gospel with the rhythmic cunning and irresistable good vibes of New Orleans. Richard was born in Macon, Georgia (also the hometown of Otis Redding, who launched his career imitating Little Richard, and JAMES BROWN) on Christmas Day of 1935, acquired his vocal and keyboard chops in church, and refined them touring with local medicine shows. In the early '50s he recorded in more-or-less conventional jump mode for Victor and Peacock, but discovered his own style cutting for Specialty Records in New Orleans. His first hit, 'Tutti Frutti', crashed both R&B and pop charts in 1955, and the rest is rock and roll history. Richard's adventures with sex, drugs, religion, make-up and The Beatles are well-documented elsewhere, so let's just cut to . . .

- **His Greatest Recordings** (Ace CDCH 109)

Ooh, my soul: twenty examples of hot-wired post-jump with tempi and volume both cranked to way past ten. Saxes honk, drums and pianos pound, and Little Richard screams his head off from start to finish. 'Ready Teddy', 'Rip It Up', 'The Girl Can't Help It', 'Good Golly Miss Molly', 'Lucille', 'Keep A-Knockin'', 'Tutti Frutti', 'Hey-Hey-Hey-Hey', 'She's Got It', 'Long Tall Sally', 'Slippin' And Slidin'' and the other eight tracks collected here are among the most galvanically exciting records of their era. Glorious novelty-blues lyrics delivered with Richard's inimitable combination of gospel fervour and camp hysteria over a band plugged directly into the mains: sounds like a good time to me . . .

Screamin' Jay Hawkins

Are you ready to get crazy? I'm not talking shed-some-British-reserve crazy, or you-don't-have-to-be-mad-to-work-here-but-it-helps crazy. I'm talking seriously-twisted crazy; I'm talking beyond-medical-help crazy; I'm talking Screamin' Jay Hawkins crazy. This is the man whose 1956 classic 'I Put A Spell On You' was barred from US radio because it allegedly sounded 'cannibal-istic' (and sold a million copies nevertheless), and who therefore followed it up with 'Feast Of The Mau Mau'. This is the man who generally began his stage act by emerging from a coffin in a blast of thunder and lightning, clutching a human skull which was smoking a cigarette, and who occasionally hired stooges to drop rubber bands onto the audience while he sang about worms. This is not a normal person. This is not even a normal '50s R&B star. This is flat-out weirdness: utterly deranged rock theatre devised while the likes of Alice Cooper and Arthur Brown were still in short pants.

Jalacy Hawkins – born in Cleveland, Ohio, on July 18, 1929 – was Alaska's 1949 middleweight boxing champion. More signifi-cantly, he spent the early '50s as a piano-playing sideman and warmup act for performers like Leroy Kirkland and, briefly, FATS DOMINO until he began recording in his own right. Hawkins has a voice somewhere between HOWLIN' WOLF, CHARLES BROWN, Luciano Pavarotti, Bela Lugosi, Tom Waits, Harry Secombe, Wilson

Pickett and a wounded grizzly. 'I Put A Spell On You' has been recorded by the likes of Nina Simone, Alan Price, Arthur Brown and Creedence Clearwater Revival: none of their versions are even in the same universe (let alone the same asylum) as the original. The Rolling Stones, who have a conscience about black music as well as a puckish sense of humour, hired him to open for them at Madison Square Gardens in 1980: as this is being written, his version of Waits's 'Heartattack And Vine' is featuring in a Levi's commercial.

- *Frenzy* (Edsel ED CD 104)

The Okeh recordings (1956–7), commencing with 'I Put A Spell On You', and getting steadily sicker from there: I mean, the very next two tracks are 'Little Demon' and 'Alligator Wine.' Then there's his epic destruction of Cole Porter's 'I Love Paris' and . . . look, I can't go on. If you think you have a taste for major dementia, check out Screamin' Jay: he's crazier than you are. If he isn't, then perhaps we'd better not meet.

- *Screamin' The Blues* (Red Lightnin' RLCD 0075)

Two batches of tracks: one from '53–4 and another from '63–'70. Taken together, they demonstrate that not only was Jay drastically ill even before 'Spell', but there was no subsequent improvement in his condition. Includes two different versions of 'The Whammy'; to date, only WILKO JOHNSON has been unwell enough to tackle that one. Oh yes . . . he also does casual violence to Paul & Linda McCartney's 'Monkberry Moon Delight.' No, I don't know why either.

- *Feast Of The Mau Mau* (Edsel ED CD 252)
- *Black Music For White People* (Demon FIEND CD 211)

Has age mellowed him? You must be crazy. *Feast* doublebacks one live and one studio album from '69/'70, and includes the epic 'Constipation Blues' (complete with cloacal saxophone from Plas Johnson) and adapts The Mar-Keys' 'Last Night' into something called 'Bite It'. Also subverted is the doowop standard 'Goodnight My Love', and what he does to the venerable 'Ain't Nobody's

Business' ain't nobody's business. 1991's *Black Music*, which finally gets him to his spiritual home, Demon Records (heh heh), is the one with 'Heartattack And Vine' on it, Levi's fans; it also includes a rap version of 'Spell'. Elsewhere: LOUIS JORDAN's 'Is You Is Or Is You Ain't My Baby', SMILEY LEWIS's 'I Hear You Knockin'', and 'Ol' Man River.' Go figure.

Elvis Presley

Elvis Presley? In a *blues book*? Ohhhhh, you're *kiiiiiddiiiiiing*! Well, if I am, so was HOWLIN' WOLF, who knew the Big El in Memphis – as did numerous other bluesmen of the time, including B.B. KING, BOBBY BLAND and JUNIOR PARKER – and as far as he was concerned, Elvis 'made his pull from the blues'. The Elvis Presley story is far too well-known to merit recounting here (if you don't know who Elvis Presley was and what he did, you've got some serious catchup to do), but fortunately many of the noteworthy blues interpretations scattered throughout Elvis Presley's recording history have actually been collected in one conveniently locatable place, and therefore we can skip straight to . . .

- *Reconsider Baby* (RCA PD 85418)

To describe Elvis Presley as 'a great blues singer' is somewhat misleading, but that is certainly one of the many things he was. This collection trawls through the immense Presley catalogue to unearth a dozen selections, cut between 1954 and 1971, borrowing from the repertoires of, among others, LONNIE JOHNSON ('Tomorrow Night'), Chuck Willis ('I Feel So Bad', also a favourite of OTIS RUSH), PERCY MAYFIELD ('Stranger In My Own Home Town'), SMILEY LEWIS ('One Night'), CHARLES BROWN ('Merry Christmas Baby', also recorded by CHUCK BERRY), Arthur 'Big Boy' Crudup ('My Baby Left Me' and 'So Glad You're Mine') and LOWELL FULSON ('Reconsider Baby' itself); the whole thing annotated by blues guru and Presley authority Peter Guralnick. Considering the not-overly-generous playing time, I'd've recommended the inclusion of Crudup's 'That's All Right Mama' (Presley's first-ever commercial recording and a significant choice, too), KOKOMO ARNOLD's

'Milk Cow Blues (Boogie)', ROY BROWN/WYNONIE HARRIS's 'Good Rockin' Tonight', and Junior Parker's 'Mystery Train': familiar Sun-era staples though they are, any trip through Presley's blues world is incomplete without them. A minor quibble, however: with them or without them, *Reconsider Baby* is an ear-opening delight.

Subjects for further investigation: Elvis Presley's blues guru was the decidedly primitive Delta bluesman Arthur 'Big Boy' Crudup (1905–1974), a limited performer but a superb songwriter. Crudup had taken up music at the comparatively late age of 35, and was street-singing in Chicago when Lester Melrose, overseer of Bluebird Records' blues line, happened by and invited him to play at a party at TAMPA RED's house. That led to a recording contract and a few regional hits, but somehow Crudup never earned enough money to be able to quit his day job. Presley's Sun-era repertoire included Crudup's 'That's All Right Mama', 'My Baby Left Me' and 'So Glad You're Mine', and Crudup is also credited with the composition of 'Mean Old Frisco' and 'Rock Me Mama', the latter being the source for B.B. King's much-covered 'Rock Me Baby'. *That's All Right Mama* (Bluebird ND 90653) collects a 22-track selection of Crudup's 1941–54 Bluebird singles, and includes the originals of all of the above titles: Crudup had a high, urgent vocal style and a somewhat restricted vocabulary of guitar riffs, and all I can say is that both Elvis and B.B. improved on their sources. For a double-whammy in which a bluesman plays Elvis rather than Elvis playing the blues, consult ALBERT KING's *Blues For Elvis* (Stax CDSXE 073).

Ray Charles

Brother Ray was the guy who took the blues to church, thereby inventing soul music: his 1954 hit 'I Got A Woman' launched the soul era as surely as ELVIS PRESLEY's 'That's All Right Mama' fired the starting gun for rock. In a culture which still observed a rigid distinction between the Lord's music and the devil's, this was sacrilege: even BIG BILL BROONZY had disapproved. Like many another blues singer who had oscillated between the church and the tavern, Broonzy didn't mind playing both musics, but he strongly objected to mixing them. What Ray Charles created was the exact opposite of the 'sanctified blues' of older singers like BLIND WILLIE JOHNSON or REV. GARY DAVIS: soul used gospel forms and blues content. 'The Genius' was a man of vast and varied gifts: a bluesman's voice, a jazzman's craft, a pop artist's commercial ear. He'd started out as a piano-playing blues-balladeer in the CHARLES BROWN vein and toured as a member of LOWELL FULSON's band, but after contributing arrangements and piano parts to GUITAR SLIM's classic 'The Things I Used To Do' he had some sort of epiphany, hired a tough post-jump band and stopped smoothing the grain out of his voice. In other words, he became Ray Charles.

Born in Albany, Georgia, on September 23, 1930, he was blinded at six and orphaned at 15. By 1949, he was on the West Coast cutting his first blues-ballad records; three years later he was recording for Atlantic, and two years after that 'I Got A Woman' forever altered the face of rhythm & blues. The success of 'What's I Say' enabled him to leave Atlantic and record for ABC during the '60s, where he cut the country records that caused a second major cultural upset. Ray Charles is still with us, though his innovating days are over; his career provides a fascinating insight into how the blues can go pop and still stay black.

- **The Birth Of Soul** (Atlantic 7 82310-2 [US])

Right now, you cannot buy a single-disk UK anthology of Ray Charles's groundbreaking seven-year hitch with Atlantic: *The Right Time* (Atlantic 241 119-2) being currently unavailable. This collection omits his in-concert recordings – if you want the brilliant *Ray Charles at Newport* live album you'll have to wait until it's reissued separately – as well as his jazz work with the Modern Jazz Quartet's Milt Jackson, and his experiments with strings and big bands – but it re-presents all of his 1952–7 R&B studio recordings for the label. The first of the three disks covers the period before 'I Got A Woman', and it depicts RC both working out his own ideas and inserting them into the Atlantic machine: adapting jump, ballads and boogie to his own ends, scoring a 1953 R&B No 5 hit with the WILLIE DIXON-styled stop-time monologue 'It Should've Been Me', and grazing the Top 10 with 'Don't You Know' and 'Blackjack.' Then comes the breakthrough: ten more

311

R&B Top 10 hits in the next five years, including four Number Ones – 'I Got A Woman', 'A Fool For You', 'Drown In My Own Tears' and 'What'd I Say', the latter his first major pop hit. *The Birth Of Soul* is expensive, sure, but it's about as much fun as a human being can take in one evening.

Subjects for further investigation: What Ray did next: **The Collection** (Castle Communications CCSCD 241) and **20 Hits Of The Genius** (Commander CD 99009) both fillet the '60s; both include 'Hit The Road Jack', 'Busted', 'Unchain My Heart' and 'One Mint Julep', and both give Brother Ray a chance to demonstrate that Paul McCartney's 'Yesterday' and 'Eleanor Rigby' can be blues tunes if a bluesman sings them.

James Brown

Aaaoooowwww! The Godfather Of Soul, The Hardest Working Man In Show Business, Soul Brother Number One and The Most Sampled Man In The History Of The Universe. Alongside JOHN LEE HOOKER and BO DIDDLEY, James Brown is one of the three artists in this book who can truly be designated as grandmasters of African-American groove. Like RAY CHARLES, he introduced elements of gospel into R&B in the mid-'50s; but whereas Charles imported gospel songs and devices wholesale, Brown concentrated on using its sheer fervour and passion to explode the traditional themes and structures of R&B. And explode they did: like Hooker and Diddley before him and John Coltrane and Ornette Coleman after him, Brown's '60s music stripped the song forms of the time of their European chord structures, and took them back to back to a one-chord African root, leaving nothing behind but the pure, pulsing rhythmic nerve we call 'funk'. It's not surprising that, by the '60s, James Brown's music had become a profound symbol of African-American cultural identity.

Born just across the Georgia state line in Barnwell, South Carolina, on May 3, 1933, JB bust loose in 1956 with the gruelling gospel-blues ballad 'Please Please Please', and maintained a double-pronged assault with rocking R&B dance tunes and ever more anguished ballads. The hits are all on the 4-CD set *Star Time*

(Polydor 849 108-2) – or its slimline single-disk equivalent *Sex Machine: The Very Best Of James Brown* (Polydor 645-828-2) – but for our purposes we need to check out . . .

● *Messin' With The Blues* (Polydor 847 258-2)

This fascinating trawl through JB's back pages firmly locates him as a child of the jump era and the heyday of blues balladry: he covers LOUIS JORDAN, BULLMOOSE JACKSON, ROY BROWN, Ivory Joe Hunter, LITTLE WILLIE JOHN and Joe Liggins, as well as GUITAR SLIM, BOBBY 'BLUE' BLAND, MEMPHIS SLIM and more. It also demonstrates exactly what separated him from his idols: both the electrifying gospel fervour he brought to material which was cool even when it was raucous; and his complete disregard for the melody of a song like 'Ain't Nobody Here But Us Chickens'. To muster the power of a JOE TURNER he must sacrifice the flexibility of a Louis Jordan. He gets the best of both worlds on a magnificently swaggering 'Every Day I Have The Blues'; and a devastating colloquy with guitarist Kenny Poole on FATS DOMINO's 'Goin' Home' which comes out sounding just like BUDDY GUY. It's all part of the grand African-American cultural continuum: Brown's music derives as directly from the R&B with which he grew up and in which he got his start as contemporary funk and hip-hop do from Brown himself.

Subjects for further investigation: While we're on the subject, allow me to recommend a few examples of other soul maestri singing the blues: Otis Redding's nuthin'-but-fine take on B.B. KING's 'Rock Me Baby' (complete with mean, aching guitar from Steve Cropper) awaits you on *Otis Blue* (Atco 7567-80318-2), and like most of that album, is recycled on *The Otis Redding Story* (Atlantic K 781 762-2). Aretha Franklin's devastatingly sensual slow-blues original 'Dr Feelgood' is included in her *20 Greatest Hits* (Atlantic 241135-2), though her glorious late-'60s interpretations of St Louis Jimmy Oden's 'Goin' Down Slow' and PERCY MAYFIELD's 'River's Invitation' remain irritatingly unavailable. Al Green's first two albums, double-backed on *Green Is Blues/Al Green Gets Next To You* (Hi HI UK CD 106), not only revisit Little Willie John's 'Talk To Me' and Junior Parker's 'Driving Wheel' but present a wonderful musical conjuring trick in which the '70s Memphis maestro turns The

Temptations' 'I Can't Get Next You' back into the blues it always really was.

8. Revival, Retro and Miscellaneous White Folks

FOLK-BLUES REVIVALISTS

When the great country bluesmen of the 20s and 30s were prised from retirement to display their magic for a new generation of listeners, one inevitable by-product was a new generation of disciples. There were quite a few of them – the names of Dave van Ronk, Spider John Koerner, Stefan Grossman and someone called Bob Dylan all spring to mind – but the recreation of rural blues a quarter-century and more gone was a much harder trick to pull off than the emulation of contemporary electric blues. Very few of the new kids played electric blues well; even fewer managed the rural blues with dignity. Herewith the honourable exceptions:

John Hammond

Much has been made of the fact that John Hammond – born in New York City on November 13, 1942 – is the son and namesake of the legendary entrepreneur/producer who recorded Billie Holiday, Charlie Christian, Bob Dylan, Aretha Franklin, Bruce Springsteen and STEVIE RAY VAUGHAN, and produced the 1938/9 'From Spirituals To Swing' concerts. In fact, John Jr's parents separated when he was a child, and about the only career advantage that he gained from his heritage was a paternal gift of a tape of the (then) unreleased ROBERT JOHNSON sides. During his teens he became fascinated by country blues, took up slide guitar and harmonica, and dropped out of college to explore his new obsession. In 1963 he signed to Vanguard Records, cut his first album and performed at the Newport Folk Festival. Gradually, his blues focus broadened to include contemporary electric styles, and he was able to attract first-class musicians: his 1965 album *So Many Roads* included members of what would – once Bob Dylan got hold of them – be known as The Band, plus MIKE BLOOMFIELD (on piano); JIMI HENDRIX served as Hammond's lead guitarist for a legendary two-week stint at a Greenwich Village club.

Over the next few years he recorded for Atlantic (including sessions with Duane Allman on slide) and Columbia (the stillborn *Triumvirate* project teamed him with Mike Bloomfield and DR JOHN; he also worked on the soundtrack for the Dustin Hoffman movie *Little Big Man*) before returning briefly to Vanguard. Many listeners – including your humble servant – find Hammond's early recordings unconvincing despite (or perhaps even because of) their remarkable fluency and fidelity to the Holy Writ of his inspirations. His music seemed over-literal, lacking both the roughneck unselfconsciousness of a PAUL BUTTERFIELD and the ironic perspective and creative misunderstandings of THE ROLLING STONES and their fellow Brit-bluesers; but over the last decade he's demonstrated that he has not only grown into his voice, but into his material. The records that he's cut for Rounder and, currently, PointBlank are far and away the best work of his entire career. John Hammond is one of the finest classicist interpreters of pre-war blues alive today: give him a National steel-bodied guitar, a slide, a harp rack and a couple of microphones, and he'll prove it to you. This man is *dangerous*.

- *Live* (Rounder CD 3074)
- *Got Love If You Want It* (PointBlank VPBCD 7)

Your two-disk crash course in current Hammond. The 1983 solo concert captured on *Live* is packed with funkily percussive acoustic guitar (not the National, unfortunately), articulately wailing harp and warm, soulful, gutsy singing; the repertoire borrows from BLIND BOY FULLER, Robert Johnson, MUDDY WATERS, BLIND LEMON JEFFERSON, CHARLEY PATTON and HOWLIN' WOLF. The 1992 studio sides on the PointBlank album surround him with empathetic accompanists who broaden the spectrum without cluttering or intrusion: extra-mural assistance comes from J.J. Cale (who produced), LITTLE CHARLIE & THE NIGHTCATS and, on a sumptuous 'Driftin' Blues', JOHN LEE HOOKER. CHUCK BERRY, SLIM HARPO and Tom Waits rub composer-credit shoulders with SON HOUSE, LITTLE WALTER and CHARLES BROWN.

Subjects for further investigation: *The Best Of John Hammond* (Vanguard VCD 11/12) covers the early years: this 2-CD set is currently in catalogue but out of stock, so you're on your own with this one. The 21-year-old Hammond performs Robert Johnson's 'Me And The Devil' at the '63 Newport Folk Festival on *Blues At Newport* (Vanguard VCD 115/16). There are more wonderful duets with Hooker on John Lee's *Mr Lucky* (Silvertone ORE CD 519) and *Boom Boom* (PointBlank VPBCD 12): other currently available Hammond albums include *John Hammond* (Rounder CD 11532), a 1987 fillet of a pair of vinyl-and-cassette-only 1980/1 albums; and 1987's *Nobody But You* (Demon FIEND CD 107).

Taj Mahal

One of the limitations of the sociological approach to the blues is that considerations of style, era or location ultimately matter far less than the personality of the individual performer. I could tell you, for example, that Taj Mahal was born – under the name of Henry St Clair Fredericks – in New York City on 17 May, 1940, to a Jamaican jazz-musician father and a gospel-singing mother from North Carolina; that he holds a B.Sc in animal husbandry from the University of Massachusetts; that he and RY COODER once co-led a band called The Rising Sons; that he plays acoustic guitar, harmonica and a little bit of piano; and that he specialises in the rural pre-war styles of SLEEPY JOHN ESTES, MISSISSIPPI JOHN HURT, ROBERT JOHNSON and BLIND WILLIE McTELL, but that wouldn't neces-sarily prepare you for the unique pleasures and treasures of his music. It's not even down to talent, though he has it by the truckload: it's a matter of sensibility, and his understanding of the often-overlooked notion that the blues is about happiness and pleasure, rather than misery and self-pity. The originators of the country blues lived in an environment where sorrow and anger did not need to be cultivated so much as escaped. Their music evolved specifically to make audience and artist alike feel better;

and sometimes it seems as if Taj Mahal is the only bluesman of his era who knows this. His blues is the happiest, warmest and most loving blues you'll ever hear.

Reinterpreters of pre-war rural blues face certain occupational hazards. Scylla is the kind of over-literal and over-reverent approach which 'preserves' the music by turning it into a period piece; Charybdis is a hamfisted drive towards heavy-rock modernism which ends up obliterating the unique character which made it valuable in the first place. Taj Mahal, about as self-effacing a performer as somone who named themselves after one of the Seven Wonders Of The World can possibly be, has devised the most elegant solution yet. His 1968 debut album was certainly rock-friendly – thanks in part to the virtuoso slide guitar of Jesse Edwin Davis – but what Taj brought to his sources that his white contemporaries didn't was a rhythmic and textural sensibility derived from soul, funk, and (later) reggae, rather than hard rock. He has absorbed the traditions to the point where he can create freely within them, and re-invent them without inhibition. The 'authenticity' question is completely by-passed: not simply because Taj Mahal is black, but because his personality is so strong and his sensibility so unique that the blues becomes a vehicle for him, rather than the other way about.

I said 'self-effacing.' That's because Taj uses his talents rather than displays them, placing his formidable skills as vocalist, guitarist and harmonicist so selflessly at the disposal of his music and the feelings that he wants to create that it can take quite a while before you notice how good he is at everything he does. His singing is warm, grainy and insinuating, and it comes with an audible smile; his harmonica work has something of HOWLIN' WOLF's squawkiness and SONNY BOY WILLIAMSON's astringency; and his plunky guitar work – most often performed on a steel-bodied National – has as driving a rhythmic undertow as that of ROBERT JOHNSON and SON HOUSE. Yet his purism is conditional: even on his earliest albums – *Taj Mahal* (1968) and *The Natch'l Blues* (1969) – he was drawing freely on country and soul hits as well as traditional blues, and the front half of his titanic double album *Giant Step/De Ole Folks At Home* titles itself after a Carole King composition that started life as a Monkees B-side.

By the early '70s, Taj had expanded his scope from neo-trad blues to an all-embracing Pan-African-Americanism, exploring

West Indian and Afro-Latin styles while never relinquishing his hold on the blues. He's never sold vast amounts of records, but he's always sold some, and despite wearing his influences on his sleeve he's continued to make music that's perfectly and distinctively his own. You need to hear this guy.

- *The Collection* (Castle Communications CCSCD 180)
- *Taj's Blues* (Columbia Legacy 471660 2)

Two competing fillets of Taj's Columbia years (1968–1977): Castle's 19 tracks and Legacy's 12 have only four cuts in common, but they're the crucial ones: Estes's 'Leaving Trunk' (originally titled 'Milk Cow Blues') done up like Howlin' Wolf would have done it if he'd just come off a three-month tour alongside JAMES BROWN; HENRY THOMAS's 'Fishin' Blues' played on banjo; a 'Dust My Broom' that's both immaculately Johnsonian and totally Taj; and his inspired reworking of McTell's 'Statesboro Blues', complete with rocking shuffle rhythms and the searing, swooping slide-guitar (played by Jesse Ed Davis and not – contrary to popular belief – by Ry Cooder, who was indeed present, but on rhythm guitar) which inspired Duane Allman to stick an aspirin bottle on his finger. Both compilations have their merits: the Legacy set concentrates more on the solo Taj's country blues redux, while Castle's spotlights more group sessions and a wider stylistic reach. I'd pick the latter as the first stop simply because it features Taj's superb takes on the truckers'-anthem 'Six Days On The Road' and the funk epic 'A Lot Of Love', plus his lovely John Hurt interpretations 'Candy Man' and 'Staggerlee' (the latter miscredited to Lloyd Price, presumably because of the title; Hurt called his 'Stack O'Lee Blues') and the majestic reggae of 'Clara (St Kitts Woman)'. Those first two albums are available separately, but *Taj Mahal* (Edsel ED CD 166) and *The Natch'l Blues* (Edsel ED CD 231) are just aching to be doublebacked.

- *Giant Step/De Ole Folks At Home* (Columbia CGK 18 [US])

This budget-price single-disk edition of my all-time favourite Taj album-as-album has been showing up in various UK stores lately; I bought it and hopefully you can do likewise. The original vinyl double contained what were essentially two separate albums:

Giant Step featured Taj's band and followed the pattern set by *Taj Mahal* and *The Natch'l Blues*, while *De Ole Folks At Home* presented Taj solo (he credits himself with 'vocals, harmonica, guitar, banjo, jive') on traditional material derived from BLIND BOY FULLER, LEADBELLY, Hurt, Thomas and Johnson. If you want to avoid the compilations and stick with albums-as-albums, this is where you find 'Staggerlee', 'Candy Man', 'Fishin' Blues' and 'Six Days On The Road'.

- *Like Never Before* (Private Music 261 679)

Taj's most recent studio effort at the time of writing, and it's a little treasure. For a start, there's 'Squat That Rabbit', a rare fusion of hip-hop and blues in which D.J. Jazzy Jeff spins a sample of SLIM HARPO's 'Shake Your Hips' into one of the most hypnotic boogies on record. Then there's an exuberant 'Big Legged Mamas Are Back In Style Again' (it's no relation to the old BULLMOOSE JACKSON tune of the same title, except in spirit; healthy-butt fans can play it – you should pardon the expression – back-to-back with Sir Mix-A-Lot's 'Baby Got Back') and a soulful take on LITTLE WALTER's 'Blues With A Feeling', both featuring Taj's delightfully idiosyn-cratic piano playing. Taj also revisits his back catalogue with new versions of 'Cakewalk Into Town' and 'Take A Giant Step', both even more beguiling than the originals. Apart from Jazzy Jeff, other guest stars include Hall & Oates, The Pointer Sisters and DR JOHN, but rest assured that they don't get in the way.

Subjects for further investigation: 1988's live-in-London *Big Blues* (Essential! ESMCD 002) is marred by an overly dinky electric piano sound and a rather nasty chorus effect on Taj's guitar, but it has some nice moments and demonstrates Taj's capacity to reinvent his material: 'Staggerlee' reappears as a band number with a pronounced reggae lilt, and 'Statesboro Blues' as an uptempo solo piano feature. Taj also pops up providing musical and moral support to Michelle Shocked on 'Jump Jim Crow', locatable on Shocked's *Arkansas Traveler* (London/Cooking Vinyl 512 189-2) and co-starring with JOHN LEE HOOKER and Miles Davis on Jack Nitzsche's soundtrack to Dennis Hopper's *The Hot Spot* (Antilles ANTCD 8755). If you still have a Taj deficiency after checking out the above, you can always hope for imminent CD reissues of *The Real Thing, Happy To Be Just Like I Am, Recycling The Blues & Other Related Stuff, Ooh So Good 'N' Blues, Mo' Roots or Satisfied 'N' Tickled Too*. The Rising Sons' solitary album, recorded for Columbia during 1966–7 but never released, was set to surface on Columbia Legacy in mid-'93.

Ry Cooder

Ryland Peter Cooder is, according to JOHN LEE HOOKER and various other folks who ought to know, the finest slide guitarist alive today. He is also a paster master of virtually all fretted stringed instruments, including mandolin, banjo and tiple; and a walking repository of American vernacular song: in other words, he's a folkie with a difference. His name will also live in eternal infamy for teaching THE ROLLING STONES' Keith Richards the open-G tuning which subsequently became The Human Riff's aural signature. Originally renowned as a studio musician – mandolin on the Stones's *Let It Bleed*; spectacular slide on Randy Newman's *12 Songs* and Jack Nitszche's soundtrack for Nicolas Roeg's notorious *Performance* – he signed a solo deal in 1970 and recorded a string of innovative, eclectic solo albums which mingled songs from the Depression era with more recent R&B favourites, and juxtaposed styles ranging from gospel and calypso to rural blues and hillbilly modes. His encyclopaedic repertoire, instrumental virtuosity, compassionate wit and rickety *homme moyen sensuel* voice gave those albums their distinctive flavour: part study aid, part party.

Cooder was born in Los Angeles on 15 March 1947; barely out of his 20s, he emerged from The Rising Sons (one of the most famous unheard bands of the era) to play on the debut album by fellow former Son TAJ MAHAL, with whom he shared a fascination with pre-war blues in general and SLEEPY JOHN ESTES in particular. His first real showcase was Captain Beefheart & The Magic Band's *Safe As Milk* (1967), which led to his rather better-publicised efforts with Randy Newman and the Stones as well as his post-'70 solo career, which peaked with 1979's *Bop 'Til You Drop*. More recently, his simmering, evocative slide has been heard on numerous movie soundtracks, including Paul Schrader's *Blue Collar*, Wim Wenders' *Paris, Texas*; and Walter Hill's *The Long*

Riders, *Southern Comfort* and *Crossroads*. He currently appears alongside John Hiatt, Nick Lowe and Jim Keltner in roots-rock supergroup Little Village, named after an obscure SONNY BOY WILLIAMSON side.

- *Into The Purple Valley* (Reprise 7599-27200-2)
- *Boomer's Story* (Reprise 7599-26398-2)
- *Paradise And Lunch* (Reprise 7599-27212-2)

The early-'70s trilogy which established Cooder as virtually an idiom in his own right, keynoted by *Purple Valley*'s opener 'How Can A Poor Man Stand Such Times And Live?'. They are, I suppose, p*st-m*d*rn in that they conjure up an air of antiquity without ever actually sounding like the actual old blues and country records from which the material derives. On *Paradise And Lunch*, for example, he's quite happy to juxtapose Bacharach & David with J.B. LENOIR, or to place a rousing reggae version of 'It's All Over Now' alongside something by BLIND WILLIE McTELL. His version of BLIND BLAKE's 'Ditty Wah Ditty' (performed as a guitar/piano duet with the sublime Earl Hines) simultaneously remains true to Blake's mischievous spirit without simply Xeroxing any specific Blake version. On *Boomer's Story*, he reinterprets Sleepy John Estes's 'Ax Sweet Mama' (a variant on the same Estes original as Taj Mahal's 'Leaving Trunk') and brings on Estes himself – unfortunately somewhat past his sell-by date in '72 – to perform his own 'President Kennedy'; and immaculately finger-picks his way through SKIP JAMES's 'Cherry Ball Blues'. You'll be in good shape with any of these three, though I'd take *Paradise And Lunch* as first pick while missing *Boomer's Story* only fractionally more than *Into The Purple Valley*.

- *Bop Till You Drop* (Warner Bros 7599-27398-2)

On its release in 1979, this was acclaimed as a masterpiece by many critics, including your correspondent; however, it hasn't aged that well. Much was originally made of the fact that it was one of the first albums to use the then brand-new digital recording technology, and, by comparison with most vinyl albums of the time, the sound literally sparkled. But the paradox – one to gladden every technophobe's heart – was that the fuzzy resolution of the vinyl and the glacial high end of the digital recording proved mutually beneficial: the digital clarity pushed the vinyl to its optimum resolution, while the soft warmth of the vinyl (if you'll pardon the expression) smoothed out those sharp digital edges. On CD, *Bop 'Til You Drop* simply sounds thin and shrill: I'm hanging on to my vinyl edition. I also have misgivings about the extravagant minstrel-show blackface of some of Cooder's vocals, which often collapse into parody: but then none of the black vocalists who join the fun seem to be worried, so why should I? With hindsight (or its aural equivalent) *Bop Till You Drop* is a purist's notion of funk recorded on an audiophile's notion of hi-fi, but the best of its reinterpretations of '50s and '60s R&B standards and obscurities still hit the mark.

Subjects for further investigation: Extra Ry: 1976's **Chicken Skin Music** (Reprise 7599-27231-2) is topped and tailed by two LEADBELLY tunes, 'Bourgeois Blues' and 'Goodnight Irene'; the post-*Bop* **Borderline** (Warner Bros 7599-23489-2) continues the R&B excursion. Most of Cooder's soundtracks, from the sublime and enormously influential *Paris, Texas* to the ridiculous *Crossroads*, are currently out of print; his latest is the menacing drone-and-rumble of **Trespass: Original Motion Picture Score** (Sire/Warner Bros 9362-45220-2) from the Ice-T/Ice Cube gangsta-rap thrilla. Cannily, the label splits Cooder's music and the movie's rap tunes (by Cube, T, Public Enemy, Sir Mix-A-Lot and more) onto separate albums: the rap disk with artwork prominently displaying the stars, and Cooder's music with Ice-free packaging. (Just so's Cooder fans don't get stuck with a rap album – or *vice versa* – please be advised that the Ices and their assorted homies are on *Trespass: Music From The Motion Picture* (Sire/Warner Bros 7599-26978-2). It's a subtle distinction, I agree.) For a more recent example of Cooder happily bluesing out, hear him sliding all over 'This Is Hip' on John Lee Hooker's **Mr Lucky** (Silvertone ORE CD 519).

Captain Beefheart's bemusing and exhilarating mutation of Delta blues, free jazz, dadaism, sex and ecology is one of life's more challenging pleasures: you can check out the gorgeous 'Rollin' And Tumblin'' variant that Cooder uses as the basis for the Captain's 'Sure 'Nuff 'N Yes I Do' on **Safe As Milk** (Castle Classics

CLACD 234); and follow some of the Captain's further adventures *sans* Ry on *The Spotlight Kid/Clear Spot* (Reprise 7599-26249).

Bonnie Raitt

In the video for 'I'm In The Mood For Love', her Grammy-winning duet with JOHN LEE HOOKER, Bonnie Raitt makes an entry worthy of Clint Eastwood: the first you see of her is a pair of cowboy-booted, bejeaned legs striding purposefully through the dust; a Blueswoman With No Name with a Stratocaster, rather than a Winchester, swinging at her side. Born into a showbiz family (her father was an actor) in Burbank, California, on 8 November 1949, she caught the blues bug at college, replacing her youthful folkie fervour for Joan Baez with a love for the blues of HOOKER, SON HOUSE and MISSISSIPPI FRED McDOWELL, and becoming a well-known figure on the Northeastern folk/blues circuit. She began recording in 1971, mixing country blues with laid-back 'mellow mafia' Los Angeles soft-rock, but her greatest successes came after her original record company, Warner Bros, dropped her in 1986. Like Tina Turner a few years before, she came back from the dead on Capitol with the highest sales of her career.

Starting out as an acoustic thumb-picker, Raitt demonstrated both love and command of her original sources, but – tutored and encouraged by Little Feat's late bottleneck whiz, Lowell George – she developed a highly distinctive electric slide style: lean, loping, stinging. She is, in a sense, a female counterpart of ERIC CLAPTON: her undeniable blues powers and the unfeigned respect in which she was (and is) held by the likes of House, Hooker and McDowell serve as validation for some fairly uninspiring exercises in AOR popcraft. I freely admit that those whose threshold for the '70s 'L.A. Bore' school is higher than mine may not find her albums as hard going as I often do, but hopefully we can agree on this: whether or not she has rotten taste in pop, Bonnie Raitt is a hell of a blueswoman and one of the finest slide guitarists around today.

- *The Bonnie Raitt Collection* (Warner Bros 7599-26242-2)

A fair cross-section of the first fifteen or so years of Raitt's recording career: a little country, a dollop of pop, a few torch songs and a fair amount of blues. The very first sound you hear is Junior Wells's harp locking in with Raitt's ringing National slide on a track from her debut album; the collection also borrows no less than four of the ten tracks from her second *Give It Up* (Warner Bros 7599-27264-2), including Chris Smither's divinely funky 'Love Me Like A Man'. Including guest shots from PAUL BUTTER-FIELD (on Jackson Browne's 'Under The FallingSky') and Raitt's mentor (mentress?) SIPPIE WALLACE (on a previously unreleased version of her own 'Woman Be Wise'), this isn't quite the all-blues Raitt collection I crave, but it'll do.

Subjects for further investigation: Raitt's 'I'm In The Mood For Love' cameo on John Lee Hooker's *The Healer* (Silvertone ORECD 508) is justifiably legendary, and it's both entertaining and instructive to compare it with the 1990 live version included on *John Lee Hooker: The Ultimate Collection 1948–1950* (Rhino R2 70572). Look for other examples of Raitt's prowess as a sittin'-in slidemeister on A.C. REED's *I'm In The Wrong Business* (Alligator ALCD), KATIE WEBSTER's *Swamp Boogie Queen* (Alligator ALCD) and BUDDY GUY's *Feels Like Rain* (Silvertone ORE CD 525).

9. Can Blue Kids Play The Whites?

UK R&B

In the early '60s, 'rhythm-and-blues' replaced New Orleans jazz as the retro fad of choice for a group of cultural dissidents who had grown equally disenchanted with insipid mainstream pop and with increasingly complex and 'difficult' modern jazz. In the US, 'rhythm and blues' was a catchall term for black popular music (or should that be 'popular black music'?) coined by Atlantic Records honcho Jerry Wexler during his days at *Billboard* magazine; in the

UK the definition was flash-frozen in the early '60s, meaning a loose conflation of South Side Chicago blues, assorted soul styles from JAMES BROWN to Motown, and the rootsier varieties of '50s rock and roll. In other words, anything from MUDDY WATERS to Marvin Gaye, from CHUCK BERRY to JIMMY REED, from Wilson Pickett to SLIM HARPO, from BO DIDDLEY to The Coasters.

UK R&B began as an underground scene, a cognoscenti's cult. The 'trad jazz' movement of the '50s had sparked an interest in pre-war blues of both the 'classic' and rural varieties, which led to British appearances by the likes of BIG BILL BROONZY and Muddy Waters. These were not without problems: the good-living, city-dwelling Broonzy was forced to pretend that he'd ambled on stage straight from a hard day behind the plough, and Muddy freaked out the sensitive jazzers and folkies with his keening electric slide and OTIS SPANN's thunderous piano. However, trad guru Chris Barber was by now devoting considerable stage time to Chicago-style blues, and soon a small but thriving blues scene sprang up in London under the aegis of ALEXIS KORNER and Cyril Davies. Their activities attracted the attention of the young would-be musicians who would soon form THE ROLLING STONES, Manfred Mann, THE YARDBIRDS, The Pretty Things and the other bands who, following in the wake of The Beatles, re-exported the blues back to the US. It is a sad comment on the ingrained nature of American racism that so much African-American music – from R&B to rap – has been unable to 'cross the tracks' from black neighbourhoods to white without taking a transatlantic detour via Britain.

Alexis Korner

Almost singlehandedly, the late singer-guitarist Alexis Korner brought the British R&B scene into being. In collaboration with harpist Cyril Davies (1932–1964), he formed Blues Unlimited during the late '50s: not only Britain's first Chicago-style electric blues band, but probably the first such white band anywhere in the world; and the one which ultimately set the pattern for UK rhythm and blues. It didn't last: Korner saw blues as common ground where jazz, folk and rock musicians could interact, while Davies adhered as solidly to the verities of Delta-gone-to-South-

Side blues as the 'trad jazzers' whom the R&B guys ousted did to the gospel according to Louis Armstrong. Nevertheless, it was the blues clubs which Korner founded which provided both meeting-place and platform for future members of bands like THE ROLLING STONES and Manfred Mann. He introduced Mick Jagger and Keith Richards to Brian Jones – the Stones played their first all-important Marquee Club gig when Blues Unlimited had to skip their Thursday night residency there to play a BBC radio show – and persuaded JOHN MAYALL to say farewell to Manchester; MUDDY WATERS and BIG BILL BROONZY were among his house-guests. A man of boundless urbanity and charm and a tireless propagandist for the blues, he was a guru to younger musicians who may have eclipsed him in worldly achievement but never lost respect for him. One of Brian Jones's last earthly acts before his death in 1969 was to beg to join Alexis Korner's latest band; Keith Richards sessioned for him as late as 1975, and ERIC CLAPTON was merely the best-known of the musicians who popped up to play at his gala 50th birthday party.

Born in Paris of Austrian and Greco-Turkish extraction on 19 April, 1928, he played jazz and skiffle banjo with trad-jazzer Chris Barber before catching the blues bug: he and Cyril Davies performed a Chicago-style blues set within Barber's band before splitting off to form Blues Unlimited. When Davies set off in his own right, Korner started singing, revealing a a richly tobacco-cured baritone and a bombastically theatrical vocal style which combined an impeccably black-and-bluesy timbre with equally impeccable patrician British vowels, but was unfortunately flawed by a persistently erratic sense of pitch. His bands and duos included the likes of Jack Bruce and Ginger Baker (Clapton's partners in Cream), future John Mayall and Free bassist Andy Fraser and even a pre-LED ZEPPELIN Robert Plant, but his greatest commercial success came in the early '70s with the jazz-rock big-band CCS, and with the numerous television-commercial voice-overs which paid his bills. He continued to perform solo, in duos and with small groups until the end of his life, as well as hosting his own R&B radio shows. Sad to say, his records haven't aged well, but Korner himself aged beautifully: he was infinitely less of an old fart than many one-third his age; and when he died – on New Year's Day of 1984 – virtually the entire British rock scene felt personally bereaved.

Ultimately, Alexis Korner made little great music, but he was the direct cause of so much great music from others that he deserves to be remembered, with affection and admiration, wherever blues is played.

- *Alexis Korner And . . . 1961–1972* (Castle Communications CSSCD 150)
- *Alexis Korner And . . . 1972–1983* (Castle Communications CSSCD 192)

These panoramic surveys of Korner's lengthy career are probably the best place to start if you want to find out what Korner actually sounded like. The first (and probably the more interesting) is currently in catalogue but out of stock; the second includes examples of Korner's satirical songwriting ('Captain America', 'Juvenile Delinquent'), a couple of warm tributes ('KING B.B.', 'ROBERT JOHNSON'), some Stones covers, guest appearances from Richards, Clapton, Chris Farlowe and Steve Marriott, and several showcases for bass monster Colin Hodgkinson.

Subjects for further investigation: The live-in-the-studio '66/'67 trio sides on *I Wonder Who* (BGO BGOCD 136) illustrate Korner's expansive personality and folk/jazz approach to the blues: its best shot is a cracklingly funky take on Percy Mayfield's 'River's Invitation'. 1968's *A New Generation Of Blues* (BGO BGOCD 102) is a mildly stoned and mildly eccentric jam (power trio with flute?), and its best moments are a rocking version of Freddie King's 'I'm Tore Down'; and 'A Flower', Alexis's sage advice to hippies, which concludes with the immortal line 'I love me, baby, better than you do yourself.' The 1975 supersession – well, Keef's on it, innee? – *Get Off My Cloud* (Sequel NEXCD 134) includes a splendidly sardonic reading of The Doors' 'The WASP (Texas Radio And The Big Beat)' and the affecting 'Song For Jimi'; it's also where 'Robert Johnson' first appeared. 'Alexis Boogie' on *B.B. King In London* (BGO BGOCD 42) demonstrates his powers of persuasion, if nothing else: he's the only person ever to convince the Big B to pick an acoustic guitar with tape rolling.

The Rolling Stones

Does the story of The Rolling Stones require retelling? I think not. Let's restrict our observations to these: when the Stones started playing blues, there were no prospects for immediate financial gain in what they were doing, which blows away the 'cynical expropriators' theory. Since the British bluesers lacked any information about the music apart from what could be gleaned from the records themselves and their skimpy, often inaccurate, liner notes, they freely mixed the styles, devices and repertoires of different schools, which is why the Stones – like ELVIS PRESLEY before them – often performed uptown material with downtown or rural instrumentation. Where Presley had tackled sophisticated jump material like the ROY BROWN/WYNONIE HARRIS 'Good Rockin' Tonight' with only a couple of guitars and a string bass, the Stones applied the instrumentation of a Chicago blues band – harp, guitars, optional piano – and the rubbery guitar and rustling maraccas of BO DIDDLEY to material derived from everybody from Buddy Holly to Solomon Burke.

At the same time, the very sedulousness with which they mimicked the intonations, both vocal and instrumental, of their models only served to emphasise both their cultural distance from those models, and their own awareness of that distance. Their defence against incongruity was irony: everthing Mick Jagger sang appeared in implied quotes. The Stones pointed a finger at African-American culture, and as a result found Anglo-American culture pointing back at them: more than any other artists, the Stones woke up the white suburbs to the blues, and this book exists almost entirely because of the audience that they created.

As David Sinclair points out in exhaustive detail in this book's companion volume *Rock On CD*, The Stones' early catalogue is currently in extreme disarray. During the early '60s British and American record companies had radically different notions of what an album ought to be. Brits aimed for 12–14 tracks, most if not all of which should be original recordings specifically cut for that album; Americans preferred 10–12 cuts, including as many singles as possible. The Beatles' catalogue has now been internationally standardised to the original UK versions; since the Stones' stuff is controlled from the US we have to put up with rejigged and shortened US albums, resulting in a whole bunch of good sides simply falling between the cracks. Even their current early Greatest Hits collection *Hot Rocks: The Greatest Hits 1964–1971* (London 820 140-2) is a half-assed version of the original *Big Hits (High Tide And Green Grass)* and *More Hot Rocks (Big Hits And Fazed Cookies)* anthologies which manages to omit 'Little Red Rooster', the epochal single with which they took a relatively unadorned HOWLIN' WOLF interpretation of a WILLIE DIXON song into the British and American charts. Since, in rock and roll terms, the Stones matter bigtime, this is a seriously screwed situation.

- *The Rolling Stones* (London 820 047-2)

Miraculously unmessed-with, this '64 dêbut is the definitive account of Model-T UK R&B. Jagger's leer, Keith's grunge and Brian Jones's narcissistic purism go to work on what they've learned from CHUCK BERRY, Bo Diddley, MUDDY WATERS, SLIM HARPO, Rufus Thomas and Marvin Gaye. Gwaaaan . . . treat yourself.

- *Beggar's Banquet* (London 800 084-2)
- *Let It Bleed* (London 820 052-2)
- *Get Yer Ya-Ya's Out* (London 820 131-2)

Mad, bad and dangerous to know: the Stones in their archetypal late-'60s prime, and reconnected to their blues roots after lengthy forays into soul, twee English art-pop and psychedelia. They returned in the wake of 'Jumpin' Jack Flash' with the authority to bend the blues form to depict an apocalyptic dreamscape of sexual terror, political corruption and social collapse. It was the period of 'Sympathy For The Devil', 'Street Fighting Man', 'Honky Tonk Women', 'Gimme Shelter' and 'Let It Bleed'; but it was also the period of their deepest engagement with rural blues. *Beggars' Banquet*'s only overt country-blues cover is 'Prodigal Son' (a near-standard most frequently associated with Rev. Robert Wilkins, who's recorded variants of it under a variety of titles), but the entire album is soaked in its spirit: look no further than the vagabond theme and lyrical acoustic slide on 'No Expectations'. *Let It Bleed* introduces Keith Richards to RY COODER, and the Stones' repertoire to ROBERT JOHNSON's 'Love In Vain' and – in an extended suite of blues settings – a creation worthy of PEETIE WHEATSTRAW himself, the predatory 'Midnight Rambler'. Both 'Love In Vain' and 'Midnight Rambler' are, however, knocked into an Uncle Sam top hat by the live versions on *Ya-Ya's*: Brian Jones' replacement Mick Taylor, who'd barely had time to unpack his guitar for Let It Bleed, had found his depth; most notably in a spare, passionate slide solo on 'Love In Vain' that almost shames Jagger into singing the song straight. Recorded in Madison Square Gardens in 1969, it documents the 'Altamont' tour on which the Stones discovered the downside of delivering on their myth.

- *Exile On Main Street* (Rolling Stones 450196 2)

The morning after the decade before: this gloriously tattered hangover album includes, among its many unappetisingly encrusted gems, versions of Slim Harpo's 'Shake Your Hips' and Robert Johnson's 'Stop Breaking Down' which are blessed with an almost irresistable scarecrow grace, rarely achieved before or since.

Subjects for further investigation: **12 x 5** (London 820 048-2) is a miserable travesty of the second Stones album, the cover artwork of which it appropriates: it's basically the *5 x 5* EP, both sides of the 'It's All Over Now' single, an outtake judged unfit for the UK market, and *four whole tracks* from *The Rolling Stones No. 2*. Still, at least 5 x 5 included one of their finest Chuck Berry covers (two, if you take into account that they learned Jay McShann and Walter Brown's 'Confessin' The Blues' from Berry's version) in 'Around And Around', and some classic Jagger 'sincerity' in their version of Wilson Pickett's 'If You Need Me.' Still, I miss their fabulous versions of Muddy's 'I Can't Be Satisfied', Chuck's 'You Can't Catch Me', and Solomon Burke's 'Everybody Needs Somebody To Love.' (Those three titles sum the Stones up rather well, as it goes.) Fifteen years later, they were still capable of playing the whoopingly carnal take on Muddy Waters' 'Manish Boy' which **Sucking In The Seventies** (Rolling Stones CDCBS 450205 2) thoughtfully rescues from an otherwise mostly undistinguished live album; if only it could also have included the cover of Bo Diddley's 'Crackin' Up' that went with it, and the raucous strum-up on MISSISSIPPI FRED McDOWELL's 'You Got To Move', which graces **Sticky Fingers** (Rolling Stones 450 195-2).

The rather nifty 27-track budget collection **Stoned Alchemy**

(Instant CD INS 5016) traces their sources by assembling the original versions – by, among others, Chuck Berry (six tunes), Howlin' Wolf (three), Jimmy Reed (two), Muddy Waters and Bo Diddley (four apiece) – of much of the early Stones repertoire. Slim Harpo's 'I'm A King Bee', a highspot of their first album, is missing; the keen-eyed will spot Tommy Tucker's name on the cover artwork even though his 'Hi Heel Sneakers' doesn't appear, and the included version of 'It's All Over Now' is a 1975 remake by its composer Bobby Womack rather than the *original* original by Womack's group The Valentinos, but hey! Whaddya want: blood?

The Yardbirds

The Yardbirds began as the ultimate post-ROLLING STONES weedy-but-smart suburban whiteboy blues band; LED ZEPPELIN – their lineal descendants – were The Yardbirds on steroids. Like JOHN MAYALL's BluesBreakers, the 'most blueswailing' Yardbirds served as a finishing school for three key '60s Britrock guitar gods, and their five-year professional career exemplified the evolution from earnest Brit R&B ('63-'65, with ERIC CLAPTON) to artful but commercial psychedelic pop ('65–'66, with Jeff Beck) and, finally, the shores of Heavy Metal ('66-'68, with Jimmy Page). Their vocalist, Keith Relf (1943–1976), sounded about as black and funky as John Major, but his flat, nasal whine and serviceable harp were juxtaposed against those raging guitars and a rhythm section given to frantic, modal-improv 'rave-ups'. When the Stones graduated to the big time, The Yardbirds inherited both their showcase residency at Twickenham's Crawdaddy club, and their fanatical local following.

After three singles and a live album, Clapton left to join John Mayall because he couldn't stand the pop direction of their first hit 'For Your Love'; he was replaced by Beck, who quit in his turn, a year and a half of skewed, druggy pop-blues hits later, because he couldn't stand touring. Page, already in the band as bassist, took over on lead guitar and, when the founder members walked out in '68, formed a 'New Yardbirds' to fulfil outstanding commitments. Said New Yardbirds then became Led Zeppelin, which is most definitely another story.

● *On Air* (Band Of Joy BOJCD 200)

The Yardbirds' meagre catalogue – three albums, one with each guitarist; a fistful of singles, and assorted demos and outtakes – is currently in CD limbo as Charly ready a new deluxe boxed set. This post-Clapton collection of '65–'68 BBC airshots, mostly featuring Beck with a few Page showcases bringing up the rear, is all you're guaranteed to find at the time of writing; it mixes up their pop hits with assorted CHUCK BERRY, BO DIDDLEY, ELMORE JAMES, Billy Boy Arnold and SLIM HARPO tunes; and privides the opportunity to hear Beck play several pieces generally associated with Clapton. Judged as 'blues' it's ridiculous; heard as an example of how liberating blues materials and attitudes were for stiff young Brits, it's a revelation, despite the BBC engineers' reluctance to allow the young brutes to turn their amplifiers up to real-life onstage levels.

Subjects for further investigation: Eric Clapton's career best-of *Crossroads* (Polydor 835 261-2) includes the A's and B's of his three 'Birds singles alongside three demos from their first studio session; copies of 1964's *Five Live Yardbirds* (Decal CD CHARLY 182) may still be in stock in some stores, though I wouldn't stake my life on it. Their key material with Beck, both pop and blues, is on Beck's collection *Beckology* (Epic Legacy 469282 2); the ingenuity, audacity and sheer venom with which he turns both sets of conventions inside out is a joy to hear. The Page stuff I wouldn't – you should pardon the expression – fret about. All three Yardbirds guitar heroes are represented on *Blue Eyed Blues* (Charly CD BM 20).

The other two significant R&B-turned-pop Britblues bands of the period were Manfred Mann and The Animals. The Manfreds (led by the South African expat jazz pianist whose name the group borrowed, and featuring singer/harpist Paul Jones, a graduate of the ALEXIS KORNER school who resurfaced in the '70s and '80s as front man for London club attraction The Blues Band) have no significant CDs available at this time; but The Animals' *The EP Collection* (See For Miles SEE CD 244) both recycles their early hits – including the groundbreaking blues-ballad 'House Of The Rising Sun' – and documents singer Eric Burdon's soulful way with his favourite RAY CHARLES, JOHN LEE HOOKER and FATS DOMINO songs.

UK BLUES BOOM

The most important thing to remember about the British Blues Boomers of the late '60s is how intense and *serious* they all were. The 'R&B' groups of the early '60s wave – THE ROLLING STONES, THE YARDBIRDS, Manfred Mann, The Animals – drew freely on '50s rock and contemporary pop-soul as well as Delta, Chicago and Memphis blues, but their inquisitive eclecticism, pop sensibility and willingness to experiment soon produced a vehement reaction from those who considered any departure from The Book Of The Law as being sacrilegious and possible grounds for a *fatwa*. ERIC CLAPTON's 1965 resignation from THE YARDBIRDS in order to sign up with JOHN MAYALL's Bluesbreakers was one profound indicator: his decision – less than a year later – to quit Mayall in order to form Cream with Jack Bruce and Ginger Baker – was another. The Blues Boomers were so serious about the 'real' blues that they regarded RAY CHARLES and JAMES BROWN as sellouts: Stax and Motown were beyond the pale and even the use of horn sections was frowned upon (presumably this meant that B.B. KING, ALBERT KING and T-BONE WALKER weren't 'real' blues singers) until Mayall bit the bullet and hired three brass players in 1967. Their featured instrumental soloists tended to be rather better than their vocalists or rhythm section players, which is why Britblues served as a hothouse for the pathological guitar fetish which it bequeathed to heavy metal.

Like their ideological predecessors, the trad jazzers of the '50s, the Blues Boomers at their best generated music of startling emotional power and idiomatic fidelity, but at their worst they exhibited a thoroughly British puritanism and an intense mistrust of the pleasure principle which placed them at diametrical odds with the great bluesmen whose every mannerism they mimicked so sedulously. The caesura between the pop R&B of the early '60s and the puritan blues boom came with one key album, and its surprising chart success canonised two major figureheads. One kept the faith, and the other soon defected.

John Mayall

Undoubtedly the greatest bluesman ever to be born in Maccles-field, Cheshire (on 29 November 1933), John Mayall was a British Army veteran (Korea 1951–5) and former graphic artist who'd picked up a taste for the boogie from his trombonist father. Beginning with mastering the piano styles acquired from a pile of early boogie-woogie 78s by the likes of Cripple Clarence Lofton, Pinetop Smith and others, he set about learning the basics of harmonica and guitar before forming his first bands. Starting out in Manchester with 'John Mayall's Powerhouse Four', he relo-cated to London in the early '60s, at the behest of Alexis Korner, to form the first of many line-ups of his Bluesbreakers. His legend had as much to do with his obsessiveness and his eccentricities as with his music – he was renowned for living in a self-constructed treehouse, his blues purism was of an almost religious intensity, and he was a notoriously strict bandleader – but he was never less than useful at any of his instruments; his compositions were canny and deeply-felt pastiches of his heroes' creations; and his voice – an eerie falsetto reminiscent of OTIS RUSH, BUDDY GUY and his hero J.B. LENOIR – carried real conviction.

Where Mayall differed from the Chicagocentric post-Stones R&B crews who had preceded him was his fondness for West Side blues, and his resulting determination that his bands should always include a featured lead guitarist well versed in the gospel according to Rush, Guy and the three KINGS (B.B., ALBERT and FREDDIE). His most celebrated groups straddled the mid-to-late '60s and were crucial showcases for, respectively, ERIC CLAPTON, Peter Green and Mick Taylor, all of whom left his band with vastly increased reputations to earn vastly increased salaries. Clapton joined in 1965, fresh from THE YARDBIRDS, whom he'd denounced as pop sell-outs, and made his mark on the extraordinary *Blues Breakers*, which set a major precedent by charting impressively without the aid of a hit single. When he departed the following year to form Cream (with former Mayall and Manfred Mann bassist Jack Bruce), he was replaced by Peter Green, eventually to depart in his turn, with Mayall's longtime bassist John McVie following not long after, to start up FLEETWOOD MAC in 1967. Green was replaced by shy young Mick Taylor, who lasted until 1969 before being headhunted for Brian Jones's slot in THE ROLLING STONES.

Tired of running a finishing school for aspiring blues-rock megastars, Mayall went to the other extreme: disbanding the BluesBreakers to form a drummerless acoustic band with guitarist Jon Mark and reedman Johnny Almond, who soon took off to form their own short-lived group, Mark-Almond (no relation to the post-punk campmeister of almost the same name). And so it went. Mayall, now a long-term resident of Los Angeles, never regained the commercial clout he'd had in the '60s, but he's long since earned his billing as The Father Of British Blues, and the odd new star still emerges from his ever-changing Bluesbreakers (the most recent being guitarist WALTER TROUT). For what it's worth, Mayall has indeed become a Real Bluesman, but what that means in the modern world is hustling around the world, cranking out the Greatest Hits and watching his best sidemen learn all they can from him and then take off when a better offer presents itself. He recorded regularly throughout the '70s and '80s, but to little effect; though his most recent efforts, 1990's *A Sense Of Place* and 1993's *Wake Up Call*, are his most convincing for years.

- **JOHN MAYALL WITH ERIC CLAPTON:** *Blues Breakers* (London 800 086-2)
- **JOHN MAYALL & THE BLUESBREAKERS:** *A Hard Road* (London 820 474-2)

Two of the finest – if not the two absolute finest – white blues albums of the '60s: simultaneously absolutely idiomatic and with a distinct ambience all their own. Producer Mike Vernon conjured up the perfect studio environment for Mayall's music: dark, murky and eerie, with Mayall's spooky falsetto and Clapton and Green's guitars gleaming out of the fog like streetlamps reflected on a rainy pavement. The Clapton album is justly celebrated for its exposure of the young God's startling blues powers, but in many ways *A Hard Road* is a better album. Mayall was on a songwriting roll with excellent originals like 'Living Alone', 'Top Of The Hill' and the title song; and Peter Green takes full advantage of his four showcases: two instrumentals (the inevitable Freddie King tribute 'The Stumble', and his own brooding sustain heaven 'The Supernatural') and two vocals (the perennial

'You Don't Love Me' and his original 'The Same Way'). As Mayall points out in his liner notes, Green had already formulated a personal style: less ferocious than Clapton but achingly lyrical, with a liquid purity of tone which drew on B.B. King and anticipated Carlos Santana. Mayall, a canny bandleader above all else, struck different sparks off Clapton and Green; he used the former to bring out the anger in his music, and the latter to highlight its melancholia.

Subjects for further investigation: For **Crusade** (Deram 820 537-2), exit Peter Green: enter Mick Taylor and a horn section. The repertoire borrows, tastefully enough, from Albert King, Buddy Guy, Freddie King, Otis Rush and Sonny Boy Williamson, and it does include Mayall's own affecting 'The Death Of J.B. LENOIR', but the overall feel is sluggish and Taylor, despite a mean, snaky turn of guitar phrase, is a far less commanding presence than either of his predecessors. Singer-songwriterismo struck on **Bare Wires** (London 820 538-2) – the last BluesBreakers album – and **Blues From Laurel Canyon** (Deram 820 539-2); a pair of song-suites respectively concerning lost love and featuring a jazzier version of the brass-laden Crusade line-up (ponderous); and an account of a holiday in Los Angeles, with a quartet spotlighting Taylor (bathetic). **Looking Back** (Deram 820 331-2) and **Thru The Years** (Deram 844 028-2) gather up assorted '65-'68 singles and outtakes featuring Clapton, Green, Taylor, Jack Bruce, Fleetwood and Mac. **Primal Solos** (London 820 320-2) collects a bunch of exceedingly lo-fi live recordings from '66 and '68 – heavy on historicity, light on listenability – featuring Clapton, Bruce and Taylor; the collection **Raw Blues** (London 820 479-2) presents more Mayall/Clapton collaborations, including the ridiculously rare single 'Lonely Years'/'Bernard Jenkins'.

Closer to the present day, **Life In The Jungle** (Charly CD BM 4) features mid-'80s live recordings from Germany: its best shot is the title track, composed by Walter Trout and later to resurface on a Trout album of the same name. If nothing else, **A Sense Of Place** (Island IMCD 167) demonstrates that Mayall's homing instinct for stellar guitarists is still in effect: nouveau slidemeister SONNY LANDRETH augments the 1990 edition of The Bluesbreakers, as does ALBERT COLLINS' stalwart rhythm guitarist Debbie Davies. Still reinterpreting J.B. Lenoir (as well as Wilbert Harrison and J.J.

Cale) alongside his own and Landreth's originals, Mayall finally becomes the blues patriarch he always wanted to be. His current album, 1993's *Wake Up Call* (Silvertone ORE CD 527), borrows Jimmy Reed's 'Ain't That Lovin' You Baby' and, puckishly, Tony Joe White's composition 'Undercover Agent For The Blues' from no less a personage than Tina Turner; it also augments the Bluesbreakers with Buddy Guy – the same duet version of JUNIOR WELLS' 'I Could Cry' which appears on Buddy's *Feels Like Rain* (Silvertone ORE CD 516) – Mick Taylor, Mavis Staples (duetting on the whomping title track) and, on two Mayall originals, the impeccably searing guitar of Albert Collins himself. These are as tough, resilient and enjoyable a pair of albums as he's made since *A Hard Road*.

Eric Clapton

The fans who eagerly and naively claimed, back in the Clapton-is-God era, that Eric Clapton is the world's greatest blues guitarist, have done him a profound disservice. The scarred, worldly Clapton of today knows, even if the fiery blues purist of the '60s didn't, that – to paraphrase MUDDY WATERS – no-one can hope to be the best, and all you could do is try to be a good 'un. Eric Clapton is a good 'un: and the bluesmen who once were his idols now consider him a peer. The journey that Eric Patrick Clapton – born March 30, 1945, in Ripley, Surrey – has taken since the early '60s transformed him from the sharply-dressed moddy-boy of THE YARDBIRDS to today's sharply-dressed Elder Statesman Of Rock. In between, the angry young man of the blues undergoes an archetypal quest for self: he discovers his powers, revels in them, is brought low by them, rejects them, and is finally reconciled to them. Along the way, he learns valuable lessons: that virtuosity is not necessarily its own reward, and that the white-hot intensity of continual bare-knuckle improvisation can be exhausting to artist and audience; that emotional pain can stimulate great art, but at considerable cost; and that if the world cannot be changed, it must be accomodated.

The foundation of Clapton's legend is his guitar work, and – after acquiring a grounding in the acoustic folk blues of BIG BILL

BROONZY – he built it playing electric guitar behind other vocalists: Keith Relf (in The Yardbirds), JOHN MAYALL (in Mayall's BluesBreakers), Jack Bruce (in Cream) and Stev(i)e Winwood (in Blind Faith). With The Yardbirds and Mayall he demonstrated his fluency, aggression and ability to adapt and customise what he learned from sedulous study of the records of BUDDY GUY, CHUCK BERRY, OTIS RUSH, Hubert Sumlin and, of course, B.B., FREDDIE AND ALBERT KING. With Cream, he attempted to apply what he'd learned to other forms: the post-Beatles art-pop songs the trio favoured in the studio, the raging open-ended improvs in which they specialised in concert, and the bulldozing rifferama common to both. As with all experimental music, the results were mixed: as the live half of Cream's 1968 double-album *Wheels Of Fire* proved, for every 'Crossroads' there is a 'Toad'. 'Crossroads' is one of Clapton's enduring masterpieces: the band charge through ROBERT JOHNSON's nightmarish Delta terrain as if they're on a nuclear-powered three-seater Harley-Davidson, yet – for all their explosive propulsion – they're as trapped as Johnson was. 'Toad', on the other hand, was a 16-minute Ginger Baker drum solo so legendarily tedious that even drummers can't bear to listen to it.

Cream's blues side came out in a mixture of Chicago and Memphis standards like Howlin' Wolf's 'Spoonful' and 'Sittin' On Top Of The World', and Albert King's 'Born Under A Bad Sign' (none of which represent any threat to the originals); and older, more esoteric tunes like Johnson's 'Crossroads' and 'Four Till Late', SKIP JAMES' 'I'm So Glad', Dr Ross's 'Catsquirrel', Blind Joe Reynolds' 'Outside Woman Blues (a.k.a. ''Fore Day Creep') and – on their 1966 debut, *Fresh Cream* (Polydor 827 576-2) – a frantic guitar-harp-and-drums workout on the Delta standard 'Rollin' And Tumblin'' which is the finest treatment the song has ever received at the hands of white folks. Their bluesier originals included Bruce's acrid 'Politician' and Clapton's 'Strange Brew', which gave a funky Albert King-style setting to an ethereal ode to a psychedelic dreamgirl.

Cream literally burned itself out: the trio collapsed, after less than two years, under the strain of its members' clashing personalities and at-odds musical agendas. After a brief detour into the ill-fated Blind Faith, essentially a showcase for Winwood which got too big too quickly, Clapton finally took over the centre-stage vocal microphone for Derek & The Dominos, a quartet augmented in the studio by guest guitarist Duane Allman of Georgia's Allman Brothers Band. The title track of the resulting double-album, *Layla And Other Assorted Love Songs* (Polydor 511 234-2), was as masterful an original as 'Crossroads' had been an interpretation, and elsewhere *Layla* added powerful versions of Broonzy's 'Key To The Highway', Freddie King's 'Have You Ever Loved A Woman' and JIMI HENDRIX's 'Little Wing' to Clapton's canon. The Dominos disintegrated in their turn, and Clapton – whose first 'solo' album had been so dominated by his friends Delaney Bramlett (of Delaney & Bonnie) and Leon Russell that he was the featured artist in barely more than name only – emerged from a bout of heroin addiction to take full charge of his own career for the first time. In revolt against the improv-based 'guitar hero' æsthetic which had dominated his '60s work, he began a series of albums, commencing with 1974's *461 Ocean Boulevarde* (Polydor 811 697-2), which included a nifty version of Robert Johnson's 'Steady Rollin' Man' and an affecting take on the staple 'Motherless Children' (a song with special significance for Clapton), but concentrated on laid-back singer-songwriterism spiced with excursions into reggae and country music. In the following decade, he enjoyed not a few hits, notably with Bob Marley's 'I Shot The Sheriff' and a reggae-based interpretation of Bob Dylan's 'Knockin' On Heaven's Door'; less notably with the woozy sentimentality of 'Wonderful Tonight'. Finally, he kicked the alcoholism which had replaced his junk habit, started wearing suits again, and embarked on the musical policy which has characterised his last decade or so: a mixture of radio-friendly AOR and blues, with a lucrative and prestigious sideline in RY COODER-ish TV and movie soundtracks.

So where does the blues soul of Eric Clapton reside? Read on.

- ● *Crossroads* (Polydor 835 261-2)
- ● *24 Nights* (Reprise 7599-26402-2)

The hulking 4-CD boxed set *Crossroads* does a sterling job of rounding up highlights from the first quarter-century of Clapton's history; the 2-CD live set *24 Nights*, recorded during his 1990 and 1991 Royal Albert Hall residencies, tells you an awful lot about how the artist regards that history. *Crossroads* opens in 1963, with the young Yardbirds cautiously feeling their way through

JOHN LEE HOOKER's 'Boom Boom' at their first-ever studio session, and closes in 1987 with Clapton rerecording his 1970 version of J.J. Cale's 'After Midnight' for a 1987 beer commercial. It contains just about every studio side he cut with The Yardbirds, a sampling of the Mayall era (not enough to justify not buying *Blues Breakers*, though), a Cream selection which concentrates on their hits and Clapton's originals rather than their blues, though it naturally includes 'Crossroads'), a saunter through the Blind Faith and Dominos catalogues which is liberally salted with outtakes – the best of which is an acoustic slide duet, by Clapton and Duane Allman, on LITTLE WALTER's 'Mean Old World' – and enough of Clapton's AOR work to choke a horse. Along the line he assays, with varying degrees of commitment, Howlin' Wolf's 'Evil' and Arthur Crudup's 'Mean Old Frisco' (with the Dominos), ELMORE JAMES' 'The Sky Is Crying' and 'It Hurts Me Too', BOBBY BLAND's 'Further On Up The Road' and Otis Rush's 'Double Trouble'. The mixture of hits and outtakes is standard box-set procedure: the well-known songs hook in the casual buyer and the esoterica appeases the buffs.

24 Nights attempts to cover several waterfronts: Clapton runs through a selection of hits from the Cream era to the present day with small and large soul-rock bands, supplies a grandstanding climax with RAY CHARLES' 'Hard Times' (first unveiled on 1989's *Journeyman*) and his *Edge Of Darkness* theme in the company of the National Philharmonic Orchestra, and performs JUNIOR WELLS' 'Hoodoo Man Blues', Little Walter's 'Watch Yourself' (miscredited to Buddy Guy), Big Maceo's 'Worried Life Blues' and the perennial 'Have You Ever Loved A Woman' with a couple of allstar blues bands which include ROBERT CRAY and Buddy Guy, though those worthies stay in the background. It's the blues tracks and 'Edge Of Darkness' which are the most effective; the rest is more elegant than hard-hitting.

● *The Early Clapton Collection* (Castle Communications CCSCD 162)

Young God in training: this 1963–66 compilation is better news for the devout Claptophile seeking to study the evolution of young EC's guitar style than it is for the general listener. Its 20 tracks divide up into three basic slices: Slice One covers The

Yardbirds (three B's and an A from their first three singles; one manky early live recording, one live cut backing SONNY BOY WILLIAMSON and one extract from the considerably more confident and professional *Five Live Yardbirds*); Slice Two is a half-dozen early-morning home jams with Jimmy Page, subsequently over-dubbed by Charlie Watts (drums), Bill Wyman (bass) and Mick Jagger (harp); and Slice Three rounds up assorted BluesBreakers sides that didn't make it onto That Album, including the 'I'm Your Witchdoctor'/'Telephone Blues' single, and the two duo tracks from *Raw Blues*. The early Yardbirds live stuff (including the track where they're thoroughly intimidated by Sonny Boy) could be any teenage tyro making a stab at the blues, but the rapidity with which Eric Clapton became *Eric Clapton* is impressive, to say the least. Some of the same material – and other material from the same sources – recurs on *Blue Eyed Blues* (Charly CD BM 20) alongside early works by Clapton's fellow ex-Yardbirds Jeff Beck and Jimmy Page; and also on *White Boy Blues* (Castle Communications CCSCD 103).

● **JOHN MAYALL WITH ERIC CLAPTON:** *Blues Breakers* (London 800 086-2)

Essentially, the Clapton-Is-God myth starts here, on the gradua-tion piece which marks his transition from apprentice to journey-man. It features his first-ever studio lead vocal (a restrained but emotional reading of Robert Johnson's 'Rambling On My Mind', backed only by Mayall's piano and his own guitar), and it's also the only album Clapton has ever recorded which is straight-up blues from start to finish. The repertoire is a mixture of Mayall originals and borrowings from Otis Rush, Freddie King and Memphis Slim, but Clapton plays throughout in what had become his own distinctive voice (anger and desire, barely suppressed) and signa-ture sound (the velvet snarl of a Gibson Les Paul guitar and a Marshall amp). It is his fluid, corrosive playing which gives the album its extraordinary tension: his best solos literally burn holes in the music. The influences of Rush, Guy, Sumlin and the inevitable Three Kings have been swallowed by many, but digested by few: Clapton was the first British bluesman to transcend plagiarism and mimicry to play the music as himself, without irony or vaudeville. If this is cultural imperialism, it's rarely sounded as good, or done as much honour to the colonised.

- *Just One Night* (Polydor 800 093-2)

This 1980 live double-CD, cut in Japan, represents Clapton's current peak of recorded blues improvisation: amongst his standard fistful of rock hits – 'Lay Down Sally', 'Wonderful Tonight', 'After Midnight', 'Cocaine' *et al* – are superb and deeply felt versions of (Big) Maceo Merriwether's 'Worried Life Blues', Otis Rush's 'Double Trouble', BOBBY BLAND's 'Further On Up The Road' and a storming medley of 'Rambling On My Mind' and Freddie King's 'Have You Ever Loved A Woman.' Recommended to anyone who felt that Clapton lost touch with the blues after his Mayall/Cream/Dominos years; and to anyone who simply loves to hear him play.

- *Unplugged* (Reprise 9362-45024)

Surprisingly, the most commercially successful album of Clapton's career was this multi-Grammied 1992 MTV acoustic session. Alongside the acoustic 'Layla' and the affecting 'Tears In Heaven' (an epitaph to his late son Conor which will be providing comfort to bereaved parents for years to come) is a spiritual return to Clapton's pre-Yardbirds beginnnings as a folkie devotee of Big Bill Broonzy and Jesse Fuller. He adds 'Malted Milk' and 'Walkin' Blues' to his Robert Johnson canon and canters through BO DIDDLEY's 'Before You Accuse Me' and Fuller's 'San Francisco Bay Blues', but the effect throughout is oddly muted. To say that these performances are smooth, deft and polished is not to imply that they are shallow or unemotional, but by comparison with the in-your-face originals, these seem to be displayed under glass. Perhaps this is the essence of Clapton's mature style: that the naked flame which once threatened to immolate artist and audience alike is now contained.

Subjects for further investigation: Clapton has periodically guested with his inspirations: the most notable of these collaborations are *The Howlin' Wolf London Sessions* (Chess CD CHESS 1004) and *Buddy Guy & Junior Wells Play The Blues* (Rhino/Atco R2 70299 [US]). His epochal 'Crossroads' has been frequently anthologised; those unwilling – with good reason – to lash out for the sprawling *Wheels Of Fire* (Polydor 827 578-2) can find it on *Q: The Blues* (The Hit Label AHLCD 1), *Rocking The Blues* (Castle Communications CCSCD 191) or *The Cream Of Eric Clapton* (Polydor 833 519-2). Of his movie scores, I'd recommend 1989's *Homeboy* (Virgin Movie Music CDV 2574) for its lingering National slide sounds as well as for the archive tracks by J.B. Hutto and MAGIC SAM; and 1992's *Rush* (Reprise 7599-26794-2), if only for the original studio version of 'Tears In Heaven' – why was such an emotionally-charged song introduced as part of the soundtrack for such a violent movie? – and for Buddy Guy's hysterically powerful ten-minute cameo on 'Don't Know Which Way To Go'. Duane Allman – the secret hero of *Layla* – probably had his finest moment with his own group on 1971's *The Allman Brothers Band: The Fillmore Concerts* (Polydor 517 294-2), which includes awesome versions of 'Statesboro Blues' (from BLIND WILLIE McTELL via TAJ MAHAL) and T-BONE WALKER's 'Stormy Monday', marred only by vocalist Gregg Allman's occasional hamminess. And maybe one day someone will get around to compiling the *Eric Clapton Sings Robert Johnson* album which EC's been cutting, on and off, since 1965. (I think I'll make a tape . . .)

Fleetwood Mac

Yeah, yeah, yeah: L.A. soft-rock soap opera, mega-squillion-selling AOR, Bill Clinton, etc., etc. Still, we're talking early, original Fleetwood Mac here: the band that former JOHN MAYALL sidemen Peter Green (guitar, harp, vocals), John McVie (bass) and Mick Fleetwood (drums) formed in 1967, alongside ELMORE JAMES clone Jeremy Spencer (slide-guitar, vocals). In the interests of group democracy, their early repertoire was split down the middle between Green and Spencer, which is yet another argument against group democracy: Green was a prodigiously gifted and soulful musician considered by many (including B.B. KING, who should know) to be at least as eloquent and distinctive a singer/guitarist than ERIC CLAPTON, whereas a little of Spencer's Elmore routine goes a very long way indeed. His knockabout exuberance provided much-needed onstage leavening for Green's pervasive melancholia, though it translated poorly to record: Spencer's limitations necessitated the 1968 addition of yet a third singer/ guitarist, Danny Kirwan, who – despite being a fairly uninterest- ing vocalist – proved a far more versatile guitar foil for Green.

The 'blues' edition of Fleetwood Mac was by no means an obscure cult band: their eponymous debut album was a Top 10 hit, and, almost by accident, they fell into the British singles chart with a succession of atmospheric 45s including the moody Latinate 'Black Magic Woman' (best-known in the US through Santana's version), a string-laden, B.B. King-derived version of LITTLE WILLIE JOHN's 'Need Your Love So Bad', and two chart-topping originals, 'Albatross' and 'Man Of The World'. They survived until 1970, by which time Green – severely disturbed both by the band's pop successes and by the mandatory late-'60s intake of psychoactive chemicals – converted to Christianity and soared off into the wild blue yonder. He was replaced by Chicken Shack's vocalist and pianist Christine Perfect (later Christine McVie), but soon Jeremy Spencer also set off in search of God, leaving Fleetwood and the two Macs to pilot the course which eventually led them into *People* magazine. The rest of the story need not concern us here, so let's leave it with this: Green's work with Fleetwood Mac is one of the (very few) genuine artistic peaks of whiteboy blues, not only demonstrating a fluent mastery of the music's stylistic devices, but a startling penetration of its emotional core. Performances like 'Love That Burns' aren't simply 'white blues', but *blues* blues of a high order; that weary, wracked voice and piercingly sweet guitar tone would honour any bluesman of any race, place or time. Green has made very little music since then, and certainly none of it matches his work with Mayall and Mac: the power of the blues can destroy those who tap it if the physical and mental vessel is unequal to the task of containing that power. Peter Green burned astonishingly bright before he burned out.

- *Fleetwood Mac: The Collection* (Castle Communications CCSCD 157)
- *The Original Fleetwood Mac: The Blues Years* (Essential ESBCD 138)

Do you want the five-minute argument or the full half-hour? Or rather: the 65-minute, 20-track single-CD, as opposed to the 3-CD completists'-wet-dream box set. *The Collection*, concentrating on the Peter Green features, is tailor-made for civilians and contains all the early hit singles (with the exception of 'Oh Well' and 'Green Manalishi') as well as a generous and thoughtful selection of MacBlues with just enough Spencer to prevent any outbreaks of wrist-slashing, including a rocking 'Shake Your Moneymaker' and the '50s rock parody 'Somebody's Gonna Get Their Head Kicked In Tonite'. *The Blues Years* collects the complete contents of Fleetwood Mac's first two UK LPs plus a few singles – everything from *The Collection*, in fact – a couple of tracks cut as backup band to Chicago pianist EDDIE BOYD, and seven excerpts from the excellent and underrated Chicago-cut *Blues Jam At Chess* (Blue Horizon, 1969, unavailable; also known in the US as *Fleetwood Mac in Chicago*), which teamed them up with the likes of WILLIE DIXON, OTIS SPANN, WALTER HORTON and (pseudonymously) BUDDY GUY. As a nod to Christine Perfect McVie's subsequent importance to F.Mac, this also includes the Chicken Shack's hit version of ETTA JAMES's 'I'd Rather Go Blind', on which she sang lead. As a nod to historicity, it also includes rather more Jeremy Spencer than most people need. This one's for obsessives (y'all know who you are); *The Collection* is for everybody else.

Subjects for further investigation: **The Blues Collection** (Castle Communications CCSCD 216) and **Boston Live** (Castle Classics CLACD 152) both draw on the same hi-octane but grungy 1970 live recordings cut during Green's final months with the band: the former has more than twice the runtime of the latter, and its 12 tracks include five of the latter's seven. Since the omitted pair are a J. Spencer traduction of E. James and a Danny Kirwan composition, I wouldn't lose any sleep over it. It's sort-of-instructive to compare the abovementioned with the later material on **The Chain** (Warner Bros 9362-45188-2), a 2-CD Greatest Hits stretching from the Green era – 'Albatross', 'Black Magic Woman' *et al* plus the otherwise hard-to-find 'Oh Well' and 'Green Manalishi' – up to the Clinton era. Christine Perfect McVie's original band Chicken Shack were basically a vehicle for guitarist/singer Stan Webb, whose flash West Side-derived guitar and onstage extroversion were the band's only real calling card apart from Perfect's occasional vocals: they're remembered on

Chicken Shack: The Collection (Castle Communications CCSCD 179). A sampling of the good, the bad and the ridiculous from all phases of '60s Britblues can be obtained on *White Boy Blues* (Castle Communications CCSCD 103) and *White Boy Blues Volume II* (Castle Communications CCSCD 142), featuring all manner of juvenalia, outtakes and 'collectors' items' by Eric Clapton, Jeff Beck, John Mayall, Jimmy Page, Jeremy Spencer, Cyril Davies, Albert Lee, Ronnie Wood, Rod Stewart, Ten Years After, Savoy Brown, Tony McPhee etc, etc. Incidentally, Peter Green's 1959 Gibson Les Paul guitar is now the proudest possession of Green's one-time protege GARY MOORE.

US BLUES BOOM

The advantage which America's white bluesers had over their British counterparts was the chance to see and learn from the great originators at first hand; their disadvantage was that their greater sense of the music's context and the lives led by the men and women behind the music inhibited them from the Brits' wilder experimentation. Mick Jagger or ERIC CLAPTON derived many of their ideas from creative misunderstandings: they could only dream of the opportunities to see their heroes in action enjoyed by Chicagoans (native or adopted) like PAUL BUTTERFIELD, MIKE BLOOMFIELD, CHARLIE MUSSELWHITE, ELVIN BISHOP and Nick Gravenites, or Texans like JOHNNY WINTER and JANIS JOPLIN. The drawback of the American approach is that, after all, no matter how much heart a white kid has, (s)he's unlikely to be better than BUDDY GUY; whereas the problem of the Brit approach was that if the music mutated sufficiently, its tenuous connection to the blues might evaporate altogether. The Brits were artier and angstier; the Americans were more fun. Plus they generally had better rhythm sections.

Paul Butterfield

Almost exact contemporaries of JOHN MAYALL's BluesBreakers, Chicago harpist Paul Butterfield's blues band provides a perfect opportunity to contrast and compare the very different approaches of Yank and Brit white blues guys. For a start, the classic mid-'60s line-up of the Butterfield band had a 'real' blues rhythm section: drummer Sam Lay and bassist Jerome Arnold (the latter being the brother of former BO DIDDLEY sideman, harpist Billy Boy Arnold) were veterans of the HOWLIN' WOLF band. For another, Butterfield and his colleagues replaced the lugubrious-ness of the Mayall bands with the whomp and punch of the music that the likes of BUDDY GUY and JUNIOR WELLS were playing in the same Chicago taverns in which Butterfield worked. And finally, while Mayall & Co had learned their stuff from records and the occasional encounter with touring US bluesmen, Butterfield and his colleagues were able to study the masters first hand.

Butterfield, born in Chicago on 17 December 1942, was a one-dimensional singer – though he had a fine, tough voice and some ability to swing – but he was a formidable harmonica player, who had studied the styles of LITTLE WALTER, JAMES COTTON, BIG WALTER HORTON, SONNY BOY WILLIAMSON and JAMES COTTON with ferocious devotion. His band had begun in 1963 as a quartet in which University of Chicago student ELVIN BISHOP joined Lay, Arnold and Butterfield himself, but they swelled to a sextet for their first album in 1965, adding an ace card in the form of lead guitarist MIKE BLOOMFIELD, one of the key players in Bob Dylan's electric experiment, who rapidly became a major-league guitar hero: Butterfield's very own ERIC CLAPTON. Bloomfield played on Butter-field's first two albums, which became accepted as an artistic high point for mid-'60s white blues, but after Bloomfield quit in 1967 to form the psychedelic soul band Electric Flag, Butterfield added a horn section (as did John Mayall at almost the same time), moved Elvin Bishop back to lead guitar, and turned his own attention to soul. The band lost direction with each successive album: the low point being the appalling 'Love March' preserved for posterity after they performed it at Woodstock in 1969. Butterfield played less and less harp, turned more and more vocals over to his band members and, when the band dissolved in the early '70s to be replaced by the ill-fated Better Days (co-featuring folkie Geoff Muldaur and guitarist Amos Garrett), it was hardly missed.

Butterfield died in Los Angeles on 3–4 May 1987; during his last decade or so he had added his commanding harp and presence to other people's projects but made few records of his own. Another white boy lost in the blues, he made some truly powerful music, but found to his cost that it's easier to get into the blues than to get out.

- *The Paul Butterfield Blues Band* (Elektra 960 647-2)
- **THE BUTTERFIELD BLUES BAND:** *East-West* (Elektra 7559-60751-2)

Right from the first few bars of 'Born In Chicago', the opening cut on the Butterfield band's 1965 debut, it's clear that that we're in the presence of people who know what they're doing. Its sheer crunch and commitment demonstrate just how hard it's possible to play the blues without metalling out: Lay and Arnold lay down a crisp, punchy groove over which Butterfield's harp and Bloomfield's guitar duel like twin banshees, and the pressure hardly lets up from start to finish. Drawing heavily on the repertoires of ELMORE JAMES (Bloomfield was deeply into slide-guitar at the time) and Little Walter (for obvious reasons), it's tough, gutsy and authentic in spirit as well as detail. (On MUDDY WATERS's 'Got My Mojo Working', Lay puts down a lead vocal so deeply Muddyesque that to this day you'll meet people prepared to swear that it's really an uncredited guest shot by Waters himself.) According to legend, the album was the result of no less than three separate attempts (including scrapped live sessions), and numeous studio edits: it's a testament to the skills of producer Paul A. Rothchild (later of Doors fame) that it sounds like it went down live in the studio in one night. *East-West*, released the following year, replaced Jerome Arnold with Billy Davenport, and found the band stretching beyond strict blues confines, juxtaposing compositions by ROBERT JOHNSON, Cannonball Adderley, Allen Toussaint and Monkee-to-be Mike Nesmith (as well as variations on themes associated with Muddy Waters and B.B. KING)with the extended raga-rock improvs of the enormously influential 13-minute title track. The fluidity with which Bloomfield, Butterfield, Bishop and organist Mark Naftalin trade fours on Adderley's 'Work Song' is as much a source of delight as the funky backbeat which underpins Johnson's 'Walkin' Blues'.

- *Paul Butterfield's Better Days* (Sequel NEX CD 128)
- **PAUL BUTTERFIELD'S BETTER DAYS:** *It All Comes Back* (Sequel NEX CD 127)

Close, but no cigar. Sadly, these albums founder on the kind of sluggishness which passed for 'laid back' in the early '70s, and also because Butterfield's colleague Geoff Muldaur is allowed to open his mouth. On the first album, a potentially wonderful version of PERCY MAYFIELD's 'Please Send Me Someone To Love' is thrown away on a teeth-grindingly 'sincere' and 'homespun' Muldaur lead vocal. Organist Ronnie Barron brings a likeable Nwawlins drawl to his vocal features, and Butterfield is fine and affecting on 'Walkin' Blues' (used as opening track presumably to evoke the past glories of *East-West*), Big Joe Williams's 'Baby Please Don't Go', and BLIND WILLIE JOHNSON's 'Nobody's Fault But Mine' (here credited to Nina Simone rather than, ahem, Page & Plant). (Trivia note: 'Buried Alive In The Blues', composed by Butter's Chicago contemporary Nick Gravenites, who also wrote 'Born In Chicago', was originally composed for JANIS JOPLIN's *Pearl* album, but she died before recording the lead vocal.) The second album has its moments, notably on Smokey Hogg's 'Too Many Drivers', DR JOHN and Ronnie Barron's 'Louisiana Flood', and MOSE ALLISON's 'If You Live', but too often the music pulls its punch: this is blues wrapped in cotton wool.

Subjects for further investigation: Butterfield is on fabulously fine form alongside his mentor Muddy Waters on *Fathers And Sons* (Chess/ MCA CHD-92522); Mike Bloomfield, also along for the ride, fares less well. He and Muddy also appear on *The Last Waltz* (WEA K266076) as guests of The Band.

Mike Bloomfield

The Most Valuable Player in the Paul Butterfield band and America's first homegrown ERIC CLAPTON-style '60s guitar hero, Michael Bloomfield – born 28 July 1944, in Chicago – was as temperamentally unsuited for stardom and leadership as he was musically qualified. Much as he loved B.B. KING or Otis Redding, he was a folkie at heart and mistrusted showbiz; he also hated to travel and suffered from chronic insomnia when away from his home in Mill Valley, near San Francisco. These problems, combined with his fondness for drugs and complete lack of self-discipline, prevented him from fulfilling the dazzling potential he displayed with Bob Dylan and Paul Butterfield.

Bloomfield was a scion of Chicago's Jewish middle-class whose folkie leanings soon led him to the blues. For a while he was BIG JOE WILLIAMS's chauffeur and accompanist, but like Paul Butterfield, ELVIN BISHOP, Nick Gravenites and CHARLIE MUSSELWHITE, he learned his trade first-hand in the bars and taverns of Chicago's South and West sides. Eventually he teamed up with Paul Butterfield's band, just in time for their 1965 debut; along with other Butterfield sidemen, backed Bob Dylan at the epochal Newport Folk Festival of that same year, playing on Dylan's 'Like A Rolling Stone' and *Highway 61 Revisited* sessions. Quitting Butterfield in '67, he teamed up with Nick Gravenites and drummer/vocalist Buddy Miles to form the 'American Music Band' Electric Flag, but after one album – *A Long Time Comin'* (CBS, unavailable) – he bailed out. His last commercial successes were with *Super Session* and *The Live Adventures Of Mike Bloomfield & Al Kooper*, both jam-oriented albums dreamed up by polymath/hustler Al Kooper, whom Bloomfield had met on Dylan's 'Rolling Stone' session. His first solo album, 1969's *It's Not Killing Me* (CBS, unavailable) was a disaster, and other flawed big-time projects included the ersatz supersession *Triumvirate* (with JOHN HAMMOND and DR JOHN) and the ersatz supergroup KGB, of whom the less said the better.

Bloomfield retreated into low-budget movie scoring, acoustic music and the golden bubble of heroin: he died of a drug overdose in San Francisco on 15 February 1981. Despite occasional flashes of subsequent brilliance, his most memorable performances are on the Butterfield and Dylan records with which he made his name.

- **MIKE BLOOMFIELD, AL KOOPER & STEVE STILLS:** *Super Session* (Essential ESSCD 951)

Having just been fired from his own band Blood, Sweat & Tears, Al Kooper had a bright idea: how about if he just, like, went into an L.A. studio with Mike Bloomfield (who'd just bailed out of Electric Flag) and a rhythm section and just, like, jammed? After recording around half an album, Bloomfield succumbed to his insomnia and did a midnight flit back to San Francisco, which is why Kooper called in Stephen Stills (then plain old 'Steve' and newly free of the disintegrating Buffalo Springfield) to finish the album. Kooper sings a pleasant version of Percy Mayfield's 'Man's Temptation', Bloomfield plays a lot of slow blues (flat on his back, according to the sleeve photo, and sounding accordingly), and while the music rarely takes off, the sales did. Bloomfield did another runner during the recording of the in-concert sequel, *The Live Adventures Of Mike Bloomfield & Al Kooper* (CBS, unavailable), which is why that album features guest shots by Elvin Bishop (alcoholically challenged, by the sound of it) and Carlos Santana (making his recording debut on a tribute to SONNY BOY WILLIAMSON written by former Manfred Mann singer Paul Jones), alongside some of Bloomfield's most powerful blues performances; most of which easily eclipse their *Super Session* equivalents.

- *I'm With You Always* (Demon FIEND CD 92)

Bloomfield in the low-key live setting in which he finally felt most at home, mingling acoustic, electric, small-group and solo-folkie performances on material ranging from CHUCK BERRY and Sonny Boy Williamson to JOHN LEE HOOKER and MISSISSIPPI JOHN HURT. Bloomfield's warm good humour, unpretentious singing and sparkling guitar make this hugely enjoyable; 'I'm Glad I'm Jewish' – a parody of Barbecue Bob's 'Chocolate To The Bone' – is undoubtedly the funniest song he ever wrote.

Subjects for further investigation: The best Bloomfield record you can't get is the hideously rare *If You Love These Blues, Play 'Em As You Please*, recorded in 1976 for the now-defunct subsidiary label of America's *Guitar Player* magazine, only briefly available and never released on CD. Ostensibly a study guide to blues guitar styles, it's actually as varied and entertaining a record as Bloomfield ever made: its covers and tributes range from B.B. King, T-BONE WALKER, GUITAR SLIM and JIMI HENDRIX through to BLIND BLAKE, LONNIE JOHNSON and Jimmie Rodgers. If someone ever resolves the legal complications which took this off the market almost as soon as it was released, snap it up. His work with Butterfield is cited immediately north of this entry: his Dylan collaboration is on *Highway 61 Revisited* (Columbia 460 953-2).

Canned Heat

Just in case it needs saying again, the blues is a risky business. Consider the case of Canned Heat, a late-'60s convocation of plug-ugly California-based blues purists who were one of the few groups able both to hear and to present rural blues as chart-busting pop music. Their two key founder-members both died young: one shy, short-sighted, bona-fide near-genius and one monstrous, extrovert Furry Freak Brother. Alan 'Blind Owl' Wilson (1943–1970) was a formidable blues researcher and musician who participated in the rediscovery of SON HOUSE (not to mention seconding him on guitar and harmonica on the sessions for his epochal 1965 comeback album), and – for what it's worth – he was the most individual and creative of all the '60s American white blues boys, as well as the one most deeply steeped in the music's rural origins. His musical trademark was an eerie, floating falsetto seemingly derived from SKIP JAMES, while his partner clearly preferred CHARLEY PATTON.

Bob 'The Bear' Hite (1945–1981) was a fanatical blues collector who at one time owned some 20,000 original blues 78s and had sung with various jug bands. Canned Heat had themselves begun as a jug band, but with the participation of guitarist Henry 'Sunflower' Vestine (a former member of Frank Zappa's Mothers Of Invention), studio bassist Larry 'The Mole' Taylor (a veteran of sessions for, among others, Jerry Lee Lewis and The Monkees) and jazz drummer Frank Cook (replaced after their first album by Adolfo 'Fito' De La Parra), they mutated into an electric blues band named after Tommy Johnson's 'Canned Heat Blues' (1928). After building a formidable reputation as a live act in the Los Angeles area, they played the 1967 Monterey Pop Festival, and debuted on record with *Canned Heat* (See For Miles SEECD 268), an overly-careful exercise in studied authenticity and cultivated raucousness. The sequel more than compensated: 1968's *Boogie With Canned Heat* (See For Miles SEECD 62) codified their likeable blend of blues purism and psychedelic populism ('Hi, kids! This is The Bear!') and produced a smash hit single in Wilson's spooky, ectoplasmic 'On The Road Again,' which adapted Floyd Jones's 1952 'Dark Road' (itself partially derived from Tommy Johnson's 1929 'Big Road Blues'). The following year the unwieldy, inconsistent double-album *Livin' The Blues* (See For Miles SEECD 97) spawned an even bigger one in 'Goin' Up The Country', Alan Wilson's inspired conflation of HENRY THOMAS's 1928 'Bull Doze Blues' and a verse from BLIND WILLIE McTELL's 'Statesboro Blues'.

They put their new-found chart clout where their taste was when they bullied their record company, Liberty, into giving the superb but (then) criminally underrecorded Texas guitarist ALBERT COLLINS a recording contract with its R&B subsidiary Imperial, but arguably their finest hour came in 1970, when they financed a double-album team-up with their hero JOHN LEE HOOKER, whose 'Boogie Chillen' groove had given them the inspiration for at least half of their live set. *Hooker 'N' Heat* (See For Miles SEECD 234) gave the boogiemeister the first chart album of his career – not to mention his biggest long-playing hit until his '90s resurrection with *The Healer* (Silvertone ORECD 508) – but sadly Wilson committed suicide on 3 September 1970, between the album's completion and release. Canned Heat soldiered on, scoring one more international hit with a reworking of Wilbert Harrison's 'Let's Work Together,' but without Wilson their music lacked light and shade; their boogie became increasingly one-dimensional, and their trajectory was irreversibly downwards. Hite died on 5 April 1981; the band continues today under De La Parra's leadership – their shifting ranks at one time included guitarist WALTER TROUT – and guested with Hooker on one track of *The Healer*. By this time, they needed Hooker more than he needed them, but The Boogie Man always pays his debts.

- *The Big Heat* (EMI CANNED 1)

As much Canned Heat as you'll ever need, if not more. This massive 3-CD set includes all their hit singles, all their flop singles, and a fair selection from their albums. *Boogie With Canned Heat* donates its obvious highlights: the masterly 'On The Road Again', the hilarious 'Amphetamine Annie' (a.k.a. 'Speed Kills'), the slippery Wilson showcase 'Owl Song' and the 12-minute 'Fried Hockey Boogie', a pothead clodhop through their pet 'Boogie Chillen' variations. The dominant sounds are Hite's grunt'n growl and Henry Vestine's fuzzed-out acid-rock guitar: it was as much of a period piece as Big Brother & The Holding Company's *Cheap Thrills*, and for much the same reasons. *Livin' The Blues* also receives a much-needed filleting: in a sort of misguided tribute to Cream's *Wheels Of Fire*, the original double-album release of *Livin' The Blues* combined a studio album with – are you ready for this? – a two-sided, forty-minute version of 'Fried Hockey Boogie', disingenuously retitled 'Refried Boogie'. In favour of more solid fare (retreads of CHARLEY PATTON's 'Pony Blues' and JIMMY ROGERS's 'Walkin' By Myself', a fine original 'Boogie Music' with DR JOHN on piano, and – oh yes – 'Goin' Up The Country') this collection excises a giant, bloated 19-minute *thing* called 'Parthenogenesis' (*Acieeeeed!*), a collage of individual improvs by the band members. Some of it is splendid – a Hite vocal accompanied only by JOHN MAYALL's '20s-style piano, an astonishing harmonica raga by Wilson – but the rest is ghastly beyond belief. Sadly, much of *The Big Heat* is devoted to documenting their post-Wilson decline, but it's a fairly detailed portrait of an idiosyncratic and likeable band.

Subjects for further investigation: Considerably more wieldy that the above are two options for a single-CD Canned Heat set: *Let's Work Together: The Best Of Canned Heat* (Liberty CDP 7 93114 2) and *On The Road Again* (Fame/EMI CDM 7 93058 2). Both contain the obvious hits plus 'Amphetamine Annie' and 'Fried Hockey Boogie': the former is rather more balanced (apart from the inclusion of Canned Heat's infamous team-up with The Chipmunks), and the latter includes *all* of 'Parthenogenesis', but if you're planning to open up *that* particular can of worms you might as well buy *Livin' The Blues*. 'We'd like to take you back to Woodstock' is a singularly unfortunate opening announcement for *Live In Australia* (Bedrock BEDLP 5 CD), especially since it is not delivered by drummer Adolfo de la Parra, the sole member of this late-'80s line-up who actually was at Woodstock in '69. A conscientious but uninspired retread of the Wilson-Hite greatest hits, it's chiefly noteworthy for the participation of the freshly-recruited Walter Trout: i.e. not very noteworthy. *Roots Of Rock* (Yazoo 1063) contains, among other 'original versions' of blues-rock standards, Tommy Johnson's 'Big Road Blues' and HENRY THOMAS's 'Bull Doze Blues'.

Johnny Winter

Johnny Winter may not be the greatest white blues guitarist who ever lived – though on his hotter nights he came close – but, as an albino, he's certainly the whitest. He plays extravagant power blues wired up to seemingly inexhaustable supplies of energy; firing off an endless chain of wiry hyperspeed blues guitar licks while hollering the blues in a gravelly high-pitched drawl. Lacking the sonic imagination to reshape the blues as did his contemporaries JIMI HENDRIX or LED ZEPPELIN, he compensated with sheer velocity and brute force. His career has oscillated between power blues and big rock; and if that means that his blues work is a touch on the metally side, it also means that his arena-rock moves have an ineradicably blue stain. It is axiomatic that the most essential qualities for a blues singer are the three f's: fervour, feel and phrasing (okay, I cheated); though Winter has all these qualities, his peculiar vocal timbre – once memorably described as resembling a 'tuneable belch' – makes his singing something of an acquired taste. He plays some of the most ferocious slide guitar you'll ever hear: a white-lightning compression of MUDDY WATERS, ROBERT JOHNSON and ELMORE JAMES sped up to an amphetamine pace that's exhilarating when it works and simply exhausting when it doesn't.

John Dawson Winter III, born in Leland, Mississippi, on 22 February 1944, came roaring out of Beaumont, Texas, in 1969, heralded by a glowing *Rolling Stone* story lauding his prowess. Growing up in Texas on a solid diet of deep blues and hard rock, he came by his music the hard way, gigging at everything from high-school dances to black bars with various bands (many of which featured his younger brother Edgar on piano and saxophone), and churning out derivative juke-box singles for small local labels, soundalikeing everyone from Bob Dylan to BOBBY 'BLUE' BLAND. By the late '60s, he was concentrating on blues, fronting a power trio including bassist Tommy Shannon (who reappeared over a decade later backing another Texan blues-rock guitar god, STEVIE RAY VAUGHAN) and drummer Uncle John 'Red' Turner. It was with this band that he made his major-label breakthrough, signing to Columbia in 1969 for what was then a spectacularly high advance. After his first two Columbia albums, his manager steered him further towards hard rock, dumping Shannon and Turner and teaming Winter up with the faded mid-'60s teen sensations The McCoys (featuring singer-guitarist/ songwriter Rick Derringer) to form Johnny Winter And. Two 'And' albums later, Winter was in rehab with a severe heroin habit.

Re-emerging with a renewed commitment to the blues, his most spectacular '70s achievement was his masterminding of Muddy Waters's post-Chess comeback albums, beginning with 1977's *Hard Again*, and his own *Nothin' But The Blues* album, recorded with the same band during the same sessions. On the expiry of the Columbia contract, he signed to the Chicago-based Alligator label to record a trilogy of '80s albums which were his best and bluesiest work since the early days. After one disastrous attempt to re-enter the Big Rock leagues – MCA's *Winter Of '88*; best forgotten – he has continued on PointBlank records with music firmly in the Alligator tradition. Unfortunately, his live performances can be tiresome for those who find clumping rock rhythm sections and fifteen-minute guitar solos less than endearing. The bottom line is this: put him with rock guys and he plays like a rock guy. Put him with blues guys and he plays like a blues guy. I prefer him with blues guys.

- *Johnny Winter* (Edsel ED CD 163)

Of Winter's first three albums, only this one – the least interesting, unfortunately – is currently available on CD. *The Progressive Blues Experiment*, predating the Columbia deal and cut live-without-an-audience in an Austin nightclub, is murky as hell but fresh and powerful in approach; and Edsel recently deleted the eclectic but authentic 'three-sided' *Second Winter* after the copyright-holders demanded more money for the licence than it was actually generating. That leaves this one, which is still excellent listening, though, at under 35 minutes, rather too little of a good thing. There's a pair of ROBERT JOHNSON tributes featuring Winter solo on a National steel, a rousing Chicago-style jam with WALTER HORTON and WILLIE DIXON on Muddy Waters's 'Mean Mistreater', a powerful Texas take on LIGHTNIN' HOPKINS's 'Back Door Friend', plenty of lashing guitar, and only one serious error of judgement: Winter's voice simply isn't up to the challenge of RAY CHARLES's 'Drown In My Own Tears'.

- **Nothin' But The Blues** (BGO BGOCD 104)

Cut back-to-back with Muddy Waters's *Hard Again* in 1977 (with the Big Mud providing a guest lead vocal on 'Walkin' Through The Park'), this eminently Chicago-approved album features not only the same band, including JAMES COTTON (harp), PINETOP PERKINS (piano) and Willie 'Big Eyes' Smith (drums), but the same spirit: the relaxed, good-humoured whomp which is Waters's trademark permeates the music, smoothing down Winter's tendency to hyperthyroid excess without diluting the music's overall punch. Winter rises to the occasion with his best featured performances of the decade, including a gorgeous, Johnsonesque 'TV Mama' (no relation to the JOE TURNER/ELMORE JAMES tune of the same name), and the West Side-styled guitar pyrotechnics of 'Everybody's Blues'.

- **Guitar Slinger** (Alligator ALCD 4735)
- **Third Degree** (Alligator ALCD 4748)

My favourite Winter albums, with the possible exception of *Nothin' But The Blues* and *Second Winter*. The Alligator trilogy – these two and *Serious Business* (Alligator ALCD 4742), the 'middle one' and only fractionally the others' inferior – draws on a trio of Chicago's finest blues sessioneers, including Johnny B. Gayden, the genius bass player from ALBERT COLLINS's Icebreakers, and they're about the most relaxed albums Winter made in his entire career. There isn't a snooze-a-thon in the bunch, though; Winter is so hyper that he's cranked even when he's laid-back. The first and third are the best: *Guitar Slinger* leavens the basic quartet with pithy contributions from Gene Barge (tenor) and Billy Branch (harp), presenting an impeccable repertoire derived from DR JOHN ('Lights Out'), Bobby 'Blue' Bland ('I Smell Trouble'), Earl King ('Trick Bag'), LONNIE 'Guitar Jr' BROOKS ('Don't Take Advantage Of Me'), Muddy Waters ('Iodine In My Coffee'), A.C. REED ('Kiss Tomorrow Goodbye') and even SCREAMIN' JAY HAWKINS ('My Soul'). The exuberantly (but not overbearingly) rocking *Third Degree* wheels on Dr John for a couple of splendid 88 cameos as well as briefly reuniting Winter with his old Texas sidemen Tommy Shannon and Uncle John 'Red' Turner, though it's the regular Alligator team who spark Winter's best blues guitar here on a searing version of EDDIE BOYD's title track. That's despite the excellence of the Elmore James cover, the JIMMY REED cover, the Dr John original, and the cool National-steel slide feature.

- *Let Me In* (PointBlank VPBCD 5)
- *Hey, Where's Your Brother?* (PointBlank VPBCD 11)

Like the Alligator albums, these were co-produced by Dick Shurman, and both feature Ken Saydak, pianist from the Alligator sessions, and Billy Branch. Dr John returns on *Let Me In*, and – appropriately enough – Edgar Winter shows up to play saxophone and organ on *Hey, Where's Your Brother?* Guess who's more welcome. *Let Me In* wins because of a better repertoire, and because of Dr John; Winter himself is at or near the top of his form on both, but I miss Alligator's rhythm section.

Subjects for further investigation: The music that put Winter into hospital is on *Johnny Winter And* (BGO BGOCD 105) and *Johnny Winter And Live* BGO BGOCD 29), respectively from 1970 and 1971. The first is an earthy Southern take on post-JIMI HENDRIX progressive blues-rock usages; the second a knock-down-drag-out metal-blues throwdown in which songs and devices borrowed from B.B. KING, SONNY BOY WILLIAMSON I, JOHN LEE HOOKER, CHUCK BERRY and THE ROLLING STONES are joyfully beaten to within an inch of their lives. Winter's decade or so with Columbia is filleted on *Scorchin' Blues* (Epic Legacy 471661 2) and *Johnny Winter: The Collection* (Castle Communications CCSCD 167). The former, better-packaged and more blues-oriented, draws heavily on *Nothin' But The Blues* (no bad thing, certainly), and showcases Winter's Delta-to-Chicago side by reprising 'Dallas' and 'Mean Mistreater' from *Johnny Winter*; but many of the tracks are hamstrung by the kind of clumping rock rhythm sections to which Winter is unfortunately drawn. The second, poorer sounding and more rockist, rescues tracks from *Second Winter*, the *And* albums, and the excellent post-therapy comeback *Still Alive And Well* (1972, unavailable), plus other productions by his former And colleague Rick Derringer, but inexplicably wastes seven minutes on a *rrrrock-and-rrroooll!* medley, from *Johnny Winter And Live*, spotlighting Derringer's vocals and lead guitar. (Perhaps the compilers didn't notice.) Winter's 1977–'80 work with Muddy Waters is justly celebrated: it's filleted on *Hoochie Coochie Man* (Epic 461186 2) and *Blues Sky* (Columbia Legacy 467892 2); of the original four albums, *Hard Again* (Blue Sky CDSKY 32357), *I'm Ready* (BGO BGOCD 108) and *Muddy 'Mississippi' Waters Live* (BGO BGOCD 109) are still available. Winter also produced and played on SONNY TERRY's wonderful swan song *Whoopin'* (Alligator ALCD 4738), and lays some smoulder on 'Susie', from John Lee Hooker's *Mr Lucky* (Silvertone ORECD 519). You can also hear him sitting in with his fellow Alligator Brother Lonnie Brooks on the title tune of *Wound Up Tight* (Alligator ALCD 4751).

Janis Joplin

Perhaps the most perceptive epitaph that Janis Joplin ever received was the observation that she paid for BESSIE SMITH's tombstone, but not for her own. Between 1967 and 1970 she was acclaimed as 'the world's greatest blues singer' – a similar millstone to that hung around ERIC CLAPTON's neck by the kind of well-wishers whom an artist can well do without – thanks to her efforts to update the 'classic blues' hard-drinkin' hard-lovin' mama tradition into the psychedelic era. Joplin (born in Port Arthur, Texas, on 19 January, 1943) first recorded as vocalist for Big Brother & The Holding Company, a San Francisco band who emerged as contemporaries of The Grateful Dead, Jefferson Airplane and Quicksilver Messenger Service. Her name soon became as much of a byword for extravagant sexual adventures as those of Mick Jagger or JIMI HENDRIX; she was a legendary drunk in a culture of professional acidheads; and her proudly frizzy hair, thrift-shop finery and open emotionalism made her a pre-feminist heroine for thousands of young women still trapped between mousewife and dollybird stereotypes.

Her admirers felt that she made up in expression for what she lacked in range: her frayed caw could travel from croon to shriek, but she was certainly no Aretha Franklin. Nevertheless, there was genuine pain in her voice, and an equally genuine desire to communicate with her audiences rather than simply throw a show at them. Her vocal charisma hauled Big Brother's 1968 *Cheap Thrills* to the top of the US charts; in the wake of subsequent criticisms of the band's musical capabilities, she ditched them in favour of Full Tilt Boogie, a more professional rock and soul outfit which, despite its slickness and musicality, nevertheless lacked Big Brother's distinctive character. She died of a heroin overdose in Hollywood on 4 October, 1970, before completing her second solo album, *Pearl*, which was eventually released with two instrumental tracks still lacking lead vocals. One of them, significantly or not, was Nick Gravenites' composition 'Buried Alive In The Blues.' She was greatly mourned, but her posthumous status only briefly rivalled that of a Jim Morrison or Jimi Hendrix. Her critical stock is currently low: Joplin's music doesn't seem to work without her physical presence.

- **BIG BROTHER & THE HOLDING COMPANY:** *Cheap Thrills* (CBS CDCBS 32004)

Big Brother were a good-natured, barely competent shambles of a band, and the out-of-tune fuzz-boxed lead guitars they favoured could set far less sensitive teeth than mine on edge. This album, though, contains four of Joplin's key performances: the lengthy bravura workout on Big Mama Thornton's 'Ball And Chain', her stomping take on Erma Franklin's 'Piece Of My Heart', the '20s-style 'Turtle Blues' (accompanied only by the band's producer John Simon on piano) and the emotional triumph of Gershwin's 'Summertime', where the sour, off-key guitars actually add to, rather than detract from, the piece's poignancy.

Subjects for further investigation: The short route to all-purpose Joplinalia is undoubtedly her *Greatest Hits* (CBS CD 32190), which contains her biggest post-Big Brother hit 'Me And Bobbie McGee'; her two solo albums *Kozmic Blues* (CBS CD 32063) and the posthumous *Pearl* (CBS CD 64188) are available either separately, or doublebacked (CBS 461020 2). *In Concert* (CBS 466838) combines amateur tapes from her Texas days with both Big Brother and Full Tilt Boogie tracks.

Charlie Musselwhite

When Charlie Musselwhite sings 'I was born in Mississippi/and raised up in Tennessee', it is not white-blues posturing but the literal truth. 'Memphis Charlie', as he was known in Chicago during the '60s, is one of those all-too-rare performers to whom the old can-white-men-play-the-blues authenticist question simply does not apply: the blues has soaked right into his bone marrow. Born in Kosciusko, Mississippi, on January 31, 1944, and raised in Memphis, he's been playing harp since he was thirteen; as a member of the original Chicago white blues clique which also included PAUL BUTTERFIELD and MIKE BLOOMFIELD, he refined his blues chops in South Side taverns under the tutelege of WALTER HORTON (with whom he made his first recordings), JUNIOR WELLS (on whom he initially modelled his vocal style), JAMES COTTON and LITTLE WALTER. Relocating from Chicago to the West Coast in the early '70s, he shared an Oakland apartment with JOHN LEE HOOKER, successfully ditched a severe alcohol habit; and is currently making the finest music of his career. Charlie Musselwhite is not a 'white blues guy': he's a bluesman, *period*.

- *Ace Of Harps* (Alligator ALCD 4781)
- *Signature* (Alligator ALCD 4801)

Musselwhite's most recent albums, both cut with his red-hot road band and featuring a characteristic mix of blues standards, snappy originals (my favourite is *Signature*'s 'Mama Long Legs', dedicated to his wife) and instrumental readings of classy pop ballads like Jerome Kerns's 'Yesterdays' and Johnny Burke's 'What's New.' Of the two, I'd pick *Signature*, if only for 'What's New', the rollicking 'Hey! Miss Bessie', the daring harmonic extensions of '.38 Special' and the wonderful closing duet with Hooker in 'Cheatin' On Me'; but *Ace Of Harps* is almost as good, which means it's as good a blues-harp album as anything cut in the past decade.

Subjects for further investigation: Musselwhite's first album as a leader was ***Stand Back! Here Comes Charlie Musselwhite's South Side Band*** (Vanguard VMD 79232), cut in 1967 with guitarist Harvey Mandel (later of CANNED HEAT and – almost – THE ROLLING STONES), keybman Barry Goldberg and veteran Chicago drummer Fred Below. Comparable to the first Paul Butterfield album, it's thicker and richer, if less sparkling; the youthful Musselwhite had still to cut loose from Junior Wells' vocal influence. ***Memphis Charlie*** (Arhoolie CD 303), which definitely has its moments, combines West Coast sessions from '72 (with Robben Ford) and '74 (with a band featuring guitarist Tim Kaihatsu and bassist Karl Sevareid, both of whom subsequently worked with ROBERT CRAY). Musselwhite also appears as a guest on John Lee Hooker's *The Healer* (Silvertone ORE CD 508) and *Boom Boom* (PointBlank VPCD 12).

J. Geils Band

This gang of tough Blues Jews from Boston made their biggest pop breakthrough with the sexist pap of their chart-topping 1981 single 'Centerfold', but they started out in the late '60s with an an incendiary stew of blues, rock and soul. Despite naming themselves after guitarist J.Geils, their principals were actually frontman Peter Wolf (David Lee Roth to Geils's Van Halen, rock fans), organist/songwriter Seth Justman, and harp wizard Magic Dick. The Bronx-born Wolf, a former R&B radio DJ, made up in jive and physicality what he lacked in vocal range; the rhythm section could swing as well as stomp, and Magic Dick virtually blew his face off every night. At their best – as on 1972's deliriously exciting *Full House: Live* (Atlantic, unavailable) – they were the missing link between Little Walter, JAMES BROWN and THE ROLLING STONES; as well as a salutory antidote to the grimness and gloom of the post-JOHN MAYALL school of British bluesers. Unfortunately, like many blues-based rock bands, their mainstream pop-rock moves were erratic and unsatisfying: after the hit, the original line-up, which had held together for over 17 years, finally gave up the ghost. Wolf launched an inconclusive solo career while the band soldiered on with Justman at the front; little has been heard of either faction since.

- *The J. Geils Band* (Edsel EDCD 300)

Ah yes, the 'eponymous' 1971 debut: recorded and mixed in 18 hours, and produced by R&B veterans Dave Crawford and Brad Shapiro; essentially a club set performed live-in-the-studio, mixing respectable originals with rather more exciting material borrowed from JOHN LEE HOOKER, ALBERT COLLINS, OTIS RUSH and Smokey Robinson. It demonstrates how much more extrovert and exuberant they were than, say, FLEETWOOD MAC, but all the cover versions included here were served up several zillion degrees hotter on *Live: Full House*; and I'd swap this for a CD copy of that any damn day of the week, Jack.

WE'RE NOT IN MEMPHIS ANY MORE, TOTO . . .

Most Heavy Metal is what's left of blues-rock when you take the blues out. The three names who complete this section were the ones who neither abandoned the blues, nor lacked the confidence to explore and transform it. If blues-rock has finally become a legit subgenre in its own right (rather than simply an exploitative travesty of 'real' blues), then these folks deserve a great deal of the credit.

Jimi Hendrix

Having devoted an entire book – *Crosstown Traffic: Jimi Hendrix And Postwar Pop* (Faber & Faber, 1989) – to an attempt to disentangle the roots and branches of Jimi Hendrix's music, I'll self-servingly point you in that direction and simply cut to the chase: Hendrix the bluesman was thoroughly steeped in both the Delta-gone-to-big-town tradition of MUDDY WATERS, HOWLIN' WOLF and JOHN LEE HOOKER; and in the Chicago West Side and Memphis-to-Texas schools of T-BONE WALKER, BUDDY GUY, OTIS RUSH, ALBERT KING, ALBERT COLLINS and B.B. KING; all topped off with a healthy dose of guitar showboating derived from CLARENCE 'GATEMOUTH' BROWN, IKE TURNER, GUITAR SLIM, JOHNNY GUITAR WATSON and, of course, Walker and Guy.

Hendrix – who was born in Seattle, Washington, on November 27, 1942, and died in London on September 18, 1970 – had a great deal more on his musical mind than simply playing the blues, but when he did approach the form he brought to it a touch which was both faithful and innovative. Scattered throughout his repertoire are both signature blues originals like 'Red House', 'Voodoo Chile' and 'Hear My Train A-Comin''; and a fistful of great covers, many of which were one-offs. The long, slow take of 'Voodoo Chile' (as opposed to the better-known funk-rock apocalypse version) included on *Electric Ladyland* (finally available in a correctly-sequenced single-disk edition on Polydor 847 233-2, thankfully bereft of its Sid-The-Sexist UK cover art) begins with the ominously rolling Delta bass-string riffs of a Waters or Hooker, evolves through the Chicago South-and-West-Side styles and finally explodes into the free-jazz-for-all of a Coltrane or Coleman. 'Hear My Train A-Comin'' was a piece with Hendrix had been fooling since 1967; no version of it was released in his lifetime, so it's safe to assume that he had not yet developed it to his satisfaction. Wish he had.

- **Variations On A Theme: Red House** (Jimi Hendrix reference Library/Hal Leonard Publishing, no discernible catalogue number)

A distinct oddity, this: an 'instructional' disc only available through musical instrument dealers rather than in record stores. However, it provides an utterly unprecedented glimpse of Hendrix the bluesman. The notion of seven versions of 'Red House' (six by Hendrix, one by John Lee Hooker with Booker T Jones on organ and one-time Hendrix sideman Randy California on rhythm guitar) may seem intimidating (not to say thoroughly redundant), but the whole point of the album is the astonishing amount of variations which Hendrix is able to bring to his single theme. The various interpretations only stretch from '68 to '70, but tempi, mood, length and instrumentation change from version to version, and it's a remarkable illustration of the sheer range of emotion with which a master bluesman can continually revitalise a single song. (The Hooker take is wonderful, too.)

'Red House' has even more history than this compilation can include: the marvellous original version appeared on the UK edition of Hendrix's first album *Are You Experienced?* (Polydor 825 416-2, deleted), but since his catalogue has now been 'rationalised' to comply with the US editions, the current release (Polydor 847 234-2) omits it, and the 'unedited' take which appears on the collections *Kiss The Sky* (Polydor 823 704-2) and *The Ultimate Experience* (Polydor 517 235-2) is ostentatiously marred by super-fluous psychedelia. The only current source for the original version is *Rockin' The Blues* (Castle Communications CCSCD 191). The fascinating but irritating 3-CD radio-show-complete-with-hideous-narration *Live And Unreleased: The Radio Show* (Castle Communications HBCD 100) contains, among other Hendrix esoterica, a fabulously taut and compact 'Red House' recorded live in Paris in October '67. A bootlegged jam-session version of the song, set to Cream's 'Crossroads' riff, is included on the 3-CD anthology *Rock Guitar Legends* (Knight RGLCD 47001). Extended live versions are also on *Hendrix In The West* (Polydor 831 312-2), *Isle Of Wight* (second edition only: Polydor 831 236-2), *Live At Winterland* (Polydor 847 238-2) and *The Jimi Hendrix Concerts* (Media Motion MEDIA CD 1).

- *Radio One* (Castle Communications CCSCD 212)
- *Jimi Plays Monterey* (Polydor 847 244-2)

Two '67 exercises in combining and recombining new and old wine with new and old bottles. Hendrix often used his radio sessions to goof around with material not featured on either his studio recordings or his live shows, and this compilation is studded with blues and R&B gems. *Primus inter pares* is an exquisite 'Catfish Blues', Hendrix's take on the Delta staple also known as 'Two Trains Running' and Muddy Waters' 'Still A Fool'; not far behind are a rollicking post-Wolf 'Killing Floor', an early 'Hear My Train A-Comin'', the blasting instrumental 'Drivin' South', and one of his two versions of Waters' 'Hoochie Coochie Man', this one with

ALEXIS KORNER guesting on slide guitar. His devastating Monterey Pop Festival show, at which he returned to the US as the conquering hero, also features 'Killing Floor' (opening his set with a funk riff that bounces around like a hand-grenade in a pinball machine), and a soul-stomp arrangement of B.B. King's 'Rock Me Baby.'

Subjects for further investigation: A lovely '69 live-at-the-Albert-Hall take on ELMORE JAMES' 'Bleeding Heart' crops up on *The Jimi Hendrix Concerts* (Media Motion MEDIA CD 1) and on the budget oddity *The Last Experience* (Bescol CD 42). The 'other' 'Hoochie Coochie Man' – a '69 studio goof in which Hendrix mimics both Muddy Waters and a Harlem drag queen – is on *Loose Ends* (Polydor 837 574-2). The gorgeous 12-string acoustic version of 'Hear My Train A-Comin'' performed in the 1973 movie documentary *Jimi Hendrix*, and included in the now-deleted double-album *Soundtrack Recordings From The Film Jimi Hendrix* (Reprise), is currently completely unavailable on CD.

Led Zeppelin

Did I earlier describe JOHNNY WINTER's music as 'power blues'? I take it back – by comparison with Led Zeppelin, Winter is as modest and restrained as MISSISSIPPI JOHN HURT. The band that began in late '68 as guitarist/producer Jimmy Page's 'New YARDBIRDS' outdid the volume (of sales as well as decibels) and influence of hard-rock predecessors like THE ROLLING STONES, The Who, JIMI HENDRIX and Cream to become the primary role-models for the '70s and '80s battalions of big-hair, big-amp bands. In collusion with Robert Plant (vocals, harp, air-raid siren impressions), John Bonham (drums: the band's most distinctive and influential instrumentalist) and John Paul Jones (bass, mandolin, keyboards), Page mingled what he called his 'CIA connection' (Celtic, Indian and Arabic influences) with Heavy Blooze. One of Zeppelin's most prominent blues attributes were an unually cavalier attitude to composer credits which some, including your humble servant, consider to be an abuse of the folk process; and others – including the erudite and persuasive Robert Palmer in his notes to their Big Box – to be a signal contribution to that process.

The other was, after the obligatory ransacking of the Chicago tradition, a classically British predilection for comparatively esoteric pre-war blues. As well as the credited covers of WILLIE DIXON's 'You Shook Me' and 'I Can't Quit You Baby' on their first album and the (uncredited) rips of his 'You Need Love' (reincarnated as the legendary 'Whole Lotta Love') and 'Bring It On Home' on their second, their blues repertoire included memorable transformations of 'When The Levee Breaks' (by MEMPHIS MINNIE and 'Kansas City Joe' McCoy), BLIND WILLIE JOHNSON's 'Nobody's Fault But Mine', MISSISSIPPI FRED McDOWELL's 'In My Time Of Dying' and ROBERT JOHNSON's 'Travelling Riverside Blues'. Personally, I could give a shit whether I ever hear 'Stairway To Heaven' again in my life, but I'd sorely miss 'In My Time Of Dying' or 'Nobody's Fault But Mine.'

● *Led Zeppelin* (Atlantic 7567-82144-2)

This 4-CD doorstop contains 54 of the band's 80-odd sides: the remainder have recently undergone the same painstaking remastering and resequencing procedure and should reappear as a second box for Christmas 1993 (maybe they'll call it *Led Zeppelin II*). It contains all the above-cited blues epics – a BBC session cut of 'Travelling Riverside Blues' appears here for the first time – as well as a previously unreleased live-at-a-soundcheck take of their one great non-derivative blues 'Since I've Been Loving You'; therefore it should take purchasing precedence over the existing CDs of their original albums. Better sound, better sequencing, better packaging – if you want some Led Zeppelin, you know it makes sense.

ZZ Top

Sometimes I think these three Texan clowns are the hippest white-blues guys in the world. Other times I think they're the hippest stadium-rock guys in the world. The rest of the time I just think they're hip. ZZ Top – Billy Gibbons (guitar, most of the vocals), Dusty Hill (bass, rest of the vocals) and Frank Beard (drums) – came out of the psychedelic end of the late-'60s white-blues scene; or maybe it was the bluesy end of the late '60s psychedelic scene. They certainly weren't the first (or the last) ones to blow the blues up to Big Rock scale, but they were the first (and only) ones to do so with wry absurdist humour and a lack of sex-god posturing. ZZ Top – the name is a complex private joke referring both to deep-soul bluesman ZZ Hill and a popular brand of cigarette papers – became Acceptably Cool in the '80s, thanks to 1984's *Eliminator* album – the one with 'Sharp Dressed Man', 'Gimme All Your Lovin'' and 'Legs' on it – and their discovery of videos and sequencers: their admirers would say that they'd been cool all along.

- *Tres Hombres* (Warner Bros 7599-27381-2)
- *Degüello* (Warner Bros 7599-27400-2)

The best and most blues-approved of ZZ's '70s albums: 1973's *Tres Hombres* boasts the sublime opening one-two punch of 'Waiting For The Bus' and 'Jesus Just Left Chicago', as well as the gospelly ballads 'Have You Heard?' and 'Hot Blue And Righteous', plus their lascivious JOHN LEE HOOKER-styled 'Boogie Chillun' rip 'La Grange'. *Degüello*, from 1979, was their return to the fray after the three-year layoff during which Gibbons and Hill sprouted their iconic chin-shrubbery, and – while it includes a couple of covers in the form of a funk-rock take on Sam & Dave's 'I Thank You' which inexplicably fails to take advantage of Gibbons and Hill's distinctive harmony singing, and a 'Dust My Broom' which isn't terribly different from anybody else's – it boasted some of the sleaziest, slinkiest blues originals of their career. 'Cheap Sunglasses', 'She Loves My Automobile' and 'A Fool For Your Stockings' are how I like *my* ZZ Top.

Subjects for further investigation: The shortest route to rounding up ZZ with their post-*Eliminator* MTV hats on is the inevitable *Greatest Hits* (Warner Bros 7599-26846-2); at 18 tracks as opposed to 10, this would seem to supercede the earlier compilation *The Best Of ZZ Top* (Warner Bros.7599-27384-2), but while it scoops up their '80s successes it loses 'Waiting For The Bus' and 'Jesus Just Left Chicago' in the process. On the other hand, the present for the ZZ fan who wants (almost) everything is *The ZZ Top Sixpack*

(Warner Bros 7599-25661-2), a sumptuous little package containing six of their first seven albums – *ZZ Top's First Album* through *El Loco*, omitting *Deguello* – all conveniently doublebacked onto three CDs: apart from anything else, it's a reasonable way to pick up a few of the better blues performances from their early years. Notables include 'Brown Sugar' (not the ROLLING STONES tune) from *ZZ Top's First Album*; 'Mushmouth Shoutin'' and 'Apologies To Pearly' from *Rio Grande Mud*; and *Fandango!*'s deadly duo of the lovely 'Blue Jean Blues' (as covered by JEFF HEALEY) and the butt-rockin' 'Tush.' Their most recent all-new album at the time of writing, 1990's **Recycler** (Warner Bros 7599-26265-2), was more notable for its blues entries, '2000 Blues' and the sublime 'My Head's In Mississippi' than for its would-be hit singles. Their spiritual doubles, Das Combo, back up RAINER on **The Texas Tapes** (Demon FIEND CD 734).

PART THREE: THE BLUES TODAY
(1975–1993)

Ludicrous as it may seem, the starting signal for the current upturn in the blues ecomomy was probably John Landis' 1980 movie *The Blues Brothers*. An urban shaggy-dog riff on the fantasy life of white R&B fans, its musical thrust had rather more to do with soul music than the blues – as indicated by the presence of JAMES BROWN, Aretha Franklin and RAY CHARLES among the featured performers, and Stax backroom legends Steve Cropper and Duck Dunn in the band – but the cult success of the movie and its big-selling soundtrack *Music From The Motion Picture The Blues Brothers* (Atlantic 7567-81471-2) did much to raise the profile of a music which, as far as the music business mainstream was concerned, had been consigned to commercial oblivion in the early '70s.

The '60s may not have been a feast of fabulous prosperity for any but a handful of blues artists, but by comparison the following decade was a time of utter famine. B.B. KING is the only bluesman who remained continuously contracted to a major record company between the early '60s and the present day. BUDDY GUY & JUNIOR WELLS were dispatched into the wilderness after the failure of their first-and-only album for Atlantic; BOBBY BLAND hung on at ABC and its inheritor MCA until the law of diminishing returns set in at the end of the '70s; ALBERT KING and LITTLE MILTON were left high and dry by the mid-'70s collapse of Stax; ALBERT COLLINS actually quit playing for several years, and when JOHN LEE HOOKER's contract with ABC expired in 1974, neither party showed much interest in renewing it. For a younger bluesman like SON SEALS, it was a long wait between albums and a lot of road hours logged before the rent was paid. Only MUDDY WATERS managed to fall on his feet, extracting himself from Chess before it folded and, with the full weight of CBS' promotion department behind him, embarking on his magnificent quartet of Indian-summer come-back albums.

In the meantime, those big-time white blues-rockers who had retained their popularity had shifted their ground to laid-back singer-songwriterism or bombastic stadium rock. The task of waving the flag and taking up the slack was left to small-time, small-town bar bands, like THE FABULOUS THUNDERBIRDS (from Austin, Texas) and GEORGE THOROGOOD & THE DESTROYERS (from Delaware, of all places) or, in Britain, DR FEELGOOD (from the Essex Delta), and to independent labels like Chicago's Alligator Records, which did its best to keep veterans like BIG WALTER HORTON and Albert Collins before the public while introducing new-to-vinyl blues talent like HOUND DOG TAYLOR and Son Seals. The break-through finally came in the mid-'80s when a couple of ten-year 'overnight-success' stories – balls-to-the-wall Texas guitar wild-man STEVIE RAY VAUGHAN and soul-blues matinee idol ROBERT CRAY – managed to convince a new, young audience that the blues was sexy after all. If I may scratch-mix my metaphors, it was their ability to connect with the rock and pop mainstreams which opened the floodgates: B.B. King, John Lee Hooker and Buddy Guy slammed into the pop charts, ERIC CLAPTON and GARY MOORE rediscovered their blues consciences, and a multitude of blues talents old and new were afforded the opportunity to strut their various stuffs. So right now, ladies 'n gentlemen, let's hear it for the guys who made it happen . . .

1. The Definitely-Ready-For-Prime-Time Players

Dr Feelgood

If pre-punk '70s Britain had been ready for a full-scale R&B revival, then Dr Feelgood, from Canvey Island in Essex, were the only ones who could have started it. Instead, the most gifted kids whom the Feelgoods inspired – like Paul Weller and Joe Strummer – derived more from their attitude than their repertoire, which is why the result was the Great Punk Rock Explosion rather than a new generation of R&B groups. A quartet of uncompromising roughnecks whose tastes in both music and clothing seemed to have been flash-frozen in 1964, they were, initially at least, sufficiently purist to insist that their first album, 1975's *Down By The Jetty*, should be released in mono. Lee Brilleaux (vocals, harp, slide), WILKO JOHNSON (guitar, vocals), John B. Sparks (bass) and John 'The Big Figure' Martin (drums) applied the classic post-ROLLING STONES Brit R&B formula of combining a hefty dose of Chess-style blues-rock with a few '50s black-pop novelties, a fistful of rock classics, a pinch of early soul and a songbook of Johnson originals. The result was a snarling, streetwise, stripped-down show which replaced late-'60s hippie-blues languor with an edge of genuine urban menace: Johnson's clattering, percussive guitar slice-and-diced a 4/4 beat with more variations than anyone since JAMES BROWN's great guitarist Jimmy Nolen: a perfect foil both for Brilleaux's feral growl and honking harp, and for a rhythm section which made the Rock of Gibraltar seem flimsy by comparison.

Within 18 months of detonating the London pub-rock scene, they had developed enough commercial clout for their live album *Stupidity* (1976) to enter the charts at No 1, but they had to wait until 1977, when Johnson-the-guitarist was replaced by John 'Gypie' Mayo – and Johnson-the-songwriter by a platoon of outside co-composers including Nick Lowe – before they hit their stride as a singles act. They had five solid hits between 1977 and 1979, including the ominous boogie 'Down At The Doctors' and the JOHN LEE HOOKER-inspired 'Milk And Alcohol'. When Mayo retired hurt in 1980 and was, in his turn, replaced by Johnny Guitar, the Feelgoods still retained their unique flavour, if not their mass audience, but it was the departure of the original rhythm section, in 1984, which reduced a once-great band to an average one with an unusually charismatic vocalist. Since then, Dr Feelgood has essentially been Lee Brilleaux-plus-three: they've retained their hold on concert audiences in Europe, Japan and Australia as well as Britain, though they never cracked the US market. They've always made money, they've cut the occasional good record and they've generally been good value on the night, but their moment of greatness has long since passed.

- *Singles: The U.A. Years*+ (Liberty CDP 7 92440 2)

It's a real testament to the gritty integrity and wacky individual-ism of the Feelgoods aesthetic that their singles collection is as thoroughly representative of their work as any of their album-as-albums. The hour-and-a-quarter of flinty raunch included here represents homegrown Britblues' only real creative achievement since Peter Green left FLEETWOOD MAC. (Speaking of F. Mac, Jeremy Spencer should have been so lucky as to be able to apply his ELMORE JAMES chops to an original as inspired as Wilko Johnson's Elmo-resque 'Back In The Night'.) With 24 tracks (six with Johnson, ten with Mayo, and four each by the Johnny Guitar and Lee-plus line-ups), this collection doesn't skimp. The emphasis is on original material: to hear them work out on the MUDDY WATERS, HOWLIN' WOLF or BO DIDDLEY songbooks you have to go to their 'regular' albums. Obviously, this has their chart hits – 'Sneakin' Suspicion', 'She's A Windup', 'Down At The Doctor's', 'Milk And Alcohol' , 'As Long As The Price Is Right', and like that – but it also includes such R&B esoterica as WILLIE DIXON's 'Violent Love' (attributed to Otis Rush, who recorded the best-known version), a crunching Coasters nod on 'Riot In Cell Block No 9', and a splendidly raw take on John Lee Hooker's 'Mad Man Blues'. Dr Feelgood were among the very small number of white blues bands who managed to create work which is distinctively personal, while remaining faithful to its sources. Anyone who suggests that Status Quo were the UK equivalent to ZZ TOP has only proved that they don't understand ZZ Top: the Feelgoods are the only British blues band who could ever match wit, funk and popcraft with the Rev Willy G. At the very least, they're the UK's answer to THE FABULOUS THUNDERBIRDS, with Canvey 'ump replacing Austin cool. In Dr Feelgood's alphabet, 'Essex' must be an anagram of 'Texas': their credentials are available for inspection right here.

Subjects for further investigation: **Case History: The Best Of Dr Feelgood** (EMI CDP 7 46711 2) is a budget-price alternative to *Singles*, six tracks lighter and covering substantially the same ground in proportionally less detail. Of their studio albums, the most satisfying are probably 1975's *Malpractice* (Grand GRANDCD09) – the second by the original line-up, including 'Back In The Night', 'Goin' Back Home', Bo Diddley's 'I Can Tell' and Johnson's self-referential 'You Shouldn't Call The Doctor (If You Can't Afford The Bills' – and 1977's *Be Seeing You* (Grand GRANDCD 14), the first with Gypie Mayo on board, including their first hit 'She's A Windup' and, appropriately enough, the BROWNIE McGHEE/Muddy Waters anthem 'The Blues Had A Baby And They Named It Rock 'N Roll'. *Stupidity* (Grand GRANDCD 18) is heartily disliked by all its participants, but those of us with fond memories of the original Feelgoods line-up love it warts and all. But after Dr Feelgood, even the best of the orthodox British blues bands – like Blues 'N Trouble and, indeed, The Blues Band – have seemed pretty mundane.

George Thorogood & The Destroyers

It's a white-blues fairytale: George Thorogood's tireless willing-ness to entertain 'til he drops and his boundless enthusiasm for his chosen music – a reductive conflation of HOUND DOG TAYLOR, ELMORE JAMES, JOHN LEE HOOKER, CHUCK BERRY and BO DIDDLEY, with a little Hank Williams and Johnny Cash thrown in for good measure – took him and his Destroyers from local Delaware bars to the world stage of Live Aid in the space of seven years. The rough-and-tumble '50s-style blues'n'roll of Thorogood and his rhythm section (bassist Billy Blough, drummer Jeff Simon) won them a recording contract with Rounder, in those days such an earnest folkie label that the liner notes of Thorogood's debut included both an apology for releasing such a vulgar album in the first place, and worry as to whether the record would sell. Endorse-ments followed from rock tastemakers like Nick Lowe, and Thorogood was launched, selling more and more records each time out, and touring first nationally and then internationally. His move from Rounder to EMI, and the massive success of *Bad To The Bone*, reinforced his position as the first real white-blues success story of the '80s. Thorogood has often – and accurately – been accused of being crass and derivative; he'd probably agree as long as it was also acknowledged that on the right night, or the right record, he's big, big fun.

- *The Baddest Of George Thorogood & The Destroyers* (EMI MTL 1070)

A thoroghly serviceable and highly enjoyable canter through a catalogue which benefits considerably from a judicious filleting. *The Baddest* melts down five albums on EMI and two from Rounder but, apart from variations in production quality and the addition of saxophone and rhythm guitar on the later tracks, it could all have been recorded at the same session. Proof that Thorogood has his heart (and his slide) in the right place can be inferred by the sleeve photos of Thorogood happily hanging out with Bo Diddley, STEVIE RAY VAUGHAN, ALBERT COLLINS, John Lee Hooker and THE ROLLING STONES.

Subjects for further investigation: **George Thorogood & The Destroyers** (Demon FIENDCD 55) was the rough, raw 1977 debut, and probably the most accurate transcription of the original bar-band shows by the closest-ever white approximation of Hound Dog Taylor's HouseRockers. Its masterstroke was Thorogood's medley of Hooker's 'House Rent Boogie' and 'One Bourbon, One Scotch, One Beer', but then that's also on *The Baddest*, even though his stomping account of Bo Diddley's 'Ride On Josephine' isn't. *Move It On Over* (Demon FIENDCD 58) was the sequel, and *Bad To The Bone* (BGO BGOCD 94) was the 1982 commercial breakthrough. It sold mainly on its title track, though if you stick with the compilation you miss out on the rocking Chuck Berry pastiche 'Back To Wentzville', the insanely speeded-up Hooker tribute 'New Boogie Chillen' and a dignified, Cash-style reading of Bob Dylan's 'Wanted Man'.

The Fabulous Thunderbirds

The pride of Austin, Texas, and the lynchpins for one of the most active regional blues scenes in the entire US, The Fabulous Thunderbirds constructed a new way for white boys to play the blues which was both as powerful and as appropriate as that contemporaneously developed by DR FEELGOOD in the UK. Though bass players and drummers would come and go, the frontline team of Kim Wilson (vocals, harp) and Jimmie Vaughan (guitar) built their approach on a sleazy, baggy-suited retro elegance and a defiantly regional Gulf Coast style which blended the Texas guitar tradition, a touch of Tex-Mex polka and a rolling swamp-blues groove – primarily derived from SLIM HARPO, Lazy Lester and the Excello Records school – with the more common Delta-gone-to-Chicago vocabulary. The Detroit-born Wilson was a jivey, charismatic frontman and a near-virtuoso blues harpist capable of handling any known harp style from LITTLE WALTER to JIMMY REED, as well as mimicking CLIFTON CHENIER's accordion or the Memphis Horns; Vaughan was considered by many to be the best white blues guitarist in America. Eschewing the manic elaboration of his younger brother STEVIE RAY VAUGHAN in favour of a minimalist approach in which only the essentials were played, he delivered those essentials with a sledgehammer assault and utter tonal purity.

They had been together for four years when they cut their first album, *The Fabulous Thunderbirds* (1979), for the small Takoma indie. Its cult success earned them a British tour, a deal with Chrysalis Records and the admiration of Brit roots-rock gurus Nick Lowe and Dave Edmunds, who were to pop up as producers and co-writers throughout their subsequent career. The Takoma/Chrysalis deal expired with '82's Lowe-produced *T-Bird Rhythm*, and it took them another four years to get back in the game: *Tuff Enuff*, cut in London in '85 with Dave Edmunds producing, was leased to Epic Records and, on its release the following year, went Top 30 (with the title-track single making the Top 10) to give them the biggest hit of their career.

What eventually did for The Fabulous Thunderbirds was the combination of misguided concessions to their new mass audience (with the over-produced, would-be radio-friendly *Hot Number* and *Powerful Stuff*), and the departure of Jimmie Vaughan, looking to spend more time with his family after almost twenty years of full-time roadwork. Kim Wilson recruited no less than two guitarists to replace Vaughan, one of whom was his good buddy, the highly-respected Roomful Of Blues veteran Duke Robillard, which meant that Austin's finest no longer contained any native-born Texans. When the resulting album, *Walk That Walk, Talk That Talk*, bombed, Epic reacted by dumping the band from the label and – to add insult to injury – deleting all their pre-*Walk* albums (even the chart-striding career-peak *Tuff Enuff*) from the catalogue. Robillard then left to return to his own post-Roomful trio, The

Pleasure Kings, and The Fabulous Thunderbirds are currently in limbo. They deserve considerably better.

- *Portfolio* (Chrysalis MPCD 1599)

T-Birds Classic: a jam-packed 73-minute, 26-track fillet of the first four albums, recorded between 1979 and 1982. The sound, on the earlier tracks at any rate, is indie-thin, but the playing isn't: the T-Birds in general, and Vaughan in particular, derive their flavour from a combination of wiry strength and relaxed cool. There's plenty of bayou funk: Slim Harpo's 'Scratch My Back' and 'Tip On In', Lazy Lester's 'Sugar Coated Love', Rockin' Sidney's 'You Ain't Nothing But Fine', the killer opener of 'The Crawl', (originated by LONNIE BROOKS back when he was still calling himself Guitar Junior), and a harp-as-accordion *tour de force* on 'Cherry Pink And Apple Blossom White'. And then there's the rougher stuff: 'Diddy Wah Diddy' is BO DIDDLEY's rather than BLIND BLAKE's, and Vaughan gets to show off his slow-blues chops on Wilson's 'Full Time Lover'. All in all, a nifty showcase for one of the most important contemporary white blues bands, cut back in the days before they realised they were important.

Subjects for further investigation: If the task of replacing Jimmie Vaughan had simply been difficult, the combination of Duke Robillard (lead) and Kid Bangham (rhythm) could undoubtedly have managed it. As *Walk That Walk, Talk That Talk* (Epic EPC 468524 2) demonstrates, it turned out to be impossible, despite creditable stabs at Junior Parker's 'Feelin' Good' (*a la* MAGIC SAM) and Homer Banks' 'Ain't That A Lot Of Love' (*a la* TAJ MAHAL). The T-Birds were no longer the T-Birds, but a new band with Wilson singing, and unfortunately, the new band wasn't nearly as interesting as the old one. Vaughan's major work since turning in his wings was his long-awaited collaboration, as The Vaughan Brothers, with younger sib Stevie Ray on *Family Style* (Epic 467014 2); he can also be heard recreating the maestro's licks on the title track of JOHN LEE HOOKER's *Boom Boom* (PointBlank VPBCD 12).

If you want to know why Duke Robillard was the pick-to-click as Vaughan's replacement, *Duke Robillard & The Pleasure Kings/Too Hot To Handle* (Demon FIEND CD 707) doublebacks a couple of

'84–5 trio albums: fine and fierce, adept and soulful, considerably better than competent and just short of inspired. Robillard's replacement in Roomful Of Blues, by the way, was Ronnie Earl, whose most recent solo shot, as Ronnie Earl & The Broadcasters, comes on *Peace Of Mind* (Demon/Black Top FIEND CD 169): bold brassy shuffles with a pronounced Texas lope and Earl's guitar poking through in the right places. Like Robillard's, Earl's work is entertaining and satisfying, if not particularly innovative: records like this tend to sell to the artist's existing following rather than helping to create a new one.

Stevie Ray Vaughan & Double Trouble

When Stevie Ray Vaughan died on 27 August, 1990, it was a mark of the respect in which he was held by the blues community that JOHN LEE HOOKER and BUDDY GUY dedicated their next albums to him. It's safe to say that no white bluesman, not even ERIC CLAPTON in his prime, ever enjoyed such a powerful combination of peer-group approval and non-specialist audience adulation as Stevie Ray Vaughan: the closest precedent was probably CANNED HEAT's Alan 'Blind Owl' Wilson. The trajectory of Vaughan's career eerily reprised the fate of Johnny Winter, who had worn the same Texas Guitar Hotshot mantle a dozen years before: a massive, sensational impact was fuelled and celebrated with an equally massive and sensational intake of assorted intoxicants, and followed by collapse and gruelling rehabilitation. Like Winter, Stevie Ray had the rock-god pretensions burned out of him by the ordeal, but unlike Winter, he didn't live long enough to put more than a fraction of his new resolutions into practice. Only minutes after he had shared the stage with Eric Clapton, Buddy Guy, ROBERT CRAY and elder brother Jimmie Vaughan, late of THE FABULOUS THUNDERBIRDS, at a Chicago-area open-air show's triumphant jam finale, his helicopter crashed into a mountain, killing all on board.

Born in Dallas, Texas, in 1955, he made his first international impact as lead guitarist on David Bowie's 1983 pop-funk master-piece *Let's Dance*; but he had considerable prehistory. As the runty kid brother of local hero Jimmie, he had become first the pet and then the peer of every major bluesman who'd ever passed through Antone's, Austin's blues mecca. Buddy Guy, John Lee Hooker, MUDDY WATERS, ALBERT KING: they all thought Stevie Ray was fantastic. His two-fisted blend of JIMI HENDRIX, Albert King, Hubert Sumlin and Lonnie Mack was, according to connoisseurs, the hottest ticket in town. Stevie Ray's band Double Trouble had started out as the Triple Threat Revue, co-starring human fireball LOU ANN BARTON and local bluesman W.C. Clark, but the band wasn't big enough for both Vaughan and Barton. When the latter scored a one-off deal with Elektra/Asylum Records in the wake of her departure from the band, former Atlantic mastermind Jerry Wexler came to Austin to see Barton, but after catching a Double Trouble show, Wexler used his considerable influence to secure Stevie Ray an appearance at the Montreux Jazz Festival.

This was unheard-of for an unsigned band, but Vaughan more than pulled his weight; John Hammond signed him for Epic, and David Bowie buttonholed him for the *Let's Dance* sessions. The Bowie/Vaughan connection expired in acrimony not long after, but the upshot was that Vaughan was free to tour in his own right with his own band to promote his own first album, 1983's *Texas Flood*. He rapidly became a rock-god guitar hero and the Great White Hope of the blues revival, but the sudden change in his circumstances and the pressures attendant on his career drove him into a spiral of cocaine and booze that ended when he collapsed during a European tour, and retired hurt to reassess his music and his life. When he reemerged, it was with a new sense of focus and commitment; suddenly the fireworks had context and purpose. His comeback album, 1989's *In Step*, was the finest work of his career to date, and provided powerful evidence that the best was, as they say, yet to come. He'd beaten the odds, beaten the dope, beaten the booze and beaten his own ego, but the laws of physics and gravity proved too much for him. His death provoked a massive outpouring of grief, and the great artists who inspired him, from Hooker and Guy to Jeff Beck and Eric Clapton, queued up to pay tribute to the little guy with the beat-up Strat and the big, big soul.

● *Live Alive* (Epic 450238 2)

The jury's still out on this '86 in-concert job: the band and their intimates always considered it their sole artistic failure, possibly because it was recorded and mixed when some of them, especially the leader, were in the throes of massive cocaine and booze abuse; and also because it's patched with overdubs from end to end. Many civilians, on the other hand, prefer it to the three studio jobs which preceded it – 1983's *Texas Flood* (Epic EPC 460951 2), 1984's *Couldn't Stand The Weather* (Epic 465571 2) and 1985's *Soul To Soul* (Epic CDEPC 26441) – because it presents some of the best of SRV's material in its optimum context. I started out with the former view and now incline to the latter, even though *Live Alive*'s nine-and-a-half-minute take on Hendrix's 'Voodoo Chile (Slight Return)' is even more of a waste of time than the eight-minute version on *Weather*. There are three slow-blues *tours-de-force*, a massive dose of Stevie-does-Jimi with both 'Voodoo Chile' and 'Say What!', a remorselessly rolling 'Cold Shot', and a few boogies. All that's missing from the original vinyl double-LP is the version of 'Life Without You', when he denounces apartheid and delivers the immortal line, 'I may be white, but I ain't stupid'. All in all, it's Early Stevie at his showboating best, and, yes, it's a hell of a lot better than the London show I saw.

Of those three Phase-1 albums, I'd recommend *Weather* as the best supplement to *Live Alive:* simply because it's packed with gems: the outrageously funky polyrhthmic chances the band take with the groove on the title track; the nifty chicken-pickin' on 'Scuttle Buttin"; the cool-jazz organ-trio pastiche of 'Stan's Swang'; the churning riff of 'Cold Shot'; the heartfelt tribute to Guitar Slim with 'The Things I Used To Do' . . . actually, that's most of the album. Apart from 'Voodoo Chile', that is. Come to that, there are also moments I'd miss if I never heard either of the other two again, but not as many.

- *In Step* (Epic EPC 463395 2)
- **THE VAUGHAN BROTHERS:** *Family Style* (Epic 467014 2)

The last records released in Vaughan's lifetime: the superb post-rehab album in which he discovered how to use his formidable vocabulary to say something that was genuinely important to him, and the long-awaited teamup with Jimmie Vaughan which was probably the most unself-conscious music he'd ever made. *In Step*, Stevie Ray's rite of passage, contains plenty of 'secular' material – it does, after all, open up with the Jerry Lee Lewis-style piano-pounder 'The House Is Rockin" and detonate itself halfway through with two Buddy Guy covers – but its core is a trio of numbers, 'Crossfire', 'Tightrope' and 'Wall Of Denial', which use addiction as a metaphor for all life's obstacles, and which infuse the entire album with a sense of power and purpose. Here the playing serves the songs rather than the other way about: the flashy white kid is replaced by the adult bluesman. *Family Style* is the other side of the coin: produced by Nile Rodgers, with whom Vaughan The Younger had worked on Bowie's *Let's Dance*, it's nothing but fun from start to finish. Freed from the restrictions of the Double Trouble and Fab T-Birds formats, the brothers swap guitar and vocal leads, fool around with soul, funk, Western swing and country grooves, and wind up the proceedings by playing a manic Albert King-style duet on the same guitar.

- *The Sky Is Crying* (Epic EPC 468640 2)

Paradoxically, this posthumous barrel-scraper ranks with *In Step* as the best studio record in Stevie Ray's catalogue. Constructed by Jimmie Vaughan from all the outtakes from SRV's four studio albums, it includes everything from the exuberant barrel through roadhouse-rock master Lonnie Mack's 'Wham!' (the first single Stevie Ray ever bought) to a version of 'Little Wing' which is easily the most soulful Hendrix tribute he ever cut, plus tributes to Muddy Waters, Howlin Wolf, ELMORE JAMES and – on the funky 'Chitlin Con Carne' – jazz guitar honcho Kenny Burrell. The closing 'Life By The Drop', performed solo on 12-string acoustic, completes the set of affecting clean-up songs originally recorded for *In Step*; all in all, a small miracle.

Subjects for further investigation: **In The Beginning** (Epic 462624 2) is prehistory: a 1980 live airshot from the vaults of a local station, for confirmed Vaughanatics only. There's a stunning Texas Flood' (here titled 'Flood Down In Texas') on **Blues Masters Vol: 3 Texas Blues** (Rhino R2 71123), taken from that 1982 Montreaux show. Bowie's **Let's Dance** (EMI America CDP 746 002 2) was Vaughan's first international showcase; JOHNNY COPELAND's **Texas Twister** (Rounder CD 11504), A.C. REED's **I'm In The Wrong Business!** (Alligator ALCD 4757) and Lonnie Mack's **Strike Like Lightning** (Alligator ALCD 4739) all find him sitting in. The Mack is probably the most intriguing, since 'Double Whammy' finds master and student duetting on a variant of 'Wham!'. A Reed/ Vaughan performance of 'These Blues Is Killing Me' reappears on *The Alligator Records 20th Anniversary Collection* (Alligator ALCD 105/6). The numerous tributes which Vaughan's death elicited from the blues community naturally included musical ones: Otis Grand and JOE LOUIS WALKER perform 'SRV (My Mood Too)' on *The Blues Guiitar Box 2* (Sequel NXT CD 185); Buddy Guy's 'Remembering Stevie' appeared on *Damn Right I've Got The Blues* (Silvertone ORE CD 516); Albert Collins contributed 'Blues For Stevie' to *The Guitars That Rule The World* (Metal Blade 9 26828-2 [US]), Robben Ford kicks off *Robben Ford & The Blue Line* (Stretch/GRP GRS 11022) with 'The Brother (For Jimmie & Stevie)', and WALTER TROUT's 'Say Goodbye To The Blues' is on *Prisoner Of A Dream* (Provogue PRD 70262).

The Robert Cray Band

Anyone choosing to enshrine the parties responsible for bringing the blues back so big in the 1980s will need to construct a pedestal wide and sturdy enough to accomodate both STEVIE RAY VAUGHAN and Robert Cray, respectively the Great White – And Black – Hopes of the decade's revival. While Vaughan evangelised blues to a young hard-rock crowd which worshipped Van Halen and Ozzy Osbourne, Robert Cray challenged the shallowness of US AOR radio with some genuinely adult pop: his music updated the heyday of Southern soul-blues with a bleak, chilly vision for the ominous '90s. Like a slim young BOBBY 'BLUE' BLAND or a Memphis Marvin Gaye, Cray sang like a soul man in the tradition of O.V. Wright or Z.Z.Hill, and spiked his mid-tempo, minor-key cheatin' songs with neatly vicious guitar solos which betrayed the influences of ALBERT COLLINS and Hubert Sumlin. He has the most impressive original songbook of any contemporary blues act, bar none; he is a vastly resourceful vocalist who can move in the space of a single note from menace to pathos, squeezing every nuance from lyrics which are invariably worth the effort; he has as distinctive and eloquent a guitar style as anyone in his generation can boast; he's old enough and experienced enough to have thoroughly mastered his craft, but he's still youthful and good-looking enough to be considered a hunk in certain quarters; plus he's a nice guy, to boot. If Robert Cray seems too good to be true, it's because he almost is.

Which is the Cray Problem for people who feel that blues ought to be dirty. Everything about Cray is *clean*: his guitar tone, his diction, the production of his records, his appearance and, for all I know, his socks. The only thing about Robert Cray that's dirty is his repertoire. I don't mean 'dirty' in the sense that Bo Carter, TAMPA RED or 2 Live Crew would understand it – Cray delivers no cussing and no double-entendres – but dirty in the sense that they explore, in telling detail, some of the nastiest emotions you can ever hope to avoid. You'll never find a beat that isn't straightforward in his music, or an emotion that is. There's rarely a shaft of light in Robert Cray's world: it's a nightmarescape of paranoia, jealousy, guilt and deceit in which Cray is always either the deceiver wondering when he's going to get found out, or the cuckold who *has* just found out. Cray's is as coherent and fully realised a body of work as anything in the blues since ROBERT JOHNSON; in fact, 'Young Bob' (Cray's on-disc alter ego) inhabits a moral universe as chill and hostile as 'Po' Bob' did a half-century or so earlier. And they say this stuff isn't the blues? Well, I'll concede that they aren't 12-bars, but that's as far as I'll budge.

And yet . . . Cray's music can be frustrating. He can play and sing in a wide variety of styles, but he sticks steadfastly with a very specific musical and emotional register. At his shows, the narrow, muted palette with which he chooses to work imposes a lack of emotional release on the audience. The classic climax of a blues show is just that: a joyous release which sends you home happy and strong enough to face the travails of the next day (or night). Cray never brings you to that point: the tension created by the power of his songs, voice and guitar remains undispelled as you leave the theatre, and the message of his music is that *there is no escape*. He once said that he only considered sad songs to be really the blues: if that's truly so, he may be the most authentic blues singer of them all. But the blues is a music which explores pain in order to vanquish it, and recognises each moment of pleasure as a victory against a system which would deny it; and soul is a music which, by virtue of its gospel heritage, carries with it an implicit belief in salvation. A bluesman denying pleasure and a soul man denied redemption, Robert Cray subverts the traditional contents of the genres in which he works as profoundly as he respects their traditional forms.

The scion of an army family, he was born in Columbus, Georgia, on 1 August, 1953, and spent some time in Germany, but he did the bulk of his growing up in Portland, Oregon, where he encountered both his most profound influence (other than his father's record collection) and his longest-serving musical partner. The featured attraction at a high school dance was, amazingly enough, Albert Collins, whose sizzling guitar had a traumatic effect on the young Young Bob; and the group which he formed in 1974 with bassist Richard Cousins often found itself backing Collins whenever The Master Of The Telecaster toured in the Pacific Northwest area. The Robert Cray Band, then featuring harpist/co-vocalist Curtis Salgado, may even have helped to inspire *The Blues Brothers*: Cray met John Belushi and director John Landis in 1977 during the making of *Animal House*, in which Cray played the bassist of the fictional Otis Day & The Knights band, and Belushi's 'Joliet Jake Blues' persona is allegedly partially based on Salgado. (Dan Aykroyd's 'Elwood Blues' is, equally allegedly, derived from harpist CHARLIE MUSSELWHITE.)

Following a rejection from Alligator Records, they cut their first album *Who's Been Talking* in 1978 for Tomato Records, who sat on the tapes for two years before celebrating the album's eventual release by promptly going out of business. It took them three years to make another record connection, this time with the small Hightone independent, run by producer/composers Dennis Walker and Bruce Bromberg. Their first collaboration, 1983's *Bad Influence*, was a sensation both within and without the blues circuit: ALBERT KING gave the young hotshot full-credibility blues-approval by making Cray's 'Phone Booth' the title song of his next album; in Britain, the album soared into the independent charts. When CLARENCE 'GATEMOUTH' BROWN ducked out of a Texas guitar summit session with Albert Collins and JOHNNY COPELAND, Cray was invited to deputise: the resulting album, 1985's *Showdown!*, won a Grammy the following year. Soon, he was opening shows for – and guesting with – the Big Rock likes of ERIC CLAPTON and Tina Turner: Clapton covered the title tune of *Bad Influence* in 1986, and enlisted Cray to play and compose on his *Journeyman* album. Poised as he was halfway between Stax-as-in-Otis-

Redding and Stax-as-in-Albert-King, it came as no surprise when he recruited The Memphis Horns as soon as he could afford them, which was when Mercury decided to distribute the next in the series, 1986's *Strong Persuader*. The album went platinum: it was probably the biggest commercial score in blues recording since Bobby Bland's *Two Steps From The Blues* made the Top 10 of the pop charts in 1963, and Cray became a *bona fide* star.

Nowadays, he's a ubiquitous presence on the blues-rock Chums' Circuit, showing up here with Clapton and Turner, there with JOHN LEE HOOKER or CHUCK BERRY. The personnel of his band seems to roll over with ominous regularity – the Walker/Bromberg production team has fissured, and even the long-serving Cousins disappeared after 1990's *Midnight Stroll* – and his most recent music exists in an uncomfortable state of transition: not quite standing its ground, not quite ready to move on. Nevertheless, he remains the key figure in contemporary blues : still a young musician with a lengthy career still ahead of him, the commercial destiny of the music depends on what Robert Cray does in the next few years.

- *Bad Influence* (Demon FIEND CD 23)
- *False Accusations* (Demon FIEND CD 43)

Since *Who's Been Talking* was more of a prologue than a first act, these – from, respectively, 1983 and 1985 – are effectively Cray's debut albums, and vastly impressive they were, too. Here are the tight, itchy grooves, the stinging guitar, the clean, rich, detailed vocals; the chilly, hellish traps which Young Bob either sets or is ensnared by. The originals are strong and memorable; the covers – JOHNNY 'GUITAR' WATSON's 'Don't Touch Me', Eddie Floyd's 'Got To Make A Comeback', William Bell's 'Share What You Got' and Peppermint Harris' uncharacteristically celebratory 'I Got Loaded' – well-chosen and well-performed. *Bad Influence* has the best-known repertoire, thanks to its one-two opener of 'Phone Booth' and the title track, but *False Accusation* is every bit as strong: 'Playin' In The Dirt', 'The Last Time (I Get Burned Like This', 'Payin' For It Now', and 'Sonny' – in which Young Bob cuckolds a blinded Vietnam vet – are full-strength, classic Cray. The production on these albums is decidedly less glossy and radio-friendly than on the subsequent pair of Cray albums, but that shouldn't prove too much of a problem for any but the most timid listener.

- **Strong Persuader** (Mercury 830 568-2)
- **Don't Be Afraid Of The Dark** (Mercury 834 923-2)

From 1986 and 1988, the breakthrough albums: despite the Big Drums and chorussy rhythm guitar which rendered _Strong Persuader_ palatable to Adult-Oriented Rock radio, the explorations of the sexual badlands were as uncompromisingly confrontational as ever; the then-current edition of the Cray band delivered the material with enormous assurance, The Memphis Horns applied a brassy supercharger whenever the songs needed a lift and Cray himself was in peak form as singer, composer and guitarist. Its radio hit was 'Smokin' Gun', but the rest of the album was, if anything, stronger: songs like 'I Guess I Showed Her', 'Still Around', 'Foul Play' and 'Right Next Door (Because Of Me)', which provided the album with its title phrase, were tougher than anything else on the radio at the time. _Don't Be Afraid Of The Dark_ bore approximately the same relationship to _Strong Persuader_ as _False Accusation_ did to _Bad Influence:_ the mixture-as-before, with a lower Title Recognition Factor but absolutely no drop in quality. As a bonus, it includes a zippy, jazzy shuffle in 'Across The Line', a welcome change-of-pace and a convincing rebuttal to those who claimed that Cray has forgotten how to play anything other than his soul-blues ballads. Think of it as a double-album released in instalments.

- **Midnight Stroll** (Mercury 846 652-2)
- **I Was Warned** (Mercury 512 721-2)

The 'transition' albums: it's kind of spooky the way Cray albums tend to come in pairs. This duo, from 1990 and 1992, brings the story more or less up-to-date. _Midnight Stroll_ sought to extend his music beyond the mid-tempo-minor-key-cheatin'-song format with which he had become so inextricably associated. It added a few new classics to the already overstuffed Cray songbook: 'The Forecast (Calls For Pain)', 'Bouncin' Back', 'Consequences' and 'Walk Around Time' are as good as anything on the earlier albums, but though we can sense Cray reaching out for something new, whatever that something might turn out to be wasn't quite yet within his grasp. With the departure of bassist Richard Cousins, *I Was Warned* completed the personnel rollover of The Robert Cray Band – apart from The Memphis Horns, producer Dennis Walker and Cray himself, no-one remained from the *Persuader* sessions – and the result balances both losses and gains. The new rhythm section groove lacked the sheer authority and the whomping solidity which were Cousins' hallmarks, but the compensation was a new flexibility: the ominous rhumba groove of the title track would have been inconceivable from the *Persuader* line-up. The songs are uniformly powerful and affecting, particularly the soul ballads like 'Our Last Time' and 'He Doesn't Live Here Any More' – Cray is probably the finest practitioner of this neglected form to emerge in the last couple of decades – though nothing as commercial and radio-friendly as 'Smoking Gun' leaped out of the album. It may take one more record for this edition of the Cray Band to settle down, but on this evidence Robert Cray is currently not only at the height of his powers, but in a position to demonstrate that his powers are greater than previously suspected.

Subjects for further investigation: Not surprisingly, *Who's Been Talking* reappeared after Cray's breakthrough; it's currently available, repackaged as **The Score** (Charly CD BM 16): a competent enough debut by a band still in search of an identity, it's only truly essential for the hardcore Cray fan. **Showdown!** (Alligator ALCD 4743) made Cray an honorary Texan and won him a joint Grammy with Collins and Copeland: his playing lacks the muscularity of the older men, but his adroit, jittery guitar lines stab into place like poisoned pinpricks. He contributes both guitar (on 'Hound Dog') and composition (a co-writing credit on the gorgeous 'Old Love' to Eric Clapton's 1989 **Journeyman** (Reprise 926 074-2), and appears, none too prominently, on Clapton's live album **24 Nights** (Reprise 7599-26420-2). He's all over John Lee Hooker's contemporary trilogy **The Healer** (Silvertone ORE CD 508), **Mr Lucky** (Silvertone ORE CD 519) and **Boom Boom** (PointBlank VPBCD 12); and adds his funky plunk to 'Who's Making Love?' on KATIE WEBSTER's **Swamp Boogie Queen** (Alligator ALCD 4766).

Gary Moore

In 1990, the Irish rock guitarist Gary Moore became a born-again bluesman. Inspired by the work of ERIC CLAPTON and PETER GREEN during their respective mid-'60s tenures with JOHN MAYALL's BluesBreakers (as well as by JIMI HENDRIX and Jeff Beck), he had begun his career as the teen-prodigy guitarist for the Dublin-based trio Skid Row (no relation to the contemporary cock-rockers of the same name), and had received his first recording contract after Skid Row had opened a Dublin show for the original edition of FLEETWOOD MAC, then under Peter Green's leadership. Green took a shine to the youngster, introduced him to Fleetwood Mac's management, and later sold him the 1959 Gibson Les Paul guitar which is now Moore's proudest posses-sion. Following Skid Row's demise, Moore carved out a successful career both as a journeyman guitarist, performing and recording jazz-rock fusion and heavy metal with Colosseum and Thin Lizzy (whose frontman, the late Phil Lynott, was a fellow graduate of Skid Row), and also as a solo artist and leader of his own band, G-Force.

Swapping his leather jackets, ripped jeans and pointy-headed shred-machine guitars for a baggy suit and his old Les Paul has proved to be Moore's smartest move in years; his two blues albums, 1990's *Still Got The Blues* and its 1992 successor *After Hours*, and their respective tours (featuring the likes of ALBERT COLLINS and Larry McCray as opening acts) revived what was a fairly stagnant career. As a bluesman, Moore wears his influences on his sleeve – the Mayall Holy Trinity of Clapton, Green and Mick Taylor – and when he appears alongside venerable titans like B.B. KING, ALBERT KING and ALBERT COLLINS, he takes on their distinctive flavourings just as milk is said to do when you park it next to something strong-tasting in the fridge. Nevertheless, his blues albums are unmistakeably passionate, deeply-felt and honourable affairs, and it'll be interesting to see how long he remains loyal to this recently reawakened old love.

- *Still Got The Blues* (Virgin CDV 260 568)
- *After Hours* (Virgin CDV 2884 (262 558))

A pastiche of a pastiche. Both Moore's sound – the thick, syrupy wail of a Gibson Les Paul guitar cranked through an overdriven Marshall amp, the earnest, husky vocal tone of a clean man trying to sing dirty – and his repertoire hark back to the mid-to-late '60s British Blues Boom: the era of John Mayall's BluesBreakers and the blues-purist incarnation of Fleetwood Mac. Despite a cameo appearance by King himself, the reading of Albert King's 'Oh Pretty Woman' which appears on *Still Got The Blues* recalls the Mayall version (with Mick Taylor on guitar) from 1967's *Crusade*, rather than King's blue(s)print; just as the same album's 'All Your Love' owes more to the 1966 Mayall/Clapton *Blues Breakers* cover than it does to the original by OTIS RUSH. *Still Got The Blues* is rocker-brash, and Moore's team-up with Albert Collins on JOHNNY GUITAR WATSON's 'Too Tired' is certainly exhilarating enough; but it's Albert King's 'As The Years Go Passing By' and Moore's own *hommage* to Albert (entitled 'King Of The Blues' – I wonder how B.B. feels about that?) which prefigure the deeper, more soulful tone of *After Hours*. The sequel brings Collins back for an engaging romp through the now-standard 'The Blues Is Alright' and wheels on B.B. King for some amiable rough-housing on 'Since I Met You Baby' (not the Ivory Joe Hunter standard, but a Moore original). Let's hope that Moore is in no hurry to return to heavy rock: apart from anything else, he looks so much better in the baggy suit.

A QUICK AND EXPENSIVE SURVEY OF THE TALENT IN THE ROOM

An awful lot of blues talent has surfaced during the past couple of decades. Some of these artists are fresh-faced newcomers (the most extreme case being Eric Gales, barely 16 when he recorded his first album) while others are grizzled veterans who've had to wait a very long time to take their best shots: the great harpist SNOOKY PRYOR didn't get a chance to cut an album as a featured artist until his eighth decade. There is an active contemporary performer representing virtually every blues style that's ever existed, ranging from the late-'60s-style power-blues-rock of JEFF

HEALEY to the '20s country blues purism of Bob Brozman; or from the pounding swamp boogie of KATIE WEBSTER to the 'classic blues' variations of DANA GILLESPIE and SAFFIRE - THE UPPITY BLUESWOMEN; or from the solid West Side electric traditionalism of SON SEALS to the radical bottleneck of RAINER or SONNY LANDRETH. You get the idea . . . but please be advised that there is also an ungodly number of white guys who play superb guitar, sing passably well and write thoroughly indifferent songs.

2. *Classicists, Lifers & Survivors*

Here's where we meet the artists who are, currently, the backbone of the blues. Some of them are relative newcomers who work firmly within the existing traditions of the music, and some of them have been 'out there' for decades, but they all exist below the high level of pop visibility afforded to the likes of B.B. KING, JOHN LEE HOOKER and BUDDY GUY, let alone ROBERT CRAY, STEVIE RAY VAUGHAN, ERIC CLAPTON and GARY MOORE. These folks do not drift in and out of the blues according to fashion or whim: they're down with it for life whether they're coining it big or not, and they'll keep going 'til they drop whether they win Grammies and MTV awards or not.

Son Seals

Singer/guitarist Frank 'Son' Seals, born in Osceola, Arkansas, on 11 August, 1942, launched himself on the Chicago scene in 1971: just a few years too late to be part of the '60s scene, and just a few years too early to qualify as part of that scene's revival. A genuine blues veteran – he served time as ALBERT KING's drummer for awhile and claims to have played on the great man's 1968 *Live Wire/Blues Power* album, though the credits say different – he's firmly in the school of A. King and OTIS RUSH, which means he has a big chesty voice, a ferocious, slicing guitar attack, limitless energy and a few good songs. He's about as good as blues journeymen get, which is to say (to paraphrase Robert Christgau) that he has everything that a great bluesman needs except greatness. The hurdle he has yet to clear is that of distinctiveness: that personal something that renders an artist instantly recognisable in a blindfold test. As it is, as soon as you hear him, you know that you're listening to someone good: you're just never quite sure who it is. Over the past twenty-odd years, he's racked up a mere six albums on Alligator, four of which are currently in catalogue. However, he's played more gigs than Roy Hattersley has had hot dinners and, on the evidence of his *Live And Burning* album and the show I saw when he opened for Albert King in London, most of them were probably superb. It's on guys like Son Seals that the blues depend upon for survival: guys who are out there playing the music whether or not it's fashionable at any given moment. If the blues boom goes down, GARY MOORE will probably rediscover his roots in fusion or metal, but Son Seals will still be playing the blues.

- *Midnight Sun* (Alligator ALCD 4708)
- *Live And Burning* (Alligator ALCD 4712)

From the late '70s, not only the definitive Son Seals albums, but definitive examples of evolved West Side blues at its biggest, boldest and brassiest. *Midnight's* first three songs set the agenda: RAY CHARLES' rolling, gospelly 'I Believe (To My Soul)', complete with dramatic stop-time guitar flourishes, is followed by two primo originals, the bass-popping funk of 'No No Baby' and the exuberant shuffle 'Four Full Seasons Of Love'. If you don't argue with *Midnight Son*, you back off and buy the appropriately titled *Live And Burning* (1978) a drink: it pops right out of the box with a snarling, definitive cover of ELMORE JAMES' 'I Can't Hold Out' and follows up with a smouldering, sax-spiced take on Junior Parker's 'Blue Shadows Falling', and the bustling boogaloo 'Funky Bitch'. Through the B.B. KING, LITTLE WALTER and JIMMY REED covers and the sprinkling of originals, this is an all-the-way-classic live blues album which wouldn't disgrace itself in the company of such landmarks as B.B.'s *Live At The Regal* and *Blues Is King*, or Albert K's *Live Wire/Blues Power*. It's not just Son and the band, either: the audience is kickin' from start to finish.

- _Living In The Danger Zone_ (Alligator ALCD 4798)

From 1991, Son Seals' post-ROBERT CRAY album. Any bluesman who expects to survive has to manage a balancing act between sticking to his (or her) guns and moving with the times, and here Son nearly pulls it off. He sounds almost as comfortable against the clean, clipped Memphis-soul groove of the opening 'Frigidaire Woman' – complete with a chorus, wonders never cease – or the hyperdramatic, _Shaft_-era stylings of 'Tell It To Another Fool' and the title track as he does with the trademarked shuffles and slow blues retained elsewhere. 'Danger Zone' itself, like JOE LOUIS WALKER's 'City Of Angels', tells us that today's urban bluesman inhabits the same inner-city turf as the gangsta rapper: he's just not as well adapted to it as an Ice-T or Ice Cube. This is an intriguing album: not as raucously immediate as its '70s predecessors, but to say that it has its moments would be to damn it with faint praise.

Lonnie Brooks

Whether you realise it or not, you've seen Lonnie Brooks innumerable times on prime-time TV: he's the '_That_ ain't the blues!' guy on the front porch in the Heineken commercials. Don't be fooled, though: he's not a country bluesman, but a Louisiana-to-Chicago transplant whose music flirts with Chi-town generica but never quite goes all the way. Brooks' 'bayou lightning' sound still retains distinct traces of country lilt and funk bounce, both appropriate to a veteran of the late-'50s Baton Rouge swamp-blues scene. Brooks got his start gigging with CLIFTON CHENIER's band and – as 'Guitar Junior' – cutting the 1958 swamp-rock landmark 'The Crawl' (as covered by THE FABULOUS THUNDERBIRDS). When he got to Chicago in 1960, he found the place already crawling (sorry!) with 'Guitar Juniors' so, instead of reverting back to his real name of Lee Baker Jr. (under which he was born in Dubuisson, Louisiana, on 18 December, 1933) he opted to become 'Lonnie Brooks'. The new incarnation's music had rather more in common with BUDDY GUY or ALBERT KING than it did with SLIM HARPO or LIGHTNIN' SLIM.

Brooks' subsequent career demonstrates, once again, that

'success' in the blues can be a long haul. He worked continuously throughout the '60s and '70s, cutting the odd session and touring the US with an occasional foray into Europe, but his career didn't really stabilise until 1978, when he contributed four tracks to an Alligator Records anthology and was thus signed to record *Bayou Lightning*, the first in his current catalogue. Since then he's done the rounds, working clubs and festivals and slowly pumping up his sales and concert audiences. Higher on solidity and good humour than either flash or content, Brooks is a hardworking, not ungifted entertainer who gets over on common-man likeability and sheer professionalism. In other words, he's a genuine footsoldier of the blues, one of the career road bluesmen who keeps the music alive until the next crossover superstar comes along, and after.

- *Live From Chicago: Bayou Lightnin' Strikes* (Alligator ALCD 4759)
- *Satisfaction Guaranteed* (Alligator ALCD 4799)

As you might expect, the live album is the one to go for, though there are a few worthwhile tracks on each of his studio albums and this selection of mostly-fresh material recycles only a few of them. Despite the band's occasional lumpiness, Brooks shows why he's still doing good business: he preaches, jives and digs deeper into the slow blues tunes than he does in the studio, winding up with a hellishly fast scamper through Freddie King's 'Hideaway'. However, the current studio album sounds almost as live as the live one. Lonnie's son Ronnie joins him for a guitar/vocal duet on 'Like Father Like Son', Lonnie borrows 'A Little Rock 'N' Roll And Some Country Blues' from country singer John Anderson, and KOKO TAYLOR sits in.

Subjects for further investigation: Prehistory: The 'Guitar Junior' persona takes centre-stage on *The Crawl* (Charly CD BM 1), recorded in Louisiana 1957-9 and including his local hits 'The Crawl' and 'Family Rule': good fun, but watch out for the hits on compilation CDs. *Sweet Home Chicago* (Black & Blue 59.554 2), recorded in Paris in 1975, features Hubert Sumlin on guitar and Fred Below on drums, but it could be just about any bunch of hardened Chicago pros barrelling through an album's worth of standards in a day's worth of studio time.

The 'audition' tracks were on *Living Chicago Blues Vol II* (Alligator ALCD 77002). Of the recent stuff, 1981's **Turn On The Night** (Alligator ALCD 4721) wins for a couple of thoughtful originals, a couple of hip covers (BOBBY 'BLUE' BLAND's 'I'll Take Care Of You' and the JOE TURNER/ELMORE JAMES 'TV Mama') and the exuberant zydeco finale; **Wound Up Tight** (Alligator ALCD 4751) brings on JOHNNY WINTER for a strafing break on the Jerry Lee Lewis-styled 'Got Lucky Last Night', and stays right in your face for much of its duration.

Johnny Copeland

All the way from Houston, Texas, comes one of the most successful bluesmen to emerge between SON SEALS and ROBERT CRAY. Copeland – born in Homer, Louisiana, in 1937 – learned his trade singing soul while chancing his arm as a boxer in Houston's Third Ward (musical cradle to LIGHTNIN' HOPKINS, JOHNNY 'GUITAR' WATSON and ALBERT COLLINS) but launched his current career in Harlem, NYC. Throughout the '80s, he's been selling hi-octane variations on brassy Texas-style blues updating the T-BONE WALKER and CLARENCE 'GATEMOUTH' BROWN tradition; he's toured Africa for the US State Department, and he's got a W.C. Handy Award, a Grand Prix du Disque de Montreaux and a Grammy (shared with Robert Cray and Albert Collins for 1986's *Showdown!*) to show for it. Nevertheless, the mass market remains resolutely uncracked: Copeland's never made a mainstream rock or pop move in his life, and probably wouldn't know how to.

While there's no denying the force and commitment of his big, grainy voice and fleet, spiky guitar, I've always admired his records more than I've enjoyed them. Unlike many other bluesmen of both greater and lesser gifts, his albums tell us more about what he can do than who he is. Maybe the problem lies in his material, which is decidedly routine. However, many authoritative commentators – who have, unlike myself, seen him in concert – disagree vehemently. Feel free to join them.

- *Texas Twister* (Rounder CD 11504)
- *When The Rain Starts Fallin'* (Rounder CD 11515)

Copeland's first four Rounder LPs, currently unavailable as separate CDs, filleted into two hour-plus compilations, the first of which confusingly shares its title and cover art with one of the original albums. *Texas Twister* comes out ahead because of its STEVIE RAY VAUGHAN cameo, and because it quotes the lion's share of Copeland's intriguing 1986 soukous experiment *Bringing It All Back Home*, which took him to the Ivory Coast to blend his blues with the local grooves. The sparkling eight-minute-plus 'Ngote' is probably the most unusual and unexpected pleasure you'll find on any blues album in this book. Major annoyance: *Bringing It All Back Home*'s vinyl incarnation split 'Djeli Djeli Blues' (co-featuring kora man Djeli Mousa) over two sides, and neither of these compilations took the opportunity to join it back up.

Subjects for further investigation: Basic rule: with journeymen, check out the live album, but *Ain't Nothin' But A Party* (Rounder CD 2055), recorded back home in Houston in 1987, unfortunately lives up to its title. It must have been a hell of a party on the night, but it doesn't get over in your living room; its best shot transforms the venerable 'Baby Please Don't Go' into an anguished slow blues. The title track of Copeland's current album, *Boom Boom* (Rounder CD 2060), has absolutely nothing to do with JOHN LEE HOOKER or even LITTLE WALTER, and the album is par for the Copeland course, which means that it's deeply felt, competently performed, and still utterly generic.

Katie Webster

Around the time that JOHNNY COPELAND was making the trek from Louisiana to Texas, Katie Webster was going the other way. Yet another long-serving vet who finally found an opportunity to surface in the '80s, the classically-trained Webster – born September 1, 1939 in Houston, Texas – was adding her rolling, muscular piano to sessions for Excello Records' swamp-blues stars like SLIM HARPO, Lazy Lester and LIGHTNIN' SLIM when she was barely out of her teens. During the '60s, she toured as the opening act in Otis Redding's revue, and the Big O was planning to produce her records before his death in 1967 derailed that project (as well as all the others). Now, as the self-styled Swamp Boogie Queen, she has attitude as well as talent to burn: if you can imagine Millie Jackson, KOKO TAYLOR and Meade Lux Lewis all rolled up into one rough-and-tough, sweet-and-salty ball of pure energy, you're already halfway there.

- *Two-Fisted Mama!* (Alligator ALCD 4777)
- *No Foolin'!* (Alligator ALCD 4803)

Do these live up to their titles? You betcha. Webster alternately pounds and tickles her piano, sings open-throated soul and gospel and talks deep-blues down-in-the-alley trash. Don't worry about guest stars (though you'll find The Memphis Horns on both albums and a LONNIE BROOKS cameo on *No Foolin'!*) or intriguing covers (though she can even make a Mark Knopfler composition sound soulful): just spend some money.

Subjects for further investigation: Despite its hard-sell come-on – reprises of her best Excello-era material (much of it unreleased at the time) like 'Sea Of Love', 'Whoo-Wee Sweet Daddy' and the caustic 'No Bread No Meat'; cameos from ROBERT CRAY, BONNIE RAITT, THE FABULOUS THUNDERBIRDS' Kim Wilson, and The Memphis Horns – Webster's 1988 solo debut *The Swamp Boogie Queen* (Alligator ALCD 4766) wastes rather too much time retreading overrecorded soul standards. Prehistory: the vintage Excello stuff is on *Katie Webster* (Flyright FLYCD 12).

Robert Ward

It is, by now, axiomatic that any 'new blues discovery' should actually be a veteran of many years of dues-paying, but even by these standards Robert Ward, from Georgia, is an extreme case. By the time his major-league debut *Fear No Evil* was released, he had some three decades of experience under his belt. In 1962, he had played guitar on 'I Found A Love', an influential hit by Detroit vocal group The Falcons, which launched a distinguished solo career for their lead singer, Wilson Pickett: later, as a featured performer, he fronted Robert Ward & The Ohio Untouchables. After Ward's departure, the Untouchables metamorphosed into The Ohio Players: one of the most popular of the street-funk bands of the early '70s, equally renowned for slippery, elasticated grooves and elaborate S&M cover art; and Ward himself played on-the-road backup guitar for The Temptations and The Undisputed Truth. After that he seemingly disappeared off the face the earth: his fans – few in number but fanatical in their devotion to his unorthodox finger-style guitar, distinctive amp-tremolo sound and gospelly voice – thought he was either dead, in jail, or fully dedicated to the church.

Not so, as one of those fans – Black Top Records boss Hammond Scott, who had already indulged his taste for brilliant guitar mavericks by recording SNOOKS EAGLIN – found when word reached Ward, who'd gone to ground in Dry Branch, Georgia, that Scott was looking for him, and Ward called Scott. Pausing only to buy an old Magnatone amp (to recreate that original sound), they rushed into the studio to cut *Fear No Evil*, one of the most eclectic and most-praised R&B albums of 1991. Since then, Ward's unique soul/blues/gospel homebrew has been knocking audiences flat: I saw him in Texas in 1992, and I'm ready to testify that he's the real deal. How big a carpet do you need to sweep a talent this large under it, let alone keep it there this long?

- *Fear No Evil* (Silvertone ORE CD 520)
- *Rhythm Of The People* (Black Top CD BT-1088)

Recorded in New Orleans in 1990 with a stellar session crew including the fabulous ex-Meters bassist George Porter Jr, *Fear No Evil* runs the gamut from deep, dirty blues to euphoric gospel soul both sacred and secular. Sometimes the lilting, tremolo-ed guitar recalls Curtis Mayfield or Roebuck 'POPS' STAPLES and the voice evokes a sweeter, less manic Wilson Pickett, but mostly it's all Robert Ward, kicking some flavour you can't find anywhere else. The 1993 sequel buries his guitar under the band rather too often for comfort on the non-blues cuts, so it's probably not the place to start. Best shot: a remake of 'I Found A Love' which offers him the chance, this time around, to be Pickett as well as himself.

Subjects for further investigation: Ward contributes five songs, four of which are on *Fear No Evil*, to **Black Top Blues-A-Rama: Live At Tipitina's** (Black Top CD BT-1089); they're served up at a high enough temperature to induce serious cravings for a full-length live album.

Pops Staples

Speaking of Pops Staples, the patriarch of gospel soul has never let the blues sink too far below the surface of his music, which is why The Staple Singers, the Chicago-based family gospel group he'd helmed since 1950, was easily the funkiest thing in its genre. (Mind you, having Pops' dynamic daughter Mavis Staples as co-lead voice didn't hurt, either.) Roebuck Staples was born in Winona, Mississippi, on 28 December, 1915, and grew up on the Delta's legendary (and notorious) Dockery plantation, literally within earshot of CHARLEY PATTON: if that ain't a blues background I don't know what is. On Vee Jay, Riverside and Epic during the '50s and '60s, the Staple Singers were one of the biggest acts in gospel: two of their songs, 'Stand By Me' and 'This Could Be The Last Time' are better known today for the successful secular derivatives recorded by, respectively, Ben E. King and THE ROLLING STONES. They refused to sing any rock and roll, but supplemented their gospel material with secular message songs: their home-based Baptist church wasn't amused, and ejected them, so they signed to Stax and went secular in earnest, still eschewing the vulgar in favour of the positive and enjoying mainstream hits like 'Respect Yourself' (Bruce Willis – *geddahdavit!*), 'Come Go With me' and 'I'll Take You There'.

In recent years, the Singers' principals, Pops and Mavis, have both diversified: Pops into acting, with appearances in David Byrne's *True Stories* and Jim Jarmusch's Memphis fable *Mystery Train*; and Mavis into the decidedly personal spiritual universe of the man they call Prince. Pops' belated solo venture marks the first real advance in gospel-blues since the death of REV. GARY DAVIS.

- *Peace To The Neighborhood* (PointBlank VPBCD 8)

Material from Jackson Browne ('World In Motion') and Los Lobos (the title song); guest shots and production from Browne, BONNIE RAITT, RY COODER and Pops' soulful offspring notwithstanding, this is no super-session but about as personal a record as you can get. The spotlight rarely leaves Pops' light, insinuating voice and spare, rubbery vibrato guitar; and the agenda is all his, too. There are four gospel pieces: one a rerun of The Staple Singers' '50s hit 'This May Be The Last Time', another, 'Pray On My Child', boasts a scorching lead vocal by Mavis; and another still presents Cooder giving it some serious Blind Willie Johnson on the traditional 'I Shall Not Be Moved'. Elsewhere, he recalls a Delta childhood behind the plough on 'Down In Mississippi' (again with Cooder on board), frets about the state of America (with good reason), comes out in favour of brotherly love and, in 'Miss Cocaine', provides a chilling counterpart to JAMES BROWN's 'King Heroin'.

Subjects for further investigation: The nearest Pops got to a 'solo' album during the group's heyday was something of a curio: 1969's *Jammed Together* (Stax CDSXE 028), a team-up with ALBERT KING and Steve Cropper, consisted mainly of jams but included one perfect gem: Pops' hushed, intimate rendition of JOHN LEE HOOKER's 'Tupelo'. The Staple Singers' early-'70s CV is *Respect Yourself: The Best Of The Staple Singers* (Stax CDSX 006); the '50s Vee Jay stuff is currently uncollected on CD, but you can find a heaping handful of their '62–'64 gospel sides on *Great Day* (Ace CDCHD 391). And, just for the record, you can virtually hear the earth move when Mavis Staples duets with Aretha Franklin on 'Oh Happy Day', included on Aretha's '87 gospel *tour de force* **One Lord, One Faith, One Baptism** (Arista 353 178); if Our Saviour ever encounters these two ladies in a dark alley he'll probably have the best night of his millennium.

Snooky Pryor

Anybody planning to challenge Snooky Prior for the Last Of The Downhome Harp Guys title must *really* be biding his time. This Delta elder statesman – one of the first Electric Downhome bluesmen to record in Chicago after World War II and the self-proclaimed pioneer of the city's amplified harp tradition – had to wait until 1991 for the release of his first custom-built solo album: anyone lurking behind him better make their move *now*. Even in (comparative) old age, there's the hard edge to Pryor's sound that comes from learning one's trade with little or no amplification: both his naturally mellifluous voice and his piercing, squawky harp are pitched to cut through the bustle of a noisy crowd. James Edward Pryor was born in Lambert, Mississippi, on 15 September, 1921, numbering JIMMY ROGERS and JOHN LEE HOOKER amongst his early playmates; learned harmonica despite his father's disapproval and was on the road to Helena, Arkansas, and beyond by the time he was 16. Emerging from the army with, among other skills, some expertise with PA systems, he settled in Chicago and set about establishing himself on the local blues scene.

During the late '40s he worked with many of the top South Side names – BIG BILL BROONZY, MEMPHIS MINNIE and others – but despite cutting a few highly regarded singles, mainly with cousins Floyd Jones and Moody Jones, for smaller labels up to and including Vee Jay, he never grasped Chicago harmonica's brass ring: the MUDDY WATERS harp chair and a deal with Chess. He went into retirement in 1962, resumed active duty in 1970 and has kept going ever since, recently cutting a superb album, *Too Cool To Move*, for the Austin-based Antone's label. Prior (sorry!) to that, his most notable contemporary work was *Back To The Country* (Blind Pig 74391), which teamed him up with JOHNNY SHINES.

- *Too Cool To Move* (Antone's ANTCD 0017)
- *Snooky Pryor* (Flyright FLY CD 20)

Snooky modern and ancient, in that order. The Antone's set was cut over a couple of years during the cusp of the '80s and '90s, shuffling visiting firemen from Chicago (a team of Muddy Waters alumni led by PINETOP PERKINS) with the pick of the Austin blues mafia, and guitarist Duke Robillard – then with THE FABULOUS THUNDERBIRDS – as an honorary Texan. The result is an absolute gem: the music has that blessed combination of loose-limbed relaxation, accidentally-right-on-purpose precision and joyful whomp which distinguishes prime-time South Side from the tourist stuff. This is one of those albums like they don't make any more, except that occasionally they do. Meanwhile, Flyright offer Snooky's early Chicago sides, recorded between 1947 and 'probably early '60s', and they're a minor revelation: Floyd Jones' 'Stockyard Blues', one of the earliest included sides, finds him matching Jones' bleak lyric with a harp solo of extraordinary passion, and his own 'Boogie', cut the following year with only Moody Jones' guitar for back-up, seems simultaneously to anticipate LITTLE WALTER's 'Juke' and to mine the same rhythmic seam as his old marbles opponent John Lee Hooker, while 'Boogie Twist' recorded a decade or so later but unissued until 1963, sounds like 'Juke' from hell. Incidentally, the 'unknown guitar' on 'My Hair Is Turning Gray' sounds remarkably like the young BUDDY GUY.

A.C. Reed

It's open to dispute whether Aaron Corthen 'A.C.' Reed is JIMMY REED's cousin or not, but it's been a while since there's been any argument about his status as one of Chicago's leading tenor saxophonists. Born in Wardell, Missouri, in 1926, his first act on arrival in Chicago in 1942 was to buy a tenor sax; he's been in continuous employment since the late '40s, touring with Willie Mabon, EARL HOOKER, BUDDY GUY & JUNIOR WELLS and, most recently, a lengthy stint with ALBERT COLLINS; plus he's made studio dates with MUDDY WATERS, ERIC CLAPTON, THE ROLLING STONES and BONNIE RAITT. Right now, he's also one of the wittiest singer/songwriters in Chicago, and I can't understand why more people haven't covered his songs. Maybe he's right – he *is* in the wrong business.

- *I'm In The Wrong Business!* (Alligator ALCD 4757)

Yeah, sure: STEVIE RAY VAUGHAN, MAURICE JOHN VAUGHN (no relation) and Bonnie Raitt put in guest shots on this 1987 album, but all you really need to know is that A.C. is singing his own songs, and that Johnny B. Gayden is playing bass. The latter fact tells you that it's as funky as any Chicago blues album has a right to be, and the former that it's much funnier than any Chicago blues album has a right to be. Some might say that A.C. doesn't have much of a voice, but he writes fabulous lyrics (for documentary evidence check out 'These Blues Is Killing Me', 'Fast Food Annie' or the title track), has more than enough attitude to put them over, and knows how to run a band that can get his attitude *and* his lyrics over. And if none of that works, he can just blow his sax.

Elvin Bishop

The early '60s blues boom was so long ago now that even some of the white guys have been playing the music for thirty-odd years. Singer/guitarist Elvin Bishop, born in Tulsa, Oklahoma, on 21 October, 1942) was one of the original members of The PAUL BUTTERFIELD Blues Band, which he joined while a student at the University of Chicago, but sharing a band with a vocalist like Butterfield and a guitarist like MIKE BLOOMFIELD (the latter hired at record company behest just before the sessions for their first album) left him with little to do but play rhythm guitar. In 1969, he left Butterfield, relocated to San Francisco and, under the guidance of entrepreneur Bill Graham, relaunched himself with an act which owed as much to his midwestern farmboy youth as it did to his apprenticeship in the South Side taverns.

In the Butterfield band, Bishop's nickname had been 'Pigboy Crabshaw': their third album, on which Bishop moved back to the lead guitar chair from which Bloomfield had displaced him, was even titled *The Resurrection Of Pigboy Crabshaw*. It was 'Crabshaw', the beer-drinkin', gone-fishin', pickup-drivin' good-ol'-boy, who dominated his solo music. The effect of Bishop's raucously bucolic mixture of blues, country rock and funk was something like a less academic RY COODER with a few drinks down him: Bishop's voice is no more prepossessing than Cooder's and his slide touch decidedly rougher, but all he's selling is the notion that there's *always* a party in Elvin's barn. Thanks to guest vocalist Mickey Thomas – subsequently embroiled in the gibbering hideousness that was Jefferson Starship – he had a 1975 Top 10 hit with 'Fooled Around And Fell In Love', but he spent most of the '80s on an extended studio vacation broken only by 1988's *Big Fun*. He's still playing

Crabshaw to the hilt, but these days Crabshaw plays pretty much strictly blues. For fun, of course.

- *Big Fun* (Alligator ALCD 4767)
- *Don't Let The Bossman Get You Down* (Alligator ALCD 4791)

The first time I heard *Big Fun*, it lived right up to its title. The second time, Elvin seemed excessively laid-back and the band excessively pushy. It has its moments, notably the yee-haw classics 'My Dog' and 'Gone Fishin'', and a lovely reading of JIMMY REED's 'Honest I Do', but 1991's *Bossman* is the one that hits the spot: Elvin works a little harder and the band ease up accordingly. You get a gorgeous slide instrumental ('Devil's Slide'), a rap over an itchy-twitchy Meters-style groove ('You Got To Rock 'Em'), a couple of crowd-pleasing good-ol'-boy monologues ('Rollin' With My Blues' and 'My Whisky Head Buddies'), a straight-up JUNIOR WELLS slowie ('Come On In This House') and plenty of blasting slide-and-horns shuffles. Bigger fun than *Big Fun*. You can also find Bishop, incidentally, strutting the proverbial stuff on *The Alligator Records 20th Anniversary Tour* (Alligator ALCD 107/108), with LONNIE BROOKS, KOKO TAYLOR, KATIE WEBSTER and LI'L ED & THE BLUES IMPERIALS as his travelling companions.

Roy Buchanan

A revealing Roy Buchanan anecdote: during the sessions for his first (and greatest) Alligator album *When A Guitar Plays The Blues*, one of the other musicians asked him how such a quiet, laid-back gent could play such nakedly emotional guitar. Buchanan replied 'But I'm screaming inside'. A second revealing Buchanan anecdote: when THE ROLLING STONES were attempting to replace Mick Taylor in 1975, Buchanan – then known as 'The Greatest Unknown Guitarist In The World' – was one of the players invited to audition. He declined on the grounds that he couldn't be bothered to learn their material. Born in Ozark, Tennessee, on 23 September, 1939, Buchanan was the son of a Pentecostal preacher, a teenage rockabilly fanatic who was on the road and in studios before he was out of his teens. By the early '60s, he'd settled down as the bar-band king of Washington DC, conjuring a huge palette of sounds from the humble Fender Telecaster guitar which was his trademark and, in the process, building an awesome reputation with his free-flowing blend of blues, country and jazz.

The buzz got started in the early '70s, and he was snapped up by Polydor Records, who decided that his reputation, rather than his music, was the commodity they wanted to sell. The label persistently shoehorned Buchanan into inappropriate contexts of their, rather than his, choosing, and the result was a series of records that depressed Buchanan sufficiently for him swear an oath of recording abstinence. It wasn't until 1985, when he signed to Alligator and decided to dig deep into the blues, that he was permitted to call the shots on his own sessions and make records that he actually liked. He later described *When A Guitar Plays The Blues*, his Alligator debut, as his 'first record'.

Buchanan was a complex man, battling both his Pentecostal upbringing and his alcoholism. He was on the wagon when he cut *Guitar*, though not during the sessions for its two sequels, and he was theoretically 'dry' when he died under mysterious circumstances on the night of 14 August, 1988. Picked up by the Virginia police on a drunk-in-public charge, he was dumped into the Fairfax County slammer and was found hanged in his cell later the same night, dying in an ambulance *en route* to the hospital. The police claimed that he'd hanged himself (possibly as an act of repentence for having fallen off the wagon); his wife and friends indignantly disputed this, counter-claiming that it was both physically impossible and psychologically improbable for him to have done so. Until such time as there is a full-scale investigation (a prospect which, at this late date, seems fairly unlikely) we'll have to concentrate on his life, and the music he made, rather than his death. Which is probably the way he'd've wanted it.

● *When A Guitar Plays The Blues* (Alligator ALCD 4741)

To date, there isn't anything specifically designated as a 'Roy Buchanan Memorial Album', so this – his 1985 Alligator debut – will have to do. The title track, basically an instrumental with commentary, is as good an explanation as any of what playing an instrument means to a person who doesn't sing but who needs to express themselves; and also of what the blues meant to Buchanan himself. You'll not only be floored by the technique, but also by the emotional revelation that makes that technique so much more than mere stuntwork. This is radical blues with the emphasis placed as firmly on 'blues' as on 'radical'. The guest vocalists include Chicago soulman Otis Clay and blues diva Gloria Hardiman, but the real singing on this album comes from Buchanan's guitar: this is as tough a blues guitar album as anybody cut in the '80s, including any Vaughans, Crays, Collinses, Guys and Kings you care to name.

Subjects for further investigation: Maybe it's because Buchanan was back on the juice when he recorded the sequels *Dancing On The Edge* (Alligator ALCD 4742) and the fractionally superior *Hot Wires* (Alligator ALCD 4756), but much of both albums falls into the trap so neatly and soulfully avoided on *When A Guitar Plays The Blues*, supplanting the overwhelming with the merely overbearing. The only guitarist Buchanan acknowledged as a rival, let alone a peer, in the mutant-bluesbilly Telecaster league was Danny Gatton, whose *88 Elmira Street* (Elektra 7559-61032-2)is a better companion piece to *When A Guitar* than either of Buchanan's own followups.

Rory Gallagher

Talk about roots: JOHNNY WINTER's separated-at-birth Irish twin was playing blues on a beat-up Stratocaster when STEVIE RAY VAUGHAN's was still hanging in the shop window, as well as wearing check shirts while Nirvana were still in nappies. With a bull-roar voice and a guitar style that adapts equally well to overamped Strat and steel-bodied National, he's a career blues-rocker who demonstrates as well as anybody the extent to which blues-rockers with taste ended up closer to blues than rock. Born in Ballyshannon, County Donegal, on 2 March, 1949, he emerged from the Cork showband scene to lead Taste, a bluesy, working-man's-Cream power trio which made a medium-sized impact during the late '60s, and finally went solo in 1971. His roots were in country blues and Celtic folk, but – as is an occupational hazard with trios – much of his '70s music was sufficiently overwrought to topple over into arena-rock. In the '80s his work mellowed enough to let the blues rise to the surface again, plus his songwriting improved considerably. Gallagher's current work boasts a neat line in back-alley urban-*noir* lyrics and the awareness of light and shade which his paste-'em-against-the-back-wall early material lacked. Rock guys tend to go off as they get older: bluesmen get better. It's one of the ways you tell 'em apart.

- *Irish Tour '74* (Demon FIEND CD 120)
- *Edged In Blue* (Demon FIEND CD 719)

The live album captures the manic, showboating extroversion of the early solo years in all its hi-energy nothing-exceeds-like-excess glory, complete with MUDDY WATERS and J.B. Hutto covers nestling amidst the originals; if you like your blues-rock seriously cranked, this has your name on it. *Edged In Blue* is the Gallagher career best-of for blues fans, and it's a honey: originals like 'Calling Card', 'Brute Force And Ignorance' and 'Loanshark Blues' demonstrate how well he's learned his lessons; his brooding JOHN LEE HOOKER-styled version of JUNIOR WELLS' 'I Could Have Had Religion' shows how far down-home he can take it when he's in the mood, and his take on SONNY BOY WILLIAMSON's 'Don't Start me Talkin'' proves that he can still remember where to find '10' on his amplifier. It also quotes the *Irish Tour '74* version of Muddy's 'I Wonder Who', in case you were worried. And the acoustic 'Seven Days' pays off his debts to Bert Jansch and SON HOUSE in one shot.

Wilko Johnson

The founding guitarist and songwriter of DR FEELGOOD is still the most original blues-based British guitar stylist to have emerged in the past two decades: if he's not a big star today, it's probably equally attributable to his decidedly-an-acquired-taste voice, and his penchant for quarreling with record company bosses. Solo since 1977, he's kept going by sheer roadwork, Feelgoods royalties and the occasional indie release. His sharp, witty songwriting, idiosyncratic taste in covers and one-of-a-kind Telecastering still provide one of the most distinctive pleasures of the UK R&B circuit, partially because Johnson has continued to refine his craft, if not his singing; and partly because, in bassist Norman Watt-Roy and drummer Salvatore Ramundo, he has his best-ever post-Feelgoods rhythm section. Wilko is unique amongst British R&B guys for his resolute refusal to sing, play or write as anybody other than himself. In my book, that makes him 'authentic' in a real sense, which is to say in the only sense that counts.

- *Ice On The Motorway* (Hound Dog BUT CD 001)
- *Barbed Wire Blues* (Jungle CD FREUD 26)
- *Don't Let Your Daddy Know* (Bedrock BED CD 21)

Respectively, a reissue-with-remixes of his second late-'70s solo album, including his totally-out-of-order live version of SCREAMIN' JAY HAWKINS' already-severely-disturbed 'The Whammy' (it's worth buying just to hear Wilko's quavering yell of 'My mind's in *noo*-tral!'); his most recent studio album, including several killer originals, and harmonica from someone not unadjacent to the author; and a live work-out which restores several Feelgoods-era originals to the composer's canon. The 13-minute-plus title track of the latter is probably the finest extant showcase for his considerable vocabulary of blues chops, as well as for the contrast between the deadly assurance of said chops and his wobbly Essex-geezer voice.

Joe Louis Walker

If any of the neo-trad blues stars-in-waiting qualifies as a genuine modern classic on legs, it's Joe Louis Walker, a nudging-forty Bay Area bluesman from the same writing/producing team which launched ROBERT CRAY. That connection aside, Walker has more in common with a traditional post-West-Side bluesman like SON SEALS than with his erstwhile stablemate: he not only lacks Cray's disciplined popcraft and emotional complexity, but also Young Bob's mistrust of pleasure and release. What he doesn't lack is blues power aplenty: voice and guitar alike display a rich, grainy depth unmatched by any of his contemporaries. He's got a distinct agenda, too: loves God, doesn't like preachers much; loves women, doesn't like his girlfriend much.

He made his studio debut in 1986 after sending a demo to Dennis Walker and Bruce Bromberg at Hightone Records; the first result was the impressive *Cold Is The Night* (Ace CDCHM 208), and he's been a very welcome addition to the circuit ever since. On the basis of current performance, JLW doesn't have a pop move in him, but watch out for his remorseless rise up the blues ladder over the next couple of decades. By the time he's of pensionable age, he'll probably be one of the top two or three blues singers in the world, and you might even find a few people to opine that he already qualifies as such.

- *The Gift* (Ace CDCH 241)
- *Live At Slims Vol 2* (Demon FIEND CD 716)

What did I tell you about going for the live album? Walker's in-person effort, and its predecessor, *Live At Slims Vol 1* (Demon FIEND CD 212), were drawn from the same late-'90 show, and all I can say is that it must've been a hell of a night. One aspect of Walker's gifts (no pun intended) is showcased to perfection on *Slims Vol 2* – and only slightly less well on *Slims Vol 1* – and it's the most extrovert and conventional aspect. This is an absolute state-of-the-art example of classy live blues, 1990-style, but it omits an awful lot of what makes Walker more than simply an ultra-competent generic bluesman, which is why you need the intimate, gospelly *The Gift*. JLW's other studio albums, *Cold Is The Night* and his latest, *Blue Soul* (Demon FIEND CD 159), also have their considerable merits: in fact, his finest studio achievements are *The Gift's* title track, and *Blue Soul's* 'City Of Angels'; the latter, which thoroughly deserves its frequently-anthologised status, proves that his L.A. is definitely the same town as Ice-T's. If you don't want to spring for *Blue Soul*, you can pick up 'City Of Angels' either on *Blue Demons* (Demon FIEND CD 714), alongside cool stuff by DR JOHN, JOHN HAMMOND, JOHN LEE HOOKER, PROFESSOR LONGHAIR, OTIS RUSH, RORY GALLAGHER, SNOOKS EAGLIN *et al*, or on *The Blues Guitar Box* (Sequel TBB CD 47555), a guitar glutton's blues blowout if I ever did see one.

Subjects for further investigation: This is as good an opportunity as any for a shout-out in favour of a few other good citizens and straight shooters of the blues: Phillip Walker (no relation) was an early client of Bruce Bromberg's Joliet Records, and *The Bottom Of The Top/Blues* (Demon FIEND CD 158) emphasises the fact by bringing together, on a single CD, an album he cut for Bromberg in 1971, and a long-delayed '88 sequel produced by Bromberg and Dennis Walker (also no relation). Interestingly enough, it includes a version of 'Don't Be Afraid Of The Dark' (yes, the Robert Cray title-track) also featuring The Memphis Horns. Fenton Robinson displays considerable songwriting chops, a heated, downhome vocal style and a cool, jazzy guitar on *I Hear Some Blues Downstairs* (Alligator ALCD 4710), with jumping funk beats and sophisticated horn lines to match.

Then there's Chicago stalwart Jimmy Johnson: he sings good, he plays good, he's even more cynical about the music business (and the blues biz in particular) than he is about relationships. *Johnson's Whacks* (Delmark DD-664) contains at least three songs which ought to have become standards; chief among which is 'Strange How How I Miss You (When I Haven't Even Lost You Yet)'. Apart from the odd strand of grey in his beard, New Orleans guitar guru Walter 'Wolfman' Washington – LIGHTNIN' SLIM's nephew, for what it's worth – doesn't look old enough to have played on Lee Dorsey's '65 cult classic 'Ride Your Pony', but I'm assured that he did. He plays a mean guitar, for sure, but his real strength is in his voice: this man is the missing link between Albert King and Isaac Hayes. You believe that? You will. At his best, he delivers cinerama-scaled blues melodrama in a late-Albert-King-at Stax bag: the earliest Wolfman Washington you can find is 1981's *Get On Up* (Charly CD BM 9), and the most recent is the rather disappointing *Sada* (PointBlank VPBCD 4), but the way to go is via *Wolf Tracks* (Rounder CD 2048), *Out Of The Dark* (Rounder CD 2068) and *Wolf At The Door* (Rounder CD 2098).

Other cool guys playing blues you can definitely use include Byther Smith, with *I'm A Mad Man* (Bullseye Blues CD BB 9527); Georgie Fame, with *The Blues And Me* (Go Jazz vBr 2104 2); Larry Davis, with *Sooner Or Later* (Bullseye Blues CD BB 9511); Robben Ford, with *Robben Ford & The Blue Line* (Stretch/GRP GRS 11022); Jay Owens, with *The Blues Soul Of Jay Owens* (Indigo IGO CD 2004); the late Zuzu Bollins with *Texas Bluesman* (Antone's

ANTCD 0018), and James 'Thunderbird' Davis who, unfortunately, barely had time to record *Check Out Time* (Demon
FIENDCD 149) before he – you guessed – checked out.

3. Post-Vaughanism: Texas and Elsewhere

As you've probably noticed unless you're reading this book from
the back, Texas blues has a long and honourable tradition: BLIND
LEMON JEFFERSON, T-BONE WALKER, CLARENCE 'GATEMOUTH' BROWN,
JOHNNY 'GUITAR' WATSON, ALBERT COLLINS, JOHNNY WINTER and more. In
the 1980s, though, Texas blues was redefined by two Dallas-born,
Austin-bred brothers: THE FABULOUS THUNDERBIRDS' Jimmie
Vaughan and his fiery younger sib, STEVIE RAY VAUGHAN. The two
archetypes thus represented – T-Birds-style 4-piece combos
fronted by jivey singer/harpists and taut, mean guitarists; and
post-Stevie take-it-tothe-limit guitar-stranglers – have spread the
modern Lone Star State blues ethos, with Cliff Antone's Austin
club as its epicentre, far beyond the state line.

However, it's worth remembering that (a) contemporary Texas
blues comes in flavours other than those favoured by Vaughan
Major and Minor, and (b) that, while the success of Stevie Ray and
the T-Birds created a commercial context in which likeminded
artists could function, these folks should not be considered as
imitators so much as fellow participants in the tradition. Our first
contestant, in fact, used to share a group with Stevie Ray
Vaughan . . .

Lou Ann Barton

. . . but, as noted elsewhere, it just wasn't big enough for both of
them. Lou Ann Barton, originally from Fort Worth, is the Texas
Bad Girl Supreme: to hear her sing like a Wanda Jackson from hell,
or to see her flick a lit cigarette away – without looking to see
where it's going – just before she steps on stage is to witness True

Style in action. She sang with early line-ups of Roomful Of Blues and THE FABULOUS THUNDERBIRDS, and the Triple Threat Revue, which she and STEVIE RAY VAUGHAN co-fronted in the '70s, splintered after a memorable occasion on which the entire band drove all the way from Austin to New York City and back (if you're not impressed, check out a map sometime) to play a $100 gig. At the end of the night, so the story goes, Lou Ann became seriously annoyed with waitresses who refused to serve her any more drinks, and began pitching glasses at them and introducing them to some of the finer points of Texan invective. So much for the Triple Threat Revue. She made a couple of previous solo albums during the '80s – *Old Enough* (Asylum, 1982) and *Forbidden Tones* (Spindletop, 1986) – but they're long-deleted. The day she cuts a follow-up to 1989's brilliant *Read My Lips*, I'll be waiting in line.

- *Read My Lips* (Antone's ANTCD 0009)

This is a wonderful album, and why its reputation never spread far beyond the Austin city limits is just one of those great mysteries of life, like where socks go in the dryer and why the Tories keep getting elected. The repertoire stretches from the patented Austin-style bayou moves (like SLIM HARPO's 'Te-Ni-Nee-Ni-Nu' and a slow, belly-rubbing 'Shake Your Hips', and a whomping take on Lazy Lester's 'Sugar Coated Love') to the Wanda Jacksonesque rockabilly retreads ('Mean Mean Man' and 'Let's Have A Party', on which she sounds like the missing link between MEMPHIS MINNIE and Minnie The Minx), plus a few soul ballads and some deep blues; some B.B. KING, a little JIMMY REED and even some Joe Cocker. The backup is provided by a veritable Austin Who's Who: naturally, the T-birds contingent (Jimmie Vaughan and Kim Wilson) are right up front, but so are lesser-known but equally respected Antonites like drummer George Rains, organist Reese Wynans and guitarists Denny Freeman and Derek O'Brien. This is about as good a contemporary blues album as you can expect from a white woman these days. Recommended!

- **MARCIA BALL, LOU ANN BARTON & ANGELA STREHLI:**
  Dreams Come True (Antone's ANTCD 0014)

Theoretically, this team-up between Austin's three R&B divas and producer Mac 'DR JOHN' Rebennack should have been exactly what the title suggests. Instead, it proves that putting three lead singers together doth not necessarily a vocal group make. Despite its great cast – Dr John himself, guitarist Derek O'Brien, drummer George Rains and bassist/polymath Sarah Brown – and its great moments – particularly when it dips into the IKE & Tina TURNER songbook for 'A Fool In Love' and 'I Idolise You', or when Barton rips her way through Brown's 'Bad Thing' – it's considerably less than the sum of its parts. Better value is the oddly-titled compilation *Antone's Women: Bringing You The Best In Blues* (Antone's ANT 9902), which samples *Dreams* plus Barton's *Read My Lips*, Strehli's *Soul Shake* (Antone's ANT CD 0006), SUE FOLEY's *Young Girl Blues* (Antone's ANT CD 0019) and potentially mouth-watering albums by Lavelle White and Barbara Lynn which don't seem to have surfaced yet. 'Long Tall Marcia Ball' – six foot one of booty-twitching bayou piano and sassy, full-throated vocals – can be heard stage-centre, not so much cutting the mustard as vaporising it, on *Soulful Dress* (Rounder CD 3078), *Hot Tamale Baby* (Rounder CD 3095) and *Gatorhythms* (Rounder CD 3101).

Sue Foley

As noted elsewhere, the contemporary blues scene is packed to bursting with white guys who are (in descending order of ability) guitarists, singers and songwriters. Now here's a woman who matches those specifications exactly: the good news is that Sue Foley, a twenty-something Canadian transplant to Austin, is still – unlike most of her thirty-or-forty-something male competitors – young enough to have plenty of time to bring her singing and composing up to the exalted level of her axepersonship. And can she play? Yes, *ma'am*.

- *Young Girl Blues* (Antone's ANT CD 0019)

Aided by Austin stalwarts including keybman Reese Wynans (from STEVIE RAY VAUGHAN & DOUBLE TROUBLE) and Kim Wilson (from THE FABULOUS THUNDERBIRDS), Foley lets her pink paisley Telecaster off the leash for some serious friskiness. She sings MEMPHIS MINNIE, TAMPA RED, SLIM HARPO and LIGHTNIN' SLIM (the latter pair apparently compulsory in Austin), and plays EARL HOOKER and IKE TURNER. The instrumentals come off best, not because Foley has an inadequate voice, but because she has yet to figure out what to do with the adequate voice she's already got. Which is not a problem for Chicago's dazzling Joanna Connor, who's a few years older and has that much more experience under her belt. Connor's sensational version of Aretha Franklin's 'Doctor Feelgood', included on *(Almost) Everybody Slides* (Sky Ranch SR 652301), is as well sung as it's played – which is considerable – and it's whetted my appetite for an eventual CD release of her Blind Pig album *Believe It*.

Omar & The Howlers

Kent 'Omar' Dykes, Austin-based but originally from BO DIDDLEY's hometown of McComb, Mississippi, is what they call a maverick. A big, bearded, black-clad hulk with a Strat and a cowboy hat, he has one of those growly hurricane-filtered-through-a-letterbox voices which recalls HOWLIN' WOLF or Captain Beefheart; in fact, the first thing you notice about him is how much he sounds like Howlin' Wolf. (Unfortunately, the second thing you notice is that he *isn't* Howlin' Wolf.) Unlike most of his contemporaries, he trades on his voice, rather than his guitar; if he didn't sing so distinctively, his clean, strong, deceptively rough-hewn playing would probably rate more compliments. Apart from Wolf and Diddley, Omar's most readily discernible influence would seem to be John Fogerty: many of his non-blues originals evoke the West Coast bayou choogle of Creedence Clearwater Revival's late-'60s hits. Omar seemingly spends his whole life on the road or in studios; and only at your peril should he be confused with the UK soulman of the same name. In the wake of the STEVIE RAY VAUGHAN/ FABULOUS THUNDERBIRDS Austin blues-rock explosion, he got a major-label shot via CBS/Epic, who released his *Hard Times In The*

Land Of Plenty; naturally, it didn't last long. Omar & The Howlers are probably playing on a continent near you right now; if they're not, have a beer, wait ten minutes and they'll probably show up.

● *Live At Paradiso* (Provogue PRD 70352)

The Live Album Rule proved once again: Omar fillets his repertoire for his catchiest tunes and delivers them at maximum impact. This is export-strength Austin blues-bar showboating; comparatively few younger bluesman, black or white, could get away with hokum like 'Mississippi Hoodoo Man'. In front of a crowd of Dutch hippies who hail Omar like a conquering hero, great early songs like 'Border Girl' and 'Magic Man' are rescued from the dustbin of history, and good new ones like 'Hard Times In The Land Of Plenty' salvaged from disappointing studio albums. Nothing you haven't heard before, but a few things you might want to hear again sopmetime. Re his other albums, the mainly solo and partly acoustic *Blues Bag* (Provogue PRD 70282) has its moments, but rather too few: not only is Omar not JOHN HAMMOND, but even John Hammond isn't SON HOUSE. The highlight of *Monkey Land* (Provogue PRD 70132) is The Beatles' 'She's A Woman' served up *a la* Wolf, and his latest *Courts Of Lulu* (Provogue PRD 70452) has, in 'Firewalker', Omar's best Fogerty pastiche so far.

Little Charlie & The Nightcats

This jivey Bay Area quartet – the absolute state-of-the-art in contemporary white club blues – is constructed on the basic T-Bird chassis, but the standard formula has been customised with a decidedly personal stamp. 'Little Charlie' is guitarist Charlie Baty, who salts his blues with bop and 'billy touches which display as much affinity with ROY BUCHANAN or Danny Gatton as with the Vaughans, but The Nightcats' frontman is Rick Estrin, whose extrovert presence, witty originals and blasting harp seem to be beamed in from a parallel universe where LITTLE WALTER was a member of The Coasters. At the very least, Estrin rolls J. GEILS BAND vocalist Peter Wolf and harpist Magic Dick into one rail-thin, baggy-suited hustler/clown. Baty and Estrin have been playing together since the mid-'70s, and had earned an enviable home-state reputation as a Grade-A live band, but they only managed to fight their way out of California when Alligator signed Little Charlie & The Nightcats in 1987. The resulting album, *All The Way Crazy*, put them over first nationally and then internationally: their combination of cartoony humour, hepcat authenticity, crowdpleasing showmanship and solid musicality makes them the most impressive – not to mention the most fun – of all the wouldbe successors to THE FABULOUS THUNDERBIRDS' crown. You can also add 'self-promotional smarts' to that list of attributes: the covers of their first three albums even tell a little story. On *All The Way Crazy* (Alligator ALCD 4753), we see the band having an impromptu party in the home of a stuffy upper-middle-class couple; by the time of *Disturbing The Peace* (Alligator ALCD 4761), they've been arrested and are pleading with cops at the precinct house. Clearly, the grovelling tactic failed, and on *The Big Break* (Alligator ALCD 4776)we find them in prison garb – naturally, Estrin's suit is baggy and double-breasted – on the lam from the Big House. The saga has been suspended on subsequent albums; I, for one, wish to register a formal complaint.

● *Captured Live* (Alligator ALCD 4794)

You guessed it: go for the live album. The other albums are all perfectly fine, and the best of the early repertoire is, not surprisingly, on *All The Way Crazy*, but here's where they bring it all on home for a big-fun, party-hearty blues bash. Estrin gets a satisfying harp and vocal workout on an almost solo version of JOHN LEE HOOKER's 'Crawling King Snake'; Batey plays eloquent tribute to BUDDY GUY on an almost-but-not-quite-too long 'Ten Years Ago' and gets to show off his bebop-blues stuff on 'Run Me Down'. However, the archetypal LC&N is found on the epigram-matic jump-based novelties like 'Dump That Chump' and 'Smart Like Einstein', which showcase not only the front guys' talents, but the ensemble punch which drives their particular bluesmobile.

- *Night Vision* (Alligator ALCD 4812)

In which LC&N move to Phase II and grapple with the science of record-making, as opposed to simply documenting their live show in the studio. Produced by JOE LOUIS WALKER, *Night Vision* expands their jumpin' jive with an ominous undertow, and the tight sparseness of the basic line-up with an augmented sound including keyboards, horns and (occasionally) the producer's guitar. The opener 'My Next Ex-Wife' gives you an idea of what ROBERT CRAY might create if he ever allowed his sense of humour into the studio. Despite the band's name, this is Estrin's show nearly all the way: he wrote or co-wrote all the material, and under Walker's guidance, his persona becomes less cartoony and more rounded. *Night Vision* isn't as immediately entertaining as its predecessors, but it's ultimately more satisfying, plus it provides the band with an alternative to spending the next few years driving their schtick into the ground.

Subjects for further investigation: While we're harpin' on it, let's consider some more recent arrivals: Mick Jagger liked the New York-based quintet The Red Devils enough to take them into the studio to cut an album's worth of blues standards, but not quite enough to release the results. Their own album *King King* (This Way Up 514 492-2), recorded live at the L.A. venue of the same name, is gritty '50s Chicago revivalism at its most fundamentalist; Lester Butler's vocals are almost as distorted as his harp. Produced by Rick Rubin for his Def American label, you could just about mistake this for a bunch of Little Walter or HOWLIN' WOLF records if you heard it through a wall. Bearing in mind that this is some kind of achievement, the fact remains that – unless you've seen the band live and fancy a souvenir – you might as well have the Walter or Wolf sides. Another reason for Höhner stockholders to be cheerful is hardworking L.A. journeyman William Clarke, a honker to be reckoned with – at the very least you'd believe that PAUL BUTTERFIELD had returned from the grave – but on the evidence of *Serious Intentions* (Alligator ALCD 4806), while he could certainly give a good account of himself in a harp battle with Rick Estrin, his songwriting is comparatively undistinguished, and he lacks Estrin's vocal charisma and distinctive persona. Plus

417

he pisses me off by allowing his overdubbed vocal and harp tracks to overlap. Wait for the live album.

Tinsley Ellis

There's no shortage of contenders for STEVIE RAY VAUGHAN's still-vacant throne, but Tinsley Ellis – born in Florida and operating out of Atlanta, Georgia – is apparently one of the more convincing. He's been fronting his group The Heartfixers for over a decade, first as lead guitarist alongside singer Bob Nelson, and then as vocalist; they first attracted attention outside their manor by backing cult jumper Nappy Brown on 1984's *Tore Up* (Alligator ALCD 4792), following up two years later with the big, brassy and blustering *Cool On It* (Alligator ALCD 3905), originally released on the local Landslide label. It demonstrated both hip choice in covers – BO DIDDLEY's 'Hong Kong Mississippi', CHUCK BERRY's 'Tulane' and the title song's MAGIC SAM rip, anybody? – and the punchy, extrovert attack which earned Ellis his considerable regional prominence. The three solo albums he's cut since signing with Alligator in 1988 are distinctly and defiantly Southwestern in flavour: Ellis ranges all the way from contemporary brass-backed funk-blues in a post-ALBERT KING style instantly recognisable to fans of SON SEALS and JOE LOUIS WALKER through T-BONE WALKER and CLARENCE 'GATEMOUGH' BROWN-ish jump-guitar novelties all the way to full-bore guitar-strangling reminiscent of SRV or JOHNNY WINTER. Sad to say, none of them match the reputation built up by his allegedly spectacular live shows. If the songwriting was as good as the singing – or if either or, better still, both were as good as the guitar-playing – Ellis would be a major performer. As it is, he's simply a good one with a lot of growing to do.

- *Trouble Time* (Alligator ALCD 4805)

The most recent, and best, of Ellis' three 'solo' albums – the others, incidentally, are *Georgia Blue* (Alligator ALCD 4765) and *Fanning The Flames* (Alligator ALCD 4778) – dispenses with the horns on all but one cut, and, with the chunky rhythm and squiddly wah-wah of the intro to 'Highwayman', dives straight into the Stevie Ray gap before it's eight bars old. Slow blues, funk blues, rockers and ballads add up to a spirited, if one-dimensional, performance which cooks up a fair head of steam, but doesn't leave an awful lot behind once the sweat dries. R.E.M. fans will note the presence of Peter Buck lending some rhythm guitar to 'Sign Of The Blues'. Where's the live album?

Bobby Radcliff

Various factors distinguish Bobby Radcliff – born in Bethesda, Maryland, in 1950 – from the rest of the plays-great-sings-okay-can't-write-for-toffee whiteboy pack. There's the combination of manic guitar and distinctive cawing voice with encyclopaedic lickology and sledgehammer delivery which raised the inevitable compasions with STEVIE RAY VAUGHAN, but there's also the love for '70s funk which led him to end his first album with Kool & The Gang's self-titled signature tune. Like most of his contemporaries, he's more an interpreter than a songwriter, but unlike most of 'em he's a resourceful enough interpreter for that to be no problem at all. Radcliff draws on the standard received vocabulary of modern blues guitar – the howling ALBERT KING two-string bend, the ALBERT COLLINS slice'n screech, the BUDDY GUY skitter – but he's no mere chameleon: each impeccably-executed quote comes with its own ironic snap. His thinnish voice is, surprisingly, equally adaptable: he can sing many people's styles without disappearing into them.

Radcliff learned his stuff first-hand on the West Side of Chicago before he was out of his teens. Just as the young Bob Dylan made a pilgrimage to the bedside of the ailing Woody Guthrie, Radcliff began his blues apprenticeship by running away from home to seek out the then-hospitalised MAGIC SAM, who took Bobby under his wing and gave him an insider's tour of the West Side clubs. He's spent most of the '70s and '80s refining his formidable craft and making terrible career decisions, but after making his first real album in 1988 he's been steadily rising up the blues ladder and – for my money – he's as far above the post-SRV pack as LITTLE CHARLIE & THE NIGHTCATS are above all the mini-FABULOUS THUNDER-BIRDS. His tributes – like the infamous 'Kool And The Gang' from *Dresses Too Short* and 'Animators' Convention', the delightful

Albert Collins pastiche on *Universal Blues* – are as wittily insightful as they are viscerally exciting, demonstrating that Radcliff is capable of bringing something of his own to *anybody's* party. Neither his repertoire nor his devices are strictly his own: where you find what is distinctively Bobby Radcliff's is the angle from which he views his sources, the fresh variations that he mines from familiar material, and the sheer exuberance with which he expresses his love for mentors and inspirations ranging from JAMES BROWN and The Bar-Kays to Roy Milton. Just another Stevie-come-lately . . . *NOT!*

- *Dresses Too Short* (Black Top CD BT 1048)
- *Universal Blues* (Black Top CD BT 1067)

And this is where you check him out. Both these albums sparkle all the way through, and each one has stuff that you'll want to hear again: it just so happens that *Universal Blues* (1991) has fractionally more moments to treasure than *Dresses Too Short* (1988). The latter ain't chopped liver, though: most white blues guys are diminished when you spot the swipes, but Radcliff invites you to share the joke every time you greet another old friend. 'Kool And The Gang' is priceless, as are the doffs of the hat to B.B. KING, Buddy Guy, and, basically, everybody who's ever recorded a noteworthy lick. Radcliff's heard 'em all, and he knows where the good stuff is. As the liner note points out, the former's title refers equally to the inclusion of the JUNIOR WELLS/EARL HOOKER adaptation 'Universal Rock', and to the fact that Radcliff plays, or alludes to, just about every school of electric-guitar blues there is. Actually, I'm exaggerating, because Radcliff rarely ventures further south than the West Side of Chicago. In other words, he doesn't play any slide, and he stays well away from the Delta-gone-to-big-town stomp tradition of MUDDY WATERS and JOHN LEE HOOKER but, on the other hand, he manages to hit most styles west of the South Side smack on the button. He starts with B.T. Express's 'Express Yourself', ends with ELVIS PRESLEY's 'Devil In Disguise', and manages to check in with Buddy Guy, The Bar-Kays, James Brown and ROY MILTON along the way. When he finally becomes seriously famous, in a few years' time, he'll have made enough albums for Black Top to doubleback these. In the meantime, you're safe with either or both, but *Universal Blues* comes first.

4. *Slide Nouveau: From Down Home to Out There*

The twin beauties of slide guitar are these: the very sound of the thing is both instantly evocative of rural 20th century Americana, and also capable of lending itself to all kinds of twisted and depraved musical purposes. The notion of freedom from the fixed pitch of the fretted (or keyed) note, with its unlimited potential for 'vocalisation', is common to both folk and moderne musics: slide thus appeals to traditionalists and avant-gardists alike, and even provides opportunities for each to explore each others' worlds.

Two current compilations enable both wings of contemporary slide to lay out their wares: to oversimplify (though not by much), *Slide Crazy!* (Sky Ranch SR 652324) showcases the serious crazies, while *(Almost) Everybody Slides* (Sky Ranch SR 652301) shelters the fundamentalists (as well as a bunch of people not playing slide at all: presumably they're the 'almost'). In truth, the distinction is misleading. Many of the slide radicals discovered their adventurous techniques while working with traditional musical materials: SONNY LANDRETH, a slide radical if ever there was one, appears on the 'traditional' collection, while the British bottleneck traditionalist Mike Cooper – the first person I ever saw actually playing bottleneck or using a National – shows up on *Slide Crazy!* with a BLIND WILLIE JOHNSON set-piece which is one of the oldest slide standards on record. Mind you, he's in the company of avantist Henry Kaiser and jazzer David Tronzo, not to mention lap-steel daredevil Freddie Roulette and English traditionalist Martin Simnpson, the latter with a haunting Celtic ballad interpreted, once again, a la Blind Willie. What emerges from a side-by-side (slide-by-slide?) comparision is that the most effective artists are those who straddle the trad/rad divide rather than take up permanent residence in one camp or the other. Unfortunately, the liner notes for *(Almost) Everybody Slides*, by one Serge K, are marred by dumb, liberal-racist remarks about how it's good news that all the participants are white, and that contemporary African-American youth are too obsessed with 'jogging suits and gold chains' to care about bottleneck guitar. African-American youth have about as much interest in bottleneck guitar as their English contemporaries have in Morris dancing: curiosity about the traditions and folkways of one's grandparents' generation generally comes later in life, if at all.

Rory Block

New York folkie Rory Block literally sings like a woman possessed: give this woman a slide, a ROBERT JOHNSON song and a nice reverberant room to perform in, and she'll scare the shit out of you. Of all the neo-Delta traddies, she's the one who makes the least effort to impersonate the timbre and weight of the post-CHARLEY PATTON school, but she is easily the spookiest and most electric because, even though she doesn't sound like anything other than a contemporary white woman, she sounds like a contemporary white woman whose physical equipment is being used by tthe spirit of a Delta bluesman. The word 'ectoplasmic', often cited in discussions of the music of Robert Johnson or SKIP JAMES, is applicable in Block's case: there's something genuinely otherworldly about her renditions of the wellworn Delta staples which she reanimates so compellingly.

Of the same mid-'60s East Coast country-blues-revival generation as JOHN HAMMOND, John Sebastian (later to lead The Lovin' Spoonful) and Stefan Grossman, she was able to study with REV GARY DAVIS and – when she was only 15 – rock SON HOUSE back on his heels with her renditions of a couple of his songs. It took until the mid-'70s before she recorded professionally, though, and until the early '80s before she recorded regularly. She's always enjoyed respect from fellow musicians (the likes of TAJ MAHAL, Stevie Wonder, The Persuasions and Mark Knopfler have contributed to her records), but she remains virtually unknown outside the folk-blues world. The obvious comparison is with the considerably more successful BONNIE RAITT, but – apart from sharing a gender, a generation, an instrument, and a taste for great blues and naff originals – they're very different performers. Raitt has the solidity and earthiness which the occasionally ethereal Block lacks: Block's work, on the other hand, has a wiry tension, a sense of risk and danger, which the more phlegmatic Raitt rarely evokes. Her albums generally split between her nonpareil pre-war blues interpretations, and her own compositions: unfortunately, too many of her non-blues originals are distressingly earnest and earthbound. She is, after all, an East Coast folkie (as opposed to Raitt's West Coast folk-rocker), so we'll leave that aspect of her work to *Sensitive And Observant Singer-Songwriters: The Essential Guide*.

- *Best Blues & Originals* (Munich MRCD 137)
- *Mama's Blues* (Munich/Network NETCD 22)
- *Ain't I A Woman* (Munich/Network NETCD 0038)

The uninspired-but-accurate title is self-explanatory: *BB&O* fillets Block's first four 'real' albums, opening with her devastating 'Walkin' Blues' and also including Robert Johnson's 'Crossroad Blues', Rev. Gary Davis' 'Sit Down On The banks', Charley Patton's 'Moon Going Down', Tommy Johnson's 'Travelin' Blues' and Willie Brown's 'Future Blues' and 'M&O Blues'. I'd've picked more blues and less originals, but must concede that most of the originals here match their surroundings, and songs like 'Send The Man Back Home' and 'God's Gift To Women' (not to mention the lovely instrumental 'Catastrophe Rag') fit into place right nice. The guest harp players are John Sebastian, Taj Mahal and – on the next-door-to-closing 'Gypsie Boy' – Stevie Wonder. The others are two of her three most recent albums: the third, *House Of Hearts* (Rounder CD 3104), is a song-cycle mourning the death of her son Thiele and, intriguingly, the least bluesy record she's ever made. *Mama's Blues* was was recorded in a church (the 'natural room sound' is actually a natural room), and brings on the choir for its gospel finale: it opens with another masterful Robert Johnson interpretation, 'Terraplane Blues', and the originals pay almost as much tribute to BESSIE SMITH and Tommy Johnson as the covers do. The ambitious *Ain't I A Woman* bounces off the famous speech by anti-slavery campaigner Sojourner Truth: it, too, boasts a Robert Johnson cover ('Come On In My Kitchen', done to a turn on a borrowed National) and a gospel finale. Archivists will note that her first recordings are available on *The Early Tapes 1975/1976* (Munich MRMCD 1). No Robert Johnson, one Willie Brown, one

Tommy Johnson, and 'Nobody Knows You When You're Down And Out'.

Roy Rogers

Northern California ex-folkie Roy Rogers claims that his parents had a sense of humour. Fortunately, so does he, which is why his albums have titles like *Chops Not Chaps*, *Blues On The Range* and *Slidewinder*. Best-known as the producer of JOHN LEE HOOKER's hit albums *The Healer*, *Mr Lucky* and *Boom Boom*, he's a veteran of Hooker's Coast To Coast Blues band but, more to the point, he's a devastating Delta-based slide stylist whose reinterpretations of ROBERT JOHNSON's themes – nine so far on his four solo albums – are, instrumentally at least, near-definitive. Working solo or pitting his trademark amplified acoustic guitars against the rocking bass and drums of his Delta Rhythm Kings, he explores pre-war country blues through the prism of the late-'40s/early '50s electric downhome of early MUDDY WATERS, ELMORE JAMES and John Lee Hooker; the period just before the Fender guitars and amplified harps arrived. He also runs a nice line in juxtaposing his Delta-isms with New Orleans polyrhythms, as his occasional collaborations with Nwawlins piano virtuoso Allen Toussaint demonstrate so beautifully. Rogers is a picker in a million: his dazzlingly expressive guitar delivers even when his light, amiable voice falters and his occasional attempts at AOR songwriting fail to get off the ground.

In a sense, Rogers is caught in a particularly annoying trap: he can do just about anything he wants with his guitar, but remains restricted by his vocal limitations. The closer he sticks to bedrock blues and R&B formats, the better he fares: a better vocalist could conceivably have animated the original compositions which make up the less interesting half of *Slidewinder* (Blind Pig BP 72687), but I doubt it. This is a shame, because that's the album which contains his glorious instrumental Toussaint duets and his memorable team-up with John Lee Hooker on Robert Johnson's 'Terraplane Blues', not to mention the fine original 'Down In Mississippi' and his grand-slam version of Johnson's 'Walkin' Blues'. However, he learns fast, and his later albums find him avoiding earlier pitfalls and writing around his voice with ever-increasing sophistication. So why can't he do for himself what he's done for Hooker? Well, firstly no matter how far you drag the Hook into the mainstream, you cannot compromise him; and secondly, Hooker's voice is one of the marvels of our age.

- *Blues On The Range* (Blind Pig BP 73589)
- *Slide Of Hand* (Liberty CDP 7810972)

To say that these albums find Rogers playing his strengths up and his weaknesses down is not to imply that they're stuffed full of instrumentals and covers; just that this time he's both written and selected stuff that he can sing comfortably. There's not much to choose between the last one for the little label and the first one for the big label except that *Slide Of Hand* benefits from bigger production sounds, and suffers from a couple of AOR ballads (someone shoot the A&R guy). Both are chock-full of rocking New Orleans grooves – sample *Blues On The Range*'s 'Crawfish City' on the *(Almost) Everybody Slides* collection discussed above – cool Delta stuff both ancient and (comparatively) modern, and plenty daredevil slide work.

Subjects for further investigation: **Chops Not Chaps** (Blind Pig BP 74892) was Rogers' first solo album and remains his most nakedly country-blues-oriented work. The Rogers-produced Hooker albums, for the *n*th time, are *The Healer* (Silvertone ORE CD 508), *Mr Lucky* (Silvertone ORE CD 519) and *Boom Boom* (PointBlank VPBCD 12); 'Terraplane Blues' is also included on Hooker's *The Ultimate Collection 1948–1990* (Rhino R2 70572 [US]). Rogers has also cut a couple of delightful duo albums with singer/harpist Norton Buffalo, *R&B* (Blind Pig BP 74491) and *Travellin' Tracks* (Blind Pig BPCD 5003): at the very least, they're the hippest acoustic guitar/harp team since SONNY TERRY & BROWNIE McGHEE.

John Mooney – a New Yorker who learned his stuff at the august knee of SON HOUSE before settling in New Orleans – shares Rogers' fascination with the interaction of the rhythmic idiosyncracies of Delta and Bayou. He plays a mean slide and better-than-okay standard lead, but his highest card is a bobby-dazzling polyrhythm guitar somewhere between SNOOKS EAGLIN and WILKO JOHNSON: his hectically exhilarating ride through the James Booker variant of 'Junco Partner' – on the live-in-Germany *Travelin' On* (CrossCut CCD 11032) – is literally breathtaking. Unfortunately, he's a somewhat mannered vocalist on the traditional repertoire which dominates the live album, cut with the young Nwawlins rhythm section currently using the 'Bluesiana' name established by DR JOHN and Art Blakey, but fares better on *Testimony* (Minor Music DOMCD 001), where he goes into the studio in the company of such hometown stalwarts as Dr John and Meters bassist George Porter Jr with a set of original material pitched halfway between RY COODER at his most frivolous and Little Feat at their most rootsy.

Another neotradder well worth some of your attention is Bob Brozman, who allegedly likes to mutter that music's been going downhill since 1928, which would make Son House a modernist radical and Robert Johnson a degenerate revisionist. I'm assured that this is an exaggeration, and that Brozman doesn't date the decline of bluesy civilisation until . . . oooh, at least 1935 (which would still make Johnson a degenerate revisionist). However, he features Johnson tunes both on the blues-specific *Truckload Of Blues* (Sky Ranch SR 635 209), but also on *Devil's Slide* (Rounder CD 11557), which sets his blues work in the context of his other preoccupations, Hawaiian music and early jazz, and beats the pants off similar exercises by Ry Cooder. His voice is more reminiscent of CHARLEY PATTON or SON HOUSE on the blues material – and of Louis Armstrong and Louis Prima on the novelties – than Johnson's, but his Johnson interpretations are by no means greatly inferior to those of RORY BLOCK, TAJ MAHAL or Roy Rogers. Incidentally, anyone noticing a Gibson Les Paul – that anachronistic implement of destruction – nestling amongst the gleaming steel-bodied Nationals on *Truckload*'s cover can rest easy: it was borrowed.

John Campbell

Louisiana-born John Campbell (1952–1993) was, essentially, ROY ROGERS with more angst, less chops, a bigger voice, auteurist songwriting ambitions and a too-bad-to-die attitude acquired the hard way. On the other hand, while Rogers' voice is unassuming to the point of anonymity, at least it's his; too often Campbell's spooky two-keys-below-his-natural-range growl sounded like he was just trying it on for size while CHARLEY PATTON, SCREAMIN' JAY HAWKINS, BLIND WILLIE JOHNSON and HOWLIN' WOLF stepped outside for a hand of poker. Some idea of his lyrical agenda can be gauged by the fact that his first album began '*Got the devil in my closet/wolves howlin' at my door*' and his second '*Taught the hellhound how to sit/cheated the devil at cards*'. Campbell was the hoodoo man for the '90s, playing the demon-haunted ROBERT JOHNSON card for all he was worth, and metaphorically bedecked with so many mojo hands and black cat bones that I'm surprised that he could stand up straight.

He got away with it because many of his songs – like 'Tiny Coffins' on the first album – were so powerful that even the occasional hokiness of his singing could not undermine them; because, while he lacked the virtuosity of a Rogers or Brozman, his amplified acoustic guitar-playing was solid and unpretentious; and because – partially as a result of the spiritual and physical traumas of the horrific teenage auto accident which required 5000 stitches worth of facial reconstruction and provided him with a hard-earned key to the inner mysteries of the blues – he resembled a 19th-century riverboat gambler from hell. Discovered street-singing and small-clubbing in New York, and produced by ROBERT CRAY honcho Dennis Walker, he got over on his live performances, which were considerably less pretentious and theatrical than his records might suggest. In fact, the gig I saw was friendly, varied and engaging enough to blow away the headlining JOHNNY WINTER, whose current idea of a show is to stand in one spot and spray the audience with guitar solos for up to fifteen minutes at a time. John Campbell had enormous potential and only lived to realise a fraction of it – which brought him rather closer to Robert Johnson than he probably wanted to be.

- *One Believer* (Elektra 7559-61086-2)
- *Howlin Mercy* (Elektra 7559-61440-2)

Sample song titles from Campbell's two albums: 'Devil In My Closet', 'Voodoo Edge', 'Tiny Coffin', 'Ain't Afraid Of Midnight' and 'Wolf Among The Lambs.' Well, alright. *One Believer* alternated his road rhythm section with moonlighting Cray sidemen like bassist Richard Cousins and keybist Jimmy Pugh and established Campbell's right to hang at that by-now crowded crossroads, while the more rock-friendly *Howlin Mercy* added a superfluous lead guitarist to the line-up and, rather too often, turned the density of Walker's production into mere clutter. Here he covers Tom Waits and Charley Patton, and works over LED ZEPPELIN's version of 'When The Levee Breaks' rather than MEMPHIS MINNIE's, a genuine populist move and a hilarious slap at the blues purists with whom he was, no doubt, distressingly familiar. Campbell never made the great blues-rock album he undoubtedly had in him, let alone the live album.

Subjects for further investigation: Campbell was the driving force behind **Strike A Deep Chord: Blues Guitars For The Homeless** (Justice JR 0003-2), an impressive all-star effort co-featuring, among others, DR JOHN, CLARENCE 'GATEMOUTH' BROWN, JOHNNY COPELAND, Odetta and SUE FOLEY. He was also frequently compared to Chris Whitley, a broodingly sensitive hunk who intones his singer-songwriterisms across a shimmering *Paris, Texas*-styled National-steel backdrop on **Living With The Law** (Columbia 468586 2).

Sonny Landreth

If you play slide and your CV includes replacing RY COODER in John Hiatt's band, you obviously know one end of an open-G tuning from the other. If you've also served time with JOHN MAYALL's BluesBreakers and contributed songs to the Father Of British Blues' permanent repertoire, then you're probably Sonny Landreth, author of 'Congo Square' – featured on Mayall's *A Sense Of Place* (Island IMCD 167) – and the unassuming master of progressive slide. Did I say 'unassuming'? His dweeby, bespectacled party-on-Garth appearance and soft, light voice make ROY ROGERS come on like JOHN CAMPBELL by comparison. However, Landreth couldn't sound more different from those worthies: he's a restless experimenter who uses both unorthodox techniques (like fretting behind his slide to achieve chord voicings unavailable to more conventional players) and extensive use of sound-processing boxes to pull every conceivable noise out of his battery of electric and acoustic guitars. Yet another player with a fondness for Louisiana beats, his performances suffer from his seeming determination to translate Nwawlins rhythms into arena-rock – some of his solo intros are so mind-boggling that it's a letdown when the rhythm section crash in – but he's as consistently surprising and inventive as any blues-rocker around today.

● *Outward Bound* (Praxis/Zoo 72445-11032)

Though the style (not to mention the quality) of the compositions varies enormously and Landreth's voice is as unmemorable as any on record – when former boss John Hiatt contributes a backing vocal, you find yourself listening to him rather than the featured artist – this album cements Sonny L's status as a one-man research-and-development lab for unique slide voicings and textures. Horns, bagpipes, overdriven amplified mouth-harp, dulcimer, even Pete Townshend's primitive sequencer at the beginning of The Who's 'Won't Get Fooled Again': all these and more are coaxed or torn into being on this appropriately-named album. Pop and rock jostle for space with the mutated blues and zydeco, but all are sparked by a degree of sonic innovation rarely encountered in a tradition-based field. Check out the title track and then try to tell me that you're not listening to a true original.

Dave Hole

The protagonist of this particular bar-band fairy-tale ahould have his own category: maybe we could call it 'radical powerslide'. Dave Hole is the grizzled Australian practitioner of a pseudo-lap-steel-style approach to the guitar which involves applying the slide from above, rather than below, the neck, and which he shares with absolutely nobody else. He cut and pressed up his own album to sell at his gigs in the general vicinity of Perth, a copy winged its way across the ocean to *Guitar Player* magazine, a rave review followed, and before Hole could say 'Blimey!' the album was licensed to Provogue in Europe and Alligator in the US, he was on tour with GARY MOORE, and the next time he plays Perth his gig fee will have gone up considerably.

- **Short Fuse Blues** (Provogue PRD 70362)

Its matched extremes are two bravura cover versions: he gives BLIND WILLIE JOHNSON's hallowed 'Dark Was The Night, Cold Was The Ground' a haunting ride through some new territory, and recreates all the signature licks (and sounds!) of JIMI HENDRIX's 'Purple Haze' with his slide. In between there's some ROBERT JOHNSON, some FREDDIE KING, some Albert King, some ELMORE JAMES, some BUDDY GUY, FLEETWOOD MAC's 'Albatross' (!?) and even a few originals. He's a fairly undistinguished vocalist and the originals aren't very, but the band swings and the guitar is consistently startling.

Rainer

Trust me: this guy can tell a hellhound from a Pekinese. Rainer Ptacek's parents brought him from what was then Czechoslovakia (where they have the best beer and the worst food in all of Europe) via what was then East Germany; he was raised in Chicago and ended up in the Arizona desert playing evolved-blues on a steel-bodied National guitar. He looks like a disshevelled version of David McCallum back in his Illya Kuryakin days, and though he eschews electricity (apart from the current necessary to power his sampler) and sticks religiously to his National, he can easily match SONNY LANDRETH as a formal innovator; while his work carries a chilly unease that's ultimately far more unsettling than JOHN CAMPBELL's received diabolism. His first album, performed solo and self-recorded on a Sony DAT recorder, became something of a cult sensation in Britain when it reached the ears of Demon Records, who released it in 1992 and promptly flew Rainer over for a series of one-man National-and-sampler showcases in which the music was all but drowned out by the sound of fellow sliders' jaws hitting the ground. Its 1993 sequel, *The Texas Tapes*, is credited to 'Rainer & Das Combo' and teams him up with a well-known Texas-based trio whose name cannot be mentioned for contractual reasons. Therefore, all I'm legally empowered to tell you is that two of the three members of Das Combo have very long beards, that they make killer videos involving a vintage car that turns into a spaceship, and that Rainer Ptacek is nobody's idea of a sharp-dressed man.

- *Worried Spirits* (Demon FIEND CD 723)
- **RAINER AND DAS COMBO:** *The Texas Tapes* (Demon FIEND CD 734)

Worried Spirits is about as good an album as any one man has cut alone with a National since SON HOUSE quit recording. Some of the less bluesy originals carry a distinct whiff of the young Bob Dylan, and though Rainer's voice is technically no richer or stronger than those of Sonny Landreth or ROY ROGERS, there's a mean, wiry, acidic undercurrent which keeps it resonating in the mind as long as that extraordinary guitar, which is to say: long after the music stops. The initial problem with *The Texas Tapes* is that, on first listening it almost sounds more ZZ – whoops, nearly let the cat out of the bag there – than it does like Rainer, but there's no need for Rainer to recut *Worried Spirits*, and if you're going to go electric, you might as well do so the company of a proven class act. And – for those hankering after a second helping of the solo Rainer – the album closes with three more one-man gems from the 'Arizona Tapes.' You need to watch this guy – he's going to be around for awhile.

5. *One Pigfoot and One Bottle of Beer, Comin' Right Up: Daughters of Bessie*

If there's any blues subgenre which seems utterly timelocked – not to mention currently utterly unfashionable – it's the 'classic blues' of the '20s and early '30s. BESSIE SMITH is the only one of its numerous stars whose name and music are known to non-specialists, and contemporary figures working in the style can be counted on the fingers of one hand even if we allocate the thumb to DANA GILLESPIE and a finger apiece to each of the founding members of SAFFIRE THE UPPITY BLUESWOMEN. The remaining finger wears a slide, because both RORY BLOCK and BONNIE RAITT have explored both its repertoire and its attitude, but the only patch of blues turf which was ever historically dominated by women remains distressingly underpopulated. The leading contemporary blueswomen, from KOKO TAYLOR to LOU ANN BARTON, work – albeit subversively – in the male-defined postwar idioms; surely *someone* wants to reclaim the women's blues for the modern agenda. Saffire reanimate this music as feminist cabaret; Gillespie as bawdy fantasia. Guess who's truer to its spirit. Now guess who's more fun.

Dana Gillespie

Considering her varied artistic background, Dana Gillespie's blues-singing would seem somewhat unlikely if she hadn't also put in a lengthy stint hosting a blues radio show in New York. She's combined a musical career that stretches from '60s folkie-dom (inspired by her childhood hero Bob Dylan) through '70s glam-provocation (orchestrated by her childhood pal David Bowie) with a dramatic career encompassing both cleavage-heaving Hammer Films bimbodom and an appearance in Nicolas Roeg's *Bad Timing* (in movies), and demanding straight-theatre work in Vienna. That doesn't even take into account her frequent appearances in musicals like *Jesus Christ Superstar* and *Tommy*, or the fact that she was once British junior water-skiing champion.

She cut three blues albums – mostly for producer Mike Vernon – in the 1980s: *Blue Job* (1982), *Below The Belt* (1985) and *Sweet Meat* (1989). As the titles might suggest, they applied a broad variety of styles – 'classic', jump, Delta, Chicago – to a single subject: men and their physical attributes. Or should that be 'attribute'? Saying that Dana Gillespie enjoys singing about sex is like claiming that Danny DeVito is under six feet tall. However, she sings about enjoying men on her terms, not theirs. No man ever is ever permitted to mistreat Gillespie in these songs; she gives, rather than gets, the blues. If, as Ida Cox's song says, 'Wild Women Don't Get The Blues', then Dana G is one of the wildest around. You got a problem with that? Didn't think so.

- *Blues It Up* (Ace CDCHD 950)

This collection fillets Gillespie's blues trilogy into as consciously salacious a 73-minute programme as anybody this side of Lucille Bogan, Millie Jackson or 2 Live Crew has ever committed to tape. Three song titles out of 23 include the word 'meat': this is where the 'One Hour Mama' meets the 'Sixty Minute Papa'; where 'Tongue In Cheek' goes 'Below The Belt'; where 'It Ain't The Meat, It's The Motion' sets a 'Big Ten Inch Record'; where 'Joe's Joint' rubs shoulders – or rubs *something*, anyway – with the 'Organ Grinder'. It's also where stellar London sidemen like slide guitarist Sam Mitchell, saxophonist Pete Thomas and the late drummer Kieron O'Connor get to show off like mad and still stay in context. It's an index of Gillespie's empathy with her material that the originals blend so seamlessly with the covers; considering that the covers include 'My Man Stands Out', 'Don't You Make Me High' (better-known as 'Don't You Feel My Leg') and items by the likes of LOUIS JORDAN, WILLIE DIXON and Leiber & Stoller, that's no mean achievement. Sung and played with both lascivious glee and casual expertise, this is a fabulous album; it literally beats the pants off anything done by a British blues*man* these last ten years.

Saffire – The Uppity Blueswomen

DANA GILLESPIE doesn't have an explicit feminist agenda – the way she frames her blues, maybe she doesn't need one – but Saffire The Uppity Blueswomen definitely do. What's surprising is how infrequently it impedes their witty, swinging, feisty statements of the love rights of fortysomething single women. They formed in Fredericksburg, Virginia, around pianist/guitarist Anne Rabson, who was teaching guitar to performance artist Gaye Adegbalola and computer programming to bassist Earline Lewis when the idea of forming an acoustic blues trio – named after a pure blue gem – struck them. With Rabson at the piano (with occasional guitar interludes) and Adegbalola playing guitar and singing the bulk of the lead vocals, they turned professional in 1988 and released their first, eponymous album on Alligator two years later. On Lewis' departure, a larger band formed around the central duo of Adegbolola and Rabson. Saffire's lyrics are considerably raunchier than their music; still, Adegbalola has a voice and a half and Rabson can hold her own with any contemporary blues pianist.

- **Saffire – The Uppity Blueswomen** (Alligator ALCD 4780)

The first album is still the definitive one: it includes their signature songs 'Middle Aged Blues Boogie', 'Even Yuppies Get The Blues' and 'School Teacher's Blues'. Their performances grew more confident on their subsequent outing *Hot Flash* (Alligator ALCD 4796), but it doesn't so much extend the debut's achievement as simply reinforce it. The brisk and lively *Broad Casting* (Alligator ALCD 4811) deftly incorporates contemporary material like LITTLE CHARLIE & THE NIGHTCATS' 'Dump That Chump' alongside new originals like Adegbalola's fabulous 'Miz Thang' and 'OBG Why Me Blues', or vintage classics like 'One Hour Mama'; and the occasional use of Hammond organ or electric guitar make me wish that Rabson and Adegabalola would go the whole hog and hire a drummer. And cut a live album, of course.

6. 'New Bluebloods' and Young Hotshots: Sweet Home Chicago and Elsewhere

One by-product of post-'60s white blues was that the music was kept alive long enough for a new generation of young black blues guys to rediscover it. The flashpoint was 1987's all-original anthology *The New Bluebloods* (Alligator ALCD 4707), subtitled 'The Next Generation Of Chicago Blues' and eminently fulfilling its brief as a successor to the massively influential *Chicago/The Blues/Today!* and *Living Chicago Blues* collections. It introduced un(der)recorded Chicago talent like THE KINSEY REPORT, LI'L ED & THE BLUES IMPERIALS and MAURICE JOHN VAUGHN to audiences outside their neighbourhoods, disproving the notion that ROBERT CRAY was the only fresh young black bluesman around. New Bluebloods may or may not play old-time blues, but they sing about credit cards and answering machines, or about how the computer took their job. When Maurice John Vaughn's woman leaves him (again!), he ruefully murmurs 'Game Over'.

Li'l Ed & The Blues Imperials

Is this a dream-come-true or what? Li'l Ed Williams, the nephew of Chicago slideman J.B. Hutto, inherited Hutto's guitar after his uncle's death. By day he worked in a carwash; by night he played West Side taverns with his half-brother on bass and one of his uncle's guitar students on rhythm, delivering exuberant, raunchy old-time slide boogie in the manner of HOUND DOG TAYLOR, ELMORE JAMES and – naturally – Hutto himself. When Alligator's Bruce Iglauer tapped him for a contribution to *The New Bluebloods*, Ed and his group virtually did their whole act in the studio, laid down thirty songs in three hours and cut a deal for an album of their own right there on the spot. Alligator were so anxious to get Ed out there that they released *Roughhousin'* (Alligator ALCD 4749) – the real live-in-the-studio deal, cut, for what it's worth, between 8pm and 11:15pm on January 24, 1986 – even before *Bluebloods* itself. Needless to say, he quit his job at the carwash, and though only he and bassist James 'Pookie' Young remain from the original group, the agenda remains the same. The only difference is that now they've taken it to the stages of every major blues festival in the US, Europe and Japan. Ed Williams was barely out of nappies when Elmore James died, but he's as strongly in the tradition as it is possible to be, and he gives that tradition more than nuf respec'.

● *Chicken, Gravy And Biscuits* (Alligator ALCD 4722)

Boy, they really took their time with the follow-up: they spent two whole evenings cutting it. If I blindfold-tested you with this, your only clue that it wasn't cut in the '50s would be the clarity of the recording, and the slightly more modern groove they hit on the cover of ALBERT COLLINS' 'Master Charge'. All the rest of the songs, bar J.B. Hutto's '20% Alcohol', are Ed's own, and they do a better job of recapturing the spirit of classic Elmore than either GEORGE THOROGOOD or the Jeremy Spencer-fronted FLEETWOOD

MAC. How you feel about the most recent Li'l Ed album, 1992's . . . *What You See Is What You Get* (Alligator ALCD 4808) depends on whether you fancy a tenor sax added to the brew, or whether you'd like to hear Ed kick off with a JOHN LEE HOOKER-style boogie. As with his avatar Hound Dog Taylor, you can't go wrong with any of Ed's albums: if you like what he does you'll want them all; if you don't, you won't need any of them. While you're waiting for the inevitable but long-overdue live album, slake your thirst with the in-concert Li'l Ed tracks that open up *The Alligator Records 20th Anniversary Tour* (Alligator ALCD 107/108).

Maurice John Vaughn

In a blues marketplace where a large number of artists are chasing what was until recently a very small pool of blues dollars, it might be considered commercial suicide to title your debut *Generic Blues Album*, and package it accordingly, complete with a stylised bar-code on the front which probably confuses the hell out of the counter staff at Tower Records. For Maurice John Vaughn – no relation to any other blues guitarists with similar-sounding names – it was a masterpiece of small-label marketing which drew considerably more attention to a flawed but intriguing record than the standard moody/jolly-guy-with-guitar sleeve could ever have done. He'd come to the blues the long way round after starting out as a soul saxophonist, and then discovering that brass players frequently got laid off in times of economic hardship, whereas rhythm section players stayed in work. He duly switched to guitar, and developed a taste for the blues in 1979, when his entire band was hired by bluesman Phil (hates to be known as brother of BUDDY) GUY.

He soon became an in-demand sideman – he still is, as A.C. Reed's *I'm In The Wrong Business!* will testify – and released the original homebrew version of *Generic Blues Album* in 1984. (Alligator reissued it in 1988 in the wake of the success of *The New Bluebloods*.) The style he developed was cool, smooth and easy; but with an underlying urban tension and urgency to prevent bland-out. His guitar is clean and jazzy; his voice deep and confidential. Vaughn is an insinuating, sweet-talking *lurrve*-man as much as he's a blues player: he sounds pretty much the way the owner of the snakeskin-covered Fender amplifier on the back of *In The Shadow Of The City* ought to. At a time when even urban blues artists play up the more down-home aspects of their work (possibly because white audiences seem to prefer it that way), that makes Vaughn as distinctive a stylist as he is a singer. In short, he's about as different from LI'L ED Williams as any contemporary Chicago bluesman could be: that the same scene supports both of them demonstrates both the variety and the vigour of the city's blues tradition.

- *In The Shadow Of The City* (Alligator ALCD 4813)

1993's long-delayed follow-up is a considerable improvement over *Generic Blues Album* (Alligator ALCD 4763): partly because Vaughn's singing and songwriting have solidified in the near-decade; partly because Alligator's heightened production values allow for some smashing horn-section arrangements (written and mostly played by Vaughn himself); and partly because he's dropped the HOWLIN' WOLF impressions which outwore their welcome so speedily on the previous album. This is cinerama-scale urban blues only slightly less heroic than ALBERT KING's *I Wanna Get Funky* or the better moments of Walter 'Wolfman' Washington's *Wolf Tracks* and Jimmy Johnson's *Johnson's Whacks*. 'I Want To Be Your Spy', 'Game Over', 'Watching Your Watch' and 'Are You Satisfied?' are genuinely powerful songs done to an absolute turn; when he manages to maintain that standard for a whole album, watch out. (Incidentally, Zora Young, the vocalist who shares the title track of *Generic Blues Album* with Vaughn, has an album of her own available: unfortunately *Travelin' Light* (Sky Ranch SR 652332) isn't the one Vaughn produced for her in 1986.)

Kenny Neal

Born into the blues as opposed to with them, Kenny Neal will, if there's any justice, eventually find himself at the forefront of an entire school of contemporary downhome blues singers. The son of harpist Raful Neal and one-time bassist for fellow Louisianan

BUDDY GUY (himself Raful Neal's former bassman), Neal was born in New Orleans, Louisiana, in 1957, and learned the music at his father's knee: on the autobiographical monologue 'Bio On The Bayou' he claims that he was given his first harmonica by SLIM HARPO. He came up through the Baton Rouge swamp-blues scene, joining his father's band on bass at 13 and moonlighting with local funk outfits until he got the call from Guy. By 1980, he was in Canada, woodshedding on harmonica and lead guitar and sharpening his chops on the Toronto blues scene. Eventually he returned to Baton Rouge to start up his own band; his debut album, *Bio On The Bayou*, was cut for the local King Snake label and picked up for reissue in 1988 by (appropriately enough) Alligator Records as the expanded, remixed *Big News From Baton Rouge!!* (Alligator ALCD 4764).

He's been steadily working his way up the blues ladder ever since, giving a good account of himself at all the major US clubs and festivals, and touring Europe to rapturous receptions. In February of 1991 he even appeared performing music written by TAJ MAHAL in a Broadway production of *Mule Bone*, a play written in the '30s by poet Langston Hughes and folklorist Zora Neale Thurston. His sessions attract sidemen of the calibre of The Memphis Horns, The Horny Horns (the brass from the great JAMES BROWN bands) and Lucky Peterson. Neal's music retains its regional roots, yet – as demonstrated by a comparison with a first-generation swamp-blues veteran like Clarence Edwards, a contemporary of Slim Harpo and LIGHTNIN' SLIM whose *Swamp's The Word* (Red Lightnin' RLCD 0090) could have come straight from Jay Miller's studio via time machine – he's absorbed the more modern influences which you'd expect from a bluesman with his particular combination of youth and experience. His warm, weathered voice and laid-back harp are still covered in swamp mud, his hardnosed, spiky guitar pays eloquent tribute to Buddy Guy (as well as to the ubiquitous influence of ALBERT KING), and his rhythms mix up every beat from Baton Rouge to Chicago. Since blues singers are generally in it for the long haul rather than the quick fix, expect to find Kenny Neal next door to ROBERT CRAY and JOE LOUIS WALKER in the front rank of 21st century blues.

- *Walking On Fire* (Alligator ALCD 4795)
- *Bayou Blood* (Alligator ALCD 4809)

If you doubt that Kenny Neal is a hard worker, check out the progressive degeneration of his Fender Telecaster, from virtually pristine to worn-out near-wreck, over the course of his four album covers. And if you also doubt that the man is on a steep learning curve, bear in mind that each of his albums is perceptibly better than the one before. These are his third and fourth albums – the second was 1989's *Devil Child* (Alligator ALCD 4774) – and *Walking On Fire* salts a mostly stimulating horn-driven post-Albert King blend of soul, funk and shuffles with a few downhome interludes, including the harp showcase 'Blues Stew' and a couple of acoustic (though lavishly overdubbed) Langston Hughes adaptations. The one to get is the richly emotional *Bayou Blood*, where he ditches the horns, features more of Lucky Peterson's Hammond and his own harp, and generally makes the most downhome sounding record of his career, including the first one, which really *was* down home. 'Gonna Put You Out Of My Misery' and the title track are set to a decidedly Nwawlins bounce; the slow blues 'That Knife Don't Cut No More' features the most intense guitar of his career; 'Do I Have To Go That Far?' marvellously evokes SONNY BOY WILLIAMSON's harp style, and the hectic instrumental shuffle 'Neal And Prey' provides both Neal and Peterson with an excuse to show off their jazz chops.

Larry McCray

When Virgin launched its PointBlank blues subsidiary in 1990, the company picked the young Detroit bluesman Larry McCray as its launch act. Bad call. McCray certainly had a voice: big, hoarse, urgent; he had an impressive guitar style: agile, forceful, sizzling; and he even had the look. Trust me: if you were in a nightclub and Larry McCray was the bouncer, you would behave yourself. The problem, as revealed on *Ambition* (PointBlank VPBCD 1) was that he had neither the songs or the vision. The title track was powerful enough, but to describe the rest of it as 'patchy' would be overly generous. Like a real blues warrior, he retreated and regrouped, performing as an acoustic solo act and biding his time.

His second effort is so much more authoritative than his first that we'll simply pretend that *Ambition* never happened, hope that he recycles its title song into a live album sometime, and act as if Larry McCray's debut album was actually . . .

● *Delta Hurricane* (PointBlank VPBCD 10)

The influence of ALBERT KING is once again writ large all over this soulful, eloquent record, from the punchy, brass-backed funk-blues arrangements to the Gibson Flying V guitar McCray sports on the cover. Using A. King – and a pinch of ALBERT COLLINS – as a lever, the 'new' McCray wedges himself into previously-unexplored space somewhere between SON SEALS and JOE LOUIS WALKER. His voice and guitar flex more muscle than an entire stageful of Mr Universe contestants, and the production – by Mike Vernon, who's made a few blues records in his time – provides him with as solid a platform as could be desired. McCray still isn't a particularly prolific songwriter: fully half the album is written by one Dave Steen (who he?) and the artist himself accounts for a mere three songs, one an instrumental but another, 'Hole In My Heart', a highlight. After a shaky start, Larry McCray is off and running.

Subjects for further investigation: In his autobiography *I Am The Blues*, WILLIE DIXON recounts how, during the early '70s, he lost the $25–30,000 he invested in the career of the then-5-year-old child-prodigy singer/organist Lucky Peterson, whom he was convinced could have been bigger than the Jackson 5. Despite a rash of successful TV appearances, Lucky's launch eventually foundered on the rock of disagreements between Peterson's father and Dixon. The young genius spent the next two-or-so decades serving his apprenticeship, sessioning and gigging on keys – he's currently a fixture behind KENNY NEAL – and working on his guitar-playing. By 1989, when Peterson emerged from lengthy stints behind BOBBY 'BLUE' BLAND and LITTLE MILTON to cut his first adult solo album *Lucky Strikes* (Alligator ALCD 4470) at the ripe old age of 24, he was the youngest veteran in the business. So he's young, he's multi-talented, he's experienced and he's connected: why isn't he a star? Both *Lucky Strikes* and its sequel *Triple Play* (Alligator ALCD 4789) reveal a seasoned pro with absolutely nothing individual to say, which is somewhat terrifying in one so gifted and still so young. The organ work is still brilliant, the voice and guitar still somewhat anonymous, and it ain't what you do, it's the way that you do it.

A hotter shot is Sherman Robertson, a Texas-born, Louisiana-seasoned guitarist who's as much a post-Vaughanist as a Blueblood. An admirer of STEVIE RAY VAUGHAN and FREDDIE KING and a veteran of the CLIFTON CHENIER and Rockin' Dopsie zydeco academies – he appeared with Dopsie on Paul Simon's *Graceland* – *I'm The Man* (Indigo IGO CD 2005) puts him over as a talent still in transition; but distinguished from the enervated Lucky Peterson by an emotional warmth which could explode his strong, committed voice and guitar as soon as some superior material provides the spark.

7. *Power Blues*

If there is any one blues idiom which can truly be said to be indigenously British, it's power blues, though it took an African-American, JIMI HENDRIX, to detonate and ultimately define it. Funnily enough, none of its current leading practitioners are British, and they're not even all white, but that's just poetic justice. 'Power blues' was the music of Cream, Hendrix, LED ZEPPELIN, JOHNNY WINTER (in arena-rock mode) and ZZ TOP; it has one foot in the blues and the other in heavy metal. The big question: where's its soul?

Jeff Healey

Toronto guitar virtuoso Jeff Healey created something of an upset when he started winning the 'Best Blues Guitarist' slot in magazine polls; not because his musicianship was anything less than astonishing, but because the ascendency which followed so rapidly after the release of his 1988 debut album *See The Light* seemed to indicate that the battle over whether blues-rock was 'really blues' seemed to have been settled with a definitive yes. Healey himself, a serious jazz and blues buff who hosts a Toronto jazz radio show when he's off the road and whose collection of vintage 78s runs into tens of thousands, has enough musical suss to know that he's less a blues guitarist than a rock guitarist who happens to play good blues and sometimes does so. His trio, The Jeff Healey Band, started out as post-Vaughanist hard rockers frequently compared to STEVIE RAY VAUGHAN & Double Trouble, and have been moving steadily rockwards ever since. Their principal calling card is Healey's extraordinary guitar technique: he plays with the instrument flat on his lap, holding it like a lap steel player but instead of using a slide, he frets the guitar from above as a pianist might. This enables him to span wider intervals, and to use the power of his thumb for broader and giddier string-bends, than would be possible with conventional techniques. His sound is genuinely galvanic: notes literally *leap* out of the speakers.

So if Healey doesn't call himself a blues player, then why do so many other people? It was that first album, the bluesiest he's ever made, which misdirected so many of his early fans: the combination of his light but huskily world-weary voice and that ear-grabbing guitar instantly recalled the Cream-era ERIC CLAPTON stripped of kitsch psychedelic trappings. One day, Jeff Healey could – if he so desired – make a wonderful blues album. Right now, he's busy doing something else. Beyond that, deponent sayeth not.

- *See The Light* (Arista 259 441)
- **ORIGINAL MOTION PICTURE SOUNDTRACK:** *Roadhouse* (Arista 259 948)

If you want to hear why Healey was acclaimed as a blues prodigy, step this way. The first album, and the band's contributions to the soundtrack of the ludicrous Patrick Swayze vehicle *Roadhouse* – in which a part as a blind guitarist who holds his instrument on his lap was specially written for Healey – are the nearest they ever got to straight blues moves. *See The Light* opens with a couple of state-of-the-art blues-rock punches, John Hiatt's 'Confidence Man' and Healey's own 'My Little Girl', and includes some bluesy originals (like the title track, 'Don't Let Your Chance Go By' and the instrumental 'Nice Problem To Have') plus a smart choice of covers: ZZ TOP's 'Blue Jean Blues' and FREDDIE KING's 'Hideaway'. Alongside licensed nuggets from Bob Seger, Otis Redding and Little Feat, the soundtrack features Healey's spirited bar-band choogles through The Doors' 'Roadhouse Blues', MUDDY WATERS' 'Hoochie Coochie Man' and F. King's 'I'm Tore Down'. There's also a vocal from Swayze . . . sorry, didn't mean to put you off.

The Kinsey Report

If any contemporary blues hotshot has a hipper pedigree than Donald Kinsey's, I'd like to hear about it. The guitar-playing son of Mississippi blues singer Big Daddy Kinsey, DK is the only musician to have worked with ALBERT KING (most notably on *I Wanna Get Funky*) and Bob Marley (hear him on *Rastaman Vibration*), not to mention Peter Tosh and ROY BUCHANAN. The Kinsey Report is a family affair formed to back Big Daddy after Donald returned to Gary, Indiana – the hometown he shares with the Jackson 5 – after his road adventures with King, Tosh and Marley. Gradually, the quartet – Kinsey's brothers Kenneth and Ralph in the rhythm section, and cousin Ron Prince on second guitar – became an attraction in their own right; after contributing to Alligator's *The New Bluebloods*, they cut two raw, funky blues-rock albums for the label before moving to Virgin's PointBlank subsidiary, where – reduced to a trio, minus Ron Prince – the Kinsey brothers are currently launching unsuccessful attempts to crack the AOR hard rock market.

As guitarist or vocalist, Donald Kinsey is more than adept at rock, reggae, funk or blues: in other words, the problem certainly isn't a talent shortage. The initial Kinsey Report combination of crunchy rock dynamics, radical Afrocentric politics, tough, compassionate ghetto-realist lyrics and trad blues virtues was an enormously exciting one; but their conservative approach to the conventions of each genre prevents The Kinsey Report from exploring the unmapped regions of their common ground, thereby reinventing blues-rock in the process and fulfilling their artistic and commercial potential as the missing link between ROBERT CRAY and Living Colour.

- *Edge Of The City* (Alligator ALCD 4758)
- *Midnight Drive* (Alligator ALCD 4775)
- **BIG DADDY KINSEY & SONS:** *Can't Let Go* (Blind Pig BP 73489)

The Kinsey posse before the rock set in. The Alligator albums are the ones which raised my hopes; the ones which dashed them were *Powerhouse* (PointBlank VPBCD 2) and *Crossing Bridges* (PointBlank VPBCD 9). 1987's *Edge Of The City* is cranked blues, ranging from the ominous 'Full Moon On Main Street' to the wry 'Answering Machine' and the soulful 'I Can't Let You Go'; 'Back Door Man' isn't the one WILLIE DIXON wrote for HOWLIN' WOLF, but an original, and 'The Game Of Love' transforms into a wracked slow blues the same song which British Invasion triviacs associate with Wayne Fontana & The Mindbenders. *Midnight Drive*, which followed two years later, takes a few adventurous steps into street-funk and hard-rock territory without ever losing its bluesy essence, which is why it remains the definitive Kinsey Report album. The autobiographical 'Big Time' has charm as well as toughness, 'Nowhere To Go, Nothing To Lose' and the title track are the most haunting songs they've ever written, and they also include a coolly swinging take on PERCY MAYFIELD's 'River's Invitation' and a powerful, impassioned 'Free South Africa'. Big Daddy takes the spotlight on the appealing *Can't Let Go*, which augments the family firm with a few guests, including Lucky Peterson on keys, and blends Big Daddy's engagingly bluff and forthright approach to raw Delta materials – including some well-chosen MUDDY WATERS and JIMMY REED tunes – with some of his sons' newer tricks.

Walter Trout

Cinders, you *shall* go to the ball: L.A. guitarist Walter Trout – a veteran of JOHN LEE HOOKER's Coast To Coast Blues Band and CANNED HEAT – was holding down the lead guitar chair with JOHN MAYALL's BluesBreakers when the Father Of British Blues came over all indisposed one night during a Scandinavian tour. Since the promotor had a philosophical objection to refunding the gate money, he asked the band to go on without Mayall, and the next thing Trout knew, he had his own record deal. The resulting records plonked Trout squarely in the no-man's-land between post-Vaughanism and heavy metal. An appallingly hammy vocalist, a formidable guitar technician and a dedicated showman with a powerful taste for JIMI HENDRIX and STEVIE RAY VAUGHAN, he comes on like gangbusters: as subtle as an air strike and as brutally effective. For all his prowess, Trout is a textbook example of power blues' classic pitfall (sometimes known as the JOHNNY WINTER dilemma): succumbing to the temptation to flatten the audience rather than reach out to them. He can play (superbly), he can sing (after a fashion), and he can even write (though John Mayall's 'Life In The Jungle' – auditionable on *his* album of the same name – shows how much more can be coaxed out of that song by a singer with a little finesse); however, his relentless assault gets old real quick. If he listens a little harder to those Jimi and Stevie records – not to mention a little more BUDDY GUY and B.B. KING – he'll eventually notice that the masters can whisper as well as roar.

- *Live: No More Fish Jokes* (Provogue PRD 70512)

You guessed it: the live album. Quintessential Trout is live Trout, so this nicely-titled 1993 effort, recorded at a couple of festivals in Denmark and Holland, re-presents Trout's pick of the most durable material from its three predecessors, 1990's *Life In The Jungle* (Provogue PRD 70202) and *Prisoner Of A Dream* (Provogue PRD 70262), and 1992's *Transition* (Provogue PRD 70442). Blistering guitar, blustering voice, blazing Hammond, and bludgeoning rhythm section: all straight in your face for 71 minutes. The sources of his style and the instrumentation of his group recall Stevie Ray Vaughan & Double Trouble, but the (almost) nonstop guitar jabbering recalls Johnny Winter at his most claustrophobically self-absorbed. When he lightens up for his virtual-definition-of-bathos version of Bob Dylan's 'Girl From The North Country' or a slow blues like 'If You Just Try', you realise why he shouts most of the time: at lower intensities, his voice thins out alarmingly. You also notice that his guitar playing spaces out, which as the 'violin' passages demonstrate, improves matters immensely. Finally you notice that even when he creates a moment of genuine light and shade, he can't resist wrecking it.

Live: No More Fish Jokes doesn't include his marathon version of Hendrix's 'Red House' – that's on *Life In The Jungle* – but hey, this is the blues. You got to make *some* sacrifices.

L.A. Blues Authority

God, this is a horror: a convocation of Big Rock Dudes from the Los Angeles Heavy Metal scene team up in various combinations to pay tribute to MUDDY WATERS, JUNIOR WELLS, B.B. KING, ALBERT KING, ROBERT JOHNSON and – um – Al Kooper and Stephen Stills, Cream, LED ZEPPELIN, STEVIE RAY VAUGHAN and JIMI HENDRIX. Shooting for blues and ending up with 'blooze' are guitarists Zakk Wylde, Brad Gillis, Steve Lukather, Richie Kotzen, Pat Thrall, George Lynch, Jeff Watson and Tony MacAlpine; singers Glenn Hughes, Kevin Dubrow (yes, from Quiet Riot), Kotzen again, and – on a half-way decent 'Rollin' And Tumblin'' featuring Lynch, which provides one of the album's only two semi-listenable moments – vocalist/harpist Little John Chrisley. Also implicated: bassists Stuart Hamm and Billy Sheehan, and drummer Greg Bissonette. If you know who all these people are, you listen to entirely too much metal.

- *L.A. Blues Authority* (Blues Bureau International BBI 2001-CD)

The ultimate *reductio ad absurdam* of power blues. Third-generation white post-heavy blues-rockers firmly rooted in second-generation white post-heavy blooze, the L.A. Blues Authority attack their material with the brute force and self-absorption that is metal's sole *raison d'être*, apparently not noticing that they're trashing every song they touch. (The vocalists are by far the worst offenders; guitarists generally don't know any better.) The first generation white blooze-rockers may not have understood the blues much better than these big-hair shred dudes, but they *wanted* to understand it. The difference between these guys and those guys is that the 3G-ers think they don't need to try and understand it, because they already do. Except that they don't. P.S. The other 'semi-listenable moment' is provided by the totally non-famous Kevin Russell, who co-produced the album, played rhythm guitar on all the tracks and was the only person allowed to perform an original. His 'Hands On You' recalls Jeff Beck and Rod Stewart's take on HOWLIN' WOLF's 'I Ain't Superstitious'; whereas the rest of it simply recalls Great Migraines Of Our Time. Thank Christ it's a one-off.

Subjects for further investigation: Also looming on the power-blues horizon is a studiedly Jimiesque left-handed guitar prodigy from Memphis, Teneessee: Eric Gales was barely 16 when *The Eric Gales Band* (Elektra 61083 [US])was released in 1991. Since all of the Jimi-Hendrix-via-JEFF-HEALEY material is composed, arranged and sung by his bass-playing elder brother Eugene, one wonders whose band it really is, but the kid in the hat, bandanas and flares certainly delivers: he's swallowed his influences even if he hasn't had time to digest them. Yet another southpaw brother, Manuel Gales, performs rather more blues-specific and commendably snappy New Blueblood stylings under the name of Little Jimmy King: 'King' for Albert, for whom he served a term as rhythm guitarist, and 'Jimmy' for Jimi. *Little Jimmy King & The Memphis Soul Survivors* (Bullseye Blues NETCD 9509) draws heavily (and lovingly, and expertly) on those worthies' towering heritages, but it's also steeped in the influence of Stevie Ray Vaughan, emphasising yet again the role which SRV's work played in reinvigorating the roots from which it originally grew.

Coda: Back Down Home

Every journey needs to finish somewhere; and if the journey is a long and complex one, the resourceful traveller remains open to the possibility that the journey may end up right back where it first began. Much has been made of the fact that the blues originated in the South before migrating across the US and across the globe, but comparatively little attention has been paid to its survival back down home in the Delta and the bayous. The standard accounts seem to suggest that when MUDDY WATERS,

HOWLIN' WOLF, JOHN LEE HOOKER and B.B. KING set off on their travels, they took the music away with them.

Yet whatever happens to the blues out there in the world – whether or not it is, at any given moment, popular or fashionable in Chicago, or Detroit, or New York, or L.A., or Austin, or London, or Paris, or Berlin – the music still lives down in the Mississippi Delta. That's because they're not producing it as a commodity for 'us'; they're playing it for themselves, because it fulfils a function and meets a need in *their* lives. Traditionally, Mississippi musicians have had to leave the Delta to get their music recorded, because the area – which boasts the richest soil and the poorest people in the USA – had no recording industry to support them. Yet the music is still there, and if there is still any such thing as 'real' blues left in an era when someone can release a compilation called *The Blues Experience* (no, I'm not going to tell you how to get it. You crazy?) and include no black artists except B.B. King (on U2's guest-list), ROBERT CRAY (because he's pals with Tina Turner and ERIC CLAPTON), and JIMI HENDRIX (because he's Jimi Hendrix), it's the music which Delta people play for themselves and their community.

- **ORIGINAL MOTION PICTURE SOUNDTRACK:** *Deep Blues*
  (Anxious 4509-91981-2)

In 1981, the critic and historian Robert Palmer published one of the half-dozen most important books ever written about the blues. *Deep Blues* was, essentially, a history of Delta blues, tracing the music from its West African origins through its modern diaspora, from before CHARLEY PATTON to after SON SEALS. In the late '80s, producer/guitarist/kibitzer Dave Stewart, best-known for his partnership with Annie Lennox in Eurythmics, financed and produced a TV documentary film based on Palmer's book and featuring performances from contemporary Delta-based artists, most of whom were virtually unrecorded and only known outside their manor to the most hardcore bluenatics. (One exception is Roosevelt 'Booba' Barnes, who can be heard at greater length on his own album *The Heartbroken Man* (Bedrock BED CD 17), as hardcore an example of electric Delta blues as anyone's cut since HOWLIN' WOLF left for Chicago.) This CD, the final artefact of the book/movie/album *Deep Blues* tryptych, contains Palmer's pick of the performances recorded for the movie, even though some of them didn't make the final cut.

Some of this music, recorded *in situ* during late 1990, is timeless, traditional Delta blues as it might have been heard in the days of SON HOUSE or ROBERT JOHNSON, and some of it is fierce, funky, hard-rocking band blues of the type which we associate with the taverns of Chicago's South Side. Barnes, Jr Kimbrough, Frank Frost and Big Jack Johnson blow up a big, rumbustious electric storm for the benefit of a vocally appreciative audience, while Jessie Mae Hemphill and R.L. Burnside commune with their souls in the privacy of their own homes; the extraordinary young player Lonnie Pitchford raises the ghost of Robert Johnson on eerily powerful versions of 'Terraplane Blues' and 'If I Had Possession Over Judgement Day', and the guitar/harp duo of Jack Owens and Bud Spires close the proceedings by penetrating the innermost pre-Christian heart of the blues, invoking SKIP JAMES and the Bentonia sound on 'Devil Blues'. The music has travelled vast distances through our century, and its odyssey is far from over; however, *Deep Blues* is invaluable because it reminds us, quite simply, what the blues sounds like when it's at home.

INDEX OF BIOGRAPHICAL ENTRIES